The Economics of
Oligopolistic Competition

Advances in Theoretical and Applied Economics
A series from the European Economics and Financial Centre
Edited by Dr Homa Motamen-Scobie

Forthcoming in the series:

Informal Financial Markets in Developing Countries
Peter J. Montiel, Pierre-Richard Agénor, Nadeem Ul Haque

Macroeconomic Information and Financial Trading
Robert I. Webb

The Economics of Oligopolistic Competition

Price and Nonprice Rivalry

Collected Papers of Robert E. Kuenne

BLACKWELL
Oxford UK & Cambridge USA

First published 1992

Blackwell Publishers
Three Cambridge Center
Cambridge, Massachusetts 02142
USA

108 Cowley Road
Oxford OX4 1JF
UK

Library of Congress Cataloging in Publication Data

Kuenne, Robert E.
    The economics of oligopolistic competition: price and nonprice rivalry: collected papers of Robert E. Kuenne.
        p.   cm.
    Includes bibliographical references and index.
    ISNB 1-55786-301-6 (alk. paper)
    1. Oligopolies.   I. Title.
    HD2757.3.K835   1992
    338.8'2 — — dc20z   91-767   CIP

A CIP catalogue record for this book is available from the British Library.

Typeset in 10 on 12 pt Times by Colset Pte. Ltd., Singapore
Printed in Great Britain by Hartnolls Limited, Bodmin, Cornwall
This book is printed on acid-free paper.

For
Janet B. Kuenne
in gratitude for long service as
companion, collaborator, and critic

Other Books by Robert E. Kuenne

The Theory of General Economic Equilibrium

The Attack Submarine: A Study in Strategy

The Polaris Missile Strike: A General Economic Systems Analysis

Monopolistic Competition Theory: Studies in Impact (ed.)

Microeconomic Theory of the Market Mechanism: A General Equilibrium Approach

Eugen von Böhm-Bawerk

Rivalrous Consonance: A Theory of General Oligopolistic Equilibrium

Warranties in Weapon Systems Procurement (with P. H. Richanbach, F. Riddell, and R. Kaganoff)

Microeconomic Theory: Theoretical and Applied, Volumes I, II, and III (ed.)

Dynamics and Conflict in Regional Structural Change (ed., with Manas Chatterji)

New Frontiers in Regional Science (ed., with Manas Chatterji)

General Equilibrium Economics: Space, Time and Money

Contents

Figures

Tables

Series Editor's Preface

The Advances in Theoretical and Applied Economics series, which stems from the European Economics and Financial Centre, is designed to capture recent advances in both theoretical and applied economics. The theme of the series has deliberately been kept broad to portray new developments in a wide range of subjects covering both macro and microeconomics.

It is intended that the series will act as a forum for new developments in various areas of economics – finance, trade, industry, labour, etc., as well as specific topics such as general equilibrium, dynamic games and rational and adaptive expectations.

During the last two decades a gap began to emerge between economists and practitioners (embracing both the policy makers within the public sector and the decision-makers within the private sector). It appeared to the non-economists that the economists had a world of their own, and it seemed as if the field was advanced for its own sake regardless of its relevance or application. As a result, economics as a discipline suffered to some extent. Perhaps this has been due to the way in which the thinking and findings of many economists have been made available to readers. The outcome and policy recommendations emerging out of many research projects have not been communicated in an effective manner – that is, in a language clear and comprehensible, particularly to those who do not possess technical expertise.

Hopefully the 1990s will be a period of consolidation, bringing to the fore the work of those economists who continued their work in the difficult atmosphere of the last two decades with the dedication and the talent necessary to advance the field.

It is one of the aims of this series to bring the work and contributions of economists closer to those of practitioners and to portray the new directions in the field.

New volumes are invited by authors whose work falls in line with the aims and objectives of the series. Contributions should be sent to the Editor at the European Economics and Financial Centre, PO Box 2498, London W2 4LE.

Finally, it is an honour to launch the series with a volume by Professor Robert Kuenne of Princeton University. His collected works on "The Economics of Oligopolistic Competition" makes an outstanding contribution to the field and is a fitting first volume in the series.

Homa Motamen-Scobie
European Economics and Financial Centre

Preface

This volume of my collected writings in oligopoly analysis contains 19 papers that have been published over the past two decades and one unpublished paper delivered in 1990. The papers have been structured into four parts with the intent of presenting an organized and integrated depiction of the emergence and evolution of major themes over that period. They are published with the hope that they may inspire economists and graduate students to go further along the paths mapped in these pages to develop new ideas and methodologies in the difficult task of devising operational frameworks with which to gain insights into differentiated oligopoly.

I believe there is a growing awareness among microtheorists and industrial organization specialists that this is the market structure of dominant interest in the explication of the economic decisions of advanced market economies. Unless we develop a general equilibrium theory that incorporates differentiated oligopoly with a welfare economics as adjunct, we are really incapable of providing worthwhile analyses to the policy community. I realize that this is a strong statement, but I am increasingly convinced of its truth. Much more progress must be made in the analysis of nonprice competition especially, with its decisions concerning choices of qualities, advertising and other marketing methods and amounts, product innovation, cost-reduction technologies, and spatial structures.

It is gratifying to see that young scholars are making good progress in these areas, moving away from the comfortingly determinate structure of the large-group case or imperfect competition to confront the major problems head-on. I detect also an increasing willingness to abandon the fetish of established methodology and experiment with new methods.

I am grateful for the opportunity of publishing the volume to Dr Homa Motamen-Scobie, who first suggested presenting a work for the series she edits, and I feel honored to inaugurate that series with this volume. She and Mark Allin, senior commissioning editor at Blackwell Publishers, have been most encouraging and supportive. I am also grateful for support in funding over the long period of the research, for fellowships from the Ford and Rockefeller Foundations, and for a research fellowship at the University of Vienna, currently from the Fulbright Commission. I must also express long-delayed appreciation to Professors Åke Andersson and Tönu Puu of the University of Umeå in Sweden for their encouragement of my efforts in oligopolistic spatial competition.

The work was edited by John Taylor with a dedication to perfection and an attention to exactitude that renders deficient any expression of gratitude I might tender.

Finally, I must pay special tribute for the patience and daily encouragement over the past 34 years of my wife and my children, Christopher and Carolyn, during periods of intense academic dedication. These familial inputs were indispensable in the production functions whose outputs are here displayed.

R. E. K.

Acknowledgments

I am grateful to the following publishers for permission to reproduce the listed materials.

De Economist for chapter 1, "Toward a Usable General Theory of Oligopoly".

Helbing & Lichtenhahn Verlag AG, publisher of *Kyklos*, for chapter 2, "Towards an Operational General Equilibrium Theory with Oligopoly: Some Experimental Results and Conjectures", and chapter 6, "Rivalrous Consonance and the Power Structure of OPEC".

Editrice Cedam, publisher of *Pioneering Economics: Essays in Honor of Giovanni Demaria*, for chapter 3, "General Oligopolistic Equilibrium: a Crippled Optimization Approach".

Oxford University Press, publisher of *Oxford Economic Papers*, for chapter 4, "Duopoly Reaction Functions Under Crippled Optimization Regimes".

Elsevier Science Publishers BV, publisher of *Regional Science and Urban Economics* and *Advances in Spatial Theory and Dynamics*, for chapter 5, "The Rivalrous Consonance Theory of Oligopoly", chapter 15, "Price-location Interdependence and Social Cost in a Discrete Market Space", and chapter 16, "The Dynamics of Oligopolistic Location: Present Status and Future Research Directions".

The Logistics and Transportation Review for chapter 7, "A Short-run Demand Analysis of the OPEC Cartel".

The Princeton Alumni Weekly for chapter 8, "The Limits of OPEC".

Butterworth Scientific Ltd, publishers of *Energy Economics*, for chapter 9, "The GENESYS Model of OPEC, 1974–1980: Structural Insights from a Non-forecasting Model".

The University of Pennsylvania Press, publisher of *Reaganomics and the Stagflation Economy*, for chapter 10, "OPEC's Role in the World Economy: Some Lessons and Conjectures".

John Wiley & Sons, publisher of *Monopolistic Competition Theory:*

Studies in Impact, for chapter 11, "Quality Space, Interproduct Competition, and General Equilibrium Theory".

Chapman & Hall Ltd, publisher of *Applied Economics*, for chapter 12, "Interproduct Distances in a Quality-space: Inexact Measurement in Differentiated Oligopoly Analysis".

The Macmillan Press Ltd, publisher of *The Economics of Imperfect Competition and Employment*, *New Frontiers in Regional Science: Essays in Honour of Walter Isard*, and *Arrow and the Ascent of Modern Economic Theory*, for chapter 14, "Advertising Competition and Information Flows in Spatial Oligopoly", and chapter 18, "Oligopolistic Uncertainty and Optimal Bidding in Government Procurement: a Subjective Probability Approach".

Pion Limited, publisher of *Environment and Planning A*, for chapter 19, "Uncertainty, spatial Proximity and the Stability of Oligopoly Pricing".

Conflict Management and Peace Science for chapter 20, "Conflict Management and the Theory of Mature Oligopoly".

Introduction to the Volume

Confronting the papers one has published over a period of some 40 years stirs many of the same conflicting emotions one feels in revisiting old friends after long lapses. Some of them one has frankly outgrown, having moved beyond their narrow horizons, and it is difficult to recall what attraction they might ever have had. Others raise fond memories of one's youth, when reality had a simpler and unambiguous meaning, and commitments had the freedom from doubt that confers a confident earnestness. And still others are the companions of one's maturity, in whom one perceives regrettable but endearing faults, but with whom one is comfortable and has a certain pride in their finding. Treating them all as a whole, however, one is grateful for the opportunity to have met each, to have benefited from each as one passed the milestones, and to have enjoyed a rich lifetime experience in their joint company.

For the 20 essays on oligopoly I have chosen from auld acquaintance in this volume I retain a great deal of fondness, and, more importantly, a strong belief in the validity of their underlying themes. My hope is that the reader will find in them some value in enriching his or her "vision" of economic reality and in enlarging the methodology he or she employs. I confess that had I the opportunity to redo some of them – especially those that are empirical – I would make changes to avoid some naivete or correct some assumptions with the lessons of subsequent history. Nonetheless, I have reproduced them all as they appeared with few changes other than typographical or grammatical. The few changes of substance are placed within brackets.

My interests in economics have had a fundamental unity since my doctoral dissertation, and the selections in this volume reflect that consistency. In my research for the dissertation, written under Walter Isard at Harvard and dealing with an input–output study of the impact of the new US Steel integrated mill in the Delaware Valley upon the region's economy, I became interested in the relation of Leontief's framework to Walrasian general equilibrium theory. At that time, before William Jaffé's erudite translation of the *Eléments* in English was available, Walras's work was not well known in Anglo-Saxon literature. Graduate education in microeconomic theory was almost wholly Marshallian partial equilibrium economics.

From that research I acquired three interests I have retained throughout my career: a dedication to general equilibrium economics and, more generally, to models that include extensive endogenous interdependence; a belief that such general frameworks must be made "operational," which is to say, capable of generating propositions with empirical bearing upon the realistic market economy; and, from Isard, an interest in spatial economics as it relates to general systems modelling. Almost all of my writing relates to these three fields, and the current volume is no exception.

During the writing of my book, *The Theory of General Economic Equilibrium*, in the early 1960s I became increasingly concerned about two aspects of the Walrasian Model and its derivatives that limited its potential operationalism. The first was its attachment to pure competition and the barriers to practicality that such adherence entailed. As a student of Edward H. Chamberlin and William J. Fellner, and later as a teaching assistant of Chamberlin's, I became convinced that developed nations' market economies must be analyzed in terms of differentiated oligopoly. In this early postwar period Chamberlin had become convinced that the "large-group case" or "monopolistic competition proper" was not a realistic framework, and he was moving to emphasize differentiated oligopoly in his teaching and writing. Also, Fellner's *Competition Among the Few* appeared and played a substantial role in stimulating interest in oligopoly, as did Joe S. Bain's work in the industrial organization field he did so much to create. One of my long-term goals was set during this decade: the incorporation of differentiated oligopoly into general equilibrium theory.

The second damning defect in Walras's schema was revealed in Samuelson's *Foundations of Economic Analysis*, to which I am hugely indebted. To me, perhaps contrary to the intent of its author, a major lesson it taught was the essential sterility of the system in its inability to generate theorems or propositions relying wholly upon the second-order conditions for extrema in convex systems or upon the conditions upon such systems emplaced by assumptions of the stability of equilibrium. Only a handful of insights could be so obtained in well-behaved systems.

Leontief's input–output analysis was a most encouraging step forward in this respect, especially in its emphasis on replacing the unspecified functions of pure theory with numerical functions, with the attendant ability to obtain solutions in quantitative rather than qualitative terms. Moreover, it provided the potential for determinate parametric displacements of many types, not limited to variation of one such datum each time. My empirical work in the dissertation with a regional input–output system gave me a solid respect for the structure, but my theoretical work with the Walrasian model in that research tempered my enthusiasm. I was led to an understanding of the extent of exclusions of variables from the internal content of the input-output model and a realization that it was a non-optimizing system depending essentially upon technological determinants which split prices off from quantities in the depicted interdependence.

Developments in general equilibrium analysis springing from the application of topological and real analysis do little to dispel my qualms concerning the defects in terms of theorem generation. Despite the admitted technical brilliance of the work, the appearance of the Arrow–Debreu model reinforced the attachment of general equilibrium theory to pure competition and did nothing (to my knowledge) to increase the number or reality of deducible theorems. I fear that I remain one of the few nonbelievers who view this departure from the Walrasian–Paretian–Hicksian–Samuelsonian development of a differentiable general equilibrium theory – with all its admitted faults – as a blind alley from the viewpoint of progress in moving the theory in needed directions. Proofs of existence, uniqueness or stability of equilibrium do little in these respects but display the mathematical virtuosity of their propounders.

My works on oligopoly theory are in the largest part steps upon the way to attempting the incorporation of differentiated oligopoly into general equilibrium theory. That task was completed in my *Rivalrous Consonance: a Theory of General Oligopolistic Equilibrium*, published in 1986. The reader will perceive better the red thread of continuity that runs through the essays if he or she understands the ultimate aim whose attempted accomplishment they point toward. However, the papers are self-subsistent and also explore nonprice competition more fully than was done in the book. Also, they include my later excursions into uncertainty and information flows in oligopoly, as well as empirical applications of the basic theory to the OPEC cartel.

As the reader will quickly see, the basic theory which unites all of the papers is the "theory of rivalrous consonance." By that term I mean to convey my belief that in mature oligopolies a blend of competition and cooperation develops among the incumbents of an industry which results in a mutual deference in their pricing decisions and a tacit collusion. As a community, the oligopoly develops a competitive–cooperative power structure which must be isolated for fruitful analysis to occur. This analysis must also be done within a framework in which general interdependence among rivals and with customers is recognized, firms are permitted to have multiple objectives, and the "sociological specifics" of an industry can be incorporated. My own model for integrating all these aspects of realistic oligopolistic decision-making – rivalrous consonance using crippled optimization techniques – is fully (and I hope not tediously) developed in parts I and II.

As each part is introduced by a separate prefatory explanation of content and goals I shall go no further at this point.

In part II the selections illustrate the operational potential of the model by applications to the OPEC cartel. Game theory, it seems to me, despite its admitted value and, indeed, indispensability in the analysis of situations in which egoistic rivalry drives agents exclusively, is not an appropriate framework with which to approach multiple-objective firms in sociological matrices that permit substantial cooperation. In saying that I must admit some personal unease: denying the theoretical omnipotence of game theory at Princeton is somewhat akin to questioning the existence of the Holy Ghost at St Peter's. And, further, because I was brought to Princeton by Oskar Morgenstern, such incapacity to share the faith is complicated by the guilt feelings of the ingrate. Nonetheless, rivalrous consonance seems to me a more promising approach to the analysis of mature oligopoly. I hope the reader will be convinced of that by the applications of it to OPEC.

The work on nonprice competition in part III develops a series of operational models which are inspired in part by my interest in spatial economics. Product differentiation since Hotelling's seminal work has been linked to location in quality-spaces, and I, too, exploit the analogy. Besides the use of a fictitious space I seek in some of the papers to investigate the role of space as an inhibitor of marketing efficiency in the new industrial structures arising in developed economies. Also, using simulation approaches, I investigate spatial location as a tool of competition in oligopoly. Rivalrous consonance, with its focus upon tacit price collusion, implicitly places new emphasis upon the notion of nonprice means of rivalry, and supports the increasing interest economists have been evincing in this difficult subject area.

My pervasive insistence upon operational frameworks has led me to use "simulative theorizing" as a tool to gain insights from models whose complexity is such as to foreclose closed solutions. Spatial location is but one example of the introduction of an extremely difficult variable into nonprice competition models. By the term I mean to denote a set of techniques that guides the choice of specifications and parameters for functions in fictitious environments for the purpose of deriving broader theoretical insights into the nature of some body of economic variation. To make progress in many areas of oligopoly analysis we must be willing to forgo the search for universal principles through closed analysis and lower our ambitions by accepting simulation techniques. For efficient application of such techniques we need to develop an "econometrics of simulation" that will provide principles for selections of functions and parameters and isolation of strategic parameters for displacements. Guy H. Orcutt and his coworkers have been instrumental in introducing simulation techniques into economic analysis and in initiating the development of such an "econometrics," and that work has been an inspiration to my own research.

Finally, in part IV the reader will find my recent first steps in introducing uncertainty and the economics of information into oligopoly theory. These involve the use of subjective probability to shape rivals' conjectural variations and views of the likelihood of competitors' price changes.

In reading the acknowledgements to publishers for permission to reprint the papers the reader will notice that a large number of them appeared in European journals. This reflects the fact that I have always felt more at home in the European tradition of economics than the American. The former, I believe, continues to stress the need for general rather than partial analysis, and to value the broader approaches to economic problems, encompassing the philosophical, sociological, political, legal, and cultural aspects and implications. It manages to balance an interest in the policy implications of economic theory with concerns for the deeper philosophical origins and meanings of theoretical concepts. The mainstream of current American economics I find much too involved with arcane mathematical irrelevance and too little concerned with the operational, too fascinated with the ideal of a scientific purity it can never attain, too narrow in restricting the scope of investigation to value-free efficiency concerns, and too impatient with analysts who seek to relate economic phenomena to the ethos, institutions, and culture of the society which they impact and are impacted by.

My debts to many teachers and coworkers are large. Foremost among them are those to Edward H. Chamberlin and William Fellner, who inspired my interest in oligopoly theory; to Walter Isard, whose teaching and thesis direction awoke my interest in spatial theory, and whose friendship I have enjoyed over more than 40 years; to Guy H. Orcutt, whose patient guidance in student days and whose published research paced my interest in simulation as a tool to extend operational theory; and to Jacob Viner, whose polymath knowledge sparked off brilliant insights into any number of subjects for a young colleague in patient and informal but thankfully long encounters in the depths of Firestone Library.

I am thankful for the hospitality that the University of Vienna has accorded me, and most particularly Professors E. Streissler and E. Weissel.

To the Guardians of the Grove of Academe, I can only intone (with apologies to Robert W. Service) a humble prayer:

> The gods above look down and grin,
> As seas of ink I spatter.
> Ye gods! forgive my academic sins –
> The other kinds don't matter!

Part I

Rivalrous Consonance Theory: a Blend of Competition and Cooperation

Introduction to Part I

The selections of part I summarize my contributions to oligopoly theory and trace the evolution of my modelling approaches. The work spans 15 years of research effort, and when one is offered the opportunity for such a retrospective one suffers some anxiety. On second reading does one encounter inconsistencies or contradictions in one's "vision" of the oligopolistic industry's decision-space or its procedures in selecting the values of variables within that space? Does one confront earlier viewpoints from which one recoils in disbelief that such naivete or error ever existed in one's professional consciousness? Alternatively, does one discern a rather surprising continuity in past and present analytical frameworks, with sufficient evolution of ideas to ward off fears of ossification or scholarly sclerosis?

On the whole I was gratified to find a reassuring unity of my basic vision of oligopolistic decision contexts over the years and of the analytical frameworks I believe most useful in formalizing firms' decisions and their joint interdependent outcomes. The distinctive features of that vision I believe will be found in all of the five papers reproduced in part I, albeit with different emphases:

1   *The existence of a "rivalrous consonance of interests" among mature oligopolists, or in most cases the recognition that the industry or product group is a community whose component units' relations are mixtures of the competitive and the cooperative.* Realistic analysis of firms' decisions must incorporate both motivations, with the cooperative strand getting greater emphasis as the industry matures.

2   *The need to incorporate oligopoly theory into general equilibrium theory to make the latter at once more realistic and more useful.* At the same time, since by its very nature any acceptable theory of oligopoly must cope with the interdependence of firms' decisions, it must retain the microeconomic detail of individual firms' relations with every other firm in the industry.

3   *The multi-objective nature of the oligopolistic firm's decision-making.*

9

Empirical evidence does not support an assumption by the analyst that firms act simply to maximize profits, ignoring other goals. Rather, firms seek to find some compromise among a set of goals in their decision-making.

4 *The futility of searching for a universal theory of oligopoly.* Every oligopolistic industry is a unique community, with history, customs, personalities and modes of behavior that distinguish it from all others. The goal of theory, therefore, must be to construct frameworks that permit tailoring to these individualities.

5 *The necessity of deriving the binary power structure of the industry.* The cultural and sociological aspects of the oligopolistic community, as listed in point 4, manifest themselves in large part in the power structure present. This must be defined for each incumbent in terms of each of its rivals, and specifically the degree of deference that must be accorded such rivals when price or nonprice variable values are chosen.

6 *The importance of "simulative theorizing".* The analytical complications implicit in the above-listed features, which I believe to be necessary for realistic operational oligopoly theories, give rise to models which are much too complex to be analyzed in closed, determinate ways. The field must make greater use of simulation methodology and develop an "econometrics of simulation" that will permit greater efficiency in deriving useful insights into firm behavior under specified industry conditions.

7 *The need to incorporate nonprice competition in oligopoly analysis.* It is well recognized that as rivalrous consonance intrudes with maturity, industries dampen price competition in favor of less destabilizing rivalry in marketing, quality, style, performance characteristics and other such competitive areas that do not directly involve price changes. In the future, greater emphasis must be given this difficult-to-analyze feature of oligopolistic competition.

All or most of these articles of analytic faith will be found in each of the included papers, but the reader will note differing emphases among them as my thinking changed *pari passu* with my research and the insights derived from criticism. The firm is viewed as an optimizer – generally as a "crippled optimizer," handicapped by its need to consider the welfare of its rivals in degrees dictated by the power structure – constrained by a set of secondary goals. The choices of a primary goal for the objective function and the set of secondary goals in the form of constraints permit the model to be tailored to industry specifics. Rivalrous consonance is incorporated in the crippled optimization by each firm including the welfare of every other firm in its objective function, when those welfares are discounted by power structure coefficients. And because of the complicated nature of the interdependence that occurs as each firm in its optimizing affects every other firm's parameters and is affected in turn by their reactions, simulation is used to gain insights into oligopolistic behavior.

Chapter 1 was my initial attempt to formulate the theory and contains a good deal of the empirical background that motivated it. The discontent with general equilibrium theory's continued allegiance to pure competition is explicit here, as is my desire to devise a theory of general oligopolistic equilibrium.[1] The model presented here was viewed as a standalone industry analysis which could form the module for such a more ambitious model. Multiple-objective nonlinear programming is used in the construction in the belief that game theory, with its stress on competition and ultra-rational, one-dimensional motivation in centralized and fully informed rivals does not capture the empirics of modern industry.

An early stress on product competition is noted here – a feature to which I give greater attention in my later work contained in part III. It was, however, a continuing interest of mine from the publication of a framework in which I believe nonprice competition could be analyzed and which is reproduced in chapter 11.

One emphasis in this paper that I lessened in my later work is the stress on target rates of return as primary objectives of the firm. It is interesting that this approach can also be used in profit maximization, but further research led me to question the notion that it was a more common goal than straightforward profit maximization.

Another distinctive difference between this paper and those that follow in part I is that although I discussed rivalrous consonance in the literary presentation I did not incorporate it in the formal models because I had not yet developed methods for its inclusion. That came a bit later in the analysis of chapter 2. The emphasis in this earlier work was on multi-objective optimization and oligopolistic interdependence. Extensive discussion of non-linear programming, the comparative statics of such models, and the SUMT algorithm for their solution – all of which were rather less widely known at the time of publication than now – was incorporated.

Finally, simulation was used for the first time to analyze a fictitious industry with features common to many such industries. One conclusion which was to be drawn from all future work with the models was the unpredictability of the results of parametric displacements because of the complicated nature of the interdependence in oligopolistic competition among $n > 2$ (in the present case, $n = 5$) firms. Two particular results of interest in this regard are the failure of products which have qualities that isolate them from other brands in "quality-space" to always benefit from such protection, and the reduction in social welfare that may result from regulation setting limits to firms' rates of return.

In summary, chapter 1 is the summarization of my earliest thinking about oligopoly and my first formalization of those thoughts. It contained most of the features that were to be included in my future work, although some changes in approach and more changes in emphasis were to occur.

Chapter 2 moves the analysis of chapter 1 in the direction of a rivalrous consonance general equilibrium among industries by assuming that a firm will take no action that yields it a profit smaller than the sum of losses that action inflicts on all other firms, including its suppliers. The theory also intrudes more interdependence among firms by taking into account the supply of intermediate inputs among industries as well as consumer demand. Power structure coefficients, however, are not yet present to permit a more discriminating rivalrous consonance among firms, but they are anticipated in note 1.

The paper is notable in expanding the role of "simulative theorizing," introduced in chapter 1. In the five-firm, two-industry model employed, the meager qualitative results obtainable from a general comparative statics approach with unspecified functions are demonstrated, and their nonderivability when models are not convex are discussed. Recourse is therefore had to finite displacements of a specified model designed to incorporate features of oligopolistic industry structure and characteristics. I remain convinced that economic theory in general and oligopoly theory in particular must employ such methods increasingly to obtain fruitful insights into a reality characterized by complex interdependence.

Another result of this paper is to demonstrate concretely the complexities that a multifirm, multi-industry rivalrous consonance model presents as an approximation to the even greater complications of the real world. One must expect that decisions are made in a "nonconvex context" so that they may lead to local extrema at best. Counterintuitive price and quantity responses to parameter changes can be quite frequent and unpredictable. Inductive methods applied to industry data to discern or summarize the causal patterns of such variable movements – most notably, regression analysis – may be inadequate to the task. This last lesson is derived by seeking to isolate the relationships of firms' price movements with changes in factor costs. Finally, an important insight derivable from the model is that the asymmetry in price responses to factor cost change – with cost increases leading to large price rises but cost decreases resulting in small price falls – may be explicable by rivalrous consonance.

The paper, expressing dissatisfaction with general equilibrium theory's purely competitive structure, takes a step in the direction of substituting oligopolistic decision-making, with the incorporation of intermediate goods supplies among industries. But the cooperative aspects of rivalrous consonance are still crude and the form of firms' objective functions rather strained.

A deeper analysis of the model in chapter 2 is performed in chapter 3, and a more thorough derivation of its economic implications obtained. Through a study of the Kuhn–Tucker conditions for an industry optimum three separable types of profit impacts are derived which the firm takes into account in its price setting. These are (1) own-profit, (2) other-firm-profit (including that of both customers and rivals), and (3) income impacts. Through the use of these components, the Lagrangean dual variables and various combinations of the constraint functions, insights into firm behavior and its implications for optimal variable values are presented.

In section 3.3 an important first step is taken on the path to explicit inclusion of the power structure of the industry. As indicated above, straight-forward treatment of the firm's optimization within the context of an industry objective function implies that the firm treats all three of the profit impact components as of coordinate importance to itself. Hence, a dollar of profit for itself is no more important than preventing its rival or customer from losing a dollar. This is, of course, unrealistically altruistic. In this selection I use the iterated solution conditions of the SUMT algorithm to eliminate or control the weights of such impacts in a rather heuristic manner. Such weights were the precursors of explicitly derived *consonance coefficients* that were introduced in chapters 4 and 6 in a more satisfactory manner. This initial treatment, however, was an important step in my own under-standing of the problem and the proper manner of its solution.

Simulative theorizing is used extensively in the paper to study the changes in price, quantity, and profits when other-firm profit components are elimi-nated. The cases studied in this portion of the work provide a rich oppor-tunity to study the effects of interdependent decision-making in detail, and thereby to gauge the importance of tacit cooperation to rivals and customers with different circumstantial profiles.

Finally, my dissatisfaction with regression analysis, explained in chapter 2, led me to experiment with factor analysis as a means of discerning the important variables acting orthogonally in the analysis to effect the solu-tions. I performed a factor analysis on the solutions to the cases used in the simulations and subjected the factors to a varimax rotation to further distill the information derived. I was impressed by the additional insights the exercise permitted and believe that economists would be wise to become more familiar with these techniques as an adjunct to their favorite tool of multi-variate analysis: regression techniques. For example, a notable result was the insight that in my simulations prices were moved predominantly by noncost factors, which is to say, by rivalrous consonance cooperation.

In the development of my theory this selection played a more important role. It provided me with important elements of the mature framework I was to present in the book quoted in note 1. The isolation of the profit com-ponents, the extensive use of combinations of such components in simu-lations, the initial insights into the explicit introduction of the power structure of the industry to the firm's optimization, and the employment of factor analysis were extremely important in the progress of my thinking.

The power structure analysis is developed in chapter 4, which finalizes the means of using that structure to incorporate selectively the other-firms profit component in a firm's optimization. The methodology was derived independently, but is linked in the paper to prior work in game-theoretic contexts.

The model used to present the theory is that of duopoly without secondary goal constraints, and "consonance" factors (or coefficients) θ_{ij}, $i = 1, 2$, $j = 1, 2$, $i \neq j$, are introduced as scalar multipliers applied to rivals' profits in the respective firms' objective functions. These factors vary between 0 (in which case the myopic Cournot-type solution is obtained) and 1 (the joint-profit maximization or Chamberlin case). Intermediate values can be interpreted as the own-profit equivalent of $1 in other-firm profit. Hence, if $\theta_{ij} = 0.25$, firm i values $1 of firm j's profit as equal to $0.25 of its own profit.

Price reaction functions are derived for given $\theta = [\theta_{ij}, \theta_{ji}]$ vectors whose intersection yields the rivalrous consonance solution for the given pair of consonance coefficients. A graphical analysis of the reaction functions is made and they are related to isoprofit contours. Within the feasible region, delimited by the limiting values 0 and 1 of the coefficients, the price solution vector will vary as the vector (or, more generally, the matrix) θ varies.

If we follow a longer run analysis in which the elements of θ are variable we may view firms as varying their consonance coefficients to maximize profits. In this context I identify a "generalized Stackelberg point" to which both firms prices will move and remain since it is a Nash equilibrium. This ability to determine the θs endogenously through optimality analysis is important, as it provides an option to analysts who disagree with my stress on the importance of sociopolitical relations in their determination.

The solutions are subjected to parametric changes in the θ_{ij} and in costs and the comparative statics results evaluated. The nature of the interdependent adjustments to such equilibrium shocks is illustrated graphically and decomposed into shift-and-slope changes in the reaction functions. The comparative statics results are evaluated as to sign, and some attention is paid to the conditions under which perverse price movements could occur.

I feel that the analysis in this selection not only fills the gap in the theory of prior chapters with respect to depiction of varying degrees of deference paid different rivals in firms' decision-making, but that it extends classic reaction function frameworks by permitting intermediate values of the θ_{ij} and hence intermediate solutions. In this sense it stands alone outside of the framework of rivalrous consonance as an extension of Cournot-type reaction function analysis.

Finally I have included as chapter 5 a lecture I delivered in 1984 to a group of European scholars with the aim of giving a concise description of the rivalrous consonance framework. Although it is somewhat repetitious of the previous selections, especially chapter 4, I feel that it is the best brief summary of the assumptions behind the model, the model's content, its relation to classic oligopoly theory, and the potential comparative statics theorems derivable from it. For a more complete explication of the theory in its mature form and extensions of these themes the reader is referred to the book cited in note 1.

In part I the reader is introduced to an alternative approach to game theory in addressing one of the major gaps in microeconomic theory: oligopoly theory. I believe it possesses advantages to the more established approach: it is designed to be flexible in its application to specific industries; it fulfills more realistically the need to treat mature oligopoly as a variable mixture of competition and cooperation; it incorporates a power structure that encapsulates the sociological characteristics of the industry; it permits a general equilibrium formulation with oligopoly, and, of great importance, it is designed to be operational. To demonstrate that applicability to real-world industries part II is dedicated to the use of the model to analyze the OPEC cartel.

Note

[1] In 1986 I published such a theory in *Rivalrous Consonance: a Theory of General Oligopolistic Equilibrium*, Contributions to Economic Analysis 157, North-Holland, Amsterdam.

1

Toward a Usable General Theory of Oligopoly

1 Desiderata

There is likely to be little professional quarrel with the assertion that it is time to move general economic equilibrium theory away from its suffocating postulate of pure competition. With exceptions that are rapidly cited, theorists active in extending that theory's classic forms or in restating them in the newer set-theoretic and topological modes have remained with this simplest market structure.[1] Indeed, it is one of the less fortunate by-products of the latter movement that it reinforced the attachment to atomism. Yet, the formal theories of monopolistic and imperfect competition have been with us for 40 years, the classic analyses of duopolistic markets are much older, and the general dissatisfaction with pure competition has been deeply ingrained for some time.

We assert as well that it is differentiated oligopoly – rivalrous competition with product differences – that must be accommodated within general equilibrium systems. It is clearly the dominant form of industrial competition in developed economies, and, indeed, much seeming nonrivalrous competition in nonindustrial fields reveals its oligopolistic character when spatial structure or the clustering of product brands into competing groups are taken into account. It provides the challenge for a new conceptual approach differing orthogonally from the forms we now have in general systems analysis, even when they have been somewhat deceptively garbed in the newer mathematical dress.

Three additional considerations tempt the model builder into a search for methods of including oligopoly in general equilibrium theory. The first is that the task requires the design of a theory at once general yet flexible enough to incorporate substantial differences in industrial folkways and structure.[2]

The second consideration is the possibility that success will permit the construction of an empirically usable model, to predict realistic sectoral price

16

impacts of wage rises for example. And the last consideration is a conjecture that despite the expectation that oligopolistic interdependence will complicate general systems, it may be that the general theory of oligopoly price behavior will simplify the interdependence of the models and thereby make them richer sources of operational theorems than unspecified purely competitive general equilibrium systems have been in the past.

This chapter attempts to take the first step down the long road to achievement of the goal by constructing the theoretical industry module that can be used as the sectoral building block. The analysis has the additional attraction that it can stand alone as a partial equilibrium framework for the depiction of a differentiated oligopolistic industry's interactions. Hence, although we shall remain wholly at the level of the industry, and confine our attentions to the theoretical, we believe the results will be of interest to those who work in the areas of general equilibrium theory and the theory of oligopoly. In [11], the "building blocks" have been integrated into a general equilibrium model.

1.1 Empirical Guide Lines

In recent years the theorist has received welcome guidance from the valuable empirical work that has been done by such investigators as Kaplan, Dirlam and Lanzillotti [7] in the United States, Fog [4] in Denmark, and Wärneryd in Sweden.[3] From this work has emerged a major theoretical guidepost: the modern oligopolistic firm follows a multiple-objective strategy. In very few cases can any simply defined profit maximization be discerned; rather, to an almost exclusive degree, the goals sought are a set of mutually constraining and conflicting aims, imperfectly conceived and articulated, uncertainly coordinated, and decentralized in administrative origin and achievement.

The set of goals frequently striven for includes the following:

1 a target rate of return on computed investment[4];
2 maintenance or expansion of market share;
3 maintenance of a profit margin over a standard cost figure;
4 stabilization of prices in the industry;
5 conformance to current antitrust trends;
6 meeting competitors' price leads;
7 minimization of customer inconvenience;
8 exclusion of potential industry entrants[5];
9 enhancing the welfare of managers.

Another major conclusion emerges by default from this recent literature: the preconditions to make formal game-theoretic approaches promising as a general analytical framework for the pricing decision do not exist. The modern corporation is a pluralistic organization with multiple, uncoordinated, and to some extent, competing, loci of decision-making.[6] Within such groups, decisions are arrived at in heuristic, informal, or nebulous manners.[7] Of course, it is possible to use game theory as a formal encapsulation of the informal procedures of rivalrous corporations, but that framework is not a likely candidate to serve this metaphoric role. For its plausible application it is difficult to escape the need for a clear-cut demonstration of a well-defined locus of decision-making authority with a comprehensive canvas of possibilities, grasp of strategic alternatives, concern with rivals' potential reactions, and constant preoccupation with firm survival or the payoffs implied by the paraphernalia of game theory.

It is difficult, therefore, to accept the war-of-survival paradigm typified by Shubik's work [16], or indeed most of the classic or modern approaches which stress the individual-firm oriented one-dimensional "reaction function" in one form or another.[8] Rather, the realistic image of rivalrous competition is one which includes competing intrafirm goals and elements of an "organic" subordination of the individual unit's welfare somewhat to the welfare of the whole. That is, there is a definite commitment of the rivalrous firm to the continued peaceful survival of the industry – a rivalrous consonance – even if that implies to some degree the foregoing of opportunities by the firm to seek greater benefit through conflict.

At one extreme of the "organic" model is the homeostasis of Claude Bernard and Walter B. Cannon, in which the organizing principle of the whole imposes its effective self-effacing constraints upon the component units to keep the vital parameters of the organism within viable limits. Certainly we do not wish to adopt this vision of oligopolistic coexistence. But, at the same time, the picture obtained from game-theoretic or games-of-survival analysis errs in the opposite direction. Our view, therefore, is that a compromise between the organic and the self-seeking is in order, as reflected in the firm's search for "reasonable" profits within an essentially stable environment.

Although we shall persist in a marginalistic approach in an optimizing framework to the equilibrium of the oligopolistic industry, I feel that the findings of these more behaviorally oriented investigators must modify the content of current models. As Koopmans has written in his *Three Essays*, the role of the theorist is to follow the empiricist, not to lead him. Theoretical advance in the social sciences lies in the direction of incorporating, enlightening, and coordinating the empiricists' discoveries, to the extent that such action does not involve too great a loss of the analytical power of formal theory. The unrealistic must yield to the realistic postulate unless the simplifying abstraction from reality can be shown to yield more fruitful results. Hence, it is always unfortunate for a field when empiricist and theoretician do not communicate in continuous fashion.

A general theory of oligopoly, suitable for the multi-industry application of general equilibrium systems, must incorporate the multi-objective nature of corporate planning at the same time that it permits different emphases among the goals. Further, it must seek to include the semi-cooperative, semi-competitive milieu of the modern industry. Although the firm's aspirations cannot be condensed into a single objective, and though the set of objectives must be constrained by an industry welfare consideration, optimization of some kind is not inconsistent with the empirical studies. The benefits which derive in theory construction from its assumption are not sacrificed lightly, and it is possible with nonlinear programming techniques to incorporate goals as constraints upon a maximizing or minimizing procedure. This is the path we shall follow below.

2 The Short-run Model

Two periods are distinguished in this analysis: (1) the *short term*, in which firms attain a sequence of temporary equilibria within the limits of existing constraints on production and price change, and (2) the *medium term*, in which they achieve a sustainable industry equilibrium. In sections 2 and 3 we shall concentrate on the short term, so defined.

Our view of the nature of oligopolistic competition diverges from the classic vision of intense interdependence: earnest attempts to anticipate rivals' reactions to hypothetical strategies, the determination of defensive policies to prevent rivals from reducing the firm's earnings below minimum levels, and the rest of the self-and-other conscious apparatus found in modern theories of rivalrous firm competition. Rather, we shall place the competitive emphasis upon product competition, and, for reasons already discussed in section 1, the rivalrous environment will be endowed with a great deal more existential unity and concern for industry welfare than is usual.[9]

In the typical oligopolistic industry we assume that firms formulate plans to seek fulfillment of a set of goals involving only incidental conflict with the similar plans of rivals. It is assumed, of course, that the plans of rivals are mutually consistent in the sense that a nonempty feasible region exists in the industry's decision space.

The interdependence among firms enters the model in two guises.

1   Each firm is assumed to have a sales function for each product it produces, containing as arguments its own price and the prices of all rival products in the group. We assume that this sales function is known with certainty by the relevant firm; it is also necessary that the firm know or form conjectures about the sales functions of its rivals.

2   Product competition reflects the closeness in a "quality space" of such

products, two goods very close to one another in "core qualities" being more closely competitive than others in the same group whose core or non-core qualities are more dissimilar.[10] We shall assume that it is possible to measure a product's distance from competitor products along a scale from 0 to 1, where 0 represents a perfect substitute and 1 the complete absence of substitutability.[11] We use this parameter, s, to determine the other-price elasticities of a firm's sales function (see section 2.1.1 below) and to shift the sales function as the number of competing products is changed.

Thus, our view of the prototypical oligopolistic interdependence is one of marked passivity and does not preclude a joint attainment of consistent if conflicting goals by rivals engaged in decision-making that can be modelled as passively anticipatory.

2.1 The Explicit Model

We assume that in the short-run each firm v defines for each good j it produces the amount of dedicated capital, K_{vj}, allocated to its production. The firm then minimizes the square of the deviation of the actual rate of return, r_{vj}, from a target rate of return, $\bar{r}_{vj}$ on that capital, subject to constraints. We define the actual rate of return as

$$r_{vj} = \frac{X_{vj}(P_{vj} - C_{vj})}{K_{vj}}, \tag{1.1}$$

where C_{vj} is taken to be constant average and marginal cost, exogenously given; P_{vj} is price; and X_{vj} is output. The firm's objective function may then be written

$$Z_{vj} = (r_{vj} - \bar{r}_{vj})^2 \tag{1.2}$$

for this good.

It is convenient to use this objective function for two reasons. First, because of the importance firms place upon achieving a target rate of return on investment for each product (see notes 3 and 12) it will be directly applicable to many industries' behavior. Second, because with it, through a judicious choice of $\bar{r}$, the target rates of return, it is possible to treat profit maximization in a convex nonlinear programming model.

In our general short-term model the firm's objective of minimizing (1.2) is constrained by five types of coordinate goals. First, the output of the good must be within the firm's capacity, B_{vj}, to produce:

$$_1L_{vj} \equiv B_{vj} - X_{vj} \geqslant 0. \tag{1.3}$$

Next, each firm aims for a minimum market share for each of its products. The desire of the firm to retain a foothold in the industry, at the expense of accepting a less-than-target rate of return or even negative profits on the good in the short run, seems well-grounded in empirical and theoretical grounds.[12] The clear preoccupation of firms with product competition, the desire to maintain plants at some viable fraction of capacity operation, and the urge to retain or enhance the market power that springs from market share, support this constraint as a general corporate goal.[13] We write it

$$_2L_{vj} \equiv X_{vj} - M_{vj}\sum_v X_{vj} \geqslant 0, \tag{1.4}$$

where M_{vj} is the target market share ratio for firm v in the production and sale of good j and the summed term is total product-group output.

The third general constraint reflects the costs to a firm of too rapid changes in prices, upward or downward. In Fog's study of large and medium-sized Danish firms, and in Haynes's study of small American firms, few cases of rigid full cost pricing were found.[14] A reluctance to raise prices the full extent of rapid cost increases coexistent with important price flexibility in response to demand were typical. The fear of adverse consumer or governmental reaction, a belief that within a certain interval of price change rivals would not react to destabilize the price structure, the desire to avoid stimulating union demands, the fear of public association of low price and low quality, a belief that within a certain interval the amount demanded does not respond appreciably to price change, and the reluctance to undergo the costs of revising and publishing price lists too frequently, are some of the important stimuli to put ceilings and floors on short-run price fluctuation.

We may state the constraint initially as

$$N_{vj} - \left(\frac{P_{vj}}{\bar{P}_{vj}} - 1\right)^2 \geqslant 0, \tag{1.5}$$

where $\bar{P}_{vj}$ is the exogenous price of the prior period and N_{vj} the square of the ratio of the maximum permitted price change. This constraint is concave, and hence consistent in a minimization problem with the convexity of the feasible region, but we may retain the linearity of the other elements in the constraint set and permit directional asymmetry by substituting constraints based upon the floor and ceiling limits. Let T_{vj}^+ be the maximum proportionate increase in price that is permissible, and T_{vj}^- the maximum proportionate decrease in price allowable. We then state:

1. $_3L_{vj} \equiv (1 + T_{vj}^+)\bar{P}_{vj} - P_{vj} \geqslant 0$

2. $_4L_{vj} \equiv P_{vj} - (1 - T_{vj}^-)\bar{P}_{vj} \geqslant 0.$
$$\tag{1.6}$$

2.1.1 Defining the Demand Function

In the interest of simplicity and the hope of empirical fitting in a domain of relevance, we assume the possibility of approximating the sales function by a linear relationship,

$$D_{vj} = a_{vj} - b_{vj}P_{vj} + \sum_{v^* \neq v} d_{vv^*j}P_{v^*j} + g_{vj}Y, \qquad (1.7)$$

where Y is an exogenously determined national income variable.

The intercept is assumed to vary with n, the number of products in the product group, and with s_{vv^*j}, the measure of closeness in quality space[15]:

$$a_{vj} = A_{vj}\left[n^{((\Sigma_v \cdot s_{vv^*j}/(n-1))-1)}\right],$$

where A_{vj} is a given parameter. If firm v were a monopolist, or if all of its rivals had products located at maximum distance 1 from its own, A_{vj} would be the amount of firm v's good the market would absorb at zero price. As more firms enter and/or as their products become closer in quality space to that of firm v's, a_{vj} is reduced - that is, sales shift left on the Marshallian grid.

The determination of d_{vv^*j} is similar:

$$d_{vv^*j} = (1 - s_{vv^*j})E_{vj},$$

with E_{vj} a parameter representing the impact upon firm v's sales of a product which is located at near-zero distance from firm v^*'s in quality space. As $s_{vv^*j}(= s_{v^*vj})$ rises toward 1, the impact is reduced and attains zero in that limit.[16]

The sales function, then, in final form, is written

$$D_{vj} = A_{vj}\left[n^{((\Sigma_v \cdot s_{vv^*j})/(n-1))-1)}\right] - b_{vj}P_{vj} + \sum_{v^* \neq v} (1 - s_{vv^*j})E_{vj}P_{v^*j} + g_{vj}Y.$$

The last pair of primary constraints assumes that the firm permits demand to exceed supply, but only within acceptable limits. That is, we permit the firm to set a price at which all of demand may not be satisfied,

$$_5L_{vj} \equiv D_{vj} - X_{vj} \geq 0, \qquad (1.8)$$

but the amount of disappointed demand is bounded:

$$_6L_{vj} \equiv U_{vj}X_{vj} - D_{vj} \geq 0, \qquad (1.9)$$

where U_{vj} is given.

We impose the usual nonnegativity constraints upon the variables:

$$X_{vj}, P_{vj} \geq 0, \qquad (1.10)$$

noting that these imply that $D_{vj} \geqslant 0$; but we permit r_{vj} to become negative. Finally, for future reference, we symbolize the right-hand sides of the constraints as follows:

$$_1R_{vj} = {}_2R_{vj} = {}_3R_{vj} = {}_4R_{vj} = {}_5R_{vj} = {}_6R_{vj} = 0.$$

2.2 The Flexibility of the Model

The model as constructed is an approach to a general theory of oligopoly, and possesses a potential for tailoring to specific industry conditions. As noted above, for the firm with a straightforward maximization-of-profits objective subject to the constraints, the $\bar{r}_{vj}$ parameter can be set in a range of upper bounds that preserves the convexity of the model.[17] Where market share goals are maxima rather than minima it is possible to state $_2L_{vj}$ as an upper bound. Where no effective limits on price change exist, as, for example in the medium-term model, the T^+ and T^- parameters may be set at levels that make constraints $_3L_{vj}$ and $_4L_{vj}$ ineffective. If market share or demand-supply constraints do not affect firm behavior, the same treatment can be afforded M_{vj} or U_{vj}.

Constraints and objective function can be interchanged to meet specific industry folkways. For example, where firms are more strongly motivated to maximize market share, $_2L_{vj}$ can be converted to become the objective function and can be maximized subject to the actual rate of return equalling or exceeding a target rate. The objective function in this case can be modelled after (1.2) with obvious modifications.

Price leadership as a pricing policy, subject to our existing constraints, can be accommodated by minimizing the deviation of the firm's price from the price of the leader (possibly adjusted for a customary differential). Because we shall extend the model to all firms in the whole product group, this interdependence can be handled with no difficulty.

Of course, no general theory will cover all empirical cases, most particularly in the field of rivalrous competition. However, one of the distinct advantages of the present theory is that it permits a great deal of flexibility in the way of changing objective functions and constraints as well as the type and intensity of interdependence.

2.3 The Industry Model

The industry's objective function is formed by summing the firms' objective functions:

$$Z_j = \sum_v Z_{vj}, \tag{1.11}$$

and the constraint set for the industry is simply the union of firm constraints $_1L_{vj}$ through $_6L_{vj}$ over firms, along with the nonnegativity constraints for all firms. Each firm seeks its equilibrium within the industry context, its actions constraining and being constrained by the prices and outputs of all its rivals, all of this mutual interdependence being prespecified in the firms' sales functions.

3 The Short-term Model under Profit Maximization

The nonlinear programming nature of the model proposed permits us to draw upon the theory and solution techniques developed in that field for the analysis of oligopoly in partial and in general equilibrium. In this section we shall make the special assumption that all firms in an industry attempt simultaneously to maximize profits subject to the the constraints. This assumption is introduced into the model by choosing an $\bar{r}_{vj}$ for each firm sufficiently high to be unattainable; however, to preserve the convexity of the model, we must set this target rate of return below an upper bound. This limitation on $\bar{r}_{vj}$ will be explained below.

3.1 The Primal Nonlinear Programming Problem: Necessary and Sufficient Conditions

In what follows we drop the subscript j to lighten notation, it being understood that we are dealing with one good (product-group). Further, we assume that the r_v variables have been eliminated from the objective function by substitution from (1.1) into (1.2), and the D_v variables have been eliminated from $_5L_v$ and $_6L_v$ by substitution from (1.7).

The Lagrangean form of the constrained problem is written

$$\mathscr{L}(\mathbf{X}_v, \mathbf{P}_v, \boldsymbol{\lambda}_v) = Z - \sum_v \sum_i \lambda_{v\,i} {}_iL_v, \tag{1.12}$$

which we minimize with respect to the primal variables $\mathbf{X}_v$ and $\mathbf{P}_v$ and maximize with respect to the dual variables $\boldsymbol{\lambda}_v$. Then $[\mathbf{X}_v^0, \mathbf{P}_v^0]$ is a local constrained optimum solution of Z, given the conformity of the constraints in its neighborhood to any of a number of sufficient conditions that guarantee the existence of finite $\lambda_v,$[18] only if a saddle point exists in $\mathscr{L}$ such that

$$\mathscr{L}(\mathbf{X}_v^0, \mathbf{P}_v^0, \lambda_v) \leqslant \mathscr{L}(\mathbf{X}_v^0, \mathbf{P}_v^0, \lambda_v^0) \leqslant \mathscr{L}(\mathbf{X}_v, \mathbf{P}_v, \lambda^0), \quad \mathbf{X}_v, \mathbf{P}_v, \lambda_v \geqslant 0.$$
$$(1.13)$$

The necessary conditions for this local saddle point are:

1. $\delta\mathscr{L}/\delta X_v = 2(r_v - \bar{r}_v)r_v/X_v \geqslant -_1\lambda_v + _2\lambda_v(M_v - 1) - \sum_{v*}{}_2\lambda_{v*}M_{v*}$

   $-_5\lambda_v + U_{v6}\lambda_v$, all v $\qquad\qquad (1.14)$

2. $X_v(\delta\mathscr{L}/\delta X_v) = 0$, all v

3. $\delta\mathscr{L}/\delta P_v = 2(r_v - \bar{r}_v)r_v/(P_v - C_v) \geqslant -_3\lambda_v + _4\lambda_v - b_{v5}\lambda_v +$

   $\sum_{v*} d_{vv*}E_{v*5}\lambda_{v*} + b_{v6}\lambda_v - \sum_{v*} d_{vv*}E_{v*6}\lambda_{v*}$, all v

4. $P_v(\delta\mathscr{L}/\delta P_v) = 0$, all v

5. $\delta\mathscr{L}/\delta_i\lambda_v \equiv {}_iL_v \geqslant 0$, all v, all i

6. $_i\lambda_v(_iL_v) = 0$, all v, all i

7. $\mathbf{X}, \mathbf{P}, \lambda \geqslant 0$.

When $0.33\bar{r}_v \leqslant r_v \leqslant \bar{r}_v$, each Z_v is convex, and therefore Z is convex.[19] For example, if we set $\bar{r}_v = 0.30$, then if r_v lies between 0.10 and 0.30 the objective function for firm v will be convex. Note that it is possible to set $\bar{r}_v$ for every v independently and in the light of its expected range of actual rates of return. When Z is convex, given the linearity of the constraints, conditions (1.14) are sufficient to guarantee that the global saddle point of $\mathscr{L}$ has been found, and, therefore, that the solution is the global constrained profit maximization solution for the model. If the condition on r_v is violated for one or more firms, a local constrained profit maximization is guaranteed by conditions (1.14). In what follows, we shall assume that we have a convex programming problem.

3.2 The Solution Where Demand Constrains

For a geometric representation of the model we assume that all oligopolists except firm 1 hold their X, P, and λ values constant at their equilibrium values. The $_iL_1$ functions in figure 1.1, therefore, are relevant for the general equilibrium of the product-group. From the viewpoint of practical expectations, we shall be interested in two cases for firm 1: the first is one in which the demand function constrains output and the second, which we shall treat briefly, is one in which it does not.

For the first case – which we expect to be the usual one in reality – we

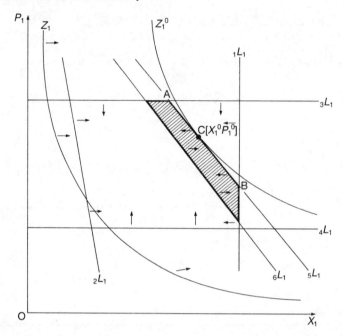

Figure 1.1   The feasible region for firm 1, objective function contours, and optimal solution.

can discern three subcases, depicted at points C, A, and B respectively on figure 1.1.

3.2.1 Subcase 1. Only Demand Constrains

At point C the contour of the objective function is tangent to the feasible region (outlined in bold lines and shaded) at a point where only the demand constraint holds as an equality with X_1 and $P_1 > 0$. We now further lighten notation by dropping the subscript 1 when no confusion results. Then, from (1.14: 1, 3, and 6) we obtain:

1. $2(r - \bar{r})r/X = -_5\lambda - \sum_{v^*}{}_2\lambda_{v^*}M_{v^*}$

2. $2(r - \bar{r})r/(P - C) = -b\,_5\lambda + \sum_{v^*}d_{vv^*}E_{vv^*}(_5\lambda_{v^*} - _6\lambda_{v^*})$ (1.15)

3. $D - X = 0.$

Remembering that the λ_{v^*} factors are treated as constants, we see that $dP/dD = -1/b$: moreover, the optimal objective function contour has slope $dP/dX = -(P - C)/X$. At point C these slopes are equal, as is demonstrated by eliminating $_5\lambda$ from (1.15:1, 2) and ignoring the λ_v. terms.

It is well known that if a constraint binds at the optimum, if $_iR$ is changed slightly, and if $\delta Z/\delta_iR$ exists at the relevant point,[20] then $_i\lambda = \delta Z/\delta_iR$. Thus

$$\delta Z/\delta_5R_1 = \delta Z_1/\delta_5R_1 = -2(r - \bar{r})r/X = _5\lambda = -\delta Z/\delta X. \quad (1.16)$$

A small rise in $_5R$ when the constraint is effective implies that supply X is reduced with demand constant, leading to a *fall* in profit of $(P - C)$, and, when $r \leqslant \bar{r}$, to a *rise* in Z.

3.2.2 Subcase 2. Demand and Upper or Lower Price Constraints Bind

We suppose now that the optimal solution occurs at A on figure 1.1, where both the demand and the upper price change constraints are effective. The point of support between the demand constraint and the contour of the objective function must occur with $dP/dX|_{z_1^0} \geqslant dP/dD$. Suppose the equality held, so that a tangency occurred: then a slight rise in $_3L$ would lead to an intersection with the demand constraint below the tangent objective function contour, and the optimal value of the objective function would be unaffected by the rise in the constraint. Hence, $\lambda_3 = 0$.

If the inequality of slope characterizes the functions at A, we may interpret a rise in $_3R$ as resulting from a slight fall in P, moving us to a higher objective function contour and hence to a rise in Z. That is,

$$\delta Z/\delta_3R = (\delta Z/\delta P)(\delta P/\delta_3)R = -\delta Z/\delta P = -2(r - \bar{r})r/(P - C) = _3\lambda.$$

These conditions are summarized in (1.14:1, 3, and 6) when we ignore the λ_v. terms:

1. $2(r - \bar{r})r/X = -_5\lambda$

2. $2(r - \bar{r})r/(P - C) = -_3\lambda - b_5\lambda$ (1.17)

3. $D - X = 0.$

Substitution from (1.16) to eliminate $_5\lambda$ in (1.17) yields

$$-_3\lambda = \delta Z/\delta P(1 - b\,dP/dX|_{z^0}). \quad (1.18)$$

But $\delta D/\delta P = -b$, and when $dP/dX|_{z^0} = (\delta D/\delta P)^{-1}$ it follows that $_3\lambda = 0$, and when the slopes are unequal the positive value of $_3\lambda$ is obtained.

When the demand and *lower* price constraints bind, the analysis is the same except that the slope of the objective function contour line must be equal to or *less than* $(\delta D/\delta P)^{-1}$.

3.2.3 Subcase 3. Demand and Capacity Constraints Bind

Suppose the optimum occurs at B on figure 1.1. At that point $dP/dX|_{z^0} \leqslant -1/b$. If the equality holds a rise in capacity will have no impact upon the optimum, and $_1\lambda = 0$, whereas if the inequality holds a smaller value of Z_1 will be attainable, so $_1\lambda \geqslant 0$. From (1.14:1, 3, and 6) once more, and again ignoring λ_{v^*} terms:

1. $2(r - \bar{r})r/X = -_1\lambda - _5\lambda$

2. $2(r - \bar{r})r/(P - C) = -b_5\lambda$ (1.19)

3. $D - X = 0$.

Substitutions of the form we have done in subcases 1 and 2 yield the expected results, and we omit the demonstration to save space.

3.3 The Solution Where Demand Does Not Constrain

On figure 1.2 is illustrated the second case of interest: the solution where firm 1's demand does not constrain. In this case we should expect the firm to produce as much as it can sell and to sell it at the highest price it can. A small

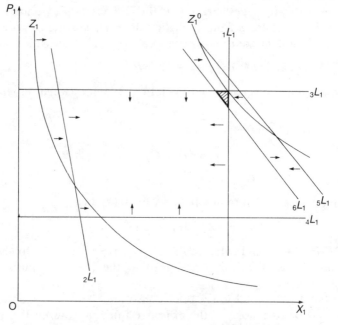

Figure 1.2 Optimal solution when the demand constraint does not bind.

rise in capacity will increase profits as will a rise in the upper price bound, so that by analyses parallel to (1.16) above we can show that $_1\lambda$ and $_3\lambda$ will be positive. The results are immediate from (1.14:1, 3, and 6), neglecting λ_{v^*} terms:

1. $2(r - \bar{r})r/X = -_1\lambda$

2. $2(r - \bar{r})r/(P - C) = -_3\lambda.$

In the interest of space conservation we neglect other cases in which the market share constraint and others bind. Note, in general, however, being upper and lower bound dual variables, at most only one of the $[_3\lambda, {}_4\lambda]$ and $[_5\lambda, {}_6\lambda]$ pairs can be positive, and we should expect in the general case that at most only one of the $[_1\lambda, {}_2\lambda]$ pair would be positive.

3.4 Equilibrium Displacement: an Extension of Classical Methods

The comparative statics of the model can be developed along two paths: an extension of existing equilibrium displacement techniques and the use of the newer methods of nonlinear parametric programming. We shall illustrate the first approach in this subsection and the second in subsection 3.5.

For small changes in parameters at an equilibrium, we may assume that (1) no constraint that is ineffective in the original position will become effective in the new position; (2) no constraint that is effective in the old solution will become ineffective in the new; (3) no variable that is zero in the old position will become positive in the displaced position; and (4) no variable that is positive in the original position will become zero in the new solution.[21]

To illustrate the method we assume a duopoly solution in which subcase 1 (only demand constrains) holds for both firms. Hence the equilibrium is described by two triads of equations (1.15), one each for firms 1 and 2, where $_2\lambda_1 = {}_2\lambda_2 = 0$. Suppose now that firm 1's costs, C_1, rises by dC_1: then, if we take total differentials of the six equations we obtain the following displacement system:

$$
\begin{bmatrix} \mathbf{A}_1 & \mathbf{B}_{12} \\ \mathbf{B}_{21} & \mathbf{A}_2 \end{bmatrix}
\begin{bmatrix} dX_1/dC_1 \\ dP_1/dC_1 \\ d_5\lambda_1/dC_1 \\ dX_2/dC_1 \\ dP_2/dC_1 \\ d_5\lambda_2/dC_1 \end{bmatrix}
=
\begin{bmatrix} a_{12}^1 \\ a_{22}^1 \\ 0 \\ 0 \\ 0 \\ 0 \end{bmatrix},
\qquad (1.20)
$$

where we define

$$a_{11}^v = 2r_v^2/X_v^2, \qquad a_{22}^v = 2r_v^2/(P_v - C_v)^2$$

$$a_{12}^v = (4r_v - 2\bar{r}_v)/K_v$$

b_{vv} is the (own-price) coefficient of P_v in v's sales function

b_{vv^*} is the (other-price) coefficient of P_{v^*} in v's sales function.

Then, for example

$$\mathbf{A}_1 = \begin{bmatrix} a_{11}^1 & a_{12}^1 & 1 \\ a_{12}^1 & a_{22}^1 & b_{11} \\ 1 & b_{11} & 0 \end{bmatrix}, \mathbf{B}_{12} = \begin{bmatrix} 0 & 0 & 0 \\ 0 & 0 & -b_{21} \\ 0 & -b_{12} & 0 \end{bmatrix}, \qquad (1.21)$$

and $\mathbf{A}_2$ and $\mathbf{B}_{21}$ are of similar form.

My pessimism concerning the "qualitative calculus" in general systems analysis is recorded at length elsewhere.[22] Our ability to progress in analytical directions depends upon the development of such frameworks as these which have hopes of empirical implementation. Note that in the bordered Hessians $\mathbf{A}_i$ the terms involve rates of return, outputs, prices, and sales curve coefficients – parameters we may have some hope of capturing from reality. Note too the lack of density of the $\mathbf{B}_{vv^*}$, which simplifies considerably the computational and data-collection tasks.

But the truth is that the simplicity of the displacement system (1.20) does permit us, with some plausible assumptions, to derive operational theorems in the absence of specification, and supports our conjecture in section 1 that oligopolistic displacement systems of this form may be richer than purely competitive as sources of theorems. By the convexity of the firms' objective functions the *unbordered* Hessians of $\mathbf{A}_v$ are positive definite or positive semi-definite. We have seen that convexity depends upon $r_v \leqslant \bar{r}_v \leqslant 3r_v$. If this is tightened to $2r_v \leqslant \bar{r}_v \leqslant 3r_v$, then $|\mathbf{A}_v| < 0$, which is of help in evaluating displacements.

However, a_{12}^v should be close to zero in realistic cases and in the present profit-maximizing case can be made arbitrarily close to zero by permitting, *ex post facto*, $\bar{r}_v$ to approach r_v. We shall set it to zero in our analysis. In addition, we may make the assumption (broadly interpreted) that own-price effects are greater than other price effects, or specifically that $b_{vv}b_{v^*v^*} > b_{vv^*}b_{v^*v}$. On the basis of these assumptions and the convexity of the firms' objective functions we can derive the following propositions for duopoly:

$$dX_1/dC_1 < 0 \qquad dX_2/dC_1 \gtreqless 0, > 0 \text{ if } (b_{11}b_{22} - b_{12}b_{21}) \leqslant 0$$

$$dP_1/dC_1 > 0 \qquad dP_2/dC_1 > 0 \text{ if } (b_{11}b_{22} - b_{12}b_{21}) \gtreqless 0 \qquad (1.22)$$

$$d_s\lambda_1/dC_1 < 0 \qquad d_s\lambda_2/dC_1 \geqslant 0 \text{ if } (b_{11}b_{22} - b_{12}b_{21}) \geqslant \frac{a_{22}^1 a_{22}^2 b_{21}}{a_{11}^1 b_{12}}.$$

Compared with the meager rewards of displacement analysis of traditional economic systems, these are rich payoffs to a few realistic assumptions.

3.5 Equilibrium Displacement: Parametric Programming

Instead of adapting the classical analysis we may adopt a formal parametric programming approach to the derivation of such theorems for specified or unspecified displacement systems. We assume:

Assumption 1. Z and $_iL_j$, all i, j, are twice differentiable functions of $\mathbf{X}, \mathbf{P}$.

Assumption 2. At the original equilibrium the necessary conditions (1.14) hold with $\mathbf{X}$ and $\mathbf{P}$ strictly positive.

Assumption 3. The problem is a convex problem, and the Hessian of Z positive definite.

Assumption 4. At the original equilibrium, the Jacobian with respect to $\mathbf{X}, \mathbf{P}$, and $\boldsymbol{\lambda}$ of (1.14:1 and 3) (equalities by assumption 2) and (1.14:6) is nonsingular;

Assumption 5. At the original equilibrium, the Jacobian of all $_iL_j = 0$ with respect to $\mathbf{X}$ and $\mathbf{P}$ is nonsingular;

Assumption 6. At the original equilibrium, strict complementarity of $_i\lambda_j$ and $_iL_j$ holds, so that when $_iL_j = 0$, $_i\lambda_j > 0$.

Assumptions 1, 2, and 4 are sufficient to assure that the initial equilibrium is a locally unique (isolated) local minimum, and assumption 3 assures that that local minimum is also a global minimum which is globally unique. Assumption 5 is a set of sufficient conditions to meet the qualification discussed in note 18. Finally, as will be seen, assumption 6 is needed to prevent the singularity of the matrix of the displacement system.

Let us now restate the model to prepare it for parametric displacement in the neighborhood of the equilibrium:

$$\text{minimize } Z + \theta\alpha(\mathbf{X}, \mathbf{P})$$

$$\text{subject to}$$

$$_iL_v + \theta_i\beta_v(\mathbf{X}, \mathbf{P}) \geqslant 0 \qquad (1.23)$$

$$X, P \geqslant 0.$$

The scalar-valued function $\alpha(\cdot)$ permits us to alter the objective function in desired ways, and θ is a small scalar which determines an equilibrium $[X(\theta), P(\theta)]$ in the neighborhood of the global minimum $[X(0), P(0)]$. The functions $_i\beta_v(\cdot)$, when bona fide functions, permit us to alter the form of the constraints, and when defined as constants change the values of the $_iR_v$. At the equilibrium, where $\theta = 0$, by assumptions 1 and 2, the necessary conditions hold:

$$\nabla Z + \theta \nabla \alpha - \sum_i \sum_v {}_i \lambda_v (\nabla {}_i L_v + \theta {}_i \beta_v) = 0$$

$$_i\lambda_v({}_iL_v + \theta {}_i\beta_v) = 0, \text{ all } i, v, \tag{1.24}$$

where ∇ denotes a (column) gradient vector of a variable with respect to all primal variables $\mathbf{X}, \mathbf{P}$. The equations (1.24) form the set of interrelationships for our new displacement system, corresponding to the set (1.15) in the older method.

Let us illustrate the method by changing C_1 again in the neighborhood of the equilibrium. If we assume that C_1 rises to $C_1 + m, m > 0$, then

$$Z_1 = (r_1 - \bar{r}_1)^2 + [m^2 r_1^2 / (P_1 - C_1)^2 + 2mr_1^2 / (P_1 - C_1) - 2mr_1\bar{r}_1 / (P_1 - C_1)]$$

$$= (r_1 - \bar{r}_1)^2 + \alpha(\mathbf{X}, \mathbf{P}).$$

Without loss of generality we may set $m = 1$, and, to deal with one parametric shock at a time, set all $_i\beta_v = 0$. The equilibrium relationships are then those of (1.24), although we shall rearrange them so that the equations obtained by differentiating with respect to firm j's primal variables (X_j and P_j) and those equations pertaining to firm j's constraints are grouped together. We then take total differentials of these equations to obtain the displacement system.

We define:

$_s\nabla \mathbf{Z}$:   A (column) vector of the partial derivatives of Z with respect to the primal variables of firm s. It is, therefore, the gradient of Z with respect to the primal variables of firm s.

$_{st}\nabla \mathbf{Z}$:   A matrix whose columns are the elements of $_s\nabla \mathbf{Z}$ differentiated with respect to the primal variables of firm t.

$_{st}\nabla \mathbf{G}_i$:   A (column) vector of the partial derivatives of the constraint $_iL_s$ with respect to the primal variables of firm t.

$_{st}\nabla \mathbf{G}$:   A matrix whose columns are $_{st}\nabla \mathbf{G}_i$ for all i.

$\mathbf{D}(\cdot)$:   A diagonal matrix whose diagonal elements are the terms in parantheses taken in natural order.

$_s\nabla \alpha$:   The gradient of α with respect to the primal variables of firm s.

T: Denotes the transpose of a matrix.

The general displacement system, therefore, can be depicted as follows:

$$
\begin{bmatrix}
{}_{11}\nabla Z & -{}_{11}\nabla G & {}_{12}\nabla Z & -{}_{21}\nabla G & \cdots \\
\mathbf{D}({}_i\lambda_1){}_{11}\nabla G & \mathbf{D}({}_iL_1) & \mathbf{D}({}_i\lambda_1){}_{12}\nabla G & 0 & \cdots \\
{}_{21}\nabla Z & -{}_{21}\nabla G & {}_{22}\nabla Z & -{}_{22}\nabla G & \cdots \\
\mathbf{D}({}_i\lambda_2){}_{21}\nabla G & 0 & \mathbf{D}({}_i\lambda_2){}_{22}\nabla G & \mathbf{D}({}_iL_2) & \cdots \\
\cdots & \cdots & \cdots & \cdots \\
\cdots & \cdots & \cdots & \cdots \\
\cdots & \cdots & \cdots & \cdots
\end{bmatrix}
\begin{bmatrix}
dX_1/d\theta \\ dP_1/d\theta \\ d\lambda_1/d\theta \\ dX_2/d\theta \\ dP_2/d\theta \\ d\lambda_2/d\theta \\ \cdot \\ \cdot \\ \cdot
\end{bmatrix}
=
\begin{bmatrix}
-{}_1\nabla\alpha \\ -{}_2\nabla\alpha \\ \cdot \\ \cdot \\ \cdot
\end{bmatrix}
$$

$$(1.25)$$

which may be symbolized as

$$
\begin{bmatrix}
\mathbf{A}_{11} & \mathbf{A}_{12} & \cdots \\
\mathbf{A}_{21} & \mathbf{A}_{22} & \cdots \\
\cdots\cdots\cdots\cdots\cdots
\end{bmatrix}
\begin{bmatrix}
d\mathbf{V}_1/d\theta \\ d\mathbf{V}_2/d\theta \\ \cdots\cdots
\end{bmatrix}
=
\begin{bmatrix}
-\mathbf{B}_1 \\ -\mathbf{B}_2 \\ \cdots
\end{bmatrix}.
\qquad (1.26)
$$

We may illustrate the simplicity of the system by reproducing $\mathbf{A}_{11}$ and $\mathbf{A}_{12}$ below:

$$
\mathbf{A}_{11} =
\begin{bmatrix}
\dfrac{2r_1^2}{X_1^2} & \dfrac{4r_1-2\bar{r}_1}{K_1} & 1 & -(M_1-1) & 0 & 0 & 1 & -U_1 \\[2mm]
\dfrac{4r_1-2\bar{r}_1}{K_1} & \dfrac{2r_1^2}{(P_1-C_1)^2} & 0 & 0 & 1 & -1 & b_{11} & -b_{11} \\[2mm]
-{}_1\lambda_1 & 0 & {}_1L_1 & 0 & 0 & 0 & 0 & 0 \\
-{}_2\lambda_1(1-M_1) & 0 & 0 & {}_2L_1 & 0 & 0 & 0 & 0 \\
0 & -{}_3\lambda_1 & 0 & 0 & {}_3L_1 & 0 & 0 & 0 \\
0 & {}_4\lambda_1 & 0 & 0 & 0 & {}_4L_1 & 0 & 0 \\
-{}_5\lambda_1 & -b_{11}{}_5\lambda_1 & 0 & 0 & 0 & 0 & {}_5L_1 & 0 \\
U_1{}_6\lambda_1 & b_{11}{}_6\lambda_1 & 0 & 0 & 0 & 0 & 0 & {}_6L_1
\end{bmatrix}
$$

$$(1.27)$$

$$
\mathbf{A}_{12} =
\begin{bmatrix}
0 & 0 & 0 & M_1 & 0 & 0 & 0 & 0 \\
0 & 0 & 0 & 0 & 0 & 0 & -b_{12} & b_{12} \\
0 & 0 & 0 & 0 & 0 & 0 & 0 & 0 \\
-{}_2\lambda_1 M_1 & 0 & 0 & 0 & 0 & 0 & 0 & 0 \\
0 & 0 & 0 & 0 & 0 & 0 & 0 & 0 \\
0 & 0 & 0 & 0 & 0 & 0 & 0 & 0 \\
0 & {}_5\lambda_1 b_{12} & 0 & 0 & 0 & 0 & 0 & 0 \\
0 & -{}_6\lambda_1 b_{12} & 0 & 0 & 0 & 0 & 0 & 0
\end{bmatrix}
$$

Once again we point to the ease of manipulation of large systems that springs from such nondense component matrices. The determinants of the matrices involved in displacement evaluations are simplified by the elimination of rows whose only nonzero element is a diagonal $_iL_j$ (always nonnegative), and by dividing out $-_5\lambda_1$ and $-_5\lambda_2$ terms. If we adopt the simplifying assumptions used in our classical displacement analysis of this problem we derive the theorems of (1.22).

Finally, it should be noted from $\mathbf{A}_{11}$ and $\mathbf{A}_{12}$ that if $_5\lambda_1$ or $_5\lambda_2$ is zero, the matrix of the system is singular, and recourse to the classical displacement methods will be necessary. This observation motivates the assumption of strict complementarity in assumption 6.

4 The Target Rate of Return: a Nonconvex Programming Model

Despite the success we have had in section 3 with a profit-maximizing model, as well as its lingering appeal to the profession, we remain stubbornly convinced that realistic attacks upon the differentiated oligopoly problem within general equilibrium frameworks demand a capability for dealing with the firm and industry that strains for a target rate of return as well.[23] It was noted in section 3 that when $\bar{r}_v$ lies within a stated interval the model may be treated as a convex profit-maximizing model. But in the real world it is not uncommon for target rates to be exceeded by actual rates, and for firms striving to get close to a target rate we must allow movements toward it from either direction.

We now alter the objective function of the firm to the following:

$$Z_v = \begin{cases} \exp(r_v - \bar{r}_v), \text{ if } r_v > \bar{r}_v \\ \log_e \bar{r}_v - \log_e r_v + 1, \text{ if } r_v \leqslant \bar{r}_v \\ 1/P_v, \text{ if } r_v < 0. \end{cases} \qquad (1.28)$$

The logarithmic branch and the branch for a negative r are convex in $\mathbf{X}$ and $\mathbf{P}$, but the exponential branch is strictly quasi-*concave* in those variables. Through the use of modern iterative solution techniques the relevant branch of each firm's objective function is always well-defined. The monotone transformations of (1.2) in the domain where $r_v \geqslant 0$ are better behaved than that function, and permit us to work with convex functions whenever $r_v \leqslant \bar{r}_v$; hence, the profit maximization model escapes the restrictions on r_v and $\bar{r}_v$ noted above. For cases other than the profit maximization model, however, when the exponential branch may be relevant, we must be reconciled to locating only local optima rather than global.

4.1 An Illustration of the Methods in a Fictional Oligopolistic Industry

To illustrate the methods we have constructed a five-firm differentiated oligopolistic product group, with data that in the largest part are wholly notional. In [10] I described methods to measure distances between products in a quality space, and illustrated them with experiments conducted with five candy bars and four sets of subjects. These results have been used in defining the sales functions below, and we have made the functions conform to Census of Manufactures, 1969, data for five and ten candy bar sales. Beyond this, however, our data are wholly fictional, and hence our results cannot be treated in any way as an analysis of the realistic candy bar product group.

The sales functions used are the following. Note that we have omitted the income term for convenience:

$$D_1 = 45000 - 70P_1 + 12.993\,(0.72P_2 + 0.45P_3 + 0.69P_4 + 0.65P_5)$$

$$D_2 = 34000 - 75P_2 + 16.463\,(0.72P_1 + 0.53P_3 + 0.74P_4 + 0.75P_5)$$

$$D_3 = 26910 - 52P_3 + 5.547\,(0.45P_1 + 0.53P_2 + 0.62P_4 + 0.64P_5)$$

$$D_4 = 29515 - 69P_4 + 12.149\,(0.69P_1 + 0.74P_2 + 0.62P_3 + 0.84P_5)$$

$$D_5 = 15500 - 35P_5 + 5.660\,(0.65P_1 + 0.75P_2 + 0.64P_3 + 0.84P_4),$$

having the form discussed in section 2.1.1 and defined in thousands of pounds of candy bars, with prices taken to be prices to wholesalers.

Other parameters adopted for the examples are listed in table 1.1. The industry contains two large-sized firms (firms 1 and 2) measured in terms of market-share goals and capacity, two medium-sized firms (firms 3 and 4), and one small firm (firm 5), whose high capitalization, low capacity, high cost, and low market share seem to mark it as a marginal unit. This pessimism is reinforced by firm 5's greater willingness to lower price and disappoint demand. For example, firms 1 and 2, as industry leaders, are more conservative on both these scores.

Table 1.1 Parameters assumed for fictional oligopoly: baseline case

Firm	P_{v0}	r_v	K_v	C_v	B_v	M_v	T_v^+	T_v^-	U_v
1	$ 725.86	0.28	$ 10.00m	$ 649	32,000	0.30	1.03	0.98	1.02
2	673.29	0.28	6.57	605	28,000	0.25	1.04	0.97	1.03
3	563.29	0.35	2.19	517	15,000	0.12	1.04	0.98	1.01
4	634.77	0.30	2.74	605	20,000	0.15	1.03	0.96	1.02
5	684.37	0.22	10.20	638	10,000	0.03	1.04	0.95	1.04

Firm 3 produces a distinctly different brand from the others, as indexed by its low cost and by the markedly low d_{3v}. coefficients in its sales function. The average of the d-coefficients (proximity is a rising function of the ds) for brand 3 is only 0.56, compared with 0.63 for brand 1, 0.69 for brand 2, and 0.72 for brand 4 and 5. Hence, in quality space, the industry leader enjoys some isolation from its competitors, but brand 3 is most isolated, whereas brands 2, 4, and 5 are relatively clustered.

4.1.1 The Short-run Model – Baseline Case

In table 1.2 are listed the seven successive short-run solutions beginning from an arbitrary state at $t = 0$ and ending with the attainment of a medium-term industry equilibrium in $t = 7$. The baseline case is a profit maximization model, the target rates of return having been set sufficiently high to assure that they bounded from above actual rates of return in all periods. The solutions were obtained using Fiacco and McCormick's Sequential Unconstrained Minimization Technique (SUMT), which employs a penalty

Table 1.2   Short-term solutions: baseline case

Var./t =	1	2	3	4	5	6	7	% initial
r_1	0.1172	0.1330	0.1561	0.1762	0.1919	0.1959	0.1900	0.1775	151
$X_1(=D_1)$	15,251	15,205	14,251	13,320	12,324	10,891	9,279	7,705	51
P_1	725.86	736.45	758.54	781.30	804.74	828.89	853.75	879.32	121
m_1	.334	0.360	0.365	0.379	0.392	0.373	0.336	0.300	99
r_2	0.1372	0.1743	0.1978	0.2112	0.2164	0.2166	0.2205	0.2229	162
$X_2(=D_2)$	13,204	11,683	10,298	8,927	7,850	7,312	7,199	6,936	53
P_2	673.29	703.04	731.16	760.41	786.15	799.60	806.28	816.16	121
m_2	0.289	0.277	0.264	0.254	0.250	0.250	0.260	0.270	94
r_3	0.1273	0.1524	0.1623	0.1849	0.1870	0.1915	0.1955	0.1991	156
$X_3(=D_3)$	6,022	5,544	5,689	4,726	3,768	3,748	3,778	3,735	62
P_3	563.29	577.20	579.49	602.67	625.72	628.89	630.32	633.73	113
m_3	0.132	0.131	0.146	0.134	0.120	0.128	0.137	0.145	110
r_4	0.0986	0.1643	0.1976	0.2231	0.2368	0.2436	0.2535	0.2617	265
$X_4(=D_4)$	9,080	7,585	6,830	6,124	5,363	5,145	5,210	5,115	56
P_4	634.77	664.35	684.28	704.81	725.95	734.75	738.30	745.18	117
m_4	0.199	0.80	0.175	0.174	0.171	0.176	0.188	0.199	100
r_5	0.0970	0.1179	0.1346	0.1582	0.1814	0.1949	0.2046	0.2159	223
$X_5(=D_5)$	2,133	2,200	1,940	2,045	2,094	2,152	2,187	2,193	103
P_5	684.37	692.64	708.77	716.89	726.33	730.39	733.43	738.43	108
m_5	0.047	0.052	0.050	0.058	0.067	0.074	0.079	0.085	181
ΣX_v	45,689	42,220	39,008	35,142	31,399	29,247	27,653	25,685	56
Σr_v	0.5773	0.7419	0.8484	0.9536	1.0135	1.0425	1.0641	1.0771	–

function approach to nonlinear programming.[24] Because the algorithm is not guaranteed to converge to an optimum for non-convex problems, our solutions below must be treated as approximations. After many trials from different initial positions, and from the internal structure of the models, we feel that the approximations are close to the global minima. However, it has been our experience that the functions are quite "flat-bottomed," so that rather large changes in the fortunes of specific firms in the neighbourhood of the minima do not change the objective function by much.

From an initial position in which prices were uniformly lower than the medium-term optimum, the industry decreased its output monotonically to about 56 percent of the initial level. The firms' rates of return rose over the adjustment period, with the upper price change and demand-supply constraints binding typically in the short-run equilibria, with an occasional holding of the market share constraint (firm 1 in $t = 7$, firm 2 in $t = 4$ and 5, and firm 3 in $t = 4$).

Most interestingly, the improvement in firms' profits was closely correlated with their general *proximity* in quality space to their rivals, not their degree of protective isolation. Brands 4 and 5 show this most dramatically, the latter increasing its price and output over time, the former increasing its price, and both recording large increases in the rate of return. On the other hand, brand 3 – which we have seen to be furthest away from its competitors in its qualities and which enjoys low costs as well – records a distinctly mediocre performance, with the next to smallest rise in the rate of return in the industry.

But the market leaders, brands 1 and 2, offer the large surprises, each sacrificing market share and enjoying rises in rates of return of only 51 percent (the lowest of all firms) and 62 percent respectively. Firm 1, with its high degree of insulation in product quality space, and its dominance of the market, obtained the lowest rate of return of any rival. Moreover, both market leaders have high (negative) own-price response coefficients and medium-high (positive) other-price sales response coefficients; yet both registered the maximum price increases of 21 percent.

Of course, in reality we would never observe such a process of medium-term equilibrium achievement from an initial position so far from the terminal one. But this does not detract from its interest. It reveals the underlying strength of firms 4 and 5, the surprising weakness of firm 3, and the vulnerability of the market leaders. It suggests a strong tendency for prices to move upward and quantity to be restricted, as well as the desirability of locating products closer to competitors rather than further away.

4.1.2 The Medium-run Model – Four Cases

We now abstract from the dynamic path of approach to a medium-term equilibrium and study finite displacements of the baseline case equilibrium after all price adjustment has been made. These medium-term equilibria are obtained by making the upper and lower price change constraints of the short-term model ineffective. We compare the results of the displacement in every case with the baseline medium-term equilibrium.

1. *Case 1. M_3 rises from 0.12 to 0.15.* In this case firm 3 strives to obtain an increase in its market share. The results, with absolute changes from the base line solution, are given in table 1.3. The m_v data are the achieved market shares of the firms.

This case is meant to approximate an infinitesimal displacement of the base line equilibrium, and the resulting absolute changes in the variables reflect this. Interestingly, this striving for market share enhancement by a rival *lowers* industry output and *raises* all prices but that of initiating firm 3. Moreover, it raises firm 3's actual rate of return, as well as firm 5's, whereas all other rates fall.

Table 1.3   Case 1 solution

Firm	r_v	Diff. from baseline	$X_v (= D_v)$	Diff. from baseline	P_v	Diff. from baseline	m_v	Diff. from baseline
1	0.1773	−0.0001	7,683	−20	$879.80	0.43	0.300	0.000
2	0.2210	−0.0018	6,830	−97	817.59	1.30	0.267	−0.003
3	0.2015	0.0024	3,842	107	631.85	−1.89	0.150	0.005
4	0.2606	−0.0012	5,066	−50	745.98	0.78	0.198	−0.001
5	0.2161	0.0001	2,190	−5	738.66	0.26	0.085	0.000

$\Sigma X = 25,611$
$Z = 1.4042$

Firm 3's product is closest in quality space to firm 5's and firm 4's, is quite distant from firm 2, and is furthest from firm 1. We should expect the competitive impacts of firm 3's price reduction to diminish in this same progression, but no simple pattern emerges. Indeed, firm 5 is all but unaffected and improves its profit position slightly by virtue of firm 3's initiative. As in the study of the short-run model, the interdependence among the products is clearly too complicated to permit easy *ex ante* conjectures.

2   *Case 2. M_5 rises from 0.03 to 0.10.* Inspired by the remarkable poise of firm 5 in the face of such challenges, I shocked the baseline case slightly by assuming firm 5 strove to improve its market position from its actual base line share of 8.5 percent to 10 percent. The results are given in table 1.4.

Table 1.4   Case 2 solution

Firm	r_v	Diff. from baseline	$X_v(=D_v)$	Diff. from baseline	P_v	Diff. from baseline	m_v	Diff. from baseline
1	0.1779	−0.0005	8,007	304	$871.15	−8.22	0.300	0.000
2	0.2195	−0.0033	7,059	132	809.28	−7.01	0.265	−0.005
3	0.1958	−0.0033	3,767	32	630.84	−2.90	0.141	−0.004
4	0.2546	−0.0072	5,186	70	739.54	−5.66	0.194	−0.005
5	0.2200	0.0040	2,670	475	772.04	−16.36	0.100	0.015

ΣX = 26,688
Z = 1.4421

In this case the results are much more in line with expectations. Firm 5's struggle to increase market share pushes all prices down and increases all firms' outputs. Moreover, the actual rates of return of all firms fall except for that of the remarkable firm 5 itself, whose rate *rises*; despite the large fall in price the move entails, the customer response is great enough to increase its profits. Hence it benefits in both market share and returns.

Enhanced competition forces industry output up, firm 1's sales rises sharply to maintain its market share at the minimum acceptable level. Firm 5's rise in market share is taken about evenly from the remaining three rivals, with firm 4 – whose product is nearest in quality space to firm 5's – suffering most in profit reduction.

Case 2, therefore, exhibits the commonly expected results of oligopolistic competition – lower prices, higher outputs, lower rates of return – with the exception of firm 5's slight profit rise.

3   *Case 3. All costs rise 10 percent.* With this case we move away from small displacements to assume that all firms undergo cost rises of 10 percent. The solution values are listed in table 1.5, the numbers in parentheses beneath price changes being the rise in prices that would have occurred had all cost change been passed along to the consumer.

Clearly, the impacts of the cost rise are quite severe on all firms, leading to reductions in rates of return from 4 to 7.5 percentage points. The industry's output falls by 15 percent, and prices rise between 3 and 5 percent – considerably less, however, than the cost increases. Once again, firm 5 demonstrates its strength by suffering the smallest rate of return reduction, lifting price the smallest percentage, and actually increasing its market share. Firm 2 is the largest loser in these same dimensions; its sales suffer from large own-price sensitivity, but beyond this there seems little else that would account for its very poor performance.

The remaining firms are intermediate in their reactions, although firm 4 does enjoy a slight increase in market share. Firm 1, despite the fact that its

Table 1.5   Case 3 solution

Firm	r_v	Diff. from baseline	$X_v (= D_v)$	Diff. from baseline	P_v	Diff. from baseline	m_v	Diff. from baseline
1	0.1249	-0.0525	6,524	$-1,179$	$906.51	27.14 (64.90)	0.300	0.000
2	0.1480	-0.0748	5,760	$-1,167$	844.78	28.49 (60.50)	0.265	-0.005
3	0.1370	-0.0621	3,120	-615	651.19	17.45 (51.70)	0.143	-0.002
4	0.1964	-0.0654	4,407	-709	767.12	21.92 (60.50)	0.203	0.004
5	0.1725	-0.0435	1,937	-258	756.87	18.47 (63.80)	0.089	0.004

$\Sigma X = 21{,}747$
$Z = 3.0492$

minimum market share constraint is binding, is forced to cut its rate of return by the least of the three. Firm 3, rather surprisingly given its remoteness from other products, is notably unable to pass its cost increases along to wholesalers, and suffers large losses in output and profits as well as market share.

In summary, case 3 presents some of the recurrent themes of our analysis to date: the strength of firm 5 amidst the appearance of weakness, the failure of product isolation to protect, and the difficult nature of the interdependence. In addition, a surprising inability of the interdependent, multiple-objective profit maximization environment to permit a large portion of the cost increase to be shifted forward, even in the medium run, must be listed as unexpected.

4   *Case 4. All target rates set at 0.12.* To obtain an example where all firms are forced to reduce their rates of return to achieve target rates, we set the target rates uniformly at 0.12. The results are presented in table 1.6.

Not surprisingly, in general it is the stronger profit performers of the previous cases who suffer most when target rates of return are reduced below potentials (say by incomes policy regulators). The losses in percentage points in case 4 are in the same order as the actual rates of return registered in case 1. For the first time we encounter a case where demand and supply are not equalized: a discrepancy arises in brand 3. Brand 3 has actually enlarged its market share by a small amount, and has registered the smallest absolute price climb of any of the rivals. Had firm 3 raised its price to eliminate the excess demand it would, in the first instance, have moved further from the target rate of return, and would have inspired upward movements in the profits of some of the other firms, which would have moved Z positively.

Table 1.6 Case 4 solution

Firm	r_v	Diff. from baseline	$X_v(=D_v)$	Diff. from baseline	P_v	Diff. from baseline	m_v	Diff. from baseline
1	0.1200	−0.0574	3,646	−4,057	\$978.10	98.73	0.337	0.037
2	0.1313	−0.0915	2,711	−4,216	923.92	107.00	0.250	−0.020
3	0.1319	−0.0672	1,609*	−2,126	696.55	62.81	0.149	0.004
4	0.1697	−0.0463	2,024	−3,092	834.77	89.57	0.187	−0.012
5	0.1481	−0.0679	833	−1,362	819.34	80.94	0.077	−0.008

$\Sigma X = 10,823$
$Z = 0.00596$ * $D_3 = 1,625$

The most interesting consequence, however, is the sharp upward price movement and downward quantity adjustment in the product group. Our solutions are in the region of elastic demand, where upward price movements are necessary to reduce profits. However, the lesson is made in such cases that an attempt to regulate oligopolistic industries by setting upper limits on their rates of return, when those firms have a set of multiple objectives to achieve, may be strongly contrary to the interests of consumers. In our case wholesalers are paying prices from 6¢ to 11¢ per pound more for candy bars and purchasing less than half their former amounts.

5 A Final Word

The theoretical framework developed in this paper has several advantages to alternative oligopoly models. First, it confronts the problems of differentiated oligopoly explicitly and absorbs them. Second, it incorporates the empirical results of recent investigators, notably the multi-objective nature of the firm's decisionmaking and the inappropriateness of frameworks centered on reaction functions. Third, it permits the exploitation of linear and nonlinear programming theory, as well as the parametric programming techniques associated with them. Fourth, the simplicity of its functions gives hope of empirical implementation of the analysis. And, lastly, its modular simplicity permits the general equilibrium theoretical task to be approached with some prospect of success and empirical usefulness.

Appendix

The Sequential Unconstrained Minimization Technique (SUMT) is a penalty function algorithm for the solution of linear and nonlinear programming problems. It was developed by Anthony Fiacco and Garth McCormick at the Research Analysis Corporation (now the General Research Corporation), McLean, Virginia, USA, from which the FORTRAN IV version is available. In the present author's opinion, it is one of the most robust, least temperamental, and generally applicable programming algorithms available. It is sparing of computer core storage and relatively rapid in execution time. Not only is it capable of solving linear and nonlinear programming problems, but it will also permit the mixing of inequalities and equalities in the constraint set. Although, like all programming routines, it is capable of finding only local constrained optima except under convex programming conditions, in our experience it performs well even in nonconvex conditions.

Penalty function approaches to solving nonlinear programming problems involve the solution of a sequence of *unconstrained* problems (with the simplifications they entail) whose solutions, in the case of a convex problem, can be shown to converge to the solution of the original constrained problem. Consider the problem

$$\min Z = f(\mathbf{X}) \tag{A1}$$

subject to

$$g_j(\mathbf{X}) \geqslant 0$$
$$\mathbf{X} \geqslant 0, \tag{A2}$$

where $f(\mathbf{X})$ is convex and all $g_j(\mathbf{X})$ are concave.

Convert the problem to subproblem 1 by defining the *penalty function*

$$P(\mathbf{X}, r_1) = f(\mathbf{X}) - r_1 \left(\sum_j \log_e g_j(\mathbf{X}) \right), \tag{A3}$$

where r_1 is a chosen positive scalar, and which may be treated as an unconstrained function to be minimized.

Moreover, $P(\mathbf{X}, r_1)$ is convex, and hence its minimum may be obtained in straightforward fashion by setting the gradient vector equal to zero:

$$\frac{\partial P}{\partial X_i} = \frac{\partial f}{\partial X_i} - r_1 \left[\sum_j \frac{1}{g_j(\mathbf{X})} \cdot \frac{\partial g_j}{\partial X_i} \right] = 0, \text{ all } i. \tag{A4}$$

The choice of an initial $\mathbf{X}^0$ interior to the feasible region assures that none of the $g_j(\mathbf{X})$ functions becomes zero (i.e. the initial $\mathbf{X}^0$ does not lie on a boundary of the feasible region) and permits a solution to system (A4) by Newton's method, Fletcher–Powell search, or other numerical iteration technique for solving systems of *equalities*.

The purpose of the negative term in (A3) is, paradoxically, to keep the solution of the subproblem away from the boundary of the feasible region

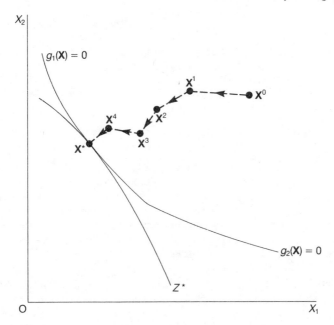

Figure 1.3   Penalty function subproblems sequence.

where (in general) the solution of the original problem which we seek lies. This can be seen by assuming that any $g_j(\mathbf{X}) = 0$, giving rise to a $+\infty$ term in (A4). Since we are minimizing $P(\mathbf{X}, r_1)$, obviously that minimum must occur at some interior point of the feasible region. Indeed, the closer we get to any boundary point of that region, the greater must $P(\mathbf{X}, r_1)$ become.

But suppose we use the solution $\mathbf{X}^1$ to $P(\mathbf{X}, r_1)$ as a new initial point, and set up the *new* penalty function $P(\mathbf{X}, r_2)$ in (A3), where $r_2 < r_1$. Reducing the size of the positive scalar r lessens the importance of the penalty term and permits $\mathbf{X}^2$ to move closer to the boundary of the feasible region. By setting up the sequence $r_1 > r_2 > r_3 > \ldots$, a sequence of penalty function subproblems is derived whose solutions can be shown to converge, for convex programming problems, upon the solution $\mathbf{X}^*$ to the original problem defined in (A1) and (A2). The sequence is demonstrated in figure 1.3, where Z^* is the optimal objective function contour, $g_j(\mathbf{X}) = 0$ are the boundaries of the feasible region, and $\mathbf{X}^i$ is the sequence of subproblem solutions derived for $r_1 > r_2 > r_3 > \ldots$.

Moreover, for the convex problem, there exists a dual whose solution forms a lower bound for the original problem as the subproblems yield upper bounds. Even though the latter never arrive at the boundary, the values of $P(\mathbf{X}, r_i)$, $i = 1, 2, 3, \ldots$, approach the boundary solution as a limit, as does the series of solutions to the dual problems. By specifying the difference between the solutions to the subproblems and duals that he is willing to tolerate, the user can control the degree of precision in the final approximation and obtains upper and lower bounds for the true answer.

Notes

* Originally published in *De Economist* , 122 (1974), 471–502, and reproduced with permission.

[1] The earliest work in this area was that of Pareto [15], pp. 224, 333, 594–8, 613, in which he dealt briefly with a world of pure monopolies. Triffin [19] wrote a classic extended consideration of the problems of incorporating product differentiation within general equilibrium contexts, pleading that oligopoly be accepted as the only worthwhile goal of such efforts. However, he did not move far from the partial equilibrium frameworks of Marshall and Chamberlin, his effort having most value in pointing up the need for a revision. Negishi [14], in a brief, formal analysis, has essentially extended the Pareto-type model to include both pure and "monopolistic" competition. Finally, in [9] I used the concept of "quality space" to build a general equilibrium model incorporating monopoly, monopolistic competition, and pure competition – that is, non-rivalrous forms of competition. The present paper is an attempt to project the methods and concepts of [9] to rivalrous competition, remaining, however, at the industry level. In [11] I have constructed a small general equilibrium model from the industry modules of the present paper. [I have since sought to incorporate oligopoly into a geneal equilibrium framework in *Rivalrous Consonance: a Theory of General Oligopolistic Competition*, North-Holland, Amsterdam, 1986.]

[2] Compare Joe S. Bain [2], p. 4: "Examination of any considerable number of concentrated industries reveals great differences in market conduct and performance among them, in spite of the fact that in each a recognized interdependence among established sellers definitely appears to be present."

[3] For a general summary of Wärneryd's work, see Johnsen [6], chapter 3.

[4] Kaplan, Dirlam and Lanzillotti [7] found this goal the most frequently stressed by the large firms in their study (p. 130), but it is typical of the poorly coordinated decision-making of the corporations that they found it to be of concern at the higher levels of management, the lower rungs of officialdom stressing profit margins on sales (p. 17).

[5] This goal is emphasized by Bain [2], Andrews [1], and Sylos-Labini [17], among others. It has not been considered explicitly in the models to follow.

[6] For example, cf. [7]: "The officials who discussed policy with the interviewers found it difficult to analyze pricing as a separate activity distinct from others entering into company policy. Pricing decisions were made or influenced by executives from production, development, engineering, accounting, finance, sales, and public relations divisions. They were usually considered part of the general strategy for achieving a broadly defined goal" (p. 3). And: "Indeed, top management frequently did not take these decisions and was surprisingly ignorant of the manner in which they were derived – that is, prices" (p. 5).

[7] Quoting from [7] again, we find: "Economists, legislators, and the public generally would like to see pricing decisions by big companies analyzed in logical fashion, with historical comparisons of competitors' prices, cost factors, and profit margins given consistent and quantitative weight in detailed memoranda of officials involved. Unfortunately for those who would insist on fully ordered business behavior, such strategic memoranda summarizing the considerations at an important conference leading to a price decision are rarely found. Perhaps the presumed formal conference was never held. Even where the people doing the pricing tended to have certain staff information placed before them while making up their minds, whether and just how that information was taken into consideration often remained obscure. There was no document tracing the steps by which the staff information could be said to account for the price decision. Repeatedly, reference was made to the 'art' or 'feel' of pricing rather than observance of a formula" (p. 5).

[8] Among modern treatments, Tun Thin's [18] typifies this "monolithic" approach. He identifies two possible motives of the oligopolist: either (1) to seek the maximum payoff for himself regardless of the impacts on his rivals, or (2) to wage a price war to kill them off even at the cost of his own profits (p. 57). This type of "vision" does not gain support from empirical study.

[9] I have discussed product competition at length in [9], pp. 225–34.

[10] In [9] I have developed the idea of a quality space and the distances of products from one another in it. Experiments with techniques for implementing the theory are described in [10].

[11] These procedures are detailed and illustrated in [10]. However, the model can be developed in terms that are not dependent upon the idea of quality space or upon the ability to measure distances in it.

[12] Lanzillotti concluded from his study of large-scale firms that market share was mentioned almost as frequently as target rate of return as a pricing motivation ([130, p. 932).

[13] Lanzillotti found that among large corporations this constraint was more frequently an upper bound on pricing policy. See [13], pp. 932–4.

[14] See [4], pp. 30, 43–5, and 103, and [5], p. 32. Haynes found full cost to be a reference point, however – typically, a floor to price.

[15] Alternatively, a_{vj} may be viewed as an econometrically determined parameter.

[16] Or, d_{vv^*j} may be viewed as an econometrically determined parameter.

[17] This case is dealt with at length in section 3.

[18] The conditions are necessary to insure that (in a minimization problem) there exists no vector in the neighborhood of the asserted optimum along which it is possible to move lower on the objective function while remaining in the feasible region. When the set of such vectors is empty (assuming the objective and constraint functions are at least once differentiable) the necessary and sufficient conditions for the existence of the dual variables hold. Any number of conditions will imply the set of vectors is empty. See, for example, [3], pp. 2–25.

[19] In section 4 I will state an alternative model which is everywhere convex.

[20] If a constraint is shifted by a change in its restraint when that constraint falls at an existing corner of the feasible region, the relevant partial derivative of the objective function with respect to the restraint does not exist. It is then necessary to specify the left-hand and right-hand derivatives of this function.

[21] For a fuller discussion of the methodology, see [8], pp. 104–7.

[22] See [12], chapter 1.

[23] We have already discussed the importance of the target rate of return in the findings of [7] and [13]. See also Fog's conclusion ([4], p. 31): "A definite impression was obtained that the conception of a reasonable profit in contrast to maximum profit plays a distinct role and that it cannot merely be rejected as an empty phrase. Industrialists are unpleasantly affected when making too big a profit, and they would definitely not like to be criticized for charging inordinate prices." We should remark, however, that Haynes did not find target rates of return stressed among the small firms he studied ([5], p. 78).

[24] An explanation of the method will be found in the appendix to this chapter. A more detailed presentation is contained in Fiacco and McCormick [3].

References

[1] Andrews, P. W. S., *Manufacturing Business*, Longman, London, 1949.

[2] Bain, Joe S., *Barriers to New Competition*, Harvard University Press, Cambridge, MA, 1956.

[3] Fiacco, Anthony V., and Garth McCormick, *Nonlinear Programming: Sequential Unconstrained Minimization Technique*, John Wiley, New York, 1968.

[4] Fog, Bjarke, *Industrial Pricing Policies: an Analysis of Pricing Policies of Danish Manufacturers*, North-Holland, Amsterdam, 1960.

[5] Haynes, W. Warren, *Pricing Decisions in Small Business*, University of Kentucky Press, Lexington, 1962.

[6] Johnsen, Erik, *Studies in Multiobjective Decision Models*, Studentlitteratur, Lund, 1968.

[7] Kaplan, A. D. H., Joel B. Dirlam and Robert F. Lanzillotti, *Pricing in Big Business: a Case Approach*, Brookings, Washington, DC, 1958.

[8] Kuenne, Robert E., *Microeconomic Theory of the Market Mechanism: a General Equilibrium Approach*, Macmillan, New York, 1968.

[9] —— (ed.), *Monopolistic Competition Theory: Studies in Impact*, John Wiley, New York, 1967. [Reprinted as chapter 8 of this volume.]

[10] ——, "Toward the Incorporation of Product Differentiation in Economic Theory: The Uses of Inexact Measurement", *Applied Economics*, 6 (1974), 255–73. [Reprinted as chapter 12 of this volume.]

[11] ——, "Towards an Operational General Equilibrium Theory with Oligopoly: Some Experimental Results and Conjectures", *Kyklos*, 27 (1974) 792–819. [Reprinted as chapter 2 of this volume.]

[12] ——, *The Theory of General Economic Equilibrium*, Princeton University Press, Princeton, 1963.

[13] Lanzillotti, Robert F., "Pricing Objectives in Large Companies", *American Economic Review*, 49 (1959), 921–40.

[14] Negishi, Takashi, "Monopolistic Competition and General Equilibrium", *Review of Economic Studies*, 28 (1961), 196–201.

[15] Pareto, Vilfredo, *Manuel d'Economie Politique*, Giard et Brière, Paris, 1909.

[16] Shubik, Martin, *Strategy and Market Structure*, John Wiley, New York, 1959.

[17] Sylos-Labini, Paolo, *Oligopoly and Technical Progress*, Harvard University Press, Cambridge, MA, 1969.

[18] Tun Thin, *Theory of Markets*, Harvard University Press, Cambridge, MA, 1960.

[19] Triffin, Robert, *Monopolistic Competition and General Equilibrium Theory*, Harvard University Press, Cambridge, MA, 1949.

2

Toward an Operational General Equilibrium Theory with Oligopoly: Some Experimental Results and Conjectures

1 The Goals

Modern general equilibrium theory suffers from two well-known shortcomings that have kept it from the mainstream of theoretical development and forced it to become a murky backwater inhabited by a covey of specialists. First, it has failed to move away from the stultifying assumption of pure competition to the more realistic forms of monopolistic competition; indeed, the application of point set topology and sophisticated real analysis during the last 25 years have reinforced its attachment to pure competition as well as other more arcane regularities and simplifications. Second, even within this antiseptic environment, little progress has been made in escaping the limitations of the pure deductive method that inhere in large scale (i.e. general) systems. *A priori* restrictions have not been sufficiently exclusive of alternative states of the economic system to permit the derivation of useful qualitative theorems with empirical content. Where unambiguous deductions have been achieved, more frequently than not highly unrealistic and restrictive assumptions have been adopted to that end.

This paper is one of a series that attempt the development of an operational framework for the analysis of differentiated oligopoly in an industry and interindustry context. In [3] I developed the notion of a *quality-space* in which the distances between goods in an industry (*product group*) could be measured. These concepts and methods were made operational in [6], and an experiment with four independent samples of subjects, five well-known

Originally published in *Kyklos*, 27 (1974), 792–819, and reproduced with permission of Helbing & Lichtenhahn Verlag AG, Basle and Frankfrut am Main.

48

brands of candy bar, and seven product characteristics (*qualities*) showed encouraging results. It was possible to "measure" the proximity of each candy bar to every other and to envision the use of these distances as parameters in the brands' sales functions.

A new approach to an operational general theory of oligopoly is stated in detail in [5], which exploits recent empirical findings concerning oligopolistic behaviour and the modern techniques of nonlinear programming. This framework permits a flexible approach to describing the equilibrating tendencies of the rivalrous industry, and constitutes the theoretical module from which the general equilibrium system of the present paper will be molded. Finally, I have employed such an industry model in [7] to show how an incomes policy can be enlightened by demonstration of the possibility of perverse moves in prices and outputs induced by straightforward regulatory restrictions on rates of return.

To save space I shall sketch in section 2 the rationale of the analyses in [5] and [6] only insofar as it is directly relevant to the general equilibrium model in the current paper. In section 3 I build a two-industry interdependence model with specified functions and obtain a "baseline solution" by nonlinear programming techniques. Section 4 attempts unsuccessfully to apply classic displacement analysis to the baseline solution and resorts to approximation by small finite cost movements. A large number of finite equilibrium displacements from changes in firms' factor costs from their baseline values was obtained; the results of these experiments are summarized in section 5, along with some attempts to apply econometric techniques to extract "laws" from the solutions. Finally, some conclusions and conjectures based upon the model and its displacement – most particularly, some persistent perversities in price and output movements with empirical interest – are discussed in section 6.

2 An Oligopolistic Industry Module

The research of empirical workers in several developed nations is yielding a tableau of realistic oligopolistic behavior at serious variance from that implicit in existing theoretical models. The typical mature oligopoly is a multi-objective planner whose reactions to rivals in the pricing decision are unexpectedly passive, which has a concern for the stability of the industry and therefore that its rivals' profits permit a viable equilibrium, and whose approach to decision-making is much more inward-looking and much less focused and purposive than those frameworks envisage. A multi-objective model incorporating these characteristics is stated in the following form, incorporating this "rivalrous consonance" in a specific manner that may be modified to accommodate different industry folkways by converting constraints to objective function and vice versa (see [5]).

We distinguish m industries in the economy, symbolized i, and within each we assume the existence of firms $j = 1, 2, \ldots, n$, where n varies from industry to industry. For convenience we assume that firms and product brands are in 1–1 correspondence so that we may identify brands and firms. To illustrate, let us choose firm $\mathcal{F}$ in group I for analysis, denoting firms other than $\mathcal{F}$ in I as the set $\mathcal{F}'$.

Suppose that firms strive in the pricing and production of their brands to minimize the deviation of the actual rate of return, r, gross or net of taxes, from a target rate of return $\bar{r}$, where the actual rate is defined in terms of sales X, price P, dedicated capital base K, and given constant unit costs C. The objective function of the firm might then be defined as

$$Z_{I,J} = \{ [X_{I,J}(P_{I,J} - C_{I,J}) | K_{I,J}] - \bar{r}_{I,J} \}^2 \qquad (2.1)$$

where K is the capital devoted by the firm to the production of brand I, $\mathcal{F}$. The industry's objective function is defined as

$$Z_I = Z_{I,J} + \sum_{J'} Z_{I,J'}$$

Unfortunately, however, (2.1) is convex in X and P only for $r \leqslant \bar{r} \leqslant 3\,r$, so that, for example, if a firm's actual rate is above its target rate that firm's function is not necessarily globally convex. It follows that Z_I is not necessarily globally convex and hence local constrained minima are not necessarily global. Therefore, we shall transform the firms' objective functions to obtain positive monotone transformations that are better (but not ideally) behaved. For firm I, $\mathcal{F}$ we employ the function:

$$Z_{I,J} = \begin{cases} \exp(r_{I,J} - \bar{r}_{I,J}), & \text{if } r_{I,J} \geqslant \bar{r}_{I,J} \\ \log_e \bar{r}_{I,J} - \log_e r_{I,J} + 1, & \text{if } 0 \leqslant r_{I,J} \leqslant \bar{r}_{I,J} \\ 1/P_{I,J}, & \text{if } r_{I,J} < 0 \end{cases} \qquad (2.2)$$

For $r \geqslant 0$, the logarithmic branch of the function is globally convex in X and P; unfortunately, however, the exponential branch is quasi-*concave* and we therefore violate a sufficient condition (given the convexity of the feasible region) for a global minimum. In the negative domain for r the objective is to minimize $(\bar{r} - r)$ by moving r to positive values if possible. With constant costs this implies that price should be raised (its inverse lowered), and in this domain $Z_{I,J}$ is once more convex.

However, an important conclusion follows: if every firm strives to maximize profits, we may set each $\bar{r}$ to an unrealistically high level; we are then assured of remaining in the convex portion of the objective function and of obtaining a global minimum. Further, Z_I as the sum of firms' functions will be convex and the industry minimum also global. In the analysis to follow I shall exploit this feature *of the industry model*, but with the understanding that straightforward attempts to attain a target rate of return or, indeed, other motivations, are possible adoptions for the approach.

The industry objective function to be minimized is then

$$Z_I = Z_{I,J} + \sum_{J'} Z_{I,J'} \tag{2.3}$$

Each firm strives for a minimum $Z_{I,J}$ subject to (1) the implicit restrictions that exist in a joint objective function, (2) seven constraints listed below, (3) the specification of sales functions for household and intermediate good usage of its brand, and (4) a specified cost function.

The joint industry objective function is our means of including in the model the strong flavor of concern for industrial stability that oligopolistic firms reveal in the real world (see [5]). This notion of "rivalrous consonance," or a quasi-harmony of actions that coexists with egoistic urges, is approximated in the model by the imposition of the necessary conditions of an industry profit maximum that no firm act marginally to increase its profits if all other firms taken together lose more than it gains, subject to the requirements of the constraints in the problem.

The first of the constraints is that output must be within the firm's capacity, B, to produce:

$$B_{I,J} - X_{I,J} \geqslant 0 \tag{2.4}$$

The firm insists that it captures at least the proportion M of its industry sales:

$$X_{I,J} - M_{I,J}\left(X_{I,J} + \sum_{J'} X_{I,J'}\right) \geqslant 0 \tag{2.5}$$

Further, the firm sets upper and lower constraints on period-by-period price changes, specified as proportions of the previous period's price, $\bar{P}_{I,J}$:

$$T_{I,J}^+ \bar{P}_{I,J} - P_{I,J} \geqslant 0 \tag{2.6}$$

and

$$P_{I,J} - T_{I,J}^- \bar{P}_{I,J} \geqslant 0 \tag{2.7}$$

The firm's total cost function is defined as the sum of (1) given unit primary factor costs times output, (2) unit intermediate goods requirements times exogenously given prices of such goods times output, and (3) dedicated capital times the given fixed rate of return paid on it. We write it:

$$C_{I,J} = F_{I,J} X_{I,J} + \sum_i \sum_j a_{i,j/I,J} P_{i,j} X_{I,J} + i_{I,J} K_{I,J} \tag{2.8}$$

with F average (and marginal) factor cost, the a coefficients average (and marginal) intermediate input requirements, and i fixed cost return on the capital base. Note that C is linear in X.

Intermediate account demand for firm I, $\mathcal{F}$'s product is defined as

$$Q_{I,J} = \sum_i \sum_j a_{I,J/i,j} X_{i,j} \qquad (2.9)$$

and is taken as exogenously given at this time. Sales to households are given as a linear function of industry prices:

$$D_{I,J} = b_{I,J} - g^I_{J,J} P_{I,J} + \sum_{J'} g^I_{J',J} P_{I,J'} + a_{I,J} Y \qquad (2.10)$$

where Y is an income term.

The relation of the g parameters to measures of interproduct distances in quality space has been explained in [5] and [6] and will be further discussed in section 3, but will not be featured in this chapter.

Each firm insists that demand be at least as great as sales,

$$D_{I,J} + Q_{I,J} - X_{I,J} \geq 0 \qquad (2.11)$$

but also that intermediate demand be met fully and that excess demand on household account be bounded from above by a given proportion U of sales:

$$U_{I,J}(X_{I,J} - Q_{I,J}) - D_{I,J} \geq 0 \qquad (2.12)$$

Finally, nonnegativity constraints are imposed:

$$X_{I,J}, P_{I,J} \geq 0 \qquad (2.13)$$

We substitute (2.8) into (2.3) to eliminate C, (2.9) and (2.10) into (2.11) and (2.12) to eliminate Q and D, leaving us with the endogenous variables X and P. The constraints – (2.4-2.7), (2.11-2.13) – are linear and hence define a convex feasible region. Therefore, for the case of profit maximization when all r are less than $\bar{r}$, we have a convex programming problem.

The model generates a succession of short-run equilibria as prices become benchmarks for the succeeding period, the series converging to a medium-term industry equilibrium characterized by stationary values for X and P. This latter solution can be obtained immediately by setting all T^+ to very large values and all T^- to zero in order to render constraints (2.6) and (2.7) ineffective. In this chapter we deal exclusively with this medium-term solution.

The use of such a model as an industry module to depict the interdependent decision-making of rivals implicitly hypothesizes that firms (1) typically aim at some target rate of return which may or may not be effectively a profit-maximization rate, subject to a set of constraints that includes notably market-share and disappointed demand limitations, and (2) act to preserve the stability of the industry by making no marginal adjustment that reduces all rivals' profits by more than its resulting profit increment, subject to the constraints.

3 The Interdependence Model

We now confront the major task of this chapter – the analysis of the problem of *interrelated* oligopolistic product groups, where the interface of such groups occurs through the supply of intermediate inputs among firms. In this chapter we simply hypothesize that firms in one product group absorb as inputs the products of specific firms in another group, and that these supply relationships are invariant to price change.

A purpose of the present chapter is to suggest the utility in general equilibrium systems analysis of "simulative theory." The acknowledged failure of large-scale pure deductive models, and the inability (which we shall illustrate below) of econometric techniques to discern the complicated causal structures that generate the price-output data of interdependent oligopoly, urge us down this new investigative route. Models must be constructed that are simple enough to be specified numerically in manners that incorporate our knowledge of the structure, conduct, and folkways of specific rivalrous industries. These models must then be subjected to finite parametric ranging in order to gain insights into price-output behaviour in the real world, to which the quantitative solutions of the models can be compared.

To illustrate the technique we have constructed two fictitious, interdependent oligopolistic product groups, whose relevant parameters for the industry modules of section 2 in the initial or *baseline* case will be found in table 2.1. For convenience, we have eliminated the income term in the demand equations, assuming that Y is constant.

In the statement of the demand functions I have included (in the parenthesized terms) the "distances" between products in quality space (see [3]). The $g^i_{j,j}$ coefficients in (2.10) are the products of such a distance term with a coefficient depicting the success of the firm in buffering itself, largely through selling costs and a choice of qualities, from products a given distance from itself in quality space. The lower the coefficient outside the parentheses, the less impact will changes in its rivals' prices have upon its own household demand function. Hereafter, we shall deal only with the g coefficients, noting, however, that the products in industry 1 are quite close together in their "objective" characteristics.

In industry 1, firm 1 is the giant in terms of dedicated capital stock, capacity, and the share of the market it strives to attain. Its cost structure features low fixed charges and the second highest primary factor costs in the

Table 2.1   Baseline case parameters

Brand	$\bar{r}_{,i,j}$	K_{ij}	$B_{i,j}$	$M_{i,j}$	$U_{i,j}$	$F_{i,j}$	$L_{i,j}$
Product group 1							
1	0.28	$10.00M	32,000	0.50	1.02	$525.00	0.09
2	0.28	6.57	28,000	0.30	1.03	318.00	0.07
3	0.30	2.74	20,000	0.10	1.02	582.00	0.06
Product group 2							
1	0.50	2.19	15,000	0.50	1.01	652.00	0.09
2	0.50	1.02	10,000	0.20	1.04	1,175.00	0.06

Demand functions

$D_{1,1} = 45,000 - 53\ P_{1,1} + 12.993\ (0.72\ P_{1,2} + 0.69\ P_{1,3}) + 0.21\ X_{2,2}$
$D_{1,2} = 34,000 - 55\ P_{1,2} + 16.463\ (0.72\ P_{1,1} + 0.74 P_{1,3}) + 0.10\ X_{2,1}$
$D_{1,3} = 29,515 - 42\ P_{1,3} + 12.149\ (0.69\ P_{1,1} + 0.74\ P_{1,2})$
$D_{2,1} = 26,910 - 32\ P_{2,1} + 5.547\ (0.64\ P_{2,2}) + 0.20\ X_{1,1} + 0.21\ X_{1,3}$
$D_{2,2} = 15,500 - 12\ P_{2,2} + 5.660\ (0.64\ P_{2,1}) + 0.27\ X_{1,2}$

Average cost functions

$C_{1,1} = 525 + 0.20\ P_{2,1} + 0.06\ (10,000,000)/X_{1,1}$
$C_{1,2} = 318 + 0.27\ P_{2,2} + 0.07\ (6,570,000)/X_{1,2}$
$C_{1,3} = 582 + 0.21\ P_{2,1} + 0.06\ (2,740,000)/X_{1,3}$
$C_{2,1} = 652 + 0.10\ P_{1,2} + 0.09\ (2,190,000)/X_{2,1}$
$C_{2,2} = 1,175 + 0.21\ P_{1,1} + 0.06\ (1,020,000)/X_{2,2}$

industry. To judge crudely its success in differentiation, we compare the coefficient outside the parentheses in its sales function with the intercept value, and see that it has succeeded more than its rivals in obtaining low demand sensitivity to its rivals' prices. Firm 3 seems the weakest rival: its capital stock is small, its market share goal is modest, and its factor costs are highest. If we use the same rough measure of demand sensitivity, we find that while it has not obtained the protection that firm 1 has, it has somewhat greater freedom from its rivals' prices than firm 2; but it does not have any intermediate demand to enjoy as its rivals have. Finally, firm 2 is the middle-sized rival, enjoying notably lower factor costs and only slightly higher charges on its dedicated capital than its competitors. It has succeeded least in "identifying" its product in the minds of consumers, however.

Industry 2 is a duopoly with firm 1 the dominant rival, given its capital base, capacity, and market share goals. It is saddled with high fixed charges on its capital base, but has a marked advantage in factor costs over its rival. Our rough measure of success in differentiation of product declares that firm 1 has not been as successful as firm 2 in acquiring independence. The latter is a small but, judging from its very high factor costs, a high-quality producer, with high fixed charges on a small capital base.

We solved the baseline case (and all of the displacements to be presented in section 4) by forming a new objective function as the sum of the two separate Z_i functions (2.3) and minimizing it subject to the union of the constraints of the five firms. This joint minimization (in effect, maximization of profits) implies the second facet of our concept of rivalrous consonance. The easy identifiability of "price-raisers" in oligopolistic supply situations, the desire not to antagonize the public, the fear of displacement by a rival in a supply market, as well as the already identified anxiety about unsettling its own industry's stability, leads the rivalrous supplier of an intermediate good not to take price actions on a wholly egoistic basis. The interindustry model approximates this hesitancy by assuming that a supplying firm will not take a marginal action that results in its gaining less profit than is lost by all other rivals in the economy. This now contains an interindustry component which, given the weakness of impacts upon non-customer firms can be taken as a supplier–customer relationship.[1]

Unfortunately, the conversion of intermediate good prices from exogenous variables to endogenous variables renders the objective function not necessarily convex, even in the profit maximization case. Therefore, solutions to the model can only be viewed as local maxima rather than global profit maxima. But if the model approaches reality, it is that reality which does not present a convex problem for solution, and modeling it enforces the grasping of the nettle of nonconvexity. The general oligopolistic equilibrium may indeed be one of a set of potentially achievable good-but-suboptimal solutions, with chance playing its part in dictating which emerges.

All solutions in this section and in section 4 were obtained by use of Fiacco and McCormick's Sequential Unconstrained Minimization Technique (SUMT) algorithm for nonlinear programming problems [2]. The baseline solution is presented in table 2.2, where (0) is used to distinguish the

Table 2.2   Baseline solution

Brand	$r_{t,j}^0$	$P_{i,j}^0$	$X_{i,j}^0$	$D_{i,j}^0$	$Q_{i,j}^0$	$M_{i,j}^0$	$C_{i,j}^0$
Product group 1							
1	0.23	$903.82	14,407	13,734	674	0.50	$747.00
2	0.13	858.98	9,883	9,156	728	0.34	774.66
3	0.25	959.29	4,524	4,524	0	0.16	807,72
			28,814				
Product group 2							
1	0.45	901.78	7,277	3,446	3,831	0.69	764.98
2	0.42	1,518.98	3,207	539	2,669	0.31	1,383.88
			10,484				

$$Z^0 = 6.44588$$

Table 2.3   Cost breakdown for the baseline solution

Type of cost	Firm 1,1	Firm 1,2	Firm 1,3	Firm 2,1	Firm 2,2
1. Average factor cost	$525.00	$318.00	$582.00	$652.00	$1,175.00
2. Averager intermediate good cost	180.36	410.28	189.37	85.90	189.80
3. Average fixed cost	41.64	46.38	36.35	27.08	19.08
Average total cost	$747.00	$774.66	$807.72	$764.98	$1,383.88

Table 2.4   Demand price elasticities at baseline solution

Firm k	$e_{k,1}$	$e_{k,2}$	$e_{k,3}$
a. Product group 1			
Firm 1,1	−3.34	0.56	0.60
Firm 1,2	1.08	−4.79	1.18
Firm 1,3	1.68	1.71	−8.90
b. Product group 2			
Firm 2,1	−3.97	0.74	–
Firm 2,2	1.01	−5.68	–

solution value of a variable.

In table 2.3 is listed the average total cost breakdown for the firms in the baseline solution.

As a final presentation, table 2.4 lists the own-price and other price elasticities of the sales functions in the neighbourhood of the baseline solution.

In the baseline solution, no firm is bound by its capacity constraint, each firm's demand equals its supply (constraint (2.11) binds for each), and only firm 1, 1 is bound by its market share constraint (constraint (2.5)). It will be recalled that the price change constraints (2.6) and (2.7) were made ineffective for all firms in the present analysis.

In product group 1, firm 3 is the star performer. It achieves the highest rate of return, attains fully 60 percent more of the market than it strove for, and has compensated for its high unit factor costs by low intermediate and fixed costs. On the other hand, contrary to initial expectations, it has the highest own-price and cross-elasticities in the industry, so that in the neighborhood of the baseline solution at least it is most sensitive to its rivals' pricing policies and has the least freedom to change its own prices. It is, nonetheless, a stronger firm than our initial information indicated.

Firm 1's solution is more consistent with expectations. It has had to hold down its price to attain its desired half of the market, but its rate of return is healthy, its costs the cheapest of the three rivals, and its advertising most successful in making its brand distinctive, as reflected in its low own-price and cross-elasticities of demand.

It is firm 2 which is the most vulnerable of the rivals. Its cross-elasticities are intermediate in buffering the firm from its rivals' price changes, and its low own-price elasticity gives it more pricing power than firm 3. But its very low factor costs are outweighed by its extraordinarily high intermediate costs, making the firm the most vulnerable to the prices of its suppliers. These factors contribute to its low rate of return.

Product group 2 meets our expectations but is a surprisingly profitable coexistence of two quite different rivals. Firm 1 is a low factor cost, low intermediate cost producer of 69 percent of the market's product, with high brand differentiation. It (like its rival) is a large producer of intermediate goods, and a large portion of the demand for its product is therefore perfectly inelastic. Firm 2 shares these demand characteristics, but is less protected from its rival's price changes and has weaker own-price power. It is even more predominantly an intermediate good producer, and its production is marked by high factor and intermediate costs. Firm 2, therefore, should be most subject to factors that affect its customer (firm 1, 2).

In the two product groups we have studiously attempted to encapsulate many of the more common features of oligopolistic industries: various own-price and other-price elasticities grouped about the generally high values which reflect close but not perfect substitutability; consumer orientation versus intermediate good orientation; high factor input versus low factor input; high intermediate good costs versus low intermediate good costs; dominant firms versus firms aiming for a small portion of the market; and high-quality producers in the presence of lower quality producers. With this mixture we shall formulate questions and seeks answers on the basis of the specified equations of the model.

4 An Approximation to Classic Displacement Analysis

The limitations of *a priori* equilibrium displacement analysis are well known, especially when the objective function of a minimization exercise is not convex. In general, what guidance can we expect from a comparative statics of the infinitesimal for interpreting reality through such models of general oligopolistic equilibrium?

Consider, for example, movements in P and X incumbent upon changes in F (factor costs) in the neighborhood of the baseline solution. We assume that (1) no constraint that binds in that solution fails to hold in the new solution; (2) no ineffective constraint in the baseline solution is effective in the new; (3) no nonzero variable in the baseline solution becomes zero in the new solution; and (4) no variable which is zero in the baseline solution becomes nonzero in the new solution (see [4], pp. 104–7). The validity of all of these assumptions in our present example is supported by the finite displacements that follow in section 5.

Six constraints bind in the baseline solution – demand equals supply for all five firms (constraint (2.11) and supply equals required market share for good 1, 1 (constraint (2.5)). These equations, along with the ten obtained by differentiating Z with respect to P and X and setting the partial derivatives equal to zero, form the 16-equation first-order conditions for determination of the baseline solution. We now shock this system by imposing five consecutive infinitesimal changes in $F_{i,j}$, to obtain the system

$$\mathbf{M} d\mathbf{V}/d\mathbf{F} = \mathbf{K} \tag{2.14}$$

where $d\mathbf{V}/d\mathbf{F}$ symbolizes the rates of change of λ, P, and X in that order with respect to a specific factor cost, $\mathbf{K}$ is the vector of partial derivatives of the equations with respect to a factor cost, and

$$\mathbf{M} = \begin{bmatrix} \mathbf{0} & \mathbf{B} \\ \mathbf{B}' & \mathbf{A} \end{bmatrix} \tag{2.15}$$

$\mathbf{A}$ is a 10×10 matrix containing the partial derivatives of the non-constraint equations with respect to P and X; $\mathbf{0}$ is a 6×6 null matrix; and

$$\mathbf{B} = \begin{bmatrix} -g_{1,1}^1 & -g_{2,1}^1 & -g_{3,1}^1 & 0 & 0 & -1 & 0 & 0 & 0 & 0 \\ g_{1,2}^1 & -g_{2,2}^1 & g_{3,2}^1 & 0 & 0 & 0 & -1 & 0 & 0 & 0 \\ g_{1,3}^1 & g_{2,3}^1 & -g_{3,3}^1 & 0 & 0 & 0 & 0 & -1 & 0 & 0 \\ 0 & 0 & 0 & -g_{1,1}^2 & g_{2,1}^2 & 0 & 0 & 0 & -1 & 0 \\ 0 & 0 & 0 & g_{1,2}^2 & -g_{2,2}^2 & 0 & 0 & 0 & 0 & -1 \\ 0 & 0 & 0 & 0 & 0 & (1-M_{1,1}) & -M_{1,1} & -M_{1,1} & 0 & 0 \end{bmatrix}$$

Let us review briefly the limited hopes we may entertain concerning the derivation of theorems from an *unspecified* system (2.14). Were Z convex, with $\mathbf{M}$ nonsingular and $(n + m) \times (n + m)$, where n is the number of primal variables and m the number of constraints, then $\mathbf{A}$ would be positive definite, for values of the variables consistent with the constraints. A sufficient condition for this result is that the last $n - m$ bordered principal minors of $\mathbf{M}$ have the sign $(-1)^m$. Were this true, if $\mathbf{K}$ met the necessary and sufficient conditions of the law of conjugate pairs (see [1]), no more than one unambiguous theorem on the direction of movement of a variable could be derived for each parameter change. In our present case, the last four such minors would be positive, but because the $\mathbf{K}$ vector has more than one term for each $F_{i,j}$ change, no unambiguous theorems are derivable.

But Z is not necessarily convex, as we have remarked, and hence these conditions on the bordered principal minors need not hold. Our analysis, therefore, must concern itself with infinitesimal moves around possibly only local minima. While disappointing, this possibility of nonconvexity should not deter us, for there is no assurance in the real world we seek to interpret that oligopolistic industries are making decisions along convex functions. As one of the costs of developing an operational large-scale systems theory it is necessary to be ready to embrace the crudities of reality and soldier on.

In this spirit, therefore, we constructed system (2.14) for the specified model with the baseline parameters of table 2.1, and with the objective function (2.2), effectively restricted to the logarithmic branch. Because the baseline solution lies on the logarithmic branches of the objective functions for each of the firms, differentiation of the first-order conditions involved ratio terms that were quite small. Unfortunately, double precision calculations on the computer were not sufficient to prevent a singular matrix from being reported out. Therefore, because objective functions of the form (2.1), where $r \leqslant \bar{r} \leqslant 3r$, are monotonic transformations of the logarithmic branch

Table 2.5 Changes from baseline solution resulting from 5 percent cost movements

Change in: Cost of firm	1,1	1,2	1,3	2,1	2,2
5% cost increases					
$P_{1,1}$	$3.72	$25.75	$21.64	$18.27	$16.12[a]
$P_{1,2}$	−0.11	29.04	23.96	20.82[a]	17.52
$P_{1,3}$	7.14	8.20	8.07	4.08	8.43
$P_{2,1}$	−2.83[a]	4.61	2.31[a]	25.52	10.33
$P_{2,2}$	0.81	2.63[a]	8.55	10.74	46.33
$X_{1,1}$	−131	−1,093	−927	−799	−764[a]
$X_{1,2}$	139	−1,225	−985	−978[a]	−702
$X_{1,3}$	−270	132	58	169	− 62
$X_{2,1}$	11[a]	−329	−217[a]	−903	−332
$X_{2,2}$	48	−345[a]	−360	−298	−350
5% cost decreases					
$P_{1,1}$	$13.97	$11.79	$13.51	$16.99	$14.29[a]
$P_{1,2}$	17.98	14.75	19.38	17.01[a]	15.11
$P_{1,3}$	1.61	8.20	−1.22	12.72	1.41
$P_{2,1}$	6.51[a]	5.84	8.03[a]	−41.78	6.78
$P_{2,2}$	7.47	12.17[a]	6.55	6.22	−56.52
$X_{1,1}$	−617	−533	−611	−701	−495[a]
$X_{1,2}$	−829	−664	−949	−462[a]	−691
$X_{1,3}$	211	141	339	−239	196
$X_{2,1}$	−261[a]	−222	−285[a]	1,168	−475
$X_{2,2}$	−290	−304[a]	−305	−350	516

[a] Row firm supplies column firm.

of (2.2), and yield the same displacement results, we changed the objective function to this form, shocked the system with changes in the five $F_{i,j}$, but obtained an ill-conditioned matrix which did not yield sufficient precision to be trustworthy.

It was necessary, therefore, to abandon classical displacement analysis and resort to small finite displacements as approximations. In ten separate analyses we changed each of the five firms' factor costs by ± 5 percent, holding all other factor costs at the baseline solution levels. It was felt that this value was in the range of realistic annual net factor cost change that industry might face. The incremental price and quantity impacts resulting from the cost changes are presented in table 2.5.

In table 2.6 we have divided the price and quantity changes by the amounts of factor cost change to obtain rates of change.

A first conclusion to be drawn from tables 2.5 and 2.6 is the asymmetry of the directions of movement in the finite analyses: rises and falls in factor costs of equal absolute values cannot be treated symmetrically. In table 2.6 positive values denote movements in the same direction as the relevant factor cost and negative values denote movements in the contrary direction. For

Table 2.6   Rates of change from baseline solution resulting from 5 percent cost movements

Change in: Cost of firm	1,1	1,2	1,3	2,1	2,2
5% cost increases					
$P_{1,1}$	0.14	1.62	0.74	0.56	0.27[a]
$P_{1,2}$	0.00	1.83	0.82	0.64[a]	0.30
$P_{1,3}$	0.27	0.52	0.28	0.13	0.14
$P_{2,1}$	−0.11[a]	0.29	0.08[a]	0.78	0.18
$P_{2,2}$	0.03	0.17[a]	0.29	0.33	0.79
$X_{1,1}$	−4.99	−68.74	−31.86	−24.51	−13.00[a]
$X_{1,2}$	5.30	−77.04	−33.85	−30.00[a]	−11.95
$X_{1,3}$	10.29	8.30	1.99	5.18	−1.06
$X_{2,1}$	0.42[a]	−20.69	−7.46[a]	−27.70	−5.65
$X_{2,2}$	1.83	−21.70[a]	−12.37	−9.14	−5.96
5% cost decrease					
$P_{1,1}$	−0.53	−0.74	−0.46	−0.52	−0.24[a]
$P_{1,2}$	−0.68	−0.93	−0.67	−0.52[a]	−0.26
$P_{1,3}$	−0.06	−0.52	0.04	−0.39	−0.02
$P_{2,1}$	−0.25[a]	−0.37	−0.28[a]	1.28	−0.12
$P_{2,2}$	−0.28	−0.77[a]	−0.23	−0.19	0.96
$X_{1,1}$	23.50	33.52	21.00	21.50	8.43[a]
$X_{1,2}$	31.58	41.76	32.62	14.17[a]	11.76
$X_{1,3}$	−8.04	−8.87	−11.65	7.33	−3.34
$X_{2,1}$	9.94[a]	13.96	9.79[a]	−35.83	8.09
$X_{2,2}$	11.05	19.12[a]	10.48	10.74	−8.78

[a] Row firm supplies column firm.

upward movements in factor costs in table 2.6 all own-price movements are positive, and all rivals' price movements are positive. In short, they are well-behaved. Further, only one quantity movement is positive for an own-cost change, and that one is only slightly positive.

Four of the five impacts upon suppliers' prices are positive, and rather strongly so, reinforcing negative supply movements in the four cases. Also, rises in factor costs in supplying firms lead in all five cases to increases in prices in the absorbing firms. We are somewhat surprised at the smallness of the own-cost passthroughs with the exception of firm 1, 2, which accelerates the cost increase.

But the analysis of 5 percent factor cost decreases reveals a strong perverse tendency in price reactions. Two of the five own-cost price reactions are negative. In general, reductions in factor costs are translated into price *increases*, as well as the *reduction* of supplies in 19 of 25 instances. Much comment has been made concerning the seeming upward price bias revealed in oligopolistic price adjustments, and our model reveals such behavior markedly for these small cost changes.

5 More Extensive Experiments and the Uses of Econometrics

Does this bias persist for large cost changes? Is the tendency for fractional cost passthroughs general for larger cost changes? Given a fairly large sample of controlled displacement results, each assumed to have a well-behaved error component, how successful would regression techniques be in isolating the "laws" of change in prices? To shed some light on the answers to such question, we changed the factor cost of each product by ± 10, ± 15, and ± 20 percent around the baseline, holding all other factor costs at the baseline level, and, in addition, permitted all factor costs to rise and fall by these same percentage amounts as well as by ± 5 percent around the baseline simultaneously. With the baseline solution for each firm, this would have given 49 observations of prices and factor cost for every brand, but this number was reduced to 45 because of the inability in four cases to find a workable initial solution for the SUMT algorithm.

We assumed that the collection of price information was subject to a normally distributed error term with spherical properties. A stepwise regression was run on each of the five sets of price observations with the following form:

$$P_{I,J} = a_{I,J} + \sum_j \sum_j b_{i,j;I,J} F_{i,j} + \sum_j \sum_j c_{i,j;I,J} F_{i,j}^2 + d_{I,J} S_{I,J} + e_{I,J}$$

$$(2.16)$$

where S is a dummy variable with a value of 0 if the factor cost generating the observation lies above its baseline value and 1 otherwise. In each case that regression was chosen that yielded the highest index of determination adjusted for degrees of freedom. The resulting equations are listed in table 2.7, with standard errors of the regression coefficients in parantheses, indices of regression adjusted for degrees of freedom, and F-distribution values.

The regression equations are disappointing. The adjusted regression indices range from 0.417 to 0.732, with four of the five below 0.613. Various peculiarities are revealed which make them suspect as interpreters of the relations between factor costs and prices that neoclassical analysis leads us to expect, even after taking into account the upward price bias detected in section 4. In the equation for $P_{1,1}$, own-factor cost, $F_{1,1}$, does not appear among the regressors; $F_{2,2}$, which is not the factor cost of an input, does

Table 2.7   Regression equations of factor costs and prices

$P_{1,1} = \quad 646.559 - 0.186F_{2,1} + 0.186F_{2,2} - 0.00041F_{2,2}^2 - 18.599S_{1,1}$
$\qquad\qquad\quad (0.075)^a \qquad (0.823) \qquad (0.00037) \qquad\quad (7.430)^a$

$\qquad\qquad \bar{R} = 0.417, F = 2.938 \ [F_{0.95} = 2.62, F_{0.99} = 3.85]$

$P_{1,2} = \quad 708.167 + 1.746F_{1,2} - 0.00258F_{1,2}^2 - 0.00009F_{2,1}^2 - 0.00006F_{2,2}^2$
$\qquad\qquad\quad (1.528) \qquad\quad (0.00244) \qquad\quad (0.00005) \qquad\quad (0.00002)^a$

$\qquad\qquad\quad -11.847S_{1,2}$
$\qquad\qquad\quad\ (5.351)^a$

$\qquad\qquad \bar{R} = 0.436, F = 2.742 \ [F_{0.95} = 2.47, F_{0.99} = 3.55$

$P_{1,3} = \quad 954.187 + 1.724F_{1,2} - 1.573F_{1,3} - 0.877F_{2,1} + 0.926F_{2,2}$
$\qquad\qquad\quad (1.354) \qquad\quad (0.739)^a \qquad (0.660) \qquad\ \ (0.616)$

$\qquad\qquad\quad +0.00016F_{1,1}^2 - 0.00291F_{1,2}^2 + 0.00140F_{1,3}^2 + 0.00052F_{2,1}^2$
$\qquad\qquad\quad\ (0.00007) \qquad\ (0.00215) \qquad\ \ (0.00064)^a \qquad (0.00051)$

$\qquad\qquad\quad -0.000042F_{2,2}^2 - 10.980S_{1,3}$
$\qquad\qquad\quad\ (0.00028) \qquad\quad (6.877)$

$\qquad\qquad \bar{R} = 0.612, F = 3.373 \ [F_{0.95} = 2.13, F_{0.99} = 2.99]$

$P_{2,1} = 3,463.284 - 0.147F_{1,1} - 5.983F_{2,1} - 1.116F_{2,2} + 0.00471F_{2,1}^2$
$\qquad\qquad\qquad (0.108) \quad\ \ (1.023)^a \quad (0.956) \qquad (0.00079)^a$

$\qquad\qquad\quad -0.00011F_{1,3}^2 + 0.00056F_{2,2}^2 - 2.817S_{2,1}$
$\qquad\qquad\quad\ (0.00009) \qquad\ (0.00043) \qquad\ (9.735)$

$\qquad\qquad \bar{R} = 0.732, F = 7.729 \ [F_{0.95} = 2.27, F_{0.99} = 3.17]$

$P_{2,2} = 3,822.776 - 4.678F_{2,2} + 0.00227F_{2,2}^2$
$\qquad\qquad\qquad (1.634)^a \quad\ (0.00074)^a$

$\qquad\qquad \bar{R} = 0.602, F = 12.425 \ [F_{0.95} = 4.07, F_{0.99} = 5.17]$

[a] Statistically significant at the level 0.95 level.

appear; and $F_{2,1}$, which is the factor cost of an input, appears with a *negative* regression coefficient.

In the equation for $P_{1,2}$, the factor cost of the input, $F_{2,2}$, exerts a statistically significant *negative* effect, whereas the own-factor cost effects, both linear and quadratic, are statistically nonsignificant. In that for $P_{1,3}$, own-factor cost is statistically significant in both linear and quadratic forms, but exerts a *negative* effect over half the domain of observation; the factor cost of a substitute, $F_{1,2}$, exerts a *negative* impact in its higher ranges; and the impact of the factor cost of the input, $F_{2,1}$ exerts a *negative* impact over its domain in the exercise. For the $P_{2,1}$ equation, own-factor cost, $F_{2,1}$, has a negative impact over the lower half of its domain, input cost $F_{1,2}$ has no impact at all, and the regression impact of changes in the cost of its rival, $F_{2,2}$, is *negative* over most of $F_{2,2}$'s domain. Finally, in the equation for $P_{2,2}$, input factor cost $F_{1,1}$ has no impact.

A closer study of the performance of the system in the experiments leads to a greater sympathy with the contortionist tasks the solutions imposed upon the econometrics, but in no sense does it reveal great hope that inductive approaches to the oligopolistic industry will uncover the paths of causation. In figure 2.1 we have graphed in the solid line the impacts of the changes in own-factor costs when all other factor costs were held at their baseline values. We shall term these the *ceteris paribus* analyses. A striking characteristic of all parts of the figure is that such impacts are simply incapable of capture by simple description, econometric or other. The complexities of rivalrous competition seem overpowering, and, to the extent our model captures some of the active forces in the far more complex oligopolistic markets of reality, discredits an empirical approach.

A first characteristic of figure 2.1 is the relatively small cost passthroughs. In table 2.8 we present the factor cost proportions for the brands in the baseline and the maximum own-price increases and decreases. Of course, the high own-price elasticities would lead us to expect less-than-full cost passthroughs, but the nonmonotonic nature of both negative and positive

Table 2.8 Baseline factor cost percentages and maximum cost-induced price changes

Firm	Factor cost as percentage of total cost in baseline	Maximum price	
		Rise (percent)	Fall (percent)
1,1	70.2	4.4%	0.5%
1,2	41.0	5.7	0.5
1,3	72.0	4.2	0.6
2,1	85.2	9.4	5.0
2,2	84.9	a	6.6

[a] Gaps in data due to inability to obtain two solutions.

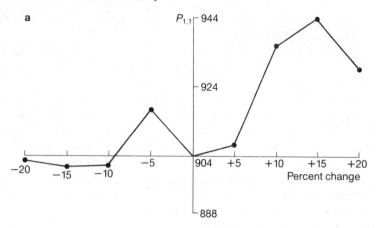

Figure 2.1(a)

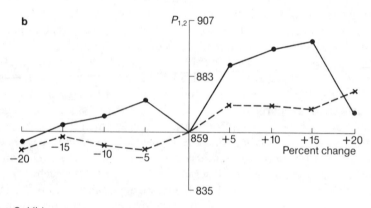

Figure 2.1(b)

Figure 2.1   *Ceteris paribus* factor cost changes.
a, $P_{1,1}$; **b**, $P_{1,2}$; **c**, $P_{1,3}$; **d**, $P_{2,1}$; **e**, $P_{2,2}$.

branches of the graphs indicates that the equilibrating process itself is involved in dictating such mild cost influences.

Secondly, the persistence of upward bias is clearly indicated. In general, the downward pressures on price are much more constrained than upward pressures: indeed, 10 of the 20 cost reductions led to *upward* own-price movements! This can be no result of simple own-price elasticities.

In the cases of $P_{1,1}$ and $P_{1,3}$ the regression results were too poor to graph, but in the other three cases we have plotted their results with the dashed line. In the cases of $P_{2,1}$ and $P_{2,2}$ the regression results have captured the U-shape of the simulation results, reflecting the perversities of the solutions. However, even in this band of controlled *ceteris paribus* and simultaneous cost movement, the richness and perversities of the behavior of the firms is

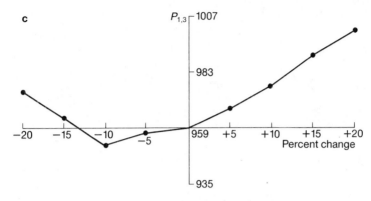

Figure 2.1(c)

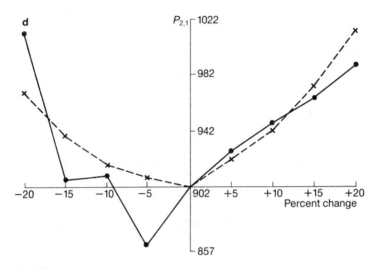

Figure 2.1(d)

simply incapable of capture by such simple econometric structures. The complexities of rivalrous cooperation seem overpowering.

These conclusions are reinforced by the study of changes in input costs upon absorbing firms' prices, as displayed in figure 2.2. In these graphs all factor costs except those of a good's input are held constant, and the impacts upon the good's price are obtained. The results are as surprising as those of the *ceteris paribus* analyses. Substantial rises in input costs have relatively small impacts on prices, and, indeed, show some perverseness in that larger input cost increases lead to smaller price rises or even to declines in prices below the baseline price.

But the greatest anomaly of the analysis is reserved for factor cost decreases. In every case, a fall in an input factor cost led to a *rise* in price

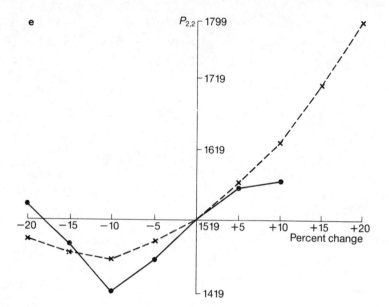

Figure 2.1(e)

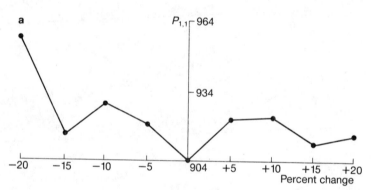

Figure 2.2(a)

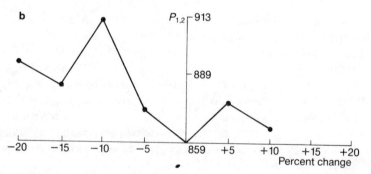

Figure 2.2(b)

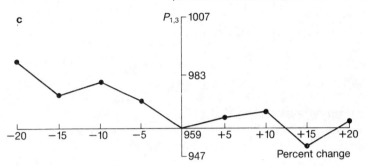

Figure 2.2(c)

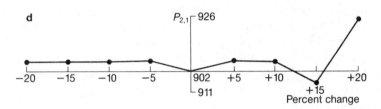

Figure 2.2(d)

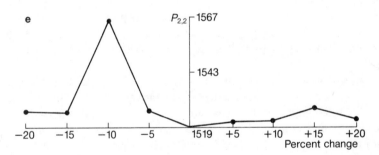

Figure 2.2(e)

Figure 2.2   Input factor cost changes.
a, $P_{1,1}$; **b**, $P_{1,2}$; **c**, $P_{1,3}$; **d**, $P_{2,1}$; **e**, $P_{2,2}$.

above the baseline. Moreover, in general the price rises were larger than those occurring for increases in own-factor cost of similar relative magnitude. And, finally, there is a marked tendency for the size of the price rises to grow with the size of the factor cost declines. Given these results, it is not surprising that in not one of the five regressions were the results sufficiently good to graph.

6 Conclusions and Conjectures

Our study has sources in several questions about present reality, the first concerning economic actuality and the second our theoretical ability to analyse it. Does there exist in modern industrial economies an upward bias in price adjustment, so that price inflation cannot be wholly caused by monetary phenomena, inflationary gaps between aggregate demand and supply, or simple cost-push phenomena, but at least partially is caused by the microeconomics of oligopolistic equilibration? Can general equilibrium theory be redesigned to explain these properties by a rivalrous quasi-harmony of aims that tempers the pure game-theoretic outlook on oligopoly?

Our proposed model of the typical oligopolistic industry stresses an aspect of rivalry which has been muted in other models: the existence in the typical oligopoly of a "rivalrous consonance" of actions that brings about a quasi-harmony of interests of the participants, born largely of the fear of destabilizing egoism, within the environment of a constrained self-interest. To our way of thinking, successful modelling of oligopoly depends upon a blending of both rivalrous and harmonistic elements.

The interdependence among oligopolistic industries inheres in supply relationships, and in these too urges toward restraint exist. The source is once more enlightened egoism. The desire to preserve customer goodwill and to retain custom tempers the extent of the price rise, and the desire to preserve stability within the industry makes the role of "cutthroat competitor" unattractive.

An approximation to both of these facets of rivalrous consonance is to assume that no firm, in its pricing decisions, makes any marginal adjustment that yields it less profit than the sum of profits lost by all other firms. The high degree of decomposability in our model assures that nonnegligible profit impacts that must be considered in a firm's actions are largely limited to its product group's rivals and the firms it supplies in other product groups. Hence, each firm's effective number of profit-limiting concerns is reasonably small.

But these characteristics are captured by the joint maximization or minimization model we have constructed in sections 2 and 3. The general equilibrium occurs "as if" all firms were acting individually to achieve a joint extremum, subject to all of the individual constraints being fulfilled. As in the perfectly decomposable conditions of pure competition, the "invisible hand" of the market mechanism seeks an extremum, but one that is constrained with indecomposability introduced via the sales functions of rivals and their intermediate good linkages to industrial customers.

Our experiments with a two-industry world involve rivals with high cross-elasticities of demand striving (in the work here presented) to maximize profits subject to individual constraints. For a series of factor cost shocks imposed upon both industries an upward price bias has been demonstrated, as well as a large component of price – cost perversity of movement. This is an alternative explanation to the "kinked-demand" theory of downward price rigidity in rivalrous competition. Cost decreases in a world of high demand cross-elasticities would lead to strong price cuts in the absence of a restrained competition that turns the situation to advantage for a majority of firms via the empathetic consideration of profit declines.

We have demonstrated that the irregularity of the separate displacement results, even when they are closely controlled in analysis, precludes an accurate representation of the price movements by econometric techniques. Our conjecture is that economic analysis of the complicated patterns of interdependence that inhere in oligopolistic general equilibrium will depend heavily upon the construction of multi-objective deductive models with operational potential of the type employed in this chapter. We have termed this technique "simulative theorizing." Fortunately, as indicated in [5], the proposed approach is flexible enough to accommodate many different patterns of rivalry; moreover, it is open to an enrichment of the patterns of interdependence permitted.

Note

[1] These "rivals'-rate-of-return" and "customers'-rate-of-return"effects can be controlled or eliminated in the firm's optimization by a technique that "cripples" the optimization. We shall report on this methodology and its application to the problems of this study in a future paper. [See the introduction of rivalrous consonance factors Θ in Chapter 4 and thereafter.]

References

[1] Archibald, G. C., "The Qualitative Content of Maximizing Models," *Journal of Political Economy*, 73 (1965), 27–36.

[2] Fiacco Anthony V. and Garth P. McCormick: *Nonlinear Programming: Sequential Unconstrained Minimization Technique*, John Wiley & Sons, New York, 1968.

[3] Kuenne, Robert E. (ed.), *Monopolistic Competition Theory: Studies in Impact*, John Wiley & Sons, New York, 1967, 219–63. [Reprinted as chapter 11 of this volume.]

[4] ——, *Microeconomic Theory of the Market Mechanism: a General Equilibrium Approach*, Macmillan, New York, 1968.

[5] ——, "Toward a Usable General Theory of Oligopoly", *De Economist*, 122 (1974), 471–502. [Reprinted as chapter 1 of this volume.]

[6] ——, "Interproduct Distances in a Quality-space: Inexact Measurement in Differentiated Oligopoly Analysis", *Applied Economics*, 6 (1974), 255–73. [Reprinted as chapter 12 of this volume.]

[7] ——, "Price Impacts of Profit Regulation in Oligopoly: Potential Perversities of Incomes Policies", Research Paper no. 3, General Economic Systems Project, Princeton, NJ, March 1974.

3

General Oligopolistic Equilibrium: A Crippled-optimization Approach

Elsewhere [4] I presented a model of general equilibrium with differentiated oligopolistic industries, featuring a flexible, multi-objective approach with a modular industrial design developed in [3]. A detailed rationale of the model will be found in the articles cited; however, it will be necessary to outline it in section 1. Section 2 analyzes the economic meaning of the necessary conditions for a general equilibrium in the model and section 3 develops techniques for altering those conditions by modifying or eliminating the terms found in them. I call these techniques "crippled-optimization analysis," and believe that they have a general applicability to optimization exercises. In section 4 they are illustrated by the two-industry example of [4] with a supplementing of its displacement analysis by two more cases using the new techniques. The results are tested against hypotheses derived from *ceteris paribus* analysis, insights are derived into the *mutatis mutandis* overriding of some of the simpler hypotheses, and in section 5 the displacement results are subjected to a varimax multivariate factor analysis rotation to discern the minimum number of dimensions in them. Finally, in section 6, a brief summary of the major results is presented.

1 The Model of Oligopolistic General Equilibrium With Rate-of-return Components

1.1 The Model of the Firm's Decision-Making

We posit a set of industries, $i = 1, 2, \ldots, m$, and, within each, a set of firms with elements $j = 1, 2, \ldots, n_j$. We assume that each firm produces one

Originally published in *Pioneering Economics: Essays in Honor of Giovanni Demaria*, Cedam, Padua, 1978, 537–77, and reproduced with permission.

good in order to identify firms with brands, and select firm J from industry I (hereafter, firm I, J) to illustrate the oligopolistic firm's behavior.

We define:

1. $X_{I,J}$: output
2. $P_{I,J}$: *price*
3. $\bar{X}_{I,J}$: output net of firm's own intermediate good usage of its product
4. $C_{I,J}$: average total cost of $X_{I,J}$
5. $C'_{I,J}$: marginal cost of $X_{I,J}$
6. $F_{I,J}$: constant unit factor cost
7. $i_{I,J}$: fixed charge per dollar of capital in current period, including depreciation
8. $K_{I,J}$: capital base dedicated to the product
9. $r_{I,J}$: actual rate of return on capital base
10. $\bar{r}_{I,J}$: target rate of return on capital base
11. $D_{I,J}$: household demand
12. $Q_{I,J}$: intermediate good demand for firm's output
13. Y : national income
14. $M_{I,J}$: firm's minimum market proportion goal
15. $T^{+}_{I,J}$: upper bound proportion on price change in current period
16. $T^{-}_{I,J}$: lower bound proportion on price change in current period
17. $B_{I,J}$: firm's capacity to produce in current period
18. $\bar{P}_{I,J}$: benchmark price for current period price change
19. $U_{I,J}$: upper bound proportion on disappointed household demand
20. $a_{i,j/I,J}$: intermediate good requirement of firm i, j's product per unit of firm I, J's product
21. $\pi_{I,J}$: total profit

Assume that the firm attempts to earn the target rate of return on its capital, and define its objective function as:

$$\min Z_{I,J} = \begin{cases} \exp(r_{I,J} - \bar{r}_{I,J}), & \text{if } r_{I,J} > \bar{r}_{I,J} \\ \ln \bar{r}_{I,J} - \ln r_{I,J} + 1, & \text{if } 0 \leqslant r_{I,J} \leqslant \bar{r}_{I,J} \\ 1/P_{I,J}, & \text{if } r_{I,J} < 0, \end{cases} \qquad (3.1)$$

before taking into account modifications of objectives because of its rivalrous competitive environment. The branches of $Z_{I,J}$ for $r_{I,J} < \bar{r}_{I,J}$ are jointly convex in $X_{I,J}$ and $P_{I,J}$ when all other $X_{i,j}$ and $P_{i,j}$ are taken as exogenous.

We define:

1. $r_{I,J} = \pi_{I,J}/K_{I,J} = X_{I,J}(P_{I,J} - C_{I,J})/K_{I,J}$

2. $C_{I,J} = F_{I,J} + \sum_i \sum_j a_{i,j/I,J} P_{i,j} + \sum i_{I,J} K_{I,J} / X_{I,J}$

3. $D_{I,J} = b_{I,J} - g'_{J,J} P_{I,J} + \sum_{j^* \neq J} g'_{j^*,J} P_{I,j^*} + g'_{J,Y} Y$ (3.2)

4. $Q_{I,J} = \sum_i \sum_j a_{I,J/i,j} X_{i,j}$

5. $Y = \sum_i \sum_j (F_{i,j} X_{i,j} + i_{i,j} K_{i,j} + \pi_{i,j})$

The firm seeks its target rate of return (hereafter, rate) subject to six constraints (symbolized $L_{k,I,J}$). First, sales must remain within the firm's capacity to produce:

$$L_{1,I,J}: B_{I,J} - X_{I,J} \geqslant 0.$$ (3.3)

Second, the firm insists on a minimum market share:

$$L_{2,I,J}: X_{I,J} - M_{I,J}\left(X_{I,J} + \sum_{j^* \neq J} X_{I,j^*}\right) \geqslant 0.$$ (3.4)

Third and fourth, the firm places upper and lower limits on price movement during the period:

$$L_{3,I,J}: T^+_{I,J} \bar{P}_{I,J} - P_{I,J} \geqslant 0$$ (3.5)

$$L_{4,I,J}: P_{I,J} - T^-_{I,J} \bar{P}_{I,J} \geqslant 0.$$ (3.6)

Fifth, the firm's consumer demand may exceed supply.

$$L_{5,I,J}: D_{I,J} - X_{I,J} + Q_{I,J} \geqslant 0,$$ (3.7)

but only within bounded limits:

$$L_{6,I,J}: U_{I,J}(X_{I,J} - Q_{I,J}) - D_{I,J} \geqslant 0.$$ (3.8)

Finally, sales and prices must be nonnegative:

$$X_{I,J}, P_{I,J} \geqslant 0.$$ (3.9)

In order to concentrate upon the medium rather than the short term, we effectively remove constraints $L_{3,I,J}$ and $L_{4,I,J}$ by setting $T^+_{I,J}$ to a very large value and $T^-_{I,J}$ to 0. In all that follows, therefore, we shall ignore these constraints. If we set $\bar{r}_{I,J}$ to an unattainably high level, (1) we obtain a profit-maximization model and (2) $r_{I,J}$ remains in the domain of the objective function where $Z_{I,J}$ is convex in $X_{I,J}$ and $P_{I,J}$, which fact, given the linearity of all constraints, is sufficient for a convex nonlinear programming problem for the firm.

1.2 The Interindustry Model

We place the firm in a general equilibrium framework by defining the objective function

$$Z = \sum_i \sum_j Z_{i,j}, \tag{3.10}$$

and we seek its minimum subject to the full set of constraints (of the forms L_1 to L_6 and the nonnegativity relations) for *all* firms. With all $\bar{r}_{i,j}$ set unattainably high in a profit-maximization mode, economic motivation is universally profit-maximizing,[1] but Z is not convex given the products of endogenous variables in its definition. Hence, we can hope only to solve for local rather than global constrained minima.

We seek to incorporate three characteristics of the typical oligopolist's decision-making we believe to be widespread in modern industry:

1 Multi-objective goal seeking by the individual firm, with maximum profits or a target rate of return a dominant consideration, but other goals such as minimum market share and limited disappointed demand constraining such quests.
2 A "rivalrous consonance" of interests felt by each firm for the welfare of its competitors owing in large part (but not entirely) to the fear that overly egoistic behavior will destabilize the industry.
3 A concern for the firm's industrial customers' profits, again born in large part of a fear that it will be displaced as a supplier if its price actions are too disturbing to its customers' costs.

We may at best hope to approximate real world behavior through such generalized modelling, especially because in oligopolistic behavior so much depends upon the specific industry in question. Formal representation of this market structure must give great priority to methods that can be tailored to specifics. This paper describes methods of controlling or eliminating effects 2 and 3 above to permit such conformance to the peculiarities of particular industries or even to make the general model conform to the investigator's general viewpoint of oligopolistic decision-making. We examine next the exact manners in which the three characteristics are reflected in the necessary conditions for a solution to the model. Because we limit our consideration to the single firm in section 2, these conditions will also be sufficient for a global constrained minimum in the model defined by (3.1)–(3.9).

2 Necessary and Sufficient Conditions for a Global Constrained Minimum for the Firm

We form the Lagrangean

$$\mathscr{L} = Z - \sum_{k=1}^{6} \sum_{i} \sum_{j} \lambda_{k,i,j} L_{k,i,j}, \qquad (3.11)$$

with X, P, and $\lambda \geqslant 0$, and with the substitutions from the identities (3.2) performed to restrict the variables to these three vectors. We assume that the $\bar{r}_{i,j}$ are unattainably high so that only the logarithmic branches of the $Z_{i,j}$ in Z are relevant as long as the $r_{i,j}$ remain nonnegative.

For this analysis we permit only firm I,J's variables to vary, the others' being given exogenously, derive the necessary and sufficient conditions for firm I,J's constrained profit maximization, and examine their economic implications.

2.1 The Conditions for an Optimum

The necessary (and sufficient) conditions for firm I,J's global constrained optimum are:

1. $\dfrac{\delta \mathscr{L}}{\delta X_{I,J}} = \left\{ \dfrac{-(P_{I,J} - C'_{I,J})}{\pi_{I,J}} + \lambda_{1,I,J} - \lambda_{2,I,J}(1 - M_{I,J}) \right.$

$$+ \sum_{j^* \neq J} \lambda_{2,I,j^*} M_{I,j^*} + \lambda_{5,I,J} - \lambda_{6,I,J} U_{I,J}$$

$$- \sum_{i} \sum_{j} \left(\lambda_{5,i,j} g^i_{j,Y} \left[P_{I,J} - \sum_{i} \sum_{j} a_{i,j/I,J} P_{i,j} \right] \right)$$

$$\left. + \sum_{i} \sum_{j} \left(\lambda_{6,i,j} g^i_{j,Y} \left[P_{I,J} - \sum_{i} \sum_{j} a_{i,j/I,J} P_{i,j} \right] \right) \right\} \geqslant 0$$

2. $X_{I,J}\{ \cdot \} = 0$

3. $\dfrac{\delta \mathscr{L}}{\delta P_{I,J}} = \left\{ \dfrac{-X_{I,J} + \Sigma_i \Sigma_j a_{I,J/i,j} X_{i,j}}{\pi_{I,J}} + (\lambda_{5,I,J} - \lambda_{6,I,J}) g'_{J,J} \right.$

$$- \left(\sum_{j^* \neq J} \lambda_{5,I,j^*} - \sum_{j^* \neq J} \lambda_{6,I,j^*} \right) g^I_{J,j^*}$$

$$- \sum_{i} \sum_{j} \left(\lambda_{5,i,j} g^i_{j,Y} \left[X_{I,J} - \sum_{i} \sum_{j} a_{I,J/i,j} X_{i,j} \right] \right)$$

$$+ \sum_i \sum_j \left(\lambda_{6,i,j} g^i_{j,Y} \left[X_{I,J} - \sum_i \sum_j a_{I,J/i,j} X_{i,j} \right] \right) \right\} \geqslant 0$$

4. $P_{I,J} \{ \cdot \} = 0$

5. $\dfrac{\delta \mathcal{L}}{\delta \lambda_{k,I,J}} = L_{k,I,J} \geqslant 0$

6. $\lambda_{k,I,J} L_{k,I,J} = 0$

7. $X_{I,J}, \ P_{I,J}, \ \lambda_{I,J} \geqslant 0$.   (3.12)

2.2 Interpreting the Conditions

In the first-order conditions note the realistic separability of firms in their decision-making, despite the convenience of minimizing Z for the economy as a whole. The interdependence of firm I, J with firms other than rivals and customers is very weak, being confined to the impacts of its decisions upon the national income and hence weakly upon the sales of all other firms. It may be safely ignored. But two types of strong and direct interdependence among rivalrous firms exist in our model:

1 a rivalrous consonance of interests that leads the firm to consider the impact of its decisions on its rivals' profits;
2 the concern of a firm for its competitive position with its customer firms by taking into account the impacts on their profits of its price decisions.

I believe that oligopolistic firms do in varying degrees consider these vertical and horizontal impacts in their constrained profit-maximizing decisions (see [3,4]). In section 3 we describe methods to "cripple" the optimal conditions by tempering or eliminating the strength of these interdependencies in order to tailor the model to the specific circumstances of firms and industries. But, presently, we stress that despite the convenience of an economy-wide, simultaneously constrained optimization model, the equilibrium conditions permit the decomposition of firms' decision-making into concerns related to realistic clusters of rivals and customers.

We assume, of course, that $X_{I,J}$ and $P_{I,J}$ are strictly positive and therefore, from (3.12–2) and (3.12–4) we study (3.12–1) and (3.12–3) as equalities. And we shall make the following assumptions (but relax them later):

Assumption C. All firms operate at the optimum strictly within their capacity restraints $B_{i,j}$. Hence, by (3.12–6), all $\lambda_{1,i,j} = 0$.

Assumption M. All firms' minimum market share goals are exceeded, so by (3.12-6) all $\lambda_{2,i,j} = 0$.

Assumption DS. All firms' total demands equal supplies in the equilibrium, so that by (3.12-6) all $\lambda_{5,i,j} \geqslant 0$, and we shall assume the strict inequality holds. When this is true the $L_{6,i,j}$ cannot be equalities for $U_{i,j} > 1$, so by (3.12-6) all $\lambda_{6,i,j} = 0$.

Assumption Y. All $g^i_{j,Y}$ are negligible.

Let us turn first to (3.12-3) under *C*, *M*, *DS*, and *Y*. It simplifies to

$$\frac{\bar{X}_{I,J}}{\pi_{I,J}} - \lambda_{5,I,J}g^I_{J,J} - \frac{Q_{I,J}}{\pi_{I,J}} + \sum_{j^* \neq J} \lambda_{5,I,j} \cdot g^I_{J,j^*} = 0 .$$

The profit term in the denominators may be eliminated by multiplying each λ by $\pi_{I,J}$ and designating these modified variables $\bar{\lambda}$.[2] Hence the condition may be rewritten

$$[\bar{X}_{I,J} - \bar{\lambda}_{5,I,J}g^I_{J,J}] - [Q_{I,J}] + \left[\sum_{j^* \neq J} \bar{\lambda}_{5,I,j} \cdot \right] = 0 .$$

Since $g^I_{J,J} = -(\delta D_{I,J}/\delta P_{I,J})$, and given *DS*, we rewrite this

$$[\bar{X}_{I,J}dP_{I,J} + \bar{\lambda}_{5,I,J}d\bar{X}_{I,J}] + [-Q_{I,J}dP_{I,J}] + \left[\sum_{j^* \neq J} \bar{\lambda}_{5,I,j} \cdot d\bar{X}_{I,j^*} \right] = 0 ,$$

(3.13)

which we symbolize

$$[OC_p] + [CC] + [RC] = 0 . \tag{3.14}$$

Assume that at the optimum the firm lowers $P_{I,J}$ slightly, inducing a rise in $D_{I,J}$ and (given *DS*) an equivalent rise in net supply. From (3.13) and (3.14) three direct and additive impacts upon *Z*, the objective function value, are apparent:

1 *Own-profit price component (OC_p)*. The fall in $P_{I,J}$ will change the relevant firm's profits at the rate shown in the first set of brackets in (3.13): the amount of its net sales in the initial optimum times price change plus the marginal profit per unit of net sales times marginal sales. It must be remembered that a reduction in profit increases *Z* so that $\bar{\lambda}$ (and λ) terms move opposite to movements in profits.

2 *Customers' profits component (CC)*. The price change will affect customers' profits at the rates shown in the second term in brackets in (3.13). Their profits will rise in the present case, hence *CC* will be positive.

3 *Rivals' profits component (RC)*. The fall in $P_{I,J}$ will reduce the demands of the relevant firm's rivals and reduce their profits by the extent of that change in amount demanded times the rate at which profits affected

by the induced reduction in supply fall. Summed over all rivals, RC yields the negative impact of a fall in $P_{I,J}$ upon industry profits after OC_p is netted out.

It follows, given C, M, DS, and Y, that the firm, in its pricing decisions, considers at the margin its impacts upon its own, customers', and rivals' profits, treating them coordinately: the gain or loss of a dollar of profits on its own account is exactly balanced by the loss or gain of a dollar of profits by its customers or rivals. Indeed, we may combine OC_p and CC in (3.13) and (3.14) to obtain.

$$[D_{I,J}dP_{I,J} + \bar{\lambda}_{s,I,J}dD_{I,J}] + \left[\sum_{j^* \neq J} \bar{\lambda}_{s,I,j} \cdot d\bar{X}_{I,j^*}\right] = 0. \qquad (3.15)$$

This implies that the relevant firm treats the subsector containing itself and its industrial customers as a unit, its own losses on existing sales springing from a reduction in price being partially offset by its customers' gains. The firm's losses on this account are viewed as springing only from its sales to household demand.

Next, let us drop Y, so that (3.12–3) is written:

$$[D_{I,J} - \bar{\lambda}_{s,I,J}g^I_{J,J}] + \left[\sum_{j^* \neq J} \bar{\lambda}_{s,I,j} \cdot g^I_{J,j^*}\right] + \left[\sum_i \sum_j \bar{\lambda}_{s,i,j}g^i_{j,Y}D_{I,J}\right] = 0,$$
$$\qquad (3.16)$$

or

$$[OC_p + CC] + [RC] + [YC_p] = 0. \qquad (3.17)$$

And we define a new component:

4 *Price-induced income component* (YC_p). The fall in $P_{I,J}$ induces a fall $D_{I,J}dP_{I,J}$ in national income, and multiplication of this value-added term by each $g^i_{j,Y}$ factor converts this to a fall in demand for that good. Multiplication by each $\bar{\lambda}_{s,i,j}$ converts this to the profits impact upon Z. Summed over all firms, including firm I,J, we obtain the aggregate impact of the reduction in $P_{I,J}$ upon aggregate profits springing from the fall in national income entailed.

Consider (3.12–3), given C, M, and DS, where we may write

$$\bar{\lambda}_{s,I,J}g^I_{J,J} = D_{I,J} + \sum_{j^* \neq J} \bar{\lambda}_{s,I,J}g^I_{J,j^*} + \sum_i \sum_j \bar{\lambda}_{s,i,j}g^i_{j,Y}D_{I,J}.$$

If we assume that all $\lambda_{s,I,j^*} \geqslant 0$, and therefore all $\bar{\lambda}_{s,I,j^*} \geqslant 0$ because $\pi_{I,J} \geqslant 0$, then the requirement that $\lambda_{s,I,J} \geqslant 0$ is met. Moreover, our interpretation of that dual variable is consistent with convex nonlinear programming theory, which tells us that it is, if it exists, the marginal change in the objective function value induced by a small change in an allowable direction of the restraint in the relevant constraint. For $L_{5,I,J}$ in the postulated equilibrium

$$D_{I,J} - X_{I,J} + \sum_i \sum_j a_{I,J/i,j} X_{i,j} = 0 ,$$

the restraint being zero. Assume that the restraint is made slightly positive by lowering $P_{I,J}$ in order to increase the amount demanded. The dual variable is the implied change in Z, or

$$\lambda_{5,I,J} = \left(\delta Z / \delta P_{I,J} \right) \left(\delta P_{I,J} / \delta D_{I,J} \right)$$

$$= \left(\delta Z / \delta P_{I,J} \right) \left(-g'_{J,J} \right)^{-1} ,$$

so that

$$\lambda_{5,I,J} g'_{J,J} = - \left(\delta Z / \delta P_{I,J} \right) ,$$

which is (ignoring all $\lambda_{5,I,j}$. terms) what we derived from (3.16) and, in the last analysis, (3.12–3).

But excess demand can be increased equivalently if $X_{I,J}$ is *lowered*, $D_{I,J}$ remaining constant – that is, if a small amount of sales is sacrificed. It is implied that $\lambda_{5,I,J}$ should equal the impact of such a change on Z if the restraint becomes positive in this manner; that is, $\lambda_{5,I,J} = \delta Z / \delta X_{I,J}$. Condition (3.12–1) under C, M, DS, and Y states this explicitly, reducing to

$$\lambda_{5,I,J} = \left(P_{I,J} - C'_{I,J} \right) / \pi_{I,J} \qquad (3.19)$$

or

$$\bar{\lambda}_{5,I,J} = \left(P_{I,J} - C'_{I,J} \right) = OC_x . \qquad (3.20)$$

The excess demand effect induced by a fall in output reduces profits by the *fall* in marginal profit and hence *raises* Z at the rate shown on the righthand side of (3.19). We have termed this the sales-induced own-profit output component, and symbolize it OC_x.

We now relax Y and assume only C, M, and DS hold. Then (3.12–1) reveals a sales-induced income component, YC_x:

$$\bar{\lambda}_{5,I,J} = OC_x + \sum_i \sum_j \bar{\lambda}_{5,i,j} g'_{j,Y} \left(P_{I,J} - \sum_i \sum_j a_{i,j/I,J} P_{i,j} \right)$$

$$= OC_x + YC_x . \qquad (3.21)$$

The interpretation of YC_x is similar to that of YC_p and need not be repeated. Note that if marginal profit is nonnegative, $\lambda_{5,I,J} \geqslant 0$, as is required by (3.12–7).

We shall now revert to C, M, DS, and Y, and, for ease of initial under-standing, assume as well that CC and RC in (3.17) are ignorable. This is the case, then, of the monopolist or the oligopolist who takes into account the impacts of his actions only on his own profit.[3] We then obtain from (3.12–3):

$$\bar{\lambda}_{s,I,J} = \bar{X}_{I,J}/g^I_{J,J}. \tag{3.22}$$

We now substitute for $\bar{\lambda}_{s,I,J}$ (remembering that $g^I_{J,J} = -\delta D_{I,J}/\delta P_{I,J}$) in (3.22) from (3.20) to obtain

$$g^I_{J,J}P_{I,J} - \bar{X}_{I,J} = g^I_{J,J}C'_{I,J} \tag{3.23}$$

or, with $\mathrm{d}D_{I,J} = \mathrm{d}\bar{X}_{I,J}$

$$P_{I,J}\mathrm{d}\bar{X}_{I,J} + \bar{X}_{I,J}\mathrm{d}P_{I,J} = C'_{I,J}\mathrm{d}\bar{X}_{I,J}. \tag{3.24}$$

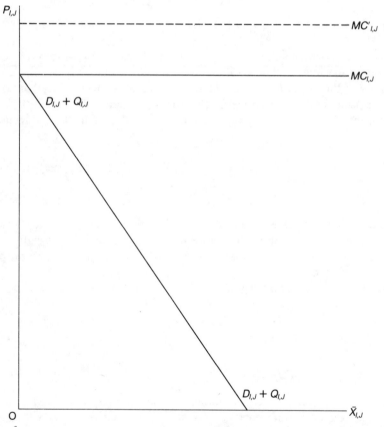

Figure 3.1   The case of null excess demand with zero demand and supply.

The lefthand side of (3.24) is marginal revenue in the traditional monopolist's sense, whereas the righthand side is the marginal cost of the price-induced demand increment. Thus, in these simplified conditions, (3.12–1) and (3.12–3) lead to the conventional profit maximization condition.[4]

It is interesting to note the conditions under which demand could equal supply when $\lambda_{s,I,J} = 0$. These results are illustrated in figure 3.1 for two possibilities: (1) when aggregate demand equals zero and marginal cost meets the demand curve at the P-axis, or (2) when the marginal cost curve's intersection with the P-axis lies above the intersection of the aggregate demand curve, at which points, from (3.23) we would set the fictitious price equal to marginal cost, given (3.19).

There remains the task of incorporating CC, RC, YC_p, and YC_x into these results. This is simply done and (3.23) is expanded to

$$
g^I_{J,J}(P_{I,J} - C'_{I,J}) = D_{I,J} + \sum_{j^* \neq J} \bar{\lambda}_{s,I,j^*} g^I_{J,j^*} + \sum_i \sum_j (\bar{\lambda}_{s,i,j} g^i_{j,Y} D_{I,J})
$$

$$
- g^I_{J,J} \sum_i \sum_j \left[\bar{\lambda}_{s,i,j} g^i_{j,Y} \left[P_{I,J} - \sum_i \sum_j a_{i,j/I,J} P_{i,j} \right] \right],
$$
(3.25)

or, as the analog of (3.24)

$$
D_{I,J} dP_{I,J} + P_{I,J} dD_{I,J} + \sum_{j^* \neq J} \lambda_{s,I,j^*} \cdot dD_{I,j^*} +
$$

$$
\sum_i \sum_j (\bar{\lambda}_{s,i,j} g^i_{j,Y} D_{I,J} dP_{I,J}) + \sum_i \sum_j \left[\bar{\lambda}_{s,i,j} g^i_{j,Y} \left[P_{I,J} - \right. \right. \tag{3.26}
$$

$$
\left. \left. \sum_i \sum_j a_{i,j/I,J} P_{i,j} \right] \right] dD_{I,J} = C'_{I,J} dD_{I,J}.
$$

Hence, in this model, the firm takes into account in its pricing decisions not only its own marginal revenue, but the marginal revenue changes its actions impose upon its customers, rivals, and via income effects, all firms including itself. The firm equates this *adjusted marginal revenue* to its marginal cost: thus if we define $MR^A_{I,J}$ as adjusted marginal revenue, (3.26) becomes $MR^A_{I,J} = MC_{I,J}$. In section 3 we shall develop methods for altering this adjusted marginal revenue to fit the firm's motivation.

2.3 Relaxing C, M, and DS

Condition (3.26) derived with C, M, and DS holding; we now relax these assumptions singly in the interpretation of (3.12). Before we do so, however, we can now remove one of the dual variables from consideration and simplify considerably the task ahead.

Our general model is constructed to permit firms to strive for bona fide target rates of return and to operate with price change constraints $L_{3,I,J}$ and $L_{4,I,J}$. The more restricted model presently under consideration eliminates the latter constraints and substitutes a modified profit maximization as a motivation for firms. These simplifications effectively remove $L_{6,I,J}$ as a constraint, as it will never bind as an equality: every firm will set demand and supply equal in equilibrium.

Formally, (3.12–1) given C, M, and Y, and $L_{6,I,J} = 0$ becomes

$$\bar{\lambda}_{6,I,J} U_{I,J} = -(P_{I,J} - C'_{I,J}),\qquad(3.27)$$

which implies that $\lambda_{6,I,J} = 0$ and, in general, $\lambda_{5,I,J} > 0$. Hence, $L_{5,I,J} = 0$ in the optimum, and DS is superfluous. This is economically rational, for suppose at $P_{I,J}$ demand exceeds supply. Then, the narrow interpretation of marginal revenue is below marginal cost, and profit maximization requires a rise in price to the optimum value. But this is also true in the case of adjusted marginal revenue, which must rise to reduce RC and raise $(OC_p + CC)$ until excess demand is eliminated. We may, therefore, set $\lambda_{6,I,J} = 0$.

2.3.1 Relaxing C

We now assume that firm I, J in the equilibrium is producing at its capacity rate $B_{I,J}$. Then (3.12–1) becomes

$$\bar{\lambda}_{1,I,J} + \lambda_{5,I,J} - OC_x - YC_x = 0.\qquad(3.28)$$

We know that $\lambda_{5,I,J} > 0$ except for the unusual cases of figure 3.1, in which cases it equals zero, and $L_{1,I,J} = 0$, implying $\lambda_{5,I,J} > 0$.

Now multiply (3.28) by $g_{J,J}^I$ and substitute from (3.18) into (3.28) to obtain, assuming $\lambda_{5,I,J} > 0$,

$$g_{J,J}^I \bar{\lambda}_{1,I,J} = g_{J,J}^I (OC_x) + g_{J,J}^I (YC_x) - D_{I,J}$$

$$-\sum_{j^* \neq J} \bar{\lambda}_{5,I,j^*} g_{J,j^*}^I - \sum_i \sum_j \bar{\lambda}_{5,i,j} g_{j,Y}^i D_{I,J}.\qquad(3.29)$$

From (3.26), when $\lambda_{1,I,J} = 0$ (no capacity constraint restrains output) the righthand side equals 0, which, as we have seen, translates into adjusted marginal revenue equals marginal cost. But when $\lambda_{1,I,J} > 0$, these two will depart from equality by the amount $\bar{\lambda}_{1,I,J} g_{J,J}^I$. For (3.29) may be written

$$\bar{\lambda}_{1,I,J}\mathrm{d}D_{I,J} = (P_{I,J} - C'_{I,J})\,\mathrm{d}D_{I,J} + \left(\sum_i \sum_j \bar{\lambda}_{s,i,j}g^i_{j,Y}\right)$$

$$\left(P_{I,J} - \sum_i \sum_j a_{i,j/I,J}P_{i,j}\right)\mathrm{d}D_{I,J} - D_{I,J}\mathrm{d}P_{I,J} - \sum_{j^*\neq J}\bar{\lambda}_{s,I,j}\cdot g^I_{J,j^*}$$

$$-\left(\sum_i \sum_j \bar{\lambda}_{s,i,j}g^i_{j,Y}\right)D_{I,J}\mathrm{d}P_{I,J}, \tag{3.30}$$

or

$$\bar{\lambda}_{1,I,J}\mathrm{d}D_{I,J} = MR^A_{I,J} - MC_{I,J}. \tag{3.31}$$

We have graphed the situation in figure 3.2, where $B_{I,J}$ binds and prevents marginal adjusted profit, $\pi'_{I,J}$, from being zero. A slight rise in $B_{I,J}$ translates into a fall in $P_{I,J}$ and a rise in $D_{I,J}$, and reflects the lefthand side of (3.31).

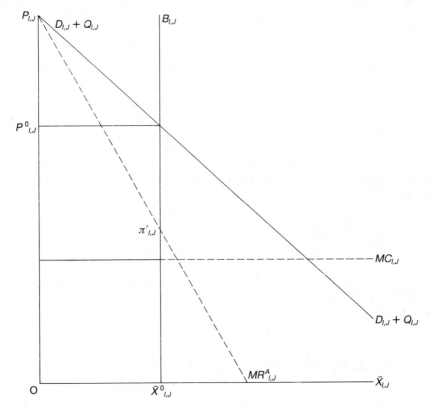

Figure 3.2   The impact of an operative capacity constraint.

2.3.2 Relaxing M

We shall now reapply C but relax M to the extent that firm I, J is bound by its minimum market share constraint, but no other firm is so bound. Then (3.12–1) becomes

$$\bar{\lambda}_{2,I,J} = (1 - M_{I,J})^{-1}(\bar{\lambda}_{5,I,J} - OC_x - YC_x) . \tag{3.32}$$

Multiplying (3.32) by $g^I_{J,J}$, substituting from (3.18), and noting that $\lambda_{5,I,J}$ can never be zero if $M_{I,J} > 0$ and industry output is positive, we may write:

$$g^I_{J,J}\bar{\lambda}_{2,I,J} = (1 - M_{I,J})^{-1} \left[D_{I,J} + \sum_{j^* \neq J} \bar{\lambda}_{5,I,j} \cdot g^I_{J,j} \cdot \right.$$

$$\left. + \sum_i \sum_j \bar{\lambda}_{5,i,j} g^i_{j,Y} D_{I,J} - g^I_{J,J}(OC_x) - g^I_{J,J}(YC_x) \right] . \tag{3.33}$$

Then, in the same manner as we used to derive (3.30) and (3.31), we obtain

$$\bar{\lambda}_{2,I,J} dD_{I,J} = (1 - M_{I,J})^{-1}[MC_{I,J} - MR^A_{I,J}] \tag{3.34}$$

$$= (1 - M_{I,J})^{-1}[\pi'_{I,J}] .$$

We have graphed the situation when $\lambda_{2,I,J} > 0$ in figure 3.3. The firm's profits are maximized (in the extended sense of adjusted marginal revenue) at $P^*_{I,J}$ and $\bar{X}^*_{I,J}$, where $\pi'_{I,J} = 0$, but the market share constraint requires production at $P^o_{I,J}$ and $\bar{X}^o_{I,J}$ with $\pi'_{I,J} < 0$. This last fact – that marginal cost lies above marginal revenue – implies that $\bar{\lambda}_{2,I,J}$ in (3.34) is positive. Also, it is seen that $\lambda_{2,I,J}$ indexes the negative marginal profit inflicted by the market share goal.

But we have yet to account for the multiplicative factor $(1 - M_{I,J})^{-1}$. Every unit increase in $D_{I,J}$ sets up a need to produce $M_{I,J}$ more units to keep the market share constraint requirement binding, which in turn sets up the necessity for $M^2_{I,J}$, and so forth in a geometric series. That is,

$$S = \Delta D_{I,J} + M_{I,J}\Delta D_{I,J} + M^2_{I,J}\Delta D_{I,J} + \ldots + M^n_{I,J}\Delta D_{I,J} + \ldots \tag{3.35}$$

With $M_{I,J} < 1$, we may reduce this series in classical fashion by multiplying (3.35) by $M_{I,J}$ and subtracting the result from (3.35), to obtain

$$S = \frac{1 - M^{n+1}_{I,J}}{1 - M_{I,J}} \Delta D_{I,J} . \tag{3.36}$$

If we take the limit by allowing $n \to \infty$, we obtain

$$\lim_{n \to \infty} \frac{1 - M^{n+1}_{I,J}}{1 - M_{I,J}} \Delta D_{I,J} = (1 - M_{I,J})^{-1} dD_{I,J} . \tag{3.37}$$

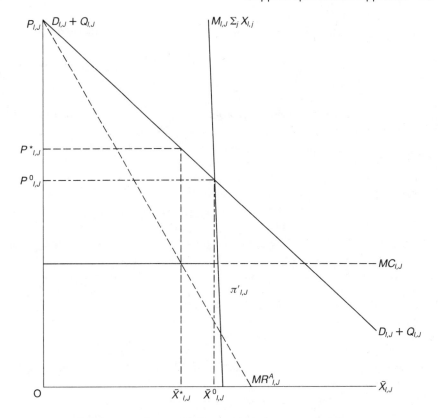

Figure 3.3   The impact of an operative market share constraint.

Hence, any need to produce extra output to meet the market share requirement generates additional amounts on that account.

If $M_{I,J}$ is reduced and $dD_{I,J}$ is the induced reduction in sales, $\pi'_{I,J}$ rises (becomes less negative) not only by the amount induced by the reduction $dD_{I,J}$ but by the amount induced by the total fall S, or $(1 - M_{I,J})^{-1}dD_{I,J}$.

Finally, suppose that some or all rivals' market share constraints bind as well, and let us denote this subset of rival firms in industry I as j^+. Then within the bracketed expression of (3.34) we add the term $(\Sigma_{j^+}\bar{\lambda}_{2,I,J^+}$ $M_{I,J^+}dD_{I,J})$. We may interpret its presence in the following manner: suppose the $\bar{\lambda}_{2,I,j^+}$ are exogenously given. Then a small reduction in $M_{I,J}$ will lead to a fall in $D_{I,J}$, which change in industry output will lead firms I,j^+ to reduce output by $M_{I,J^+}dD_{I,J}$. Multiplication by $\bar{\lambda}_{2,I,j^+}$ converts the output fall into the impact upon firm I,J's profit. Hence the marginal costs to firm I,J will be reduced by $C'_{I,J}dD_{I,J}$ directly and indirectly because of the induced fall in output caused by rivals' reactions via market share constraints to its fall in marginal costs.

3 The Methodology of Crippled Optimization

In this initial model of general oligpolistic equilibrium the firm takes into account own-profit, customers'-profit, rivals'-profit, and income components of its actions, and weights each equally, a dollar of profits gained or lost via any of them being treated as the equivalent of a dollar gained or lost through any other. Is this an adequate depiction of realistic decision-making processes in the general oligopolistic market structure? If not, or if it is in general a true vision but fails in particular industry instances, can the effects be eliminated or modified in the solution of the model?

In considering the first question, let us remember that the strength of the impact of these components in the firm's marginal reasoning is subject to the set of constraints which intrudes the firm's other goals into that reasoning. As we have seen, for example, marginal profit in the equilibrium may be negative if the firm is forced to meet its minimum market share goal. Hence, profit-maximization in any narrow or broad sense is not an absolute objective of the firm but is tempered by coordinate goals in the light of our knowledge of the frequently rather muddled pluralism of the modern corporation [3]. We accept the legitimacy of the own-profit component in that it surely represents *one* of the typical oligopolists's major goals, although the model can be altered to one featuring a search for a bona fide target rate of return or other objective should that goal not characterize any particular industry.

We have argued at length in [3] and [4] that the firm in rivalrous competition does take into account the impacts of its decisions upon its rivals' welfares, in large part because of the fear of disrupting industrial stability and thereby bringing harm upon itself, but not wholly for that reason. "Good citizenship" in an industry implies a recognition of a rivalrous consonance of long-term interests, so that rivalry coexists with strivings for harmonistic coexistence. In this light, we have sought to capture both elements by inclusion of the rivals'-profit component.

This is not to argue that *RC* is a perfect substitute for other types of reasoning about interdependence: it will not, in general, yield the same results as game-theoretic decision-making, for example. But no other manner of treating such interdependence promises to be operational in an industrial, or even more importantly, in a general equilibrium context. We deem it essential, therefore, to retain *RC*, but to develop means of controlling the magnitude of its impacts on particular firms' decision-making or even to eliminate it to meet the conditions of specific firms or industries. Ideally, we should like to discriminate for each firm in each industry, and to allow the strength of RC to vary between 0 and full-strength, the latter level as defined by the unmodified component discussed in section 2.

Similar statements are in order concerning the customers'-profit component. We believe that oligopolistic firms do concern themselves with the welfare of their customers, in largest part to assure the continuance of the supplier relationship in the face of competition, but also from feelings of pride and responsibility that develop over the years of relationship. In periods of general price advance no doubt these compunctions are dampened by the belief that cost increases can be passed through in price rises with lessened damage, but some residuum of consideration of the effect of price changes upon customers' profits persists. Once again, however, it behooves us to develop methods for eliminating or tempering CC when circumstances dictate.

Finally, we make no brief for income components: it is simply not credible that firms take into account in their pricing and output decisions the impact upon national income, because even for the largest firm in a developed economy it is negligible. In our model they will also be negligible and therefore can be safely permitted to remain, or we can eliminate them in manners to be shown for RC and CC. Therefore, we will not develop methods of explicitly removing them, on the grounds that the cost exceeds the benefit in realistic relevance.

3.1 The Sequential Unconstrained Minimization Technique (SUMT)

The solution of our oligopoly model by using a penalty function algorithm, which converts the problem to one of a sequence of unconstrained minimization problems with gradient vectors equated to zero at each solution, permits the modification or elimination of the four components, and most particularly CC and RC. As we have done in previous work, we shall employ the Fiacco – McCormick SUMT routine [1] for solution. Our work appears in [3] and [4], and a description of SUMT in its specific relevance to the present oligopoly model may be found in the appendix to [3].

The penalty function $F(\mathbf{X}, \mathbf{P}, r)$ for our model in the SUMT algorithm is written

$$F(\mathbf{X},\mathbf{P},r) = Z - r \left(\sum_k \sum_i \sum_j \ln L_{k,i,j} \right), \qquad (3.38)$$

where r is a positive exogenous parameter. Where the constraints L are all concave and Z is convex F is a function jointly convex in $\mathbf{X}$ and $\mathbf{P}$. In our general equilibrium model (as distinguished from the model of the single firm in section 2) Z is not necessarily convex, and hence we do not have a convex nonlinear programming model. We seek to minimize F as an unconstrained function with calculus techniques by setting the gradient vector of F to zero:

$$1. \quad \frac{\delta F}{\delta X_{i,j}} = \frac{\delta Z}{\delta X_{i,j}} - r \sum_k \sum_i \sum_j (L_{k,i,j})^{-1} \frac{\delta L_{k,i,j}}{\delta X_{i,j}} = 0$$

$$\text{all } i,j. \quad (3.39)$$

$$2. \quad \frac{\delta F}{\delta P_{i,j}} = \frac{\delta Z}{\delta P_{i,j}} - r \sum_k \sum_i \sum_j (L_{k,i,j})^{-1} \frac{\delta L_{k,i,j}}{\delta P_{i,j}} = 0$$

The purpose of the penalty term in parentheses in (3.38) is to prevent the penalty function problem from having a solution on the boundary of the feasible region defined by the intersection of the constraint sets. By setting up a strictly decreasing sequence $r_1 > r_2 > r_3 > \ldots > 0$, we assure that the influence of the penalty term declines without limit and the feasible region boundary is approached from the interior of the set at the point of solution to the original problem, where that solution lies on that boundary. In the absence of convexity, the local minimum to the original problem stated in (3.1)–(3.10) is not guaranteed to be the global minimum.

Consider, now, the customers'-profit component, which we desire to control or eliminate. As in (3.12–3) it occurs only in (3.39–2) in its penalty function counterpart, and it results from the partial differentiation of the $Z_{i,j}$ with respect to the relevant firm's $P_{I,J}$, and, specifically, the cost functions $C_{i,j}$ within those $Z_{i,j}$. If we control or eliminate those partial derivatives in (3.39) which are taken from the $C_{i,j}$, the solution series to the penalty functions approaches the solution to the original problem where those customers'-profit components have been controlled in or eliminated from the firms' decision-making. We are, in a real sense, copying the firms' motivation patterns.

In the SUMT algorithm, equations (3.39) are solved by iterative techniques, and control or elimination of the CC partial derivatives is accomplished by weighting the numerical differentiation process in desired ways. In the generalized algorithm we have defined the cost functions for each firm in two ways at two points in the routine: (1) in standard form, as defined in (3.2–2) above, everywhere but in the portions of the routine where differentiation is employed, and (2) in these latter routines where intermediate costs are defined as the sum of intermediate inputs times price times the weight which the supplying firm attaches to that particular customer's profits in the supplying firm's optimization procedure. We term these weights the CC *valuations*, and, of course, if they are all zero we have eliminated the CC

components from the optimizing. Again, this second definition is used only when the differentiation routine is employed, and permits the partial derivatives of the $Z_{i,j}$ with respect to intermediate input costs to be defined as desired.

Exactly similar techniques are used to control or eliminate the rivals'-profit components which intrude into (3.39-2) via differentiation of constraints $L_{5,i,j}$. These constraints are defined in two ways, the first manner again standard, and the second manner being one with weights that yield an expression used only in differentiating. The *RC valuations* express the importance each firm attaches to the impacts its decisions have upon each rival taken singly, or the analyst's estimate of such judgements, and the algorithm gives the solution to the original problem that would occur if the valuations were in effect.

The technique of crippling an optimization in this manner to eliminate or control CC and/or RC (as well as YC_x and YC_p if desired) gives our approach to modelling oligopolistic general equilibrium even more flexibility for tailoring to the specific needs of an industry or firms within an industry.[5]

4 A Methodology of Simulative Theorizing

We illustrate these techniques in detail with the results of the solutions to 45 factor cost displacements of a baseline solution for cases which contain OC (i.e. OC_p and OC_x), CC, and RC; OC and RC only; and OC only. In table 3.1 we list the baseline case parameters, sales functions, and average cost functions for firms in two industries, the first of which contains three firms and the second of which has two. The firms and industries are strictly notional.

In [4] we solved this model for the baseline case and then proceeded to obtain 44 factor cost displacement solutions by subjecting each firm taken singly to factor cost changes of ±5, ±10, ±15, and ±20 percent, and then all firms simultaneously to the same eight percentage factor cost displacements. Of these 48 solutions, four could not be obtained because of our inability to locate a feasible initial solution; therefore, 45 solutions were available – the baseline plus 44 displacement solutions. In this study we shall term these the case 1 solutions:

Case 1. Every firm seeks a constrained joint profit maximum, taking into account an own-profit component (OC), customers'-profit component (CC), and a rivals'-profit component (RC).

For the present study we solved two crippled-optimization models with the same 45 parameter sets:

Table 3.1   Baseline case parameters and functions

Firm$_{i,j}$	$\bar{r}_{i,j}$	$K_{i,j}$	$B_{i,j}$	$M_{i,j}$	$U_{i,j}$	$F_{i,j}$	$i_{i,j}$
1,1	2,00	$10,000,000	32,000	0.50	1.02	$525.00	0.06
1,2	2.00	6,570,000	28,000	0.30	1.03	318,000	0.07
1,3	2.00	2,740,000	20,000	0.10	1.02	582,000	0.06
2,1	2.00	2,190,000	15,000	0.50	1.01	652,000	0.09
2,2	2.00	1,020,000	10,000	0.20	1.04	1,175,000	0.06

Demand functions

$D_{1,1} = 45,000 - 53P_{1,1} + 9.355P_{1,2} + 8.965P_{1,3} + 0.21X_{2,2}$
$D_{1,2} = 34,000 - 55P_{1,2} + 11.853P_{1,1} + 12.183P_{1,3} + 0.10X_{2,1}$
$D_{1,3} = 29,515 - 42P_{1,3} + 8.383P_{1,1} + 8.990P_{1,2}$
$D_{2,1} = 26,910 - 32P_{2,1} + 3.550P_{2,2} + 0.20X_{1,1} + 0.21X_{1,3}$
$D_{2,2} = 15,500 - 12P_{2,2} + 3.622P_{2,1} + 0.27X_{1,2}$

Average cost functions

$C_{1,1} = 525 + 0.20P_{2,1} + 0.06(10,000,000)/X_{1,1}$
$C_{1,2} = 318 + 0.27P_{2,2} + 0.07(6,570,000)/X_{1,2}$
$C_{1,3} = 582 + 0.21P_{2,1} + 0.06(2,740,000)/X_{1,3}$
$C_{2,1} = 652 + 0.10P_{1,2} + 0.09(2,190,000)/X_{2,1}$
$C_{2,2} = 1,175 + 0.21P_{1,1} + 0.06(1,020,000)/X_{2,2}$

Case 2.   Every firm seeks a crippled constrained joint profit maximum by taking into account only *OC* and *RC*.

Case 3.   Every firm seeks a crippled constrained joint profit maximum by taking into account only *OC*.

We omit income terms from the demand functions of table 3.1, thus excluding income components from the analysis, and implicitly assuming *Y* to be fixed for all solutions.

A second goal is to analyse the results of these three cases as a start in the development of a body of methods for "simulative theorizing" (see [4]). Only if we become willing to design and specify numerically specified models of prototypical industries, to perform scientifically designed sensitivity analyses with such models, and to seek insights through deduction and multivariate inductive techniques from the results of such manipulations, will we progress in the large-scale modelling field.

4.1 *Ceteris Paribus* Analysis of the Cases

We may analyse the differential implications of the three cases at two levels of complexity. The pure *ceteris paribus* analysis studies a rival's decisions before any changes have been wrought upon his demand or marginal cost functions by adjustments of other firms. In an oligopoly context this is of limited usefulness, and we shall move to *mutatis mutandis* studies which do take these induced rivals' adjustments into consideration, as well as the accommodations made by customers. But a preliminary glimpse of the problem from the less elevated viewpoint yields initial hypotheses with which to seek perspective on the higher ground.

In the *ceteris paribus* environment, consider first the firm in case 3 equilibrium, as shown in figure 3.4a. Its price–output solution is found at the marginal revenue–marginal cost intersection. If we move from a case 3 solution, where the firm takes only *OC* into account, to an equilibrium where *OC* and *CC* are considered, all other firms' prices being unchanged, it takes the decline in its industrial customers' profits attendant upon its own price rises as equivalent to losses for itself. Hence, it is led to a price below the case 3 price, as shown in figure 3.4b. On the other hand, in moving from case 3 to case 2 equilibrium, as in figure 3.4c, where the firm considers *OC* and *RC*, it treats rivals' profit declines resulting from its price reductions as its own losses, therefore pricing higher than the case 3 equilibrium. Thus, *CC* exerts downward and *RC* upward price pressure upon the firm (see equations (3.13) and (3.14) above), and case 1 equilibrium involves simply a summation of the three component effects at the margin. In this *ceteris paribus* or *partial* context, *CC* and *RC* taken separately exert downward pressures on profits and rates.

Let us relax the pure *ceteris paribus* postulates slightly to take into account the impact upon the firm's marginal cost function when *all* rivals follow the same decision rule as the firm under consideration. The inclusion of *CC* should reduce the firm's marginal costs via reductions in intermediate goods prices, which reinforces the pure *ceteris paribus* effect displayed in figure 3.4b. Combining *OC* and *CC* in this new environment should lead to a reinforced fall in price. Profits should tend to fall least for those firms which are large users of intermediate goods and small suppliers of such goods. On the other hand, when *RC* is combined with *OC*, as in figure 3.4c, marginal cost hikes should reinforce both the upward price movement and the fall in profits. Both movements should be most severe for firms that are large users of intermediate goods.

In terms of intermediate good usage and supply, industries 1 and 2, by design, present contrasting profiles. Table 3.2 shows industry 1 to be a heavy consumer and light supplier. In the baseline solutions for cases 1 and 2 – which are completely representative in these respects of the 135 solutions we have generated – its firms sell only 4–7 percent of output to other firms, but have intermediate good costs constituting 23–53 percent of total. In opposite array, industry 2's firms sell 53–83 percent of output to industrial customers, whereas their intermediate costs are only 11–14 percent of total.

This *ceteris paribus* analysis and the data of table 3.2 lead us to formulate

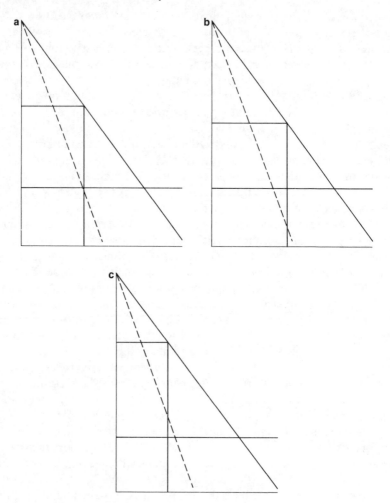

Figure 3.4   Equilibrium in the *ceteris paribus* environment. a, Case 3 equilibrium; b, equilibrium with *OC* and *CC*; c, case 2 equilibrium.

the following list of tentative hypotheses as a first step in our simulative theorizing:

1 Industry 1 rates are greater under case 1 than case 2 since as a large intermediate goods user it benefits when *CC* is universally present.
2 Industry 1 prices under case 1 lie below those of case 2 because *CC* lowers both input and output prices.

Table 3.2   Firms as intermediate goods users and suppliers, baseline solutions

	Case 1		Case 2	
	Int. demand (% sales)	Int. costs (% costs)	Int. demand (% sales)	Int. costs (% costs)
Firm 1,1	4.7	24.1	3.8	25.0
Firm 1,2	7.2	52.8	7.1	53.1
Firm 1,3	0.0	23.4	0.0	24.1
Firm 2,1	52.6	11.2	63.7	11.0
Firm 2,2	83.2	13.7	83.2	12.8

3 Industry 2 rates are smaller under case 1 than case 2 because CC injures large intermediate good suppliers and small users.

4 Industry 2 prices are lower under case 1 than case 2 (see hypothesis 2).

5 Industry 1 rates are greater under case 3 than case 1, as strong RC and weak CC yield a resultant that pulls firms away from simple maximizing levels.

6 Industry 1 prices are greater under case 1 than case 3 because RC is expected to be stronger than CC.[6]

7 Industry 2 rates are greater under case 3 than case 1 (see hypothesis 5).

8 Industry 2 prices are greater under case 1 than case 3 (see hypothesis 6).

9 Industry 1 rates are greater under case 3 than case 2 because RC pulls firms away from simple profit maximization.

10 Industry 1 prices are greater under case 2 than case 3, since RC is price-boosting.

11 Industry 2 rates are greater under case 3 than case 2 (see hypothesis 9).

12 Industry 2 prices are greater under case 2 than case 3 (see hypothesis 10).

As a first step toward validation or rejection of the hypotheses, we present table 3.3, which contains average rates and prices, as well as standard deviations, for the 45 solutions of each case. At this highly aggregate level,

Table 3.3   Means and standard deviations of rates of return and prices, 45 solutions, three cases

$Firm_{i,j}$	Case 1				Case 2				Case 3			
	r	σ_r	P	σ_p	r	σ_r	P	σ_p	r	σ_r	P	σ_p
1,1	0.24	0.05	$925.01	$21.36	0.22	0.06	$897.37	$17.36	0.22	0.06	$892.02	$18.66
1,2	0.14	0.04	880.51	18.58	0.12	0.04	857.58	15.64	0.13	0.05	851.87	18.94
1,3	0.26	0.07	968.90	17.65	0.26	0.09	951.71	10.14	0.26	0.09	946.58	17.88
2,1	0.44	0.10	914.22	32.25	0.49	0.14	920.41	20.33	0.48	0.14	898.79	28.66
2,2	0.41	0.15	1,518.31	48.55	0.50	0.19	1,528.04	29.65	0.47	0.20	1,495.14	34.08

hypotheses 2 and 5 are the only ones that are not supported by the data of table 3.3. Hypothesis 2 postulates the exact converse of the truth as revealed in the table, and hypothesis 5 is contradicted for firms 1,1 and 1,2. The dispersion of prices for case 2 is markedly smaller than for the other two cases, whereas for rates it is smallest for case 1. Hence, CC seems to scatter prices and RC to narrow their dispersion, while CC narrows the scatter of rates.

To the extent the data of table 3.3 can validate the hypotheses, our *ceteris paribus* analysis gives us some insight and leverage, but the existence of troublesome exceptions points up the need to consider the general oligopolistic interdependence and to look at the solutions in greater detail.

4.2 *Mutatis Mutandis* Analysis of the Cases

The firm's decision processes are affected by several types of interdependent feedback from the economy:

1 Changes in suppliers' prices will affect its (constant) marginal costs.
2 Changes in rivals' price will shift its sales function through their impact on household demand.
3 Changes in price throughout the economy will change the intermediate demand for its product.

These paths of interdependent causation afford a rich potential for price and profit movements that are "perverse" in the sense of *ceteris paribus* expectations.

4.2.1 *Hypotheses Validated in the Aggregate*

We shall look first at the hypotheses of section 1 that were consistent with the aggregate data of table 3.3 to see if they are validated in detail. We shall then turn our attention to the hypotheses that were not borne out by the aggregate data.

Hypothesis 1 holds up well under detailed scrutiny. Tendencies for perverse rate relationships occur only for the larger positive or negative percentage cost changes, with firm 1,3 the most pronounced transgressor. In the complete solution sets, firm 1,1 violates the hypothesis in only three of 45 solutions, firm 1,2 only twice, and firm 1,3 12 times. Hence the firm in industry 1 that sells no intermediate output, and does not benefit from the compensating downward price pull of CC in case 1, enjoys the largest number of *mutatis mutandis* profit excesses of case 2 over case 1.

These "perverse" profit movements are not readily explained by *mutatis mutandis* marginal cost changes, for such changes were positive in case 2 solutions seven times for firm 1,3 fell by small amounts three times, and fell by significant amounts only twice. Moreover, firm 1,3 has the smallest fixed costs in either industry and thus benefits least from falling average fixed costs. In only two cases, therefore, can movements on the cost side explain the perverse profit movement. It is rather on the revenue side that we must seek explanation: each of the 12 perverse movements was perverse also in price change, in that case 2 price was less than case 1 price.

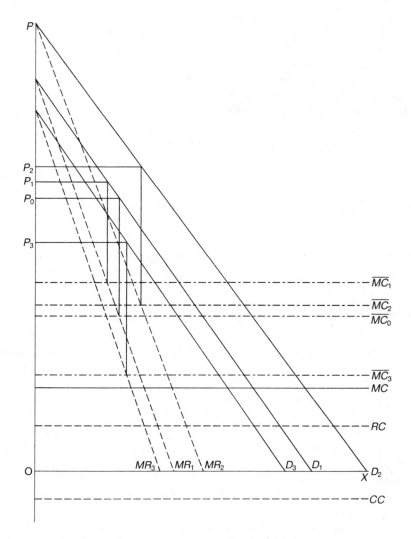

Figure 3.5   An illustration of *mutatis mutandis* adjustment.

Hypothesis 4 leads us to expect higher case 2 prices than case 1 for industry 2. For all 45 solutions firm 2, 1 reveals 15 perverse relations and firm 2, 2 fully 14, so the hypothesis is supported about two-thirds of the times.

We have reached the point where we must indicate the nature of the *mutatis mutandis* changes that can override such expected *ceteris paribus* movements, although it is often impossible to assess their specific importance for given cases. On figure 3.5 we graph a case 1 solution for firm I, J with D_1 and MR_1 the standard *ceteris paribus* sales and marginal revenue functions in an initial industry equilibrium. The CC is $-Q_{I,J}dP_{I,J}$, which, for convenience, we treat as a subtraction from marginal cost, MC, rather than as an addition to marginal revenue, and it is drawn neglecting induced changes in customers' outputs.

The RC is $\Sigma_{j} \cdot (P_{I,j} \cdot - C'_{I,j} \cdot) g'_{J,j} \cdot dP_{I,J}$, and, neglecting impacts of $P_{I,[J}$ upon $P_{I,j} \cdot$, we graph it as a constant positive increment to marginal cost: a fall in $P_{I,J}$ leads to a rise in sales by rivals and an increment of profit treated as negative cost in our analysis. The relative magnitudes of CC and RC will vary with equilibrium $P_{I,J}$, customers' outputs and input coefficients, and rivals' profit margins and other-price demand function coefficients.

We add CC and RC to MC to obtain the adjusted marginal cost, $\overline{MC}_0$, and determine the firm's initial equilibrium to be at the intersection of MR_1 and $\overline{MC}_0$, with price P_0. Suppose now, we move suddenly from general case 1 equilibrium to a general case 2 environment where all firms ignore CC. The immediate impacts on the firm will be (1) a rise in MC via intermediate inputs as suppliers ignore CC, and (2) a rise in $\overline{MC}_0$ induced by the firm's elimination of its own CC. In figure 3.5 $\overline{MC}_1$ takes both initial movements into account, giving an initial movement of price to P_1. These are the modified *ceteris paribus* movements predicted above.

But a succession of *mutatis mutandis* interactions begins to modify this initial solution. First, because all firms in industry 1 raise prices, the firm's sales function shifts to the right to D_2. Second, as marginal costs rise for all firms, and prices rise less than the full amount of this rise, profit margins $(P - C')$ fall. For the firm in our analysis, RC is the sum of *all* rivals' induced profit changes as defined above, and hence can be quite sizable. We assume, therefore, that $\overline{MC}$ falls to $\overline{MC}_2$, and price therefore to P_2. But with a general fall in prices in the industry, the firm's sales function shifts leftward to D_3, $\overline{MC}$ shifts to $\overline{MC}_3$, and we assume a final case 2 equilibrium price at P_3. Contrary to *ceteris paribus* expectations, case 2 price is lower than case 1 and case 2 output is higher than case 1.

Hence the paradox that all firms, by making decisions that keep prices lower to protect customers may in their interdependent decision-making be following policies that raise prices and reduce output. Industry 2, when compared with industry 1, is characterized by (1) relatively small intermediate input costs and hence small shifts in marginal costs, (2) very large intermediate demand for its products and small household demand, and therefore inelastic total demand functions, and (3) relatively small other-price demand function coefficients. We should expect, on these bases, "perverse" price movements in the solutions of industry 2 to be fewer than in industry 1, and this is indeed true. But about one-third of the price movements for firms 2,1 and 2,2 are perverse, giving some testimony to the strength of these forces in our model specification.

Hypothesis 6 asserts an expectation that for industry 1 prices in case 1 would be above case 3 prices because RC is believed to be stronger (in the figure 3.5 sense) than CC, even though we recognize the large intermediate good component of costs in the industry. Firm 1,1 shows only three perverse relationships in the set of 45, firm 1,2 reveals six, and firm 1,3 has 11. Although firm 1,3 reveals the smallest potential for CC, it also has the smallest RC potential, so that its greater demonstration of perversities may be explained on these grounds. In general, for these perverse movements, price differences are quite small and are partially explained by case 1 marginal cost reductions.

Hypothesis 7 asserts the expectation that case 1 rates will lie below case 3 rates for industry 2: that is, that CC and RC will typically work to the disadvantage of both firms, given their heavy reliance on intermediate demand and the relative weakness of their rivalry relations. The aggregate data of table 3.3 reveal that the scatter of rates in both cases is large, and in the light of our knowledge of the existence of price perversities, we expect the detailed data to contain perversities. The 45 solutions show 11 perversities for firm 2,1 and 17 for firm 2,2. Because both firms are about equally rivalrous (as measured by their other-price coefficients in the sales functions), but firm 2,1 is a supplier to two firms and firm 2,2 to only one, we are not surprised that the former suffers more than the latter from price-depressing CC. However, the hypothesis is broadly substantiated for both firms in detail.

Hypothesis 8 is strongly validated in detail. The aggregate data of table 3.3 show that both firms move from case 3 to case 2 with large price rises, and then they move from case 2 to case 1 with small price falls. We expect, therefore, to find RC stronger than CC in industry 2 price formation. The 45 solutions reveal firm 2,1 perversities in 12 instances and firm 2,2 perversities five times.

Hypothesis 9 implies that the typical industry 1 firm will not benefit net from its rivals' holding a price umbrella over its head. Table 3.3 reveals, in the aggregate, a positive benefit for firm 1,2, but only 1 percentage point, whereas firms 1,1 and 1,3 are unaffected. Firm 1,2's greater showing is not surprising, given that it is most affected by rivals' pricing actions in the industry.

The detailed data validate the hypothesis. Firm 1,1 is, with few exceptions, injured by RC; firm 1,2 is injured only slightly less frequently; and firm 1,3 is the least frequently injured, but still sufficiently often to accept the hypothesis. The full detail yields perversity 12 times for firm 1,1 and nine times each for firms 1,2 and 1,3. The hypothesis is accepted: *RC* is in almost every instance an interference with the profits of two or three firms in industry 1.

Hypothesis 10 leads us to suspect that industry 1's case 2 prices are greater than case 3's because of the price-boosting tendencies of *RC*. But, as in the case of hypothesis 9, study of the data indicates that this is by no means an unexceptionable rule. But firm 1,1 does conform to it in 30 of 45 times, firm 1,2 in 29, and firm 1,3 in 30. *RC* certainly biases the industry's prices upward, but in a significant fraction of the times *mutatis mutandis* movements reverse this tendency. Of the 21 solutions where one or more prices moved perversely, ten showed universal perverseness, five revealed pairs of such movements, and six were single firms' movements. In the interpretation of hypothesis 10 it should be remembered that firm 1,1's market share constraint was binding in each solution. This may well have operated to hold down price rises and profit gains for firm 1,1, and, through competition, for its rivals as well.

Hypothesis 11 asserts the same expectation concerning case 2 and case 3 rates for industry 2 as hypothesis 9 does for industry 1, this time with compelling nonvalidation. Both firms benefit from rivalry, firm 2,1 showing expected relations in ten of the 45 cases and firm 2,2 only six times. Of the six potential occasions when both firms might have shown conformance to the hypothesis, only two in fact did. Hence, in general, industry 2 benefited at the expense of industry 1 when generalized *RC* or both *CC* and *RC* (see hypotheses 5 and 7) are present.

Hypothesis 12 asserts that industry 2's prices are greater in case 2 than case 3. Only six of 45 solutions are perverse for firms 2,1 and only four for firm 2,2. Of the seven solutions in which perversity occurred, only two saw it revealed by both firms. The hypothesis is strongly validated in detail.

4.2.2 Hypotheses Invalidated in the Aggregate

Hypothesis 2 says that for industry 1, case 1 prices should lie below case 2 prices, given the strong *CC* effect. The aggregate data of table 3.3 do not support this, and the solutions in detail do nothing to contradict this perverse result. Firm 1,1 shows perversity 43 times, firm 1,2 shows it 42 times, and firm 1,3 shows it 35 times. The hypothesis is the reverse of the truth: *CC* raises prices above their *OC* and *RC* values. The *mutatis mutandis* explanation illustrated in figure 3.5 seems to be the explanation: reductions in marginal cost attendant upon introduction of *CC* raise *RC* by enlarging profit margins and result in the alchemy of the general interdependence in higher prices and lower outputs.

Table 3.4   Hypotheses accepted

	Industry 1	Industry 2
Rates	Case 1 > Case 2	Case 2 > Case 1
	Case 1 > Case 3	Case 3 > Case 1
	Case 3 > Case 2	Case 2 > Case 3
	Case 1 > Case 3 > Case 2	Case 2 > Case 3 > Case 1
Prices	Case 1 > Case 2	Case 2 > Case 1
	Case 1 > Case 3	Case 1 > Case 3
	Case 2 > Case 3	Case 2 > Case 3
	Case 1 > Case 2 > Case 3	Case 2 > Case 1 > Case 3

Lastly, hypothesis 5 – the expectation of case 3 rates above case 1 for industry 1 – was not true in the aggregate for firms 1,1 and 1,2. A study of all 45 solutions shows perversity in 30 for firm 1,1 and 24 for firm 1,2. Moreover, firm 1,2 is also a nonconformist, revealing 26 such perversities. Thus, case 3 rates show strong tendencies to lie above case 2 rates, leading us to reinforce the conclusion we have already arrived at that universal RC hurts industry 1.

Table 3.4 summarizes the evidence as revealed by the simulations. Notice that each of the four sets reveals transitivity, and hence an elementary consistency. For industry 1, the rate relationships imply that CC exerted a positive impact on rates, RC a negative impact and that CC was stronger than RC in *mutatis mutandis* results. For prices in this industry, CC and RC exerted positive *mutatis mutandis* impacts. Rivalrous consonance, therefore, hurt industry 1's profit rate but raised prices, and customer effects aided the rate of return by more than rivalrous consonance hurt it. On the other hand, both components pushed prices upward. For industry 2, rates were negatively affected by CC, positively affected by RC, with CC having greater absolute strength. The same relations hold for price impacts, except that RC outweighs CC absolutely, so that they combined to yield an upward bias to prices. Rivalrous consonance, therefore, benefited industry 2's rates, whereas concern for customers tended to lower them. Hence, there does exist an upward price bias in the economy depicted by our model, as we predicted in [4].

5 A Multivariate Analysis of the Three Cases

In this section we shall approach the *mutatis mutandis* analysis through the techniques of multivariate statistical analysis. Can we find support for the hypotheses we have accepted (or rejected) in section 4 and perhaps detect significant relationships we have missed through such objective methodology? I have expressed in [4] for case 1 a skepticism of employing multiple regression analysis of prices on factor costs when the interdependence is so tortuous. Multivariate methods are, for our needs, more powerful by virtue of their elimination of correlation among the factors selected for analysis. We have subjected the 45 observations of rates, prices, and factor costs for each case to a principal components factor analysis, and then subjected the factor loadings to a varimax orthogonal rotation of the axes to clarify the nature of the factors. We then combined the three cases into a single sample of 135 observations to see which relations persist as factors through the three different decision-making environments.[7]

We retained all factors whose eigenvalues are in excess of unity or which add at least 5 percent to the amount of explained variation in the correlation matrix of the 15 variables. The factor loadings of the resultant varimax factors are the correlation coefficients of the original variables (standardized to have zero mean and unit standard deviation) with the relevant factors, and we interpret the results for each factor taken separately. In this manner we are able to discern the dominant independent relations among rates, prices, and factor costs for each case and for all cases combined, and to compare these relations among cases. Finally, given the relative smallness of our sample sizes (45) in the three case studies, we have leaned on the conservative side to insist that only those factor loadings in excess of 0.350 in absolute size be considered significant. For the combined sample we have relaxed this value to 0.300.

5.1 The Case Studies

The factor loadings of the three sets of seven factors are given in table 3.5, with starred entries for those accepted as significant. Figures in parentheses under the headings are the cumulative percentages of variation explained by the factors.

5.1.1 Own-Factor Cost/Rate Relation, Firm 2.1

The strongest factor across the three cases is that between the factor cost of firm 2,1 and negative rate movements for that firm. In cases 1, 2, and 3 it explains 34, 40, and 10 percent respectively of the variation. Moreover, in all three cases, the only significant loadings for those variables occur in these factors, and in every case their absolute values are 0.890 or more. In none of the cases is $P_{2,1}$ significantly correlated with these two variables, so that $r_{2,1}$ and $F_{2,1}$ are associated without the intermediation of price. Price,

Table 3.5 Varimax factor loadings

Variable/Factor	1	2	3	4	5	6	7
Case 1	(34)	(56)	(66)	(75)	(83)	(90)	(96)
$r_{1,1}$	0.190	0.088	0.006	0.950*	0.145	−0.142	−0.041
$r_{1,2}$	0.163	0.352*	0.084	0.163	0.151	−0.850*	−0.148
$r_{1,3}$	0.132	0.008	0.045	0.199	0.949*	−0.098	−0.022
$r_{2,1}$	0.932*	−0.071	0.035	0.208	0.175	−0.126	−0.138
$r_{2,2}$	−0.011	−0.079	0.985*	−0.010	0.024	−0.043	−0.094
$P_{1,1}$	0.057	0.989*	−0.011	−0.003	−0.025	−0.068	−0.095
$P_{1,2}$	−0.018	0.936*	0.010	0.145	0.051	0.009	−0.148
$P_{1,3}$	0.185	0.835*	−0.150	−0.217	−0.139	−0.180	−0.085
$P_{2,1}$	−0.073	−0.250	−0.094	0.003	0.102	0.034	0.949*
$P_{2,2}$	0.003	−0.582*	−0.138	−0.223	−0.252	0.192	0.378*
$F_{1,1}$	−0.165	0.061	−0.018	−0.944*	−0.180	0.151	−0.122
$F_{1,2}$	−0.156	0.051	−0.025	−0.160	−0.149	0.955*	−0.047
$F_{1,3}$	−0.179	−0.040	−0.022	−0.123	−0.944*	0.173	−0.122
$F_{2,1}$	−0.904*	−0.244	0.025	−0.168	−0.157	0.184	−0.054
$F_{2,2}$	−0.178	−0.194	−0.473*	−0.263	−0.303	0.276	−0.015
Case 2	(40)	(54)	(64)	(73)	(81)	(88)	(94)
$r_{1,1}$	0.157	0.091	0.145	−0.928*	0.156	−0.104	0.068
$r_{1,2}$	0.191	0.130	0.166	−0.178	0.884*	−0.127	−0.025
$r_{1,3}$	0.180	0.116	0.910*	−0.158	0.149	−0.046	−0.163
$r_{2,1}$	0.920*	−0.063	0.190	−0.175	0.179	−0.067	−0.120
$r_{2,2}$	0.181	−0.003	0.226	−0.232	0.269	−0.131	−0.041
$P_{1,1}$	−0.052	0.942*	−0.011	−0.031	0.033	0.000	0.253
$P_{1,2}$	0.017	0.932*	−0.040	0.052	−0.063	0.123	−0.189
$P_{1,3}$	−0.114	0.052	−0.186	−0.040	−0.051	−0.096	0.960*
$P_{2,1}$	−0.157	0.119	−0.027	0.077	−0.090	0.931*	−0.112
$P_{2,2}$	−0.213	−0.125	−0.171	0.212	−0.170	0.337	0.171
$F_{1,1}$	−0.159	0.108	−0.148	0.940*	−0.143	0.007	0.021
$F_{1,2}$	−0.159	0.139	−0.144	0.141	−0.936*	0.013	0.043
$F_{1,3}$	−0.158	0.075	−0.942*	0.143	−0.148	0.005	0.081
$F_{2,1}$	−0.940*	−0.022	−0.147	0.147	−0.154	0.130	0.034
$F_{2,2}$	−0.172	−0.182	−0.200	0.149	−0.209	0.150	0.086
Case 3	(34)	(56)	(66)	(75)	(83)	(90)	(96)
$r_{1,1}$	0.234	0.222	0.179	−0.152	−0.880*	−0.159	0.139
$r_{1,2}$	0.392*	0.301	0.147	−0.153	−0.189	−0.793*	0.163
$r_{1,3}$	0.250	0.176	0.224	−0.893*	−0.163	−0.137	−0.087
$r_{2,1}$	0.105	−0.005	0.937*	−0.215	−0.150	−0.147	−0.097
$r_{2,2}$	0.904*	0.066	0.098	−0.195	−0.146	−0.252	−0.033
$P_{1,1}$	0.101	0.839*	0.003	−0.023	−0.074	−0.055	0.522*
$P_{1,2}$	0.132	0.983*	0.069	−0.062	−0.070	−0.038	0.031
$P_{1,3}$	−0.052	0.227	−0.037	0.067	−0.028	−0.059	0.956*
$P_{2,1}$	−0.214	−0.056	−0.289	0.029	0.128	0.087	−0.176
$P_{2,2}$	0.841*	−0.039	−0.127	0.168	0.198	0.050	−0.009
$F_{1,1}$	−0.179	0.035	−0.147	0.157	0.946*	0.143	0.059
$F_{1,2}$	−0.155	0.077	−0.171	0.157	0.152	0.942*	0.013
$F_{1,3}$	−0.184	0.053	−0.160	0.947*	0.142	0.140	−0.003
$F_{2,1}$	−0.164	−0.099	−0.913*	0.159	0.162	0.137	−0.058
$F_{2,2}$	−0.890*	−0.208	−0.144	0.197	0.189	0.216	0.021

therefore, is more prone to move in directions dictated by such forces as rivalry and concern for customers.

5.1.2 Industry 1 Price Rivalry Relation

The positive intercorrelations among the prices of firms in industry 1 explain 22, 14, and 15 percent of the variation in the cases respectively. In case 1, however, $P_{1,3}$ receives a high loading which drops to insignificance in cases 2 and 3 and, in addition, the rivalry relation is muddied by the coexistence of a strong positive relationship between $r_{1,2}$ and $P_{1,2}$, as well as high negative loadings (significant for $P_{2,2}$) for industry 2 prices. In the other two cases, however, the price rivalry effects are not so complicated, and the loadings of $P_{1,3}$ in them fall to nonsignificance.

In case 3, when firms are consulting OC only, $P_{1,1}$ and $P_{1,2}$ move in step, whereas $P_{1,3}$ moves independently of them. We should note perhaps a near-significant positive association of $r_{1,2}$ with (no doubt) $P_{1,2}$, that may account for some of $P_{1,2}$'s high loading. As we move to case 2, with firms considering rivals' welfares, firm 1,3's maverick nature exerts itself more strongly, its price moving strongly independent of the other two. In our discussion of hypothesis 6 we have noted the lower potential of firm 1,3 for both RC and CC, and this result confirms that tendency. Finally, we inject CC into firms' decision-making in case 1 and firm 1,3's prices are strongly correlated with its rivals'. We have noted in hypothesis 2 that CC tends to raise prices in industry 1 contrary to *ceteris paribus* intuitions. Given the different postures of the three firms in respect to their intermediate good supplies and demands, we now isolate the fact that CC increases their general tendency to fluctuate together, no doubt by virtue of its common impact on cost structures.

In all three of these cases the strong loading given $P_{1,2}$ is probably reflective of the close association in all three cases that it reveals for $r_{1,2}$ and $P_{2,2}$ (the price of firm 1,2's supplier). The gross correlation coefficients for $P_{1,2}$ and $r_{1,2}$ in the three cases are -0.623, -0.528, and -0.509. In case 1, $P_{1,2}$ and $P_{2,2}$ have a correlation coefficient of -0.682, but in cases 2 and 3 when CC has been eliminated r falls to -0.192 and -0.184. The *mutatis mutandis* movements of the system have obviously swamped the *ceteris paribus* impulses of CC and lead to perverse movements of customers' prices.

Interestingly, a positive association of $P_{1,1}$ and $P_{1,3}$, which excludes $P_{1,2}$, asserts itself in factor 7 of case 3 and seems to be trying to emerge in factor 7 of case 2. Each of these factors explains only 6 percent of the variation of their correlation tables, and so they depict relations which are considerably weaker than those we have just discussed, but they do assert the strongest factor loadings $P_{1,3}$ receives in the varimax rotations. Firm 1,1 does tend to be the strong rival in the industry, and firm 1,2 tends to follow weakly its lead whatever firm 1,3 may do to its price. In case 1, when price changes are computed between neighboring displacements (baseline and 5 percent, 5 percent and 10 percent, and so forth), all three firms' prices moved in the same direction 33 of 44 times. In the 11 cases when unanimity was not achieved, firm 1,1 was never the erring sister; firm 1,2 got this distinction six times and firm 1,3 the remaining five times. For cases 2, 32 unanimous movements occurred, with firm 1,1 always in the majority, firm 1,2 out of step four times and firm 1,3 eight times. In case 3, however, unanimous movements have fallen to 25, with firm 1,1 again on the side of the majority in each case of nonunanimity, and firm 1,2 being out of step only six times, firm 1,3 out 13 times. It is a heavy balance towards independence from one another that cases 2 and 3 are featuring for firm 1,2 and 1,3, with accompanying dependence on firm 1,1's prices.

5.1.3 Own-factor-cost/Rate Relation Firm 1,1

This relation is revealed in factor 4 of cases 1 and 2 and factor 5 of case 3, explaining 9 percent of the variation in the first two cases and 8 percent in the third. The relations appear about equally strong in all three cases, and in each of the cases the loading is the only significant one received by the two variables.

5.1.4 Own-factor-cost/Rate Relation, Firm 1,3

We find that this relation is of about equal strength with the last discussed, constituting factor 5 in case 1, factor 3 in case 2, and factor 7 in case 3, explaining 8, 10, and 8 percent of the variation respectively. It is weakest in terms of factor loadings in case 3, where the greater freedom given the firm through the absence of RC and CC permits it to exploit more fully its maverick propensities. In all the cases, however, these two variables receive their only significant loadings in these factors.

5.1.5 Own-factor-cost/Rate Relation, Firm 1,2

In cases 1 and 3 we find this relation in factor 6, explaining 7 percent of the variation in each, and in case 2 we find it in factor 5, explaining 8 percent. In all three cases the loading of $r_{1,2}$ is weaker than the rates in other such relations, so that the firm's rate is somewhat less sensitive to own-factor cost changes than the other firms'. Table 3.2 reveals that intermediate costs tend to account for more than half of its costs – distinctly higher than the remaining four firms – which makes this result plausible. Moreover, in case 3 $r_{1,2}$ attains significance in factor 1, related to $F_{2,2}$, the factor cost of firm 1,2's supplier, when that supplier is not restrained by *CC*. This is another aspect of the high impact of intermediate costs on firm 1, 2.

5.1.6 Own-factor-cost/Rate Relation, Firm 2, 2

This dependence reveals itself as factor 1 of case 3, though combined with positive relations with $P_{2,2}$ and a negative relation with the rate of its customer, firm 1, 2, and in case 1 as factor 3. The explanatory strengths are 42 and 10 percent respectively. *The case 3 result is the only significant positive impact upon prices that we have isolated in the three cases.* Evidently, the impacts of *CC* and *RC* upon prices in general dominate the movements dictated by factor cost. In case 2, introduction of *RC* seems to have eliminated significant impacts of factor cost for this firm upon rate.

5.1.7 Industry 2 Price Rivalry Relation

In only one case do we find a significant positive relation among the prices of industry 2: in case 1, factor 7 explains 6 percent of the variation by this relation. Seemingly, therefore, it is *CC* which leads the industry's prices to fluctuate together rather than any rivalry relation among the firms. We have seen in section 5.1.2 that at least for firm 1, 3 this seems also to be true of industry 1, although the case 2 loadings for firms 1, 1 and 1, 2 were quite high in the factors discussed there.

5.2 The Combined Cases

For the combined sample of 135 observations we have designated seven factors as revealing significant explanatory strengths. In table 3.6 we present the loadings of these factors, with the significant loadings starred.

In general, the combined sample sharpens the important relationships that tend to persist throughout the quite different circumstances of the three cases; that is, the major loadings tend to stand out from the minor loading even more clearly than in the case studies. The own-factor-cost/rate relationship for firm 1, 3 dominates the combined sample, explaining 37 percent of the variation in the correlation matrix, as factor 1. Factor 2 explains 18 percent via the covariation of industry 1's prices, and isolates the maverick position of firm 1, 2 quite clearly. Factor 3, explaining the positive covariation of industry 2's prices and with them a 9 percent contribution to explaining variation, brings out this tendency much more clearly than was done in the case studies. Factor 4 captures the own-factor-cost/rate relation of firm 2, 1, factor 5 the same relation for firm 1, 1, factor 6 for firm 1, 2, and factor

Table 3.6 Varimax factor loadings: combined sample

Variable	Factor						
	1	2	3	4	5	6	7
	(37)	(55)	(64)	(73)	(81)	(88)	(93)
$r_{1,1}$	0.150	0.172	−0.101	0.165	0.919*	−0.155	0.149
$r_{1,2}$	0.160	0.283	−0.130	0.156	0.184	−0.832*	0.229
$r_{1,3}$	0.916*	0.119	−0.047	0.186	0.172	−0.130	0.188
$r_{2,1}$	0.195	−0.104	−0.099	0.924*	0.163	−0.138	0.125
$r_{2,2}$	0.154	−0.086	−0.116	0.109	0.126	−0.169	0.930*
$P_{1,1}$	0.001	0.925*	−0.029	−0.019	0.044	−0.063	−0.012
$P_{1,2}$	0.053	0.987*	0.003	0.014	0.053	−0.021	0.051
$P_{1,3}$	−0.098	0.530*	−0.103	−0.012	−0.009	−0.087	−0.117
$P_{2,1}$	0.022	−0.021	0.953*	−0.151	−0.030	0.065	−0.117
$P_{2,2}$	−0.166	−0.136	0.300*	−0.097	−0.161	0.136	−0.257
$F_{1,1}$	−0.160	0.059	−0.045	−0.161	−0.944*	0.145	−0.121
$F_{1,2}$	−0.154	0.088	−0.001	−0.167	−0.155	0.943*	−0.143
$F_{1,3}$	−0.946*	0.064	−0.058	−0.164	−0.141	0.150	−0.120
$F_{2,1}$	−0.158	−0.100	0.095	−0.927*	−0.167	0.159	−0.104
$F_{2,2}$	−0.231	−0.185	0.053	−0.176	−0.222	0.231	−0.788*

7 that for firm 2,2. They explain 9, 8, 7, and 5 percent of the variation respectively.

In summary, the combined sample varimax rotation isolates two sets of significant relations: that between firms' factor costs and their rates of return, and that between prices in the two industries. The first is a negative relation, the second positive. These are the only relations to come through all three cases in a significant way. Most interestingly, no price/factor-cost relation revealed itself, nor did any price/intermediate-good-price relationship show. These results support broadly those derived from the varimax rotations of the case studies, with some changes of emphasis.

In both the case studies and the combined sample the inability of the factors to discern any systematic relation of prices to factor costs or intermediate good prices provides a positive body of evidence to support the hypothesis that in our model, and in all three cases, prices are moved by non-cost factors to a dominant degree. In [4] regression analysis could only provide a negative basis for that hypothesis.

Let us define a positive relation between price and own-factor-cost as existing when the loadings for both have the same sign and a negative relation when they have opposite signs. In case 1, in the 35 such relations of the seven factors, 21 were positive and 14 negative; in case 2, 26 were positive and nine negative; in case 3, 21 were positive and 14 negative; and in the combined sample, 24 were positive and 11 negative. From this evidence –

and it is not the firmest, given that all of the loadings were nonsignificant in our own definition – between 26 and 40 percent of the relations were not only insignificant but perverse in sign. If we perform the same operation for output prices and the price of supplier goods, we obtain 28 negative relations for case 1, 17 for case 2, 32 for case 3, and 24 for the combine sample. In case 1, further, where two instances of such loadings are significant, both cases were negative; in no other case or the combined cases were significant loadings revealed.

6 The Results of the Simulative Theorizing

What major conclusions may we derive from these operations with our prototypical but fictional model?

First, prices and variable costs – own-factor-costs and intermediate input costs – are not closely linked in any of the three cases. In the general oligopolistic interdependence modelled here, the variables are highly likely to move perversely, cost impulses being swamped by the pressures of the constrained competitive process. Regression analysis in [4] led us to this conclusion for case 1, and our multivariate results permit us to extend it to cases 2 and 3.

Second, and on the other hand, profits and rates are closely related to own-factor costs in all three cases, but only weakly to intermediate good costs. Indeed, principal components analysis isolated only seven "dimensions" for the three cases in the 15 variables we analyzed, a result which persisted into the combined sample. Five consist of these own-factor-cost/rate factors. They are, therefore, the most persistent forces in the model. For industry 1, it is of about equal strength across all cases and all firms, whereas for industry 2 it is quite different. Firm 2,1 reveals the strongest and firm 2,2 the weakest such relationships of all firms, despite the latter's very large factor costs.

Third, there exists some tendency, across the cases, for the prices of industry rivals to vary together. This is quite strong relation for industry 1 – whose rivalrous qualities are more pronounced – and of secondary importance for industry 2. In industry 1, firm 1,3 is a notable maverick in this regard, becoming most so in case 1 where CC enters to reinforce OC and RC. We suspect, therefore, that CC is a strong contibutor to this consociation, although it is already powerful in cases 2 and 3. This is reinforced by the fact that this relationship for industry 2 is revealed only in case 1, and is of negligible power in cases 2 and 3.

Fourth, in most instances, the directions of impact of OC, RC, and CC on rates and prices predicted by *ceteris paribus* reasoning are revealed on a strong majority basis. *Mutatis mutandis* interdependence led to an upset of these expectations in two notable instances. For industry 1, we expected case 1 prices to lie below case 2 prices because we believed *CC* should exert a strong downward force on prices in this industry. Exactly the opposite was true, and as yet we have no adequate understanding of the *mutatis mutandis* nexus for this result. Also, for this industry, case 3 rates lay below case 1 rates in many instances, contrary to our expectations. This result was not as surprising as the former, but given the closeness of the rivalrous relations of the firms, we felt a rivalrous tacit collusion would tend to benefit all of them, and that this would be supported by reductions in marginal cost owing to the presence of *CC*. The firms, however, tend to do better by going their own myopically egoistic ways.

Our results have been sufficiently rich to convince us that no general, deductive approach to general oligopolistic interdependence will be successful, in the absence of such simulative exercises as those performed in this study, in the derivation of badly needed insights into realistic economic functioning. An integrated, rationalized body of parametric techniques and multivariate tools must be developed to yield these. And models of the form displayed here must be carefully tailored to the empirical evidence of oligopolistic functioning to provide the raw material for this methodology. In short, simulative theorizing is a promising but underdeveloped field at the time of writing.

Notes

[1] Although we use the term "profit-maximizing," this is modified by the log-linear formulation of the objective function, which introduces a greater tendency toward equalization of rates than straightforward constrained profit maximization would entail. Effectively, this means that rivals and suppliers will exercise some restraint with rivals and customers in order to make rates less disparate. Because we emphasize "rivalrous consonance," I believe this has some realistic content. If the reader disagrees, he or she may define Z as the straightforward sum of $(\bar{r}_{i,j} - r_{i,j})$ and eliminate this levelling effect. For the individual firms such objective functions will be convex only within the limits noted above, but with the introduction of interindustry shipments convexity need not hold.

[2] The λ variables are expressed in the units in which Z is measured, or in our case natural logarithms of rates of return. Had we employed $Z_{i,j}$ functions defined as $(\bar{r}_{i,j} - r_{i,j})$, the only formal differences in the first-order conditions (3.12) would have been that the denominators of the first terms in (3.12-1) and (3.12-3) would have been $K_{I,J}$ rather than $\pi_{I,J}$, that is, $K_{I,J}$ instead of $r_{I,J}K_{I,J}$. Of course, the λ terms would be different, reflecting the measurement of Z in natural rate units. The modified λ variables in this latter case will also be in absolute profit units, but note that (3.13) will differ because $\bar{\lambda}$ includes an $r_{I,J}$ term which the modified λ does not. It is via this factor that the tendency towards levelling rates, discussed in note 1, enters the model.

[3] In section 4 we identify this motivation as underlying case 3 in the displacement analysis.

[4] It is worth noting that the treatment of P and X as independent variables does not prevent the marginal revenue of a price change from entering into the firm's decisions. The derivation of (3.24) indicates clearly that price policy takes into account the negative slope of D.

[5] The mathematical implications of these procedures are presented in [5].

[6] See (3.13) and (3.14) for the definition of RC, which shows that it is summed over all rivals. For this reason, and the rather strong cross-elasticity relations in the baseline solution for industry 1, we hypothesize initially that RC tends to greater strength than CC.

[7] See [2] for a detailed description and interpretation of these techniques.

References

[1] Fiacco, Anthony V. and McCormick, Garth, *Nonlinear Programming: Sequential Unconstrained Minimization Technique*, New York, John Wiley, 1968.

[2] Horst, P., *Factor Analysis of Data Matrices*, New York, Holt, Rinehart and Winston, 1965.

[3] Kuenne, Robert E., "Toward a Usable General Theory of Oligopoly", *De Economist*, 122 (1974), 471–502 [Reprinted as chapter 1 of this volume.]

[4] ——, "Towards An Operational General Equilibrium Theory With Oligopoly: Some Experimental Results and Conjectures", *Kyklos*, 27 (1974), 792–820. [Reprinted as chapter 2 of this volume.]

[5] ——, "Crippled Optimization: a Theoretic and Algorithmic Approach", Research Memorandum No. 7, General Economic Systems Project, Princeton, New Jersey, 1976.

4

Duopoly Reaction Functions under Crippled-optimization Regimes

1 Introduction

Elsewhere I have argued for an all-firm-inclusive, multi-objective, non linear programming approach to the study of realistic price-output decision-making in oligopoly analysis and modelling [11, 12]. Within a general equilibrium framework, this implies that each rival takes into account, within the limits of relevant constraints, the impacts of his decision-making on the profits of his rivals and his industrial customers [13]. To permit a greater flexibility in fitting the methodology to specific power structures within industries, I employed the technique of "crippled optimization," which modifies the first-order conditions for a constrained joint-profit maximum, permitting each rival to discount at varying rates the impacts of his decisions on each of his competitor's and customers' profits.

When this technique is lifted out of its constrained optimization, programming, n-firm context, it may be seen to be closely linked to some prior work in unconstrained game-theoretic duopoly theory by R. L. Bishop [1], J. W. Friedman [5, 6, 7], A. Hoggatt [9, 10], and R. M. Cyert and M. H. DeGroot [3,4].

This paper has several purposes. Section 2 explores the earlier approach as a simpler case of crippled optimization within this simplest of contexts using traditional Stackelberg duopoly reaction functions. In so doing it determines a new Nash equilibrium – a generalized form of the Stackelberg point – and suggests it as a possible long-run non-collusive equilibrium in mature oligopoly. Section 3 demonstrates and discusses some interesting comparative statics propositions and interprets them in the light of the hidden implications of this simplest crippled optimization reasoning. Section 4 contains a brief summary and conclusion.

Originally published in *Oxford Economic Papers*, 32 (1980), 224–40, and reproduced with permission.

2 The Duopoly Model

2.1 Reaction Functions in Crippled Optimization

We consider the case of differentiated duopoly with linear sales functions $a_i - b_i p_i + c_i p_j$, constant unit costs k_i, and no constraints upon the firms' decisions. We assume realistically that the firms are price-setters rather than output-setters. As a starting point, consider the objective of maximizing joint profit in perfect collusion,

$$\max Z = \sum_i (p_i - k_i)(a_1 - b_i p_i + c_i p_i), \qquad i = 1,2,\, j \neq i, \quad (4.1)$$

whose first-order conditions are

$$\partial Z/\partial p_i = [X_i - b_j\,(p_i - k_i)] + c_i\,(p_j - k_j) = 0, \qquad i = 1,2,\, j \neq i. \quad (4.2)$$

The term in brackets in (4.2) is the rate at which rival i's own profit is changing with respect to a small own-price change (own-profit component) and the second term is the rate at which its rival's profit is affected by the change (rival's-profit component). At the margin each firm sets the price at which marginal change affects its own profit by an amount equal but opposite in sign to its rival's profit change. Alternatively, each rival adds the impact upon its competitor's profit to its own marginal cost and equates this *adjusted marginal cost* (AMC_i) to its marginal revenue. For $p_i > k_j$, AMC_i will be higher than unadjusted, and hence both rivals will have higher prices than they would if they neglected the rival's-profit component. We shall term this solution the *Chamberlin point* in price space, signalizing that economist's suggestion that mutual interdependence recognized led to this outcome ([2], pp. 46–55).

A necessary and sufficient condition for (4.1) to be strictly concave (given b_i and b_j are positive) and hence the solution of (4.2) to be a unique global joint profit maximum is that $b_i b_j \geq 0.25(c_i + c_j)^2$, or, broadly, that other-price coefficients in the sales functions be substantially smaller than own-price coefficients. If $c_i = c_j$, for example, the restraint is merely that the product of the own-price coefficients must be no less than the square of that common other-price term. We assume in the analysis that the strict concavity condition is met throughout.

Solving equations (4.2), we obtain P^1, the vector of Chamberlin prices:

$$p_i^1 = - [2b_j K_i + (c_i + c_j)K_j]/(4b_i b_j - (c_i + c_j)^2), \qquad i = 1,2,\ \ j \neq i, \quad (4.3)$$

where $K_i = c_j k_j - a_i - b_i k_j$. We shall treat this solution as a limiting case of "rivalrous consonance" in which both competitors completely suppress rivalry and treat their rivals' gains and losses as of coordinate importance with their own.[1]

But, typically, rivals do not treat competitors' gains as equivalent to their own: the industry power structure perceived by firm i leads it to modify the importance of its impact upon firm j's profit by some factor θ_{ij} (in duopoly we can simplify the notation to θ_i). We term these coefficients "consonance factors" because they define for any short-run period the degree of tacit regard for rivals' welfares that characterizes the industry. When θ_i is positive and less than 1, the firm treats \$1 of firm j's profit as equivalent to less than \$1 of its own profit. When $\theta_i > 1$, firm i values firm j's profits more than its own, perhaps being forced by a dominant rival to defer to its wishes. When $\theta_i < 0$, firm i takes a predatory stance against its rival, being willing to undergo losses of its own to inflict losses on firm j, perhaps in a short-run price-war test of strength. And, when $\theta_i = \theta_j = 1$, the Chamberlin case of pure joint-profit maximization occurs.

We believe that realistic oligopolistic decision-making can be fruitfully studied within such a framework when complicated by a set of constraints defining goals for each rival, as explained in [11], [12], and [13]. If we remain with the simpler case of two rivals and no constraints, the firm may be viewed as maximizing the objective function

$$Z_i = (p_i - k_i)(a_i - b_i p_i + c_i p_j) + \theta_i (p_j - k_j)(a_j - b_j p_j + c_j p_i)$$
$$i = 1,2, \ j \neq i,$$

and the first-order conditions for both (all) firms are solved simultaneously:[2]

$$\partial Z_i / \partial p_i = [X_i - b_i (p_i - k_i)] + \theta_i c_j (p_j - k_j). \tag{4.4}$$

I have referred to such maximization when subject to a set of inequality constraints as "crippled optimization" to connote the fact that it is an imperfect joint-profit maximization [13]. The solutions to the first-order conditions then generalize from (4.3) – where $\theta_i = \theta_j = 1$ to

$$p_i^\theta = \frac{-[2b_j K_i + (c_i + \theta_i c_j) K_j]}{4 b_i b_j - (c_i + \theta_i c_j)(c_j + \theta_j c_i)} \equiv \frac{N_i^\theta}{D^\theta}, i = 1,2, \ j \neq i, \tag{4.5}$$

where $K_i = \theta_i c_j k_j - a_i - b_i k_i$.

Thus, P^θ is the vector of prices that results when the joint-profit maximization is crippled by the consonance factor vector $\theta = [\theta_i, \theta_j]$. We have noted that P^1 is the Chamberlin joint-profit maximization solution. When rivals ignore the impacts of their price actions upon their competitors' profits, $\theta = 0$, and the resulting price solution vector P^0 is the Cournot solution (or, more accurately, the price-setting counterpart of Cournot's quantity-setting duopoly).[3]

The first-order conditions (4.4) generalize to the following reaction function form when solved explicity for one price as a function of the other:

$$p_i^\theta = (0.5/b_i) \left[a_i + b_i k_i - \theta_i c_j k_j + (c_i + \theta_i c_j) p_j \right], \qquad i = 1,2, \; j \neq i.$$
$$\text{(4.6)}$$

The necessary and sufficient conditions for a unique price equilibrium for both firms to exist, given θ, are that

$$(\mathrm{d}p_j^\theta / \mathrm{d}p_i^\theta)_i > (\mathrm{d}p_j^\theta / \mathrm{d}p_i^\theta)_j, \qquad\qquad\qquad \text{(4.7)}$$

where $(\mathrm{d}p_j^\theta / \mathrm{d}p_i^\theta)_k$ is the slope of k's reaction function (4.6), with $k = i,j, \; j \neq i$, and the slopes of both functions are positive. Suppose firm i sets a price p_i^1. Firm j's response with p_j^1 on its reaction function leads firm i to set p_i^2. Then, p_j^2 and p_i^3 follow in response. Condition (4.7) requires that $|p_i^3 - p_i^2| < |p_i^2 - p_i^1| < p_i^3 - p_i^2|$. Since both functions (4.6) are linear, if a solution exists it is unique. From (4.6)

$$(\mathrm{d}p_j^\theta / \mathrm{d}p_i^\theta)_i = b_i / (0.5(c_i + \theta_i c_j)), \qquad (\mathrm{d}p_j^\theta / \mathrm{d}p_i^\theta)_j = 0.5(c_j + \theta_j c_i)/b_j,$$
$$\text{(4.8)}$$

and hence (4.7) implies

$$4b_i b_j > (c_i + \theta_i c_j)(c_j + \theta_j c_i). \qquad\qquad\qquad \text{(4.9)}$$

For $\theta = [1,1]$, this is implied by the strict concavity of (4.1), and, *a fortiori*, will hold for all θ in the unit square.

2.2   A Geometric Interpretation

On figure 4.1 we relate the crippled optimization analysis to the firms' isoprofit curves, the Stackelberg reaction functions derived from them, and the solutions for various θ. We graph p_i and p_i on the axes in accordance with our desire to deal with price-setting duopoly. One isoprofit contour – I_1 and J_1 – is drawn for each firm. Along the line $X_j = 0$ firm j's price reduces its sales to zero, so that isoprofit contours I become vertical lines above that line of no sales for firm j. Similarly, along the line $X_i = 0$ firm i suffers zero sales and to the right of the line firm j's contours become horizontal lines. The dotted lines k_i and k_j are the given marginal costs of the firms.

Within $ABCD$ – the region of nonnegative sales and profits for both firms where prices remain relevant – the joint-profit contours (not shown) are portions of concentric ellipses which converge with rising joint profits to that

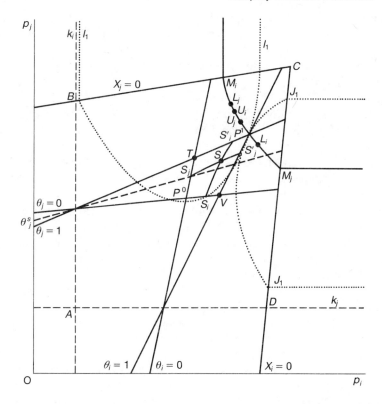

Figure 4.1   Isoprofit contours, reaction functions, and solution regions in duopoly.

center, P^1, the Chamberlin joint-profit maximum point. The locus of tangencies of firm i's and firm j's isoprofit contours, M_iM_j, passes through P^1, touches the lines of no sales at M_i and M_j, and represents a negotiation price set for the firms under collusion, because on that locus one rival's profits can be raised only if the other's suffers. M_j is the monopoly price for firm i, and the vertical segment drawn through it is its monopoly profit contour line towards which the isoprofit contours I converge as profits rise. Similarly, M_j is firm j's monopoly price, and the horizontal line its monopoly isoprofit contour. Hence, for each firm, a higher profit level is represented by a move inward (i.e. toward M_i and M_j) on the isoprofit contour map.

We have drawn the reaction functions defined by (4.6) for $\theta = [0,0]$ and $\theta = [1,1]$. For the latter, the intersection P^1 depicts the Chamberlin joint profit solution; for the former we obtain the "Cournot" solution P^0. The reaction function of $\theta_i(\theta_j) = 0$ – the Stackelberg function – intersects the $I(J)$ isoprofit contours at their minimum points; i.e. where they are tangent to horizontal (vertical) lines depicting given p_j (p_i). The reaction function for $\theta_i(\theta_j) = 1$ intersects the joint-profit isocontours where the slopes dp_j/dp_i (dp_i/dp_j) are 0.

We are interested in interpreting the "longer-run" pricing behavior in "mature" oligopoly. That is, we assume that neither rival will operate at negative profit levels and that the rivals, while sensitive to industry power structure in their adoption of θ, do not engage in warfare. In this framework, when $\theta < 0$, firm i is waging war, being willing to accept reduced profits or actual losses to inflict reduced profits or losses on firm j. In our opinion, much too much attention has been paid to the pathological behavior potential in duopoly and too little to the "peaceful coexistence" aspects of mature duopoly behavior. Therefore, our analysis adopts the unit square for θ as the region of relevance for realistic solutions; if industry mores permit tacit collusion, these limits for θ set the bounding points on the contract curve M_iM_j within which the solution occurs. Hence, our region of admissible solutions is the polygon P^1VP^0T with the possible addition (if collusion is allowed) of the negotiation set M_iM_j.

When $\theta_i = 0$ and $\theta_j = 1$ we obtain T, where firm i acts myopically and firm j acts philanthropically. But suppose that firm j guesses correctly in its judgement of firm i's power-based attitudes and assumes $\theta_i = 0$. Then it can increase its profits by moving to its *Stackelberg point*, S_j, where its profits are maximized (graphically, $\theta_i = 0$ is tangent to a J contour). Firm j no longer naively responds to a given p_i by accepting it as fixed, but by guessing θ_i correctly anticipates price adjustments by its rival. Note that in the original Cournot–Stackelberg analyses firm j was forced to form its expectations of firm i's behavior wholly from observations of i's reactions. In our analysis firm j assumes firm i is performing a crippled optimization and can base its expectations of θ_i on its own perceptions of the industry power structure. This is a gain in realistic interpretation of oligopolistic behavior, for firms in this market structure are forever engaged in striving to perceive the limits of maneuver against one another which the perceptions of power structure define.

Indeed, we may interpret firm j's movements away from T as a search for a new θ_j which – given $\theta_i = 0$ – maximizes its profits. This will, of course, be that θ_j whose reaction function intersects $\theta_i = 0$ at S_j. That function – θ_j^s on figure 4.1 – appears as a dotted line. With this step we have moved from a short-run analysis with fixed θ to a longer-run view in which rivals vary their consonance factors on the basis of their perceptions of their rivals' factors, performing crippled optimizations with the new factors until the optimal θ value is found.

Suppose, now, firm j finds this θ_j and attains S_j. The profit contour J which is tangent to the firm i reaction function for $\theta_i = 0$ (not drawn) is the *minimum* profit firm j need accept in bargaining tacitly or overtly with firm

i as long as $\theta_i = 0$. Assume the intersection of that isocontour with the M_iM_j negotiation set is at L_j, and that the I contour line passes through S_j intersects the negotiation set at U_i. Then L_j is a lower bound on the profits firm j can be forced to accept and U_i is the upper bound on profits firm i can obtain.[4] A joint price movement to a P between these two limits in a quantum leap via collusion will benefit both, but can be accomplised only by a collusive move outside the framework of crippled optimization that includes the freezing of θ at the values implied by S_j.

Of course, our reasoning is fully symmetrical for $\theta_j = 0$ and firm i seeking that θ_i that maximizes its profit at its Stackelberg point S_i. Similarly, a lower bound L_i and an upper bound U_j can be located on the negotiation set reflecting the new assumptions.

But in the long run θ_i and θ_j can take any values between 0 and 1 as firms' perceptions of their and their rivals' power change and as they experiment, so that duopoly behavior can lead to reaction functions which intersect anywhere within the admissible polygon (before considering possible collusive movement to points on M_iM_j). Similarly, any point within the polygon can be obtained as the intersection of reaction functions defined by a unique θ in the unit square. Effectively, the Stackelberg point S_j is obtained by choice of a θ_j^s intermediate between 0 and 1 (as drawn) intersecting firm i's $\theta_i = 0$ function as shown in figure 4.1. But the Stackelberg strategy must be generalized, since θ_i also can take any value between 0 and 1. Hence S_j will lie on a locus of Stackelberg tangencies S_jS_j' as shown, every point on which reflects an optimal price strategy by firm j for a given θ_i between 0 and 1. Similarly, S_iS_i' depicts the locus of Stackelberg strategies for firm i as θ_j varies. When Stackelberg points occur in the interior of the feasible polygon for either or both of the rivals the limits to tacit collusion agreements on the contract curve can be narrowed to some set of limits illustrated by L_j, U_j, L_i, and U_i on figure 4.1.

At point S on figure 4.1 the loci of Stackelberg solutions for both rivals intersect, and a Nash equilibrium point occurs. That is, at the intersection neither rival has an incentive to change its θ-value to improve its position given that the other has adopted the θ-value relevant to the point S. Before this point is reached, when one rival determines a Stackelberg strategy on the basis of a rival's θ-value, this latter rival will change that θ-value in its own Stackelberg play. But this will lead the first rival to adopt a new θ-value to obtain a new strategy on his Stackelberg locus, and so forth. Such reactive Stackelberg adjustments cease at S because choices by either rival of new consonance factors are harmful to their profit positions.

The point S is a Nash equilibrium when the dimension of optimally variable θ is added to the duopoly problem. Whether firms do or do not perceive that their rivals are adjusting their θ-values to their own changes in θ is not important to the interpretation of S. If both rivals perceive immediately that their opposite numbers are adjusting their consonance factors, the point S should be attained instantanesouly. If they do not, a series of movements to that point will occur. Only the path of attainment of S will change.

In our interpretation P^0 – the Cournot point – is a Nash equilibrium only if θ is fixed at O. But in this respect it differs not a jot from the intersection of reaction functions for any other fixed $\theta \in [0,1]$. In the usual interpretations of the Cournot point as a Nash equilibrium the conditions are that each rival expects his counterpart to hold price constant at current values (which implies that neither perceives the other is moving along a reaction function). In this interpretation, if rival i perceives that rival j is *actually* moving along $\theta_j = 0$, rival i moves to his Stackelberg point S_i, and the Nash equilibrium vanishes. But with this change the whole concept of rival i's reaction function also breaks down, since only one point on it is relevant, revealing the difficulty of depicting oligopolistic behavior with the usual interpretation of reaction functions. In our framework, a movement to S_i reflects a change in θ_i, and with it a new Nash equilibrium relevant for the new fixed θ.

The generalized Stackelberg point, S, has a strong attraction to both rivals *in the long run when θ is taken to be variable*. If tacit or overt collusion occurs, the relevant isoprofit contours intersecting at S provide the bounds on tacit bargaining on the negotiation set. For, suppose both rivals start with θ_i and θ_j equal to 1, and hence are at the Chamberlin point P^1. Firm i discovers it can increase its profit by reducing its price to try to get to S_j' on firm j's reaction function. It experiments to see if firm j will react to a reduction in its concern for j's profits. Similarly, firm j attempts to get to S_j' Each effectively reduces its θ factor to some value less than 1. But these new functions yield different Stackelberg points, which lead to further modifications of θ, and so forth, until S is reached with appropriate θ factors. At this point such strivings cease since no incentive exists to upset the status quo except by collusive attempts to reach $M_i M_j$.

Similarly, if the rivals begin from the Cournot point they will also approach point S. The line $S_i S_i'$ shows the optimal θ_i for any given θ_j, hence in the long run it will never serve firm i's purposes to adopt a θ_i less than that of the reaction function that intersects $\theta_i = 0$ at S_i. Similarly, it will never be to the advantage of firm j to adopt a θ_j less than the value relevant at S_j. In a succession of moves from $\theta = [0,0]$, therefore, it will profit both firms to increase their θ factors until S is reached, at which point both will lose from uncoordinated moves. Hence, S is approached from $\theta = [0,0]$ as well as $\theta = [1,1]$.

In the longer run, when θ is variable, even in conditions when information and perceptions of the rivals are imperfect, we expect that both firms will be led to solutions that fall outside the area $P^0 T S_i' S S_j' V$ within the polygon of feasible solutions. Consider, for example, firm i: for any given allowable $\theta_j \in [0,1]$, θ_i will be pulled rightward on figure 4.1 toward the intersection of θ_j with $S_i S_i'$. This movement increases the prices and profits of both rivals, because the movement is toward J isocontours that represent higher profit levels. Hence, firm i's self-motivated strategies benefit firm j as well, and that perception of greater benefit should be reflected in the tendency to rule out solutions in the area $P^0 T S_i' S_i'$. A reversal of roles for firms i and j leads to a symmetrical proscription of $P^0 T S_j' S S_j' V$ in which the pressures to escape are generated by the ability of both firms to improve profits even if one of the firms is passive and does not change its θ factor.

The existence of an interval in which a $\theta_i > 0$ increases firm i's profits for a given θ_j occurs for the following reason. As θ_i rises, θ_j constant, p_i and p_j both rise. As p_i rises for a time in the inelastic portion of the demand curve, profits rise, and these are enhanced even more by the shift outward owing to the responsive rise in p_j. At the relevant Stackelberg point the reduction in profit brought about by the rise in p_i in the elastic portion of the curve is just balanced by the increase in profits caused by the induced sales increase springing from the induced rise in p_j. Beyond this point a further rise in θ_i benefits the rival but harms firm i's profits, and rivalrous consonance begins in earnest.

The reduced region of high probability for the solution, therefore, is $SS_i' P^1 S_j'$. For a given θ_j which intersects this set, firm i is led to adopt a θ_i which drives the solution leftward toward $S_i S_i'$ and therefore reduces firm j's profits. Similarly, improving moves by firm j for given reaction functions for firm i push solutions downward and toward lower profits for firm i. Therefore, noncollusive movements in this region cannot benefit both rivals, and duopolistic struggle should drive the solution into this sector (plus, of course, the relevant portion of $M_i M_j$ if collusive agreements, tacit or overt, are permitted into the feasible set). It is in this region that the doctrine of rivalrous consonance has meaning, because only for such solutions need a compromise of profits be truly sought.

2.3 Crippled Optimization and θ

The distinctive nature of our approach consists in the belief that duopolists' (and, more generally, oligopolists') pricing actions are conditioned in a mature industry relationship by a perceived power structure that varies with each firm and that can be closely approximated in the short run by a con-sonance factor at which it values in terms of its own profits the profit impacts upon rivals of its pricing decisions. It is not necessary, of course, that firm managements actually frame their power considerations in such terms, nor that they literally devise θ estimates. It is sufficient that their attitudes, however determined, can be approximated by such terms in predicting their actions. The treatment of power structure in this disaggregated, if unidimensional, manner has the attraction of being based upon profit considerations – surely a crucial factor in the firm's thinking – and permitting all pairwise relations in the pecking order to be included.

Our analysis also assumes a mechanism by which θ adapts through experimentation to attain long-run solutions in the mature industry, and permits us to focus upon a subset of potential long-run solutions wherein realistic price decisions are expected to lie. At the same time we recognize that the wholly rational, full-information basis on which the theory is based (at least ideally) may not conform to realistic duopoly (oligopoly) conditions, and consequently that the intersection of reaction functions may occur outside that set of expected solutions. Moreover, as we have argued elsewhere [11, 12, 13] firms usually have multiple objectives expressed in the form of constraints upon acceptable solutions, which complicate the analysis of this chapter in ways discussed in those references.

It may be, therefore, that firms' consonance factors are more rigid even in the long run than our analysis implies. Realistic long-run behavior in some or most industries may be characterized more closely by rather fixed θ, with experimentation by rivals to determine the implicit values of the other firms' θ values – that is to say, others' perceptions of the power structure. Our short run analysis may be quite characteristic of the long run in settled or lethargic industry structures.

Our purpose is to design methods for oligopoly analysis that are operational. It is hoped that θ for industries can be formally or informally estimated by the study of price data and industrial history. With these estimates it is our hope to formally model such industries in order to gain insight into their pricing structures.[5]

3 Comparative Statics Propositions

Clearly, from figure 4.1, for the reaction functions under consideration, a rise in θ_i raises both p_i and p_j. More exactly, if $p_i > k_i$ and $p_j \geqslant k_j$, $dp_i/d\theta_i$ and $dp_i/d\theta_j$ are positive. From (4.5)

$$\frac{dp_i}{d\theta_i} = \frac{(a_j c_j - b_j c_j k_j - \theta_j c_i c_j k_i) + p_i(c_j^2 + \theta_j c_i c_j)}{D^\theta} \quad (4.10)$$

The assumed strict concavity of (4.1) (see 4.9) assures that $D^\theta > 0$; hence, for (4.10) to be positive it is necessary and sufficient that

$$(a_j - b_j k_j)c_j + p_i(c_j + \theta_j c_i)c_j > \theta_j c_i c_j k_i \quad (4.11)$$

or

$$\left(a_j - b_j k_j\right)\frac{1}{k_i} + \frac{p_i}{k_i}c_j + \left(\frac{p_i}{k_i} - 1\right)\theta_j c_i > 0, \tag{4.12}$$

all terms of which will be nonnegative and at least one positive for $p_j \geqslant k_j$, $p_i > k_j$. Hence, $dp_i/d\theta_i > 0$.

Similarly,

$$\frac{dp_i}{d\theta_j} = \frac{-\left(c_i^2 k_i + \theta_i c_i c_j k_i\right) + p_i\left(c_i^2 + \theta_i c_i c_j\right)}{D^\theta} \tag{4.13}$$

which is positive if and only if

$$\frac{p_i}{k_i}\left(c_i^2 + \theta_i c_i c_j\right) > \left(c_i^2 + \theta_i c_i c_j\right), \tag{4.14}$$

for which $p_i > k_i$ is necessary and sufficient.

Hence, as we should suspect, for profitable duopolists, as one or both rivals increase their consonance factors θ_k, both prices rise monotonically (and, of course, quantities sold are reduced). And, as is seen in figure 4.1, for θ in the unit square *both* firms attain their price maxima where $\theta = [1,1]$.

Consider now the somewhat less clearcut case of the price impacts of cost increases and their relation to fixed consonance factors in the short run. In what follows, therefore, we assume that θ_i and θ_j are fixed. As a preliminary, consider the modified reaction functions (4.6). The slope terms for those linear equations do not contain cost factors, and hence a rise in k_i will result in new reaction functions for both firms parallel to the old. Let A_i and A_j be the intercept terms in those equations. Then

$$\begin{aligned}1. \quad & dA_i = 0.5dk_i \\ 2. \quad & dA_j = \left(-0.5d\theta_j c_i/b_j\right)dk_i\end{aligned} \tag{4.15}$$

For an own-cost change the reaction function R_i shifts to the right by half the cost change as shown in figure 4.2; however, R_j – firm j's reaction function for a fixed θ_j – shifts down, reducing the rise in p_i that would occur if R_j remained fixed. It will be useful to work through the adjustments in p_i and p_j.

In phase 1, R_i shifts by one-half the rise in k_i to R_i' and firm i taking p_j constant at p_j^1 (in P_1) on figure 4.2 raises p_i to p_i^2, thereby moving the price vector to P_2. But the rise in p_i shifts firm j's sales function to the right and increases firm j's adjusted marginal cost (AMC_j) as the rival's-profit component in its first-order condition rises (see 4.4 and 4.2 above). Both of these movements lead firm j to raise its price to p_j^3, and the price vector to P_3. Obviously, the amount of price raise will depend upon the slope of R_j (see

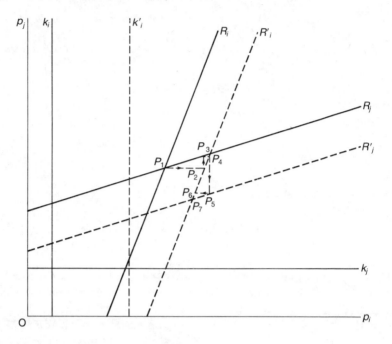

Figure 4.2   Comparative statics of a cost change.

4.8). The rise will be greater the less sensitive the sales function is to own-price (the smaller is b_j), the more sensitive it is to rival's-price (the larger is c_j), the more concerned firm j is for firm i's profits (the larger is θ_j), and the more sensitive firm i's sales are to the rise in p_j (the larger is c_i). It is important to note that rivalrous consonance is playing its usual role of boosting prices, or holding a price umbrella over the rival's head.

However, the rise in p_j to p_j^3 shifts firm i's sales function to the right and raises AMC_i by an amount dictated by the slope of R_i'. From (4.8) it is seen that the slope is dependent upon b_i, c_i, θ_i, and c_j in the manner already described for firm j's movement of P_3. After a sucession of such moves, phase 1 ends with the attainment of P_4, with p_i and p_j higher than at P_1. Moreover, if rivalrous consonance did not exist ($\theta = [0,0]$) the slope of R_j would be smaller and the slope of R_i' larger (see figure 4.1) and therefore P_4 would contain smaller values than shown in figure 4.2 (though still larger than P_1). Hence, rivalrous consonance in phase 1 has served as a net price booster.

At the start of phase 2, however, firm j finally perceives the reason for firm i's initiating move to P_2 and includes the larger k_i' in its first-order condition (4.4). This *lowers* the rival's-profit component because every sale firm j takes from firm i now causes firm i to lose less profit. At this point rivalrous consonance is a two-edged sword for firm i, for AMC_j falls and shifts R_j to R_j'. Since this shift occurs *only* because rivalrous consonance exists ($\theta_j > 0$) it will vary directly with the strength of the consonance coefficient θ_j (see (4.15–2)) and the sensitivity of firm i's sales to a reduction in p_j (c_i). Firm j must take into account, however, the "elasticity" of its sales function to own-price: the larger b_j, the less will it have to reduce price to compensate for the fall in the rival's-profit component. Firm j, therefore, will move P from P_4 to P_5, and the interaction of phase 2 will ultimately carry P to its final equilibrium at P_7.

Note that the shift of R_j is a reflection of a *downward* pressure on prices brought about by rivalrous consonance, as opposed to its *upward* pressure in the iterative adjustments through the slopes of fixed reaction functions. In this instance, therefore, a rise in one rival's cost will lead to price changes which include two opposing component forces caused by rivalrous consonance: broadly, a *slope* component which is price-increasing and a *shift* component which is price-decreasing.

The net resultant on P is the sum of these forces. Indeed, we can depict the outcome in exactly these terms. In figure 4.3 we have magnified the crucial area of adjustment of figure 4.2 in order to depict the movement more clearly. For p_1, the change from p_i^1 to p_i^7 is equal to the amount of the shift in $R_i(P_1M)$ less MN, which is simply the slope of R_i' times

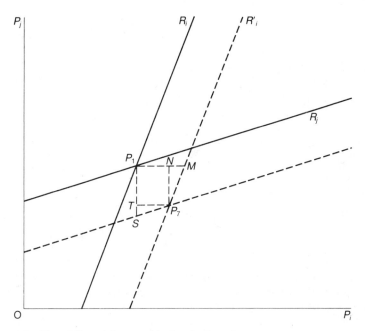

Figure 4.3   The shift-and-slope analysis of price change.

the change in $p_j(P_1T)$. The same reasoning holds for $(p_j^1 - p_j^7)$. We may write:

1. $\mathrm{d}p_i = $ shift of $R_i + $ slope of $R_i \times \mathrm{d}p_j$
2. $\mathrm{d}p_j = $ shift of $R_j + $ slope of $R_j \times \mathrm{d}p_i$.

$$(4.16)$$

From (4.15) and (4.8)

1. $\mathrm{d}p_i = 0.5\mathrm{d}k_i + [0.5(c_i + \theta_i c_j)/b_i]\mathrm{d}p_j$
2. $\mathrm{d}p_j = [-0.5\theta_j c_i/b_j]\mathrm{d}k_i + [0.5(c_j + \theta_j c_i)/b_j]\mathrm{d}p_i$

$$(4.17)$$

or

$$\begin{bmatrix} 1 & [-0.5(c_i + \theta_i c_j)/b_i] \\ [-0.5(c_j + \theta_j c_i)/b_j] & 1 \end{bmatrix} \begin{bmatrix} \mathrm{d}p_i/\mathrm{d}k_i \\ \mathrm{d}p_j/\mathrm{d}k_i \end{bmatrix} = \begin{bmatrix} 0.5 \\ [-0.5\theta_j c_i/b_j] \end{bmatrix}$$

$$(4.18)$$

and, therefore,

1. $\mathrm{d}p_i/\mathrm{d}k_i = [2b_ib_j - \theta_j c_i(c_i + \theta_i c_j)[/D^\theta$
2. $\mathrm{d}p_j/\mathrm{d}k_i = [b_i(c_j - \theta_j c_i)/D^\theta]$.

$$(4.19)$$

These expressions may be derived directly, of course, by differentiating system (4.5) totally, but the method we have used casts maximum light on the shift-and-slope nature of the adjustment process after a cost change under rivalrous consonance.

An immediate question arises: can rivalrous consonance ever lead to the perverse case where $\mathrm{d}p_i/\mathrm{d}k_i < 0$? From (4.19-1), because $D^\theta > 0$ by strict concavity of the objective functions, the sign of this expression depends upon the sign of the numerator. It will be negative if and only if

$$\theta_j c_i(c_i + \theta_i c_j) > 2b_ib_j. \qquad (4.20)$$

From strict concavity we have the additional necessary condition that

$$2b_ib_j > 0.5(c_i + \theta_i c_j)(c_j + \theta_j c_i). \qquad (4.21)$$

Together (4.20) and (4.21) imply that, in the perverse case,

$$\theta_j c_i > c_j, \qquad (4.22)$$

which in turn implies, because θ_j is in the unit interval, that $c_i > c_j$.

We shall show that the perverse case is possible, but only under unusual and improbable circumstances. First, let us express cross-price coefficients as multiples of own-price coefficients:

$$c_i = m_ib_i, \qquad c_j = m_jb_j. \qquad (4.23)$$

Then (4.20) can be reduced to

$$b_i/b_j > (2 - \theta_i\theta_j m_i m_j)/\theta_j m_i^2, \tag{4.24}$$

and by substituting (4.23) into (4.22), the condition of (4.24) can be tightened further to

$$b_i/b_j > 2/m_i^2. \tag{4.25}$$

Perversity can occur, therefore, in a duopoly where one rival controls a much larger share of the market than the other; indeed, if $m_i < 1$, as we would expect for a dominant rival, that necessary predominance may be a large multiple of 2. Moreover, for the perverse result, the weak rival's position is reflected in a very high rival's-profit component $(\theta_j c_i)$ which leads to a large shift downward in R_j, also, the small, absolute cross-price sensitivity of the weak rival to the strong rival's price actions (c_j) insures that the slope of R_i is steep.

The improbability of these conditions in a closed duopoly system hinges upon the notion that if a rival with very large sales lost a large quantity through a rise in its price, a sole small rival will fail to benefit from the action by experiencing a large increase in sales. A great leakage from the system is implied. Therefore, the possibility seems most likely when the primary competition of a strong duopolist exists abroad among exogenous exporters and a weak domestic rival acts under strong consonance motivation to exploit a large fall in his AMC.

The improbability of its occurrence for rivals of approximately equal size in a closed system can be investigated for the case where $b_i = b_j = b$, $c_i = c_j = c$. Perversity has its best chance of occurring under (4.20) when $\theta_i = \theta_j = 1$, and we therefore set them to that value. Then, from (4.20) and (4.21) we obtain the contradiction

$$c > b > c. \tag{4.26}$$

Hence the perverse case cannot arise under these best conditions: however, even the condition derived from (4.20) standing alone implies the realistically unacceptable proposition that cross-price sensitivity is larger than own-price sensitivity.

On the other hand, a rise in k_i may move p_j up or down, depending upon the sign of the numerator of (4.19–2). Specifically, p_j will fall if

$$c_j < \theta_j c_i. \tag{4.27}$$

When this occurs, the downward shift of R_j to R_j' on figure 4.2 outweighs the upward pull exerted by the slope of R_j'. Note, from (4.22), that if the perverse case of dp_i/dk_i occurs, p_j must also fall, but the converse is not true. When firm j's rival's-profit component shifts AMC_j down greatly and c_j does not move its sales curve much rightward, it may indeed pay firm j to lower the price umbrella it had been holding over its rival's head and thereby constrain the rise in p_i.

The negative net impact upon prices that rivalrous consonance can inspire is not as paradoxical as might appear at first sight. A fall in the profit margin of a rival can be viewed as the equivalent of a reduction in his power base, and will lead the other firm to lower the price protection afforded previously. This will be tempered, and in the normal case, will be outweighed, by the shift rightward of the sales function of firm j set off by the initial rise in p_i, but where cross-price elasticities are weak, the net effect of a fall in p_j and (though much less likely) a responding fall in p_i may occur.

4 Conclusions

Crippled optimization, with or without constraints, is one path toward a necessary integration of rivalry and cooperation in oligopoly theory. It has the advantages of preserving the identities of individual firms and their pairwise relations with each other, providing a flexible framework to accommodate industry specifics, and approximating the crucial impact upon profits of the firms' different views of the power structure. The technique permits a short-run analysis where the consonance coefficients are treated as fixed and a long-run analysis where they are adaptive. The former analysis permits us to extend and unify classic reaction function analysis. The latter isolates a generalized Stackelberg point which provides an interesting Nash equilibrium in the long-run interactive game.

The theory also casts light upon the contradictory impulses that a unilateral cost increase radiates among oligopolists. On the one hand, the unfortunate rival's attempt to pass through the increase in price rises leads rivals to increase their own prices as their demands strengthen. But on the other hand, the decline in the profit margin of the firm suffering a cost increase leads its rivals to reduce the price protection formerly afforded it. Net price changes in the industry are net resultants of these two forces.

Notes

[1] Our assumption throughout (unless specifically indicated to the contrary) is that effective legal prohibitions exist forbidding the overt collusion necessary for side payments. The "consonance" of interests that we believe is accepted in mature oligopolies is reflected in greater or lesser degree by tacit understandings that become encoded in industry folkways.

[2] The second term in Z_i is linear in p_i. Hence, when own-profit functions are concave, Z_i remains concave in p_i even when $\theta_i < 0$.

[3] Note that our procedure permits us a clearer characterization of the nature of joint-profit maximization versus Cournot behavior than Chamberlin's classic interpretation and terminology gives ([2], chapter 3). The distinction is not that of recognizing or ignoring mutual interdependence: the presence of c_i and k_j in (4.6) for any θ assures that this interdependence is present. It is rather the valuation attached to rivals' adverse profit experiences, i.e. θ, that is the crucial difference.

[4] We follow A. Henderson [8] here.

[5] For an application of the theory to the determination of an $11 \times 11\ \theta$ matrix for the OPEC cartel, see [14].

References

[1] Bishop, Robert L., "Game-Theoretic Analyses of Bargaining", *Quarterly Journal of Economics*, 77 (1963), 559–602.

[2] Chamberlin, Edward H., *The Theory of Monopolistic Competition*, Harvard University Press, Cambridge, MA, 1933.

[3] Cyert, R. M. and DeGroot, M. H., "Multiperiod Decision Models With Alternating Choice as a Solution to the Duopoly Problem", *Quarterly Journal of Economics*, 84 (1970), 410–29.

[4] ——, "An Analysis of Cooperation and Learning in a Duopoly Context," *American Economic Review*, 63 (1973), 24–37.

[5] Friedman, J. W., "Individual Behavior in Oligopolistic Markets: an Experimental Study", *Yale Economic Essays*, 3 (1963), 359–417.

[6] ——, "Reaction Functions and the Theory of Duopoly", *Review of Economic Studies*, 35 (1968), 257–72.

[7] ——, "On Experimental Research in Oligolopy", *Review of Economic Studies*, 36 (1969), 319–415.

[8] Henderson, Alexander, "The Theory of Duopoly," *Quarterly Journal of Economics*, 68 (1954), 565–81.

[9] Hoggatt, Austin, "Measuring the Cooperativeness of Behavior in Quantity Variation Duopoly Games", *Behavioral Science* 12 (1967), 109–21.

[10] ——, "Response of Paid Student Subjects to Differential Behavior of Robots in Bifurcated Duopoly Games", *Review of Economic Studies*, 36 (1969), 417–32.

[11] Kuenne, Robert E., "Toward a Usable General Theory of Oligopoly", *De Economist*, 122 (1974), 471–502. [Reprinted as chapter 1 in this volume.]

[12] ——, "Towards an Operational General Equilibrium Theory with Oligopoly: Some Experimental Results and Conjectures", *Kyklos*, 27 (1974), 792–820. [Reprinted as chapter 2 in this volume.]

[13] ——, "General Oligopolistic Equilibrium: a Crippled-optimization Approach". In *Pioneering Economics: Essays in Honor of Giovanni Demaria*, Cedam, Padua, 1978, 537–77. [Reprinted as chapter 3 in this volume].

[14] ——, "Rivalrous Consonance and the Power Structure of OPEC', *Kyklos*, 32 (1979), 19–35. [Reprinted as chapter 6 in this volume.]

5

Rivalrous Consonance: A Theory of Mature Oligopolistic Behavior in a General Equilibrium Framework

1 Introduction

The theory of rivalrous consonance as a framework within which to analyze the strategies of mature oligopolistic industries incorporates a body of assumptions that appear to me to be widely accepted. Indeed, they receive such common acceptance as to seem trite. Yet, in my view, they have not previously been employed as the formal, postulational basis for an operational theory of oligopolistic decision-making. The following are among the most important.

Assumption 1. Mature oligopolies, or rivalrous industries with a substantial industrial history, are *communities* in important respects. Individual units within such communities have important competitive interests which make them rivals in their goal seeking. But as members of an acknowledged community they have common interests which imply cooperative relations. Their actions, therefore, will be motivated by a blend of rivalrous and cooperative goals in mutual recognition of a *rivalrous consonance of long-run interests.*

Assumption 2. Each such community, in which individual actors are few enough in number to impact the industry in personally identifiable ways, has a power structure, or a web of perceptions among firms that has an important bearing upon their decisions. The binary, firm-to-firm, combination of rivalry and cooperation that constitutes an important component of their decision-making is the operational expression of that power structure.

Originally published as chapter 8 in A. E. Andersson, D. F. Batten, B. Johansson and P. Nijkamp (eds), *Advances in Spatial Theory and Dynamics*, North-Holland, Amsterdam, 1989, 107–18. The paper was originally delivered as a lecture at the European Summer Institute, University of Umeå, Umeå, Sweden, July 1986.

Unless that sociological matrix of power relationships is incorporated in the analysis of industry decision-making little hope exists for useful insights.

Assumption 3. Because these industrial communities and their power structures are the result of unique historical evolution energized by unique individuals and framed by unique industry and product characteristics, each is marked by distinguishing patterns of behaviour. A universal theory of oligopoly is therefore unattainable. Analytical ambitions must be limited to studies of industries *sui generis* with the goal of gaining insights into their functioning and structure, and with cautious generalizations arising from limited commonalities such industries may reveal.

Assumption 4. Corporations consistently reveal risk aversion in their attitudes to uncertain events, and this must project into the conditions of decision stability in their industries. The role of the cooperative motivation in tempering the rivalrous drive is thereby strengthened to the extent the latter threatens those stability conditions. Indeed, one of the social functions of the power structure is to exercise such restraining influences.

Assumption 5. Corporations are multi-objective entities making decisions in a multidimensional target variable space incorporating price, quality, and advertising dimensions. They consist of sub-bureaucracies with their selfish goals, many of which clash with like goals of their fellow groups. Corporate policy, therefore, reflects these goals with different priorities, and is frequently ill-defined or even inconsistent. The goals, therefore, are distinct to the firm, and must be isolated to approximate the firm's motivation in a formal model.

Assumption 6. Few market structures are characterized by pure competition or monopoly. Most mixtures of competition and monopoly reveal themselves to be clusters of oligopoly. Therefore, if general equilibrium theory is to approach a realistic and operational form it must incorporate in an extensive manner oligopolistic decision-making. By assumption 3, such incorporations must have limited aims for generality. The extensive use of mathematical theorem deduction must give place to simulation analyses with numerical structure. The goal must no longer be the derivation of universal theorems from mathematically manipulable but pitifully unrealistic models, but of insights into the functioning of models provided with parametric scenarios of efficient design to yield useful insights.

If these assumptions approach the realistic, frameworks must emerge to encompass them. But oligopoly theory today is dominated by game theory, which only partially and rather imperfectly captures the essence of this environment. Its primary focus is upon the rivalrous implications of oligopolistic interdependence, even when it deals with cooperative aspects of such relationships. It is a single-objective analysis; it neglects industrial power structures as well as other sociological aspects of the decision-making, and is not well suited to general equilibrium analysis.

The rivalrous consonance framework is an attempt to move analysis in the indicated directions and, unfortunately, given the almost exclusive attachment of present analysis to it, away from game theory in vital ways. It is experimental, but at least it is designed for application to realistic oligopolies and is therefore testable. I shall present it in its most rudimentary form in the present paper, but even at its most complicated it is a "middle-brow" theory in terms of complexity of structure.

2 The Oligopoly in Rivalrous Consonance

Assume an oligopoly with n rivals producing differentiated brands in a product group. Suppose their strategy consists of setting price with the primary goal of maximizing profits subject to (1) industry ties to rivals, (2) groups of subsidiary goals unique to each firm, and (3) demand and cost functions. If we focus upon rival i's motivation, rivalrous consonance views its objective function as an "extended profit function", E_i:

$$\text{Max}_{P_i} E_i = \sum_{j=1}^{n} \theta_{ij} (p_j - k_j) x_j, \qquad (5.1)$$

subject to a set of constraints, where

P_j = price of rival j's product

$x_j = a_j - b_{jj} p_j + \sum_{j \neq k} b_{jk} p_k + B_{jq} Q$ = rival's j's demand function

Q = a vector of unspecified variables (other than industry prices) affecting demand

k_j = average cost, assumed constant, of product j

θ_{ij} = binary consonance factors for firm i relevant to rivals j, $\theta_{ii} \equiv 1$.

The distinctive terms in the objective function are elements in the binary consonance matrix, θ, which specifies the effective power structure of the industry. Rival i maximizes his profits and the profits of his rivals when those rival profits are discounted by θ factors. $\theta_{ij} \in \theta$ is the dollar amount rival i values a \$1 profit or loss for rival j. Thus, if θ_{ij} = \$0.25 a dollar change in rival j's profit is the equivalent of \$0.25 in rival i's own profit. The ith row of θ defines rival i's attitudes to each of its competitors as those attitudes impact on its decision-making. The ith column of θ, of course, defines rivals' power structure attitudes to rival i. Hence, rival i's perception of rival j's ability to retaliate against it should rival i's price decisions impact too severely rival j's profits is included in rival i's decision-making. But it also includes rival i's concern for rival j's welfare on more altruistic grounds as well, perhaps with some concern for the peaceful stability of the industry. Of course θ_{ij} need not equal θ_{ji}, since rivals' perceptions of each other's position in the power structure can be quite disparate.

The subsidiary goals of rival i are incorporated in the model as constraints. To illustrate, let us use a set of common goals exhibited by firms in oligopoly. First, output must be within the firm's capacity to produce, q_i:

$$C^1 : x_i - q_i \leqslant 0. \tag{5.2}$$

Second, the firm insists upon attaining a minimum level of sales, m_i, set perhaps by an expected target share proportion:

$$C^2 : m_i - x_i \leqslant 0. \tag{5.3}$$

Third, the firm sets upper and lower bounds, t_i^+ and t_i^- respectively, on price changes in the period, specified as proportions of previous period price $\bar{p}_i$:

$$C^3 : p_i/\bar{p}_i - t_i^t \leqslant 0, \tag{5.4}$$

$$C^4 : t_i^- - p_i/\bar{p}_i \leqslant 0. \tag{5.5}$$

Last, price is bounded away from a specific lower limit which we will assume to be zero but may not be:

$$C^5 : u_i - p_i \leqslant 0. \tag{5.6}$$

The rivalrous consonance framework includes such "crippled optimization" submodels that consist of nonlinear programming models. Each is solved sequentially assuming all rivals' prices are temporarily fixed so that if each rival submodel is convex in own price the sufficient condition for a global constrained maximum will be achieved. Since all constraints are linear they are convex. The objective function yields

$$d^2 E_i/dp_i^2 = -2b_{ii} < 0, \tag{5.7}$$

and hence it is (strictly) concave in p_i. Hence, each submodel is a convex nonlinear programming model.

It should be noted that such firm models may not be convex and this must be accepted as a possible reflection of the real oligopolistic world. Local maxima may therefore be all that can be attained realistically. Convexity is convenient, to be sure, but is has no claim upon exclusive consideration by the theorist. I have solved rivalrous consonance models which were not convex for five and eleven firms using the Fiacco-McCormick Sequential Unconstrained Minimization Technique (SUMT) with no problems.

For this paper I will remain with the simple profit maximization model limited to one industry given in (5.1)–(5.6) above. However, let me indicate the flexibility and extendability of the approach briefly. First, different objective functions may be adopted to accommodate firms' differing goal sets. For example, a firm's major objective may be to attain a target rate of return, or to maximize market share, and different rivals in the same industry may have different major objectives as well as subsidiary objectives. This causes no problem to the modelling. Price leadership and followership are easily included for relevant firms as major objectives.

Second, general equilibrium is attained by linking an industry to its suppliers and its customers. Rival i's industrial customers as well as its rivals are given consonance factors and included in the extended profit function. In this manner patterns of price behavior among client industries can be studied given parametric shocks (see [1] for an extended presentation).

3 A Graphic Presentation

In order to depict some important characteristics of the pricing let us simplify by assuming a duopoly under rivalrous consonance and let us ignore constraints. Then reaction function depictions of some limiting cases are possible that serve to unify certain aspects of classic oligopoly theory by revealing them to be limiting cases of rivalrous consonance.

Figure 5.1 illustrates some basic concepts and implications of rivalrous consonance for the case of duopoly. For rival i, first order necessary conditions for a crippled optimization price solution, given the price for rival j, p_j, are

$$\partial E_i/\partial p_i = (x_i - b_{ii}(p_i - k_i)) + \theta_{ij}b_{ij}(p_j - k_j), \ i = 1,2; \quad j \neq i, \quad (5.8)$$

and, solving the pair of equations for p_1 and p_2, we obtain

$$p_i^\theta = \frac{-(2b_{jj}M_i + (b_{ij} + \theta_{ij}b_{ji})M_j)}{4b_{ii}b_{jj} - (b_{ij} + \theta_{ij}b_{ji})(b_{ji} + \theta_{ji}b_{ij})} = \frac{N_i^\theta}{D^\theta}, \ i = 1,2; \quad j \neq i, \quad (5.9)$$

where $M_i = \theta_{ij}b_{ji}k_j - a_i - b_{ii}k_i$. Solving in terms of price interactions, we get

$$p_i^\theta = (0.5/b_{ii})[a_i + b_{ii}k_i - \theta_{ij}b_{ji}k_j + (b_{ij} + \theta_{ij}b_{ji})p_j], \ i = 1,2; \quad j \neq i$$
$$(5.10)$$

These are the reaction functions for the two firms given the consonance factor vector $\theta = [\theta_{ij}, \theta_{ji}]$. Their values yield $p^\theta = [p_i^\theta, p_j^\theta]$, the joint extended profit equilibrium.

For the mature oligopoly we hypothesize that $\theta_{ij} \in [0,1]$ and $\theta_{ji} \in [0,1]$. If a θ-value becomes negative the rival adopting it is waging price war, valuing his rival's loss at a positive own profit value. At $\theta_{ij} = 1$, rival i

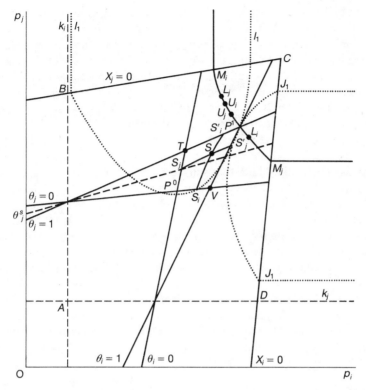

Figure 5.1   Isoprofit contours, reaction functions, and solution regions in duopoly.

values rival j's profit as equal to his own. It is difficult to imagine conditions in which he might value his rival's profit at a greater value than his own. Hence the lower and upper bounds are adopted, although no conceptual problem arises if the consonance factors are allowed to broach these limits.

If $\theta_{ij} = \theta_{ji} = 0$, we have the case where each rival makes his pricing decision in myopic disregard of its impact upon his rival. I have called the resulting P^0 vector the *Cournot point*, in the extended sense that each rival ignores the impact of his actions upon his competitor's objective function. The fact that Cournot used quantity instead of price as the firm's target variables is unimportant. The truly interesting fact is that we can reinterpret Cournot behavior to be equivalent to ignoring the impacts of one's decisions upon the welfare of one's competitor. This behavior is a more credible interpretation than the standard one of assuming one's rival's price (or quantity) will remain unchanged as one alters one's own.

If we go to the other extreme and assume $\theta_{ij} = \theta_{ji} = 1$, we have P^1, which I have called the *Chamberlin point*, in honor of that economist's suggestion that mutual interdependence recognized leads to a joint-profit maximization. Rivalrous consonance also permits a reinterpretation of Chamberlin behavior: it is not mutual interdependence recognized that distinguishes this limiting case from the Cournot case. System (5.8) makes it quite clear that both cases force the rival's parameters into the decision-making of the firms. The true distinction is the degree of valuation placed by each firm upon its rival's profit welfare. In this sense, rivalrous consonance is at once a unifier of classic oligopoly theory and an extension of it.

Figure 5.1 graphs the price space for duopoly and the P^0 and P^1 limiting solutions. The dashed lines depict the constant average costs, k_i and k_j, of the rivals. The straight lines that start at the axes and terminate at C are the loci of price vectors at which x_i and x_j become zero. Hence, the relevant price space for decisions is found in the polygon $ABCD$, since we assume that neither firm will operate in the long-run where profits are negative.

Isoprofit functions for the firms, of which we have drawn only two, I_1 and J_1, are ellipses in the relevant region and become horizontal or vertical lines beyond that region. Consider now the straight line reaction functions (defined in (5.8)) when $\theta_{ij} = \theta_{ji} = 0$, labelled θ_i and θ_j to simplify notation in the figure. These intersect the firms' isoprofit contours at their minimum points, i.e. where they are tangent to horizontal or vertical lines for firm i and j respectively. Their intersection at P^0 yields the Cournot solution. At the other extreme, consider the reaction functions where $\theta_{ij} = \theta_{ji} = 1$: if we draw the joint profit isocontours (which we have not in figure 5.1) these reactions functions would intersect them where dp_j/dp_i or dp_i/dp_j are zero. The intersection of these reaction functions yields P^1, the joint profit maximum.

Consider the set of points M_iM_j on which P^1 lies. M_i is the monopoly profit point for rival i, or the P at which rival j is eliminated from the market and rival i is maximizing its profit. It is the point upon which successively higher I isoprofit contours converge. M_j is the monopoly point for rival j with similar interpretation. The line M_iM_j is the locus of tangencies of I and J contours, or all points such that rival i cannot be bettered in profit receipts without harming rival j, and vice versa. P^1 lies on this locus at the point where the sum of such tangent contours is a maximum. If collusion were allowed, we would expect a negotiated bargain to be struck somewhere on this "negotiation set" between the exclusive beneficiary limiting points M_i and M_j. We will narrow the expected limits of negotiated solutions further below.

The important potential of rivalrous consonance, however, lies in its ability to permit θ-factors to assume intermediate values between 0 and 1, and thereby depict the pricing results of less extreme power structures. In figure 5.1 the dashed reaction function for $0 \leqslant \theta_j^s \leqslant 1$ has been drawn to illustrate the new flexibility. Where collusion is ruled out of consideration, so the negotiation set (other than P^1) can be ignored, we can set tighter bounds on the feasible solution region. When rival i acts myopically and rival j altruistically the P-solution occurs at T, and when roles are reversed at V. Hence, the region P^0TP^1V is the region of feasible solutions for the mature oligopoly as we have interpreted it.

Let us now suppose that in the very long run the consonance factors are variable and will come to reflect more accurately the egoistic profit drives of the rivals tempered by their competitors' power and acumen in the competitive process. One of the important desires of each opponent will be to assess the θ-factor that governs his competitor's strategy and to use such knowledge to improve his profit position. For example, let us start with $\theta = [0,1]$ with consequent $P = T$. Suppose rival j surmises that rival i has $\theta_i = 0$ and that it will for long periods retain that perception of its role in the industry power structure. Then it will pay rival j to find his *Stackelberg point* on $\theta_i = 0$ where he reaches the innermost J contour he can attain – say at S_j where his effective $\theta_j = \theta_j^s$. That J profit contour is the minimum profit that rival j need accept as long as rival i adopts θ_i, and, since $\theta_i = 0$ is by our assumption the lowest value rival i can adopt, this is the minimum profit rival j need accept under any condition. Hence, if we move along that J contour to its intersection with the M_iM_j negotiation set (say at L_j) this places a lower bound on the negotiated distribution of joint profit to rival j. Also, if the I contour that goes through S_j is followed to its intersection with M_iM_j (say at U_i) we have the maximum amount of joint profit that rival i can obtain by negotiation.

Symmetrically, if we start with $\theta_i = 1$ and $\theta_j = 0$, and $P = V$, and rival i seeks its Stackelberg point (say at S_i), we can locate L_i and U_j on the negotiation set. It would then benefit both parties to arrive at a P on M_iM_j between U_i and U_j by collusion, and were such action admissible this segment of M_iM_j would hold strong interest for us. But we have ruled out the possibility of collusion and must return to the rivals' Stackelberg points.

Arbitrarily, suppose that is S_j. If rival i surmises that rival j will move along the reaction function θ_j^s, it will find that point on θ_j^s that is its new Stackelberg solution, different from S_i. That implies a new θ_i^s (not drawn) and rival j will use it to obtain yet another Stackelberg point. If we plot the loci of each rival's Stackelberg points we obtain their *Stackelberg functions*, plotted on figure 5.1 as S_jS_j' and S_iS_i'. These may be viewed as their long run reaction functions, and their intersection at the point S I have termed the generalized Stackelberg point. It is a Nash equilibrium.

The point S within the feasible solution region P^0TP^1V has a strong appeal because from any point in the subset $P^0S_jSS_i$ it is possible for both firms to improve their profits by moves toward S, until S is achieved. For any P in the subset $SS_iP^1S_j'$ it will always benefit one of the noncolluding rivals to move toward S at the expense of the other – a one-sided benefit game that ends at S. Hence, in the very long run, when power structures alter under the motivating force of profit maximization, we should expect P to lie in the subset $SS_i' P^1 S_j'$ with S as the point of gravitational pull.

In the short run, however, θ is fixed and we return to the short-run reaction functions.

4 Comparative Statics Propositions

Trivially, $dp_i/d\theta_i > 0$ if $p_i \geqslant k_i$ and $dp_i/d\theta_j > 0$ if $p_i > k_i$. Consider now the impact of cost increases with fixed θ. Let us rewrite the reaction function (5.10) as

$$p_i^\theta = A_i + B_i p_j^\theta, \tag{5.11}$$

where $A_i = 0.5(a_i + b_{ii}k_i - \theta_{ij}b_{ji}k_j)/b_{ii}$ and $B_i = 0.5(b_{ij} + \theta_{ij}b_{ji})/b_i$. Then, for the intercept terms

1. $dA_i = 0.5dk_i$

2. $dA_j = -(0.5b_{ij}\theta_{ji}/b_{jj})dk_i.$ $\tag{5.12}$

For an own-cost change the reaction function R_i on figure 5.2 shifts to the right by one half the rise in cost; however, R_j shifts down, reducing the

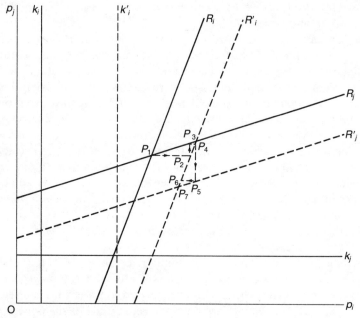

Figure 5.2   Comparative statics of a cost change.

rise in p_i that would occur if R_j remained fixed. The adjustments are shown in figure 5.2, and it will be useful to work through the adjustment process in achieving the new equilibrium.

R_i shifts by one half the cost increase to R_i' and firm i, assuming p_j constant at p_j^1 moves the price vector to P_2 from P_1. For the moment R_j remains fixed, and with p_i changed induces firm j to move to P_3, further inducing firm i to move the solution to P_4. Obviously, the amount of price movement to this point depends upon the slope of R_j. The rise is greater the less sensitive x_j is to p_j (i.e. the smaller is b_{jj}), the more sensitive it is to p_i (i.e the larger is b_{ji}), and the larger is θ_{ji}. Rivalrous consonance boosts prices, holding an umbrella over rival i's head. Phase 1 ends with P_4, which implies p_i and p_j higher than in P_1.

At the start of phase 2 firm j perceives the reason for firm i's initiating move to P_2 and includes the larger k_i in its first-order condition (5.8). Every sale firm j takes from firm i causes firm i to lose less profit than before, so R_j shifts to R_j' – a shift due solely to rivalrous consonance and varying directly with the size of θ_{ji}. Also, the more sensitive firm i's sales to a reduction in p_j (i.e. the larger b_{ij}) and the more sensitive its own sales are to p_j, the less will p_j have to be reduced to compensate for the fall in extended profits. Firm j, therefore, moves P from P_4 to P_5, and interactions along the new reaction functions will carry the new equilibrium price to P_7.

Rivalrous consonance then has two opposing price tendencies. Because of the increased *slope* it gives reaction functions, prices tend to increase with rivals' cost increases. But a shift component which is similar to a change in θ_{ji} caused by a decline in rival profits exerts downward pressure on prices.

On figure 5.3 we analyze the net resultant of these two components. For p_i, the change from p_i to p_i^7 is equal to the amount of the shift in R_i (P_1M) less MN, which is simply the slope of R_i' times the change in p_j (P_1T). The same reasoning holds for P_j^1 to P_j^7. That is,

$$\text{1. } dp_i = \text{shift of } R_i + \text{slope of } R_i \times dp_j$$
$$\text{2. } dp_j = \text{shift of } R_j + \text{slope of } R_j \times dp_j \tag{5.13}$$

From (5.12)

$$\text{1. } dp_i = 0.5dk_i + [0.5(b_{ij} + \theta_{ii}b_{ji})/b_{ii}]dp_j$$
$$\text{2. } dp_i = (-0.5\theta_{ji}b_{ji}/b_{jj})dk_i + (0.5(b_{ji} + \theta_{jj}b_{ij})/b_{jj})dp_i$$

or

$$\text{1. } dp_i/dk_i = (2b_{jj}b_{ii} - \theta_{ji}b_{ij}(b_{ij} + \theta_{ij}b_{ji}))/D^\theta$$
$$\text{2. } dp_j/dk_i = (b_{ii}(b_{ij} - \theta_{ji}b_{ij})/D^\theta). \tag{5.14}$$

Can rivalrous consonance lead to the perverse case where $dp_i/dk_i < 0$?

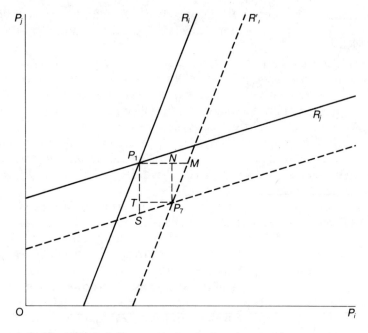

Figure 5.3   The shift-and-slope analysis of price change.

Because $D^\theta > 0$ by the strict concavity of the objective functions, the sign of (5.14–1) depends upon the sign of the numerator. It is negative if and only if

$$\theta_{ji}b_{ij}(b_{ij} + \theta_{ij}b_{ji}) > 2b_{ii}b_{jj}. \tag{5.15}$$

From strict concavity the additional necessary condition is that

$$2b_{ii}b_{jj} > 0.5(b_{ij} + \theta_{ij}b_{ji})(b_{ji} + \theta_{ji}b_{ij}) \tag{5.16}$$

Together (5.15) and (5.16) imply that in the perverse case

$$\theta_{ji}b_{ij} > b_{ji}, \tag{5.17}$$

which in turn implies, because θ_{ji} is in the unit interval, that $b_{ij} > b_{ji}$.

We will show that the perverse case is possible but unlikely. Define the other-price coefficients as multiples of own-price coefficients:

$$b_{ij} = m_i b_{ii}, \, b_{ji} = m_j b_{jj}. \tag{5.18}$$

Then (5.15) reduces to

$$b_{ii}/b_{jj} > (2 - \theta_{ij}\theta_{ji}m_i m_j)/\theta_{ji}m_i^2, \tag{5.19}$$

and by substituting (5.18) into (5.17), the condition of (5.19) can be tightened to

$$b_{ii}/b_{jj} > 2/m_i^2. \tag{5.20}$$

Perversity can occur in a duopoly where one rival controls a much larger share of the market than the other; if $m_i < 1$, as we expect for a dominant rival, that necessary predominance may be a larger multiple of 2. Moreover, for the perverse result the weak rival's position is reflected in a very high rival's profit component (i.e. $\theta_{ji}b_{ji}$), which leads to a large shift downward in R_j. Also, the small absolute cross-price sensitivity of the weak rival to the strong rival's price actions insures that the slope of R_i is steep.

The improbability of these conditions in a closed duopoly hinges upon the notion that if a rival with very large sales lost a large quantity through a rise in its price, a sole small rival will fail to benefit from the action by experiencing a large increase in sales. A great leakage from the system is implied. Therefore, the possibility seems most likely when the primary competition of a strong duopolist exists abroad among exogenous exporters and a weak domestic rival acts under strong consonance motivation to exploit a large rise in rival cost.

The improbability of its occurrence for rivals of approximately equal size can be investigated for the case where $b_{ij} = b_{ji} = b$ and $k_i = k_j = k$. Perversity has the best chance of occurring when (from (5.15)) $\theta_{ij} = \theta_{ji} = 1$, and we adopt that value. Then, from (5.15) and (5.16), we obtain the contradiction

$$c > b > c. \tag{5.21}$$

Hence, the perverse case cannot arise under the best conditions. Even the condition derived from (5.15) alone implies the realistically unacceptable proposition that cross-price sensitivity is larger than own-price sensitivity.

On the other hand, a rise in k_i may move p_j up or down depending on the numerator of (5.14-2). Specifically, p_j will fall if

$$b_{ij} < \theta_{ji}b_{ij}. \tag{5.22}$$

The downward shift of R_j to R_j' in figure 5.2 outweighs the upward pull exerted by the slope of R_i'. Note from (5.17) that if the perverse case of dp_i/dk_i occurs, p_j must also fall, but the converse is not true.

The negative net impact upon prices that rivalrous consonance can inspire is not as paradoxical as might appear at first sight. A fall in the profit margin of a rival can be viewed as a reduction of his power base and will lead a rival to lower the price protection previously afforded. This will be tempered, and in the normal case outweighed, by the rightward shift of firm j's sales function set off by the initial rise in p_i. But where cross-price sensitivities are weak, the net effect of a fall in p_j may occur.

5 Conclusion

Rivalrous consonance, with or without constraints, is one path toward a necessary integration of rivalry and cooperation in oligopoly theory. The theory isolates an interesting Nash equilibrium at the generalized Stackelberg point. And it casts light on the contradictory impulses that a unilateral cost increase inspires among oligopolists. On the one hand the unfortunate rival's attempt to pass through the increase by a price rise leads rivals to increase their own prices as demand strengthens. But the decline in the initiating firm's profit margin leads rivals to reduce the price protection formerly afforded it. Net price changes in the industry are the net resultants of these two forces.

Reference

[1] KUENNE, R. E., *Rivalrous Consonance: a Theory of General Oligopolistic Equilibrium*, North-Holland, Amsterdam, 1986.

Part II

Price Competition in Oligopoly:
The Case of OPEC

Introduction to Part II

One of the consistent goals for which I have striven, as emphasized in the selections of part I, is to construct an *operational* theory of oligopoly, which is to say, one that can be fitted to real-world industries and specified numerically. This would allow the testing of the assumptions of rivalrous consonance and permit the analyst to gain useful insights into the structure and functioning of actual industries. My hope for such a theory has never been to employ it for numerical forecasting of prices, sales or profits, since my belief is that the complexity of real-world oligopolistic decision-making forecloses that possibility. A good theory should be helpful in giving qualitative notions of movements in such variables in answer to "what if" hypothetical changes in industry parameters, however.

From the beginning of the construction of rivalrous consonance theory, therefore, I sought an industry to whose decision-making the framework could be applied. The Organization of Petroleum Exporting Countries (OPEC) was a logical choice because it offered the greatest prospect for data availability and for the discernment of power structure. Because of the topicality of its decisions and the wealth of analysis of their consequences it also afforded the hope of empirical guidance by experts in petroleum economics to one who was not so informed. Finally, OPEC's major concern was with a product that was not differentiated by producer and whose variations could be readily standardized by measures based upon specific gravity.

The most difficult problem in applying rivalrous consonance theory empirically for short-run analyses is the isolation of the industry power structure. As noted in part I's selections, the matrix of consonance coefficients which quantifies this structure is the result of a complex of economic, historical and sociological factors, complicated in the case of OPEC by political interplay. Existing oligopoly theory tends to avoid this difficult task by reducing such considerations to simple market structure assumptions. For example, in the present case, most economic models of OPEC of which I am aware simply assumed that Saudi Arabia was a monopolistic price setter

141

which determined a price that maximized its long-run profit, that the other 12 producing members were followers, and that Saudi Arabia maintained the desired price by acting as a "swing" producer, adjusting output up or down as required.

Such descriptions struck me as much too simple a depiction of an organization whose decisions were hammered out in periodic confrontations of all members, when such members were sovereign states with substantial capability for tacit or overt noncompliance, and when their decisions had such immense importance for the well-being of member states. No assemblage of this nature that included regional political powers like Iran and Iraq and large producers like Kuwait, the United Arab Emirates, Libya, Venezuela, and Nigeria could be viewed as containing such passive participants. I must say that I believe time has borne me out in that judgement, and that the insistence of rivalrous consonance theory upon a total detailing of binary power specifications is well-justified.

That forces the analyst to address the difficult problem of "measuring" the admittedly nebulous qualitative attributes of the cartel. My belief has been for some time (see chapters 11 and 12 in part III) that economists must emulate researchers and practitioners in such fields as psychology and education and engage in "fuzzy" measurement. The same economists who, as teachers, grade students from 0 to 100 in revealed knowledge or subject comprehension, treat such "measures" as unique up to a positive multiplicative constant by adding and averaging them, then permit interpersonal comparisons of such grades among colleagues, recoil in horror at "unscientific" procedures for measuring more readily discernible features that contribute to deference in pricing behavior. The fact is that educational "measures," unscientific as they are, work in practice, giving us better indexes of student abilities that we would have in their absence. The same criterion for other fuzzy measures should be adopted by economists.

Chapter 6 is a rather bold exercise in the application of these ideas to OPEC, and, I must admit, it has had a rather small effect in convincing fellow economists. But it was a necessary first step in applying rivalrous consonance theory to OPEC. In all of my modelling of the petroleum cartel I have eliminated Gabon and Ecuador because of a lack of data and of the nonimportance of their output relative to the total. This reduces the matrix of consonant coefficients, θ, to be derived to size 11×11.

I isolated five nonmarket related quantitative measures of relatively independent factors that I hypothesize to be dominant in the deliberations of OPEC insofar as power or deference structure is concerned and have normalized them as ratios to 1. A cross-factor analysis is used to derive weights for each such factor according to a scheme detailed as method C in chapter 12. The method permits a controlled usage of expertise – perhaps by employment of a Delphi exercise – to guide the necessarily subjective process of "pseudo-measurement."

From these normalized final weights of the factors and the normalized scores of each member with respect to the factors, an aggregate nonmarket power score is derived, measuring that nation's overall bargaining power in this area. The aggregate consonance factors, depicting the overall willingness of members to consider the welfare of others considered as a group, are assumed to be related to the inverses of these power scores, and are derived by combining them with measures of market power based upon own- and other-price elasticities. Finally, these aggregate scores are disaggregated over other member countries row by row to obtain the binary consonance coefficient matrix θ with elements θ_{ij}.

The methodology for deriving the consonance coefficients of chapter 6 depends upon measures of market power based upon the elasticities of the demand functions for the member states of OPEC. Chapter 7 contains an econometric estimation of these demand functions from monthly data extending from the third quarter of 1974 to the second quarter of 1977 (74Q3–77Q2), for a total of 42 months. This period splits rather neatly into a phase of declining prices that followed the chaotic price rises incident to the assertion of power by OPEC and the embargo by the Arab members (January, 1974 to February, 1975) and the period of price rise from March, 1975 through June, 1977.

The deficiencies of the data, the techniques used, the results of the econometric fitting, and the caveats appropriate to the interpretation of those results are quite complicated and presented in some detail. However, several interesting results of a general nature are derived with some confidence. One is that little short-run sensitivity to changes in tanker rates or developed nations' industrial production levels is revealed in the demand functions derived. This is a consistent characteristic for all 11 nations analyzed. Another result is that the major geographical groupings of OPEC nations – Gulf, African, South American and Asian – seem quite insulated from one another in their pricing, although some overlapping competition exists between Libya and the Gulf group. And, lastly, short-run own-price elasticities of demand functions for OPEC members tend to be surprisingly large.

The period selected does not include the 1979 price surge caused by the Iranian revolution, nor does it take into account the rapid development of alternative sources and the substantial conservation success of importing nations that occurred in the 1980s. Hence, the specific results of the selection may be somewhat outdated. However, the detailing of the problems involved in isolating demand relations and the methodology used should still be of value, and the hypotheses should serve as starting points for updated investigations.

Chapter 8 is an article that was published in Princeton University's magazine for alumni, faculty and students. Therefore, it minimizes the technical background of the GENESYS model of OPEC that was constructed in Princeton's General Economic Systems Project with the rivalrous consonance theory of part I, the demand functions of chapter 7 and the consonance coefficients of chapter 6. The model is presented in detail in chapter 9. In this paper the emphasis was placed upon presenting the results of model runs focusing on 1980.

The exercise is to project the average price of OPEC crude, national outputs, and member nation profits for 1980 if three assumptions concerning Iranian and Saudi Arabian production, growth in world demand, and worldwide inventory drawdowns were fulfilled. The runs were made in the winter of 1979, the paper was written in February, 1980 and was published in October, 1980. Given the power structure and the demand functions, and assuming a constraint set that bounded members' outputs between capacity restrictions and half those quotas, the model projected a price of $34.85 per barrel, or about a $7 increase over 1979's February price. The actual maximum price in 1980 was about $34 a barrel.

More important than the precision of the forecast, however, from the viewpoint of using the model to analyze structure, the model projected a Chamberlin joint-profit maximization price (i.e. all $\theta_{ij} = 1$) of about $35 and a Cournot price (all $\theta_{ij} = 0$) of about $30. Hence, the power structure captured in the θ derived in chapter 6 kept prices near the monopoly level, and well above the value that would occur if OPEC disbanded. These upper and lower bounds indicated that OPEC was indeed effective and that its demise would not reduce price below $30, given demand and hypothetical supply conditions at that time.

To my way of thinking the model was validated, both in its short-run projection and in its "what-if" solutions. Before the Iraqi invasion of Kuwait in 1990, after a decade's substantial increases in non-OPEC supply, surprisingly effective conservation measures by major consuming countries, and a substantially changed power structure that reduced Saudi Arabian power to the point where it accepted output quotas which it firmly opposed in the 1970s and 1980s, the price of crude fluctuated around $20 a barrel, indicating a substantial decline in OPEC's power relative to the rest of the world. These changes I believe are fully capable of explaining a decline of $10 to $15 a barrel before adjusting the dollar for inflation.

The essential validation of the model was encouraging to me in my insistence that analysis of OPEC required a depiction of binary power constructions, rather than one that treated Saudi Arabia as a monopolistic price fixer and other members as followers. I continue to believe, as is made clear in the selections of parts I and II, that the need to capture such relations is a strong one in oligopoly modelling.

Another distinctive point made in the paper was its depiction of OPEC structure as permitting a flexible approach to pricing of various qualities of crude, which permitted members a good deal of leeway to adjust prices within the markets for their specific grades. My point was that the flexibility of OPEC's rules permitted the organization to function in the face of fierce national rivalries and perceived revenue needs. This contradicted the view of many analysts that OPEC could not survive as a cartel given such conflict, and would soon dissolve. I believe this vision of OPEC as setting a purposely ill-defined price *pattern* rather than "a" price for marker crude in order to survive the inner strains it was subjected to has also been borne out by time.

Chapter 9 extends the number of observations from which the demand functions were derived from the 42 data points of chapter 8 to 72 monthly observations for the period January, 1974 to June, 1980. This includes the period of rapid price rise and reduced supply in the "second oil shock" occurring after Iran's revolution. In retrospect, I think the decision to include the data of this 1979–80 upheaval was a mistake, because it introduced an upward bias in the regression coefficients. Average cost functions were derived for five geographical submarkets in another departure from the analysis of chapter 8 and incorporated into the national objective functions, and non-OPEC, non-communist production was included as a regressor in the demand functions. Finally, the base case parameters featured substantial increases in tanker rates and the industrial output index for developed nations in an attempt to project for a more normal 1981 than was actual.

The new demand functions, cost relations, and assumptions concerning tanker rates and economic growth yield substantially more disturbing results than the projections for 1980 in chapter 8. The average price of OPEC oil would have been roughly double its actual 1980 price under the modified conditions had only short-run considerations been operative, and output would have fallen to 22.5 million barrels per day from 1980 liftings of 28 million barrels per day. African crudes would reach $86 per barrel under these conditions had such suppliers as Saudi Arabia and the UAE not followed long-run strategies aimed at keeping prices down by sustaining liftings. The results indicate a substantial potential pressure on such nations to restrict output and permit prices to rise. Such higher prices could only be obtained, however, if the African producers (Libya, Nigeria and Algeria) consented to reduce output by about 40 percent below 1980 liftings, thereby restricting market share.

Interesting structural insights occur when the power structure is modified to the joint-profit maximization case. Iraq benefits immensely in this scenario and Saudi Arabia is its benefactor through its large output reductions and subsequent price increase. On the other hand, were OPEC to dissolve and the Cournot case arise, Saudi Arabia and Iran would see profits drop by 22 to 23 percent below base case levels, whereas Iraq, free to reduce price and expand output at will, would see profits rise over 60 percent above base case levels. Iraq's profits would be substantially below its joint-profit levels, however.

The basic explanation of the results from this application of the GENESYS model lies in the fact that, member nation by member nation, the negative own-price coefficients in the demand regression equations equal approximately in absolute value the sum of the positive other-price coefficients in the equations. Hence, if all nations raise prices together sales do not decrease much, so that the effect is to yield a very inelastic aggregate OPEC sales function. The inherent motivation to act in concert is very strong under these conditions, therefore, *given short-run considerations only*. These characteristics of the demand functions were not so marked in chapter 8, when those functions were fitted to only about half the observations available for the present analysis, but, again are probably unduly affected by the 1979–80 data which, as it turned out, did not continue into the 1980s.

Once more, therefore, I must stress the disclaimers that accompany the results. Only qualitative results of comparative analyses should be given much credence. Specification errors in all econometric models used, as well as data deficiencies and multicollinearity among the regressors, make the use of the model for quantitative forecasting extremely hazardous. As noted above, the time period included an extremely abnormal market situation in which panic buying occurred, and its observations may well have warped the regression coefficients for prices in the equations. The proper use of the model is to gain insights into structure and the relative strengths and direction of stresses within that structure.

The results of the runs of the GENESYS model, particularly with respect to the relatively small differentials between actual prices and Cournot prices in the analyses of chapters 8 and 9 lead me to believe that OPEC's role in the stagflation of the 1970s has been exaggerated, and that the monetary and fiscal excesses as well as the weak economic growth pressures of the period have been underestimated as causal factors. These conjectures are expressed in chapter 10, which begins with a review of a group of studies addressed to the impact of oil price increases upon US and OECD price levels and growth rates and which gives support to these hypotheses.

The paper also looks at the then looming 1980s, predicting the survival of OPEC, the failure of Saudi Arabia to obtain consensus for a long-run pricing policy, and the pressures that emerged in the decade for limitations on output to raise short-term prices. It also projected pressures to increase the quality differentials between lower and higher grades of petroleum, but these projections did not seem to occur, perhaps because of conservation measures and the construction of refineries which were more flexible in their acceptance of lower grades as inputs. And, finally, it foresaw the continuing power of OPEC as a pricing force, but did not correctly guess the extent of consumer conservation and the strength of the short-term orientation within OPEC that was caused in large part by Iraq's economic distress resulting from its eight-year war with Iran.

Viewing in retrospect the five papers forming part II, I believe the aims with which I began the empirical analysis of OPEC were broadly achieved, although I gained new respect for the difficulties encountered by empirical researchers and the skills which they have developed to overcome them. I began the work with the limited aim of validating the theory of rivalrous consonance; most importantly, not the construction of a forecasting model for OPEC. I feel broadly that I succeeded in that task, and especially in gaining new confidence in the need to isolate a binary power structure for fruitful study of oligopoly.

My skepticism concerning the analytical power of regression analysis was reinforced, however: I think the economist is the only professional who has placed such great faith in its efficacy in extracting underlying relationships among variables. In part, I believe, this springs from a misconceived allegiance to the notion that empirically derived results incapable of being expressed numerically are deficient, even if data limitations or the crudeness of techniques in the face of complex interdependence argue strongly for the inability to derive such measures. Realistic restraint on such unattainable ambitions would conduce to an acceptance of qualitative results, and the acceptance of such multivariate methods as factor analysis and – horror of horrors – historical analysis.

6

Rivalrous Consonance and the Power Structure of OPEC

1 The Theoretical Context

In previous work [5–8] I have developed a "crippled-optimization" theoretical model with which to analyze oligopolistic decision-making operationally. That methodology is motivated by several observations about the environment from which pricing strategies emerge in mature oligopolistic industries.

1 Oligopolies are blends in different degrees of the rivalrous and the cooperative, the egoistic and the communitarian, the desire to gain at the expense of fellow industry members and the desire to coexist peacefully with them. Realistic analysis of the decisions emerging from such "rivalrous consonance" requires a recognition of *both* elements in the decision-making. Existing frameworks such as game theory do not permit a proper balancing of these attitudes.

2. Rivalrous consonance becomes effective in realistic oligopolistic decisions when rivals take into account the impacts of their decisions upon the profits of others in the industry (and possibly upon customers' profit as well). As an approximation to the resultant of a set of complex attitudes toward rivals, it is assumed that each rival "values" what it will "pay" in sacrifice of its own profits to avoid inflicting $1 in loss upon a rival. These "consonance coefficients," symbolized as θ, must be defined for every rival relative to every other rival to depict the power structure of the industry. Without such a complete depiction, analyses of the decision-making of the oligopoly will be deficient.

3. A manner of incorporating such detailed rivalrous consonance into the analysis and the modelling of oligopoly is to assume that each rival attempts

Originally published in *Kyklos*, 32 (1979), 695–717, and produced with permission of Helbing & Lichtenhahn Verlag AG, Basle and Frankfurt am Main. The project was funded in full by the Rockfeller Foundation.

to maximize his own profits plus the profit of each rival multiplied individually by its consonance coefficient and subject to a set of constraints he places upon the manner or outcomes of the decision-making. This simultaneous constrained profit maximization we have called "crippled-optimization" and we have developed a nonlinear programming approach to model design and solution.

At this stage, published work has remained at the theoretical or fictitious simulation level. Presently, however, we are engaged in an effort to model the pricing process of OPEC by crippled-optimization methods in order to experiment with the practical usefulness of the procedure as well as to seek insights into the cartel's pricing behavior. To date, two tasks in the project have been completed: first, short-run demand or sales functions have been estimated for 11 of the 13 OPEC nations as a step toward defining objective functions for the optimization [9, 11]; and presently we summarize the derivation of an 11 × 11 matrix of "consonance factors" mesuring the power structure of the cartel, again as a step toward defining crippled-optimization objective functions [10].

Sections 2 and 3 describe the procedures used to estimate the relative decision impact of each OPEC rival which is based on nonmarket factors. Section 4 employs these measures to calculate *aggregate consonance factors* for each nation relative to the other ten as a group. In sections 5 and 6 these aggregate coefficients are disaggregated into the individualized 11 × 11 matrix of binary consonance factors by incorporating the market power of each rival relative to every other rival's product. Finally, section 7 presents a brief summary and conclusion.

The power structure of an oligopolistic industry is a tangled complex of perceived threats, desires for stability, personality idiosyncracies, legal and other social sanctions, competing sub-unit bureaucratic goals, and industry mores emerging from historic process. When rivals are nations cultural value-and-belief systems intrude with implied allegiances and antagonisms. Methods of "measuring" the net resultant of such complexes by a unidimensional index are admittedly, at this stage of theoretical and empirical development, crude, but I am convinced a start must be made in bringing these attitudes to bear formally upon oligopoly theory in richer and more explicit manners than have been done to date. This paper is presented as a beginning of such necessary effort.

2 Decision Impact Power Bases

Power in modern industrial society is a curious blend of strength and weakness. The very weak may inspire contempt, paternalistic concern (perhaps by an external legal or social system), or a blend of both. The very strong may be effectively constrained in the exercise of that strength by a fear of resentment that may weaken the cooperative threads in some social fabric in whose intactness they have a selfish interest. Hence, to treat the dominant member of a cartel as a monopolist to whose self-regarding decisions other members adjust passively may be to oversimplify seriously.[1] Further, because oligopoly by definition features nonignorable mutual interactions among all participants, I feel that aggregation of participants into "homogeneous" groups is at least a suspect projection of valid technique for atomistic power structures into a quite different environment.[2]

Acting on that belief, we isolate in this section the "decision impact index" values for 11 of the 13 OPEC nations.[3] After study of the public record on OPEC Conference meetings and Economic Commission deliberations, as well as expert speculation about disputes among members, we identified five bases that seem to be implicit or explicit factors underlying the degree of general impact upon OPEC that the nations possess.[4]

2.1 Base 1: Current Levels of Crude Petroleum Production

Current market share is the most obvious component of a power base in any oligopoly. It is directly correlated with a participant's stake in the group's pricing decision and with his ability to disrupt group sales by shading price or offering *sub rosa* discounts or ancillary advantages to customers. In the absence of external protective measures (e.g. antitrust legislation) the smaller rival is not likely to inspire much sympathy on these grounds alone, since his right to benefit from the group's actions is poorly established if his stakes are low.

We measure this base for OPEC members by petroleum liftings in the first quarter of 1977 (77Q1) in millions of barrels per day (mmb/d). These data, stated as levels and normalized as ratios to the total eleven-nation output, are found in column 1 of table 6.1.

On the basis of this factor alone, Saudi Arabia is clearly in a class by itself, accounting for about one-third of the group's production. Iran occupies a clear and similarly isolated secondary position, and together with Saudi Arabia controls about one-half of the cartel's liftings. A third-tier group includes Iraq, Kuwait, Libya, Nigeria, Venezuela, the United Arab Emirates (UAE), and Indonesia. Finally, Algeria and Qatar form a small group with little impact base in production.

Table 6.1 Decision impact data bases, OPEC cartel

Nation	Base 1: production 77Q1 mmb/d	Base 2: excess installed capacity 77Q1 mmb/d	Base 3: proved reserves 77Q1 billion barrels	Base 4: per Capita GNP, 1977 US dollars deviation from maximum	Base 5: oil Exports as percent of total exports 1976	Base 5: decision impact scores (DIS)
1 Saudi Arabia	9.5/0.31	2.4/0.31	113/0.28	8,490/0.11	100/0.10	0.28
2 Iran	5.7/0.19	1.0/0.13	63/0.16	10,060/0.13	93/0.09	0.15
3 Iraq	2.1/0.07	1.0/0.13	34/0.08	10,220/0.13	99/0.10	0.10
4 Kuwait	1.8/0.06	1.6/0.21	70/0.18	0/0.00	74/0.08	0.16
5 UAE	1.7/0.05	0.4/0.05	31/0.08	1,020/0.01	97/0.10	0.06
6 Qatar	0.4/0.01	0.3/0.04	6/0.01	3,180/0.04	96/0.10	0.03
7 Libya	2.1/0.07	0.4/0.05	26/0.07	6,420/0.08	100/0.10	0.06
8 Algeria	1.1/0.04	0.0/0.00	7/0.02	10,720/0.14	80/0.07	0.02
9 Nigeria	2.2/0.07	0.2/0.03	20/0.05	11,190/0.14	94/0.10	0.05
10 Venezuela	2.3/0.08	0.3/0.04	15/0.04	9,280/0.11	65/0.08	0.06
11 Indonesia	1.7/0.05	0.1/0.01	11/0.03	9,320/0.11	69/0.08	0.03
	30.6/1.00	7.7/1.00	396/1.00	–/1.00	88[a]/1.00	1.00

[a] Arithmetic mean.

2.2 Base 2: Excess Installed Capacity

Total capacity is highly correlated with production, and to include it as an independent base would be to double count base 1 in large measure. Moreover, it is *idle* capacity that indexes a rival's ability to disrupt markets if unsatisfied, the pressure upon him to seek more market share aggressively, and his ability to instill sympathetic hearings for the opportunity cost of foregoing its use. Therefore, we locate a second base in the excess installed capacity in place in April, 1977, when measured against average daily production in 77Q1. In column 2 of table 6.1 we list levels and ratios to total excess capacity of 7.8 mmb/d in OPEC this month.

Saudi Arabia and Kuwait emerge from the data as the *"swing"* producers who absorb the excess supplies of crude in periods of slack demand and increase supply to neutralize excess demand in times of active demand. Iran and Iraq have secondary quantities of excess capacity, but all others can be seen in this period to have been operating at nearly full capacity.

It should be noted that this base does not index a member nation's willingness to reduce output in slack periods rather than reduce price. Libya, for example, has proven in the past to be quite ready to shut down capacity despite the existence of excess demand for its oil, and is generally viewed as one of the nations which absorbs slack in off-peak demand periods. We feel this willingness is reflective of a nation's time preference for revenues and we plan to capture that contributor to decision-making in the discount rate we assign the nation's objective function in the modelling that lies ahead.

2.3 Base 3: Proved Petroleum Reserves

In addition to the contribution of excess capacity, which we treat as a short-term and medium-term factor in determining decision impact in OPEC, we include proved reserves of petroleum as a long-run factor. Of course, proved reserves are a notoriously inexact measure of future productive potential: unproved reserves, perhaps, should be included in the measure despite their ambiguity, and some allowance should be made for secondary and tertiary recovery potential for each nation's fields. We feel, however, that the more conservative measure is the best current index of long-term power possessed by each cartel member *in the perceptions* of those members.

The most important impact of this base is upon the direction and intensity of a member's pricing motivation. In general, we expect a nation with a long-term interest in oil pricing to assert a different point of view to short-run price decisions than nations with short-range stakes. The latter are more prone to push in OPEC counsels for higher prices in order to maximize the value of their short-term resources with no desire to take such long-range possibilities as price-induced energy good substitution or development of alternatives into account. However, their voices must be weaker because of their shorter-range threat potential. Moreover, in the medium run, the threat of increasing capacity for future confrontations must enhance the power of nations with large reserves.

2.4 Base 4: Per Capita Gross National Product

It is difficult to select a measure of the short-term pressures upon nations to engage in economic development and, therefore, of the pressures upon them in OPEC bargaining sessions to press or gain sympathy for their strategy positions. Development expenditures are hard to obtain because of data quality and the inability to denote clearly the nature of their goals. In the end we have been forced to settle for gross national product per capita in 1977 as an index, with the assumption that members with lower values will be led to assert more forceful roles in OPEC on this ground than nations with larger incomes, *ceteris paribus*.

Hence, we do not view GNP as a weapon to impose solutions from power positions in a simple *Realpolitik* sense. OPEC has not featured the making of side payments by rich to poorer nations to gain their consent.[5] Rather, the per capita income base seems to be effective in a manner that is negatively correlated with this measure: low-GNP-per-capita nations are granted greater voice than other bases would permit out of a general communitarian recognition of the internal pressures upon their governments and of the strength of the temptation to break the pricing ranks for monetary advantage. In column 4 of table 6.1, therefore, we list per capita GNP as deviations from the maximum (Kuwait $11,510) in 1977. These are normalized by (1) converting these (absolute) deviations to ratios to the maximum and (2) dividing by the sum of these ratios.

In this dimension of decision impact, with the exception of the three highest per capita members – Kuwait, Qatar, and the UAE – power is about evenly dispersed. Rather surprisingly, except for these exceptionally rich members, no OPEC nation stands out as an extreme deviation. Therefore, the poorer eight nations exert about equal demands for increased decision impact upon the three richest nations.

2.5 Base 5: Dependence Upon Oil for Export Income

As a last dimension of impact we have been able to catalog, we seek to define the importance of oil in obtaining foreign exchange; that is, the degree of reliance upon oil for external currencies. With this variable we hope to capture a degree of impact weight accorded to nations whose vulnerability to movements in the international oil economy is high, and the discounting of power accruing to nations having alternative sources of exchange earnings. In table 6.1, column 5, we list the proportions of exports constituted by petroleum and petroleum products in 1976, and normalize on the sum of these proportions. Venezuela, Indonesia, and Kuwait are least dependent on petroleum exports, with Algeria in an intermediate position and the remaining seven extremely dependent upon oil resources.

3 Cross-factor Analysis

In section 2 we have isolated five relatively independent factors that are correlated positively with decision impact in the OPEC cartel. Each has been normalized to sum to unity over all members. The task now facing us is to employ these factor scores to obtain a single measure summarizing the relative impact of these bases as they exist for the individual OPEC nations. This information will then be used in section 4 to construct the *aggregate consonance factors*.

There is, of course, no method of doing this that is well-grounded in the theory of measurement. We have chosen to determine the weights to be accorded each of the five bases by the use of a cross-factor analysis and a "pseudo-measurement" technique described elsewhere.[6] The technique permits the analyst to derive the implied weights from a series of pairwise comparisons between factors in terms of importance in decision impact. The method permits these differences to be quantified, but the final results are highly subjective and the procedures should not disguise the fact.

In table 6.2 we construct the matrix by listing the five bases or factors in the same order in the rows and columns. Moving along a row i we stop at

Table 6.2 The cross-factor matrix

| Factor | Factor | | | | | Initial weights | Final weights |
	Output	Capacity	Reserves	GNP	Percent exports		
Output	2	1	3	3	4	0.72	0.29
Capacity	3	2	3	4	4	0.89	0.44
Reserves	1	1	2	3	3	0.56	0.17
GNP	1	0	1	2	1	0.28	0.04
Percent exports	0	0	1	3	2	0.33	0.06
							1.00

each column j and ask: is factor i more or less important than factor j in determining an OPEC member's decision impact? Beginning with a value of 0, which we assign when factor i is of negligible importance compared with factor j, we constructed the following arbitrary scale values:

0: factor j is much more important than i
1: factor j is more important than i
2: factor i is equal in importance to j
3: factor i is more important than j
4: factor i is much more important than j.

This construction, with a natural zero, yields a derived measurement unique up to a multiplicative constant. If we divided the values by 4 we would have a scale which ran from factor i's relative insignificance (0) to its perfect dominance (1). However, the measures we determine will not be invariant to the number of classes chosen. Therefore, the number selected should bear some relation to the degree of qualitative discrimination the analyst feels he is capable of exercising in the comparisons.

For obvious reasons all cells along the main diagonal in table 6.2 contain the value 2. We need, therefore, only consider comparisons above the main diagonal, since the cell i,j entry plus the cell j,i entry must equal 4. The results of our examination are given in table 6.2. Initial weights are obtained by summing values across rows and dividing by the maximum attainable row score (18). We then take into account the fact that 2 of the factor score points are achieved "easily" by a self-comparison. This is done by weighting all points by the proportion of the perfect score actually achieved. This has the effect of raising slightly the weights of high scores and lowering slightly those of low scores to offset the bias. We then normalize the weighted row sums by their total to obtain the final weights in the last column of table 6.2.

The result of this assisted judgmental procedure is to assert that 44 percent of the weight accorded these five factors at the OPEC bargaining table is determined by excess capacity possessed, 29 percent by market share, and 17 percent by extent of reserves. Per capita GNP and dependence on oil exports are distinctively less important at 4 and 6 percent respectively.

With these weights we can derive the global measure of decision impact – that is, those measures which are not tied directly to relative market performance – for each nation by multiplying each normalized column entry for the nation in a row of table 6.1 by the relevant factor weight of table 6.2, summing across the row, then normalizing these row sums by expressing them as ratios to their sum. The results are recorded in the last column of table 6.1 as the decision impact scores (*DIS*).

On the basis wholly of these power factors and the relative weight accorded them we can divide the 11 rivals into five groups. Group 1 contains only Saudi Arabia, which has about twice the impact of its closest rivals

Kuwait and Iran, which we place in group 2. Iran's weight is reduced somewhat by its smaller capacity (relative to production) and reserves, whereas
Kuwait gains strength on both these counts but suffers slightly from its high
per capita income attainment. Iraq's power is somewhat less than that of
group 2 members but still substantial at about one-third of Saudi Arabia's,
reflecting in large part its existing capacity and therefore its ability to
threaten market stability. We place it in group 3. Group 4 members – Libya,
United Arab Emirates, Venezuela, and Nigeria – possess power only half
that of Iraq and hence about one-sixth of Saudi Arabia's, being rather
accurately reflected in base 1 (current production levels). Finally, group 5
contains nations that are truly weak in bargaining impact. Indonesia's
production alone would lift her to group 4 status, but her small excess
capacity and reserves detract from that strength. Qatar, on the other hand,
is strong on the latter grounds but weak on other important ones. Lastly,
Algeria suffers from her weakness in both capacity and reserves.

4 The Aggregate Consonance Factors

We approach the determination of the binary confluence factors in two
steps. First, we ask for each nation what degree of willingness to cooperate
with partners in OPEC taken as a whole it evidences, in the sense of how it
values (in terms of its own profits) a dollar of profit earned by its partners
jointly. Second, we then break down the aggregate consonance factors into
individualized, nation-to-nation component consonance factors. Symbol-
ically, in the first step we determine for OPEC nation i an aggregate consonance factor θ_i. In the second we distribute θ_i over all of the other OPEC
nations j to obtain θ_{ij}, where $\theta_i = \Sigma_j \theta_{ij}$. In this section and *section 5* we
perform the first step and in *section* 6 we derive the θ_{ij}.

We start with the hypothesis that the amount of consideration that must
be afforded the profit impacts upon other cartel members of a given nation's
pricing decisions is inversely related to the *DIS* determined in table 6.1. The
nature of that relationship must also be hypothesized.

A simple linear relationship does not capture the complexity of rivalrous
consonance. A nation whose *DIS* approaches zero will have an upper bound
on its willingness to temper its pricing decisions to the joint welfare (i.e.
aggregate consonance factor), set in large part by its judgement about the
point at which it would be more profitable to leave the cartel. At the other
extreme, the dominant *DIS* nations – in the case of OPEC, Saudi Arabia –
set the tone of cartel consonance by adopting values (implicitly by their
actions, of course) of their aggregate consonance factors. The minimum of
these becomes the lower bound on such factors, and intermediate *DIS*
nations will be distributed between these two extreme values.

In the lower reaches of the *DIS*, the θ_i should fall slowly at first, since discrimination among various degrees of extreme weakness should be slight. At some break point, when the *DIS* attains the lower limit of the intermediate rankings, θ_i should begin to fall, at first more than linearly and then as the nations' decision impact grows and approaches dominance, less than linearly.

To represent this profile we chose to use the polynomial form

$$\theta_i = a + b \cdot DIS_i^2 + k \cdot DIS_i^3 \tag{6.1}$$

We specify the upper bound (U) reached when $DIS_i = 0$, the lower bound (L) for the Saudi Arabian *DIS*, and that the first derivative of θ_i in (6.1) be zero at L. This latter condition recognizes the lowest θ_i attainable for the cartel. To establish the fourth condition necessary to fit (6.1) various choices were possible, but we settled upon the determination of that *DIS* at which the point of inflection in (6.1) occurs, i.e. where the second derivative of (6.1) is zero. After study of table 6.1 we decided that the distribution of *DIS* logically should reflect the sharp transitional value associated with Iraq as a group 3 nation. We therefore specified the inflection point to occur at $DIS_i = 0.10$. When (6.1) is fitted under these assumptions we obtain

$$\theta_i = U - (U - L)(3.3078\,DIS_i + 14.7667\,DIS_i^2 - 49.2223\,DIS_i^3) \tag{6.2}$$

To determine U and L we argued in the following vein. For nations whose *DIS* approaches zero, we feel an aggregate consonance factor θ_i between 0.40 and 0.60 brackets realistic attitudes toward the value of remaining within cartel discipline. These values imply that the very weak nation will believe it to be to its advantage to remain within the cartel even though it is asked to treat a dollar of profit (loss) accruing to other members of the cartel as equivalent to 40 to 60 cents of its own profit (loss). We feel that this is about the limit of sacrifice such nations can be expected to bear for a commodity as readily marketable as crude oil is likely to be over the foreseeable future. Such nations always have the opportunity to leave the cartel to play an independent role without the obligation of maintaining prices in periods of slack markets.

The bracket within which realistic estimates of θ_i for Saudi Arabia was set was 0.20 to 0.40, which we felt depicts adequately its power and its desire to hold the cartel together for its own selfish interests. In the high end of the range, Saudi Arabia treats a loss of $1 accruing to other OPEC nations as a result of its decisions as a loss of $0.40 to itself – surely a high degree of concern for the welfare of OPEC. The low end of the bracket we feel is an underestimate of Saudi Arabia's solicitude for the cartel's welfare but we adopt it to bound solutions.

We define, therefore, three consonance cases by the choices of U and L. The high consonance case assumes the high estimates in the brackets stated

Table 6.3   *DIS* and aggregate consonance factors for high, moderate, and low consonance cases

Nation	DIS	θ_i for consonance case		
		Moderate	High	Low
1 Saudi Arabia	0.28	0.30	0.40	0.20
2 Iran	0.15	0.37	0.47	0.27
3 Iraq	0.10	0.41	0.51	0.31
4 Kuwait	0.16	0.36	0.46	0.26
5 UAE	0.06	0.45	0.55	0.35
6 Qatar	0.03	0.48	0.58	0.38
7 Libya	0.06	0.45	0.55	0.35
8 Algeria	0.02	0.49	0.59	0.39
9 Nigeria	0.05	0.46	0.56	0.36
10 Venezuela	0.06	0.46	0.56	0.36
11 Indonesia	0.03	0.46	0.56	0.36

above: $U = 0.6$, $L = 0.4$. The low consonance cases on the other hand adopt the conservative estimates: $U = 0.4$, $L = 0.2$. The moderate consonance case, which we shall treat as the most likely case, we define by taking the midpoints of the two brackets: $U = 0.5$, $L = 0.3$. In table 6.3 we list the *DIS* and the aggregate consonance factors θ_i for the three cases computed from (6.2).

These factors place Saudi Arabia, Iran, and Kuwait in a cluster of dominance, with Iraq continuing to occupy its intermediate position. The remaining seven members are close to the upper bounds for their cases. The grouping into dominant, intermediate, and weak members on the basis of their concern for the impacts of their pricing decisions on rivals' profits is tighter than the *DIS* score categories. This follows, of course, from the nonlinear relationship between *DIS* and θ_i which we have hypothesized. It offers us, in our future modelling efforts, the prospect of meaningful aggregation of nations if the need to do so should arise.

5 Binary Market Power Relationships

The aggregate consonance factors measure the overall power structure of OPEC members as derived from five important general and overriding bases for decision impact in cartel counsels. They are stated in terms of an individual nation's need to take into account the impact of its decisions upon other members as a group. These θ_i must now be disaggregated to derive for each member i, the specific consonance factor θ_{ij} at which it values the profit dollar impact of its decision upon *each* of its fellow members j. These we term the *binary consonance factors* to distinguish them from the aggregate factors.

We hypothesize that this disaggregation must be based upon the relative market sensitivities of two nations to changes in the prices of their respective products. That is, member i's binary consonance coefficient relevant to member j is determined by the impact of p_i upon rival j's sales x_j, taking into acount its effect upon x_i and the ability of j to punish i by a change in p_j. To capture this limitational market interdependence we define a *market power index (MPI)*:

$$MPI_{ij} = \frac{e_i + e_{ji}}{e_j + e_{ij}} \cdot \frac{p_j}{p_i} \qquad (6.3)$$

where e_i and e_j are the (absolute) own-price elasticities of the sales functions faced by members i and j at current prices p, and e_{ij} and e_{ji} are the cross-elasticities of the first subscript nation's sales curve with respect to the second's price.

Consider the relative pricing power of nations i and j with respect to each other. The *greater* the proportionate expansion in nation i's sales with a reduction in its price and the greater the *proportionate* fall in j's sales with that reduction, the *greater*, ceteris paribus, the market power of nation i. But should nation j retaliate, the *smaller* the *proportionate* expansion in its own sales and the *smaller* the proportionate impact on nation i's sales, the *greater*, ceteris paribus, the relative power of nation i. The *MPI* adds the first two proportionate measures and places the sum in the numerator, while it adds the second pair and puts the sum in the denominator.

A value of unity for MPI_{ij} indicates a parity of market power for i and j; because $MPI_{ij} = 1/MPI_{ji}$, the range of MPI_{ij} is the interval $[0,\infty]$. An important feature of the *MPI* is that it is dependent upon the *relative* importance of each nation's price impacts upon the other nation's sales. This is a welcome feature of the measure when we consider the fact that the sales functions which are truly relevant to the pricing decisions of the cartel are no doubt longer run than those we have been able to estimate statistically in [9] and [11]. Our hope must be that these sensitivities, were they derivable, would reveal the same *relative* structure as our short-run functions reveal. Our assumptions must be that the *MPI* measure stable relationships over time reflected in elasticities, and that the structure of these elasticities is similarly stable over short-run and long-run periods.

The elasticities isolated in [9] and [11] for current own-prices and average other-prices are summarized in table 6.4. The rows display own-elasticities, e_i and $e_{i,j,}$ or the elasticity of member i's product with respect to j's price. The resulting *MPI* derived from (6.3), are presented in table 6.5.

On the basis of market power alone as we have estimated it from the

Table 6.4 Own-price and cross-elasticities of sales functions, measured for average prices, January 1974 to June 1977

$i\backslash j$

e_i and e_{ij}

$i\backslash j$	Saudi Arabia	Iran	Iraq	Kuwait	UAE	Qatar	Libya	Algeria	Nigeria	Venezuela	Indonesia
Saudi Arabia	−3.340	0.278	0.300	0.249	0.165	0.250	0.057	0.062	0.087	0.000	0.000
Iran	0.068	−2.100	0.066	0.055	0.046	0.063	0.019	0.021	0.029	0.000	0.000
Iraq	0.327	0.304	−1.660	0.296	0.180	0.235	0.121	0.132	0.193	0.000	0.000
Kuwait	0.180	0.169	0.198	−1.290	0.900	0.118	0.062	0.068	0.094	0.000	0.000
UAE	0.043	0.049	0.040	0.027	−3.020	0.071	0.198	0.215	0.301	0.000	0.000
Qatar	0.374	0.429	0.358	0.271	0.480	−2.320	0.490	0.533	0.744	0.000	0.000
Libya	0.780	0.826	0.788	0.751	0.878	0.861	−5.650	0.208	0.184	0.421	0.000
Algeria	0.000	0.000	0.000	0.000	0.000	0.000	0.194	−0.800	0.458	0.000	0.000
Nigeria	0.047	0.050	0.047	0.045	0.053	0.052	0.099	0.131	−1.530	0.000	0.000
Venezuela	0.053	0.056	0.053	0.051	0.059	0.058	0.001	0.196	0.032	−0.690	0.405
Indonesia	0.053	0.056	0.053	0.051	0.059	0.058	0.063	0.070	0.098	0.676	−0.630

Table 6.5 Market power index (MPI) values and market sensitivity index (MSI) values in parentheses

i/j	Saudi Arabia	Iran	Iraq	Kuwait	UAE	Qatar	Libya	Algeria	Nigeria	Venezuela	Indonesia
Saudi Arabia	–	1.49 (0.12)	1.95 (0.09)	2.35 (0.08)	1.12 (0.17)	1.55 (0.12)	0.86 (0.22)	4.82 (0.04)	2.45 (0.08)	5.44 (0.03)	3.42 (0.05)
Iran	0.67 (0.19)	–	1.40 (0.09)	5.31 (0.02)	0.71 (0.18)	1.10 (0.12)	0.60 (0.23)	5.73 (0.02)	1.38 (0.09)	3.33 (0.04)	5.58 (0.02)
Iraq	0.51 (0.71)	0.71 (0.12)	–	1.15 (0.08)	0.55 (0.16)	0.81 (0.10)	0.49 (0.18)	1.78 (0.05)	1.11 (0.08)	2.63 (0.03)	2.93 (0.03)
Kuwait	0.43 (0.13)	0.19 (0.30)	0.87 (0.07)	–	0.43 (0.13)	0.67 (0.08)	0.42 (0.14)	1.80 (0.03)	0.94 (0.06)	2.09 (0.03)	2.33 (0.03)
UAE	0.89 (0.24)	1.41 (0.15)	1.87 (0.12)	2.31 (0.09)	–	3.49 (0.06)	3.13 (0.07)	3.51 (0.06)	1.86 (0.12)	4.69 (0.05)	5.22 (0.04)
Qatar	0.65 (0.16)	0.91 (0.11)	1.23 (0.08)	1.49 (0.07)	0.29 (0.35)	–	2.04 (0.05)	2.01 (0.04)	1.14 (0.08)	3.55 (0.03)	3.95 (0.03)
Libya	1.16 (0.10)	1.67 (0.07)	2.05 (0.06)	2.40 (0.05)	0.32 (0.36)	0.49 (0.24)	–	2.38 (0.05)	3.27 (0.04)	4.69 (0.02)	8.50 (0.01)
Algeria	0.21 (0.19)	0.17 (0.22)	0.56 (0.07)	0.56 (0.07)	0.28 (0.14)	0.44 (0.07)	0.42 (0.09)	–	0.44 (0.09)	1.28 (0.08)	6.25 (0.03)
Nigeria	0.41 (0.19)	0.73 (0.10)	0.90 (0.09)	1.07 (0.07)	0.54 (0.14)	0.88 (0.08)	0.31 (0.24)	2.27 (0.03)	–	2.14 (0.03)	2.49 (0.03)
Venezuela	0.18 (0.18)	0.30 (0.11)	0.38 (0.09)	0.48 (0.07)	0.21 (0.15)	0.28 (0.12)	0.21 (0.15)	0.78 (0.04)	0.47 (0.07)	–	1.34 (0.02)
Indonesia	0.29 (0.09)	0.18 (0.15)	0.34 (0.08)	0.43 (0.06)	0.19 (0.14)	0.25 (0.11)	0.12 (0.23)	0.80 (0.03)	0.40 (0.07)	0.75 (0.04)	–
(Mean)	(0.16)	(0.15)	(0.08)	(0.07)	(0.19)	(0.11)	(0.16)	(0.04)	(0.08)	(0.04)	(0.03)
(Standard deviation)	(0.05)	(0.08)	(0.02)	(0.02)	(0.09)	(0.05)	(0.07)	(0.01)	(0.02)	(0.02)	(0.01)

MPI_{ij} and the demand functions of [9] upon which they are based, Saudi Arabia has greater than unitary binary power relationships with all members but Libya, and even in this case it is quite close to unity. The intense competition of the premium crudes of Qatar, UAE, and Libya is mirrored in the MPI as well. Iraq and Kuwait are revealed to be weak in market power within their own Gulf submarket, whereas Libya dominates the African submarket. Nigeria and Algeria possess true market power only over distant Venezuela and Indonesia, these latter nations being vulnerable in their market relationships with OPEC rivals. It is Saudi Arabia and Libya which reveal the strongest market positions extending beyond their own proper submarkets.

The market sensitivity indices (MSI) which relate market power to binary consonance levels are inversely linked to the MPI: the greater the market power nation i has relative to nation j the less will it feel constrained to take the impacts of its decisions on nation j's profits into account on market power grounds alone. We adopt the simplest hypothesis in treating the relation as linear with the inverse of the MPI, with values of 0 when $MPI^{-1} = 0$ and 1 when $MPI^{-1} = 1$ after the MPI^{-1} have been normalized on their sum for each nation. The results are tabulated (in parentheses) in table 6.5.

Taken row-wise the MSI in table 6.5 display the relative concern the row nation has for its rivals' market power relative to its product, as isolated in (6.3). Column-wise, of course, the coefficients index the market power a given nation exerts against its rivals, measured against the total market power exercised against each of the rivals.

As a means of obtaining insights into these market power relationships we have computed simple arithmetic means and standard deviations for the columns. The mean of a column is the average proportion of other nations' market sensitivity captured by the column nation. For example, Saudi Arabia tends to capture on the average about 16 percent of other nations' sensitivities to market competition. On the basis of these simple measures four groups emerge: Saudi Arabia, UAE, Libya, and Iran as members of the dominant market power aristocracy; Qatar in a strong market position but markedly less powerful than the first group; Iraq, Kuwait, and Nigeria in an intermediate group; and Algeria, Venezuela, and Indonesia in a quite weak class.

Saudi Arabia's market power is strong across all rivals, the dispersion among the relatives being the smallest in the dominant group. Universally, it is a strong rival in every other OPEC member's markets. Within the Gulf area it is especially powerful in the UAE's market, less so in Kuwait's. It is a strong market factor in the African submarket as well, although Libya derives a good deal of independence from it by virtue of its Mediterranean location and very high quality crude.

In terms of the market power exercised against Saudi Arabia, its concerns are much more concentrated: the dominant influence is that exercised by

Libya, with the UAE's something less, and Iran's and Qatar's still smaller though large. Remaining members are markedly less worrisome to its sense of market ascendance.

The UAE's major market impacts are upon light crude producers like itself – Libya and Qatar – although the competition with its crude was felt in every other nation's market in terms comparable to Saudi Arabia's. Its own worries on market power account were located in the Gulf area – primarily Saudi Arabia and Iran – with only Nigeria outside that area a substantial threat.

Libya's power is most strongly felt by Saudi Arabia, Iran, Nigeria, and Indonesia, but its impacts upon other nations are as importantly pervasive as those of Saudi Arabia and the UAE. On the other hand, within its own market it is concerned most with the market power of the UAE and Qatar to an extremely concentrated degree.

Iran's market power is strong in the Gulf market, most notably *vis-à-vis* Kuwait and the UAE; moderately strong in the African market, where we have isolated a substantial market presence for Algeria; and lastly, important in Indonesia's markets, notably the Japanese. In its own markets Iran feels most acutely the competition of Saudi Arabia, the UAE, and Libya.

Qatar's pattern of market threat in the Gulf region is a relatively evenly distributed one of mild threat to its five rivals. As noted above, only for Libya does it afford a substantial competitive threat, like that of the UAE for that nation, because of their high quality crudes. Also, like the UAE and Iran it poses some threat to Indonesia's markets. Its own major competitors are the UAE and Saudi Arabia, the former an understandably greater presence. Other rivals are not important taken singly in its markets.

Iraq, Kuwait, and Nigeria – members of the third group – are similar in that they impose moderately important threats to their ten rivals. They are background presences in all markets. They are similar as well in facing Saudi Arabia and Libya as major market threats to them, but are dissimilar in the threat Iran poses to Kuwait's markets.

The weak power group – Algeria, Venezuela, and Indonesia – pose negligible threats to all rivals. Algeria's major market threats lie outside the African market in Saudi Arabia, Iran, and the UAE. Surprisingly, Libya is not a dominant worry. Venezuela's concerns are spread more broadly: from the Gulf it feels competition from Saudi Arabia, Iran, and the UAE, although its major competitive concern is Libya. Indonesia's major competitors are Iran, the UAE and, predominantly, Libya.

It must be pointed out that these market power relationships hinge upon the validity of the demand analysis that was performed in [9]. The difficulty of fitting sales functions to a limited set of monthly observations and other econometric problems that arose in that process are described in detail in that work. Again, our market power relationship are sensitive only to the *relative* elasticities isolated in that exercise, but the possibility that our demand function results might be misleading for some of the nations must be accepted as a risk.

6 The Binary Consonance Factors, θ_{ij}

The final step is to derive the binary consonance factors, θ_{ij}, by distributing the aggregate θ_i among rivals j on the basis of the market power relationships we have isolated in section 5. The interpretation placed upon θ_{ij} is that it depicts the valuation rival i places, in terms of its own profits, on a \$1 impact of its own pricing decisions on rival j's profits. Its importance for the future stages of the current project is that it will be used as a multiplicative term that firm i applies to firm j's profits when firm i chooses a price that maximizes joint cartel profits after all rivals' profits have been "discounted" by such consonance factors. Elsewhere, I have termed this "crippled optimization" and have described its use to model oligopoly in great detail [4, 6–8].

However, the factors have an independent interest because they depict the power structure of an oligopoly on a detailed pairwise basis. These consonance factors contain the information of overall power bases underlying decision impact as well as the specific market power enjoyed by individual nations. Although such information cannot be viewed as exhaustive in defining the intricate and shifting power structure of as complicated an organization as OPEC, nevertheless it is believed to be of great importance in that definition.

The binary consonance factors are derived by multiplying a nation i's aggregate consonance factor in table 6.3 by the row i *MSI* of table 6.5. Because we defined moderate, high, and low consonance cases for aggregate consonance factors, we derive three sets of θ_{ij}. To conserve space only those for the moderate consonance case are tabulated in table 6.6.[7]

As a supplementary comparative measure of overall relative power we have computed the ratio of column sums of table 6.6 to the row sums – these latter being the aggregate consonance factors for the three consonance cases. This yields the ratio of the sum of the consonance factors used by a nation's rivals in its favor to the aggregate consonance factor which is the degree of consonance granted by it to its rivals. We have tabulated these consonance factor relatives in table 6.7.

As would be expected, the high consonance case tends to decrease the consonance relatives of the more powerful rivals and increase those of the weaker, whereas the low consonance case does the opposite. The column sums of table 6.6 for the moderate consonance case are closer to the column sums of the high consonance case (not listed) for powerful and intermediate

Table 6.6 Binary consonance factors, θ_{ij}, moderate consonance case

i\j	Saudi Arabia	Iran	Iraq	Kuwait	UAE	Qatar	Libya	Algeria	Nigeria	Venezuela	Indonesia
Saudi Arabia	–	0.04	0.03	0.02	0.05	0.04	0.07	0.01	0.02	0.01	0.01
Iran	0.07	–	0.03	0.01	0.07	0.04	0.09	0.01	0.03	0.01	0.01
Iraq	0.07	0.05	–	0.03	0.06	0.04	0.07	0.02	0.03	0.01	0.01
Kuwait	0.05	0.11	0.02	–	0.05	0.03	0.05	0.01	0.02	0.01	0.01
UAE	0.11	0.07	0.05	0.04	–	0.03	0.03	0.03	0.05	0.02	0.02
Qatar	0.09	0.05	0.04	0.03	0.17	–	0.02	0.02	0.04	0.01	0.01
Libya	0.05	0.03	0.03	0.02	0.16	0.11	–	0.02	0.02	0.01	0.00
Algeria	0.10	0.12	0.03	0.03	0.08	0.03	0.04	–	0.04	0.01	0.01
Nigeria	0.10	0.05	0.04	0.03	0.08	0.04	0.11	0.01	–	0.01	0.01
Venezuela	0.08	0.05	0.04	0.03	0.07	0.05	0.07	0.02	0.03	–	0.01
Indonesia	0.04	0.07	0.04	0.03	0.06	0.05	0.11	0.01	0.03	0.02	–
Totals	0.76	0.64	0.35	0.27	0.73	0.46	0.66	0.16	0.31	0.12	0.10

Table 6.7   Consonance relatives

Nation	Moderate consonance	High consonance	Low consonance
Saudi Arabia	2.53	2.28	2.90
Iran	1.73	1.62	1.70
Iraq	0.85	0.86	0.87
Kuwait	0.75	0.76	0.88
UAE	1.62	1.85	1.80
Qatar	0.96	0.95	0.89
Libya	1.47	1.44	1.43
Algeria	0.33	0.34	0.33
Nigeria	0.67	0.73	0.69
Venezuela	0.26	0.32	0.31
Indonesia	0.22	0.29	0.22

rivals and closer to the low consonance case sums (not listed) for weaker rivals. The result of forming consonance relatives is to enhance the relatives of the powerful and intermediate strength rivals and diminish the scores of the weak. In general, however, the relatives for all three consonance cases reveal the same pattern.

Foremost in the power structure, and in a class by itself, is Saudi Arabia. Iran, UAE, and Libya form a strong group, with the first two close together and Libya somewhat weaker. These four nations have scores well above unity. A third group of nations, intermediate in strength, consists of Kuwait, Iraq, and Qatar, somewhat tightly bunched with scores close to unity. Nigeria is in a fourth group, not possessing the same degree of strength as Kuwait, Iraq, and Qatar, but well above the weakest. Lastly, this weakest group contains Algeria, Venezuela, and Indonesia.

7   Conclusion

We have sought in this paper to formalize and quantify the power structure of the OPEC cartel on a binary basis. This analysis is necessary to proceed with an attempt to model the economic decision-making of the cartel, but has an independent interest to those concerned with the functioning of this powerful economic bloc.

It need not be stressed that the obstacles to the accomplishment of this task are many and difficult, in both the conceptual and data planes. We feel, however, that the exercise itself raises useful questions, even where the final result may be subject to debate. Moreover, it is our deep-seated belief that economists must move toward the development of techniques that permit the quantitative manipulation of such attributes and intangibles as those we have dealt with if they are to make progress in the development of a useful, operational theory of oligopoly.

Notes

[1] See, for example, the optimal control theoretic model of OPEC pricing in [12], which effectively treats Saudi Arabia as a monopoly.

[2] While admitting the attraction of simplification it offers, I feel Gately's model of OPEC in [3] using a tripartite partition into moderate, price-pusher, and fringe groups, and treating one group or coalition as price-setters and the other(s) as price-takers, is not an accurate tableau of OPEC's power structure.

[3] Lack of data forced us to eliminate Gabon and Ecuador from consideration when we fitted short-run demand functions [9]. In the first quarter of 1977 their combined output was only 1.3 percent of total OPEC crude oil production.

[4] An analysis of the stability of the OPEC cartel and the amounts of implicit transfers from richer to poorer nations which has some common features with our study can be found in [1,2]. In this work, Danielson concentrates attention upon the tacit permission granted weaker nations to lift oil in amounts more than proportionate to their capacity or reserves.

[5] But see [1,2] for an argument that income transfers have occurred from higher to lower income rivals by a passive permission to withdraw oil faster than capacity or reserves shares would permit.

[6] See [4], where the technique and its limitations are discussed. The specific method used is method C in this reference.

[7] The θ_{ij} for high and low consonance cases may be found in [10], pp. 29–30.

References

[1] Danielsen, Albert L., "The Theory and Measurement of OPEC Stability", mimeographed, no date.

[2] ——, "The Estimation of Implicit Income Transfers Within OPEC", mimeographed, no date.

[3] Gately, Dermot, *Opec Pricing and Output Decisions*, Center for Applied Economics, New York University, No. 78–109, May 1978.

[4] Kuenne, Robert E., "Interproduct Distances in a Quality-space: Inexact Measurement in Differentiated Oligopoly Analysis", *Applied Economics*, 6 (1974), 255–73. [Reprinted as chapter 12 in this volume.]

[5] ——, "Toward a Usable General Theory of Oligopoly", *De Economist*, 122 (1974), 471–502. [Reprinted as chapter 1 in this volume.]

[6] ——, "Towards an Operational General Equilibrium Theory with Oligopoly: Some Experimental Results and Conjectures", *Kyklos*, 27 (1974), 792–820. [Reprinted as chapter 2 in this volume.]

[7] ——, "General Oligopolistic Equilibrium: a Crippled-optimization Approach".

In *Pioneering Economics: Essays in Honor of Giovanni Demaria*, Cedam, Padua, 1978, 537–77. [Reprinted as chapter 3 in this volume].

[8] ——, "Duopoly Reaction Functions under Crippled Optimization Regimes", *Oxford Economic Papers*, 32 (1980), 224–40. [Reprinted as chapter 4 in this volume.]

[9] ——, *Short-run Crude Petroleum Demand Functions for OPEC Cartel Members*, OPEC Cartel Modelling Project, Research Monograph No. 1, General Economic Systems Project, Princeton University, Princeton, NJ, 1978.

[10] ——, *Measuring the Power Structure of Oligopoly: the Case of OPEC*, OPEC Cartel Modelling Project, Research Monograph No. 2, General Economic Systems Project, Princeton University, Princeton, NJ, 1979.

[11] ——, "A short-run Demand Analysis of the OPEC Cartel", *Journal of Business Administration*, 10 (1979), 129–64. [Reprinted in the *Logistics and Transportation Review*, 17 (1981), 231–67, and as chapter 7 in this volume.]

7
A Short-run Demand Analysis of the OPEC Cartel

1 Introduction

The recent interruption of crude petroleum production from Iran highlights the importance of short-term response analysis of OPEC members' sales to modified demand conditions. A prerequisite of that analysis is a set of demand (or sales) functions for crude petroleum for each OPEC member nation.[1] This paper presents the results of data collection and equation-fitting in that enterprise. Section 2 discusses some peculiarities inherent in the time period analysed. Section 3 is concerned with data availability, the sources from which they were derived, their deficiencies, and the caveats that must accompany their usage and interpretation. Section 4 presents the methodology that was used in fitting the demand functions and the reservations that are in order because of the vulnerability of the econometric techniques employed. Section 5 discusses (and the appendix displays) the individual demand functions selected as the best estimating equations, and then considers (and the appendix displays) estimates of aggregate OPEC output derived from a regression on the aggregated data and from sums of the eleven nations' econometric equations.[2] Section 6 contains a summary and conclusion.

2 The Choice of Time Period

Although OPEC has existed as an organization since 1960, the period of active price-setting cartelization of interest to our study began only in October 1973, and extends to the present. The task of data collection and processing was begun in September 1977 but, because of the elimination of

Originally published in the *Logistics and Transportation Review*, 17 (1981), 231–66, and reproduced with permission. The author is indebted to the Rockefeller Foundation for funding the project in full.

dual pricing in July of that year and its lagged effects upon sales, it was decided to terminate the period of analysis at the end of the second quarter of 1977 (77Q2).

The choice of an initial point for the period was somewhat more difficult. Active price setting began at the start of 73Q4, as did the embargo imposed by the Organization of Arab Petroleum Exporting Countries (OAPEC). The suddenness of both actions produced a disequilibrating shock wave in the international oil market, with rampant uncertainty, hysterical trading, and prices that did not reflect the true underlying product availability at the time.

Although the embargo continued until March 1974 (7403), and hence through most of 74Q1, by January of that year the market was becoming better informed, panic buying was subsiding, the high prices of 73Q4 were falling, the international oil majors were distributing non-Arab oil to boycotted nations, leakages were appearing in the embargo, and an approach to the new "normal" began. From the viewpoint of eliminating residual short-run market instability it would have been advisable to eliminate 74Q1 and perhaps 74Q2. We decided against this foreshortening, however, on the basis of the limited number of observations available to us for fitting. It was decided to risk some degree of heterogeneity in these respects to preserve the precious degrees of freedom in the data and to counter some of the multicollinearity that exists in them. Further, a study of the price–output data for the 11 nations showed that these two quarters were continuous in configuration with 74Q3 and 74Q4, so that no sharp breaks in regime were visible.

Therefore, the period of analysis was chosen to be the 42-month period January 1974 (7401) through June 1977 (7706). The sharp division of the whole period into two subperiods can be seen clearly from the graph of OPEC sales in figure 7.1. The strong decline from the heady output levels of the early activated-OPEC period 73Q4 is clearly evident. The trough is reached in 7502, after which there starts a rather steady climb back towards the levels of 74Q1. Hence, OPEC output (disregarding rather sharp monthly movements which anticipate price increases or constitute rebounds from such pricing decisions) is U-shaped and reaches its minimum in 7502.

Period 1, associated with the falling portion of the U, is defined as 7401 through 7502, and is distinguished by the recessionary reduction of world purchases of OPEC oil. OPEC real price behavior – the sum of the deflated prices[3] of petroleum of each of the 11 members multiplied by its relative share of the total output each month – shows no distinguishing behavior in this period. The pattern is one of periodic nominal price increases which are rather rapidly attrited in real terms by excess supply-induced nominal price reductions and by inflation in customer nations. However, if we look beneath the aggregate price behavior to the individual nations' price movements, it will be seen that the African members (Libya, Algeria, and

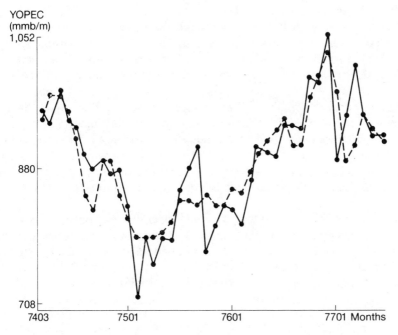

Figure 7.1   OPEC (less Ecuador and Gabon) actual (———) and estimated (–––-)
monthly production, millions of barrels per month, aggregate data estimates, March
1974 through June 1977.

Nigeria) and some Gulf nations reduced their prices substantially over this
period. Period 1 was a time of internal adjustment and attainment of relative
stability in pricing by the OPEC cartel. It was, so to speak, a period of simultaneous "shakedown" of the newly activated OPEC price policies as well as
a period of adjustment to demand forces from outside the cartel that were
reactions in large part to those early policies.

Period 2, on the other hand, which we define as 7503 through 7706, is one
of recovering output and relative real price stability both in the aggregate and
for the individual members. We do not assert, of course, that the shakedown
cruise of period 1 had instilled common price–output policies or expectations
or that the individual nations acted in complete disciplined concert. The
contention is much more modest: that, compared with the turmoil of period
1, the rising aggregate output of period 2 lessened the need for sharply
divergent price actions on the part of individual nations and permitted the
cartel to function in a markedly more effective way.

The distinguishing characteristics of these two subperiods are supported
by the behavior of two important demand determinants in our analysis. The
steep decline in tanker rates that resulted from excess supply in the face of

falling demand is clearly marked in our index of single voyage tanker rates (SIVO) for period 1, with a trough reached in 7503.[4] Period 2, on the other hand, shows some climb back toward prior levels (without attaining them) through most of this period, but with an abrupt fall in 77Q1 and 77Q2. Broadly, however, the distinction we have made between periods 1 and 2 is revealed in this index – that of decline amid disorder on the one hand, and greater stability and some recovery in period 2. Since changes in transportation rates have their greatest impact by shifting demands *within* OPEC – declines favoring distant fields at the expense of producers nearer the markets – the movement of SIVO also lends support to our conclusion that period 1 was characterized by more individualistic price and output adjustment with consequent internal strain within OPEC than was period 2.

The variable IND constitutes a weighted index of industrial production by five leading Organization for Economic Cooperation and Development countries: the United States, the United Kingdom, West Germany, France, and Japan. In our judgement IND provides the best available monthly index of economic activity as it is peculiarly relevant to demand for OPEC petroleum.[5] Although less sensitive to OPEC price movements than SIVO because of its greater causal independence, it, too, reveals the same pattern of movement as OPEC output. Abstracting from the marked summer seasonal dips in IND, we can denote a trend downward from 7401 through 7502, and then a steady recovery over period 2. Although IND as an aggregative index does not permit the spotlighting of important shifts in demand within OPEC – the rising dependence of the United States upon African oil, or the shift of Japanese demand away from Indonesian toward Gulf oil, for example – nonetheless, the pattern at the OPEC-wide level is supportive of our dichotomization of time periods.

These characteristics of periods 1 and 2 had important statistical consequences for our tasks, as will be discussed below. Briefly, in period 1 we faced the formidable task of attempting to isolate classic static demand functions in a period with declining prices *and* quantities and with only imperfect measures of declining world economic activity. In period 2, short-term movements in price and output that were not dominated by trends permitted a greater opportunity to isolate the price–sales relationship, but the greater coordination of nations' price changes led to more serious multicollinearity problems than the period 1 data, and the smaller variances of real price changes elevated the standard errors of the regression coefficients. These problems with period 2 data, along with the fact that observations for only 42 months existed, led to a decision in the general case not to eliminate the period 1 data on the basis of the problems endemic in it. Some truncation was practical, however, when the analysis required it.

3 The Data

As a preliminary to the discussion of the derivation of the data and its deficiencies, a brief introduction to the economic organization and operation of
the OPEC cartel is required as background. The cartel is an organization of
13 diverse countries with a substantial stake in oil exports who have agreed
as sovereign nations to coordinate the prices they quote to buyers. Because
petroleum is a non-homogeneous product distinguished importantly by
sulfur content, specific gravity, and distance to markets, OPEC has wisely
realized that attempting to fix rigidly the prices of each participating nation's
various grades of crude would be unworkably tight and lead speedily to
pressures that would disintegrate the organization. It has, therefore, evolved
a rather loose and informal pricing arrangement that has thus far survived
rather divergent national goals and viewpoints as they relate to the international market for oil. That arrangement has a great bearing upon our tasks
in this chapter and we will outline its basic features.

Fully 30 percent of OPEC's crude petroleum production originates in
Saudi Arabia, and about 80 percent of her output in recent years[6] has been
light crude with 34° specific gravity and sulfur content of 1.63 percent –
so-called "Arab light" or "marker" crude. Further, about half of Iran's
output of crude is "Iranian light" 34°, 1.4 percent sulfur content grade.
Therefore, about one-third of OPEC's output is essentially marker crude,
and thus it is by far the dominant grade in non-communist world oil markets.
The "price decision" arrived at semi-annually or quarterly by the OPEC
nations is the price fixed for this marker crude f.o.b. the Saudi port of
Ras Tanura.[7]

The prices of other crudes, with different gravity and sulfur scores and in
different locations, are permitted to fluctuate above and below that of
marker crude essentially as the market dictates. Attempts in OPEC to
regulate these differentials by gravity–sulfur–location formulae have not
succeeded to date, although a regularity in the price structure certainly exists
in these respects.[8] But, at the present writing, one of the more pressing
disputes among the Gulf nations is the issue of whether Saudi Arabia is
pricing its heavy crudes too low relative to such nations as Kuwait and Iraq,
and therefore whether further adjustments in differentials are needed.

Despite the failure to achieve a rigid formula for regulating these interproduct price differentials – indeed, most probably because of it – the
OPEC price discipline has proved to be acceptable to the member nations.
In periods of slack demand, when temptation has arisen to widen the
differentials on the part of hard-pressed nations, relatively few instances
of ruinous price cutting have occurred. The arrangement has permitted
rather broad shifts in demand among member nation markets to be

accommodated as freight rates or refining needs have changed. It has also permitted rapid local adaptations to OPEC-wide month-by-month demand or supply changes to take place within the necessary cartel discipline.

Much of the credit for the workability of the OPEC scheme must accrue to its dominant member, Saudi Arabia. Because OPEC is a price-setting cartel, it must be prepared to expand or contract supplies as the market requires. In periods of active demand for oil, Saudi Arabia possesses the only major excess capacity in OPEC, and its willingness to expand output has prevented prices from rising above the present level for marker crude. Even more importantly, in periods of slack demand, its willingness to contract its supply and reduce its revenues *pari passu* to absorb most of the excess supply has been amply demonstrated up to the present time.

These accommodating stances by Saudi Arabia are not wholly altruistic, of course. Her opposition has been the major roadblock to various output prorationing schemes that have been sought by such nations as Venezuela and Iraq. Any such preset output prorationing would lessen Saudi Arabia's power in the cartel, since it would neutralize its frequently used threat to enforce a price unilaterally in the absence of cartel agreement.

Indeed, were capacity to produce crude more equally distributed among the cartel members, the economics of oil production would argue strongly for a supply-setting rather than a price-setting regime from the narrow viewpoint of the cartel's welfare. Crude oil, once lifted, must be sold, as it can be stored only in limited amounts in steel tanks. Since the aggregate OPEC short-run demand function has limited price elasticity (unitary in our calculation), short-run excess supplies can lead to large price reductions and even larger proportionate revenue losses, or at least to zero revenue gains. These reactions cannot be confined to a single market because – given the already discussed adjustments for specific gravity, sulfur content, and location – the product is relatively non-differentiable and the market very well informed. Moreover, our results lead us to believe that the demand functions faced by the individual OPEC nations in the short run are more elastic than has been believed heretofore, intensifying the temptation within the cartel to cut prices in times of slack demand to the detriment of the aggregate revenue. Hence, as the history of the oil industry attests, small excess supply overhangs can cause widespread and large price–revenue disruptions, and the history of the international oil industry is largely writ in terms of gaining effective control of the supplies offered on the market, either via physical control or by formal or informal agreement.

It seems clear, therefore, that the continued existence of a price-setting cartel without formal and enforceable production agreements will remain contingent upon the willingness of Saudia Arabia to reduce or increase output and revenue receipts unilaterally. On the persistence of the willingness, which is based upon the leverage it gives her as the power within OPEC and her relative economic ability to postpone income flows, rests the basis for OPEC's *modus operandi*. As a barrier to a different mode which seems more attuned to the economies of the industry, it also serves as a key to the understanding of the potentially disintegrating conflicts within the cartel. In this regard, the major insight obtained is that of understanding the relatively flexible deviation of prices from that of marker crude that is tolerated by OPEC.

This multiprice structure forces us to seek the effective market prices of each nation's crude petroleum in each of the 42 months of the analytical period. But this is only the beginning of our problems of data collection. Most of the 11 nations produce more than a single grade of crude oil, so that "the" market price for each nation's crude that we seek is a weighted average over these different crudes. Frequently it is difficult to get the quantities of each type of crude produced in order to weight the prices rationally. Consequently, we have had to use period-wide estimates of the relative proportions of each nation's output that constituted specific grades.

Determining the market prices of those blends is itself a formidable problem, given the institutional pricing arrangements that characterized this period and the confidentiality of much of the information. Three different officially declared prices have been quoted over the analytical period with greater or lesser relevance to market price:

1 *Posted price*   These are national prices used in the calculation of royalties and taxes in those nations where and for those years when the old concession system operated with oil companies or consortia in control of production. They bore no significant relation to true cost to the companies and have been largely eliminated by the nationalization movements that characterize our period.

2 *Official sales price*   This was generally specified as a percentage of posted price – usually 93 per cent – at which state companies stood ready to sell in direct sales contracts. But, in fact, the same price was not quoted to all buyers, so that this cannot be taken uncritically as an effective price to customers.

3 *Buy-back price*   This is the price paid by the oil companies for oil purchased from the state, whether they have an equity interest in the nation's oil industry or work wholly on a contractual operating basis. It was usually – but not always – lower than the official sales price quoted to other buyers.

A great deal of discrimination among buyers existed, therefore, on an officially quoted basis. But this complicated structure of prices was rendered even more complex by the existence of spot and futures prices; by changes in the status of the oil companies over the period, with associated changes in the proportions of state-owned and equity oil in their purchases; by effective price changes through alterations in the period of payment or other credit conditions; and by unreported and jealously guarded discounts in periods of slack demand.

The estimation of "the" market price, therefore, required a determination for the month in question of the proportions of production accruing to the companies as equity oil; how much was sold to them under buy-back contracts and at what prices; how much state-owned oil was sold to other purchasers at what sales prices; and how much state-owned oil was bought by them at what official sales prices. It was not possible to obtain this information in full detail by crude petroleum grades, and even that available in lesser detail is of indeterminate accuracy. On the basis of monthly price data given over most of the period by the *Petroleum Economist*, with adjustments from reports contained in it and the *Middle East Economic Survey*, we have pieced together the estimated market prices.[9]

The quantities of crude petroleum produced each month by nations are in most cases taken from data in the *Petroleum Economist*.[10] A few instances of allocating semi-annual or quarterly data over constituent months did occur; however, the output data are less conjectural and complex than price information, and it is believed that the OPEC nations did not intentionally misreport production. All output and sales data are measured in American barrels of 42 American gallons. For marker crude's 34° API specific gravity this converts to about 7.37 barrels per short ton.

For price deflation purposes we used the consumer price index of the OECD.[11] It was felt that this index was the best available measure of relative prices in the major customer nations and therefore the best available deflator of nominal oil prices to real prices for consumers. We have based the price index on January 1977, as 100, and hence the deflated oil prices are stated in dollars of that month and year. Note that we did not attempt to adjust prices for changes in exchange rates – that is, for fluctuations in the external values of customer currencies in US dollars. It was felt that the period of analysis was too short and the relative stability of currencies sufficiently great to warrant the omission of these extremely complex corrections.

As a measure of transportation charges we adopted the single voyage tanker rate (SIVO) as computed by the London Trade Brokers on the fifteenth of each month to be used by all oil companies for pricing purposes in the following month. The rate as published in the *Petroleum Economist* is stated as a percentage of Worldscale freight rate schedules (worldwide tanker nominal freight scale). This index has been chained back to a common basis after abrupt changes in Worldscale in December 1974 and 1975, and then was converted into an index with January 1977 equal to 100.[12]

The adoption of this SIVO rate as the transport rate variable in our demand functions reflects an element of arbitrariness and deserves an explanation. All crude oil prices are quoted f.o.b. various export ports.

Tanker freight rates are determined in an open, competitive market which is independent of the international majors, and in which fluctuation is frequent as market forces vary. These rates are determined as percentages of Worldscale, which is a theoretical reference scale of basic rates for round trips between pairs of ports. A set of alternative tanker rates to SIVO, computed also as percentages of Worldscale, are the AFRA (average freight rate assessments) for five categories of ship: (1) general purpose, (2) medium, (3) large 1, (4) large 2, (80,000 to 160,000 tons deadweight), and (5) very large (160,000 to 319,000 tons deadweight). These rates reflect all tanker rates paid in any one month and therefore move more slowly than SIVO and, while one or two categories are more representative of the types of tankers used by the various submarkets of OPEC (Gulf, African, South American, and Indonesian), no one of them reflects the general short-run OPEC transport circumstances as well as SIVO. After some experimentation with the AFRA general purpose rate, which is most representative of all submarkets, we were confirmed in our belief that SIVO was a slightly more powerful explanatory variable, although they moved rather closely together.

Four sets of data, therefore – prices and quantities by nation, a tanker freight rate index (SIVO), and an industrial production index (IND) already discussed, all for the months 7401 through 7706 – constitute the raw materials of our demand analyses. Also, an OECD consumer price index was used instrumentally to deflate prices.

4 Model Specification

The OPEC cartel, as the supply apparatus for a major portion of the total world petroleum market, constitutes a single entity with interdependent constituents and, ideally, should be treated as such in the isolation of its individual sales or demand functions. In econometric terms, the specification of the OPEC nations' demand structures should recognize the simultaneous-equation nature of the relevant individual functions and the fitting of those equations to the data should be done with that causal characteristic recognized.

An attempt was made to do this. Our belief is that as a cartel of price-setting members, each of whom has some constrained flexibility to vary prices with the market's changes, the best theoretical specification for the demand structure of the typical nation i is the following. First, in month t, price (P_i) is a function of sales (Y_i) the previous month and of transport rates (SIVO) the previous month:

$$P_{i,t} = f_i(Y_{i,t-1}, SIVO_{t-1}). \qquad (7.1)$$

Transport rates are important because they index the ability of the member nation to exploit locational advantages or overcome the burden of distance from markets.

The demand function, then, is a function of own-price, other member nations' prices $(P_j, P_k, \ldots)$, $SIVO_{t-1}$ (because $SIVO_t$ affects demand in $t + 1$), and industrial production which we assume operates with a one-month lag (IND_{t-1}). Thus,

$$Y_{i,t} = g_i\left(P_{i,t}, P_{j,t}, P_{k,t}, \ldots, SIVO_{t-1}, IND_{t-1}\right). \qquad (7.2)$$

Systems (7.1) and (7.2) yield a model with 22 endogenous variables, 11 lagged endogenous and two exogenous variables, or 35 variables in total. There are 22 equations in the model. The system has the attraction of being exactly identified (meeting the rank condition for identifiability).

We attempted to fit the model by two-stage least squares to the six Gulf nations' data, but obtained very bad fits because the extreme multi-collinearity among the lagged endogenous and exogenous variables in the first stage yielded ill-conditioned matrices. The use of first differences did not improve results, and we therefore reluctantly abandoned the preferred theoretical specification for a more straightforward if slightly less acceptable specification.

In general, we fitted equations (7.2) to the data for each nation treating all prices as exogenous. In an important sense, if prices are set at the start of the month on the basis of immediate past experience of the month before (à la 7.1), and those prices are held rigidly during the month before change at the start of the following month, we have lost nothing in the proper specification of the demand equation. It is true that we no longer have an explanation for prices, but we are not interested at this stage in price determination, and in that sense the lack of price equations constitutes zero sacrifice. If these conditions hold, therefore, the specification of (7.1) and (7.2) is closely approximately since that system is recursive.

We have already indicated two basic problems that hindered the fitting and that seriously condition our results. We seek to isolate the (essentially static) sales functions from data which are subject to many dynamic perturbations: price change expectations, anticipatory buying and subsequent rebound effects, uncertain potential supply restrictions, and the general anxieties of politically based government action. These perturbations, complicated by the more usual market disturbances, as, for example, weather conditions which make ports unusable for significant periods, contribute a large element of variation our regressors cannot be expected to explain. These dynamic unsettling phenomena were especially marked in period 1, as we have noted, resulting in large excess supplies that set off movements downward in prices and quantities in a disequilibrium phase. In several cases we were forced to truncate the data to eliminate these "perverse" movements, which is to confess inadequacies in both the specification of the model and the explanatory power of the chosen regressors in representing the factors they purport to represent. In all cases, we will find the fit of our equations to the period 1 data is less good than to period 2 data. Of course, because our interest in the sales functions is for use in explaining the behavior of a settled, mature cartel in the future, the poorer fits in period 1 are less worrisome.

The second problem concerns the power of IND, even with "best" lag structure, to net out of the data the "shifts" in demand that occur with changes in world economic activity. That index does not include household consumption, and it excludes as well all industrial activity but that of the five largest OECD nations. A more comprehensive and sensitive index of world economic activity on a monthly basis could not be found, and we feel our analysis has suffered somewhat for it.

With the limited number of observations available, it was not possible to preserve a specification with 11 prices as regressors, especially when quadratic terms and multiperiod lag structures are incorporated. Moreover, price fluctuations within the relevant submarkets (Gulf and African) were in very close correlation, so that considerations of multicollinearity as well argued for the compression of detail. For each of the Gulf and African countries, therefore, we constructed a synthetic price by taking a weighted average of the prices of the other members of its submarket and a second weighted average of all the prices of the other submarket.

For example, in deriving the demand function for Saudi Arabia, we constructed a weighted average of other Gulf nations' prices (Iran, Iraq, Kuwait, UAE, Qatar) called POGSA (price of other Gulf nations' oil relevant to Saudi Arabia) and used it as a regressor in the regression equation. Moreover, we constructed a "price of African oil" (PAF) by taking a weighted average of Libyan, Algerian, and Nigerian price observations, and employed it as an independent regressor. Similarly, for Libya we constructed an "own submarket" variable POAL (other African nations' oil prices relevant to Libya) and used a weighted average of all Gulf prices (PG).

The weighting system used attempted to capture the degree of substitutability among the nations' petroleum grades by using an extension of a methodology developed in previous work [2]. For POGSA, for example, we chose the values of 24° API and 40° API as effective lower and upper bounds for the specific gravities of Gulf nations' crudes. These points become 0 and 100 limits on a scale, along which the six nations' average crude specific gravities were spaced proportionately along the line. Next the Saudi Arabian scale value was subtracted from each of the other five values, and the absolute values of these increments was deducted from 100. These differences were summed and used as a base to convert them to proportions. These five values were then used as measures of the "nearness" in the specific gravity quality of "other Gulf" crudes to that of Saudi Arabia. For PG, all six of the Gulf states were included in the analysis.

A similar analysis in every respect was performed for sulfur content. The final weights used in the POGSA calculation were derived by combining the two sets of proportions that measure nearness of the Saudi Arabian product to that of the other five Gulf nations in specific gravity and sulfur content quality space. Because of the greater weight given sulfur content in the oil markets – as indexed, for example, by the formula for price differentials discussed in section 3 – we weighted sulfur content proportionate values by 0.6 and specific gravity proportions by 0.4 to get the final weights applied to the five "other Gulf nations relevant to Saudi Arabia." These final weights for Gulf and African submarkets are displayed in Table 7.1. It is hoped that we have captured in the final synthetic prices constructed with these weights a measure of the price of rivals' products. The weights serve to give crudes most competitive with the product of the nation under analysis a greater influence in the calculation of the aggregate price.[13]

In general, for the Gulf nations, our substitutability measures reveal that Saudi Arabian, Iranian, and Iraqi crudes are rather close in quality competition, as are UAE and Qatar crudes, with Kuwaiti crudes closer to the first group but at a noticeable intermediate position. In the African submarket, Libyan and Algerian crudes are close with Nigerian noticeably distanced from them. The scalings for Gulf nations in table 7.1 can be roughly depicted in the following way. Let the reader imagine a scale of quality going from lowest to highest left to right. The ordering of the crudes from left to right is Kuwait, Iraq, Saudi Arabia, Iran, Qatar, and UAE. This ordering is consistent with the six "other Gulf" scalings of the table. In the case of the African nations the crudes are very close to each other in substitutability.

Lastly, close study of the nations' sales figures failed to reveal any important seasonal pattern in the months studied. Such practices as anticipatory buying and slow steaming seem to have ironed out a noticeable, stable movement, and consequently the data have not been de-seasonalized.

5 The Results of the Analysis

We have reproduced the estimating equations derived from our analysis, along with a key to the symbols used, in the appendix. For each regression equation given there we have listed a coefficient of multiple determination adjusted for degrees of freedom ($\bar{R}^2$), the Durbin–Watson statistic (DW), and the number of observations (N).[14] In table 7.2 we display the own-price, other-price (i.e. cross-), transport rate, and industrial activity elasticities derived from the equations for mean values of these variables (except where noted in the discussions to follow). In our selection of these equations

Table 7.1 Substitutability measures applied to prices in construction of price composites

Nation weighted	Weights relevant to										
	Saudi Arabia	Iran	Iraq	Kuwait	UAE	Qatar	All Gulf	Libya	Algeria	Nigeria	All African
Gulf											
Saudi Arabia	–	0.234	0.249	0.248	0.193	0.200	0.164	–	–	–	–
Iran	0.230	–	0.227	0.227	0.215	0.224	0.170	–	–	–	–
Iraq	0.247	0.221	–	0.265	0.173	0.186	0.161	–	–	–	–
Kuwait	0.208	0.188	0.223	–	0.120	0.143	0.156	–	–	–	–
UAE	0.135	0.151	0.132	0.106	–	0.247	0.178	–	–	–	–
Qatar	0.180	0.206	0.169	0.154	0.299	–	0.171	–	–	–	–
Africa											
Libya	–	–	–	–	–	–	–	–	0.516	0.500	0.277
Algeria	–	–	–	–	–	–	–	0.516	–	0.500	0.291
Nigeria	–	–	–	–	–	–	–	0.484	0.484	–	0.432

Table 7.2 Mean value elasticities

1 Gulf

	Own-price	Other Gulf	African-price	SIVO	IND
1 Saudi Arabia	-3.39	1.21	0.20	0.29	0.29
2 Iran	-2.10	0.30	0.07	0.40	-0.38
3 Iraq	-1.66	1.34	0.43	-0.37	0.47
4 Kuwait	-1.29	0.76	0.22	0.61	-0.46
5 United Arab Emirates	-3.02	0.23	0.71	-0.16	0.99
6 Qatar	-2.32	1.90	1.76	-0.01	0.74

2 Africa

	Own-price	Other Africa	Gulf	Venezuela	SIVO	IND
1 Libya	-5.65	4.87	0.40	0.42	0.31	0.24
2 Algeria	-0.80	0.31	0.31	–	0.00	1.05
3 Nigeria	-1.53	0.03	0.03	–	0.16	0.81

3 South America

	Own-price	Gulf	Africa	Indonesia	SIVO	IND
1 Venezuela	-0.69	0.29	0.08	0.48	0.26	0.63

4 Indonesia

	Own-price	Gulf	Africa	Venezuela	SIVO	IND
1 Indonesia	-0.63	0.33	0.22	0.55	-0.04	0.41

OPEC (aggregate data)

	Own-price	SIVO	IND
OPEC	-1.04	0.19	0.62

as "best" we did not always choose the equation that yielded the highest proportion of "explained variation" after correction for degrees of freedom ($\bar{R}^2$): rather, our interest focused upon its power of correct prediction in period 2, for the reasons of settled decision making discussed in sections 2 and 4.

One of the rather surprising characteristics of our regression analysis for all 11 nations was a general failure of the transport rate variable SIVO, with or without a lag structure, to contribute much to the explanation of inter-OPEC shifts in sales as the literature seems to believe is appropriate. The drastic decline in tanker rates duly recorded by SIVO is supposed to result in a relative advantage to Gulf sales and relative disadvantages to African, reducing as it does the penalty of greater distance to major markets. In general, the data do not consistently support this hypothesis for Gulf states: such role as tanker rates had in shifting sales among the geographic sub-markets of OPEC in the short run does not appear to have been major. Indeed, in some instances the sign of the term was counterintuitive as, for example, in the case of Saudi Arabia. In table 7.3 we list the regression coefficients obtained and their t-values.

Table 7.3 Regression coefficients and t-values for lagged and unlagged SIVO variables for OPEC nations' sales functions (millions of barrels/mouth)

	SIVO	$SIVO_{t-1}$	$SIVO_{t-2}$
Saudi Arabia		0.836^a −(2.30)	
Iran			0.785^a (3.47)
Iraq		−0.325 (−1.20)	0.048 (0.28)
Kuwait		0.436 (1.75)	
UAE	−0.064 (−1.11)	−0.026 (−0.28)	
Qatar		−0.001 (−0.04)	
Libya			0.176 (1.11)
Algeria		0.001 (0.03)	
Nigeria			0.123^a (2.10)
Venezuela			0.209 (1.98)
Indonesia			−0.022 (0.35)

^{a} Significant at the 0.05 level.

Note, first, that one- or two-month lag structures characterize such impacts as SIVO does have upon OPEC demands, but that only three of the eleven nations have statistically significant regression coefficients. In the Gulf market, three nations' coefficients are in the expected negative direction, but none of these is significant and only Iraq's could be said to be non-negligible. In the African submarket, all coefficients are in the expected positive direction, but only one is significant and all are small in absolute terms. Venezuela, with its proximity to the large Caribbean-American market, would be expected on the basis of this reasoning to have a positive coefficient, and does, but it too is small and not statistically significant.

In general, therefore, our analysis does not warrant the importance of tanker transport rates as an important shaper of the intra-OPEC demand structure in the short run. Several possible sources of error springing from methodology come to mind but, we feel, must be dismissed. First, SIVO may be unrepresentative of tanker rate movements in the respective submarkets and therefore we may not, in our desire to use a single representative freight rate variable, have chosen wisely. But two points cast doubt upon this. A study of the other AFRA alternatives as indices show broadly the same movements, and most of them do not have the same intensity of fluctuation that SIVO reveals. And we experimented with the general purpose rate as a regressor only to get even smaller impacts with less impressive t-values.

More importantly, one may suspect that multicollinearity of SIVO and other regressors is a culprit, spreading the standard errors of the SIVO regression coefficients to reduce statistical significance on the one hand, and distributing its true causal impact to other highly correlated regressors. In table 7.4 we present the crude correlation coefficients of SIVO with the other major regressors of our demand analysis. There it can be seen that there is little basis for this concern. Specifically, the case of IND does not present much serious worry but, even were it worrisome, that regressor also is one that disappoints in terms of expected impacts. If, therefore, SIVO's true effect is distorted by registering in IND's regression coefficients, that true causal force is a weak one.

Table 7.4   Correlation coefficients of SIVO with major regressors in demand analyses

Variable	Coefficient	Variable	Coefficient
Saudi Arabian price (PSA)	−0.703	Nigerian price (PN)	0.411
Iranian price (PIN)	−0.672	Venezuelan price (PV)	0.491
Iraqi price (PIQ)	−0.609	Indonesian price (PI)	−0.158
Kuwaiti price (PK)	0.417	Gulf price (PG)	−0.656
United Arab Emirates price (PU)	−0.591	African price (PAF)	−0.603
Qatari price (PQ)	−0.535	IND	0.578
Libyan price (PL)	0.614		
Algerian price (PA)	0.604		

In general, we must conclude that the existence of long-term contracts with shippers and the commitment of refineries to specific types of crude significantly limit the ability of crude purchasers to shift *among* OPEC submarkets wholly on the basis of lower freight rates in the short run. We shall see that long-term contracts to lift oil are not so binding, and that buyers do have the ability to shift sources *within* submarkets with price changes to an important degree.

Table 7.5   Regression coefficients and t-values for lagged and unlagged IND values for OPEC nations' sales functions (millions of barrels/mouth)

	IND	IND_{t-1}		IND_{t-2}	
Saudi Arabia		1.146	(1.16)		
Iran				−0.677	(−1.46)
Iraq		−0.352	(−0.96)	0.671	(1.74)
Kuwait		−0.463	(−1.09)		
UAE	0.064 (1.20)	0.456[a]	(2.44)		
Qatar				0.108	(1.42)
Libya				0.125	(0.36)
Algeria		0.330[a]	(5.09)		
Nigeria		0.572[a]	(4.28)		
Venezuela		0.499[a]	(2.44)		
Indonesia		0.191	(1.68)		
Total	0.064	2.379		0.227	

[a] Significant at the 0.05 level.

Consider the general pattern of IND's importance in nation-by-nation detail. In table 7.5 we list IND's regression coefficients and relevant t-statistics. On a percentage point basis they do in general reveal a stronger importance than SIVO, as we would expect on theoretical grounds. However, in two cases the net effects of the regression coefficients are non-significantly negative, and in the remaining non-perverse instances only four are statistically significant. Nonetheless, even in the cases where significant impact is recorded, the absolute effect on sales is disappointingly small. A once-for-all sustained rise of 10 percentage points in IND – a 10.2 percent rise over its average value in the analytical period of 42 months – leads to a rise of about 27 million barrels per month (mmb/m) for all 11 nations, or a 3 per cent rise in OPEC-wide average monthly output of 888 mmb/m. This seems a very small elasticity of sales with respect to major industrial production – it implies an elasticity coefficient of 0.3 at mean levels of OPEC-wide output. In our regression on aggregate OPEC data this elasticity for mean values of regressor variables doubles to 0.6 (table 7.2), which is a more realistic value for a world striving to economize on oil and with sources alternative to OPEC.

It seems quite possible, therefore, as we noted above, that IND does not capture the full impact of world income changes upon nations' oil sales in our individual nation analyses. It may not have sufficient sensitivity to extract all of this income impact before (notably) prices' effects are isolated by our regression methods. But the choice of an index of economic activity for the world is severely restricted because of our need for monthly observations: indeed, we know of no other available index. Hence, our defence

Table 7.6   Correlation coefficients of IND with major regressors in demand analyses

Variable	Coefficient	Variable	Coefficient
PSA	−0.264	PA	0.204
PIN	−0.163	PN	0.459
PIQ	−0.087	PV	0.358
PK	0.138	PI	−0.291
PU	−0.242	PG	−0.189
PQ	−0.152	PAF	0.255
PL	0.176	SIVO	0.578

for its usage or failure to experiment with other such variables is their non-availability.

As in the case of SIVO, the problem does not reside in an excessive direct intercorrelation with the other regressor variables. We list in table 7.6 the correlation coefficients involved: in no case does an extreme correlation value intrude.

We now turn to a brief consideration of the individual analyses whose equations are given in the appendix with relevant fit statistics.

5.1 Saudi Arabia

We judged the sales function (1A) to depict most accurately the underlying forces in the more settled period 2, and thus to be the best projector for the future. It was fitted to the months 7502 through 7706 and performed noticeably better than did functions fitted to the whole period. We note, first, the negative results that we could not uncover any noticeable impact of Venezuelan or Indonesian prices (PV and PI) upon Saudi sales (YSA). The result reflects a well-marked independence that we shall note throughout this study of the Gulf, South American, and Indonesian submarkets. Of course, this result is for the short term only and must be somewhat discounted for the lack of extreme sensitivity in regression methodology and the small number of observations. Nonetheless, we believe the conclusion is broadly true: the Gulf submarket has a noticeably important degree of independence from the South American and Indonesian, accounted for in large part by differences in specific gravity and sulfur content of their notional crudes.

The own-price regression coefficient of 73 mmb/m for a $1 *ceteris paribus* change in Saudi price (PSA) reflects a mean values elasticity of −3.39 (table 7.2) – the highest in the Gulf submarket – which may well reflect Saudi Arabia's responsiveness with its excess capacity. The other-Gulf price (POGSA) regression coefficient of 25.5 mmb/m reveals that Saudi Arabia's

Gulf rivals are the major OPEC source of competition, yielding a cross-elasticity for mean values of +1.21, quite large for the very short run.

This POGSA result is slightly obscured by an uncertain relation of YSA and PAF (African composite price), because of the rather high intercorrelation of POGSA and PAF ($r = 0.839$). The PAF regression coefficient of 3.8 mmb/m may be somewhat higher if we believe some of our alternative sales function fits. The mean value elasticity of +0.20 is in line with the results of four other Gulf nations' PAF cross-elasticities. There is, then, a large degree of independence of Saudi Arabia from the African market, even if we have substantially underestimated the PAF regression coefficient in (1A): even were the coefficient doubled our conclusion of substantial market independence would not alter.

5.2 Iran

The best fitting estimating equation for Iran is equation (2A) fitted to the period 7407–7707. The own-price impact upon sales yields an elasticity for mean values of -2.10, revealing, as in the case of Saudi Arabia, a quite sensitive response. The other-Gulf price elasticity is only +0.30, which is suspiciously low in view of the Saudi Arabian counterpart value which was four times this value. The prices, PIN and POGIN respectively, are rather closely intercorrelated ($r = 0.820$) so that their regression coefficients may be the result of faulty individualization of the separate price influences.

Once more we could denote no significant relation to PV and PI, and the relation to PAF is also a weak one (elasticity only +0.07). This reinforces our findings concerning Saudi Arabia: significant short-run independence from other submarkets for these two dominant producers is a definite indication of our study.

5.3 Iraq

Our results for Iraq, given in equation (3A), are among the most disappointing of all the nations studied. Its case offers a host of special problems. Output over the period was extremely unstable, subject to large short-run buffetings, and reflecting, among other things, the tendency for Iraq to vary prices *sub rosa* as market conditions warrant. Moreover, in 7604, Iraq suspended trans-shipment of oil through Syria to the Mediterranean from its Kirkuk field, an action which constituted a sharp disruption of markets for several months. Iraq is among the more secretive in its price and sales data, and frequently our price data reflect rumours of current pricing policies. It is, moreover, less dependent upon longer term contracts, refusing to deal with large Western oil companies since its nationalization of the majors' properties in 1975. As a consequence it is much more subject to the short-run vagaries of demand or barter deals with communist nations.

All of these elements combine to yield an unsettled picture. However, the fit of our equation is somewhat better than $\bar{R}^2$ reveals. If we eliminate 7702 and its aftermath of the dual price introduction by OPEC the month before, $\bar{R}^2$ rises to 0.446 and if, in addition, we eliminate 7512 it rises to 0.527. It is, therefore, the disturbing presence of these extreme items that yields the low value noted above.

Most interestingly, the quite sensitive nature of Iraq's sales to the prices of her Gulf neighbors is quite apparent. Iraq has at several points in recent years insisted that Saudi Arabia and Iran increase the price of their heavy crudes to make her own relatively heavy product more attractive. On the other hand, Iraq's low sensitivity with respect to African crudes reflects the same independence from this submarket that Saudi Arabia and Iran revealed, although at +0.43 the PAF elasticity is somewhat higher.

The picture of Iraq's market presented by the equation is conformant to the informal evidence in the literature. It is quite sensitive to the pricing policies of her Gulf rivals, to its own price, and substantially independent of the African submarket, although less so than her strong rivals Saudi Arabia and Iran. Although its sales expand as tanker freight rates decline, the effect is not strong, nor is the response to industrial activity in the major economies of the world.

5.4 Kuwait

Kuwait offers some singularities that present challenges to obtaining a good fit to the data. Its oil revenues are far beyond its internal needs, and so constant pressure has existed to restrict production below what could be sold at going prices. On the other hand, because its internal industry is fuelled by natural gas and because it has long-term contracts to supply butane and propane, its output cannot drop below about 30 mmb/m. With long-term contracts for oil, the floor is probably closer to 40 mmb/m. Nearly all of her output is in heavy grades of crude, and hence she has been prone to discount to get her contract customers to fulfill their contracts in periods of slack demand. Thus, nonmarket limitations to response in periods of booming demand and not-easily-captured discounts in times of slack demand have clouded the data.

Nonetheless, a reasonably good fit was obtained over the whole of the period with equation (4A). This is the first of several instances in which quadratic terms are introduced into the estimating equation. Their presence gave rise to a complication in the higher price domain because period 1's pecularities caused perverse movements in the second-order polynomials. For example, in the case of Kuwait, the contribution of PK to YK becomes positive at PK $\geq$ 12.09: that is, in the partial demand curve sense, the curve becomes backward bending at that point. For $POGK_{t-2}$ the contribution to YK becomes negative (and hence perverse) when $POGK_{t-2} \geq 13.03$. These are impermissible idiosyncracies of our data and must be corrected in our final fitting process.

The manner of correction, which we will illustrate for PK, involved the fitting of a logistic curve through two points of the partial demand function for PK and adopting that function's predictions in the domain PK $\geq$ 12.09 rather than the original functions (as long as $POGK_{t-2} \leq 13.03$). First, we set all regressors except PK at their average values for the period. The function then becomes the partial relation

$$YK = 3358.397 - 546.231PK + 22.598PK^2. \tag{7.3}$$

We choose two widely separated prices to determine two points on the non-perverse portion of (7.3), [5.00, 1192.192], [12.09, 57.571], and through them we fit the logistic function

$$YK = \beta / (1 + \exp(a + bPK)), \tag{7.4}$$

where β is an upper bound on YK approached asymptotically as PK approaches zero, and where a and b are two parameters to be determined. By rearranging terms in (7.4) we obtain

$$\ln \left(\frac{\beta}{YK} - 1 \right) = a + bPK, \tag{7.5}$$

which relationship we used to derive two linear equations in a and b using the two PK–YK pairs chosen above. We then obtain, when β is chosen as the value of YK when PK = 0 in (7.3):

$$YK = 3358.397 / (1 + \exp(-1.836 + 0.487PK)), \tag{7.6}$$

which must be corrected for departures of the other regressors from their means. When this is done we obtain the logistic branch (5A). By similar techniques, which are detailed in [3], we obtain the branches (6A) and (7A) for domains defined in their statement.

In the original estimating equation (4A) own-price elasticity for mean values is -1.29, other-price elasticity for Gulf rivals' crudes is $+0.76$, and other-price elasticity for African crudes is $+0.22$. The elastic own-price contribution and severely inelastic other-price contribution for African crudes are consistent with the analysis of the other five Gulf states. The price elasticity of other-Gulf crudes is a bit lower than for Saudi Arbia and Iraq, but higher than Iran's coefficients. Kuwait's heavy crudes are in closer competition with Saudi Arabian, Iranian, and Iraqi heavier crudes and, no doubt, had we restricted the other–Gulf categories to these crudes this coefficient would have been higher. In terms of all other Gulf crudes, however, the result is consistent with the low-substitutability nature of Kuwaiti crude for lighter crudes.

5.5 United Arab Emirates

These seven states were brought together in 1971 when Britain withdrew from the Gulf area, but for purposes of analyzing crude oil only three are relevant: Abu Dhabi, Dubai, and Shahjah in that order of importance. Abu Dhabi, being the dominant oil producer, is also the dominant power in the federation. In all that follows we combine the outputs of the three named states.

The best fit to the data was judged to be equation (8A). The own-price elasticity for mean variable values is -3.02, or close to that revealed by Saudi Arabia. We have seen in our derivation of weights for the "other–Gulf" prices that UAE and Qatar (see table 7.1) are closest to each other in terms of the higher quality of their product compared with their Gulf neighbours. This is reflected in the higher prices of their crude as well as in their relative independence from the African crude market. For the UAE, the mean variable elasticity with respect to $POGU_{t-2}$ is only $+0.23$ – the lowest value for Gulf nations yet attained whereas for PAF it is $+0.71$, the largest value attained. Thus, although UAE crude is still relatively well insulated in the short run from the African submarket, closer substitutability of its product for the fine African crudes is revealed in the analysis.

Because of our major interest in period 2, and the bias downward exerted on (8A) by the disarray of period 1, we have shifted the intercept term upward to obtain (9A) which dramatically improves the fit to period 2 data.

5.6 Qatar

Qatar is a small producer of a higher grade crude and is under considerable pressure to sell because of an ambitious ten-year development plan. The best fitting equation is that given in (10A). The own-price elasticity of the function for mean variable values is -2.32, and other-price elasticity for other Gulf nations is $+1.90$. The own-price magnitude is in the range of values for Gulf nations which have a substantial amount of light crudes (Saudi Arabia, Iran, and UAE) but the other-Gulf value is the highest of the Gulf states. This greatest sensitivity to Gulf prices is projected into that for African submarket prices. The reason for this position in the sensitivity rankings is not clear from the literature and may reflect the basic specification and data deficiencies already reported. On the other hand, tanker rate and industrial activity elasticities of -0.01 and $+0.74$ are entirely in keeping with our prior results.

5.7 Libya

The data for period 1 were most disturbing for the three nations in the African submarket, and in each case we have attempted to correct for the distortions by substituting logistic branches of the functions for extreme prices. These results are consistent with the conclusion in the literature that these nations experienced the greatest corrective adjustments of any of the OPEC nations following the distortions of the embargo.

Libyan output fell rather continuously from 7401 through 7502, then rose rapidly from 7503 through 7508 to prior levels. During this first period prices fell from \$20.65 to \$13.77 and in the second fell from \$13.67 to a low of \$12.39. Thereafter, prices essentially levelled off and moved modestly upward. The sharply contradictory price-output relations of these two periods have made it especially difficult for our regression techniques to reproduce the relation of high own-prices to sales, and we have been forced to overrule its results. We were constrained, therefore, to abandon the first sixteen months in our period to obtain acceptable results, so that the equation is based on a small number of observations. The equations adopted are (11A) and (12A).

Own-price and Gulf-price elasticities for mean values are quite large: -5.65 and $+4.87$ respectively. On the other hand, the other-price elasticity with respect to African prices is low at $+0.40$. If one adds the six regression coefficients for PAF from the six regression equations for the Gulf states, one obtains a sum of 12.190, which compares with a regression coefficient of 20.952 for the notional Gulf price in (11A). Hence, a rise of one dollar in the "Gulf price" will increase Libyan sales more than a rise in PAF will increase Gulf sales. This would indicate that the insensitivity of individual Gulf nations' sales to the African market price that we have noted (with the exception of Qatar) is reciprocated by the African market as a whole but is not shared by Libya. This result is notably blurred by the very high multi-collinearity of PL and PG, so that we may be capturing some own-prices sensitivity in the PG coefficient. However, own-price elasticity is so high that we are skeptical this has occurred. Libyan crude seems particularly linked to the Gulf market; on the other hand, its cross-elasticities with other African and Venezuelan oil are in the low 0.40's, so that from the evidence of our analysis its competitive position – quality of product and geographical location aside – mark it as part of the Gulf submarket rather than the African. In the same vein, we could discern no relation of Libyan crude to

Indonesian – a crude whose quality is similar to Libya's.

These last points may explain the positive regression coefficient for SIVO: because of its eastern Mediterranean location it shares in lesser degree some of the disadvantages of the Gulf in distance from major markets for its very light, low-sulfur crudes. In any event our analysis cannot discern any strong short-run impact of changes in tanker rates upon her sales. Further, she continues in the pattern we have noted of being unresponsive to industrial activity – indeed, the elasticity, though of the expected sign, is lower than that of any of the Gulf nations. This may reflect the peculiarly high quality of her crude and the continuation of a substantial demand for it in periods of industrial recession.

5.8 Algeria

Algeria is in a number of respects in a rather special OPEC category. Her light, sweet crude has in the past enjoyed great demand, but her reserves of it are low. The longer run future of Algerian development lies with her large reserves of natural gas; indeed, by 1990 most of her petroleum production may be required to fuel her own development. Thus, her role as a large exporter of oil is a short-run role, and her aggressive stance toward price increases within OPEC and to buyers reflect this short-term horizon and an inelastic demand function with respect to own-price. Finally, the ties to France remain strong if troubled and tend to obscure her true ability to act independently in the market. On the other hand, in early 1978 she proved to be remarkably quick in shaving prices by $0.20 in order to maintain output slightly above 1977 levels.

The best econometric fit we obtained to the Algerian data is equation (13A), which we have modified by logistic branches (14A–16A). The fit is a good one in part because Algeria's output has been a bit smoother in time profile than other OPEC producers. Nonetheless, the excellent fit of the curve to the early data of period 1 has been purchased at the price of backward-bending properties in the higher reaches of PA and $POAA_{t-2}$, which we have corrected with logistic functions.

Perhaps the most gratifying result among the regression coefficients is the statistically significant value for IND_{t-1}: a one point rise in the industrial production index expands sales by more than one percent of their mean value. This yields an elasticity of $+1.05$, the highest achieved so far, and indicates that Algerian premium crude is closely tied in its demand to the activity of highly industrial nations, notably the United States and France. On the other hand, $SIVO_{t-1}$ has a totally negligible impact on Algeria's sales.

Own-price elasticity is -0.80 – an inelasticity that compares with Libya's

−5.65 or Saudi Arabia's −3.39. This result places Algeria in a most protected market position − at least before high quality crudes began to flow from the North Sea. Other-African price elasticity is +0.31 and other-price elasticity with respect to Gulf crude is effectively zero, as we obtain a regression coefficient for PG which approximates that value. The prices of Venezuelan and Indonesian crudes had no perceptible impact upon Algerian sales. Hence, the picture of a highly protected market, most sensitive to industrial activity fluctuations, is complete.

5.9 Nigeria

Nigeria has several advantages in the OPEC cartel which have served it well in the past, notably the possession of light, low-sulfur crude and proximity to the United States and European markets. In the recent period, however, low tanker rates have dissipated much of the locational advantage and the competition of similar grade North Sea oil has eliminated much of its market. Ambitious development plans, based on expected sales of 90 mmb/m may have to be slashed if the 1977 rate of 60 mmb/m continues or if the possible fall to 45 mmb/m feared by government officials materializes.

Over our period of fitting, North Sea oil was not yet much of a factor in the picture and her sales averaged 62.3 mmb/m. The best equation we obtained by econometric fitting had to be modified by logistic patching as indicated in (17A) through (20A). The dependence of Nigeria upon her location and upon industrial markets is reflected in the significant SIVO and IND regression coefficients. The elasticity coefficients are +0.16 and +0.81 respectively which are, nonetheless, indicative of the general pattern of low demand sensitivity to these variables.

Own-price elasticity is −1.53, so that demand is quite sensitive to this variable, and other-African price elasticity is only +0.03. Nigeria and Algeria have clashed in the past over the differential that should be charged for their premium crudes, which would seem to indicate higher cross-elasticities for other-African prices than we get for either nation. On the other hand the low Gulf-price elasticity of +0.03 continues the provision of evidence that the African submarket other than Libya is surprisingly independent in the short run of Gulf prices.

5.10 Venezuela

Venezuela was one of the leaders urging the formation of OPEC in the hope that prices would be kept up and a control over production could be established. Its reserves of good quality crude are dwindling and it introduced "conservation restrictions" in 1976 to keep its light and medium crude production under 66 mmb/m. Unlike most OPEC nations, Venezuela exports much of its oil as refined product, mainly fuel oil for the United States. Hence, it is peculiarly dependent on that market and does badly when US refiners are in an overstocked position. Nonetheless, its need for domestic gasoline makes it difficult to shut down fuel oil production in such periods. Venezuela, therefore, because of its aging fields, the low own-price elasticity of its demand curve, and its experience with the price impact of distress oil products, is a strong advocate of reduced oil production.

The best fitting equation obtained in our analysis was (21A) modified by the logistic branches (22A–27A). Own-price elasticity is −0.69, rather low given the attitudes toward interdependence of OPEC oil supplies expressed by Venezuelan officials. Moreover, the market was well-protected from foreign rivals, as the other-price elasticities of +0.29 for Gulf, +0.08 for African, and +0.48 for Indonesian crude attest.

SIVO gratifyingly yielded the properly signed regression coefficient at a significant level but with an elasticity of only +0.26. The coefficient of IND was statistically significant and yielded a relatively high elasticity of +0.63.

5.11 Indonesia

The last nation whose sales were analyzed in this study is Indonesia – an OPEC outlier almost wholly dependent upon the Japanese and United States markets. Currently fully 18 percent of its production is used domestically, and this usage is expected to rise to perhaps 67 percent by 1987. In the past it has tied its price closely to Gulf prices (plus low-sulfur and light crude premia), but because of her extreme dependence upon Asian markets and increased Japanese purchases from the Persian Gulf, it has been tempted to cut prices below OPEC levels to retain sales in times of reduced demand and low tanker rates.

The best fitting equation is (28A). That regression reveals that Venezuela is an extremely important competitor for Indonesian oil, presumably for American markets, with Gulf (reflecting the shift of Japanese sales) and African markets following in that order of rivalry. This ordering conforms to our geography-based expectations, although the size of the Venezuelan regression coefficient, when compared with the own-price coefficient, is suspect. The mean price own-elasticity is −0.63, on the order of that for Venezuela. The mean other-price elasticities are +0.33 for Gulf crude, +0.22 for African oil, and +0.55 for Venezuelan output. Hence, the analysis reveals a market as isolated from other prices as Venezuela's and with marked inability to stimulate sales by price reduction.

5.12 Aggregate OPEC Regression Analysis

As a final exercise we estimated aggregate OPEC output in two ways: (1) in an independent regression of this variable (YOPEC) on an average price (POPEC) consisting of national prices weighted by monthly output shares, SIVO and IND; and (2) by summing the 11 individual econometric equations. The results were hearteningly similar for both analyses and we present them in turn.

The best fitting regression equation for the aggregate data is given in (29A). A visual depiction of the fit of estimated to actual data is given in Figure 7.1. Aggregation has ironed out the severity of the individual national fluctuations and permitted a better fit, indicating that much of the monthly movements in the national data are intra-OPEC shifts. The constant and all of the regression coefficients are statistically significant at the one percent level. The quite significant $\bar{R}^2$ is a conservative index of fit, warped downward by the four severely speculative movements captured in the short-run data.

The aggregate data are confirmatory of the national regressions in several respects. The best lag structure obtained after substantial experimentation was a uniform one-month lag in all variables. This confirms the common one- or two-month lags found in the individual regressions. Moreover, the impacts of SIVO and IND are comparable. Of course, in the national regressions these variables capture intra- as well as extra-OPEC changes in amounts demanded, whereas only the latter should remain in the aggregate figures. The elasticity for mean variable values of $SIVO_{t-1}$ in the aggregate equation was $+0.19$, which was in most instances substantially below the individual national analogues. A rise in tanker transport rates on net benefited OPEC in the short run. The netting out of intra-national shifts resulting from IND does not result in as uniform a downward shift in elasticity, but an elasticity of $+0.62$ does confirm a moderately sensitive response of OPEC output to industrial activity changes in the short run.

The own-price elasticity of OPEC oil in this period is essentially unity at -1.04 – a substantially higher estimate for the short run than those contained in the literature. Once again, however, this aggregate result lends credence to the relatively high own-price elasticities for the individual nations. Oil consumers showed unexpected and unacknowledged short-run ability to restrict demand and/or seek other sources outside the OPEC cartel.

The ability of crude purchasers to shift among sellers in the short run, even when they operate under long-term contracts, is not generally appreciated in the literature on OPEC. All long-term contracts today are non-rigid instruments which permit the following types of modifications [1], p. 85:

1   Volumes lifted *over the contract period* may vary by 5 to 10 percent from the contractual amounts;

2   *Monthly* purchases may vary by substantially more than 5 to 10 percent within the contract period;

3   A three-month re-opener clause permits price and volume to be adjusted to conform to market movements.

Hence, large national own-price elasticities are not as surprising as a surface notion of long-term contractual ties leads one to expect, and the relatively large aggregate OPEC own-price elasticity also receives credence from this analysis.

5.13   Sum of Individual Nations' Econometric Equations

If we sum the 11 econometric sales functions chosen for the OPEC nations we obtain equation (30A). These estimates are plotted against actual OPEC sales on figure 7.2, and visually the fit is about as good as the aggregate equation plotted on figure 7.1. When we correlated the actual with the estimated figures from this equation we obtained the listed r^2 (uncorrected for degrees of freedom). Its value is about the same as $\bar{R}^2$ obtained from (29A) for the aggregate analysis. The mean residual is a bit above that for the aggregate estimates, but on the whole the estimating equations yield very close results.

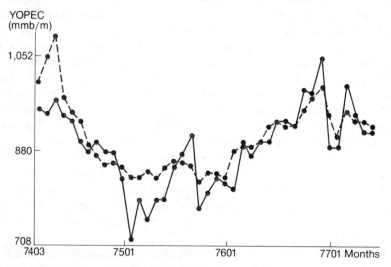

Figure 7.2   OPEC (less Ecuador and Gabon) actual (————) and estimated (- - - -) monthly production, millions of barrels per month, built up from individual nations' econometric estimates, March 1974 through June 1977.

6 Summary and Conclusion

We must stress, in briefly summarizing the results of this extensive study, several important points we have made.

First, the sales functions are short-run functions and they do not purport to reveal longer term adjustment effects. We believe that in the longer run own-price and other-price elasticities are smaller and tanker rate and income elasticities larger than in the short run. These long-run values will reflect the need to restore depleted stocks, limited storage capacity, the ties of long-term contracts, and the passage of sufficient time for adjustment to variable changes.

Second, we have insisted on an attempt to isolate the conceptually specified sales functions. Because our goal is not forecasting, we have forgone the inclusion of lagged sales as regressors, regarding their employment as generally suspect in a regression analysis that seeks to isolate causal patterns.

Third, we have also insisted that the statistical data be permitted to shape the results of the analysis, with the exception of using logistic branches of functions to overrule distorted fits ascribable to known causes. In this case, the disequilibrium conditions in period 1 were to blame and caused an identifiable distortion.

Consistency of results among the 11 OPEC nations studied reveals the following short-run characteristics of the market.

First, the lag structure of prices, tanker rates, and industrial production is a simple one, being one or two months in general. Complicated distributed lag calculations did not improve the fit of the equations.

Second, the own-price elasticities of OPEC nations taken singly, and the own-price elasticity of OPEC as a whole, in the short run, are found to be unexpectedly high. Of course, given the small number of observations and the generally high multicollinearity among important price regressors, we cannot assert that the actual magnitude of any particular own-price coefficient in the eleven equations is as estimated. But the *general* tendency for own-price elasticities to be unity or above for eight of the eleven nations, and unity for the aggregate equation, puts some credence in the result. OPEC nations, jointly and severally, even in the short run, face elastic demand functions. The international oil companies, within the surprisingly elastic provisions of long-term contracts, are operating efficiently in their purchasing activities.

Third, three of the four nations most desirous of prorationing production and/or stiff price hikes have short-run own-price elasticities less than unity: Algeria, Venezuela, and Indonesia. The fourth, Iraq, has the lowest own-price elasticity in the Gulf market, and the next-to-highest other-Gulf price elasticity. In these senses, therefore, our results conform to observation.

Fourth, submarkets within OPEC are largely independent of one another in the short run. Libya's close relationship with the Gulf market seems the only notable exception. We find consistently small price cross-elasticities among such sectors, leading us to conclude that the large own-price elasticities reflect an ability of consumers in the short run to find alternative petroleum sources outside OPEC, to substitute other energy sources, to use inventory potential, and to conserve.

Fifth, and less surprisingly, the long-term tanker contracts imply low sensitivity of oil shipments both within OPEC and for OPEC as a unit to large falls in freight rates in the short term. Universally, this variable has little significant impact in the sales functions. As opposed to contractual agreements to lift oil, which prove to be remarkably flexible in the short run, tanker commitments seem quite rigid and the monthly margin very restricted.

Sixth, the short-term responsiveness of OPEC nation sales to industrial production changes in the five largest non-communist industrial powers is unexpectedly small in the short run. It may well be that this variable is a poor index of changes in world income, so that the failure to find an expected sensitivity is truly due to the lack of a sufficiently representative variable to index it.

The hypotheses that emerge from our study are that OPEC has less market power in the pricing sense in the short run than is generally expected and is more immune from movements in world income than believed. Hence, short-term gluts are more the result of inflexible supply than income-sensitive demand movements and, from the viewpoint of OPEC's economic welfare, even more importance should be given production programming by the cartel. On the other hand, potential price rivalry within OPEC sub-markets is more endemic than often implied in the literature, and tanker freight rate changes less disruptive of markets than generally believed.

Appendix

The Estimating Equations

The following symbols have been used throughout the study:

Y**   : output of nation**'s oil
P**   : price of nation**'s oil
-SA   : Saudi Arabia
-IN   : Iran
-IQ   : Iraq
-K   : Kuwait
-U   : United Arab Emirates

-Q   : Qatar
-L   : Libya
-A   : Algeria
-N   : Nigeria
-V   : Venezuela
-I   : Indonesia
-OPEC : Organization of Petroleum Exporting Countries
-OG** : Other-Gulf omitting nation**
-OA** : Other-African omitting nation**
-G   : all Gulf nations
-AF   : all African nations
SIVO   : Single Voyage Tanker Rate
IND   : OECD Industrial Production index, January 1977 = 100
CPI   : OECD Consumer Price Index, January 1977 = 100

The equations fitted to the data are the following (*t*-values in parentheses):

1 Saudi Arabia

$$YSA = 570.603 - 73.187 \text{ PSA} + 25.463 \text{ POGSA} + 3.772 \text{ PAF}$$
$$\quad (3.06) \quad (-3.36) \quad (0.65) \quad (0.15)$$
$$+ 0.836 \text{ SIVO}_{t-2} + 1.146 \text{ IND}_{t-1},$$
$$\quad (2.30)$$
$$\bar{R}^2 = 0.711, \text{ DW} = 1.99, N = 26 \tag{1A}$$

2 Iran

$$YIN = 470.044 - 30.230 \text{ PIN} + 4.286 \text{ POGIN} + 0.856 \text{ PAF}$$
$$\quad (4.92) \quad (-2.82) \quad (0.29) \quad (0.19)$$
$$+ 0.785 \text{ SIVO}_{t-2} - 0.677 \text{ IND}_{t-2},$$
$$\quad (3.47) \quad (-1.46)$$
$$\bar{R}^2 = 0.358, \text{ DW} = 2.14, N = 36 \tag{2A}$$

3 Iraq

$$YIQ = 51.115 - 8.984 \text{ PIQ}_{t-2} + 7.349 \text{ POGIQ}_{t-2} + 2.073 \text{ PAF}_{t-2}$$
$$\quad (-1.21) \quad (0.53) \quad (0.34)$$
$$0.325 \text{ SIVO}_{t-1} + 0.048 \text{ SIVO}_{t-2} - 0.352 \text{ IND}_{t-1} + 0.671 \text{ IND}_{t-2},$$
$$\quad (-1.20) \quad (0.28) \quad (-0.96) \quad (1.74)$$
$$\bar{R}^2 = 0.013, \text{ DW} = 2.98, N = 32 \tag{3A}$$

4 Kuwait

When PK ≤ 12.09, $POGK_{t-2}$ ≤ 13.03: $YK = 3033.497 - 546.231 \text{ PK}$
$$\quad (2.06) \quad (-2.70)$$
$$+ 22.598 PK^2 + 48.961 \text{ POGK}_{t-2} - 1.879 \text{ POGK}_{t-2}^2 + 1.047 \text{ PAF}$$
$$\quad (2.64) \quad (0.29) \quad (-0.27) \quad (0.19)$$

$+ 0.436 \, \text{SIVO}_{t-1} - 0.463 \, \text{IND}_{t-1}, \; \bar{R}^2 = 0.378,$
    (1.75)   (−1.09)
$\text{DW} = 1.97, N = 40$ (4A)

Define:

$$\text{LKI} = (3358.397/(1 + \exp(-1.836 + 0.487 \, \text{PK})))$$

$$\text{LK2} = (101.887/(1 + \exp(5.079 - 0.442 \, \text{POGK}_{t-2})))$$

Then:

When $\text{PK} > 12.09$, $\text{POGK}_{t-2} \leqslant 13.03$: $\text{YK} = -324.900 + \text{LK1}$
$+ 48.961 \, \text{POGK}_{t-2} - 1.879 \, \text{POGK}_{t-2}^2 + 1.047 \, \text{PAF} + 0.436 \, \text{SIVO}_{t-1}$
$- 0.463 \, \text{IND}_{t-1}$
(5A)

When $\text{PK} \leqslant 12.09$, $\text{POGK}_{t-2} > 13.03$: $\text{YK} = 3284.81 + \text{LK2}$
$- 546.231 \, \text{PK} + 22.598 \, \text{PK}^2 + 1.047 \, \text{PAF} + 0.436 \, \text{SIVO}_{t-1} - 0.463 \, \text{IND}_{t-1}$
(6A)

When $\text{PK} > 12.09$, $\text{POGK}_{t-2} > 13.03$: $\text{YK} = -73.581 + \text{LK1} + \text{LK2}$
$+1.047 \, \text{PAF} + 0.436 \, \text{SIVO}_{t-1} - 0.463 \, \text{IND}_{t-1}$
(7A)

5 United Arab Emirates

$\text{YU} = 11.530 - 4.214 \, \text{PU} + 0.977 \, \text{POGU}_{t-2} + 2.628 \, \text{PAF} - 0.064 \, \text{SIVO}$
           (−2.06)   (1.94)   (1.24)   (−1.11)
$- 0.026 \, \text{SIVO}_{t-1} + 0.064 \, \text{IND} + 0.456 \, \text{IND}_{t-1},$
    (0.28)   (1.20)   (2.44)
$\bar{R}^2 = 0.191, \bar{R}^2(\text{less } 7501\text{-}17504, = 0.621, \text{DW} = 1.94, N = 40$ (8A)

(9A) is the same as (8A) with intercept term changed to 19.091 to conform to period
2 data more closely

6 Qatar

$\text{YQ} = 15.330 - 2.655 \, \text{PQ} + 2.271 \, \text{POGQ}_{t-2} + 1.814 \, \text{PAF}$
    (−0.85) (−2.25)   (2.08)   (2.09)
$-0.001 \, \text{SIVO}_{t-2} + 0.108 \, \text{IND}_{t-2}$
    (−0.04)   (1.42)
$\bar{R}^2 = 0.417, \bar{R}^2(\text{less } 7506, 7507, 7512) = 0.573, \text{DW} = 1.77, N = 40$

(10A)

7 Libya

When $\text{PL} \leqslant 14.00$: $\text{YL} = 11.126 - 21.033 \, \text{PL} + 20.952 \, \text{PG}$
                        (−2.10)   (1.33)
$1.452 \, \text{POAL}_{t-2} + 1.70 \, \text{PV} + 0.176 \, \text{SIVO}_{t-2} + 0.125 \, \text{IND}_{t-2},$
(0.37)   (0.30)   (1.11)   (0.36)

$\bar{R}^2 = 0.012, \bar{R}^2(\text{less } 7505) = 0.514, \text{DW} = 2.00, N = 25$ \hfill (11A)

Define: $LL1 = (332.316/(1 + \exp(-2.340 + 0.314\,\text{PL})))$

Then:

When PL > 14.00: $YL = -321.190 + LL1 + 20.952\,\text{PG} + 1.700\,\text{PV}$
$+ 1.452\,\text{POAL}_{t-2} + 0.176\,\text{SIVO}_{t-2}$
$+ 0.123\,\text{IND}_{t-2}$ \hfill (12A)

8 Algeria

When $PA \leqslant 13.98$, $\text{POAA}_{t-2} \leqslant 11.47$: $YA = 138.526 - 29.153\,\text{PA}$
$\quad\quad\quad\quad\quad\quad\quad\quad (2.70) \quad\quad (-2.31)$
$+ 1.043\,\text{PA}^2 + 11.424\,\text{POAA} - 4.980\,\text{POAA}^2 - 0.028\,\text{PG}$
$\quad (2.40) \quad\quad (1.06) \quad\quad\quad (-1.26) \quad\quad\quad (-0.02)$
$+0.001\,\text{SIVO}_{t-1} + 0.330\,\text{IND}_{t-1},$
$\quad (0.03) \quad\quad\quad (5.09)$
$\bar{R}^2 = 0.689, \text{DW} = 1.79, N = 40$ \hfill (13A)

Define:

$$LA1 = (232.173/)1 + \exp -1.007 + 0.213\,\text{PA}))$$
$$LA2 = (41.25/(1 + \exp(1.718 - 0.207\,\text{POAA}_{t-2})))$$

Then

When $PA > 13.98$, $\text{POAA}_{t-2} \leqslant 11.47$: $YA = -93.647 + LA1$
$+ 11.424\,\text{POAA}_{t-2} - 0.498\,\text{POAA}^2_{t-2} - 0.028\,\text{PG} + 0.001\,\text{SIVO}_{t-1}$
$+ 0.330\,\text{IND}_{t-1}$ \hfill (14A)

When $PA \leqslant 13.98$, $\text{POAA}_{t-2} > 11.47$: $YA = 169.366 + LA2 - 29.153\,\text{PA}$
$+ 1.043\,\text{PA}^2 - 0.028\,\text{PG} + 0.001\,\text{SIVO}_{t-1} + 0.330\,\text{IND}_{t-1}$ \hfill (15A)

When $\quad PA > 13.98 \quad$ and $\quad \text{POAA}_{t-2} > 11.47$: $YA = -62.807 + LA1 + LA2$
$- 0.028\,\text{PG} + 0.001\,\text{SIVO}_{t-1} + 0.330\,\text{IND}_{t-1}$ \hfill (16A)

9 Nigeria

When $PN_{t-1} \leqslant 13.52$, $\text{POAN}_{t-2} \leqslant 16.19$: $YN = 424.407 - 78.527\,PN_{t-1}$
$\quad\quad\quad\quad\quad\quad\quad\quad\quad (1.46) \quad\quad (-1.70)$
$+ 2.905\,PN^2_{t-1} + 10.363\,\text{POAN}_{t-2} - 0.320\,\text{POAN}^2_{t-2} + 1.512\,\text{PG}$
$\quad (1.69) \quad\quad\quad (1.14) \quad\quad\quad (-1.07) \quad\quad\quad (0.70)$
$+ 0.123\,\text{SIVO}_{t-2} + 0.572\,\text{IND}_{t-1},$
$\quad (2.10) \quad\quad\quad (4.28)$
$\bar{R}^2 = 0.827, \text{DW} = 1.84, N = 39$ \hfill (17A)

Define:

$$LN1 = (591.828/(1 + \exp(-1.004 + 0.234\,PN_{t-1})))$$

$$LN2 = (89.674/(1 + \exp(1.447 - 0.146 \, POAN_{t-2})))$$

Then:

When $PN_{t-1} > 13.52$, $POAN_{t-2} \leqslant 16.19$: $YN = -167.421 + LN1$
$+ 10.363 \, POAN_{t-2} - 0.320 \, POAN_{t-2}^2 + 1.512 \, PG + 0.123 \, SIVO_{t-2}$
$+ 0.572 \, IND_{t-1}$ (18A)

When $PN_{t-1} \leqslant 13.52$, $POAN_{t-2} > 16.19$: $YN = 444.294 + LN2$
$- 78.527 \, PN_{t-1} + 2.905 \, PN_{t-1}^2 + 1.512 \, PG + 0.123 \, SIVO_{t-2}$
$+ 0.572 \, IND_{t-1}$ (19A)

When $PN_{t-1} > 13.52$, $POAN_{t-2} > 16.19$: $YN = -147.534 + LN1 + LN2$
$+ 1.512 \, PG + 0.123 \, SIVO_{t-2} + 0.572 \, IND_{t-1}$ (20A)

10 Venezuela

When $PV \leqslant 13.16$, $PG_{t-1} \leqslant 11.44$, $PAF_{t-2} \leqslant 13.93$: $YV = 686.134$
$- 169.471 \, PV + 6.438 \, PV^2 + 52.185 \, PG_{t-1} - 2.280 \, PG_{t-1}^2$
$\quad (-1.50) \qquad (1.46) \qquad (0.29) \qquad (-0.31)$
$+ 15.411 \, PAF_{t-2} - 0.553 \, PAF_{t-2}^2 + 2.303 \, PI + 0.209 \, SIVO_{t-2}$
$\quad (0.49) \qquad\quad (-0.50) \qquad\quad (0.70) \qquad (1.98)$
$+ 0.499 \, IND_{t-1}$,
$\quad (2.44)$
$\bar{R}^2 = 0.187$, $\bar{R}^2(\text{less } 7502, 7603) = 0.478$, $DW = 1.99$, $N = 39$ (21A)

Define:

$$LV1 = (1189.214/(1 + \exp(-1.155 + 0.294 \, PV)))$$

$$LV2 = (98.01/1 + \exp(2.888 - 0.365 \, PG_{t-1})))$$

$$LV3 = (98.01/(1 + \exp(1.812 - 0.222 \, PAF_{t-2})))$$

Then:

When $PV > 13.16$, $PG_{t-1} \leqslant 11.44$, $PAF_{t-2} \leqslant 13.93$: $YV = -503.080$
$+ LV1 + 52.185 \, PG_{t-1} - 2.28 \, PG_{t-1}^2 + 15.411 \, PAF_{t-2} - 0.553 \, PAF_{t-2}^2$
$+ 2.303 \, PI + 0.209 \, SIVO_{t-2} + 0.499 \, IND_{t-1}$ (22A)

When $PV \leqslant 13.16$, $PG_{t-1} > 11.44$, $PAF_{t-2} \leqslant 13.93$: $YV = 907.950 + LV2$
$- 169.471 \, PV + 6.438 \, PV^2 + 15.411 \, PAF_{t-2} - 0.553 \, PAF_{t-2}^2 + 2.303 \, PI$
$+ 0.209 \, SIVO_{t-2} + 0.499 \, IND_{t-1}$ (23A)

When $PV \leqslant 13.16$, $PG_{t-1} \leqslant 11.44$, $PAF_{t-2} > 13.93$: $YV = 716.888 + LV3$
$- 169.471 \, PV + 6.438 \, PV^2 + 52.185 \, PG_{t-1} - 2.28 \, PG_{t-1}^2 + 2.303 \, PI$
$+ 0.209 \, SIVO_{t-2} + 0.499 \, IND_{t-1}$ (24A)

When $PV > 13.16$, $PG_{t-1} \leqslant 11.44$, $PAF_{t-2} > 13.93$: $YV = -472.325 + LV1$
$+ LV3 + 52.185 \, PG_{t-1} - 2.28 \, PG_{t-1}^2 + 2.303 \, PI + 0.209 \, SIVO_{t-2}$
$+ 0.499 \, IND_{t-1}$ (25A)

When $PV \leqslant 13.16$, $PG_{t-1} > 11.44$, $PAF_{t-2} > 13.93$: $YV = 938.704$

$$+ LV2 + LV3 - 169.471 \, PV + 6.438 \, PV^2 + 2.303 \, PI + 0.209 \, SIVO_{t-2}$$
$$+ 0.499 \, IND_{t-1} \tag{26A}$$

When $PV > 13.16$, $PG_{t-1} > 11.44$, $PAF_{t-2} > 13.93$: $YV = -250.510$
$$+ LV1 + LV2 + LV3 + 2.303 \, PI + 0.209 \, SIVO_{t-2} + 0.499 \, IND_{t-1} \tag{27A}$$

11 Indonesia

$$YI = 7.486 - 2.230 \, PI_{t-1} + 1.272 \, PG + 0.777 \, PAF_{t-2} + 2.029 \, PV_{t-2}$$
$$ (-1.05) \quad\quad (0.74) \quad\quad (0.55) \quad\quad\quad (1.37)$$
$$ -0.022 \, SIVO_{t-1} + 0.191 \, IND_{t-1},$$
$$ (-0.35) \quad\quad\quad (1.68)$$
$$\bar{R}^2 = 0.364, \bar{R}(\text{less } 7603) = 0.476, \, DW = 2.50, N = 24 \tag{28A}$$

12 Aggregate Regression

$$YOPEC = 1091.303 - 74.707 \, POPEC_{t-1} + 1.850 \, SIVO_{t-1} + 5.623 \, IND_{t-1},$$
$$ (3.47) \quad\quad (-3.09) \quad\quad\quad (3.10) \quad\quad\quad\quad (3.67)$$
$$\bar{R}^1 = 0.709, \, DW = 1.92, N = 40 \tag{29A}$$

13 Sum of Individual OPEC Nations' Demand Functions

$$
\begin{aligned}
YOPEC = {} & 5389.138 - 68.313 \, PSA + 8.558 \, PSA_{t-1} + 12.540 \, PSA_{t-2} \\
& - 20.242 \, PIN + 8.871 \, PIN_{t-1} + 11.445 \, PIN_{t-2} + 11.129 \, PIQ \\
& + 8.402 \, PIQ_{t-1} + 2.447 \, PIQ_{t-2} - 535.244 \, PK + 8.141 \, PK_{t-1} \\
& + 2.401 \, PK_{t-2} + 22.598 \, PK^2 + 5.840 \, PU + 9.289 \, PU_{t-1} \\
& + 7.825 \, PU_{t-2} + 7.453 \, PQ + 8.924 \, PQ_{t-1} + 8.609 \, PQ_{t-2} \\
& - 12.991 \, PL + 10.242 \, PL_{t-2} - 26.896 \, PA + 11.247 \, PA_{t-2} \\
& + 1.043 \, PA^2_{t-2} + 8.879 \, PN - 78.527 \, PN_{t-1} + 8.596 \, PN_{t-2} \\
& + 2.905 \, PN^2_{t-1} - 167.771 \, PV + 2.029 \, PV_{t-2} + 6.438 \, PV^2 \\
& + 2.303 \, PI - 2.230 \, PI_{t-1} - 1.879 \, POGK^2_{t-2} - 0.498 \, POAA^2 \\
& - 0.320 \, POAN^2_{t-2} - 2.280 \, PG^2_{t-1} - 0.553 \, PAF^2_{t-2} \\
& - 0.064 \, SIVO + 0.064 \, SIVO_{t-1} + 2.176 \, SIVO_{t-2} + 0.064 \, IND \\
& + 2.379 \, IND_{t-1} + 0.227 \, IND_{t-2}, \bar{R}^2 = 0.692, \, DW = 1.98, \\
& N = 40
\end{aligned}
\tag{30A}
$$

Notes

[1] Two of the 13 nations in OPEC - Ecuador and Gabon - have been excluded from consideration in this study on the bases that their production is a negligible fraction of total OPEC output (about 1.3 percent) and their price–output data are not available for a sufficient period.

[2] The term "OPEC" throughout this chapter refers to the slightly truncated set of members including Saudi Arabia, Iran, Iraq, Kuwait, the United Arab Emirates,

204 Price Competition in Oligopoly: OPEC

Qatar, Libya, Algeria, Nigeria, Venezuela, and Indonesia, but excluding Gabon and Ecuador.

[3] The nature of the index used for deflating is discussed in section 3. It should be noted at this point, however, that since we are attempting to isolate demand functions, the "price of petroleum" we are interested in is that faced by buying nations. Therefore, the deflating index represents price movements in customer countries.

[4] Its derivation is discussed in section 3, as well as the reasons for its choice over several alternatives. Its values are tabulated in table A.3 of [3] and its graph is displayed there on figure A.2.

[5] Its derivation and the weights employed are discussed in section 3. Its values are listed in table A.3 and its graph displayed in figure A.3 of [3].

[6] See *Middle East Economic Survey*, February 25, 1977, p. ii. In 1975 the proportions were 80.8 percent for Arab Light, 3.2 percent for Arab Medium, 9.9 percent for Arab Heavy, and 6.1 percent for Berri. Saudi Arabia has tried in recent years to increase its sales of the heavier grades through discriminatory pricing in their favor, but Arab Light has maintained its dominance. Most recently, however, Saudi Arabia has restricted Aramco's production of light crudes to no more than 65 percent of total offtake.

[7] In general, light crudes are favored over heavier crudes because they yield higher proportions of the more expensive distillates like gasoline. However, European refiners are more oriented to heavier crudes because of a greater demand for fuel and residual oil than American refiners, whose facilities are constructed to use lighter, low sulfur crudes such as the African. Hence, the prices of lighter and heavier crudes can move in opposite directions, depending upon the movements of the United States and European economies. Similarly, American refineries are more sensitive to high sulfur content than European and cannot accommodate "sour" crudes. "Specific gravity" as measured in the industry is the American Petroleum Institute measure:

$$\text{API specific gravity}° = \frac{141.5}{\text{specific gravity}} - 131.5.$$

Hence, API specific gravity moves inversely with true specific gravity, so that heavier grades of crude have *lower*, not higher, API gravity scores.

[8] A continuing effort by the OPEC organization to obtain greater formal agreement on price differentials has characterized its operation. The issue is of particular concern to Saudi Arabia, Iran, Iraq, Kuwait, and the United Arab Emirates, which tend to produce heavy crudes with more sulfur content than do other members. In September 1975, a formula was almost agreed to at the OPEC Economic Commission level but did not obtain final approval. Its provisions, nonetheless, illustrate the order of magnitude of differentials that characterize the different crudes, and there is some evidence that Gulf crude prices were maintained for a period in accordance with the formula, although Mediterranean and African crudes have not conformed:

1 A symmetric basic gravity differential of 3¢ per barrel per API degree above (premium) or below (penalty) marker crude's 34°.

2 An additional penalty of 1¢ per barrel for crudes below 34° API.

3 A premium of 3¢ per barrel for each 0.1 percentage point sulfur content below

1.7 per cent, and a penalty of 1¢ per barrel for each 0.1 percentage point above 1.7 per cent.

4   Some minor freight differentials within the Gulf area. See [5], p. 1.

These differentials are broadly consistent with the patterns that Rifai found holding in the Gulf market's actual operation in early periods of OPEC's functioning See [6], pp. 60-1.

[9] These prices are tabulated in table A.2 of [3].

[10] Quantities produced are listed in table A.1 of [3].

[11] This index is found in table A.3 of [3].

[12] The values are tabulated in table A.3 of [3].

[13] All of these synthetic prices are listed in table A.2 of [3].

[14] A more extensive presentation of these regression results, as well as visual displays of them against the original data, will be found in [3]. We have relied upon the tables of Durbin–Watson d_L and d_U for extended numbers of regressors compiled in [7].

References

[1] *The Banker*, March (1978).

[2] Kuenne, Robert E., "Interproduct Distances in a Quality-space: Inexact Measurement in Differentiated Oligopoly Analysis", *Applied Economics*, 6 (1974), 255-73. [Reprinted as chapter 12 in this volume.]

[3] ——, *Short-run Crude Petroleum Demand Functions for OPEC Cartel Members*, OPEC Cartel Modelling Project, Research Monograph No. 1, General Economic Systems Project, Princeton University, Princeton, NJ, 1978.

[4] *Middle East Economic Survey*, February 25 (1977), ii.

[5] *The Petroleum Economist*, November 14 (1975), 1.

[6] Rifai, Taki, *The Pricing of Crude Oil*, Praeger, New York, 1975.

[7] Savin, N. E. and K. J. White, "The Durbin–Watson Test for Serial Correlation with Extreme Sample Sizes or Many Regressors", *Econometrica*, 45 (1977), 1989-91.

8

The Limits of OPEC

To the economic theorist, the Organization of Petroleum Exporting Countries (OPEC) holds a special interest beyond its unfortunate grip on a choke point of the world economy. The cartel's pricing decisions, and the organizational structure which produces them, offer an example of "oligopolistic" decision-making that is peculiarly open to public scrutiny. By analyzing the way it operates, we may gain fruitful insights into the way other important industries exercise the pricing discretion they possess–even though they do not enjoy the enormous power of OPEC or engage openly in price collusion. Thus Princeton's General Economic Systems Project (GENESYS), funded by the Rockefeller Foundation, has spent three years constructing and testing an econometrically fitted optimization model of the organization which can be manipulated to give us a better understanding of how OPEC works.

1 Price and Supply Projections

Despite the painful impact that OPEC has had upon our personal and national lives, the GENESYS study has found that the cartel is supplying us with more oil and charging less for it than one would expect if OPEC were taking full advantage of its leverage over the oil-importing countries. Moreover, our findings indicate that if the cartel were to break up, its demise would make relatively little difference in world oil prices. The popular perception of OPEC as a monolithic organization with unlimited economic power over the West is quite exaggerated. In reality, internal conflicts arising from the varying goals of its members have consistently prevented OPEC from maximizing its potential as a cartel.

Originally published in the *Princeton Alumni Weekly*, October 6 (1980), 30–4, and reproduced with permission.

These conclusions emerged last winter when we used the GENESYS model to project OPEC's 1980 pricing decisions. Our primary interest was in analyzing a short-run "normal" benchmark year with 1980's basic outlines. For this purpose, we postulated that (1) Iran would be willing to raise its production to pre-revolution levels, (2) Saudi Arabia would keep its output constant, and (3) the demand for OPEC oil would rise by 2 percent over the year, allowing for some drawdown of already high inventories but assuming a non-recessionary world economy.

Under such conditions (to be realized perhaps in 1981?), were the cartel's decisions motivated wholly by the drive to maximize short-run profits, constrained only by its internal power structure and its members' insistence on holding production levels within acceptable limits, we would expect average OPEC oil to be priced at $34.85 (compared with last February's $28.01). Even if the cartel were to disintegrate, so that each nation went its own myopic way in seeking profit, the average price would settle at $30.23. Accordingly, the consumer has little basis for dreaming of much price relief (as opposed to supply relief) from the "breaking up" of OPEC. On the other hand, were OPEC to increase its cartel power to approach perfect collusion among producers, the price would rise to only $34.92. We conclude, therefore, that OPEC's prices are currently below the level that would fully exploit its economic advantage under "normal" conditions, though its operational structure exploits almost all of its potential overall pricing power.

It is on the supply side that differences in the cartel's operating conditions matter. If economic gain alone were to dictate OPEC's decisions, we would expect production to decline from last February's 31 million barrels per day (mbpd) to 25.4 mbpd. Disintegration of the cartel would raise that to about 30 mbpd. The closest collusion possible, given the various power conflicts among OPEC's members, would result in an output of about 27.7 mbpd. Consequently, we are led to project that for the immediate future most of the consuming nations' conflict with OPEC will center about the provision of adequate supplies at higher but essentially stabilized prices in the neighborhood of $35 (in today's dollars).

2 Functional Considerations

Since 1973, when OPEC began functioning effectively as a market force, the cartel has aimed at setting a flexible price *pattern* for its members' products. Crude petroleum is not a homogeneous product: it varies by specific gravity, sulfur content, and geographic location relative to markets. OPEC has cleverly anchored the price pattern by setting the price (f.o.b. Saudi Arabia) of so-called "marker" crude, or Arabian Light with a sulfur content of about 1.6 percent. Because at least half of OPEC's output is rather close in composition, marker crude may be treated as "crude petroleum in general," or a convenient typifying product.

Ideally, the price of marker crude is set by OPEC with the aim of equating the demand for "oil" with an "appropriate" supply. No formal agreement exists among cartel members on what constitutes an acceptable output level for this grade, but informal acquiescence by OPEC nations is sought each quarter in the light of available capacity, historic liftings (i.e. production), non-OPEC supply, world inventory levels overhanging the market, and international economic conditions.

This anchor price is then accepted by each member nation and a premium (or discount if negative) is applied to the marker crude price depending upon the special qualities of that nation's product. These premia also have never been formally adopted by OPEC – although they almost were in 1975 – but they are nonetheless rather rigorously set by historic precedent.

Let us suppose, however, that when a member nation adds (or subtracts) this quality premium surcharge to the price of marker crude, its sales would (prospectively) be less than its "acceptable level of output." Then the nation is permitted to apply a discount which allows the price to fall to the level where demand equals this acquiesced-in lifting. On the other hand, if the price of marker crude plus the quality premium results in a demand which exceeds the acceptable output, the nation is permitted to add a super-premium bringing the price up to a figure that reduces demand to the "proper" level. Once more, each nation's "acceptable level" of sales has never been formally agreed upon by the cartel: to keep OPEC viable, a healthy but nonetheless bounded ambiguity in this respect is preserved.

From OPEC's viewpoint, then, its decision-making ideally results in a price pattern in which (1) demand equals supply for crude oil in general, (2) better or worse crudes receive their customary quality premia or discounts, and (3) the specific demand-supply situation in each member's market is balanced by a superpremium or superdiscount that results in that nation selling what is accepted by all members as an appropriate amount in the light of cartel discipline.

This goal of setting a price *pattern* is frequently obscured as the limelight is cast upon the bargaining at quarterly OPEC conferences over the appropriate price for marker crude. Nonetheless, debates concerning appropriate quality premia and specific-market superpremia have come increasingly into the open in recent years.

The advantages and disadvantages to OPEC of this manner of making decisions are well displayed by our analysis. On the one hand, the price pattern is flexible, adaptable on a short-term basis to changes in market conditions for "crude in general" or a specific type of crude. No member nation need feel locked into a rigid price agreement, as it retains an important degree of independence both in pricing its product and determining its lifting levels. OPEC continues to work because it can adjust flexibly to the pressures of its market environment without bursting at the seams.

But strains are increasingly evident. It is not possible to separate unambiguously an unbalanced demand for crude in general from an unbalanced demand for a specific crude that springs from an outmoded quality premium or an inappropriate superpremium. Recently, a great deal of bickering has occurred in these terms, with strong pressure exerted upon Saudi Arabia to close an asserted excess demand gap for oil in general with a rise in the price of marker crude.

Even more potentially divisive, however, is the informality of agreement about the lifting levels to which members are entitled, and which are important in defining the superpremium. It has proved impossible to achieve formal agreement upon an output prorationing scheme, the latest suggestion by Iran in these terms being rejected out-of-hand at the December 1979 conference at Caracas. Nonetheless, the most ominous development for consuming nations has been the increasing discussion among OPEC members of output limitations.

No issue is so closely linked to the differences that challenge the unity of OPEC as this one, and member nations have wisely skirted any attempts to obtain formal commitments. The ability of Saudi Arabia to vary its output as a "swing" producer is the basis for her dominant power over the general price of oil. Consequently, the Saudis have opposed prorationing, instead seeking agreement on price premia and superpremia. But it is difficult to see how they could retain their predominant role if they were to refrain from using output variation as a disciplinary device, as their actions at this fall's OPEC meetings seem to reflect.

In an oligopoly structured around price rather than output, it should not be surprising that in periods of supply stringency or panic inventory stockage the price pattern can fluctuate within wide limits without life-threatening disagreement among members of a cartel as elastically structured as OPEC. Indeed, as we have seen, ambiguities have been built in or permitted to persist that are designed to allow this to happen. Two-tiered or three-tiered patterns – reflecting disagreements over one or more of the three price components – must be expected in times of excess demand or supply. A unified price level in which the ideal pattern prevails is just that – an OPEC ideal equilibrium – which will not be achieved in an imperfect world driven by the short run. We have heard too much to the effect that the current price pattern disorder may signal the imminent breakup of OPEC or the "disintegration" of its control.

Rather, recent developments reinforce a long-standing contention of GENESYS that too much attention has been focused upon Saudi Arabia's supposed dominant or even monopoly position within OPEC. A much wider diffusion of effective power characterizes the cartel, and an understanding of its operation requires that the complex power structure be isolated. That Saudi Arabia possesses the *potential* power to set the price of oil in general, and thereby to affect the prices of all other crudes, cannot be doubted. But, like the US and Soviet posture with nuclear weapons, power that cannot be exercised without self-destructive consequences is not truly power. As we shall see, the GENESYS model demonstrates clearly that Saudi Arabia would be a major loser should OPEC disintegrate and hence must compromise with the goals of its fellow members.

3 Demand Elasticities

Our studies of demand, for example, indicate that in general the sales of OPEC nations are very sensitive to price changes in fellow members' crudes. That is, if one member raises the price of its product while its fellow members do not raise theirs, the price hike leads to a rapid fall-off in the output of the initiating member. This sensitivity is rooted in three characteristics of the petroleum market and one behavioral trait which we are convinced will not change materially in the future:

1 The availability of near-substitute crudes for each nation's grades of oil, making switching of markets possible;
2 The multinational operations of the major oil companies and the short-term flexibility to vary liftings within their long-term contacts with producing nations;
3 The ability to use measures like inventory drawdown, slow-steaming tankers, and product allocation to customers to delay the impact of narrow-gauged price actions;
4 A tendency by OPEC nations – despite brave ex ante facto threats – to protect historic lifting levels by lowering price when necessary to retain customers. Cutbacks in output have been motivated largely by falloffs in demand or conservation considerations for producing wells.

Present developments in the market seem to heighten the sensitivity of nations' sales to their prices. Alaskan, North Sea, and Mexican oil, as well as alternative fuel sources and conservation in consuming countries, are one group of factors pushing in this direction. Moreover, the increasing importance of the short-term markets – both the Rotterdam spot market and those within the producing countries – and the decline of term contracts with the major oil companies will increase market flexibility. Thus we expect that in the future the price pattern will tend to conform more closely to the "ideal." For example, in the coming year, should demand for OPEC oil fall below our projected "normal" levels, as for example if worldwide recession continues or presently swollen inventories are drawn down, we believe African suppliers (Libya, Algeria, and Nigeria) will be forced to reduce their super-premia to maintain sales, and that they will in fact do so to protect their lifting levels as they have in the past.

4 Structural Characteristics

With this view of OPEC's goals, the GENESYS modelling effort turned to the cartel's anatomy and physiology. Like any oligopolistic industry, OPEC is a community of sellers in "rivalrous consonance." That is, members are simultaneously competitors with conflicting interests and cooperators with mutual interests. The effects of those egoistic–communitarian strivings work their way into the pricing structure via each member's perception of the industry power structure.

Weaker rivals must consider more intensely than the stronger members what impacts their pricing decisions will have upon the profits of the rest of the group. Each nation, therefore, in searching for a price that maximizes its profits, is "crippled" self-protectively by the need to consider its competitors' reactions. Finally, this crippling is enhanced by the fact that each nation has other goals besides profit maximization whose implementation lessens direct money gain; for example, a member may be willing to protect its long-run power position within the cartel by sacrificing short-run profits to retain its market share.

The GENESYS model incorporates these structural characteristics by assuming that each nation (1) maximizes its own profits plus the profits of every other member when the latter have been reduced by a specific "consonance factor" reflecting that nation's perceived strength relative to the maximizing nation, but (2) is subject to constraints in the interest of its other goals besides maximizing profits. In both of these senses, GENESYS is a "crippled-optimization rivalrous consonance" model.

The power structure of the 11 major OPEC members (excluding Ecuador and Gabon, which account for less than 3 percent of the cartel's output) is isolated by determining how each values the profits of each rival. For example, Saudi Arabia might value a $1 profit loss that its pricing decisions inflict upon Libya as the equivalent of a 25¢ loss in its own profits, whereas a like loss inflicted on Iraq may be valued at only 10¢ in its own profits. These different valuations reflect (among other factors) the relative ability of Libya and Iraq to reduce Saudi profits by price-cut retaliations. These valuations are the consonance factors that modify each rival's profit in a given nation's decision-making. We have determined 110 of these factors (11 × 10) by combining the broadly based power of each rival (grounded in production levels, excess capacity, alternative exports, and so forth) with the market sensitivity of that rival's sales to the prices of the other 10 members.

The constraints upon each rival are two: that sales not exceed its capacity to lift oil on a sustained basis and that those sales not fall below one-half of this sustained capacity.

5 Price, Output, and Profit Implications

To gain some insight into what may be expected of OPEC in the coming year and the importance of the power structure in influencing price patterns, we have run the GENESYS model with three different degrees of rivalrous consonance:

1 *Moderate consonance*   In this case the consonance factors reflect our best estimate of the actual power structure of OPEC. The price projections and expected outputs are our "most likely estimates" for a nonrecessionary year with other "normal" characteristics, as enumerated earlier – that is, our *base case*.

2 *Perfect Consonance*   For this case we asked the model to project OPEC's decisions if the cartel maximized total profits, regardless of their distribution among members. This is the case of joint-profit maximization with all consonance factors equal to 1, which implies that every rival treats a dollar of any other rival's profit as the equivalent of a dollar of its own.

3 *Perfect Rivalry*   In this case we went to the opposite extreme to assume that each rival maximizes its own profit in absolute myopic disregard for the impacts of his decisions upon other members' profits. That is, all consonance factors except his own are set at zero. This case permits us to gauge which rivals benefit most from the existing power structure.

In table 8.1 we list actual OPEC prices and estimated sales and profits as of last February 1 (before the onset of recession) as well as prices, quantities, and profits projected by the GENESYS model for the three cases. Again, these projections must be qualified in four particulars: they are based upon the "normal" assumptions that Iran would return to traditional sales levels if it were in her best interests, that Saudi Arabia would continue to be willing to produce up to 9.5 mbpd, and that the world economy would be non-recessionary; they do not take into account the possible drawdown of the world's huge inventory levels that presently exist. In its current form GENESYS is a short-run model, but it assumes normal operations and petroleum stocks within that context.

Compare, first, the actual with the base-case projections. Last February's prices were considerably below what our analysis leads us to suspect would prevail in a nonrecessionary, "normal" year with 1980's outlines. Overall, we project that OPEC prices would rise from $28 to about $35 per barrel, in dollars of present purchasing power. Persian Gulf prices would increase by about $9, although Saudi prices would rise by only $4. The fine African

Table 8.1 OPEC price pattern for three consonance cases

Area	Actual February 1980			Base case			Perfect consonance			Perfect rivalry		
	Price	Sales	Profit	Price	Sales	Profit	Price	Sales	Profit	Price	Sales	Profit
Saudi Arabia	26.00	9.522	88.104	30.02	9.389	100.681	30.88	9.792	108.073	27.61	9.435	92.851
Iran	28.50	5.021[c]	51.032	32.54	4.808[c]	55.985	31.93	5.497	62.782	29.58	5.191[c]	54.804
Iraq	27.96	3.029	30.196	40.57	1.819	26.515	45.57	1.551	25.434	29.89	2.966	31.651
Kuwait	27.50	2.073	20.311	34.48	1.694	20.923	39.23	1.400	19.723	32.70	1.600	18.714
United Arab Emirates	29.56	1.867	19.702	38.81	1.416	19.726	44.17	1.201	19.084	41.16	1.351	19.975
Qatar	29.22	0.596	6.216	41.39	0.386	5.742	47.74	0.301	5.174	32.54	0.584	6.798
Persian Gulf	27.36[b]	22.108	215.561	36.35[b]	19.512	229.577	39.98[b]	19.742	240.273	32.36[b]	21.127	224.794
Libya	34.72	1.823	22.040	47.10	1.250	20.777	41.76	2.200	32.256	36.32	1.993	24.460
Algeria	32.99	1.055	12.089	49.93	0.654	11.546	55.35	0.552	10.833	34.27	1.034	12.299
Nigeria	29.99	2.310	22.020	45.25	1.396	21.084	49.56	1.201	20.025	31.29	2.269	22.706
Africa	32.26[b]	5.188	56.150	47.13[b]	3.300	53.408	49.09[b]	3.953	63.115	33.55[b]	5.296	59.467
Venezuela	24.51	2.119	17.092	33.20	1.394	15.516	28.60	2.200	21.034	25.99	2.054	17.679
Indonesia	27.50	1.602	14.754	35.95	1.229	15.112	28.46	1.800	17.210	29.55	1.534	15.278
OPEC Total[a]	28.01[b]	31.017	303.551	34.85[b]	25.434	313.775	34.92[b]	27.693	341.632	30.23[b]	30.011	317.219

Price in dollars per barrel, sales in million barrels per day, profits in billions of dollars per year.
[a] Excludes Ecuador and Gabon. [b] Weighted by sales. [c] Under normal conditions.

crudes would increase their superpremia by about $15, whereas Venezuelan and Indonesian crudes would increase about $8.50.

At these higher prices, after demand had time to adjust, we would expect OPEC sales to fall to about 25.4 million barrels per day, as higher prices, slower growth, conservation, and alternative supply sources acted to reduce demand. Within the context of OPEC's power pattern, it would be in the best interest of each member acting selfishly to reduce outputs collectively by about 5.5 mbpd. But this is a demand-driven reduction: each member stands ready to deliver at the cited price as much as the market will take within the limits of the constraints we have set. Higher prices and reduced supply would hike OPEC profits by about $10 billion. Thus, OPEC would be doubly blessed with a larger immediate profit and greater reserves left for future sales.

The model projects that Iraq, the United Arab Emirates, and Qatar would be under peculiar stress to break their moderate stance of recent times and raise prices substantially above those of their Gulf colleagues. These changes would increase Gulf profits at the expense of African nations as Gulf area power was exerted in the market. Weak rivals Venezuela and Indonesia would neither suffer nor benefit much from the expected pattern. Note also that Saudi Arabia's traditional role as a price moderate would remain in her self-interest, given the structure of demand for its product, its quality characteristics, and the power structure it faces.

Were OPEC to move from base-case rivalrous consonance to perfect cooperative price setting in short-run "normal" conditions, price changes, while mainly upward, would be remarkably constrained. OPEC seems to be enjoying most of its potential pricing power under base-case consonance. Surprisingly, perhaps, the consuming world would suffer little overall price increase and would enjoy some rise in availability if OPEC became a tighter cartel. The distribution of price and output changes among the 11 nations happens to bring this result about. But OPEC's overall profits would rise substantially.

The profit shifts within the total permit us to see which areas and rivals benefit most from consonance. The Gulf area's profits rise from $230 to $240 billion with little increase in sales. Almost all of this profit increase accrues to Saudi Arabia and (a normal) Iran, the most powerful members of the cartel. African profits rise a like amount, although only with a substantial need to increase sales, and the gain is wholly enjoyed by Libya, as Algerian and Nigerian profits decline. Lastly, Venezuelan and Indonesian profits rise under this hypothesized larger umbrella, but again only if those nations are willing to increase their liftings substantially. Broadly, then, the clear gainers are the power bases in OPEC: Saudi Arabia, Iran, and Libya. It is they who have a strong interest in increasing the community feeling among OPEC rivals.

From a narrow profits standpoint, the African nations have the least to fear should OPEC's unity disintegrate into thorough noncooperation. Each of them actually increases profits under perfect rivalry, although to do so they would have to draw down their reserves substantially faster. Cooperation permits them to sustain high profit levels with reduced outputs, and in this important sense benefits them. Venezuela and Indonesia are in a similar position: as in the case of the African nations, perfect rivalry so reduces their prices that they are led to increase output in their myopic search for maximum constrained profit.

On the other hand, Saudi Arabia and Iran suffer smaller decreases in price and sales, with only slight falls in profit levels. In the sense of conserving output, therefore, it is they who are protected against disintegration of the cartel.

Nonetheless, the GENESYS model predicts that if OPEC's discipline were to dissolve, its overall prices would fall only $2.23 below February levels and $4.62 below the projected base case. Output would increase, however, by a substantial 5.4 million barrels a day above projected levels at very little cost to consuming nations in terms of transferred revenue. Obviously, it is to the very strong advantage of oil importers to encourage rivalrous behavior among OPEC nations.

Even so, the consuming world cannot expect OPEC prices to fall substantially if the cartel dissolves. With producing nations rather than the oil companies firmly in control of prices and outputs, they would be led under the most anarchic oligopolistic structure to keep prices quite high. Still, consumers would benefit substantially when compared to the base case in terms of the quantities they would enjoy at roughly equivalent transfers of income to OPEC.

The state of economic modelling remains a parlous one for the policy maker, and great faith should not be placed in the numerical accuracy of the GENESYSs model's projections. Rather, what this study shows is the *qualitative* movements that prices, outputs, and profits would take under the postulated environments. Moreover, as presently constructed, the model assumes that OPEC nations make decisions wholly in the short run, neglecting the future except as their attitudes are depicted in the constraints. Our next step is to refine the component mathematical functions of the model and extend it into a longer time-frame.

9

The GENESYS Model of OPEC, 1974–1980: Structural Insights from a Non-forecasting Model

Since 1977 the General Economic Systems Project (GENESYS) at Princeton University has been constructing a model of OPEC with short-term motivation based upon a specific "vision" of the nature of oligopolistic functioning which I have called "rivalrous consonance".[1] It is necessary, therefore, to present that viewpoint briefly before proceeding to an explanation of the model's structure and goals.

1 The Industry's Power Structure

Mature oligopolistic industries are characterized by pervasive attitudes of mutual rivalry constrained by a communal desire for industrial peace and concern for the welfare of the industry. Industry by industry, different mixtures of the competitive and the cooperative – a rivalrous consonance of interests – rule, and the distinctive blend in each case is captured in the power structure of that industry. An analysis of oligopolistic decision making must attempt the isolation of these mutual perceptions of competitors' threats and weaknesses with their inspirations of fear and sympathy. Moreover, that power structure can only be fruitfully incorporated in the analysis of industrial decision making by a complete determination: in an oligopolistic industry with n firms, an $n \times (n - 1)$ matrix must be obtained to define each rival's power posture relative to every other.

Our approach to determining this power structure is to estimate rival i's willingness or lack of willingness to treat rival j's profits as his own. This is

Originally published in *Energy Economics*, 4 (1982), 146–58, and reproduced with permission. The author is indebted to the Rockfeller Foundation for funding this project in part.

done by obtaining θ_{ij}, a "consonance factor," which is the discount factor by which rival i reduces \$1 of rival j's profits to an equivalent amount of his own. If $\theta_{ij} = 0.25$, firm i treats a dollar of firm j's profits as equivalent to \$0.25 of its own. Similar consonance factors are derived for firm i's attitudes towards all of its other rivals, and by letting i take all values $i = 1,2,\ldots,n$, we obtain θ, an $n \times n$ matrix (with main diagonal $\equiv 1$) of consonance factors that describes the industry's power structure in detail and comprehensively.

This power structure becomes operational in the GENESYS model by the assumption that the firm prices its product to maximize its own profits plus the profits of its rivals reduced to equivalent own-profits by the consonance factors. Hence, firm i maximizes

$$Z_i = \sum_{j=1}^{n} \theta_{ij}\pi_j,$$

$$\theta_{ii} \equiv 1,$$

where π denotes profits, subject to the simultaneous maximization of every other firm in the industry. The objective function value, Z_i, is the *extended profits* of firm i, including its own and those of its rivals translated into own-profit equivalents. We have a termed this search for a maximum which takes account of others as "crippled optimization," for the firm's attainment of an optimum is tempered by a perceived necessity to take the welfare of other firms into account.

When firm i contemplates reducing its price by \$1 to increase its profit by $\Delta\pi_i$, its deducts from that *gross* own-profit impact the own-profit equivalent of the negative profit effect on its rivals, or

$$\sum_{j \neq i} \theta_{ij}\Delta\pi_j,$$

to obtain the *net* extended profit impact of its action. It seeks to arrive at a marginal price adjustment with marginal net extended profit equal to zero.

2 The Multi-objective Firm

A second characteristic of real-world oligopolistic industries is the multi-objective decision making that typifies their members' price setting. Firms may desire to maximize long- or short-run profits, or to seek target rates of return on their products, but such goals usually coexist with a desire to conserve or increase market share; to keep price changes within set limits; to assure that output falls between set limits; or to attain another set of such subordinate goals.

These goals are constraints upon each firm's decisions in its search for crippled optimization. Hence, each firm seeks to maximize its extended profits subject to its own set of constraint objectives. Formally, firm i sets a price p_i in such manner as to

$$\text{Max } Z_i = p_i \cdot f_i(P, r, y, w) + \sum_{j \neq i} \theta_{ij} p_j \cdot f_j(P, r, y, w) \qquad (9.1)$$

subject to

$$g_{ik}(x_i, p_i) \leqslant b_k, k = 1, 2, \ldots, s$$
$$x_i - f_i(P, r, y, w) = 0 \qquad (9.2)$$
$$p_i \geqslant 0$$

where $g_{ik}(\cdot)$ are constraint functions and x_i is the sales of the firm's product as a function f_i of the prices of all rivals (P), the transportation rate r, the income of purchasers, y, and non-OPEC, non-communist supplies, w. Finally, prices are bounded away from negative values.

3 The Flexibility of the Model

Within this framework it is possible to tailor the analysis to fit the specifics of the industry under scrutiny. Firms may be assumed to price so as to maximize crippled industry profit (as assumed in equation (9.1)), to attain target rates of return, to follow price leadership patterns, and so forth, all subject to the specific constraint objectives believed to best reflect each firm's multifaceted goal pattern. All of these actions are conditioned by the power structure of the industry as depicted by θ, the matrix of θ_{ij}s.

In the specific case of OPEC we have assumed that each rival seeks to maximize short-run crippled joint industry profits subject to two constraints: an upper and a lower limit on output (expressed in millions of barrels per day, bbl/day). It would admittedly be more realistic to employ a longer-term profit horizon than one year for such optimization, but the size and complexity of the model have made this infeasible at the present stage of analysis.

Because of the unavailability of data and their relative insignificance in terms of output, Gabon and Ecuador were excluded from the model. Together they account for only about 1.5 percent of OPEC crude oil liftings. We therefore seek to determine the prices that would be set by each of the 11 remaining nations upon a notional crude (constructed for each by a quantities-sold weighted average of the various qualities of crude it produces). This assumes that such nations would set those prices *to maximize short-run crippled extended profits*, given the perceived binary power relations among them and their output constraints.

Our model attempts to incorporate other-than-economic motivations or power bases in the power structure and the constraint sets. Political and social considerations that cannot be so captured must be viewed as altering the model's predictions in auxiliary analyses.

It is emphasized that the GENESYS model is not a forecasting model, because we realize that OPEC members do not set prices within a wholly short-run context. Rather, its use yields insights into the strengths and directions of short-term price pressures, the extent of the tempering of pricing decisions by longer-term considerations, and into the stresses within OPEC that arise from the short-run horizon of most of its members. Our use of the model, therefore, is designed to obtain structural hypotheses about OPEC, not to project actual prices. This limited ambition reflects our belief that economic models can at best yield insights into a reality, the complexity of which can never be captured in its entirety.

4 The Solution of the Model

The model is solved by nonlinear programming techniques. We have modified the sequential unconstrained minimization technique, designed by Fiacco and McCormick [1], and employ a penalty function approach, to permit it to solve crippled optimization problems.[2] The model solution yields a Nash equilibrium for the prices of OPEC members: given the constraints on each nation it is doing the best it can in terms of extended profits in the face of the pricing decisions of all its rivals. The constraints are linear (and therefore convex) and the objective function for each rival is concave in own-price. Hence, each firm attains a global crippled constrained maximum as the algorithm holds its rivals' prices constant, iteration by iteration, and it determines own-price optimally.

5 An Overview of the OPEC Cartel: The Search for Ideal Price

Since the start of its effective functioning as an important market force in 1973, OPEC has aimed at setting a flexible price *pattern* for its members' products. Crude petroleum is not a homogeneous product, varying by specific gravity, sulphur content, and location relative to markets. OPEC has anchored the price pattern by setting the price (fob Ras Tanura) of marker crude. Because at least half of OPEC's output consists of crude that is close in composition to marker crude (specific gravity of 34°, sulphur content of about 1.6 percent), it may be treated as "crude petroleum in general" – a dominant, typifying product.

Ideally, the economic goal of OPEC is to set the price of marker crude at a level that equates the demand for "oil" with an "appropriate" supply. The term "appropriate" is difficult to define or even conceptualize. It includes the profit motives of OPEC members constrained by the perceived power structure, the ruling constraints on each member's production, and broader geopolitical, nationalistic, religious, and regional considerations, with many of which GENESYS cannot deal. No formal agreement among cartel members on what constitutes an acceptable supply level for this grade exits, but informal acquiescence by OPEC members is sought by debate each quarter in the light of diverse long-run factors and shorter-term information on available production capacity, non-OPEC supply, world inventory levels, and international economic conditions.

In an ideally functioning OPEC, this anchor price is then accepted by each member nation and a premium (positive or negative) is added to marker crude's price to reflect the special qualities possessed by that nation's specific crudes in the dimensions previously mentioned. These premia and discounts have never been formally adopted by OPEC – although they almost were[3] – but they are nonetheless set rather rigorously by historic precedent, tending to a maximum discount of about $2 and maximum premium of perhaps $4.

Suppose, however, that when a member nation adds (or subtracts) this quality premium surcharge to the price of marker crude its prospective sales would be less than its "acceptable level of output." The nation is then permitted (however grudgingly, perhaps) to add a (positive or negative) superpremium which allows price to attain a level that equates demand for its crude to this "acceptable" supply. Once more, each nation's acceptable sales level has never been agreed formally by the cartel from the viewpoint of keeping OPEC viable, a healthy but nonetheless bounded ambiguity is preserved.

A short-term "ideal type" of price pattern, therefore, which provides a framework within which to analyse the real patterns that emerge, is one in which

- demand equals supply for crude oil in general;
- better or worse crudes receive their customary quality premia or discounts;
- the specific demand–supply situation in each member's market is balanced by a superpremium (or superdiscount) that permits that nation to sell what is accepted by all members as an appropriate amount in the light of cartel discipline.

In the longer run, an equilibrium is achieved in which the superpremia become zero.

The fact that OPEC's ideal goal is that of setting a price *pattern* is frequently obscured as the limelight is often cast upon the bargaining at quarterly OPEC conferences over the appropriate price for marker crude. Nonetheless, debates concerning appropriate quality premia and specific-market superpremia have come increasingly into the open in recent periods.

6 Strengths and Weaknesses of the *Modus Operandi*

The advantages and disadvantages to OPEC of this manner of making decisions are well displayed in this framework. On the one hand, the price pattern is flexible, adaptable on a short-term basis to changes in market conditions for "crude in general" or a specific type of crude. No member nation need feel locked into a rigid price or supply agreement, as it retains an important degree of independence both in pricing its product and determining its lifting levels. OPEC is viable in large part because it can adjust flexibly to the temperature of its market environment or the special needs of its members without breaking up.

But strains are increasingly evident. This manner of adjustment biases most members to a short-run pricing view which drives their decision making. Nor is it possible to separate unambiguously an unbalanced demand for crude in general from an unbalanced demand for a specific grade of crude springing from an outmoded quality premium or an inappropriate superpremium. In the period 1979–81 a good deal of bickering occurred in these terms, with strong pressure exerted upon Saudi Arabia to close an asserted excess demand gap for oil in general with a rise in the price of marker crude or to reduce excess supply by curtailing liftings.[4]

Even more potentially divisive is the informality of agreement about the bracket of lifting levels to which members are entitled, and which are important in defining the superpremia. It has proved impossible to achieve formal agreement upon an output prorationing scheme, the most recent suggestion (by Iran) being rejected out-of-hand in the December 1979 conference at Caracas. However, an ominous development from the viewpoint of consuming nations in the post-Iranian stringency was the frequency of discussion among members concerning output limitations.

No issue is so closely linked to the differences that challenge the unity of OPEC as this one, and member nations have wisely skirted any attempts to obtain formal commitments. The ability of Saudi Arabia to vary its output as a "swing" producer is the basis of its dominant power in the cartel over the price of crude in general. Consequently, Saudi Arabia has in the past opposed prorationing agreements, seeking instead harmony on price premia and superpremia. In the longer run it is difficult to see how it can retain a predominant role in the power structure in the face of challenges that are highly probable if Saudi Arabia refrains from use of reserve capacity as a disciplinary device. However, if we are correct in believing that most fellow members are driven by the short run, it is doubtful it will be successful in obtaining agreement on a long-term pricing agreement or that, if it is obtained, it will last long.

7 The stability of OPEC

In an oligopoly where decision-making is structured around price rather than output, it should not be surprising that in periods of supply stringency or panic inventory stockage the price pattern can fluctuate within wide limits without life-threatening disagreement among members of an organization as elastically structured as OPEC. Indeed, as pointed out above, ambiguities have been built in, or permitted to persist, that are designed to allow this to happen. Two-tiered or three-tiered patterns – reflecting disagreements over one or more of the three price components – must be expected particularly in periods of excess demand.

These patterns may be distressing, especially as they are interpreted as challenges to the current power structure. But a unified long-term price pattern in the sense of the ideal is just that – an OPEC ideal equilibrium – which will not be achieved in an imperfect world driven so largely by the short run. We have heard too much of the price pattern disorder that existed in the 1979–81 period as signalling the imminent breakup of OPEC or the disintegration of its control over the world price of oil.

Rather, recent developments reinforce a long-standing position of GENESYS that too much attention has been focused upon Saudi Arabia's supposed dominant or even monopoly position within OPEC. A much wider diffusion of effective power characterizes the cartel, and an understanding of its operation requires that the complex power structure be isolated and made explicit in analysis. That Saudi Arabia possesses the *potential* power to set the price of oil in general, and thereby to crucially effect the prices of all other crudes, cannot be doubted. But – like that based upon the possession of strategic nuclear weapons – power that cannot be exercised without self-destructive consequences is not truly power. The GENESYS model demonstrates clearly that Saudi Arabia would be a major loser should OPEC disintegrate or short-run motives dominate price decisions; hence, she must compromise with the goals of her fellow members.

Our studies of demand functions [2, 4] indicate that in general the sales of OPEC nations are sensitive to *ceteris paribus* price changes in those nations' crudes.[5] This sensitivity is rooted in three characteristics of the petroleum market and one behavioural trait we believe will persist in the future:

- the availability of near-substitute crudes for each nation's grades of oil, making product competition potentially severe;
- the multinational operations of the major international oil companies and the short-term flexibility to vary liftings within their long-term contracts with producing nations;
- the ability to use measures such as inventory drawdown, slow-steaming, and product allocation to consumers to delay the impact of narrow-gauged price actions;
- a tendency by OPEC nations – despite brave *ex ante facto* threats – to protect historic lifting levels by lowering price when necessary to retain customers.

Present developments in the world petroleum market will heighten this sensitivity of sales to prices. Alaskan, North Sea, and Mexican oil, as well as alternative fuel sources and conservation in consuming countries, are one group of factors pushing in this direction. Moreover, the increasing use of the short-term markets – both the Rotterdam spot market and those within the producing countries – and the decline of term contracts with the oil majors will increase flexibility. Therefore, we expect that in the future the price pattern will tend to greater conformity to the ideal pattern.

8 The GENESYS Model

The GENESYS model examines the hypothetical functioning of OPEC if short-term crippled extended profit maximization were followed by all members. Of course, compared with realistic present policy this assumption is too simple, failing, for example, to adequately reflect Saudi Arabia's longer-run attitudes and actions. Moreover, greater consideration may be given longer-run pricing policy in the future. However, we feel that the short run has strongly influenced most OPEC members in the past, although its impact has been held in check by Saudi policy. To measure the *potential* impact of these unrestrained forces is to isolate some of the stresses that exist in the organization's functioning and to gauge the success of Saudi policy.

The basis for the sales curve derivation was laid in an extensive very short-run demand analysis of the crudes of the 11 OPEC nations [2, 4]. Further analysis of different specifications of the sales functions from those of these studies over a somewhat longer time period was performed. As presently constructed, the GENESYS model projects on an annual basis with sales functions estimated for the period January 1974 to June 1980.

Each of the 11 nations' sales functions was included in the model. They can be grouped for convenience of presentation into four regional areas, and typical forms reproduced (see table 9.1). (See table 9.4 for numerical specifications.) Explanations of the methodology, variables, and derivations of the equations and variables are discussed in detail in [2, 4], although specifica-

Table 9.1   Regional demand function forms

Persian Gulf (Saudi Arabia, Iran, Iraq, Kuwait, United Arab Emirates, Qatar)

(a) We denote:

  GN: surrogate for any of the six Persian Gulf nations (GN = SA, IN, IQ, K, U, or Q)
  PGN: price of nation GN's crude
  $POGGN$: weighted price of other five Persian Gulf nations' crudes
  PAF: weighted price of African nations' crudes
  PV: price of Venezuelan crude
  PI: price of Indonesian crude
  $SIVO$: index of single voyage tanker rate computed by London Trade Brokers
  IND: weighted index of industrial production in the USA, UK, West Germany, France, Japan, and Canada
  $YNCW$: non-communist world, non-OPEC production in million bbl/day
  XGN: sales in million bbl/day by Persian Gulf nation GN

(b) All prices have been deflated to January 1977, levels by the consumer price index of the OECD.

(c) The typical Persian Gulf nation sales function is:

$$XGN = AGN + b_1 \cdot PGN + b_2 \cdot POGGN + b_3 \cdot PAF + b_4 \cdot PV + b_5 \cdot PI + b_6 \cdot SIVO$$
$$+ b_7 \cdot IND + b_8 \cdot YNCW \tag{9.3}$$

Africa (Libya, Algeria, Nigeria)

(a) We denote:

  R: surrogate for any of the three African nations (R = L, A, or N)
  PR: price of nation R's crude
  $POAR$: weighted price of other two African nations' crudes
  PG: weighted price of Persian Gulf nations' crudes
  XR: sales in million bbl/day by African nation R

(b) The typical African nation sales function is:

$$XR = AR + b_1 \cdot PR + b_2 \cdot POAR + b_3 \cdot PG + b_4 \cdot PV + b_5 \cdot PI + b_6 \cdot SIVO + b_7 \cdot IND$$
$$+ b_8 \cdot YNCW \tag{9.4}$$

Venezuela

(a) The Venezuelan sales function is:

$$XV = AV + b_1 \cdot PV + b_2 \cdot PG + b_3 \cdot PAF + b_4 \cdot PI + b_5 \cdot SIVO + b_6 \cdot IND + b_7 \cdot YNCW$$
$$\tag{9.5}$$

Indonesia

(a) The Indonesia sales function is:

$$XI = AI + b_1 \cdot PI + b_2 \cdot PG + b_3 \cdot PAF + b_4 \cdot PV + b_5 \cdot SIVO + b_6 \cdot IND + b_7 \cdot YNCW$$
$$\tag{9.6}$$

---

tions were changed to the present form when the equations were fitted to the longer period.

Average cost functions for five regions (*not* for each of the 11 nations) were estimated as quadratic functions of cumulative output. The five regions were the Persian Gulf, North Africa, West Africa (Nigeria), North Central Latin America (Venezuela), and Southeast Asia (Indonesia). Where regions contained more than one nation, the model augments cumulative output by current projected output for all nations in the region, and the resulting average cost is used for each of the relevant nations. For the Persian Gulf, for example, average cost (*ACPG*) had the form

$$ACPG = BPG + b_1 \cdot CXPG + b_2 \cdot CXPG^2 \qquad (9.7)$$

where *CXPG* is cumulative output. These costs include amortized investment costs, operating costs, and a 15 percent "normal" rate of return on discounted cash flow.

The objective functions for the 11 OPEC nations analysed were, by regions, and using a Persian Gulf nation to illustrate,

$$\begin{aligned}
ZGN_i = XGN_i \, (PGN_i - ACPG) \\
+ \sum_{GN \neq i} \theta_{i,PG} \cdot XGN \, (PGN - ACPG) \\
+ \sum_{R} \theta_{i,R} \cdot XR \, (PR - ACNA) \\
+ \theta_{i,N} \cdot XN \, (PN - ACN) \\
+ \theta_{i,V} \cdot XV \, (PV - ACLA) \\
+ \theta_{i,I} \cdot XI \, (PI - ACSA) \qquad (9.8)
\end{aligned}$$

where Nigeria (*XN*,*PN*) has been split away from other African nations because its cost function is different.

The θ_{ij} factors are the consonance coefficients as already explained and estimated for OPEC in [3, 5]. Methodology is discussed in detail in these references. We have used the moderate consonance case coefficients listed in table 9.2 in all of the projections made to date.

The constraint set we have used in our projections is a simple one; we have forced each nation's output to be less than or equal to its estimated present lifting capacity (*CAP*) and to be greater than or equal to half of that capacity:

1. $0.5\,CAPGN \leqslant XGN \leqslant CAPGN$
2. $0.5\,CAPR \leqslant XR \leqslant CAPR$
3. $0.5\,CAPV \leqslant XV \leqslant CAPV$
4. $0.5\,CAPI \leqslant XI \leqslant CAPI$

$$(9.9)$$

The lower limits were placed as base case parameters in the belief that broaching such lifting levels would in general result in unacceptable economic harm to the nations and interfere with development plans. For base case – or "normal" – conditions we set upper (and, therefore, lower) bounds on output in the light of estimated 1981 sustainable capacity.

9 Base Case Parameters and Solution

Our base case is designed to be a "short-run normal" case for 1981 in directions that depart substantially from actual 1981 experience. We are primarily interested in the hypothetical pattern of prices that OPEC would set under crippled-optimization assumptions if the world economy were on a course that reflects a steady growth in demand for OPEC crude reduced from historic levels by conservation, lower economic growth, and alternative supply sources. That demand level reflects normal inventories of crude and refined product, so that the base case demand does not project drawdowns from swollen stockage. Finally, we project that Iraq and Iran would be *willing* and *able* to sell at levels of sustainable capacity above current capabilities and unwilling to sell less than half of this. This departs significantly from their current predicaments and policies, assuming enhanced deliveries over their 1982 levels.

As noted above, our primary use of the GENESYS model is to gain insights into OPEC's structure and functioning, not to forecast. This leads us to ignore transient conditions in defining the model's environment. It must also be emphasized again that it is predominantly short-run economic forces that motivate the model. The θ matrix, that reproduces the complex power structure within the cartel, is determined by economic forces in its explicit derivation, and the constraint sets for the base case also are based upon sustainable economic capacity. We recognize the desirability of modifying GENESYS output by political and social conditioners, but we feel we are not qualified to perform that task.

9.1 Base Case Consonance Factors

In table 9.2 we have reproduced the moderate case consonance coefficients for the base case (and all displacements to date). These are to be interpreted as the dollar equivalent in row nation's profit of a dollar of column nation profit. For example, Saudi Arabia values a dollar gain by Libya as equivalent to 7¢ in its own profit, whereas a dollar gain by Kuwait is valued at only 2¢. Row sums, therefore, index the consideration a nation extends to its rivals as a group, and differ inversely with power. Column sums index the con-

Table 9.2 The consonance factors, moderate case

	SA	IN	IQ	K	U	Q	L	A	N	V	I	Sum
SA	a	0.04	0.03	0.02	0.05	0.04	0.07	0.01	0.02	0.01	0.01	0.30
IN	0.07	a	0.03	0.01	0.07	0.04	0.09	0.01	0.03	0.01	0.01	0.37
IQ	0.07	0.05	a	0.03	0.06	0.04	0.07	0.02	0.03	0.01	0.01	0.39
K	0.05	0.11	0.02	a	0.05	0.03	0.05	0.01	0.02	0.01	0.01	0.36
U	0.11	0.07	0.05	0.04	a	0.03	0.03	0.03	0.05	0.02	0.02	0.45
Q	0.09	0.05	0.04	0.03	0.17	a	0.02	0.02	0.04	0.01	0.01	0.48
L	0.05	0.03	0.03	0.02	0.16	0.11	a	0.02	0.02	0.01	0.00	0.45
A	0.10	0.12	0.03	0.03	0.08	0.03	0.04	a	0.04	0.01	0.01	0.49
N	0.10	0.05	0.04	0.03	0.08	0.04	0.11	0.01	a	0.01	0.01	0.48
V	0.08	0.05	0.04	0.03	0.07	0.05	0.07	0.02	0.03	a	0.01	0.45
I	0.04	0.07	0.04	0.03	0.06	0.05	0.11	0.01	0.03	0.02	a	0.46
Sum	0.76	0.64	0.35	0.27	0.85	0.46	0.66	0.16	0.31	0.12	0.10	

[a] All diagonal elements are 1.00, but are omitted from row and column sums.
Sources: [3, 5].

sideration granted by all rivals to the column nation's profits, and vary directly with power.

Some interesting insights into OPEC's power structure are displayed in table 9.2. The UAE, for example, is accorded more aggregate consideration than Saudi Arabia. This appears peculiar until it is noted that almost 40 percent of this deference is rendered by Libya and Qatar, whose high-quality crudes are in severe competition with that of the UAE. The coefficient of variation (i.e. standard deviation divided by mean) of the UAE's column is 0.51, compared with 0.32 for Saudi Arabia's, indicating the latter's power base is more consistently dispersed. In the setting of price patterns the relevant power relations are contained in the complex pattern of *binary* consonance factors.

Moreover, to view column sums without taking into account row sums is misleading because an element of aggregate power coordinate in importance is the row sum, since it displays the degree of consideration each nation must afford all others in its search for a profit maximum. In table 9.3 we display the consonance relatives, obtained by dividing column by row sums. When considering aggregate power relationships – which are not meaningful for the purposes of the GENESYS model but may have some independent interest – these seem preferable to row or column sums taken alone. From these it is clear that Saudi Arabia's power is foremost and in a class of its own. Iran, UAE, and Libya form a strong group, with the latter somewhat weaker than the other two. These four nations have relatives above unity. Iraq, Qatar, Kuwait, and Nigeria form a third group, a full cut below the first two groups but markedly above the weakest which contains Algeria, Venezuela, and Indonesia.

Table 9.3 The consonance relatives

Nation	Relative
Saudi Arabia	2.53
Iran	1.73
Iraq	0.90
Kuwait	0.75
United Arab Emirates	1.89
Qatar	0.96
Libya	1.47
Algeria	0.33
Nigeria	0.65
Venezuela	0.27
Indonesia	0.22

Source: table 9.2.

9.2 Sales Function Coefficients

Base case regression coefficients for each nation's sales function are given in table 9.4. In general our major finding is that OPEC nations' sales functions in the short run are quite sensitive to own-prices. Uncoordinated or unilateral price changes under "normal" demand conditions will lead to serious sales declines. Hence, a good deal of internal pressure to coordinate price movements exists; that is, the OPEC cartel has a solid basis in the nature of the sales functions for crude petroleum. We have indicated the structural reasons for this sensitivity, and also pointed out its implications for pressures towards a unified price structure in normal or slack demand periods.

Further, note that for each of the 11 nations, the sum of other-price coefficients is close to the absolute value of the own-price coefficient. Hence, in general, OPEC members are quite sensitive to the prices of their rivals. Therefore, if *all* prices rise by $1, sales will decline by small amounts. This sets the stage for very large price rises in a short-run profit maximization regime.

Responsiveness in the short run to transport rates on crude is not great. We should expect positive coefficients for nations which are nearer to major markets (African and Venezuelan) and negative coefficients for products more distant from major markets (Gulf region and Indonesia). In the nine cases where nonzero coefficients were obtained, four revealed an unexpected sign. However, the impacts of short-term tanker rate charges on oil sales are not great.

Multicollinearity – which plagued the attempt to separate price impacts on sales – was also present in the covariation revealed by income changes and movements in non-OPEC, non-communist oil production. We have preserved both variables even when signs were not intuitively proper, in the belief that their joint result was generally correct and that the multicollinearity would persist. The joint impacts of the income and other production variables are generally small, however.

9.3 Constraint Restraints

For the base case we assumed the upper and lower limits on sales listed in table 9.5. These are, of course, the values relevant to the system of equations (9.9).

9.4 Other Base Case Parameters

The index of developed economies' economic activities. *IND*, is set equal to 121 in the base case (actual value on average, January–April 1981: 115.7);

Table 9.4 Base case sales function regression coefficients (million bbl/day)

	Constant	Price regressors ($1977)					Other regressors		
Persian Gulf		Own-price	Other Gulf	African	Venezuelan	Indonesian	SIVO	IND	YNCW
(a) Saudi Arabia	4.523	−0.247	0.028	0.027	0.165	–	0.010	0.010	0.121
(b) Iran	6.753	−0.257	0.030	–	–	0.086	−0.009	0.035	−0.164
(c) Iraq	−0.727	−0.295	0.255	–	–	–	0.006	–	0.192
(d) Kuwait	2.268	−0.110	0.022	–	–	–	0.006	0.013	−0.034
(e) UAE	0.332	−0.113	0.058	0.027	–	–	−0.002	0.010	0.026
(f) Qatar	0.552	−0.038	0.020	0.013	–	–	–	−0.002	0.007
Africa		Own-price	Other African	Gulf	Venezuelan	Indonesian	SIVO	IND	YNCW
(a) Libya	0.528	−0.050	0.021	0.014	–	–	0.001	−0.001	0.091
(b) Algeria	0.867	−0.043	0.018	0.012	–	–	–	0.001	0.019
(c) Nigeria	1.192	−0.109	0.052	0.035	–	–	0.003	0.003	0.030
South America		Own-price	Gulf	African	Indonesian		SIVO	IND	YNCW
(a) Venezuela	3.087	−0.095	0.050	0.044	–		0.002	0.005	−0.088
Southeast Asia		Own-price	GUlf	African	Venezuelan		SIVO	IND	YNCW
(a) Indonesia	1.105	−0.026	0.016	0.005	–		0.001	0.001	0.015

Table 9.5 Base case upper and lower limits to sales (million bbl/day)

	Upper limit	Lower limit
Persian Gulf		
(a) Saudi Arabia	10.50	5.25
(b) Iran	2.75	1.38
(c) Iraq	3.10	1.55
(d) Kuwait	2.50	1.25
(e) UAE	2.40	1.20
(f) Qatar	0.60	0.30
Total	21.85	10.93
Africa		
(a) Libya	2.20	1.10
(b) Algeria	1.10	0.55
(c) Nigeria	2.40	1.20
Total	5.70	2.85
South America		
(a) Venezuela	2.30	1.15
Southeast Asia		
(a) Indonesia	1.80	0.90
OPEC total	31.65	15.83

the index of tanker rates, $SIVO$, is 130 (actual average value, January–July 1981: 89); and non-OPEC, non-communist world output, YNCW, is 21.5 million bbl/day (actual average value January–April 1981: 21.0 million bbl/day). The motivations for the first two values are developed fully in [2, 4], whereas the value of $YNCW$ is set close to present values.

9.5 Base Case Solution

In table 9.6 we list the optimal short-run normal solution to the base case, as well as the actual prices in August 1980 and output rates for the first half of 1980.

Overall, the model projects on the basis of the following three assumptions. First, assuming 1981 had been a "normal" year, in that industrial world economic activity had grown at about 3 percent, single voyage tanker rates had settled to a pre-Iranian revolution level, Iran's and Iraq's productive capacity and willingness to supply had improved substantially, and Saudi Arabia had continued to be willing to supply at near-capacity rates. Second, the power structure within the OPEC cartel, taking into account both market and extra-market factors were as depicted in tables 9.2 and 9.3. Third, the

Table 9.6 Base case solution with actual prices (August 1980)[a]

Regions and nations	Model solution values			Actual values	
	Prices ($)[b]	Output (million bbl/day)	Profit (10^6 $)	Prices (8/80)	Output[c]
Persian Gulf					
(a) Saudi Arabia	69.44	10.50	264	29.56	9.78
(b) Iran	61.61	2.75	61	37.03	2.10
(c) Iraq	66.84	1.58	38	34.06	3.52
(d) Kuwait	49.05	1.25	22	33.45	1.86
(e) UAE	62.06	1.20	27	33.47	1.72
(f) Qatar	68.58	0.30	7	35.40	0.48
Regional	63.05	17.58	419	32.08	19.46
Africa					
(a) Libya	94.33	1.10	37	39.06	1.90
(b) Algeria	84.36	0.55	16	39.29	1.00
(c) Nigeria	81.90	1.20	34	39.32	2.16
Regional	86.06	2.85	87	39.22	5.06
South America					
(a) Venezuela	87.26	1.15	36	34.73	2.11
Southeast Asia					
(a) Indonesia	99.99	0.90	32	33.45	1.56
OPEC total	68.68	22.48	574	33.57	28.19

[a] Prices and profits in January 1981 $.
[b] Quantity-weighted average.
[c] Average for first half of 1980.

OPEC nations had acted to maximize, in a crippled fashion, short-run extended profits subjected to considerations as expressed in maximum and minimum sales constraints. Then the following aggregate results would have occurred.

The average OPEC barrel of oil would have been priced at $68.68 in January 1981 dollars, compared with an August 1980 price of $33.57 (in January 1981 dollars), or about a 105 percent deviation from the August 1980 values.

Equally disturbingly, the model projects that optimal liftings of crude by OPEC – following only short-term profit advantages and in periods of moderate growth with normal inventories – would decline from August 1980 levels of 28 million bbl/day to 22.5 million. That is, OPEC has a *short-run* as well as a long-run interest in striving to reduce output by price rises. Hence, GENESYS projects an OPEC demand that is more elastic in the short-run than some other analyses.

Marker crude's optimal price would be $69.44, or about 135 percent above its August 1980 price. The sum of quality premia plus specific market super-premia are, for regional submarkets:

	Projection ($)	Actual, 8/1980 ($)
Persian Gulf	− 6.39	+2.52
African	+16.62	+9.66
South American	+17.82	+5.17
Indonesia	+30.55	+4.01

Hence, the overall strength of the urges to establish a two-tiered price pattern is well-grounded in short-run economic motives during normal demand periods. The African submarket – with its high quality crudes and advantageous locations – reveals a substantial degree of independence from other submarkets. A price of $86 is projected. Similarly, the substantial protection from other markets enjoyed by Venezuela and Indonesia permit substantial premia to arise. These premia are sustained by the incentives of most OPEC nations to reduce output to their lower limits. On the other hand, at the aggregate submarket level, pressures on the unified price pattern are strong but seem to be no threat to the cartel's functioning. We anticipate widely based pressure on Saudi Arabia, therefore, to reduce liftings from current high rates and to lift the price of marker crude.

In the Gulf region, GENESYS's projections indicate that Kuwait would be forced to accord a substantial discount from marker crude and other Gulf prices. This $49 price is required to sell the minimum acceptable quantity, and basically reflects the lower quality of Kuwait crude. This very large discount, however, may indicate that our econometric techniques did not capture the demand function accurately.

Those who gain the most from a move to extended-profit motivated prices would be the non-Gulf nations. Indonesia and Libya would be especially benefited by large price hikes *and* substantial reductions in output levels. Indeed, half of the lifting level declines below August 1980 values would result from African cutbacks. The African submarket would supply only 12.7 percent of total OPEC production compared with output percentages of about 20 percent at that time. American and European refiners and consumers, therefore, will be under peculiarly strong price and supply pressures if the GENESYS normal projections were to eventuate.

10 The Structural Cases

To attain structural insights into OPEC, we ran the GENESYS model for two parameter sets designed to discern how the distribution of benefits from, and consequent stresses in, a short-run extended profit maximization as depicted in the base case would change with the changing power structures implied by different modes of operation. Before we present these fundamental structural cases, however, it will be useful to examine some characteristics of crippled optimization models as they manifest themselves in the causal interdependence they contain.

10.1 Mechanisms of Parametric Displacements

It will be helpful in interpreting the outcomes of the cases we analyse to consider some of these matters. Consider rival i's pricing decision, when all other rivals' prices are held fixed. It is then possible (for given r, y, and w) to draw a sales or demand curve DD' on figure 9.1 for rival i's product, as well as its marginal cost curve MC. At every hypothetical price, p_i, the other-profit term

$$E_i = \sum_{j \neq i} \theta_{ij} \pi_j$$

in rival i's objective function Z_i will change. As p_i falls, x_i rises, but E_i will fall as rivals' sales and profits fall. If we graph E_i as a function, not of p_i, but of the x_i implied by p_i, it would fall as x_i rose. However, if we obtain the marginal impact on E_i of a fall in p_i (rise in x_i),

$$dE_i = \sum_{j \neq i} \theta_{ij} \cdot \frac{\delta f_j}{\delta p_i} (p_j - c_j) dp_i$$

and we may graph it also in function of x_i as the *marginal other-profit term*, ME_i.

Graphically, it is more convenient to consider E_i as a negative cost rather than a benefit, and ME_i as an addition to the firm's marginal cost MC_i. That is, firm i's first order condition for extended profit maximization is

$$\frac{dZ_i}{dp_i} = MR_i + ME_i - MC_i = 0$$

where MR_i is conventional marginal revenue. We simply think of this as

$$MR_i = MC_i - ME_i$$

where ME_i is negative, and depict this condition in figure 9.1, where EMC_i (extended marginal cost) is the sum of MC_i and ME_i.

If firm i took no consideration of the impacts of its prices upon rivals' profits into account, its price p_i would be set initially (i.e. before other firms reacted) at p_i' on figure 9.1. Rivalrous consonance dictates a positive ME_i, so that the price set by the extended profit first-order condition, p_i, will be higher than that set in its absence. In general, the larger the values of θ_{ij} in an oligopoly and the larger the impacts of rivals' prices upon each others' sales, the higher will prices be set relative to what they would be if

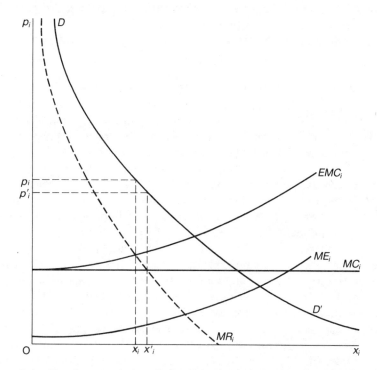

Figure 9.1   Firm i's extended-profit maximization solution in crippled optimization.

all θ_{ij} were identically zero (and, hence, $ME_i \equiv 0$).

Now, let us suppose rival j lowers p_j in response to a reduction in p_i. Two impacts are felt by rival i. First, DD' shifts downward as firm i loses sales to rival j. Second, if linear sales functions have an elasticity with respect to the profit margin $p_j - c_j$ that is greater than 1 in absolute value at the initial price, firm j's profits will *rise* with a responsive fall in p_j (and hence ME_i will shift upward). For sales functions with high own-price elasticities, therefore, ME_i, and hence EMC_i, will rise with a responsiveness fall in p_j.

In our OPEC model, as can be seen from table 9.4, own-price elasticities are high in present price ranges. Hence the expectation is that a reduction in p_j will both shift DD' downward and EMC_i upward. The net impact upon p_i and x_i, therefore, will depend upon the relative strengths of these two factors. In general, any parameter change that shifts DD' downward, thereby tending to induce a fall in p_i, can be offset by an induced rise in EMC_i, so that the fall in p_i will be partially or totally offset. Indeed, if DD' responds sluggishly to the parametric change, but EMC_i responds energetically, p_i may rise with a fall in x_i.

Hence, causal flows within the model can become quite complicated and difficult to trace. Oligopolistic reactions in such circumstances may be "perverse" when judged against the expectations extrapolated from straightforward competitive models that can abstract from recognized interdependence, as we shall see in the following analyses.

10.2 The Joint-profit Maximization Case

The first structural case we examine is that of joint profit maximization, in which each of the 11 members maximizes extended profits when each rival's profit is treated as of coordinate importance with his own. We do this readily in the GENESYS model by setting all consonance factors, θ_{ij}, to unity. All other base case parameters are unchanged. The solution is presented in table 9.7, along with percentage changes of the solution from the base case.

The purpose of this exercise is to obtain insights into the short-run stresses and benefits that exist internally to push OPEC to become more cartel-like in the strict sense of the word – that is, the implications if OPEC were conducted as a single firm with multiple "plants." Note that we are concentrating on short-run profit opportunities under the "normal" conditions of the base case (unconstrained by the longer-term aims of Saudi Arabia) and the rivalrous consonance depicted by θ.

At the *aggregate* OPEC level the most striking conclusion is that the OPEC price level is predicted to rise only about 5 percent. Hence, overall, the base case OPEC power structure under short-run normal conditions would be exploiting its self-serving pricing power at about the limit. Were

Table 9.7 Joint-profit solution, with base case comparisons[a]

Regions and nations	Model solution values			Percentage changes from base case (%)		
	Prices ($)	Output (million bbl/day)	Profit (10⁶ $)	Prices	Output	Profits
Persian Gulf						
(a) Saudi Arabia	85.92	8.16	254	+23.7	−22.3	−3.8
(b) Iran	63.03	2.75	62	+2.3	0.0	+1.6
(c) Iraq	63.83	3.10	71	−3.9	+96.2	+86.8
(d) Kuwait	50.07	1.25	23	+2.1	0.0	+4.5
(e) UAE	64.71	1.20	28	+4.3	0.0	+3.7
(f) Qatar	71.36	0.30	8	+4.1	0.0	+14.3
Regional	66.62	16.76	446	+5.7	−4.7	+6.4
Africa						
(a) Libya	96.23	1.10	38	+2.0	0.0	+2.7
(b) Algeria	86.25	0.55	17	+2.2	0.0	+6.3
(c) Nigeria	84.07	1.20	35	+2.6	0.0	+2.6
Regional	88.07	2.85	90	+2.3	0.0	+3.4
South America						
(a) Venezuela	90.21	1.15	37	+3.3	0.0	+2.8
Southeast Asia						
(a) Indonesia	102.84	0.90	33	+2.9	0.0	+3.1
OPEC total	72.20	21.66	605	+5.1	−3.6	+5.4

[a] Prices and profits in January 1981 dollars.

OPEC cooperation in the sense of joint profit maximization to become much tighter, consumers would have little to fear *in a macro-price sense*. Indeed, except for two members – Saudi Arabia and Iraq – prices rise only between 2 and a little over 4 percent in the new regime. In addition only these two members will be led to change their outputs. Saudi Arabia reduces output by about 22 percent and Iraq raises output by 96 percent. Saudi price rises 24 percent and Iraq's price falls 4 percent. Saudi Arabia, no longer deferred to by the power structure and forced to treat other rivals as equals, is led to hold an umbrella over them by raising price.

Interestingly, therefore, for joint-profit maximization, which describes a power structure where all firms have equal weight, Saudi Arabia would raise her price to the level set by African nations, suffering a large reduction in output, essentially to benefit Iraq. Iraq's strong sensitivity to other Gulf prices leads her to expand output in response. The net result is a slight reduction in Saudi profits but a large increase in Iraqi profits and small rises in all other rivals' profits. Hence, the base case solution reflects a power structure that benefits Saudi Arabia largely at the expense of Iraq. It pays the Saudis to keep price well below the level that would maximize OPEC's profits.

Aggregate sales of OPEC petroleum would decline by less than 1 million bbl/day and weighted price would rise by about $3.50. Hence, were OPEC to become cooperative in a pure cartel sense, the consuming world would not be much more inconvenienced than it would if OPEC operated with its present power structure in a purely profit-maximizing manner.

10.3 The Cournot Case

As a second structural case, let us move to the opposite extreme and assume that essentially the OPEC organization dissolved and each nation priced with total neglect of its impacts upon other nations' profits. This Cournot-type myopia can be achieved in the GENESYS model by setting all consonance factors (expect the $\theta_{ii} \equiv 1$) to zero. In this fashion we approach a world in which OPEC producers have pricing power over their own crudes and exercise that power in anarchic manner to their own joint detriment.

In table 9.8 we present the solution with percentage changes from the base case. The most important overall hypothesis is that a breakup of the OPEC cartel would have only a relatively moderate overall price effect: OPEC price would decline about 9 percent below the base case price and profits would fall about 12 percent. However, consumers would benefit from a 9 percent rise in crude supplies, lifting amounts supplied to 24 million bbl/day.

The present base case power structure in OPEC, therefore, would not reduce potential price competition among members by very large amounts

Table 9.8 Cournot solution, with base case comparisons[a]

Regions and nations	Model solution values			Percentage changes from base case (%)		
	Prices ($)	Output (million bbl/day)	Profit (10^6 $)	Prices	Output	Profits
Persian Gulf						
(a) Saudi Arabia	54.36	10.46	205	−21.7	−0.4	−22.3
(b) Iran	62.45	2.09	47	+1.4	−24.0	−23.0
(c) Iraq	54.75	3.07	61	−18.1	+94.3	+60.5
(d) Kuwait	47.58	1.25	22	−3.0	0.0	0.0
(e) UAE	58.14	1.20	25	−6.3	0.0	−7.4
(f) Qatar	64.08	0.30	7	−6.6	0.0	0.0
Regional	57.08	18.37	367	−9.5	+4.5	−12.4
Africa						
(a) Libya	91.25	1.10	36	−3.3	0.0	−2.7
(b) Algeria	81.27	0.55	16	−3.7	0.0	0.0
(c) Nigeria	78.53	1.20	32	−4.1	0.0	−5.9
Regional	82.85	2.85	84	−3.7	0.0	−2.3
South America						
(a) Venezuela	65.67	2.23	34	−24.7	+93.9	−5.6
Southeast Asia						
(a) Indonesia	93.86	0.94	31	−6.1	+4.4	−3.1
OPEC totals	62.30	24.39	506	−9.3	+8.5	−11.8

[a]Prices and profits in January 1981 $.

in the aggregate, nor, as we have seen in table 9.7, would extremely large enhancements of cooperation lead to large price increases. *In the overall price sense, the most important structural occurrences in the world petroleum market seems to have been the assumption of independent pricing power by the producing nations, not the formation of OPEC as an organization fostering cooperation.* GENESYS casts considerable doubt upon the proposition that in the macro-sense much price reduction payoff is to be expected from policies aimed at the breakup of OPEC or hindering of its urges to greater cooperation.

However, in this same overall sense, consumers do have an important stake in lessening OPEC's power when the benefits of greater crude consumption are considered. With the elimination of OPEC, we project a 9 percent rise in supplies above the base case by almost 2 million bbl/day.

When we look more closely at the distribution of gains and losses within OPEC from dissolution and among customers using the various submarket crudes, other hypotheses emerge. For example, only Iraq benefits unconditionally, in that it lowers its price 18 percent and almost doubles output to increase its profit by about 60 percent. From table 9.4 the reasons seem relatively clear: in the sales functions, Iraq's sales are the most sensitive to own-price and to other-Gulf prices. Its ability to lower price, coupled with the small fall in other-Gulf prices, permits her to almost double sales. Hence, Iraq would tend to benefit most from greater pricing freedom.

All of the other nations have strong to very strong incentives to continue OPEC in its base case depiction. Saudi Arabia – without the deference shown it in the base case – would see its profits decline by 22 percent, but its output would be essentially unchanged. Iran similarly suffers a profit decline of 23 percent and a loss of about a quarter of its market. The UAE suffers only moderately from the need to lower price, whereas Kuwait and Qatar are essentially unaffected. Overall, in the Gulf area, price drops about 10 percent, output rises 5 percent, and profits decline about 12 percent.

The African region is only marginally affected, being forced to reduce prices by 3 or 4 percent, but retaining output levels at minimum values. This region is the least affected by OPEC's passing. Venezuela, on the other hand, is forced to lower price 25 percent, and prevents a profit decline of more than 6 percent only by essentially doubling sales. Indonesia suffers a price drop and output rise of minor dimensions, with a profit fall of only 3 percent.

11 Summary

The GENESYS OPEC model has the virtue of seeking to explain virtual cartel behaviour by a general equilibrium mechanism incorporating rivals as individual decision makers and the explicit power relations among them taken pairwise. We feel this notion of rivalrous consonance is the distinctive feature with general theoretical validity for the analysis of oligopolistic market structure.

The major defects of the model that foreclose its use as a forecasting tool are its short-term nature, its failure to incorporate the different discount rates that the rivals apply to future revenue, and its uncertain ability to incorporate non-economic factors. Given the complexity and time required for solutions to such a large nonlinear optimization model, it is difficult to perceive the possibility of extending the time horizon for any distance into the future. Of practical necessity, GENESYS, if it is to remain a microeconomic general equilibrium framework, must limit itself to one or two time periods.

The failure to incorporate the probabilistic nature of relationships in the model also constitutes a limitation with greater hope of elimination. At least, we feel, future investigation should include some study of the feasibility of movement in this direction.

Finally, all of the crucial parameters of the model are subject to large estimation errors and to rapid change in the structure of the petroleum market. For example, the period of fit for our parameters did not allow us to capture what may be important breaks in consumption regimes in developed nations. Hence, it is more realistic to interpret the results of the analyses in qualitative terms rather than to place extreme faith in magnitudes.

Notes

[1] Two monographs during the research have been published. Condensed versions of these reports have appeared in [2] and [3]. Theoretical work which investigates the implications of the rivalrous consonance framework may be found in [6]–[9].

[2] Currently, the GENESYS model, with 22 variables and 22 inequality constraints takes about 20 minutes of IBM 3033 computer time.

[3] In September 1975, the OPEC Economic Commission achieved near-agreement on a formula, but failed ultimately to get formal approval.

[4] Note that in our framework such debate occurs when an actual excess demand or supply characterizes the markets. If all markets have attained their ideal short-term equilibrium prices – so that the pattern is the ideal – debate concerning an upsetting of the status quo involves quarrels about the power structure or the constraint sets, which we take to be exogenous and parametric in the short-run.

[5] The demand analysis of Kuenne [2, 4] was based upon only 42 monthly observations and therefore was limited to functions with constant elasticities. This analysis was superseded by the refitting of the demand functions in this paper to 78 monthly observations with specifications that permitted elasticities to vary. The own-price sensitivity, however, was captured in both fittings.

References

[1] Fiacco, A. V. and G. P. McCormick, *Nonlinear Programming: Sequential Unconstrained Minimization Technique*, John Wiley & Sons, New York, 1968.

[2] Kuenne, Robert E., *Short-run Crude Petroleum Demand Functions for OPEC Cartel Members*, OPEC Cartel Modelling Project, Research Monograph No. 1, General Economic Systems Project, Princeton University, Princeton, NJ, 1978.

[3] ——, *Measuring the Power Structure of Oligopoly: the Case of OPEC*, OPEC Cartel Modelling Project, Research Monograph No. 2, General Economic Systems Project, Princeton University, Princeton, NJ, 1979.

[4] ——, "A Short-run Demand Analysis of the OPEC Cartel", *Journal of Business Administration*, 10 (1979), 129–64. [Reprinted in the *Logistics and Transportation Review*, 17 (1981), 231–67, and as chapter 7 in this volume.]

[5] ——, "Rivalrous Consonance and the Power Structure of OPEC", *Kyklos*, 32 (1979), 19–35. [Reprinted as chapter 6 in this volume.]

[6] ——, "Toward a Usable General Theory of Oligopoly", *De Economist*, 122 (1974), 471–502. [Reprinted as chapter 1 in this volume.]

[7] ——, "Towards an Operational General Equilibrium Theory with Oligopoly: Some Experimental Results and Conjectures", *Kyklos*, 27 (1974), 792–820. [Reprinted as chapter 2 in this volume.]

[8] ——, "General Oligopolistic Equilibrium: a Crippled-optimization Approach", in *Pioneering Economics: Essays in Honor of Giovanni Demaria*, Cedam, Padua, 1978, 537–77. [Reprinted as chapter 3 in this volume].

[9] ——, "Duopoly Reaction Functions under Crippled Optimization Regimes", *Oxford Economic Papers*, 32 (1980), 224–40. [Reprinted as chapter 4 in this volume.]

10

Lessons and Conjectures on OPEC

---

1 The Passing of the "Energy Crisis"

Eight years have now passed since the effective activation of the pricing power of the Organization of Petroleum Exporting Countries (OPEC) in the international petroleum market. Fortunately, the initial sense of outrage, helpless frustration, and panic has subsided. Little is heard now of the wisdom of achieving energy independence. It has given way to sounder goals of conservation through market pricing, forcing those who benefit from oil to confront its market cost; of permitting those who seek to enhance domestic supply to reap typical market rewards; and of diversifying foreign sources.

Talk of an "oil crisis" is more restrained. These purported phenomena were never well defined, but they frequently implied imminent depletion of the planet's empowering resources, with bleakness beyond. One senses that such visions are being replaced by more gradualist expectations of rising energy prices into the future with attendant reductions in usage, substitution among types, and development of alternatives.

A calmer view of OPEC's strengths and weaknesses, and its capacity to afflict the economies of oil-consuming nations, is emerging. Fewer extreme views of the organization's potential stranglehold, on the one hand, or imminent dissolution, on the other hand, are being expressed. And recent research is revising downward the estimates of OPEC's part in stagflation in the short and medium run and emphasizing longer-term problems such as financing less-developed countries' oil-related balance-of-payments deficits, measurement of the social cost of oil imports, and the income distributional implications of alternative policies.

Originally published as chapter 12 in Sidney Weintraub and Marvin Goodstein (eds), *Reaganomics and the Stagflation Economy*, University of Pennsylvania Press, Philadelphia, PA, 1983, and reproduced with permission.

One may also be optimistic enough to believe – and admittedly with the aid of hope – that free market enthusiasts are learning the notion of "externality"; that environmentalists are approaching an appreciation of the meaning of "cost"; and that nuclear energy foes are grasping the concept of "alternative risk."

In short, the energy field today seems much quieter on a number of fronts. Indeed, as far as OPEC's future market power is concerned, we may have become too sanguine. The time seems ripe, therefore, to reassess OPEC's future implications for the international economy in the light of past impacts and its current nature. This is a formidable task, and I do not pretend to do the job definitively. Some ideas, however, seem to be central to understanding our present situation and medium-term petroleum prospects.

2 OPEC and Stagflation in the 1970s

To what extent did OPEC's price–output strategies contribute to the stagflation of the 1970s? The answer is a difficult one for a variety of reasons. Inflation is a *process* which includes vitally within its dynamic induced money creation to support induced cost-push and price pressures, direct and indirect, initiated by external price increases. Its relation to real factors like growth is not as well understood as the Phillips curve once led us to believe. Hence, to be meaningful, our simple question becomes quite complex. What role did the nominal price increases of petroleum play in enhancing credit creation, inflationary expectations, income leakages, and responsive cost pressures during the decade? How did these induced price pressures, coupled with aggregate demand effects of international and national income redistribution, react upon jobs and output?

Answers become even more complicated when it is recalled that OPEC's disturbances were not inflicted upon an industrialized world at full employment with mild inflation and neutral monetary–fiscal policies. Industrialized nations were struggling to contain inflationary forces in 1972 and 1973; in general, fearing the inflationary tinder of the sharp petroleum price increases of 1973 more than the recessionary impacts of such increases, they actually tightened their monetary and fiscal stance in 1974. The doubling of oil prices in 1979 came in a world embattled against inflation. Therefore, the assessment of OPEC's stagflation impact in a world of neutral economic policy can only be made hypothetically.

Yet another problem in framing an answer is whether the OPEC impacts are to be measured only in the year or so that follow their introduction, or over their life cycle. A petroleum price rise transmits an immediate price shock upon refined petroleum products and spawns recessionary income leakages by shifting income to oil exporters and to domestic oil producers.

However, over time, oil-producing nations will increase their imports from consuming nations, and domestic oil producers will step up investments in oil production. Over an even longer time frame, capital equipment will be altered to efficient configurations, reducing energy usage and making the national factor complex more efficient in goods production than it was in the immediate aftermath of the price shocks. Hence substantial "rebound" effects will offset immediate impact effects.

I do not think the definitive investigation of these complex questions has been published. Since 1977, however, my own suspicions have been that we have, in general, overestimated OPEC's stagflation effects and that we could focus more profitably on microeconomic aspects: conservation, supplies of energy goods, and international and national distribution effects. In a study for the Federal Energy Administration of the "optimal drawdown strategy" for the Strategic Petroleum Reserve in a period of oil embargo, we had used the INFORUM model of the US economy to derive a gross national product (GNP) response function for oil deprivations [5]. As we simulated six-month supply interruptions to measure GNP impacts, we were surprised by the income rebound effects in the outyears, caused primarily by investment stimuli set in motion by the embargoes. Certain problems in detail with the answers led us to ignore the outyear impacts, but the strength of the rebound persuaded me that they were not negligible.

Early studies clearly foresaw the potentiality of rebound but could only speculate about its quantitative outlines [2]. However, some current studies are seeking to estimate the time patterns of a "permanent" adjustment to an OPEC price shock. John Tatom finds that a change in energy prices relative to the price of business output impacts the price level for four quarters, with a net effect of raising prices about 0.075 percent for each 1.0 percent rise in relative energy price [9]. His equation holds the supply of money and "high-employment" government expenditures constant and reveals a negative rebound effect in the third quarter after the price rise. Business output tends to decline about 0.09 percent for each percentage point rise in relative energy price. Hence, Tatom's equations show that a 10 percent rise in relative energy prices would raise the price level permanently by about 0.8 percent and contract business output by about 0.9 percent. The output reduction is the result of a direct productivity loss aggravated by an induced fall in the capital–labor ratio [8].

Studies by the Organization for Economic Cooperation and Development (OECD) estimate that a 10 percent rise in oil prices decreases world industrial output about 0.3 percent and increases world inflation about 1 percent.[1]

The *Economist* Intelligence Unit, and the Wharton Econometric Forecasting Associates, forecast that if the nominal price of oil rises 20 percent in 1982, inflation in OECD nations would rise 1 percent, and GNP growth would fall 0.4 percentage points from their base case projections [6]. If we project a 10 percent inflation rate in these nations, the 20 percent hike in oil prices implies a real rise of about 10 percent.

Despite the variance of these estimates, they at least provide order-of-magnitude informed guesses as to direct and indirect impacts. From January 1974 through April 1979 – a period of relative calm after the quadrupling of price in 1973 and before the doubling in 1979–80 – the weighted price of OPEC oil in 1972 dollars rose from \$9.59 a barrel to \$14.40, or at an average annual rate of 7.9 percent. The OECD consumer price index (CPI) advanced at an annual rate of 9 percent. On the basis of the studies quoted, cumulatively, of the price index's rise by 57 percent over this period, only 3.5–4.5 of those percentage points were attributable to the rise in oil price. Even if the studies underestimate by a factor of five, we are still able to account for only 18–23 of those 57 points of rise.

We have constructed an index of weighted industrial production for six OECD nations: the United States, Japan, West Germany, the United Kingdom, France, and Canada. It rose during this period at an annual rate of 3.5 percent. In the absence of the OPEC price rises at an average of 7.9 percent each year, the quoted studies imply that the industrial production of these nations would have run slightly higher, at about 3.7–4.2 percent.

These estimates are crude, and they apply to a period of modest OPEC price action. But they do serve to undermine the proposition that OPEC was a major factor in the past stagflation; by implication, they also challenge the notion that if OPEC's pricing power weakens in the 1980s, a major force will be in motion in overcoming the stagflation experience.

These conclusions do not dismiss OPEC as of negligible economic significance, even in terms of stagflation. An organization that can take advantage of supply reductions, and consuming nations' mistakes, to ratchet the price of oil up by 100 percent in a year can wreak short-run macroeconomic havoc. However, we may hope that 1979–80 has taught us that prices in the short run are driven by consumers' inventory policy and that the seeds of cooperation among consuming nations to avoid panic stockage, planted in the wake of that period of price runup, will take root. Quantum price leaps can then be avoided in the 1980s; price rises, if they occur, will be relatively smooth and restrained.

If so, then the worries about OPEC in the 1980s should focus upon: (1) its ability to tax world income for its own benefit, (2) the welfare loss inflicted upon consuming nations in adjusting to a price that is above marginal cost plus scarcity rent, and (3) the means of financing less developed countries' oil imports. Whether OPEC can survive does therefore matter. An answer requires an analysis of the anatomy and physiology of that organization.

3 Can OPEC Survive?

OPEC is an elastic collusive oligopoly whose dominant policy is the setting of a price pattern for petroleum. It is important to stress that OPEC does not set *the* price of oil or a minimum price of oil. It concerns itself with the pattern of prices of a commodity that is differentiated in quality and location. It anchors this price pattern by setting the price of "marker" crude – Arabian Light 34° oil f.o.b Ras Tanura – which in effect determines the price of the most common quality at a dominant location.

After this price has been negotiated, each nation adds a (positive or negative) quality premium reflecting the specific gravity, sulfur content, and nearness to markets of each type of crude that it sells. If the demand for its oil thereafter exceeds or falls short of a fuzzily determined market share acquiesced in by the organization, a country may add or subtract a market superpremium to bring its liftings close to its "just" share.

OPEC is a price-patterning oligopoly, not a cartel controlling members' outputs. It has never succeeded in obtaining agreement on prorationing, because to do so would demand an unacceptable sacrifice of freedom of action by member nations. To the extent stability of market shares has characterized OPEC's operations – at least until the Iranian revolution – it has been the result , I surmise, of such price patterning constrained by allowable sales restraints.[2] Saudi Arabia, in particular, would lose much of her power within the consortium if she accepted quantitative restrictions on her liftings.

Occasions have been rare, therefore, when member nations have announced autonomous restrictions on output unrelated to conservation or other rational usage restrictions. Rather, prices have been set and market demand satisfied at those prices, and when the amount lifted has encountered reduced demand in a soft market, real prices have been under great pressure to undergo reduction in order to protect pumping levels.

This point is demonstrated in table 10.1, which lists the average daily liftings of 11 of the 13 OPEC members for 1974 into the first five months of 1981.[3] From 1974 through 1979, OPEC output remained between 30 and 31 million barrels per day (mmb/d) with the exception of the deep recession year 1975. The slide in output that began in April 1980 and has accelerated since is wholly a result of reductions in amount demanded. The use of declines in real price per barrel to preserve the lifting level of about 30 mmb/d, and rises when demand strengthened, are also apparent in the data through 1979. The recent market disturbance is putting severe pressure on the superpremia whose expansion ran prices up in 1979–80.

Because OPEC sets price patterns, and because each member in it has a considerable amount of price flexibility, it has proved surprisingly durable.

Table 10.1   Average daily liftings of OPEC, less Ecuador and Gabon, and average weighted OPEC price, 1974–1981 (in real terms)

	Average daily liftings (millions of barrels)	Average price per barrel (1977 dollars)
1974	30.084	12.59
1975	26.603	12.37
1976	30.208	12.12
1977	31.018	12.36
1978	29.885	11.45
1979	30.442	13.89
1980	26.624	21.16[a]
1981 (Jan.–May)	24.133	n.a.

[a] For first half of the year only.

Source: Outputs from *Petroleum Economist*, various issues. Price data are listed prices quoted in *Petroleum Economist*, various issues. Crude types are weighted by estimated proportion of each nation's output to obtain a notional price for each member; national prices are weighted by nations' liftings; and weighted average price is deflated by OECD CPI.

Two- and three-tiered pricing structures have emerged amid predictions that the organization would dissolve, yet it has been able to readjust patterns in the past with a good deal of flexibility. Thus I believe OPEC can survive severe price-pattern strains, because its fuzzy consensus on share entitlements gives it a blend of autonomy and cooperation that would be difficult to achieve among sovereign governments were it to seek rigid market prorationing.

My projection, therefore, is that OPEC can survive the prospective petroleum market conditions of the 1980s and exercise a substantial impact on price. By the same token, I doubt that the majority of members will sacrifice their ability to vary price and exploit short-run market conditions in favor of Saudi Arabia's proposed long-run pricing strategy which seeks quarterly price adjustments on the basis of OPEC's import prices, the foreign exchange value of the dollar, and the growth of industrialized nations' GNP. The Saudi proposal violates what I have interpreted as the functional essence of the organization; if Saudi Arabia should succeed in distress conditions in obtaining reluctant consent, I suspect the strategy will not long survive.

4   The GENESYS Model

The General Economic Systems Project (GENESYS) model of OPEC at Princeton University is a microeconomic model that seeks insights into the structure and decision-making of the organization. It is *not* a forecasting model, but rather tries to project the price pattern that would emerge if each rival sought to maximize its own short-term profit plus the profits of its rivals discounted by factors that aim to catch each rival's potential to affect its own profits. In short, the model attempts to build in the oligopoly power structure as well as the maximum and minimum bounds on output, nation by nation.

Based on my belief that very strong forces exist in OPEC to exploit the short run, our base case seeks to measure whether, in fact, it has done so to its full capability or whether longer-term noneconomic factors have tempered its myopic urges. I envision a short-run normal in which world industrialized activity returns to a prosperous level, inventories are drawn down to normal, and Iran and Iraq resume most of their lifting capacity. Under such conditions, what would the pattern of prices and output be?

The model projects that the average OPEC price would rise to about $69 in current dollars, or roughly *twice* the going price, and that production would fall to 22.520 mmb/d. Saudi Arabian marker crude's price would rise to about $67, but her production would continue at its maximum sustainable level.

Several caveats are in order in interpreting the model. Demand functions for member nations' sales were fitted to only 78 monthly observations available at the time. Those data do not reflect recent conservation moves by industrialized nations, which we consider later. The power structure was included by methods as objective as we could devise, but the process was inescapably judgemental.[4] And the lower bounds on sales were taken to be, rather arbitrarily, at one-half sustainable capacity.

Recognizing the shortcomings, I shall limit myself to qualitative conjectures that arise from large quantitative differences in the model's solution.

First, there is a great deal of short-term profit pressure in normal periods to raise prices substantially higher than the present figures – high enough for most producers to reduce sales to their lower bounds. The magnitudes of these lower bounds therefore become important to consuming nations. Programs that commit OPEC nations to large-scale development are to be welcomed.

Second, although Saudi Arabia's short-term interest is to keep the price low enough to set sales at her capacity output, the country has a collusive profit incentive to roughly double price.

Third, the differentials between the prices of Gulf crudes on the one hand, and African, Venezuelan, and Indonesian crudes on the other, can be substantially higher than they are at present. Hence the pressures that revealed themselves in 1979 and 1980 to widen the quality premia margins, and as market superpremia seem to be endemic in the price structure, the forces that make multitiered price problems probable should persist. New refineries, and the retrofitting of old refineries that are more tolerant of sour crudes, may weaken these forces, but they should persist through the 1980s.

Longer-term tempering of OPEC's pricing power has occurred, largely under the aegis of Saudi Arabia, at some cost in short-run profits. If most OPEC members are driven to the extent I believe by the short-run, and if world demand for OPEC oil approaches the 30 mmb/d at current prices that it experienced in most of 1974–9, we may anticipate a continuation or intensification of upward price pressures and price-pattern conflicts in OPEC's operation. But by the nature of its structure, OPEC should hold together as an entity, especially because Saudi Arabia's own short-run gains in compromising tend to allay somewhat what it perceives as its longer-term losses as prices rise.

5 Conjectures on Future OPEC Power

Will world demand for petroleum in the 1980s afford OPEC the same opportunity for price hikes that it had in the 1970s? The question springs from an optimism concerning a demand reduction for energy in general in the industrialized nations, substitution toward natural gas and coal specifically, and increased supply from non-OPEC sources.

Table 10.2 lists some relevant data for 1979 and 1980 on petroleum product usage. It is worth noting that the reduction in total petroleum consumption in 1980 below 1979 was about 2.76 mmb/d and that the industrialized world's 3 mmb/d reduction was offset by an increase in that of the industrializing nations. From table 10.1, OPEC's liftings fell by 3.18 mmb/d over this time period, which would imply that the drawdown of world stocks, the increase in non-OPEC, non-communist world production, and a cutback in communist-world consumption accounted for a net decrease of about 0.42 mmb/d in this period.

Non-OPEC, non-communist world output rose by 1.02 mmb/d during this period. If we assume the communist world's production and consumption were in balance, this would indicate a build-up of world stocks of about 0.6 mmb/d, or about 219.0 mmb over the year. Although accurate data on total world oil stocks are not available, 5.0–5.5 billion barrels is a useful order-of-magnitude estimate, indicating about a 105-day supply. Hence, on balance over the year, world oil stocks were enhanced by about a 5-day supply. Because this magnitude is negligible, we shall ignore it.

Therefore about one-third of OPEC's output reduction in calendar 1980 resulted from an oil substitution and two-thirds reflected recession and price- and other-induced conservation. Fully 56 percent of the total consumption cutback occurred in the United States; however, much of this must be viewed as a once-for-all reaction to an average price for crude that rose under decontrol from $19.87 to $32.69 per barrel during the year.

Table 10.2   Consumption of petroleum products, 1979 and 1980, with percentage changes

	All petroleum products (mmb/d)[a]		
	1979	1980	Percentage change
Industrialized nations			
USA	17.130	15.580	−9.0
Canada	1.730	1.680	−2.9
W. Europe	13.930	12.950	−7.0
Australasia	0.730	0.710	−2.7
Japan	5.130	4.650	−9.4
Subtotal	38.650	35.570	−8.0
Industrializing nations			
Latin America	4.080	4.150	+1.7
Africa and Middle East	2.670	2.870	+7.5
Indian subcontinent	0.790	0.810	+2.5
Other Asia	1.920	2.010	+4.7
Subtotal	9.460	9.840	+4.0
Total inland consumption	48.110	45.410	−5.6
Total bunker oil usage	2.190	2.130	−2.7
World total	50.300	47.540	−5.5

[a] Million barrels per day.

Source: Petroleum Economist, August 1981, pp. 329–30.

A weighted industrial production index for six major OECD nations, used earlier in this chapter, reveals that an output slump began in April 1980, continuing to the present. For 1980 as a whole, the index slumped 0.9 percent, but for the second half of the year the index was down 3.5 percent from the second half of 1979. Recession must be responsible for a sizeable amount of the decline in consumption.

In the first five months of 1981 the drop in OPEC liftings continued. Output averaged 24.13 mmb/d, down 4.47 mmb/d from the same period in 1980. The industrial production index was off 2.8 percent for the same intervals, while non-OPEC, non-communist world output *expanded* by 0.22 mmb/d. The greater severity of the current experience seems, in good part, the result of inventory decumulation because of very large holding costs brought on by record interest rates, and the widespread fear of falling oil prices. An estimate by the Petroleum Institute Research Foundation is that worldwide inventories (October 1981) are being depleted at rates as high as 1.25 mmb/d when they normally climb by 2.00 mmb/d, for a 3.25 mmb/d net reduction in demand for current output [7].

To summarize, short-run factors – once-for-all price pass-throughs in the

United States, the rise in the exchange value of the dollar, recession in industrialized nations, and cost-induced inventory depletion – seemed to dominate the petroleum market in late 1981. With their passage it is quite possible to envisage on OPEC sales rebound in 1982, or 1983, to 26 or 27 mmb/d with steady growth to 30 mmb/d (or more) in the remainder of the decade. That seems to be a level at which substantial OPEC pricing power will exist, within which non-OPEC, non-communist world production will be content to shelter as it rises.

OPEC in the 1970s has functioned as a price pattern-setter in the world petroleum market, with a longer-run cautionary Saudi Arabian policy constraining the short-run motivation of most other members. The inevitable frictions between these goals have created considerable divisiveness in the organization's operation, but it seems well designed to tolerate these strains.

OPEC should therefore function into the 1980s as an effective pricing power, with the overly sanguine hopes for its demise being born of the shorter-run demand slump. Nonetheless, OPEC's impact on world inflation and recession has been exaggerated in the past. Even if it pursues a steady target real price increase of 4 or 5 percent per year, the macroeconomic impact on the world economy will be tolerable in most economies. Microeconomic impacts, however, may well call for greater international coordination.

Notes

[1] Cited in [1], p. 19.
[2] This stability of market shares has been made the basis of a Markov process approach to the explanation of OPEC behavior by Richard F. Kosobud and Houston H. Stokes. See, for example, [3].
[3] Data limitations in earlier periods forced me to exclude the outputs of Ecuador and Gabon. Their combined lifting is only about 1.5 percent of the OPEC total.
[4] For the derivation of the power structure, see [4].

References

[1] Banks, Ferdinand E., *The Political Economy of Oil*, D.C. Heath, Lexington, MA, 1980.
[2] Fried, Edward R. and Charles L. Schultze (eds), *Higher Oil Prices and the World Economy*, Brookings Institution, Washington, DC, 1975.
[3] Kosobud, Richard F. and Houston H. Stokes, "Short-run OPEC Market Share Behavior and Its Implications", *Energy Economics*, 2 (1980), 66–80.
[4] Kuenne, Robert E., "Rivalrous Consonance and the Power Structure of OPEC", *Kyklos*, 32 (1979), 695–717. [Reprinted as chapter 6 in this volume.]

[5] ——, Jerry Blankenship and Paul F. McCoy, "Optimal Drawdown Strategy for Strategic Petroleum Reserves", *Energy Economics*, 1 (1979), 3–13.
[6] *The Economist*, September 15, 1981.
[7] *New York Times*, September 15, 1981.
[8] Tatom, John A., "Energy Prices and Capital Formation: 1972–1977", *Federal Reserve Bank of St Louis Review*, May (1979), 2–9.
[9] ——, "Energy Prices and Short-run Economic Performance", *Federal Reserve Bank of St Louis Review*, January (1981), 3–17.

Part III

Nonprice Competition in Oligopoly:
Quality, Marketing, and
Spatial Location

Introduction to Part III

In parts I and II the analysis of oligopoly was concerned with determination of prices and quantities of well-defined, undifferentiated or mildly differentiated products where the differentiation was an act of nature and easily standardized. But the very nature of rivalrous consonance implies restrictions on use of price as a competitive variable, and suggests the use of less destabilizing means of competition. My interests for some time, therefore, have been concerned with nonprice competition, and, within it, with quality, marketing, and spatial means of differentiating products.

Incorporating such dimensions into oligopoly theory, and especially general equilibrium models with oligopoly, presents the analyst with very difficult problems, admittedly. Still, I believe microeconomics must turn its attention in earnest to the means of doing so if it is to cope with realistic competitive behavior. And the concept of nonprice competition must be expanded from the three forms listed above to include product innovation as well.

My efforts in meeting this challenge are admittedly only first steps and are displayed in the seven papers of part III. In them I have tried to develop an operational framework with which to organize one's thinking about these matters and to use it to attack specific forms of such competition in oligopoly. One paper is concerned with experiments to test some of the theoretical approaches suggested, but in the other papers I have remained at the conceptual level. My fondest hope would be that these ideas and methods might stimulate others to make progress on this most difficult terrain.

Chapter 11 contains the framework I suggest as a means of incorporating product differentiation into general equilibrium theory. It is an alternative to the Lancaster approach of treating some product qualities as capable of being combined linearly in a quality space, proposing instead that goods within an industry be defined by their possession of a common set of "core" qualities or attributes and variations in a fringe of "noncore" qualities or attributes. It rejects Triffin's suggestion of dropping the concept of the industry in favor of the "product group" defined by cross-elasticities on the grounds that the industry is too valuable an analytical construct to sacrifice. Definition of products by physical attributes independent of consumer preferences seems to me to be a more fruitful approach to use in operational practice. *Interproduct* rather than *interfirm* competition when the former is extended to firms *within* an industry as well as *between* industries seems to me a more natural extension of general equilibrium theory and more practical as well when oligopoly systems are considered.

In my formal treatment of interproduct competition within a general equilibrium framework, however, I remain within a monopolistically competitive economy, rather than introducing the complications of differentiated oligopoly, and concentrate upon product qualities (where such qualities can include spatial location) to the exclusion of marketing costs. In order to "measure" the intensity of such product qualities I assume that scalings of the qualities are possible on the unit interval. With this assumption my concern with "fuzzy" or "pseudo" measurement is initially broached, and, as indicated in the introduction to part II, it has remained a continuing interest of mine (see chapter 12). This implies a willingness to ignore the theory of measurement and its demands upon uniqueness up to an affine transformation or a positive multiplicative constant in order to derive empirically justified "cardinal" measures when intensities can only be ranked or when they are 0, 1 attributes. In modern nonprice competition I view attributional competition – possession of brand names or patents, for example – as extremely important.

Every actual or potentially feasible product can be depicted as a point in multidimensional quality-space and its distance from every other such product in that space is derivable. Core and fringe qualities can be defined for each product and product groups or industries derived as those products possessing core qualities. A rather elaborate process of choice by firms of a product in quality-space on the basis of expected profits enfolds, and supply functions for the product and demands for inputs emerge. Consumer preference functions over all actual and potential products are the basis for demand functions for such products and supply functions for factor services. Prices, products in production, and quantities of products and inputs are then determined in a general equilibrium.

The remaining six selections attempt to develop these ideas more fully within less ambitious contexts. As in the case of depicting the power structure in an oligopoly, discussed in parts I and II, until operational measures of product differentiation can be obtained substantial progress in incorporating it in microeconomic theory will be lacking. Chapter 12 devises such a methodology and experiments with it to see whether consistent results are obtained for such "measures" from a succession of such trials with different subjects. I have already introduced a similar technique for isolating OPEC's power structure in chapter 6, but the motivation and explication of the methods there employed are presented here in greater detail, and other complexities are confronted as well. As a preparation for this work, and as a means of explaining its scientific limitations, a brief excursion into relevant measurement theory is included.

Beginning with Hotelling's seminal work on location of firms in a linear market, the notion of using distance metrics in a quality-space to define differentiated products has been used frequently. In chapters 1 and 11 I have used the notion of such distance measures in theoretical frameworks that confront product differentiation in a multidimensional product space, and in the remaining selections of part III I extend these methods in a variety of directions. Location in a two-dimensional space is an important application of product differentiation, and, of course, the ability to use the Euclidean or metropolitan metric to measure such differentiation raises no problems since they conform to the dictates of the theory of measurement. But with other forms of product differentiation where other qualities and attributes are in question the "measurement" of distances in quality-attribute n-dimensional space becomes most controversial because one must venture beyond the comforting confines of measurement theory.

As noted in my discussions of chapters 6 and 11, my belief is that economists must develop "fuzzy" or "pseudo" measurement scalings whose justification must be wholly empirical and practical: i.e. that they perform their tasks acceptably and better than any other tool available for these tasks. Chapter 12 makes this argument, I hope convincingly.

Scaling methods introduced in chapter 6 are employed to obtain these measures of distance. Cross-factor analysis, also presented in chapter 6, is used to derive the relative weights of each quality in defining the product. To demonstrate the method and test its consistency among different groups of subjects, I chose five brands of candy bars with seven different qualities, most of which were quite subjective and abstruse in nature (e.g. packaging, external color, chewiness). I present three different methods of deriving weights reflecting the "importance" of the qualities in product definition, and the results of four different experimental runs are presented. Also, scalings were derived for each quality and each sample of subjects, and analysis of variance was performed on the results to measure consistency of outcomes.

The results were that subjects' *scalings* over brands and qualities varied significantly and nonrandomly and that scalings among subjects for given brands and qualities varied only randomly. Hence the results of the scaling experiments were most encouraging in suggesting that these methods yield consistent perceived distances for qualities along normalized axes and for product differentiation involving quite challenging qualities. With respect to the *weights* derived over the samples, the three methods yielded almost identical results. Finally, *interproduct distances*, which combined scalings and weights, conformed closely over samples. Indeed, the consensus was surprising, given the abstruse nature of most of the qualities.

As noted in the selection, consistency of the results among subjects is no guarantee that we have "measured" that which we set out to measure. But I feel it is encouraging to the degree that such distances can be incorporated in the demand functions for products with hope of empirically demonstrated usefulness.

Chapter 13 was written as a contribution to a Joan Robinson *Festschrift* and begins with a discussion of her desire to preserve the Marshallian industry as a theoretical construct by associating differentiation with the seller of a homogeneous product rather than heterogeneous products. The analysis moves to a suggested operational manner of incorporating price and product differentiation decisions in rivalrous and nonrivalrous contexts. In the oligopoly analysis, both rivalrous consonance and noncooperative market structures are considered.

The manner of measuring products in quality-space differs somewhat from the techniques suggested in chapters 11 and 12, although it draws upon the distinction between core and noncore qualities made in the former and the notion of distance in a quality-space developed in both papers. It gauges such distances by posing questions to consumers that evaluate quality differences in dollar amounts (positive or negative) that would make them indifferent between hypothetical brands. This yields a ratio scale measure of distance for quality-space calculations. Moreover, these same dollar measures can be used to derive the weights accorded to each quality, permitting distance measures for brands to be calculated. Some disadvantages attach to the method, of course. The dollar indifference values are assumed to be additive, for example, and they are also assumed to be independent of the amounts consumed.

Using these measures of product quality and the costs of changes in such qualities, the firm maximizes profits with respect to price and quality. Comparative statics are used to study the nature of the interaction between the two decision variables and the nature of the trade-offs between them. This is done successively for isolated firms (pure competition or monopoly), for firms in myopic, Cournot-type oligopoly, and for oligopolistic firms in rivalrous consonance. The propositions derived are quite complicated and become more so as movement is made from the first to the last of these industry structures. They depend, for example, upon such characteristics as the second derivatives of the demand curves for the firms. Hence, the trade-offs between price and quality changes are most difficult to predict in the absence of a good deal of specific qualitative information about relevant functions. It will be necessary to resort to simulative theorizing to get definitive answers for interesting types of oligopolistic market structure.

For me, however, the method of measuring product differentiation and of incorporating it in the oligopolistic firm's decision-making simultaneously with price policy is an important step in the right direction for microeconomic theory. That it complicates the theorist's frameworks and may force abandonment of simple general theories with determinate solutions in favor of simulation is an unfortunate fact of analytical life that must be faced.

Chapters 14 and 17 form a closely linked body of research that focuses upon recent developments in the economies of developed countries, which will be discussed in greater detail below. The former selection constructs a model which introduces space as an impediment to the flow of information from producers to consumers. Advertising and marketing expenditures by firms, therefore, decline in their effectiveness both in increasing own-sales and in reducing other-sales as distance from the customer increases. A simple model is constructed to study the manners in which price, profits and advertising expenditures on the part of differentiated oligopolies react to a variety of situations, such as changes in the distance between producers, changes in the parameters for advertising effectiveness, and cases in which one, both, or neither of the firms advertise. The research paths that are suggested in the conclusion are explored in chapter 17, and will be discussed below, after the introduction of some other concepts that will make the discussion richer.

In chapter 15 I begin a series of papers which deal with firm location as a variable in oligopolistic nonprice competition. This paper analyzes the optimal locations, prices and allocation of markets in a two-dimensional space, when those markets are points and the distance metric used is "pseudo-Euclidean." The latter is a extended form of the Euclidean distance measure which allows the power to which the sum of the squares of the distances of latitude and longitude is raised to differ from 0.5. This permits the distance metric to adjust for the characteristics of realistic transportation rate schedules.

One of the points I make in this paper – and which is a common theme in prior selections – is the inability to obtain closed solutions in many oligopoly problems, especially in spatial contexts, in the absence of simplifying assumptions that seriously limit the usefulness of the results. I urge the development of an "econometrics of simulation" to be applied to the use of that technique in deriving insights into decision-making in oligopolistic market structures. This need is eminently demonstrated in the present paper because of the extremely complex nature of the interdependence displayed even in relatively simple location problems. In order to arrive at solutions to the set of models discussed in this paper it was necessary to use jointly nonlinear programming and branch-and-bound combinatorial methods requiring a numerical specification of relevant functions.

The two algorithms used in these solutions – SUMTOL, an adaptation of the SUMT nonlinear programming algorithm developed by Fiacco and

McCormick which was discussed in chapter 1's appendix, and SPATOL, a multisource Weber problem solution method using combinatorial techniques developed by Kuenne and Soland – were applied sequentially in an iterative manner to permit solutions to converge from initial estimates to optimal values. The method is applicable to any polygon formed by the convex hull of the variable number of markets, and permits any number of firms to be specified, although branch-and-bound algorithms require extremely large storage space for numbers of firms in excess of 12. Also, the method permits a rivalrous consonance oligopoly environment with subgoal constraints to be specified. However, for the present paper I adopted arbitrarily a square with area 100, eight markets at corners and midpoints of the boundaries of the square, and from one to four rivals, and analyzed the purely competitive Cournot case and Chamberlin joint-profit cases.

I have also used the model to specify the social cost in lost consumer and producer surplus of moving from pure competition to the various oligopoly solutions. In the simulation experiments social cost declines quite rapidly as the number of firms is increased, and, in general, for these problems is quite small.

An independent contribution of the selection is the definition of a measure of compactness for the polygonal convex hulls of market points. The *index of circular compactness* employs the area and perimeter of the polygon to give a measure of the dispersion of these markets with values on the unit interval bounded by 0 for a straight line and 1 for the circle. I feel that this index may have other uses in spatial economics.

The selection is introduced by a discussion of various forms of the Hotelling problem of location in a linear market and the difficulties arising when some of his simplifying assumptions are altered.

The concern with the economics of spatial location in oligopoly is continued in chapter 16, with some repetition but with a broader purview as well. It reviews the state of research in the field and finds that its relative stagnation springs from an increasing realization of the complexity of the problems inherent in the interdependence. Increasingly, resort to simulation is seen to be necessary for analysis of the existence of equilibria and the potential for reactive processes to converge to them. If the same or a limited number of steady-state solutions are reached from a large variety of initial positions, one can hypothesize that optimal solutions exist. In this manner the questions of whether a solution exists and whether the reactive process allows it be achieved merge into the same problem.

The paper suggests several research directions for the field. Predictably, two of them are simulative theorizing and rivalrous consonance, and little more need be said about them. They are indicated by the revealed and unavoidable sterility of traditional frameworks available to the theorist. A third route is the incorporation of stochastic process theory. All three suggested extensions reinforce the conclusion that simulation is the fruitful approach to oligopolistic location research in the future.

As noted in the discussion of chapter 14, chapter 17 constitutes an attempt to broaden the scope of the term "marketing" (or "advertising," which I have used synonymously) developed in chapter 14 to include activities that evolve from the structural changes in industry that are emerging worldwide. The growing importance of small to medium-sized firms, competing intensely with a small number of rivals for the sale of highly specialized, technically advanced, customer-specific components, where such firms are capable of rapid retooling and small-lot production to meet changing demands, is clear. Mass production runs of a limited variety of standardized products are a declining portion of industrial activity in advanced countries. Sales efforts in the future will concentrate more upon maintaining close personal and impersonal contacts with potential and actual customers, aiding them in production design, helping them to perceive the implications of technological advances, and working closely to achieve and maintain desired product quality. In short, information flow will grow in importance, and the role of space as an inhibitor of such flows will enlarge relative to its classic imposition of barriers to goods movement, as "nearness" to customers in a broad informational sense becomes important.

Incorporating this form of nonprice competition in a spatially specific oligopolistic framework is the subject of the paper, and seeking insights from comparative statics exercises using simulation analysis suggested in chapter 14 is a major purpose. The model constructed in chapter 14 is improved and used as model 1 in this paper. The model features duopolistic competition in a linear market where firms' sales are functions of own- and other-prices, transport rate, distance from customers, and the size of marketing budgets for both rivals. That is, in addition to boosting its own sales, firm i's marketing expenditures have negative attrition effects upon firm j's sales. Marketing effects of both types are assumed to decline exponentially with distance from the firm, while transport costs are proportionate to distance.

Three simulation cases are defined, two of them based on the relative importance of the spatial effects on marketing effectiveness and transport costs, and the third with firms capturing some of the loss in sales they inflict upon their rivals by their marketing. For each of the three cases four variants are run, depending upon whether both firms engage in marketing, only one does, or neither does. In general, the solutions suggest marketing budgets should rise to substantial proportions of revenue. Finally, a large number of parameter changes are introduced to obtain induced changes in prices, sales, marketing budgets, and profits.

The striking feature of the comparative statics analysis is that firms move prices and sales expenditures in parallel fashion rather than countering rises in a competitor's marketing budget with reduced prices. That is, even when no overt collusion occurs the firms act in a seemingly cooperative manner. The weaker firm almost invariably follows the lead of the stronger when it increases price and/or marketing budget. This is a most interesting support for my notion of rivalrous consonance: the drives in such industries to tacit cooperation would be quite strong.

Some of the less satisfying features of model 1 led me to construct a more sophisticated model 2, which is reproduced in section 3 of the paper. However, in the simulation runs I could not get consistent convergence, whether because of structural defects or algorithmic problems I have not discerned. However, the relationships introduced into model 2 are those which I believe should somehow be included in future work. Beyond these changes, more simply obtained improvements include the introduction of a larger number of firms and of rivalrous consonance in model 1.

11

Quality-space, Interproduct Competition, and General Equilibrium Theory

1 Some Problems of Introducing Monopolistic Competition into General Equilibrium Theory

The Chamberlinian revolution has not imposed on the body of Walrasian microgeneral analysis the valuable reconstruction that the Keynesian revolution forced on Ricardian macrogeneral systems. The enlightened confusion that the concept of the product group introduced into particular-equilibrium analysis – as these groups affect consumers' choice, the firm's decisions in isolation, and the interrelationships among firms – has been most embarrassing to the existing microeconomic general frameworks. For the most part, however, practitioners in the field have met the challenge somewhat in the manner of the staunch old Scottish Presbyterian minister who urged his flock to face up courageously to the unsettling modern dogma of free will by grasping the doctrinal bull firmly by its dilemma-shaped horns, looking it squarely in the eyes, and then walking resolutely around it.

J. R. Hicks, for example, in one and a half pages of his 340-page classic, noted that the introduction of monopolistic competition "must have very destructive consequences for economic theory," and concluded that the danger of using purely competitive theory in general-equilibrium analysis must be run.[1]

There is (alas!) much to be said for this position, and I have taken a similar stand on the more general question of the uses of simplicity [4]. The *corpus* of analysis that we may refer to as the "original neoclassical general-equilibrium theory" – most particularly the labors of Walras and Pareto, but

Originally published as chapter 10 of Robert E. Kuenne (ed.), *Monopolistic Competition Theory Studies in Impact*, John Wiley & Sons, New York, 1968 and reproduced with permission.

including the relevant work of Fisher and Wicksell – was a step backward from the "general" macroeconomic system of Ricardo and the classical economists in at least one important feature, which explains much of the historical impact[2] of the latter model and the success of its Keynesian reaction. We shall borrow terms from the field of medicine which, although not fully descriptive of the distinction we seek to develop, do serve to bring out its major features.

Walras and Pareto were most successful in those aspects of general systems analysis that I will call *anatomical* or *morphological*, by which I mean a concern with depicting the *structure* of the large-scale market system at rest. This led them to adopt the market as the elemental "organ" of *general* systems analysis and to produce an anatomical chart of that system in a steady state by listing the conditions describing the organs taken separately in that state. Although the vital, functional interrelationships *within* the market as well as the course of the adjustments they enforce – what I shall call the *physiology* of the market – were described in detail, and although these men were extremely desirous of tracing out the functioning of each market as it acted on and reacted to other markets, the physiology of the market *system* remained uncharted in the works of Walras, Pareto, Fisher, and Wicksell.

On the other hand, Ricardo, when the occasion demanded, fell back from a cost-of-production theory of value to a labor-quantity theory of value to simplify the anatomy of his economic model. By assuming that all sectors had the same period of production, that working capital and fixed capital were employed in a rigid proportion throughout the economy, that the elasticity of substitution between labor and machinery was universally zero, that diminishing returns existed in the land and resources sectors whereas constant returns ruled in manufacturing, and that the production of human beings occurred under the regime of the Malthusian response to income change – Ricardo produced a model with a simple physiology as well. The interdependent functioning of sector with sector could be traced in relevant detail to yield propositions with meaningful empirical content and social significance.

In general, the simpler the anatomy of the organism, the easier the physiological examination and the more numerous (though not necessarily the more valuable – few economists were so consistently misleading as Ricardo) the propositions derived on its vital responses to changes in its environment or its functioning by virtue of its own inner logic. The fewer the organs – consumption–investment–goverment sectors, for example, in lieu of product and factor service markets – the more discernible their patterns of systemic functioning, even if their own internal physiology is less discernible. The choice of the market (including markets for all inputs and outputs of an economy) as the organ of the system might be to approach real-world decision-making more closely. Moreover, the development of marginalism might allow the physiological workings of the organ itself to be better mapped than if the organs were consumption, or investment, or government sectors. But the very realism of such detailed anatomical charts and physiology in the small militates against discerning the flows of causation and association among the organs, and debars the derivation of theorems dependent on this discernment. On these rocks the original neoclassical general-equilibrium analysis foundered.

A revivified interest in the physiology of large-scale systems occurred in the 1930s and 1940s, led by such men as Hotelling, Hicks, Leontief, and Samuelson. Through the use of Slutsky effects, second-order extremum conditions, stability-of-equilibrium conditions, and linearity of production relationships, some progress was made. However, their efforts – brilliant and innovating as they were – have not yielded any dramatic breakthroughs. During the past 10 or 15 years the current of interest has set against these efforts to trace the qualitative characteristics of the adaptations of large-scale systems to changes in their environments via scraps of knowledge concerning their anatomies or components' physiologies. It is true that efforts to establish the stability of *tâtonnement* and *nontâtonnement* processes in multiple exchange, to introduce expectations into the study of the stability of equilibrium in a dynamic multiple-exchange model, and to determine the peculiarities of growth paths in constrained and unconstrained von Neuman dynamic linear models have yielded some insights into the physiology of market systems. Indeed, the renewed interest in microdynamic models itself evinces a concern for system physiology.

But, to a greater extent, newer mathematical advances in point-set topology and linear systems analysis have been adapted by investigators to redraw the anatomical chart with finer lines, or to design models to be filled with data for specific solutions. Perhaps of greatest importance in this line of endeavor has been the study of the necessary and sufficient conditions on the data and postulates of the model to assure the existence (and sometimes the uniqueness) of stationary solutions in both static and dynamic models, the latter efforts somewhat misleadingly termed the study of "the stability of systems." Some of the advances in drawing a more accurate anatomical chart, such as the recognition of the frequent occurrence of corner solutions rather than interior solutions to a system, have yielded, along with the greater realism of the chart, a more complicated and less fruitful system physiology when data cannot be poured into the model.

1.1 Neoclassical Anatomy

In the anatomy of neoclassical general-equilibrium theory, a good case may be made for viewing the "good" as the most fundamental unit of interest for the system, using that term to include all inputs and outputs. The physiology of those general systems sought to depict the vital process of competition among these goods for production and use. Products were substitutes among themselves for usage among consumers (and among firms if intermediate products were included in the model), whereas factor services were substitutes within firms, either directly or via product mixes in the case of fixed coefficients (and among consumers if factor services were placed in the domain of consumer choice).

These goods were distinguished on the basis of physical qualities alone, because the number and types of distinct goods were part of the data set and could not be distinguished by properties that depended on values of the variables not yet determined. Along with other implications of the (illegitimate but simplifying) assumption of interior solutions it was tacitly postulated that all potentially producible goods were in fact produced and consumed in nonzero quantities, although indeed there were some clumsy attempts by Walras and Pareto to meet the problem of corner solutions. The variables whose values were sought in solutions, therefore, were nonzero values for prices and quantities associated with goods.

These values were determined by a set of interrelated "organs" of the system: the markets. By a simplification firms were assumed to produce a single good, to be thereby unambiguously associated with a single industry, and to be sellers in a single market. Intermarket relations reflected interproduct competition, and these intermarket relations were derived from the maximizing actions of the two decision-making units of the model, consumers and firms. Their existence and functioning provided (1) the dynamics of the physiology of each market taken separately and (2) the anatomical features that integrated the markets into an organic whole.

But their existence also led to a danger for a determinate physiology in each market and for a determinate anatomy for the whole system. Underlying interproduct competition, of course, was the competition of consumer with consumer, firm with firm, and consumer with firm, which provided the energy for the dynamics of each market and of the whole system. Indeed, interproduct or intermarket competition could be abstracted as a fictitious force only if this underlying competition took a specific form – nonrivalrous competition. Only if every consumer and every firm were completely isolated from unpredictable external feedbacks of their own decision-making, so that no case of conscious rivalry among decision-makers existed within any market or between markets, could the interproduct competition yield solutions which were anonymous in terms of the actors on the stage. From the viewpoint of the anatomy of the neoclassical general system, seen from this vantage, there were only two types of "interunit" competition – rivalrous and nonrivalrous.

Pure competition in all markets, of course, was a sufficient condition for the nonrivalrous variety of interunit competition, but so was so-called "pure monopoly." In fact Pareto succeeded in constructing an economy with two products and two monopolists, exploiting the only other known nonrivalrous form at the time. If interunit competition were nonrivalrous in every market the physiology of each market could grind out determinate results when presented with price information summarizing the relevant information concerning all other goods from all other markets. The physiology of the *system* could be vaguely depicted in the form of iterative conceptual experiments, beginning with some arbitrary set of prices, confronting one market with it to get an equilibrium price to be substituted in the price set, moving to the second market for a similar operation, and so forth, until, it is hoped, after a number of such cycles a steady state would emerge. Such halting first steps as Walras's *tâtonnement* process and the rather simple explanation he gives of the multitude of forces active in its dynamics will illustrate at once the method and sketchy nature of the physiology.

To my way of thinking – and it is admittedly biased in the direction of general-equilibrium methodology – the most important innovation of the Chamberlinian revolution was to alter the nature of the interproduct competition while retaining the postulational basis for ignoring interunit competition or, realistically, interfirm competition. In Chamberlin's treatment of the latter nothing vitally new was said when it became rivalrous; rather, the important changes were to alter significantly a separable product competition within an anonymous context. The product group replaces "the product"; markets are decomposed into clusters of closely competing submarkets in nonrivalrous firm competition; variation of the product becomes a potential; and variable selling costs are introduced as a major force in interproduct competition. Through it all, however, insofar as this major contribution is concerned, nonrivalrous firm competition keeps interproduct competition determinate.

In this chapter 1 take the next step, which seems not yet to have been taken, to construct a general-equilibrium system in which all interproduct competition is composed of product groups of closely competing products physically similar to each other but dissimilar from others. The "large-group case" of Chamberlin, therefore, or, more generally, any form of nonrivalrous interfirm competition, is built into the general-equilibrium system. Let it be said at once that my analysis remains wholly at the anatomical level, and, in the absence of empirical material to fill in the model, it becomes almost impossible to derive operational theorems from it concerning its systemic functioning. Conceptually, corner solutions are unavoidable, and parametric programming methods that might permit limited "shocks" to be evaluated are not yet developed. All of the insights that the model provides, therefore, must derive from the anatomical features of it – its functional form at rest. Although it is hoped that these features will possess some interest and value, the position stated by Hicks is not challenged by its creation.

2 Triffin's Pioneering Efforts

The most celebrated and justly honored consideration of the implications of Chamberlin's analysis for general-equilibrium theory is that of Robert Triffin [10]. Although he regarded the rigorous formulation of a more complete general system incorporating monopolistic competition as one desideratum, Triffin did not essay the task, preferring instead to define some of the problems as he saw them and to prepare some necessary conceptual ground. I believe, however, that in so doing Triffin took a misleading position in the interpretation of both the core of Chamberlin's contribution and the nature of existing general-equilibrium analysis, thereby pointing out a more difficult route than the inner logic of both theories requires for their integration.

To Triffin the central contribution of monopolistic competition theory was its promise of focusing theoretical attention on the external relationships of the firm with other firms and on the constraints these relationships impose on the firm's behavior. To work these relationships into the body of Walrasian theory, and thereby to restate that theory, is the goal as he sees it. Monopolistic competition theory, constructed by Chamberlin and Mrs Robinson within the framework of Marshallian partial-equilibrium theory, incorporates in its original form only intra-industry firm relationships and isolates the firm from extra-industry firms; but it is a potential bridge over the canyon separating Marshallian analysis from the Walrasian incorporation of *all* interfirm relationships.[3]

My pair of objections to Triffin's position is derived from the analysis presented in the previous section of this paper. They are not unrelated, but both bear heavily on the tasks ahead of us and are therefore worthy of detailed and separate treatment. First, I would dispute his belief that the basic approach of the Walrasian and Paretian analysis was to incorporate in some meaningful way the extra-industry interfirm competition that he believes Marshall's analysis omits; and second, I believe it to be not so much the prospect of working revolutionary types of interfirm competition into the general-equilibrium framework that Chamberlin's analysis affords as it is the injection of interproduct competition into that system with the same nonrivalrous interfirm competition as existed in it originally.

We have seen that the elemental analytical unit of Walras's system was not the firm but rather the market.[4] Because each firm was assumed to produce only one product, homogeneous with the products of other firms, it could be unambiguously assigned to a distinct industry and forgotten. Far from providing the major focus for Walrasian analysis, the firm is merged into the body of the industry as an indeterminate, shadowy entity, as Walras's fixed coefficients and constant costs forced him to the industry. The industry – in a one-to-one correspondence with markets and products – became the production entity of sole concern, because only its output quantity was determinate. Although he treated the case of the firm's equilibrium in greater detail than Walras and included pure monopoly in his analysis, Pareto also made the purely competitive market the core of his *system* analysis. When he introduced monopoly into the general system it was the completely isolated type of pure monopoly, whose major implication for systemic relations was to eliminate interfirm competition.[5]

The interrelationships of these industries through markets in Walras were, of course, universally nonrivalrous, and, indeed, purely competitive. Pure competition is used within the market and between markets to abstract from the very interdependence Triffin seems to detect in Walras and Pareto. The anatomies of markets in Marshall's long-run particular-equilibrium analysis and in Walras's general-equilibrium analysis are alike: price equals average and marginal cost. In the physiological attainment of this structure Marshall's *ceteris paribus* froze other-market price reactions at zero levels, whereas general-equilibrium analysis allowed these other-market price reactions to influence the functioning of the disequilibrated market. But it was in just such physiological analysis that general-equilibrium theorists were so weak. This abstract freedom of other prices to vary was largely academic, because its major use was merely suggestive of potential variation by virtue of the presence of all prices in the anatomical functions depicting the economy at rest. Qualitatively, the same type of solution in every market was attained as in particular-equilibrium analysis, and such quantitative differences as existed in the market's price-output solutions with both methods were not analyzable.

But even if we were to view the achievement of the general-equilibrium theorists more generously, Triffin's position is still not supported. The industry in Walras is treated as a myopic decision-maker that ignores the negative slope of its sales curve and is isolated from all rivalrous competition with other such fictitious decision-makers. The interdependence that existed in such a world of industries through market prices was unrecognized because it appeared to industries only as their own prices fluctuated, was nonrivalrous, and was unanalyzable by the theorist in general terms. And firms are *ignes fatui*.

Therefore, when Triffin writes the following passage, I believe it to be misleading in any "physiology of the system" sense and only partially true in an "anatomy of the system" interpretation. Indeed, the second paragraph of the passage may reveal some of his own doubts:

As for the "industry" or "group," it could only appear to general equilibrium theorists as a far too timid substitute for a fuller recognition of the generality of economic interdependence throughout the system, permeating all the "industries" composing the collectivity as well as the firms composing any one of these industries. The general equilibrium approach, however, was from the start and remains to this very day, dominated by the purely competitive assumptions of the Walrasian system. [10], p. 10

Triffin's interpretation of particular-equilibrium analysis as the study of relations among firms in one industry (or group) and of general-equilibrium analysis as the study of interrelations among all firms is therefore a distortion [10], p. 67. We have seen that the neoclassical general theory was, rather, one of interdependent markets linking goods primarily and firms and consumers only incidentally in anonymous patterns. There was no yawning canyon separating Marshallian and Walrasian theory in these senses: both theories were structured with markets in the foreground and with a simple correspondence between products and industries. Walras took into explicit account in his morphology the interdependence of these markets but speedily abandoned most of it in his limited search for a physiology; Marshall simply skipped the first step in his anatomizing. And, indeed, in a judgement of which of the two theorists spent more time in the analysis of the firm and its relations with other firms, certainly it is Marshall, not Walras, who must be given the palm.

By interpreting general-equilibrium analysis as a system that emphasizes firm interdependence, Triffin concludes that monopolistic competitive techniques must be used to build into that theory thorough-going interfirm competition with product differentiation. The "industry," "group," and "commodity" must go:

> In the general pure theory of value, the group and the industry are useless concepts. The new wine of monopolistic competition should not be poured into the old goatskins of particular equilibrium methodolgy. When the study of competition is freed from the narrowing assumptions of pure competition, only two terms remain essential for the analysis: the individual firms, on the one hand; the whole collectivity of competitors on the other. It is out of these materials that a general theory of economic interdependence can be built most simply and conveniently.[6] [10], p. 89

At this point I have reached the second area of disagreement with Triffin. It does not seem to me that these materials provide the means for the simple and convenient introduction of the Chamberlinian complication into general-equilibrium theory. We have seen that the original general-equilibrium theories was also anatomized around the goods market, and that competition among these goods was featured. It was *interproduct* competition in the peculiar environment defined when firms (1) produced only one good, (2) produced goods homogeneous with other firms' goods, and (3) bought and sold negligible proportions of goods. An important function of these three assumptions was to prevent the theory from becoming one of interfirm competition in a rivalrous sense, that is, in the only way that could make interproduct competition inseparable from interfirm competition. Triffin seems, at times, entirely ready to embrace oligopolistic competition in a general system with all the anatomical and, more importantly, physiological complications it entails.[7] This is certainly a rational position, and may in the end prove to be the only useful construction. But by insisting on the *ad hoc* model it forestalls an attempt to employ existing frameworks. Abjuring the palimpsest, Triffin wants to burn the classic parchment.

Moreover, in my judgement – and here many will disagree – the core of the Chamberlin contribution is concerned with a significant alteration in interproduct competition, while interfirm competition remains incidental and analytically uninteresting. This is true, I believe, despite Chamberlin's generalization of his concepts to include rivalrous firm competition. In the first edition of the work "monopolistic competition" was defined to mean the existence of differentiated products with large or small numbers of producers [2], p. 8. Pure oligopoly was not included. But see also pp. 8–9 of the sixth edition, where the large-group case is introduced with the concept of product differentiation, and differentiated oligopoly is a footnoted second thought concerning the blend of monopoly and competition. In the core chapter of the book, chapter V, the large-group case receives 36 of the 46 pages. Therefore only in his later work did Chamberlin extend the concept of monopolistic competition to rivalrous firm competition with homogeneous products, but in this case as in the case of oligopoly with differentiated products he added interesting refinements but little of great novelty to existing duopoly theory, unless a new source of indeterminateness may be so classified for the second case.

In effect, Mrs Robinson remains with the large-group case, her market "imperfections" being very close (but importantly nonidentical[8]) to Chamberlin's "product differentiation." She did formally assume that the sales curve of the firm included the effects of any rivalrous competitors reacting to its policies [8], p. 21, but despite this bow to oligopolistic competition Mrs Robinson at other points in the analysis ignores it to deal exclusively with the large-group case. For example, in discussing the determinants of the elasticity of the firm's sales curve she mentions only the number and substitutability of competing products, not reactions of other sellers of close substitutes (pp. 50–1). At another point she says that competition may be imperfect either because a few firms sell a homogeneous product or because the large-group case exists but she ignores the former in talking of the relation of price and marginal revenue in imperfect competition

(p. 86). And, later, her statement of the equilibrium conditions for imperfect competition is readily interpretable only for the large-group case (p. 94).

Triffin at one point asserts that the successful introduction of monopolistic competition theory into general-equilibrium theory depends on the adoption of a device to limit monopolistic tendencies, such as that found in the large-group case of Chamberlin, and, indeed, asserts that this case is a "most essential contribution" to general-equilibrium theory [10], pp. 10–11.[9] But if this type of assumption is made, interfirm competition is pushed into the background. Unless in fact he is willing to embrace rivalrous firm competition in a general system, his criticism of Chamberlin for remaining within the large group instead of generalizing his analysis to an interdependence of all firms seems misplaced, given the context of his aims at some places in his book [10], p. 77. In the large-group case product competition is featured and interfirm competition is ancillary.[10] The problems of which specific forms of product to produce, how much of what types of advertising to buy for each product, and so forth, now exist for the multiproduct firm in a rivalrous product group but a nonrivalrous interfirm competitive position. Building these into a general system may move us a step farther in economic theory.

In view of the preceding argument, I believe that the "product group" does make good analytical sense, just as "the product" did in neoclassical general-equilibrium analysis. To my way of thinking, Triffin is much too ready to overthrow the idea that it is possible to partition products into groups that possess a core of physical qualities involving them in intense competition with one another for production, sales, and factor services. If the major contribution of Chamberlin and Mrs Robinson was to single out this inter-product competition and to intensify it in ways that minimized interfirm competition in order to keep the analysis determinate,[11] retention of the essential outlines of the "industry" or "group" and the "market" may afford the most promising methods of extending the newer techniques to general-equilibrium theory. The interrelation of nonrivalrous firms via product markets is the "natural" extension of monopolistic competition into general-equilibrium theory, and should be tried before ambitions are extended to introduce rivalrous types of interfirm competition as well.

Besides, Triffin's alternatives have a basic flaw as concerns their use in a *formal* general-equilibrium setting. He desires to classify goods and the rivalrous or nonrivalrous relations of the firms producing them by cross-elasticities involving quantity reactions of other firms to a given firm's price adjustments, and price adjustment of the given firm to these other firms' reactive quantity adjustments. But these measures involve variables in the solutions to the general system, not the data, for presumably the partial derivatives, prices, and quantities involved in their calculation are to be taken in the neighborhood of a general-equilibrium solution. They are part of the set of characteristics of the model to be determined in the neighborhood of that equilibrium, and although such measures may be applicable in the world of particular equilibrium Triffin is criticizing, they cannot be used easily in the classification of goods in a formal general-equilibrium model.

In these respects we shall follow the lead of Sraffa, as did Mrs Robinson. His classic article tends to retain the idea of the commodity and views the homogeneous market to pure competition as broken into a group of related, distinct submarkets carved out because of consumer preferences for *producers* rather than products [9].[12]

We shall, in the general-equilibrium model to follow, introduce monopolistic competition by accepting the physically defined product group as meaningful analytically, by studying interrelated product markets, by adopting the assumption of nonrivalrous interfirm competition, and by employing the "industry" or "group" – all in the neoclassical tradition of general equilibrium. We shall correct the retention in Chamberlin of the single-product firm, for it is much more fraught with limitations in his case than in the case of the neoclassical general-equilibrium theorists. The adoption of this device led Chamberlin to ignore – except for some attention to the case of discrimination – the isolated firm's decisions as to how many "model variations" of a given product to produce, or what kind of a differentiated-product-group slice to adopt. Also, in these first efforts we shall abstract from the complications of advertising and other selling costs, although these should not be too difficult to include in later work.

Lastly, we shall remain (unfortunately) at the level of system morphology, and shall not attempt those simplifications in the structure that might allow displacements to be evaluated, if indeed this kind of analysis is possible with the model. The results, therefore, are quite limited, but, I believe, may be important as initial steps in extending the domain of static general-equilibrium systems in such a way as to improve our system physiology.

3 Quality and Product Space

Let us assume, in the freedom of the perfect abstraction that will characterize this effort to fit monopolistic competition theory into a general-equilibrium system of interproduct competition, that A is the exhaustive set of all possible "qualities" that products can possess in the relevant period. We define a quality simply as a physical attribute of a good capable of ascription to it by a set of defined operations whose results are objective and repeatable. In this discussion, let us limit our set of products, and therefore the set of implied qualities, to products with consumer and intermediate uses, so that we may eliminate capital goods. Then, for example, $a_i \in A$ might be the degree of sweetness in a product; the color of blue decorating the product; the spatial coordinate designating the location of a product's manufacture or sale measured with respect to a certain suitable coordinate axis and in suitably chosen units; the possession of a specific brand name or a particular identifying type of package, and so forth. Let us assume that A contains n elements, denoted $a_i, i = 1, 2, \ldots, n$.

For each a_i we postulate an *index of intensity* $q_i \in Q$ which may take some or all values over the real interval $[0,1]$, and which denotes the varying degrees to which a given product possesses the qualities a_i. The indexes of intensity are taken to vary in three degrees of uniqueness of measurement:

1 *Uniqueness up to a monotonic transformation, or ordinal measurement.* In this familiar manner of measuring such economic phenomena as consumer preferences, index values attached to objects are significant only as to the sign of the increments between them, not their absolute values. Such indexes of ranking must be used to denote darker or lighter color tones of products, various flavor qualities, and so forth.

Our constraint that all ordinal index values lie between zero and unity inclusive does not add any meaningful uniqueness to the measure. However, at one point we shall violate the logic of such measurement and essentially convert it arbitrarily to a cardinal index. In constructing a metric space over Q, which we shall use to measure "product distance," we shall assume that these measurements are cardinal. Arbitrarily, if between white and darkest blue we designate 100 shades ranked in order of possession of "blueness," we shall designate the distance from zero to the second-ranking object, the distance from unity to the next-to-highest-ranking value, and the distances of successive index values in the array from each other, as equal. That is, if m positions are occupied in the rankings, we shall divide the interval $[0,1]$ into $1/(m + 1)$ segments, with the first nonzero ranking at the end of the first segment and the last nonunity ranking at the beginning of the last segment.

Those readers who are horrified by this procedure may be assured at this point that it is a nonintegral part of the analysis, used at only one point in the study, and is easily removed without damage to the results.

2 *Uniqueness up to a positive multiplicative constant, or cardinal measurement.* We have used up the two degrees of freedom in a linear transformation by our definition of origin and length of interval, and we may measure in this way dimensions of products, location in spatial coordinates, and, perhaps, such qualities as sweetness.

3 *Attributive indexes, which indicate the presence or nonpresence of the given quality.* For example, the possession or nonpossession by a product of a given brand name or given package must be indicated by such an index. Arbitrarily, we give a value of zero to the index when the quality is not possessed, and a value of unity to the index when it is.

The attributive index, which assumes a peculiarly important role in the interproduct competition of a modern industrial economy, must be used in three important situations. First, when by nature a quality does not vary, continuously or discretely. An automobile does or does not possess the name Rolls Royce; the name Bentley even for the diffident is not a less intensive representation of the former considered as a quality. Second, when, although the quality may be conceived as varying along a continuum or by discrete steps, no ordinal or cardinal measurement procedure has yet been devised to index this variation. Then, for example, instead of placing "robin's-egg blue" and "royal blue" along the "blueness continuum," each such color becomes a separate quality a_i that is or is not possessed in full measure by a product. Lastly, it must be used where the indexes available to establish numerical measures along a continuum by ordinal or cardinal methods are dependent on consumer or firm preferences, as for example the "atmosphere" or "tone" of a restaurant or store.

In realistic interproduct competition these qualities indexed by attributive indexes are most frequently protected by institutional constraints such as copyrights and trademarks, are most difficult to approach closely in product similarity because they are often not variable in any simple way, and, of course, are the very characteristics that advertising is directed to distinguish in the consumer's preferences. Indeed, in the modern, sophisticated market economy, *attributive competition* among products may be the most vital form of competition as interfirm price competition in the classic senses diminishes.

We construct the product space $S = q_1 \times q_2 \times \ldots \times q_n$, a point in which is an n-tuple of quality intensities. Let σ be a relation carrying S into $R \cup [\Phi]$, or the union of commodity space R, and Φ, the null product, in which any element r_j is either a product or the null product, Φ. That is, for any point $q_j = [q_1, q_2, \ldots, q_n] \in S$, there exists an image set $\sigma(q_j)$ which we denote R_j, and which is a subset of R. The set R is then the union of the images of $\sigma(q_j)$ or the image of S under the relation σ. We shall assume that every product, actual or potential under the given technology of the period, may be uniquely described by a point q_j in quality-intensity space S, and further, that every point $q_j \in S$ maps into a unique element $r_j = R_j$ in R. Further, we may assume the following characteristics of this topology to hold.

First, we may assume that *all* points in the interior of S, or $\mathring{S}$, are mapped by σ into Φ, the null product: that is, no product possesses *all* quality intensities to positive degrees. Every potential or actual product lies on the boundary of S insofar as its qualities description is concerned. Second, we may assume that many points on the boundary of S will be mapped into the null product, because they will denote inconsistent or contradictory quality-index properties. It is impossible for a product to be both a Ford and a Chevrolet, to be both a light and a dark beer, and so forth. Therefore, we may restrict the set S to

$$S^* = \{q_j^* | q_j^* \in S, \sigma^*(q_j^*) \neq \Phi\} \qquad (11.1)$$

which is the domain of the mapping σ^*, and the set R to

$$R^* = \sigma^*(S^*) = \bigcup_j \sigma^*(q_j^*) \qquad (11.2)$$

which is the range of the mapping σ^*.

We assume that S^* is finite, and therefore that R^* is finite. Because any mapping between finite sets is continuous, σ^* is continuous, and because finite sets are compact, S^* and R^* are compact. Further, S^* and R^* are *homeomorphic* (topologically equivalent) because they are related by the continuous mappings σ^* and σ^{*-1}.

We have, therefore, constructed a continuous one-to-one mapping from a compact quality-intensity set S^* into a compact goods space R^*. *Any* actual or potential good can be located as a bundle of quality-intensity index values; *any* allowable bundle of quality-intensity index values is contained as an element in S^* and is mapped into a feasible product in R^*; no infeasible good is contained in R^*; and no infeasible n-tuple of quality-intensity index values is contained in S^*.

Lastly, we may create a metric space over S^* and the metric d over $S^* \times S^*$ by taking the Euclidean distance between any two elements of S^*, quality-intensity space. By the equivalence relation between homeomorphic sets, this metric is also associated with the products r_j^* into which the elements q_j are mapped by σ. Because there are n qualities q_i in the product space S^*, the metric d takes values from zero to $(n)^{1/2}$ and is a continuous numerical function on this topological product $S^* \times S^*$. Thus, for any two products r_j^*, r_k^*, elements of R^*, we may obtain the "distance" d_{jk} between them in $S^* \times S^*$.

4 The Product Group

Let S_j^* be a closed subset of S^*, and let R_j^* be the image set of S_j^* in R^* under the mapping σ. Then we define R_j^* to be a *group* of products if and only if there is a meaningful *core* of qualities a_i for which every member of R_j^* has positive values, although there may or may not exist a *fringe* of qualities for which some members may contain positive values and others may not. In determining the structure of the core qualities there is no sense in pretending to a scientific precision that is not possible. It was one of the desiderata of our analysis in defining product groups that it employ a completely physical basis for such distinctions. Similar consumer uses and

similar technological production conditions are important in such discrimi-
nations too, and despite Triffin's useful reminder that interproduct competition exists between such groups as well as within them it is our view that an
emphasis on interproduct competition within the group is a valuable one.

If we let A_j be the core set of qualities for which all members of the product group have nonzero values, we could obtain a concept of *core distances*
in $\Pi_j S_j^*$ for all members of the group, but this construction seems of little
value in defining product groups because it assumes the decisions concerning
the content of the core qualities have been made. Also, if we sought to carve
out neighborhoods of proximity using d, the Euclidean distance measure
assures that we would cross group boundaries and obtain many most
dissimilar products in such a wide-meshed net. We elect to remain, therefore,
with a definition of the core set of qualities which is arbitrary in some
respects.

A homogeneous subgroup of products, denoted $R_{j/a}^* \Leftrightarrow S_{j/a}^*$, contained
within R_j^*, is defined to contain at least two elements and to meet
further sets of conditions:

1 If *fringe* qualities exist in members of the subgroup they are *neutral*, in
 that they do not lead to violations of 2 and 3 below.
2 At any fixed income distribution among consumers, for any set of positive
 prices in which the prices of all $r_{j/a}^* \in R_{j/a}^*$ are equal, every consumer c is
 indifferent among all goods in the subgroup. That is, if in these conditions
 only one product in the subgroup were available for purchase, consumers
 individually would purchase the same quantity of whatever member in the
 subgroup was offered, and the same quantities of all other goods not in
 the subgroup.
3 At any fixed set of output and input prices, where all $r_{j/a}^*$ are priced identically, for any firm v producing and/or purchasing one such good in
 optimal quantities, denying it the ability to produce and/or purchase the
 good will lead to the production or purchase of any other member of the
 subgroup in the same quantities, though all other outputs and inputs
 remain unchanged.

We have prescribed a quite rigorous set of conditions for the homogeneous subgroup within the product group. Note that it combines the qualities
of physical similarity (the possession of core qualities A_j), of perfect consumer substitutability, and of perfect technological substitutability.[13] Also,
the criteria allow physical dissimilarity if it does not interfere with perfect
substitutability, so that members of the homogeneous subgroup need not be
at a distance of zero from each other in $S^* \times S^*$ or in $S_j^* \times S_j^*$. Moreover,
within any group R_j^* there may exist more than one subgroup of homogeneous products. However, only if these three sets of conditions hold does
"perfect economic homogeneity" characterize the subgroup, for only then

can the subgroup be reduced to a single member with no actual or potential economic impact on any actual or potential solution to the system. In a general-equilibrium setting this definition provides the basis for classifying a set of products as a decomposable economic entity, taking into account not only direct consumer and producer substitutability among members of the subgroup, but also substitutability and complementarity in both consumer and producer senses for all other products and for inputs.

The rigor of the requisites for product homogeneity, however, assure that it will characterize few product subsets. Therefore, we define a hetero-geneous subgroup of products as a subset of a product group with or without a fringe of noncore qualities whose members are not elements of any homo-geneous subgroup and for which one or more of the conditions in 2 and 3 above are violated. We shall denote this type of subset $R^*_{j/b} \Leftrightarrow S^*_{j/b}$ and its nature will be sufficiently clear from our discussion of the implications of the definition of homogeneous subgroups of products. It is, in fact, the com-plement in R^*_j of the union of sets $R^*_{j/a}$.

It follows, then, from the set of definitions that the product group is the union of homogeneous and heterogeneous subgroups:

$$R^*_j = \left(\bigcup_a R^*_{j/a} \right) \cup R^*_{j/b} \tag{11.3}$$

It also follows from the definition of the product group that it must contain more than one product. Therefore, we complete the partition of R^* by defining the *singular product* for which no meaningful core of qualities in common with any other product can be defined. We define such singular products, denoting them by $r^*_{j/c}$, and it follows that

$$R^* = \left(\bigcup_j R^*_j \right) \cup \left(\bigcup_j r^*_{j/c} \right) \tag{11.4}$$

If we define $\overline{S^*_j}$ as the set of core quality-intensities of any product r^*_j, and if for any two products r^*_j and r^*_k it is true that $\overline{S^*_j}$ and $\overline{S^*_k}$ are not iden-tical, we define the distance in core-space as infinity, so that core distances between goods in different product groups, between goods in product groups and singular goods, and between singular goods, are infinite (or, more accu-rately, undefined). On the other hand, in $S^* \times S^*$ all of these goods are finite distances apart, between the limits already noted.

5 The Technology

Let all actual and potential firms be defined as $v \in V$, and let us further sup-pose that every firm is capable, taking into account technological factors only, of producing every product $r^*_j \in R^*$. We shall designate outputs of r^*_j by firm v as the vector $\overline{\mathbf{X}}_{vj}$, using the capital subscript throughout this chapter to distinguish r_j^* as an output from its use as an input on intermediate account. We denote the firm's vector of demand for inputs of primary factors by $\mathbf{X}_{vz}$, and its vector of demands for intermediate inputs by $\mathbf{X}_{vj}$. For each firm a transformation function is given:

$$T_v(\bar{\mathbf{X}}_{vJ}, \mathbf{X}_{vz}, \mathbf{X}_{vj}) = 0, \; r_j^* \in R^* \qquad (11.5)$$

We assume also that the firm has determined an anticipated sales curve for each product, which defines the expected price at which the firm can sell any quantity of any product, given the outputs of all goods it produces and given the expected reactions of other firms $v\cdot$ which are elements of the complement in V of v (symbolized $V\cdot = C_v V$) to these outputs. That is, the firm's sales curves may be presented in the following manner:

$$\begin{aligned}
&1. \; P_j^* = F_{vJ}(\bar{\mathbf{X}}_{vJ}, I_{vJ}) \\
&2. \; I_{vJ} = G_{vJ}(\bar{\mathbf{X}}_{vJ}, \bar{\mathbf{X}}_{v\cdot J})
\end{aligned} \qquad (11.\mathrm{I})$$

The I_{vJ} are *interaction factors*, summarizing the expected impact on the price of a product of actions taken by all other firms in response to the output levels chosen by the firm v for all of its outputs. For firm v, I_{vj} summarizes the interfirm competition that it takes into account in those markets in which it is an actual or potential seller. To simplify our analysis, we shall assume that $v \in V$ are insignificantly small buyers of primary factor services and intermediate products.

We shall assume initially that the conditions of production are such that some form of institutional or cultural protection is extended to every $r_j^* \in R^*$. That is, the privilege of producing every product – whether a singular product, an element in a homogeneous subgroup of a product group, or an element in the heterogeneous subgroup of a product group – is appropriable by individuals and is protected effectively by usage or by legal copyright, trademark, or patent restrictions. We shall separate these ownership privileges from the firms producing the goods, and view their owners as receiving royalty payments, L_J, from a single firm producing r_j^*. Of course, if the firm is indeed the owner of the privilege of production, we view it as making payments to itself at the imputed market value for the privilege of production. The use of a particular brand name on a particular product, the production of a particular product at a particular location, or the use of a special recipe or formula are qualities or bundles of qualities in specific intensities that must be leased at a cost of L_J per period. In our analysis, profits will always be net of such royalties unless specifically noted to the contrary. We define profits for the firm as:

$$M_v = \sum_J \bar{X}_{vJ} P_j^* - \sum_z X_{vz} P_z - \sum_j X_{vj} P_j - \sum_J L_J \qquad (11.\mathrm{II})$$

The method we shall use to arrive at a general equilibrium for all firms is a conceptual experiment through analytic time employing iterative procedures in a manner reminiscent of a Walrasian *tâtonnement* procedure. The essential questions concerned with such an experiment are whether the set of dynamic solutions are paths that converge to limiting or stationary values, whether more than one such stationary value set exists so that the one obtained (if any is obtained) is dependent on the initial position and, perhaps, the order in which the adjustments are made. Further, because the sales curves and interaction functions of (11.I) are expectations of firms, which will be revised after each step of the procedure, the convergence of the process will also be dependent on the manner of adapting these expectations to the emerging values as they unfold.

These problems are ordinarily discussed under the somewhat misleading title of "process stability," meaning by this the stability of a system of adjustment rather than that of an equilibrium point. In this terminology we must ask whether or not the process is "globally stable" – whether or not it achieves some equilibrium whatever its starting point and order of adjustment or whether it is "locally stable," attaining an equilibrium from some initial positions and orders of adjustment; and whether the equilibrium is unique or multiple. At this stage of our analysis we have not been able to investigate these properties and will confine the model to the presentation of the adjustment process. It is recognized that the market itself could not conduct these experiments, and, therefore, that we can only hope to show that the results of the real economic process are similar to these results, so that we gain some insights into the product competition of reality by their use.

We shall assume that T_y is smooth, continuous, and globally concave: that is, that all partial derivatives through at least the second order are well defined at all points on the function in the interior of its domain, and that if a tangent or support hyperplane touches the function at any point all points of the function will lie on or below the plane. Further, we shall assume the same properties to hold for the functions M_y of (11.II) and G_{vJ} of (11.I-2), and that T_y and G_{vJ} possess the Constraint Qualification regularity properties of the Kuhn–Tucker theorem [5].

Then we begin the equilibrating process by assuming that all royalties are identically zero. Under these conditions, if we substitute the appropriate sales curves for the P_j^* in (11.II) from (11.I-1), we may obtain the following Lagrangean form:

$$_0E_v = {}_0M_v + \lambda_v\left(T_v\left(\bar{\mathbf{X}}_{vJ}, \mathbf{X}_{vz}, \mathbf{X}_{vj}\right)\right) + \sum_J \pi_{vJ}\left(I_{vJ} - G_{vJ}\left(\bar{\mathbf{X}}_{vJ}, \bar{\mathbf{X}}_{v'J}\right)\right) \quad (11.6)$$

where the subscript $t = 0,1, \ldots$ to the left of the relevant symbols will be used to denote the time-sequence steps of the process under analysis.

With the $_0L_J = 0$ for all r_j^* the production of a good by any firm does not entail the payment of a lump sum that may be escaped by dropping the good from the product mix. This fact simplifies the determination of the firm's maximum-profit position considerably: we may place the following restrictions on the partial derivatives in order to obtain a critical point of the function:

$$
\begin{aligned}
1.\quad & \delta_0 E_v/\delta \bar{X}_{vJ} \equiv C_{vJ}^\circ = P_J^* + \bar{X}_{vJ}(\delta F_{vJ}/\delta \bar{X}_{vJ}) \\
& \qquad + \sum_{J' \neq J} \bar{X}_{vJ'}(\delta F_{vJ'/\delta \bar{X}_{vJ}})(\lambda_v(\delta T_v/\delta \bar{X}_{vJ})) \\
& \qquad - \sum_{J' \in R^*} \pi_{vJ'}(\delta G_{vJ'}/\delta \bar{X}_{vJ}) \leqslant 0
\end{aligned}
$$

$$
\begin{aligned}
2.\quad & \delta_0 E_v/\delta X_{vz} \equiv C_{vz}^\circ = -P_z + \lambda_v(\delta T_v/\delta X_{vz}) \leqslant 0 \\
3.\quad & \delta_0 E_v/\delta X_{vj} \equiv C_{vj}^\circ = -P_j + \lambda_v(\delta T_v/\delta X_{vj}) \leqslant 0 \\
4.\quad & \delta_0 E_v/\delta I_{vJ} \equiv C_{vJ^\circ}^\circ = \bar{X}_{vJ}(\delta F_{vJ}/\delta I_{vJ}) + \pi_{vJ} \leqslant 0 \\
5.\quad & \bar{X}_{vJ}^\circ C_{vJ}^\circ = 0 \\
6.\quad & X_{vz}^\circ C_{vz}^\circ = 0 \\
7.\quad & X_{vj}^\circ C_{vj}^\circ = 0 \\
8.\quad & I_{vJ}^\circ C_{vJ^\circ}^\circ = 0 \\
9.\quad & \lambda_v^\circ(T_v(\bar{X}_{vJ}^\circ, X_{vz}^\circ, X_{vj}^\circ)) = 0 \\
10.\quad & \pi_{vJ}^\circ[I_{vJ}^\circ - G_{vJ}(\bar{X}_{vJ}^\circ, \bar{X}_{v'J}^\circ)] = 0 \\
11.\quad & \lambda_v^\circ \geqslant 0,\ \pi_{vJ}^\circ \geqslant 0
\end{aligned}
$$

(11.7)

These conditions are necessary and sufficient to maximize $_0M_v$ for $\bar{\mathbf{X}}_{vJ}$, $\mathbf{X}_{vz}$, $\mathbf{X}_{vj} \geqslant 0$ subject to the constraints $T_v(\bar{\mathbf{X}}_{vJ}, \mathbf{X}_{vz}, \mathbf{X}_{vj}) \geqslant 0$ and $I_{vJ} - G_{vJ}(\bar{\mathbf{X}}_{vJ}, \bar{\mathbf{X}}_{v.J}) \geqslant 0$. As we shall do throughout this chapter, we have placed degree marks on values that refer to the solution.

Conditions (11.7–1) assert that at the equilibrium for the firm, for every output, the "own marginal revenue" plus or minus the marginal revenue impacts of the output upon every other output of the firm, plus or minus the impacts of the output on its own revenues from its interaction effects with all other firms and products in the economy, must be less than or equal to the output's marginal cost. Conditions (11.7–5) require that when the inequality holds, output of the good by the firm by zero, whereas if the equality holds, output may be positive.

Conditions (11.7–2) and (11.7–3) assert that, for every input employed by the firm, marginal revenue product be no greater than the price of the input. Where the inequality holds, conditions (11.7–6 and 7) require that the firm use none of the input, whereas if the equality holds it may buy positive quantities.

Condition (11.7–4) is actually a dummy condition including the inequality in order to fulfill the Kuhn–Tucker conditions formally. It says that the "marginal interaction revenue" used to reduce or increase marginal revenues in condition (11.7–1) must be no less than the impact of a slight change in the interaction term on revenue. Condition (11.7–8) asserts that this can happen only when $I_{vJ} = 0$, and in that case condition (11.7–10) sets "marginal interaction revenue" to zero. Thus, in effect, the equality holds in (11.7–4).

We have assumed that in the technology function, T_v, outputs are treated as negative inputs. Therefore, in stating the function as a possible inequality, we have allowed for the possibility that the firm may use more inputs than it needs to use. Condition (11.7–9) assures that if this inequality does hold, the equilibrium marginal cost is zero – which is to say that all inputs are costless. Effectively, therefore, the equality will always hold true.

Let us assume, therefore, that every firm v has determined its maximum-profit equilibrium vectors of outputs and inputs. Now, we shall choose any good, say r_1^*, and for every firm determine $_0M_{v/1}$, which is the maximum profit firm v can earn under the conditions of $t = 0$ *if it is denied the opportunity of producing r_1^**. For each firm we compute $_0D_{v/1}$, the difference between $_0M_v$ and the new constrained profit:

$$_0D_{v/1} = {}_0M_v - {}_0M_{v/1} \tag{11.8}$$

which is nonnegative because the firm has the option not to produce at all. Let the set V_1^* with elements v_1^* contain the firms for which $_0D_{v/1}$ is a maximum, and for convenience let us assume it has but one element: a single firm to whose profits the opportunity to produce r_1^* makes the largest contribution. Competition among firms for the unique ability to produce this good will lead to a royalty payment for this opportunity which is equal to or greater than $_0D_{v/1}$ for $v_1^{**} \in V_1^{**}$ which is that subset of firms that has the second highest $_0D_{v/1}$. We shall assume that the royalty for the privilege of producing r_1^* is equalized to the value of the opportunity of producing r_1^* to $v_1^{**} \in V_1^{**}$, so that

$$_1L_1 = {}_0D_{v^{**}/1} \tag{11.9}$$

and the opportunity to produce the good is now restricted to some one firm v_1^*. This restriction may require that some firms $v \notin V_1^*$ go out of business, and will require that others stop producing the good, both of which actions may affect $I_{v_1^*1}$ as well as other interaction factors in the economy, thereby affecting sales curves. It also means that the successful firm v_1^* must now deduct the royalty from its profits. We may redefine maximum potential profits as follows:

$$1. \quad _0M_v' = {_0}M_v - {_1}L_1, \qquad v_1^* \in V_1^{**}$$
$$2. \quad _0M_v' = {_0}M_{v/1}, \qquad v \notin V_1^*$$
$$(11.10)$$

We allow sales curves to readjust to the new situation, and then move to any other product, say r_2^*. We compute for every firm $_0M_{v/2}'$, or the maximum profit it could now obtain if it were denied the right to produce r_2^*, and compute

$$_0D_{v/2} = {_0}M_v' - {_0}M_{v/2}' \qquad (11.11)$$

Once more we array these differences and determine $v_2^* \in V_2^*$ (which we again assume to be a single-element set) and v_2^{**}, which are firms that receive the greatest and second-greatest advantage from the opportunity to produce the good, after taking into account the outcome of the competition for good r_1^*. We set

$$_1L_2 = {_0}D_{v^{**}/2} \qquad (11.12)$$

and restrict production of r_2^* to v_2^*. Then, we define

$$1. \quad _0M_v'' = {_0}M_v - \sum_{J=1}^{2} {_1}L_J, \qquad v \in \cap V_j^*$$
$$2. \quad _0M_v'' = {_0}M_{v/J}'' - {_1}L_{J'}, \qquad v \notin V_j^*, \quad v \in V_{j'}^*, \quad \cap V_j^* = \Phi$$
$$3. \quad _0M_v'' = {_0}M_{v/1,2}, \qquad v \notin \cup V_j^*$$
$$(11.13)$$

This adjustment process is repeated for goods $r_3^*, r_4^* \ldots r_n^*$ at the last of which steps we have determined $_1L_J$, $J = 1, 2, \ldots, n$, an allocation of products among firms, optimal firm demand for inputs, optimal output quantities, and firm profits. We then define

$$_1M_v = {_0}M'''^{\cdots(n)} \qquad (11.14)$$

and we start the process over again by considering all contracts made in $t = 0$ subject to abrogation if either party finds it to his advantage, and on the basis of the changed expectations for sales curves and interaction effects we repeat the whole analysis once more, using the same order of goods adjustment. When this step has been completed we repeat the whole operation for $t = 3, 4, \ldots$ until that step is reached (if ever) at which the solution to the previous step is merely repeated to some very close order of approximation, or, at least, the step solutions reveal cluster points within which the variation remains bounded.

The properties of such solutions are not at all evident from the mere statement of the procedure. About all that seems to be clear on the surface is that each firm is doing as well as it can when the order of goods adjustment is in the arbitrarily determined manner depicted. Had another order of adjustment been taken the solution in all respects might be quite different, but, again, one in which all firms were optimizing given that order of adjustment. Would it be possible for a planning authority to redistribute inputs among the firms in such a manner as to increase the net outputs of at least one of the products produced (or of substitute products in their homogeneous subgroups) without reducing the net outputs of any products (or of substitute products in their homogeneous subgroups)? The extension of welfare economics to monopolistic competition theory must answer such questions. Or would the market mechanism lead to such Pareto-optima? A closer study of the process than I have been able to perform in this paper is necessary to shed light on these questions.

From this process, in the equilibria for varying price vectors, we may derive the supply and demand functions for the firm:

1. $\bar{X}_{vJ} = H_{vJ}(\mathbf{P}_j, \mathbf{P}_z), \qquad r_j^* \in R^*, v \in V$

2. $X_{vz} = H_{vz}(\mathbf{P}_j, \mathbf{P}_z)$ \hfill (11.III)

3. $X_{vj} = H_{vj}(\mathbf{P}_j, \mathbf{P}_z)$

6 Interfirm Competition

For $v \in V$ and $v' \in V'$, where $V' = C_v V$, let $\bar{\mathbf{X}}_{vJ}^o$ and $\bar{\mathbf{X}}_{v'J}$ be equilibrium output vectors in the sense described in the previous section. When $I_{vJ} = 0$ for a good r_j^* and a firm v in the neighborhood of the equilibrium we say that the firm enjoys *locally nonrivalrous interfirm competition* in the sale of this good. A change in the firm's output of the product by a small amount, after all interproduct relations have been taken into account, will not induce any change in the price of the product by virtue of others' reactions to the quantity change: only the direct price reaction in the market to the firm's output change will occur.

When the function G_{vJ} is undefined in this neighborhood we may say that the firm is engaged in *locally indeterminate rivalrous interfirm competition* in the sale of this product. At the given constellation of firm outputs, firm v cannot determine what the net resultant of its small quantity changes will be on its price via interfirm competition: the inability to define the interaction factor implies the inability to define the firm's sales curve.

When I_{vJ} is defined and is nonzero, we shall say that the firm is engaged in *locally determinate rivalrous interfirm competition*, for the neighborhood of the equilibrium of a product's output. As I indicated in the first and second sections of this chapter, in my opinion the Chamberlin contribution did not include much of the novel in this case. Indeed, as I asserted at those points, the revolutionary contribution of Chamberlin was in the analysis of that competition which assumed $\mathbf{I}_{vj}$ to be zero for *all* relevant output constellations of the firms: that is, a situation we may term *global non-rivalrous interfirm competition*.

This situation can occur in our analysis in three environments for the firm. It should be borne in mind that firms producing goods in the same product group may have zero, nonzero, or indeterminate I_{vj} factors, so that to refer to a "market" as purely competitive or oligopolistic is an oversimplification. The firm environments are the following familiar ones:

1 *Pure competition*. The firm is producing a good in a homogeneous subgroup of a product group, and cost conditions are such that entry into the subgroup dictates that the firm's output is sold at a price set parametrically. Note that the fact of production in the homogeneous subgroup does not imply pure competition, even in the "long run" with which we are concerned because our model includes all potential firms. The location of a product's image in quality-intensity space S^* does not dicate the nature of interfirm competition.

2 *Monopolistic competition proper*. This is the case Chamberlin refers to as the large-group case, and in my interpretation constitutes the core of his original contribution. It is characterized by a large number of firms producing members of a product group in such fashion that no firm feels any impact on its sales curves for products in the group that it produces from reactions of other such products. The firms may be producing outputs in a homogeneous subgroup if they are protected institutionally or, more typically, protected goods in the heterogeneous subgroup, when the *direct* impact of the firm's output on price is nonzero.

3 *Pure monopoly*. In this classic case a firm is producing a singular product whose qualities are sufficiently distinguished that its production changes are not affected by any other firm's reaction in any other product. In the previous two cases I_{vj} is zero by virtue of the anonymity of the crowd, whereas in the present case it is zero because of the firm's splendid isolation.

In our model of monopolistic competition we shall assume that all firms, for all products in their output mixes, within the feasible domain of (11.I-2), have I_{vj} defined and equal to zero. That is, we postulate universal global nonrivalrous interfirm competition. This postulate actually assumes illegitimately that the realistic solutions to the model will occur in the output domain of (11.III-1) functions, where such an assumption can be accepted. It was this type of competition that is so brilliantly clarified by Chamberlin's large-group case. Therefore we assume:[14]

$$\mathbf{I}_{vJ} \equiv 0, \qquad v \in V, \qquad r_j^* \in R^* \tag{11.IV}$$

With the absence of rivalrous interfirm competition at all feasible output constellations, the economy will attain its equilibrium in the entrepreneurial sector by the competition among products for adoption by firms and the competition among firms via royalty payments to produce them, given the institutional protection afforded products by the society.

7 The Consumer Sector

In this idealization we shall assume that each consumer $c \in C$ can construct a complete weak ordering over a field of choice containing all $r_j^* \in R^*$, and that this ordering can be represented by a smooth, continuous, quasi-concave, real-valued function unique up to a monotone transformation. The consumer's expenditures are made from receipts from the sale of primary inputs he controls, from his receipts of product royalties, and from his share of the distribution of firm profits. Let α_{cj} be the proportion of the royalties from the production of r_j^* received by consumer c, where

$$\sum_{c \in C} \alpha_{cj} = 1, \qquad \alpha_{cj} \geqslant 0.$$

Also, let β_{cv} be the proportion of firm v's profits received by consumer c, where

$$\sum_{c \in C} \beta_{cv} = 1, \qquad \beta_{cv} \geqslant 0.$$

We assume also that at the start of each period the consumer inherits stocks $\mathbf{Q}_{cz}$ of inputs that are given among the data of the model.

The preference function is written

$$U_c = U_c(\mathbf{X}_{cj}, \mathbf{X}_{cz}), \qquad r_j^* \in R^*, c \in C \tag{11.15}$$

where the arguments are amounts consumed of products and of any primary inputs that might have alternative consumer uses. The consumer's income is defined as[15]

$$Y_c = \sum_z \bar{X}_{cz} P_z + \sum_J \alpha_{cJ} L_J + \sum_v \beta_{cv} M_v \tag{11.16}$$

where

$$\bar{X}_{cz} = Q_{cz} - X_{cz} \tag{11.17}$$

The consumer's choices may be predicted by maximizing U_c subject to the constraint that expenditures not exceed Y_c. We construct the Lagrangean form T_c and assume that U_c is globally strictly quasi-concave. We then place the following conditions on the partial derivatives, after defining T_c:

$$T_c = U_c(\mathbf{X}_{cj}, \mathbf{X}_{cz}) - \phi_c \left(Y_c - \sum_j X_{cj}P_j \geqslant 0 \right) \qquad (11.18)$$

Then:

1. $\delta T_c / \delta X^o_{cj} = \delta U_c / \delta X^o_{cj} - \phi^o_c P_j \leqslant 0$

2. $\delta T_c / \delta X^o_{cz} = \delta U_c / \delta X^o_{cz} - \phi^o_c P_z \leqslant 0$

3. $X^o_{cj}(\delta U_c / \delta X^o_{cj} - \phi^o_c P_j) = 0$

4. $X^o_{cz}(\delta U_c / \delta X^o_{cz} - \phi^o_c P_z) = 0$ $\qquad (11.19)$

5. $\phi^o_c \left(Y_c - \sum_j X_{cj}P_j \right) = 0$

6. $\phi^o_c \geqslant 0$

where $P_j > 0$, $P_z > 0$, and where $P_j = \infty$ when product r_j^* is not available.

Note that if $\phi^o_c > 0$, so that general satiation has not occurred, satiation in any one good is denied by (11.19) unless the consumer does not want a first unit of the good. This latter kind of "satiation" is the only kind of partial satiation we allow at positive prices.

From these conditions we may solve out conceptually to obtain the demand and supply functions for the consumer:

1. $X_{cj} = J_{cj}(\mathbf{P}_j, \mathbf{P}_z; \mathbf{Q}_{cz}, \alpha_{cj}, \beta_{cv})$, $r_j^* \in R^*, c \in C$ $\qquad (11.\text{V})$

2. $\bar{X}_{cz} = Q_{cz} - J_{cz}(\mathbf{P}_j, \mathbf{P}_z; \mathbf{Q}_{cz}, \alpha_{cj}, \beta_{cv})$

And from these we may obtain the aggregate functions:

1. $X_j = \sum_c X_{cj}$ $\qquad (11.\text{VI})$

2. $\bar{X}_z = \sum_c \bar{X}_{cz}$

8 Interproduct Competition

We shall start with a product group that has only homogeneous subgroups of products and no heterogeneous subgroup. Suppose it were possible to obtain institutional protection for some or all of the quality intensities in the core or for one or more of the neutral quality intensities, so that each $r^*_{j/a}$ is protected and is held by a different licensor. Then, by the definition of the homogeneous product subgroup, the royalty payments accruing to each product must be equal in equilibrium:

$$L^o_J = D^o_{v**/J} = K^o_{J/a}, \qquad \text{for } r^*_{j/a} \in R^*_{j/a} \qquad (11.\text{VII}')$$

where $K^o_{J/a}$ is some common value. If we assume that demand for products in the group is very great relative to the number of elements in $R^*_{j/a}$, royalties can be positive; if the number of elements in $R^*_{j/a}$ is potentially very large, then competition among licensors will bid royalties down to zero. Therefore we specify that in equilibrium

$$K^o_{j/a} \geqslant 0 \qquad (11.\text{VIII}')$$

In equilibrium, under any conditions, the firm's profits must be nonnegative:

$$M^o_v \geqslant 0, \qquad v \in V \qquad (11.\text{IX})$$

Under our assumptions all primary inputs are of equal efficiency anywhere in the economy, so that profits to the firm are returns to differential efficiency of management *after* the "differential efficiency" of quality-intensities is accounted for through royalty payments. For any firm the contribution of any good in the subset $R^*_{j/a}$ must be the same:

$$M^o_v - M^o_{v/J} = C^o_{v/J}, \qquad r^*_{j/a} \in R^*_{j/a} \qquad (11.\text{X}')$$

and if we allow differential management abilities,

$$C^o_{v/J} \geqslant 0, \qquad r^*_{j/a} \in R^*_{j/a} \qquad (11.\text{XI}')$$

If, more realistically, we assume that none of the products in the homogeneous subgroup receives institutional protection, then of course

$$K^o_{j/a} = 0 \qquad (11.\text{VIII}'')$$

Consider now the heterogeneous subgroups of the economy. We define the equilibrium condition

$$L^o_J = D^o_{v**/J}, \qquad \text{for } r^*_{j/b} \in R^*_{j/b} \qquad (11.\text{VII}'')$$

where

$$L^o_J \geqslant 0 \qquad (11.\text{VIII}')$$

Also, no longer are the contributions to profits of all elements in the subgroup the same for each firm:

$$M_v^o - M_{v/J}^o \geqslant 0, \qquad \text{for } r_{j/b}^* \in R_{j/b}^* \tag{11.X''}$$

Lastly, for the singular commodity,

$$L_J^o = D_{v**/J}^o, \qquad \text{for } r_{j/c}^* \tag{11.VII'''}$$

where

$$L_J^o \geqslant 0 \tag{11.VII''''}$$

Further,

$$M_v^o - M_{v/J}^o \geqslant 0, \qquad \text{for } r_{j/c}^* \tag{11.X'''}$$

For all firms and all products, if $M_v^o - M_{v/J}^o > 0$, so that the contribution to the firm's profits is positive after paying equilibrium royalties, the firm must produce the good; if this magnitude is zero, either the firm did not include the good in its unconstrained profit maximum, or it did but the good adds nothing to its profits after payment of equilibrium royalties. In either case we require its output to be zero:

1. $\bar{X}_{vJ}^o > 0 \Leftrightarrow (M_v^o - M_{v/J}^o) > 0, \qquad r_j^* \in R^* \tag{11.XII}$

2. $\bar{X}_{vJ}^o = 0 \Leftrightarrow (M_v^o - M_{v/J}^o) = 0$

9 The Market Equilibrium

Lastly, let us state the conditions that must rule in all markets throughout the economy. First, we choose as *numéraire* a good whose price in any conceivable equilibrium, when expressed in some outside *numéraire*, will lie in the open interval $]0, \infty[$. Then, if this product is $r_{j=1}^*$, we define

$$P_{j=1} \equiv 1 \tag{11.XIII}$$

We define aggregate firm input demands as

1. $X_j' = \sum_v X_{vj} \tag{11.XIV}$

2. $X_z' = \sum_y X_{vz}$

We define excess demands as follows:

1. $E_J = X_j + X_j' - \bar{X}_J \tag{11.XV}$

2. $E_z = X_z' - \bar{X}_z$

Because we are treating each of our firms as the sole supplier of the goods
it produces, we view each of them as determining a given amount to be
supplied that is thrown on the market and sold at the market clearing price.
We require the markets for all goods, therefore, to be exactly cleared in
equilibrium, except when the firm has so miscalculated that this may be done
only at a negative price. Therefore:

$$\text{1.}\quad E_j^o \leqslant 0, \qquad P_j^o E_j^o = 0 \qquad (11.\text{XVI})$$

$$\text{2.}\quad E_z^o \leqslant 0, \qquad P_z^o E_z^o = 0$$

For firms, however, these are not sufficient to induce them to retain their
current supply policies. From (11.I) the current supplies are seen to be based
on an expectation of the price at which given quantities of goods can be sold,
and from the relations of (11.7), which lie behind (10.III), supply will be
determined with an eye toward obtaining that expected price, P_j^*, which
maximizes profit. If, in the event that the firm has not chosen its supply
optimally, the solution price P_j^o and the expected profit maximizing price
P_j^* will be unequal. Therefore, we impose as an equilibrium condition

$$P_j^o - P_j^* = 0 \qquad (11.\text{XVII})$$

Lastly, we must define away a price ambiguity for goods that are not produced. If a good is not produced in equilibrium, the desire to supply it must
be zero at all nonnegative prices for which the desire to consume it is positive.
Zero excess demand for it must occur where $\bar{X}_j^o = 0$. In such circumstances
price is not uniquely defined. Therefore we impose the following condition:

$$P_j^o = \min P_j \text{ for which } (X_j + X_j') = 0, \text{ when } \bar{X}_j^o = 0 \qquad (11.\text{XVIII})$$

Then, with conditions (11.I) through (11.XVIII) we have described the
"anatomy" of a general equilibrium, in which all markets are purely or
monopolistically competitive in the nonrivalrous sense.

Notes

[1] See [3], pp. 83–5. A notable exception to this general position is that of Takashi
Negishi, who has built a general-equilibrium system incorporating both pure and
"monopolistic" competition. Negishi uses a Uzawa mapping to demonstrate the
existence of a fixed point that is an equilibrium, after (1) placing essentially the
Arrow–Debreu restrictions upon consumption and production sets; (2) assuming
the expected price of monopolistically competitive goods to be a function of all prices
and of their own quantities offered and demanded; (3) making these inverse sales
curves linear or composed of linear segments; and (4) assuming one monopolistic
competitor at most in each market. Further, under conditions of strict gross substi-

tutability for purely competitive goods and for a similar condition on the prices of monopolistically competitive goods, he adapts his own proof to show that the equilibrium is locally stable, and the Arrow–Block–Hurwicz proof that the system is globally stable. See [6].

Negishi does not cope with the problem of product differentiation in any satisfactory way. He assumes a set of distinct goods exists, all elements of which are held as positive stocks by every consumer (a condition that is sufficient to eliminate a certain potential discontinuity in consumer demands). Interproduct competition is eliminated in its rivalrous form and ignored in its nonrivalrous aspects, because no restrictions on nonnegative profits are discussed. The model best fits the conditions of a world of pure monopolistic markets or markets with one dominant seller and a fringe of pure competitors in which products are essentially isolated from one another. In this sense perhaps it is best regarded as a generalization of Pareto's model of general monopoly.

2 The strength of this influence on policy and thought has been questioned recently by M. Blaug, in [1], chapters 10 and 12.

3 [10], p. 3. See also pp. 5–7, where Triffin specifically rejects the essence of the contribution of Chamberlin and Mrs Robinson as that which I accept: the novel aspects for the firm's isolated adjustment introduced by product groups within a nonrivalrous competitive environment.

4 Cf. [10], pp. 9–10: "In Walras and Pareto, the whole system of general equilibrium is made explicitly to hinge upon the individual entrepreneur and his efforts to maximize profits."

5 See, for example, V. Pareto, [7], pp. 224, 333, 594–8, 613.

6 Cf. also: "Instead of the vague, ill-defined, 'industries' and undifferentiated 'commodies' of traditional economics, we proposed to build up from the elementary maximizing units (firms and households) and from commodities narrowly and unequivocally defined with reference not to 'industries,' but to those elementary maximizing units" [10], p. 141.

7 See, for example, his concluding paragraphs, where he asserts: "Instead of [economics] drawing its substance from arbitrary assumptions, chosen for their simplicity and unduly extended to the whole field of economic activity, our theory may turn to more pedestrian, but more fruitful methods. It will recognize the richness and variety of all concrete cases, and tackle each problem with due respect for its individual aspects. More advantage will be taken of all relevant factual information and less reliance will be placed on a mere resort to the passkey of general theoretical assumptions" [10], p. 189.

8 See note 12.

9 But see also p. 77, where he asserts that "to be useful, Professor Chamberlin's formulation needs to be broadened beyond the realm of a hypothetical group of symmetrical firms." And see note 7.

10 "With ... the breaking up of the industry into firms, the old problem of equilibrium within a relatively large economic unit fades into the background before the now all-important problem of the relationships *between* relatively small economic units. The attention passes from the equilibrium of supply and demand within an industry to the conditions of equilibrium external to the firm. By virtue of definition, the latter question cannot be successfully attacked with the tools of particular

equilibrium, forged as they are for the study of one economic unit (the industry yester-day, now the individual firm) in isolation from the rest of the system" [10], p. 12.
[11] Triffin seems to agree with this: "One common feature of both *The Theory of Monopolistic Competition* and *The Economics of Imperfect Competition* is their insistence on the maximizing problem of the individual seller and their summary treatment of the problem of the interrelationships between the firms" [10], p. 49.
[12] See also J. Robinson, [8] p. 307, where she asserts that her analysis deals with the isolated industry, a group of related monopolists. The Sraffa outlook is further reflected in the short shrift she gives to problems of selling costs and product variation.

It is interesting to compare the lists of quotations that Triffin has compiled from Chamberlin and Mrs Robinson to show the similarity of their concepts of mono-polistic competition and imperfect competition. In Mrs Robinson's writings the belief that the seller rather than the product is differentiated seems clear; indeed, in only one phrase – "guarantee of quality provided by a well-known name" – does she mention a possible product quality. Triffin also points to the fact that she does not mention patents in her list. See [10], pp. 38–42, and [8], pp. 88–90.

This rather subtle difference in outlook may explain some of Professor Chamberlin's belief that the theories are quite different. It helps to explain, for exam-ple, the greater role of the tangency solution in Mrs Robinson (see Chamberlin's criticism, [2], p. 210), and it explains her use of the expression "firm's output" rather than "firm's product" throughout the work. See [2], p. 209n., where he comes very close to sensing this difference in outlooks.
[13] Chamberlin does not seem to include product differentiation in the eyes of the firm. See, for example, [2] p. 56.
[14] Negishi states the condition that each goods market have at most one mono-polistic competitor and asserts that by so doing he aims to exclude oligopoly and other rivalrous relations. But this is insufficient. In effect he adds the condition that all interaction effects are zero by defining sales curves for monopolistically competitive goods as unrelated to the amounts of all other goods sold and by assuming that no interaction effects exist to make such sales curves indeterminate. See [6].
[15] More exactly, because consumers share firm profits but not losses, income is defined as

$$Y_c = \sum_z \bar{X}_{cz} P_z + \sum_J \alpha_{cJ} \bar{L}_J + \sum_v \max \left[0, \beta_{cv} M_v \right]$$

However, because the null vector is in the domain of each firm's production func-tions, negative profits will not occur. However, in proofs of existence of equilibrium and in stability analysis, where arbitrary nonnegative price vectors may be used, the above formulation may be relevant.

References

[1] Blaug, Mark, *Ricardian Economics*, Yale University Press, New Haven, CT, 1958.

[2] Chamberlin, Edward H., *The Theory of Monopolistic Competition*, 1st edn, Harvard University Press, Cambridge, MA, 1933.

[3] Hicks, J. R., *Value and Capital*, 2nd edn, Oxford University Press, Oxford, 1946.

[4] Kuenne, Robert E., *The Theory of General Economic Equilibrium*, Princeton University Press, Princeton, NJ, 1963.

[5] Kuhn, Harold W. and A. Tucker, "Nonlinear Programming", in J. Neyman (ed.), *Proceedings of the Second Berkeley Symposium on Mathematical Statistics and Probability*, University of California Press, Berkeley, CA, 1951.

[6] Negishi, Takashi, "Monopolistic Competition and General Equilibrium", *Review of Economic Studies*, 28 (1961), 196–201.

[7] Pareto, Vilfredo, *Manuel d'Economie Politique*, Giard et Brière, Paris, 1909.

[8] Robinson, Joan, *The Economics of Imperfect Competition*, Macmillan, London, 1933.

[9] Sraffa, Piero, "The Laws of Returns Under Competitive Conditions", *Economic Journal*, 36 (1926), 544–6.

[10] Triffin, Robert, *Monopolistic Competition and General Equilibrium Theory*, Harvard University Press, Cambridge, MA, 1949.

12

Interproduct Distances in a Quality-space: Inexact Measurement in Differentiated Oligopoly Analysis

Despite the passage of some 40 years since the formal introduction of the notion of differentiated products by Chamberlin [1], chapters 4 and 5, and Robinson [6], pp. 21, 88–90, little progress has been made in its rigorous incorporation into economic theory.[1] If the experience of other areas of economic theory is relevant, until some means is found to "measure" qualitative differences among products substantial advance is not to be expected. It is incumbent upon the theorist, therefore, to find operational methods for the achievement of the goal.

In presenting a model of general economic equilibrium that included monopolistic competition, I put forward the concept of a "quality-space" in which members of a product group were located, and of the "distance" in some metric between pairs of them [3], pp. 232–5. In that work all goods in a product group are assumed to have certain "core qualities" in varying extensive, intensive, or attributive degrees, and some brands to possess "non-core" qualities variably. The former set of qualities demarcates the goods as a product group.

In a later paper concerned with constructing a theoretical module for use in a general equilibrium model of differentiated oligopoly, I used a measure of interproduct distance between the goods of firm v and a rival v^*, or s_{v,v^*}, defined on the unit interval, in the statement of the firm v sales function [4]:

$$D_v = a_v - b_v P_v + \sum_{v^*} d_{v,v^*} P_{v^*} + g_v Y, \qquad (12.1)$$

the P-terms being brand prices and Y a national income variable. The intercept parameter is defined as

Originally published in *Applied Economics*, 6 (1974), 255–73, and reproduced with permission.

$$a_v = A_v \left\{ n^{[\Sigma_{v^*} s_{v,v^*} / (n-1)] - 1} \right\}, \tag{12.2}$$

where n is the number of firms (brands). Further,

$$d_{v,v^*} = (1 - s_{v,v^*}) E_v, \tag{12.3}$$

with E_v being a parameter depicting the impact upon firm v's sales of a product located at a near-zero distance from its own. From equations (12.1) to (12.3) the final form of the oligopolist's sales function is

$$D_v = A_v \left\{ n^{[\Sigma_{v^*} s_{v,v^*} / (n-1)] - 1} \right\} - b_v P_v + \sum_{v^*} (1 - s_{v,v^*}) E_v P_{v^*} + g_v Y, \tag{12.4}$$

which incorporates the interproduct distance measurements explicitly.

The current paper presents a theory of graphic scaling of interproduct quality distances with the aim of defining the s_{v,v^*} numerically: an operational method of measuring imprecise and introspective concepts. Through the use of a cross-impact matrix, weights are derived that reflect the importance in subjects' minds of the relevant quality in defining the product group. The measurement of interproduct distances between pairs of goods is accomplished by summing the interproduct quality distances multiplied by the normalized weights. Finally, we illustrate the technique and establish some experimentally based hope for its success by presenting the results of four sample experiments measuring interproduct distances among five candy bars in seven quality dimensions.

1 Some Preliminaries on the Theory of Measurement

Formal measurement of the degree to which empirical objects possess a given property entails two problems, whose solutions imply the proof of two types of theorem.[2] We discuss each in turn briefly.

1.1 The Representation Problem

This problem is that of establishing that the empirical relational system relevant to the given property possesses a similar structure (is isomorphic or homomorphic) to a relational system defined (for practical purposes) on the real number line. The empirical relational system consists of the set of objects possessing the property to be measured and one or more relations between objects with respect to the property. For example, let the set A be a group of laboratory mice, the property of interest their weight, and the relation chosen the binary relation " $\geqslant$ " or "at least as heavy as." The empirical relational system may then be defined as

$$\mathscr{A} = [A, \geqslant].$$

It is possible with such a system to place the objects in descending sequence of weight through the use of a laboratory balance, with animals of the same weight placed in the same group as their fellows. To measure the empirical objects with respect to the property, however, a numerical relational system

$$\mathscr{N} = [N, R_1, R_2, \ldots],$$

on the set of real numbers N and employing the indicated relations R_i, must be established, and a function f defined to map the elements in A on to N in a one-to-one (isomorphic) or, in the case where f^{-1} is not one-to-one, in a homomorphic (permitting ties) manner, such that $f(a) \geqslant f(a')$ if $a \geqslant a'$. For the case at hand, the numerical relational system

$$\mathscr{N} = [\text{positive integers, } \geqslant]$$

can be shown to be homomorphic to the elements of A, and

$$\mathscr{N} = [\text{positive integers, } >]$$

to be isomorphic to the sequenced *groups* of like-weight mice. Hence, f is defined as a functional assignment of integers to the sets of objects such that heavier animals get larger numbers than lighter and equi-weight animals get the same number. The representational problem is solved when the proof that $\mathscr{N}$ is isomorphic or homomorphic to $\mathscr{A}$ is completed.

1.2 The Uniqueness Problem

The three-tuple $[\mathscr{A}, \mathscr{N}, f]$ defines a *scale* of measurement characterized by its "uniqueness," which is to say by the kinds of transformations of f that do not affect the structure of the measurement. To economists, three types of scales so characterized have been of theoretical interest:

1 *Uniqueness up to a monotonic transformation.* The economist is accustomed to this degree of uniqueness which merely preserves ranking in his usage of ordinal utility functions.
2 *Uniqueness up to a linear transformation.* The measurement of time and temperature are classic examples of this scale: the non-existence of a natural zero origin for the ordinary (non-Kelvin) measurement of temperature means that an arbitrary origin can be chosen (say 32°F for the freezing point of water) and an arbitrary value chosen higher on the scale (say 212°F for the boiling point of water), with the interval divided into equal units. Such measurement yields meaningful *intervals*, and measurement specialists term such scales *interval scales*, but ratios of such measurements are not meaningful.

3 *Uniqueness up to a similarity transformation.* When a scale possesses a natural zero origin any function f derived differs from all potentially derivable f^* only in the choice of unit; i.e. $f^* = b \times f$, $b \geqslant 0$. Such a scale is characterized by the meaningfulness of ratios, and is termed a *ratio scale* for this reason.

In summary, exact measurement techniques rest upon the clear and precise definition of the property being measured; the choice of appropriate relations; the proof that an empirical relational system has an exactly defined structural similarity to a numerical relational system; and the proof of a uniqueness theorem to establish the scale type.

2 The Practicalities of Scaling in the Social Sciences

In the social sciences frequent occasions arise when one or more of these procedures are impossible, and progress in quantification depends upon the use of techniques with only an empirically-demonstrated usefulness. For example, psychologists seek insights into attitudes, ask subjects to scale handwriting in terms of "pleasingness," and require raters to score candidates in such qualities as "cooperativeness," "leadership," and "acting ability." None of these properties is truly susceptible to exact definition, or capable of meeting the other preconditions described in section 1 for rigorous measurement.

The methods to be employed in this paper for the ends of economic theory are also those of "subjective estimate" [9] p. 62 – blends of the scientific and intuitive – and our results must be considered experimental. We frankly embrace the intuitive when the objective fails us: for example, we shall ask if the "flavor" of brand 1 is closer to that of brand 2 or brand 3 and by how much, where "flavor" is the primitive concept. It seems fruitless to search for more primitive concepts in which to define "flavor" or "aroma," and yet we hypothesize that the consumer will be able to answer such questions within the confines of subjective probability theory consistently with his fellows, to the extent that the scale constructed may be treated as similar to an interval scale with useful results.

The use of "inexact" measurement for practical scaling purposes has a long history in such fields as psychology and education, and we may appeal for an extended example to a procedure with which we are all familiar: grading in or being graded by an educational system in many course dimensions. Consider the scoring of students' achievements in a course of study on a scale from 0 to 100. The characteristic to be "measured" is notable for its lack of precise definition: it is a connotative quality, drawing upon the experience, intuition, and introspection of the grader for meaningfulness. Attempts to give it simple meaning lead one to balk: for example, conversion to the proportion of objective questions answered correctly in a series of examinations leads to the objection that there is no readily plausible relation between percentage points on the correct-answer scale and percentage points of achievement.

What degree of uniqueness does such a student scoring system have? Is it at best unique up to a monotonic transformation? If so, the usual arithmetic operations performed upon such grades are illegal: they cannot be added to other grades or averaged or weighted. Are they equivalent to points on an interval scale, so that the 0 mark corresponds to no natural origin but distances between individuals on the scale are meaningful? This would permit us to perform arithmetic operations of the weighted-average variety, in certain circumstances, but would forbid such procedures as standardizing grades by the use of standard deviations. Or is the 0 on the scale indeed a natural zero in some definable sense, and do we in fact have a ratio scale: is a student who earns 60 considered to have achieved 60 percent of a definable range of 100 units, and a student who received a grade of 30 in that sense only half the beneficiary?

To ask these questions is to seek for a clear definition of the characteristic, a representation theorem, and a uniqueness theorem. In all respects that search will fail. We are enmeshed in "quasi-measurement" or "inexact measurement" which possesses only a surface resemblance to exact measurement. Is it, therefore, a useless or misleading procedure which would be best discontinued?

I suggest that an interpretation of the following type would validate the procedure. A teacher acquires through experience and training a good conception of the performance of an idealized student who has passed through the course or some segment of it with no practicably measurable accretion of knowledge. This idealized notion of null accomplishment he places at the 0 mark of his scale, and we shall interpret it as a "natural" zero for the individual teacher. On the other hand, the idealized student who has mastered the material in a manner that could not be effectively surpassed in the time available is also present in the teacher's professional subconscious, and anchors the scale at the 100 mark. Hence the grading scale may be interpreted as *percentages of effective range (ER) of accomplishment*, and may be manipulated as a ratio scale.

If the "standards" of a teacher – the idealized definitions at 0 and 100 – are similar in some inevitably intuitive sense to the standards of other teachers, the grades may be averaged among courses over the academic lifetime of the student with meaningful results. Decisions of great importance to individuals, universities, and society are made on the basis of such scaling and in the faith that their assimilated uniqueness is that of a ratio scale. The indefinable quality of academic excellence or achievement is scored in a "measurement" procedure reflecting intuitive–introspective knowledge, without formal proofs of representation or uniqueness, and with no scale validations by means of controlled stimuli.

Is it possible to project such techniques into the measurement of distances among goods in a quality dimension and in a quality space of many dimensions? We turn to methods for answering the question affirmatively, and to do so we shall distinguish the following types of qualities that present somewhat distinctive problems:

1 qualities that are measurable with a high degree of uniqueness in natural units;
2 qualities without natural units that vary in an absolute sense;
3 qualities without natural units that vary in a relative sense;
4 qualities that are attributes.

We shall deal with each of these categories independently.

3 Qualities Capable of High-uniqueness Representation

Suppose a quality is capable of objective measurement unique up to a linear or similarity transformation – length, weight, or maximum velocity, for example. For the product group in question we must establish an effective lower bound for the quality as manifested in the group. If the brands of a product group can vary realistically in length between 18 and 24 inches, we place these values at 0 and 100 respectively and transform intermediate values to percentages of an ER of 6 inches. If brand 1 is 21 inches and brand 2 is 19 inches, their "quality grades" are 50.00 and 16.67 respectively, and their Euclidean interproduct distance in this quality dimension is $D_{1,2} = 33.33$. Their absolute distance of 2 inches is thus transformed to a distance of one-third of ER.

If the quality is the recommended temperature at which different wines are served, so that the natural scale is an interval scale, we proceed in the same manner. We conceive of a maximum lower bound below which it is inconceivable that a wine will be served – say 42°F – and a minimum upper bound above which it normally never is served – say 80°F. These values are transformed to 0 and 100 respectively, and intermediate values are given the grade $G = 2.6317\,(T - 42°)$, where T is the recommended serving temperature of a wine in degrees Fahrenheit. If brand 1 is served at 48°F it receives a position of 15.79, and if brand 2 is served at 50°F a score of 21.05 is recorded. Therefore, $D_{1,2} = 5.26$, and the two types of wine vary in temperature at serving by about 5 percentage points of ER. Such measurements are invariant to the change of origin and unit of the original temperature scale: degrees centrigrade will yield the same results.

How meaningful is such measurement? The answer hinges upon the ability to define meaningful least upper and greatest lower bounds for the product group's possession of the properties. These bounds should not be the lowest and highest values for *existing* products: the notion of a product group and the possibility of introducing new brands into it without disturbing existing distance measures require that the limits be defined in terms of potential as well as existing brands.

4 Qualities of Varying Intensities that Differ Absolutely

A quality which can be viewed as contained in a given brand in greater or lesser intensity, though objective measurement techniques do not exist to calibrate that intensity in other-than-ordinal fashion, we shall speak of as having qualities that differ *absolutely* among members of the product group. We envision the interproduct distance between goods on that quality's axis as a consensual magnitude for the relevant decision-makers of an economy at a particular time, reflecting their individual conceptual and perceptual differences and subjective uncertainties.

To be more explicit, we shall formalize the state of mind of each relevant individual as a subjective probability distribution over an ER scale, the probability value defining a degree of belief for each potential position of a brand on the quality scale. The expected values of these distributions for all relevant individuals, in turn, form a distribution whose own expected value we shall treat as the valid intensity of this quality for the brand in question. By asking the individual to locate three grades on an ER scale, we shall attempt to estimate his subjective probability distribution and its expected value, and by averaging expected values over a sample of individuals we shall estimate the universe expected value.

On a linear scale with 0 and 100 at the endpoints, and with the 25, 50, and 75 points also marked at the quarters, the individual is asked to place three points graphically:

1 L: a lower bound of intensity below which he is in effect certain the given good does not contain the relevant quality;
2 H: an upper bound of intensity above which he is in effect certain the given good does not contain the relevant quality;
3 M: the best point estimate he can make of the number of percentage points of ER at which the given good is located on the quality scale.

Obtaining such estimates from each subject permits us to take into account the uncertainty he feels concerning his scaling as well as his best judgement of a good's score on a quality scale. Moreover, we have found from experience that the mechanics of the decision-making by the subject are facilitated when this sequence of marking points is followed.

To obtain a single scale value reflecting both aspects of judgement, we shall assume that L and H are the end-points of a domain over which the subjective probability distribution is defined, and for ease of handling we shall assume that the form of the distribution is that of a beta-distribution:

$$B(X) = \left[\frac{\gamma(\alpha + \beta + 2)}{[\gamma(\alpha + 1)\gamma(\beta + 1)(H - L)^{\alpha+\beta+1}]} \right] (X - L)^{\alpha} (H - X)^{\beta}.$$

Further, we shall assume that M is the mode of the beta-distribution, and shall seek to estimate the expected value $E(X)$ of that distribution for use as the individual's scaling of the brand in the relevant quality.

The value of $E(X)$ for a beta-distribution is

$$E(X) = \frac{L + (\alpha + \beta)M + H}{\alpha + \beta + 2}, \tag{12.5}$$

where M is the mode of the distribution:

$$M = \frac{\alpha H + \beta L}{\alpha + \beta}. \tag{12.6}$$

Our approximation procedure is as follows. Note from equation (12.5) that $E(X)$ is a function of $Z = \alpha + \beta$, so that we may rewrite equation (12.6) as

$$\alpha = Z \left(\frac{M - L}{H - L} \right) \equiv ZK, \tag{12.7}$$

where we have defined K as the expression in parentheses. We then use equation (12.7) to transform equation (12.5) to

$$E(X) = \frac{L + ZM + H.}{Z + 2} \tag{12.8}$$

The task has now become one of estimating Z, for which we need another independent relation. This we find in the expression for the variance of the beta distribution:

$$\sigma^2 = (H - L)^2 \frac{(\alpha + 1)(\beta + 1)}{(\alpha + \beta + 2)^2(\alpha + \beta + 3)}$$

$$= (H - L)^2 \frac{Z^2 K - Z^2 K^2 + Z + 1}{(Z + 2)^2(Z + 3)}. \tag{12.9}$$

The value $(H - L)$ we know to be the domain of the distribution, and we shall assume that the beta-distribution follows closely the normal distribution in that practically all of its domain is included in an interval of 6σ. This is exactly true only for three sets of values $[\alpha, \beta]$, but it is a reasonably good approximation for the range of Z values that will concern us.[3] From equation 12.9 we then obtain

$$1 = 36 \frac{Z^2 K - Z^2 K^2 + Z + 1}{(Z + 2)^2 (Z + 3)}, \tag{12.10}$$

from which Z may be treated as a function of K. For the range of values for K and Z which have relevance for the unimodal beta distributions of our analysis, we list below the relation between standard deviation and $(H - L)$ as well as v^*, the value of $(H - L)$ at which the 6σ relation holds exactly:

$$K = 0.25 \text{ or } 0.75$$
$$Z = 2: \sigma = 0.22(H - L), \; v^* \approx 27$$
$$Z = 3: \sigma = 0.14(H - L), \; v^* \approx 43$$
$$Z = 4: \sigma = 0.17(H - L), \; v^* \approx 35$$
$$Z = 5: \sigma = 0.37(H - L), \; v^* \approx 16$$
$$K = 0.50$$
$$Z = 2: \sigma = 0.22(H - L), \; v^* \approx 27$$
$$Z = 3: \sigma = 0.19(H - L), \; v^* \approx 30$$
$$Z = 4: \sigma = 0.19(H - L), \; v^* \approx 32$$
$$Z = 5: \sigma = 0.12(H - L), \; v^* \approx 50$$

In our experience to date, K in the range of 0.30 to 0.50 and Z in the 3 to 4 range have proved to be most relevant, and the spread between H and L of 30 to 40 a quite frequent response from subjects. The estimate of range as 6σ, therefore, seems workably accurate.

From equation (12.7) it may be seen that K is the ratio of distance from the mode to the lower bound divided by range, and if the subject is reasonably symmetrical in his uncertainty this should approximate 0.50. If we assume this, so that $K - K^2 \approx 0.25$, equation (12.10) may be solved and yields $Z \approx 6.00$. Substitution of this into equation (12.8) gives

$$E(X) = \frac{L + 6M + H}{8}, \tag{12.11}$$

which may be used as an approximation to the expected value. We have chosen to sharpen the approximation somewhat as follows. Z reaches its maximum for $K = 0.50$ and its minimum for $K = 0$ or 1, at which latter values $Z \approx 2.85$. Further, when $K = 0.25$ or 0.75, $Z \approx 4.80$. By fitting a least squares regression to these three points, we obtain

$$Z \approx 2.85 + 9.30G - 6.00G^2, \; G = \begin{cases} K, & \text{if } K \leqslant 0.50 \\ (1 - K), & \text{if } K > 0.50, \end{cases}$$

which we substitute into equation (12.8) to obtain better estimates than those from equation (12.11). $E(X)$ so estimated is the scale value for the subject which we seek.

Let us review briefly the characteristics of this measurement procedure that should not be blinked. First, it will frequently be true that the quality can be named but not defined, so that the conceptualizations of the subject must be relied upon. Of course, this immediately raises the questions of common standards among the subjects and the uniqueness of the natural origins for ER. Second, the subject is not responding to any external stimulus under the control of the experimenter and capable of being varied continuously. Therefore, methods of scaling using fractionalization or equi-sectioning are denied us: the stimulus is wholly subjective, cannot be related functionally to a controlled stimulus, and the resulting scale, therefore, cannot be operationally validated to assure that equal distances along it reflect equal intervals of the stimulus.

Third, it is unclear the extent to which we can exclude personal preferences from the definition of the product qualities, or, perhaps worse, the extent to which it is desirable. Much as we should like to be able to describe all members of product groups with vectors of such objective qualities as length, color, weight, temperature, and the like, there are qualities whose gradings involve personal preferences intimately, and it is with a consensual judgement that we seek to locate the quality's measure. The "tone" of a restaurant's customers, the quality of service it offers, the diversity of its menu, and so forth, involve personal value judgements. Where it is desirable to minimize their impacts, the methods to be discussed in section 5 may be applicable; but frequently this will not prove to be undesirable, as the degree of excellence is not the same as the degree of similarity.

5 Qualities of Varying Intensities that Differ Relatively

In many cases the measurement of a quality can be accomplished only by comparing the intensity attainment of the property by one product relative to another. For example, the design of the container for brand 1 may be more or less similar to the design of brand 3's package than the design of brand 2's container. Hence the quality "similarity of package design" is graded on the basis of closeness to some arbitrarily chosen product as standard. The standard is then placed at 100 on the graphic scale as an upper anchoring agent, and the individual is asked to imagine a package design which is as far away from the design of the standard as possible if the package continues to be relevant to the product group. He associates 0 with this lower anchoring agent. All brands are then located on a scale from 0 to 100 by the three-grade procedures of section 4, so that inter-product distances in this quality dimension are measured in percentage points of ER.

This type of measurement employing quarternary relations in its empirical relation system – "the difference between A and B is no greater than the difference between C and D: true or false" – is frequently used in psychological scaling theory, usually with a controllable stimulus which varies continuously or in small discrete steps over the entire continuum of the scale. For example, suppose the stimulus is the frequency of a tone in cycles per second, and the scale is being constructed for the subject's awareness of pitch. Arbitrary maximum and minimum frequencies are selected to anchor the scale, and the subject is asked to choose a frequency that bisects the whole interval. He is then asked to choose a frequency that bisects the interval between the minimum point of the scale and the midpoint, and so forth. The equal-interval assumption permits a scale unique up to a linear or similarity transformation, depending upon one's interpretation of the 0 origin.

Note the fact that this procedure in psychometrics depends only upon the subject's ability to *rank* differences between the stimuli values, for it depends solely upon this discernment that the distance of a variable stimulus from one end-point is greater than, equal to, or less that the distance to the other end-point. This is the basis for the frequent assertion that cardinal measurement depends upon the ability to rank differences between stimuli values, but the crucial ability to control the stimuli in continuous or quasi-continuous ways over the whole continuum is often omitted. However, such procedures might be used experimentally to measure an individual's utility-of-income function over an income domain that is relevant to his experience.

Of course, similarity is not an operationally definable concept, and our attitude to it is the practical one of Luce and Galanter [5], p. 251:

> The word "similar" used in the instructions is vague, and it is left that way because neither the experimenter nor the subject can verbalize very precisely what he means by it. Nonetheless, subjects respond non-randomly when instructed in this way. That reproducible data can arise from a vague criterion should not surprise us when we think of how often we use equally vague criteria in everyday life, but in the long run a science is not likely to let reproducibility alone substitute for well analyzed and controlled experimental design.

Moreover, we must face the complications of uncontrolled stimuli and the great demand upon the subject implicit in asking him to imagine a polar antithesis. But the only scientific manner to proceed in the face of an unscientific problem is to experiment to see if indeed the hypothesized consensual consistency is demonstrated.

6 Attributes

In the case of pure attributes – qualities which are present or absent and in which presence no gradations are possible – we arbitrarily assume that the interproduct distances between brands possessing different categories of attributes are 100. If one brand is blue and another is red, and only one shade of each is available, we record the interproduct distances in the color dimension as 100. Actually, the number of pure attributes is not so large as one might think at first sight; many qualities that seem to fit the category can be interpreted as qualities which vary along a scale.

Where attributes show this potential for variation we permit the grading of an attribute falling within a given category but retain the treatment of pure attributes between categories. For example, if brand 1 is dark red and brand 2 is light red, whereas brand 3 is blue, we will grade brands 1 and 2 along the same scale by the methods of sections 4 and 5, depending upon appropriateness, and compute their interproduct distance in the color dimension straightforwardly. However, we measure the distance of each from brand 3 as 100.

7 Weighting the Qualities

Qualities cannot be assumed to be of equal importance in *defining* the product group, and therefore we are faced with the need to derive the relative weights to be applied to the interproduct distances in the various quality dimensions to obtain interproduct distances in the quality-space. In this enterprise we again depend upon a probe of individual attitudes, and with it accept the risk of mixing individual preferences among qualities with the importance of the qualities in defining the product groups. A consumer might find that color was of large personal importance in his choice of automobile, and at the same time believe that it was of secondary importance in defining the groups of products that form the automobile complex. But, on the other hand, he may not distinguish the two aspects in his answers, and despite briefings of the subjects, it will be difficult to assess to what degree the judgements rendered are free of consumer preferences as we would desire them to be. Nevertheless, the stress must be upon defining product groups rather than stating individual preferences over the qualities they possess.

We use a cross-factor matrix method that assures the comparison of every quality with every other quality in the determination of the weights. An $n \times n$ matrix of the n qualities is established as a tableau, as illustrated in table 12.1 for $n = 4$. The diagonal items are ignored, and the subject is asked to consider only those cells that lie above the main diagonal. Across row i,

Table 12.1   The cross-factor matrix: method A

	Quality					
Quality	1	2	3	4	Sum	Weighting factor
1	–	3	0	1	4	0.17
2	1	–	4	3	8	0.33
3	4	0	–	2	6	0.25
4	3	1	2	–	6	0.25
					24	

quality i is compared with the qualities $j, k, \ldots$, and the subject is asked to indicate the importance of qualities $j, k, \ldots$, and to score his judgements in the relevant cells.

Two methods of scoring are recommended, the choice depending upon the number of qualities in the quality-space and the fineness of discrimination among quality weights required.

7.1 Method 1

The method used in the illustrations of this section is based upon scores of 0 to 4, and it has also been adopted in the experiments to be described in section 8. The subject is asked to consider row quality i versus column quality j and to grade as follows:

4: Quality i is much more important than quality j in the definition of the product group.
3: Quality i is more important than quality j.
2: Quality i and quality j are of equal importance.
1: Quality j is more important than quality i.
0: Quality j is much more important than quality i.

The cells below the main diagonal are graded by the experimenter on the basis that the value in cell (i, j) plus the value in cell (j, i) must sum to 4.

We have illustrated the method in table 12.1. Each row sum is computed to obtain the absolute score of the relevant quality, and then is divided by the total of the row sums $[2n(n-1)]$ to obtain the set of *weighting factors*.

7.2 Method 2

A finer discrimination among the qualities in determining weighting factors may be obtained by asking the subject to divide 100 points between qualities

i and j in cells (i,j) and (j,i). Again, of course, only the cells in the main diagonal need be scored.

To obtain the final weights we have experimented with three different methods, the results of which are presented separately in section 8.

7.3 Method A

The weighting factors in table 12.1 are adopted as the final weights. While this may be an acceptable procedure in many cases, a difficulty with it should be noted: no quality can attain a weight greater than $2/n$, and this upper bound is independent of the sum distributed between cells (i,j) and (j,i). In smaller problems – for example, that of table 12.1 – this may be acceptable, because the limit is rather high. But as n rises it becomes increasingly restrictive, as may be seen in table 12.2, so that for a seven-quality study no single quality can be more than 28 percent in total importance.

Table 12.2 Maximum quality weights

			n		
Method	3	4	5	7	10
A	0.67	0.50	0.40	0.28	0.20
B	1.00	0.75	0.60	0.43	0.30
C	0.86	0.68	0.56	0.41	0.29

7.4 Method B

This limitation of method A can be overcome, as revealed in table 12.2, by the method illustrated in table 12.3. Each row sum is divided by its maximum potential value of $(n-1)/4$ so that the weighting factors are row scores as ratios to perfect scores. These weighting factors are then used as multipliers on the row's relevant column entries, and a new row sum thereby computed. The normalized values of these sums are final weights. The maximum weight attainable by a quality is given by

$$\frac{(n-1)(n-2)}{1 \times 2 + 2 \times 3 + 3 \times 4 + \ldots + (n-2)(n-1)},$$

from which the values of table 12.2 have been computed for the B row. The calculation of the weights for the problem of table 12.1, using method B, is illustrated in table 12.3.

Table 12.3   The cross-factor matrix: method B

| | Quality | | | | | | | |
Quality	1	2	3	4	Sum	W.F.	W. sum	Weights
1	–	3	0	1	4	0.33	2.50	0.22
2	1	–	4	3	8	0.50	3.83	0.34
3	4	0	–	2	6	0.67	2.32	0.20
4	3	1	2	–	6	0.67	2.67	0.24
							11.32	

Table 12.4   The cross-factor matrix: $n = 5$

| | Quality | | | | | Weights | | |
Quality	1	2	3	4	5	A	B	C
1	–	3	0	1	4	0.20 (0.17)	0.20 (0.22)	0.20 (0.21)
2	1	–	4	3	4	0.30 (0.33)	0.34 (0.34)	0.33 (0.32)
3	4	0	–	2	4	0.25 (0.25)	0.22 (0.20)	0.23 (0.22)
4	3	1	2	–	4	0.25 (0.25)	0.24 (0.24)	0.24 (0.25)
5	0	0	0	0	–	0	0	0

In addition to permitting some release from the tight restriction on maximum weight that method A imposes, another advantage of method B is that it enhances the independence of weights from irrelevant qualities. Suppose for example, we introduce a fifth quality into the example of table 12.1 which is of no importance in defining the product group, as illustrated in table 12.4. Ideally, such a quality should have no impact on the weights derived for $n = 4$, but unfortunately some impact cannot be avoided. Method B, by taking into account the "easy victory" of qualities 1 to 4 over 5, will soften the impact, as shown in table 12.4 by a comparison of the weights for $n = 5$ with the $n = 4$ weights in parentheses for the three methods.

7.5 Method C

Method C permits an even greater freedom for quality weights, and is recommended in studies where one or more row sums approach zero. It differs from method B only in that a unity value is placed in each diagonal cell before the weighting factors are applied to the column entries in each row. This permits the row quality's own weighting factor to enter the weighted sum, giving weaker-scoring qualities a greater weight than obtained in method B, but permitting a zero-scoring quality no weight at all. The maximum weight attainable by this method is

$$\frac{2n - 3}{0.5n + 2(n - 1)^{-1}(1 \times 2 + 2 \times 3 + 3 \times 4 + \ldots + (n - 2)(n - 1))},$$

which can be seen to be less than that of method B, but by an amount that approaches zero rapidly for $n > 10$, as is evident in table 12.2. The weights for $n = 4$ and 5 are given in table 12.4, where the greater stability in the face of an irrelevant quality is demonstrated.

8 An Illustrative Experiment

To illustrate our methods and to experiment with their workability we attempted to determine the interproduct quality distances of five well-known brands of American ten-cent candy bars, employing a seven-quality space. The candy bars were the following: brand 1, plain Hershey Bar; brand 2, Milky Way; brand 3, Life Savers, assorted fruit flavors; brand 4, Mounds; and brand 5, Baby Ruth. The seven qualities forming the dimensions of the quality space were: quality 1, net weight; quality 2, package; quality 3, external color; quality 4, shape; quality 5, sweetness; quality 6, chewiness; and quality 7, flavor.

Two samples of male adults between 40 and 45 years of age and two samples of young adults between 20 and 25 years were polled independently in the experiment. For qualities 2, 4, and 7 (package, shape, and flavor) the subjects were presented with a horizontal scale 10 cm long with the 0, 25, 50, 75, and 100 points calibrated. They were instructed to place the Hershey Bar at the 100 mark in their mind's eye, and to scale the other brands with L-M-H marks in terms of similarity of those brands in the relevant quality to the standard, as discussed in section 5. As there indicated, they were asked to imagine at the 0 point a candy bar as different from the Hershey Bar in the relevant quality as it was possible to be and yet remain in the candy bar product-group.

For qualities, 3, 5, and 6, following the methods of section 4, we asked the subjects to imagine the highest and lowest possible attainment in candy bars of brownness of color, sweetness, and chewiness, and to mark L-M-H scores for each brand. For the color quality only brownness was scaled, and Life Savers were ruled to be at distance 100 from the other four brands, as discussed in section 6.

For quality 1 (net weight) we scaled the brands directly in the manner of section 3, and they were given scores of 64, 88, 45, 82, and 80 respectively. Finally, a 7 × 7 cross-factor matrix was presented to the subjects and they were asked to divide four grade points between quality pairs on the basis of the importance in defining the product-group, in the manner of the discussion of section 7.

Sample 1 contained 22 subjects, sample 2 had 14 subjects, sample 3 contained 17 subjects, and sample 4 had 16 subjects. It was interesting that no

Table 12.5   Mean quality scalings for brands, with standard deviations, samples 1, 2, 3, 4, and C

Brand	Quality	Mean					Standard deviation				
		1	2	3	4	C	1	2	3	4	C
1	1	64.00	64.00	64.00	64.00	64.00	0.00	0.00	0.00	0.00	0.00
	2	100.00	100.00	100.00	100.00	100.00	0.00	0.00	0.00	0.00	0.00
	3	63.53	65.39	60.01	62.64	62.83	12.35	11.88	11.99	9.76	11.59
	4	100.00	100.00	100.00	100.00	100.00	0.00	0.00	0.00	0.00	0.00
	5	66.49	60.48	60.26	64.85	63.35	17.60	15.26	17.05	10.51	15.16
	6	33.37	35.63	37.65	33.57	34.93	10.98	14.28	15.39	18.40	15.68
	7	100.00	100.00	100.00	100.00	100.00	0.00	0.00	0.00	0.00	0.00
2	1	88.00	88.00	88.00	88.00	88.00	0.00	0.00	0.00	0.00	0.00
	2	57.65	52.53	58.00	62.85	57.90	15.42	15.06	16.06	12.94	15.13
	3	46.50	56.31	36.27	48.51	46.44	17.27	16.00	12.11	14.58	15.92
	4	58.15	47.30	53.96	55.14	54.22	18.09	15.23	18.69	15.62	16.25
	5	66.65	65.90	67.23	70.45	67.52	15.33	15.82	12.83	11.83	14.36
	6	58.83	63.93	69.92	63.12	63.52	14.28	14.92	12.09	11.60	14.01
	7	70.09	71.84	65.44	63.51	67.77	11.55	14.97	13.11	20.04	16.20
3	1	45.00	45.00	45.00	45.00	45.00	0.00	0.00	0.00	0.00	0.00
	2	28.13	40.50	18.94	22.09	26.98	28.25	25.48	13.16	8.54	20.94
	3	0.00	0.00	0.00	0.00	0.00	0.00	0.00	0.00	0.00	0.00
	4	15.43	15.19	10.98	26.84	16.93	13.77	10.27	6.67	20.97	14.17
	5	55.72	64.66	55.40	49.89	56.10	22.35	21.78	25.19	19.30	22.46
	6	25.29	17.13	10.95	27.68	20.65	19.33	22.91	5.16	28.17	22.37
	7	18.20	18.65	10.40	21.90	17.23	13.01	11.38	5.97	22.17	14.41
4	1	82.00	82.00	82.00	82.00	82.00	0.00	0.00	0.00	0.00	0.00
	2	58.65	56.95	61.69	59.81	59.32	14.92	15.10	10.82	13.69	13.91
	3	79.14	85.79	78.77	80.23	80.65	9.11	12.19	7.11	11.46	11.05
	4	42.48	43.48	40.37	50.39	44.02	17.27	16.74	11.13	14.36	15.42
	5	56.25	52.19	56.03	58.61	55.92	16.61	16.15	20.99	16.46	17.61
	6	52.55	52.86	52.32	51.24	52.25	10.27	15.10	14.74	13.19	14.60
	7	50.66	53.98	47.48	51.10	50.65	21.55	19.26	16.32	18.61	18.52
5	1	80.00	80.00	80.00	80.00	80.00	0.00	0.00	0.00	0.00	0.00
	2	44.08	50.62	46.37	47.56	46.78	17.80	19.02	12.55	12.36	16.22
	3	53.02	59.83	55.12	59.21	56.35	13.92	13.72	10.96	9.14	12.26
	4	45.62	38.50	37.40	49.15	42.97	15.75	15.78	13.85	16.30	15.98
	5	50.19	62.85	52.88	48.54	53.04	13.95	14.90	18.80	10.55	15.35
	6	68.68	67.23	68.67	65.86	67.75	11.35	15.00	15.07	11.04	14.23
	7	45.48	47.59	51.64	55.50	51.78	14.94	16.43	13.45	14.12	15.37

subject balked at scaling any of the brands or qualities, so that we concluded tentatively that the tasks possessed intuitive–introspective meaning for them. The results are summarized in tables 12.5, 12.6, and 12.7 for the four samples and for the 69 observations of the combined samples (labelled sample C).

Table 12.6   Analysis of variance, quality scalings, samples 1, 2, 3, 4, and C

	Sum of squares	D.F.	Variance	F	$F_{0.05}$
1 Sample 1					
Brand-quality					
Between brands	93,286	4	23,321	118.98	2.37
Between qualities	175,438	6	29,240	149.18	2.10
Interaction ($B \times Q$)	140,997	24	5,875	29.97	1.52
Within sets	144,222	735	196		
Brand-subjects					
Between brands	93,286	4	23,321	35.87	2.37
Between subjects	12,695	21	605	0.93	1.57
Interaction ($B \times S$)	18,886	84	225	0.34	1.27
Within sets	429,076	660	650		
Quality-subjects					
Between qualities	175,438	6	29,240	43.51	2.10
Between subjects	12,695	21	605	0.90	1.57
Interaction ($Q \times S$)	18,946	126	150	0.22	1.22
Within sets	346,864	516	672		
2 Sample 2					
Brand-quality					
Between brands	55,866	4	13,967	66.82	2.37
Between qualities	98,141	6	16,357	78.26	2.10
Interaction ($B \times Q$)	109,473	24	4,561	21.82	1.52
Within sets	95,239	455	209		
Brand-subjects					
Between brands	55,866	4	13,967	202.42	2.37
Between subjects	7,276	13	560	0.69	1.73
Interaction ($B \times S$)	5,853	52	113	0.16	1.36
Within sets	289,724	420	690		
Quality subjects					
Between qualities	98,141	6	16,357	27.03	2.10
Between subjects	7,276	13	560	0.92	1.73
Interaction ($Q \times$)	16,108	78	207	0.34	1.28
Within sets	237,194	392	605		
3 Sample 3					
Brand-quality					
Between brands	83,579	4	20,895	130.59	2.37
Between qualities	158,888	6	26,481	165.50	2.10
Interaction ($B \times Q$)	123,948	24	5,165	32.28	1.52
Within sets	89,568	560	160		

Table 12.6 Continued

	Sum of squares	D.F.	Variance	F	$F_{0.05}$
Brand-subjects					
Between brands	83,579	4	20,895	30.01	2.37
Between subjects	7,407	16	463	0.66	1.65
Interaction ($B \times S$)	9,955	64	156	0.23	1.30
Within sets	355,042	510	696		
Quality-subjects					
Between qualities	158,888	6	26,481	45.55	2.10
Between subjects	7,407	16	463	0.79	1.65
Interaction ($Q \times S$)	12,432	96	130	0.22	1.27
Within sets	277,256	476	582		
4 Sample 4					
Brand-quality					
Between brands	96,987	4	24,247	126.95	2.37
Between qualities	49,554	6	8,259	43.24	2.10
Interaction ($B \times Q$)	102,838	24	4,285	22.43	1.52
Within sets	100,234	525	191		
Brand-subjects					
Between brands	96,987	4	24,247	48.40	2.37
Between subjects	3,006	15	200	0.39	1.67
Interaction ($B \times S$)	9,185	60	153	0.31	1.32
Within sets	240,435	480	501		
Quality-subjects					
Between qualities	49,554	6	8,259	13.28	2.10
Between subjects	3,006	15	200	0.32	1.67
Interaction ($Q \times S$)	18,580	90	206	0.33	1.27
Within sets	278,473	448	622		
5 Sample C					
Brand-quality					
Between brands	312,238	4	78,060	319.92	2.37
Between qualities	456,996	6	76,166	312.16	2.09
Interaction ($B \times Q$)	377,340	24	15,722	64.43	1.52
Within sets	580,614	2 380	244		
Brand-subjects					
Between brands	312,238	4	78,060	122.93	2.37
Between subjects	39,417	68	580	8.92	1.43
Interaction ($B \times S$)	61,357	272	226	0.36	1.13
Within sets	1,314,176	2 070	635		
Quality-subjects					
Between qualities	456,996	6	76,166	129.09	2.03
Between subjects	39,417	68	580	0.98	1.49
Interaction ($Q \times S$)	91,087	408	223	0.38	1.14
Within sets	1,139,688	1 932	590		

Table 12.7   Quality weights, computed by methods A, B, and C, for samples 1–4 and C

Quality	Mean					Standard deviation				
	1	2	3	4	C	1	2	3	4	C
1 *Method A*										
1	0.14	0.10	0.10	0.11	0.11	0.05	0.05	0.06	0.06	0.06
2	0.08	0.10	0.12	0.10	0.10	0.05	0.06	0.06	0.04	0.05
3	0.10	0.11	0.12	0.10	0.11	0.03	0.06	0.04	0.03	0.04
4	0.08	0.10	0.11	0.10	0.10	0.02	0.04	0.04	0.04	0.04
5	0.18	0.19	0.16	0.19	0.18	0.04	0.03	0.06	0.04	0.04
6	0.18	0.17	0.17	0.17	0.17	0.04	0.05	0.05	0.05	0.05
7	0.24	0.24	0.22	0.23	0.23	0.05	0.06	0.06	0.03	0.05
2 *Method B*										
1	0.13	0.09	0.10	0.10	0.11	0.06	0.04	0.06	0.06	0.06
2	0.08	0.10	0.11	0.09	0.09	0.05	0.07	0.07	0.04	0.06
3	0.09	0.10	0.12	0.09	0.10	0.04	0.08	0.05	0.04	0.05
4	0.08	0.09	0.11	0.09	0.09	0.03	0.04	0.05	0.04	0.04
5	0.18	0.19	0.16	0.20	0.18	0.05	0.05	0.07	0.05	0.06
6	0.18	0.17	0.17	0.18	0.18	0.07	0.06	0.07	0.07	0.06
7	0.27	0.27	0.23	0.25	0.25	0.07	0.09	0.08	0.03	0.07
3 *Method C*										
1	0.13	0.09	0.10	0.10	0.11	0.06	0.04	0.06	0.06	0.06
2	0.08	0.10	0.11	0.09	0.09	0.05	0.07	0.07	0.04	0.06
3	0.09	0.10	0.12	0.09	0.10	0.04	0.07	0.05	0.04	0.05
4	0.08	0.09	0.11	0.09	0.09	0.03	0.05	0.05	0.04	0.04
5	0.18	0.19	0.16	0.20	0.18	0.05	0.05	0.07	0.05	0.05
6	0.18	0.17	0.17	0.18	0.18	0.04	0.06	0.07	0.07	0.06
7	0.26	0.26	0.23	0.25	0.25	0.07	0.09	0.08	0.03	0.07

8.1 Quality Scaling

In table 12.5 we list, brand by brand, the average scale values on each quality scale, derived as the expected value of beta distributions, for the four samples and the combined sample. Standard deviations are also recorded. The degree of correspondence among the four samples is surprisingly good. We performed an analysis of variance on each of them, as well as the combined sample C, with the results shown in Table 12.6. It can be seen that we have chosen pairs of the three factors in the experiment – brands, qualities, and subjects – eliminating one of them in order to provide variation within the sets. For example, for the brand–quality analyses, the variation among subjects is ignored and the observations are treated as replications by the same individual of the quality scalings for each brand. In the brand–subjects analyses, qualities are ignored and the observations are treated as replications by subjects of the scaling of brands in a single quality. Finally, in the

Table 12.8 Interproduct distances in quality-space using method B weights

Distance of brand i to brand j	Sample				
	1	2	3	4	C
$D_{1,2}$	27.75	27.69	32.31	28.83	29.11
	(5.47)	(8.45)	(8.04)	(5.24)	(7.06)
$D_{1,3}$	53.18	56.87	61.41	52.39	55.77
	(6.61)	(10.57)	(10.43)	(7.48)	(9.45)
$D_{1,4}$	31.86	30.72	35.13	30.81	32.19
	(10.13)	(7.20)	(5.52)	(5.32)	(7.77)
$D_{1,5}$	37.07	32.26	36.75	33.32	35.14
	(8.12)	(8.80)	(5.87)	(6.34)	(7.67)
$D_{2,3}$	46.28	47.07	51.70	46.45	47.82
	(8.08)	(8.69)	(7.46)	(10.21)	(8.89)
$D_{2,4}$	25.97	25.21	27.98	23.34	25.70
	(8.17)	(9.36)	(5.35)	(7.41)	(7.84)
$D_{2,5}$	27.04	21.41	26.09	25.48	25.30
	(7.81)	(8.50)	(7.54)	(5.38)	(7.68)
$D_{3,4}$	36.90	39.95	40.71	34.01	37.79
	(8.65)	(8.20)	(6.38)	(9.90)	(8.77)
$D_{3,5}$	34.83	38.40	40.81	35.04	37.08
	(9.44)	(9.67)	(7.34)	(9.75)	(9.44)
$D_{4,5}$	15.70	12.25	17.36	15.45	15.96
	(5.73)	(5.71)	(5.09)	(2.98)	(5.12)

quality–subject analyses, brands are ignored, and the observations are treated as replications of subjects scaling a single brand in the set of qualities.

The statistical testimony is dramatically unambiguous. In all cases, the differences between subjects' scalings over brands ignoring qualities and qualities ignoring brands are statistically nonsignificant, as are the potential nonadditive interaction effects. On the other hand, the scaling differences between brands and qualities as well as the interaction effects between them are significant in every instance. Hence, we may conclude that (1) the subjects' scalings over brands and qualities varied systematically in an other-than-random fashion, and (2) the scalings among subjects given brand and quality varied only randomly.

8.2 Quality Weights

The quality weights were computed by cross-factor methods using methods A, B, and C, as discussed in section 7. The resulting means and standard deviations of the four groups are given in table 12.7.

The weights are very similar, among samples and methods. Method B, which does not include own-weights, tends to yield the largest weight for quality 7 (taste) and lower weights for the less important qualities, but method C for the combined sample provides exactly the same weights, with one exception. The only noticeable difference among the methods is a slight tendency of method A to lessen the standard deviations among individuals. Overall, however, in this experiment, it seems immaterial which quality weighting method was used. In view of this, we shall employ only the weights obtained from method B to compute interproduct distances, in order to save space.

8.3 Interproduct Distances

Finally, the interproduct distances of the individual scalings were weighted by method B weights, and the means and standard deviations of the distributions computed. The results are given in table 12.8, with the means listed in the upper row and the standard deviations in parentheses below them. The median distances were also computed but differed so little from the means that in the interest of saving space they are excluded.

It is gratifying to note the close conformity of the distance measures among samples 1, 2, 3, 4, and C, *in every interproduct distance* as well as the quite reasonable standard deviations. The subjects revealed a truly astonishing consensus concerning the distances of products in an abstract quality-space, given the abstruse nature of many of the qualities considered. These initial experiments are encouraging, although they are meant as illustrations of the methods developed, and it must be recognized that such revealed consistency even among a larger number of samples is not a sufficient condition to establish that we have in fact "measured" what we have set out to measure.

We convert the distances of table 12.8 into the s_{v,v^*} of equations (12.2, 12.3 and 12.4) simply by dividing each D_{v,v^*} by 100. They are then ready for use in the sales functions for the differentiated oligopolists.

9 Conclusion

A call for the relaxation of scientific standards to make progress in a problem area cannot hope to be as ringing as a heroic summons to embrace their sterile if comforting rigor. It is our hope, however, that such experimental scaling methods as those discussed will make it possible to introduce differentiated products into economic theory on an empirically demonstrated basis. No doubt refinements and complications of such methods will be necessary, but a rich literature on psychometric scaling techniques awaits the investigator.

Though admittedly small-scale and inconclusive, our initial experiments have proven to be encouraging.

Notes

[1] Elsewhere, I have offered the opinion that Robinson's differentiation is that of producer rather than product, and that perception of this difference was an important factor in Chamberlin's belief that the two analyses were quite different. See [3], pp. 231–2.

[2] I draw heavily upon the work of Stevens [7] and Suppes and Zinnes [8] in this section.

[3] The relation is exact for $[\alpha,\beta]$ equal to $[2 + \sqrt{2}, 2 - \sqrt{2}]$, $[2 - \sqrt{2}, 2 + \sqrt{2}]$, and $[3,3]$.

References

[1] Chamberlin, Edward H., *The Theory of Monopolistic Competition*, 6th edn, Harvard University Press, Cambridge MA, 1948.

[2] Kuenne, Robert E., *The Theory of General Economic Equilibrium*, Princeton University Press, Princeton, NJ, 1963.

[3] ——, "Quality Space, Interproduct Competition, and General Equilibrium Theory", in Robert E. Kuenne (ed.), *Monopolistic Competition Theory: Studies in Impact*, John Wiley & Sons, New York, 1968, chapter 10. [Reprinted as chapter 11 in this volume.]

[4] ——, "Toward a Usable General Theory of Oligopoly", *De Economist*, 122 (1974), 471–502. [Reprinted as chapter 1 in this volume.]

[5] Luce, R. Duncan and Eugene Galanter, "Psychophysical Scaling", in R. Duncan Luce, R. Bush and Eugene Galanter (eds), *Handbook of Mathematical Psychology I*, John Wiley & Sons, New York, 1963.

[6] Robinson, Joan, *The Economics of Imperfect Competition*, Macmillan, London, 1933.

[7] Stevens, S. S., "Mathematics, Measurement, and Psychophysics", in S. S. Stevens (ed.), *Handbook of Experimental Psychology*, John Wiley & Sons, New York, 1951, chapter 1.

[8] Suppes, Patrick and Joseph L. Zinnes, "Basic Measurement Theory", in R. Duncan Luce, R. Bush and Eugene Galanter (eds), *Handbook of Mathematical Psychology I*, John Wiley & Sons, New York, 1963, chapter 1.

[9] Torgeson, Warren S., *Theory and Methods of Scaling*, John Wiley & Sons, New York, 1958.

13

Price–quality Competition in Oligopolistic Interdependence

1 Introduction

The nature of product differentiation in Joan Robinson's *Economics of Imperfect Competition* remains unclear fifty-odd years after its publication. Her thinking was shaped by the cost disputes in the British literature of the 1920s that reacted to the recently formalized analysis of the firm in pure competition. Because, it was asserted, decreasing costs were experienced in industry more frequently than not, the limits to the size of the firm must be dictated by a declining demand curve, not rising marginal cost and horizontal demand functions. As Sraffa [13] argued explicitly in the most influential article in the debate, the analysis of the firm's decision-making must be reformulated in a universal theory of monopoly. Implicitly, the decreasing cost advocates urged that if the inspired fuzziness of Marshallian economics had to be formalized, the monopoly model, not that of pure competition, was the more relevant tool. Robinson's debt to Sraffa is amply recorded in her book.[1]

This must surely be the point of departure in seeking an understanding of the role of product differentiation in her work. Robinson's primary interest lies in the nature, functioning, and – typically – social evils of monopoly. Book IV, V, VI, VIII, IX, and X are devoted exclusively to it and its comparison with pure competition, and they constitute almost 50 percent of the work. Other chapters, including much of the analysis of perfect (i.e. pure) competition, was to prepare for the departure therefrom of monopoly. Monopoly was the extreme of imperfect *competition*, and the provision and use of tools for its analysis were her primary interests.[2]

The conceptual scaffolding of Robinson's work may be sketched in the following terms. Market structures may be divided into two classes: perfect

Originally published as chapter 13 in George Feiwel (ed.), *The Economics of Imperfect Competition and Employment*, Macmillan, London, 1989, and reproduced with permission.

(i.e. pure) competition and imperfect competition. The two classes are distinguished simply by the firm's demand curve possessing a zero or negative price slope (p. 18). All firms are monopolists of their own output, but when, in the production of a "commodity," they are large in number and "buyers are all alike in respect of their choice between rival sellers" (pp. 18, 170) the first class exists. A commodity is "a consumable good, arbitrarily demarcated from other kinds of goods, but which may be regarded for practical purposes as homogeneous within itself" (p. 17).

Imperfect *competition* is embodied in two types of *markets*: *imperfect* markets, in which buyers reveal preferences for individual firms in well-defined, nonhorizontal demand curves, and (borrowing non-Robinsonian terminology) *oligopolistic* markets in which numbers of firms are so small that demand curves are not defined in the absence of explicit reaction patterns (pp. 21, 86n.). With these patterned responses such curves may be defined, *mutatis mutandis*, but Robinson explicitly rules out the analysis of oligopoly in the work (pp. 21, 86n.). Rather, it is the analysis of imperfect markets by marginalism that constitutes the book, and a more accurate title would have been *The Economics of Imperfect Markets*. As an analysis of *markets* rather than *firms* the focus of her interest was rather definitely the industry, as will be developed below, and it was this dominant interest that led Chamberlin to assert that she failed to meld competition and monopoly at the firm's level.

Imperfect markets span the spectrum in her analysis from Chamberlin's large-group tangency structure through classic monopoly, in each case with buyers expressing their preferences for firms' commodities in demand curves that are not destroyed by fewness. But it is the classic monopoly extreme, as noted above, that is her major interest. Most of the analysis of the large-group case is contained in chapter 6, sections 1 and 2, consisting of only six pages!

Since the basis of existence of imperfect markets is consumer partiality for firms' commodities, what was the nature of these distinctions? The striking feature of Robinson's discussions of these qualities is that they almost invariably are associated with the *seller* rather than the *seller's product*. It is interesting to speculate on the reasons for this view of the phenomenon that seems, to an American economist, to neglect the more prominent product-associated reasons for consumer's distinctions. This neglect of the many dimensions of product qualities and the bases for most advertising efforts[3] constitutes a deficiency when her analytical contributions are compared with those of Chamberlin.[4]

One contributing factor to this analytical viewpoint may be that 50 years ago branded products in Great Britain were not as dominant a presence in consumer products as they were in America. A more important reason, however, inheres in Robinson's Marshallian indoctrination and the importance it placed upon the industry as a unit of analysis. She realized, more clearly than Chamberlin did at this time, the threat to its existence that non-homogeneous commodities posed. By associating the differentiation with the sellers of an essentially physically similar commodity she did not eliminate that challenge, but in her own mind it substantially lessened it. It permitted her to move from the analysis of the firm in imperfect markets to the analysis of industry demand and supply curves for "essentially" homogeneous goods.

It was understandable, therefore, that Chamberlin found in Robinson's imperfect market analysis a standard industry monopoly case with essentially competitive firms selling homogeneous products with implied neglect of the firm's product and selling cost decisions. It is, however, another matter to assert, tirelessly and tiresomely, as Chamberlin did, that she failed to meld the concepts into new market structures as he had in the concept of monopolistic competition.[5] It was a difference in emphasis – with a purpose of self-deception – not an omission. The Chamberlinian large-group symmetry case with its tangency solution for the firm is developed explicitly by Robinson, with free entry the profit eliminating mechanism (chapter 7). Monopolists fill in the interstices among slightly protected markets for physically homogeneous products, their impacts upon "industry" demand diffused over their cohabitants. I find Chamberlin's more patient and deeper probing into product differentiation, selling costs, group equilibrium, and oligopoly richer in analytical insight and polished with greater scholarly care. More importantly, it has greater realistic content, once he moved away from the large-group case as he did in his later career.[6] But as a step along the route from perfect (i.e. pure) competition to the monopolized industry analysis that was admittedly her goal, and with the stubborn but pointed refusal to associate differentiation with product, Robinson paused at the market structure featuring the mixture of competition and monopoly that was in essentials indistinguishable from Chamberlin's core large-group case.

This chapter investigates manners of incorporating product differentiation in the decision-making of the firm simultaneously with the price decision. It ignores selling costs, however, to focus upon product qualities. The market structure envisioned is that of differentiated oligopoly under both Cournot neglect of rivals' reactions and a mode of interdependence I have termed "rivalrous consonance." In this excursion I am following the lead of Chamberlin in both the choice of variable and market structure, as explained above, but with the guidance of Joan Robinson who saw deeply into the complications of both factors and illuminated them.

Section 2 contains an initial framework for classifying and measuring qualities and attributes of products as they are varied about certain nonappropriable core features. Section 3 analyzes the firm's price–quality decisions in an environment that anticipates no rival reactions, focusing particularly upon the circumstances under which firms move closer together or farther apart on quality scales, and on the tradeoffs between price and quality policies.

Section 4 places the firm within an oligopolistic setting to the limited extent of forcing it to adjust to a rival's enhancement of quality. Section 5 moves these decisions into the context of mature differentiated oligopoly using rivalrous consonance as a framework to capture the mixture of competition and cooperation that characterizes such industries. As Chamberlin viewed the pressing task of his period of microeconomic analysis to be the blending of competition and monopoly, I feel that the greatest need of price theory currently is to search for flexible frameworks for the analysis of differentiated oligopoly that permit the fusion of rivalry and tacit cooperation which characterizes such industries. An initial investigation of this quest as it includes both price and quality complexes is contained in this section. Finally, section 6 contains a brief summary and some conclusions.

2 An Initial Framework for Product Differentiation Analysis

In prior work, I have quarrelled with the Triffin–Chamberlin notion that the "product" is not a useful tool of analysis, and that categorization by cross-elasticities that ignores physical properties is preferable.[7] The point is simply that the product is too useful a concept to be abandoned in operational analysis. Joan Robinson's notion of an effectively homogeneous cluster of goods produced by an "industry" could be defined by isolating a set of goods containing certain "core" qualities in common, among them physical similarity, as well as diverse "noncore" qualities which they may or may not possess in common. Certain of these noncore qualities may be *nonappropriable* by rivals – e.g. brand name – but most will lie within the area of competition by imitation. This viewpoint constitutes the point of departure for this paper.

Suppose that in such an industry – or "product group" – there exist n firms, each associated with a single "brand," where n is small enough to yield an oligopolistic market structure. Each brand has a complex of nonappropriable qualities, so that no brand can ever merge its identity completely with another through its choice of a quality complex. Through analysis, let us assume we have isolated relevant appropriable qualities $i = 1, 2, \ldots, m$, the first r of which are variables which can be measured cardinally[8] and the remainder of which are attributes.

2.1 The Derivation of Quality Indifference Premia

Arbitrarily, let us choose firm (brand) 1 as an anchor for the analysis. To a large sample of potential customers for the product we address the following set of questions:

> Suppose you were given a unit of brand 1 at no cost to you. If you were offered brand j instead, how many dollars would you have to receive or give up to make you feel as well off as you feel with brand 1?

Let us choose some measure of central tendency for the sample responses for $j = 2, 3, \ldots, n$, and term these the *indifference premia*, I_j, where $I_1 \equiv 0$ and $I_j \gtrless 0$. Next, let us attempt to decompose these I_j into additive components, I_{ij}, $i = 1, 2, \ldots, m$, by pursuing the following line of questioning for each of the m appropriable qualities:

> Suppose once more you are given a unit of brand 1. Assume brand 1's quality i were changed from its present state to that of brand j's quality i state. How much would you have to receive or pay to feel equally well off as you feel with unchanged brand 1?

A representative measure of central tendency is once more chosen for the sample responses. We can then record the information obtained in table 13.1 as the *quality indifference matrix*.

If we assume additivity of the *indifference components*, I_{ij}, and the exhaustiveness of the list of m appropriable qualities, then, for the individual we hypothesize that

$$I_j \equiv \sum_i I_{ij} + I_{ej}, \tag{13.1}$$

Table 13.1 The quality indifference matrix, I, brand 1 base

Quality (i)/Brand (j)	1	2	$\ldots$	n
1	0	I_{12}	$\ldots$	I_{1n}
2	0	I_{22}	$\ldots$	I_{2n}
.	.	.	$\ldots$	.
.	.	.	$\ldots$	.
.	.	$\ldots$		.
m	0	I_{m2}	$\ldots$	I_{mn}
Nonappropriable (I_{ej})	0	I_{e2}	$\ldots$	I_{en}
Indifference premia	0	I_2	$\ldots$	I_n

where I_{ej} is the indifference component for the nonappropriable qualities. We assume the identity of (13.1) will be approximated for the central tendency measures of the sample and will neglect sampling error, treating the aggregates as deterministic and consistent (in the sense of identity (13.1)) measures.

2.2 Conceptual Content

The goal of the exercise in deriving the quality indifference matrix, I, is to obtain an index over qualities which is a ratio scale, i.e. is unique up to a positive multiplicative scalar, measured in monetary units, and to derive it in an operational manner. The derivation of I is independent of prices, but it does mix with quality preferences the attitudes of responding individuals to money, as affected predominantly by money income levels. Because the purpose of isolating the preferences is to gain insights into the firms' decision-making, the intrusion of income into the consumer's quality preferences is not unwelcome since it will influence his decision to buy. However, such preferences do not have the unsullied psychological purity of the indifference map. They are more akin to the preference curve over alternatives under conditions of risk, capturing a relevant attitude to the purpose for which they will be used.

The indifference components, I_{ij}, may be shifted to a base other than brand 1, say brand k, by subtracting or adding I_{ik} from each row i element in table 13.1, so that the brand k column contains zeroes. Also, several meaningful and potentially useful measures can be obtained from I because of the uniqueness of the measurement. The Euclidean metric may be used to obtain the distances of brands j and k from each other in quality space:

$$d_{jk} = \left[\sum_i (I_{ij} - I_{ik})^2 \right]^{0.5},$$ (13.2)

which may be useful in clustering brands into subgroups containing close substitutes in consumers' preferences. A relative measure of qualities' importance can be defined as

$$s_i = \sum_j |I_{ij}| \bigg/ \sum_i \sum_j |I_{ij}|,$$ (13.3)

which may be used to obtain a weighted distance measure in quality space:

$$d_{ij}^w = \left[\sum_i s_i (I_{ij} - I_{ik})^2 \right]^{0.5}.$$ (13.4)

Several other characteristics of the preference measurement framework are also appealing. It is possible, for example, to include as a brand in table 13.1 a hypothetical product which does not exist but can be described as a quality complex to consumers. Also, qualities that may not be capable of independent consideration by consumers, being significantly associated physically or psychologically, may be combined into a single quality. And, lastly, the underlying qualities' intensities may be measurable ordinally or cardinally, or may be attributes describable only with a binary 0–1 index: I_{ij} indifference components will be capable of expression in all cases.

But deficiencies in the method provide some drawbacks. First, we have assumed a type of "additive transitivity." For quality i, if the consumers indicate that moving from brand 1 to brand 2 requires a subsidy of x, and moving from brand 2 to brand 3 requires a subsidy of y, then a move from brand 1 to brand 3 requires a subsidy of $x + y$. Even if this held for the individual consumer, it is not necessarily true that it will hold for the aggregate measures. And it might not hold for the individual if quality i interacts with other qualities in his preferences. Combining qualities may be useful in such cases, as noted above, but may not always be possible.

Second, we are assuming that the I_{ij} are independent of the quantity taken by consumers. This is a simplification which may or may not be an acceptable approximation, but it is a hypothesis that is at least initially desirable to retain an operational framework.

Third, we have been treating the I_{ij} as aggregate deterministic values obtained by an averaging process. They are more realistically seen as sample estimators of a population value, distributed as a sampling distribution with expected value and variance.

2.3 Quality Scales with Quality-Dollar Units

Consider the row entries of I for quality i. In quality preference space each brand has a location calibrated in dollars for quality i as a distance from brand 1. When appropriable quality i is a variable that can vary continuously, define

$$I_i = \max_j I_{ij} - \min_j I_{ij}, \qquad (13.5)$$

so that any location for brand 1 on the scale may be defined as

$$_1x_i = {}_1y_i I_i, \qquad (13.6)$$

where $_1x_i = 0$ for brand 1's initial state for quality i.

When appropriable quality i is an attribute which can take values only as recorded for existent or hypothetical brands, then acceptable points on the scale for brand 1 are defined as

$$_1x_i = \sum_j y_{ij}I_{ij}, \text{ where } y_{ij}(1 - y_{ij}) = 0, \sum_{ij} y_{ij} = 1. \qquad (13.7)$$

Arbitrarily, again, let us consider brand 1, and assume the first h appropriable qualities are variables and the remainder are attributes. Then any feasible location for brand 1 in quality space may be given by the vector $_1X$, with elements defined by (13.6) and (13.7).

3 The Firm's Decision in an Assumed Nonreactive Context

Assume that firm 1 must decide upon a price–quality policy on the assumption that its rivals' prices, p_j, and quality complexes, $_jX$, $1 < j \leqslant n$, will remain unchanged. The demand for brand 1 may be written

$$D_1 = D_1(P, X, Y), \qquad (13.8)$$

where $P = [p_1, p_2, \ldots, p_n]$, $X = [_1X, _2X, \ldots, _nX]$, and Y is a vector of unspecified exogenous variables affecting demand that we will treat as fixed over the period of analysis. The average cost of production is a function of the level of output and $_1X$:

$$C_1 = C_1(_1X, D_1). \qquad (13.9)$$

Suppose the first h appropriable qualities are variables as before. Then the firm seeks to

$$\underset{p_1, _1X}{\text{Max}} Z = D_1(p_1, _1X; p_2, p_3, \ldots, p_n, _2X, _3X, \ldots, _nX, Y) \quad (p_1 - C_1(_1X, D_1))$$
$$(13.10)$$

subject to

$$1. \quad _1x_i = y_iI_i, \quad 1 \leqslant i \leqslant h \qquad (13.11)$$

$$2. \quad _1x_i = \sum_j y_{ij}I_{ij}, \quad h + 1 \leqslant i \leqslant m$$

$$3. \quad y_{ij}(1 - y_{ij}) = 0, \quad h + 1 \leqslant i \leqslant m, \quad 1 \leqslant j \leqslant n$$

$$4. \quad \sum_j y_{ij} = 1, \quad h + 1 \leqslant i \leqslant m.$$

Relations (13.10) and (13.11) form a nonlinear integer programming problem and may be solved by an algorithm such as SUMT in combination with branch and bound combinatorics. It will not, however, be convex due to the lattice on which the y_{ij}, $h + 1 \leqslant i \leqslant m$, are defined, and may be too large for practical solution by branch and bound.

To pursue the analysis theoretically, let us therefore assume that all qualities are variables (i.e. $h = m$), and, to reduce notational clutter, let us suppress the subscript 1 on all variables. The first-order conditions for firm 1's maximum-profit solution are then

1. $\delta Z/\delta p = D(1 - C_D D_p) + (p - C)D_p = 0$ (13.12)

2. $\delta Z/\delta x_i = (p - C)D_i - C_i D - C_D D_i D = 0, \quad 1 \leqslant i \leqslant m,$

where $D_p = \delta D/\delta p$, $D_i = \delta D/\delta x_i$, $C_D = \delta C/\delta D$, and $C_i = \delta C/\delta X_i$. These conditions may be rewritten

1. $p - C - C_D D = -D/D_p$ (13.13)

2. $p - C - C_D D = C_i D/D_i, \quad 1 \leqslant i \leqslant m.$

The left-hand sides of these equations are the marginal profit per unit of sales expansion by any policy before considering the marginal cost of that policy. The right-hand sides are the marginal costs of the price and quality policies, respectively, per unit of expanded sales by that policy. System (13.13) implies that a necessary condition for a profit maximum is that the marginal cost of a unit of sales increase be equal for all policies. Therefore, we may rewrite (13.13) as

1. $C_i D/D_i = -D/D_p, \quad 1 \leqslant i \leqslant m$ (13.14)

2. $p - C - C_D D = -D/D_p.$

The second-order sufficient conditions for $m = 2$ are that the following Hessian be negative definite either in the neighborhood of the optimum for a local maximum or everywhere for a global maximum:

$$\begin{bmatrix} 2D_p - C_D D_p^2 - D_{pp}D/D_p & D_i - C_D D_p D_i - D_{pi}D/D_p \\ D_i - C_D D_p D_i - D_{pi}D/D_p & -(2C_i D_i + C_D D_i^2 + C_{ii}D + D_{ii}D/D_p) \\ D_k - C_D D_p D_k - D_{pk}D/D_p & 0 \end{bmatrix}$$

$$\left.\begin{matrix} D_k - C_D D_p D_k - D_{pk}D/D_p \\ 0 \\ -(2C_k D_k + C_D D_k^2 + C_{kk}D + D_{kk}D/D_p) \end{matrix}\right]$$ (13.15)

We assume:

1. $D_p < 0$

2. $D_{pp} < 0, \quad D_{pi}, D_{pk} \gtrless 0$

3. $D_{ii}, D_{kk} < 0, \quad D_{ik} = 0$

4. $C_D > 0, \quad C_{DD} = 0, \quad C_i, C_k > 0, \quad C_{ii}, C_{kk} \geqslant 0.$

Under these conditions, Z is concave in p, x_i, and x_k taken singly, so that the second-order conditions can be overruled by the interaction of the variables only. If all second-order derivatives are assumed near zero in absolute value, p and x_1 and p and x_2 form concave subsystems. Only x_1 and x_2 interactions jointly interacting with p could upset the conditions, and this is highly unlikely. We conclude that concavity of Z is a highly probable occurrence when second derivatives are not large relative to first-order derivatives.

Let us rewrite (13.14) in the more convenient form

$$1. \quad D_i/C_i = -D_p, \quad 1 \leqslant i \leqslant m. \tag{13.16}$$

$$2. \quad p - C - C_D D + D/D_p = 0.$$

For graphic presentation let us assume hereafter that $m = 1$. Then, equation (13.16–1) yields curves $MBCE$ (policy marginal benefit–cost equality) on figure 13.1 along which policy pairs $[p, x]$ have achieved equal marginal cost per unit of marginal sales. $MCBE$ has the slope

$$\left(\frac{dp}{dx}\right)_{MBCE} = \frac{D_{xx} + C_{xx}D_p + C_xD_{px}}{-(D_{xp} + C_xD_{pp})}, \tag{13.17}$$

which, when $D_{px} \approx 0$ and is ignored, becomes

$$\left(\frac{dp}{dx}\right)_{MBCE} = \frac{D_{xx} + C_{xx}D_p}{-C_xD_{pp}}. \tag{13.18}$$

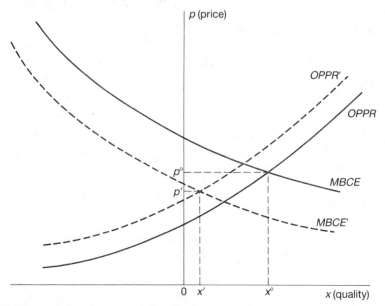

Figure 13.1   The firm's optimal price–quality policy, $D_{pp} < 0$.

Where $D_{xx} < 0$ and $C_{xx} \geqslant 0$ as assumed above, the sign of dp/dx depends upon D_{pp}. It will be negative when $D_{pp} < 0$ and positive when $D_{pp} \geqslant 0$, so that the concavity or convexity of D with respect to p is of great importance to the analysis. As recorded above, we shall assume the normal case is diminishing sales returns to price reductions $(D_{pp} < 0)$.

Equation (13.16-2) yields marginal price policy profit which is zero at the optimum. It shows, in its optimum mode, for any x, the value of p which just equates marginal profit to zero. We will term it the *OPPR* (optimal price policy relation) on figure 13.1 and, if we continue to ignore D_{px}, its slope will be

$$\left(\frac{dp}{dx} \right)_{OPPR} = \frac{C_x + C_D D_x - D_x/D_p}{2 - C_D D_p - D_{pp}/D_p^2} = \frac{2C_x + C_D D_x}{2 - C_D D_p - D_{pp}/D_p^2}, \quad (13.19)$$

every term of which will be positive when $D_{pp} < 0$. For $D_{pp} \geqslant 0$, convexity would have to be extreme to make the slope negative.

On figure 13.1 we have drawn the firm's *MBCE* and *OPPR* functions and its achieved policy optimum. The meaning of these conditions is worth developing. Curve *MBCE* requires that the marginal sales response to the last dollar spent on quality enhancement be equal to the marginal sales response to the last dollar of price reduction. From an initial equality position (expressed algebraically in (13.16-1)) suppose x is increased with a consequent fall in D_x (since $D_{xx} < 0$) and rise in C_x (because $C_{xx} \geqslant 0$). The absolute value of D_p must fall. With diminishing sales returns to price reductions $(D_{pp} < 0)$ price must fall to attain the diminished $-D_p$, and hence *MBCE* will slope negatively. But when increasing sales returns to price reductions rule $(D_{pp} \geqslant 0)$ – the "non-normal" case in our presentation – price must rise to reduce $-D_p$, and *MCBE* will be positively sloped.

The slope of *MBCE* reflects the relative effectiveness of price and quality policies as reflected in their marginal benefit–cost ratios displayed in (13.16-1). When D_{xx} is large absolutely and/or C_{xx} is large, a small rise in x will cause a large fall in the quality policy ratio. When $|D_{pp}|$ is large, a small change in p will restore balance, and the slope of *MBCE* will be shallow. Economically, the numerator of dp/dx is the net effective change in *marginal* sales per unit of dx, consisting of the direct reduction in $D_x(D_{xx})$ and the effective reduction in sales imposed by the rise in cost $(C_{xx} D_x/C_x = -C_{xx} D_p)$. This, divided by C_x in the denominator of dp/dx, converts it to the rate of marginal sales change per dollar spent on quality enhancement. The $-D_{pp}$ in the denominator compares this magnitude with the rate of marginal sales change per dollar of price reduction.

The *OPPR* function reveals the price for any x value that will equate marginal profit to zero. When x rises, D rises and C rises, price constant. From (13.16-2), marginal profit from existing price will fall. Price must therefore rise, to raise p and $-D_p$ (when $D_{pp} < 0$) until marginal profit reaches zero. When $D_{pp} \geqslant 0$, D/D_p will become larger in absolute value as p rises, offsetting the direct positive impact of the price rise. Only when this indirect effect outweighs the direct effect will price have to fall to bring the expression back to zero. Hence, OPPR will usually slope upward, but may slope downward under "pathological" circumstances.

Consider, now, comparative static parameter displacements. Suppose a rise in C occurs that affects only C_x, the marginal cost of quality improvement. Since $D_{pp} < 0$, and because (from 13.16-1) the term $-D_p$ must fall for a given D_x, p must fall. Hence, MBCE will shift downward to MBCE' on figure 13.1. The shift will be greater the more responsive demand is to price, the greater the rise in C_x, the smaller is the original C_x, and the closer D is to linearity ($D_{pp} = 0$). If the demand function is strictly convex in price ($D_{pp} \geqslant 0$) the shift in MBCE will be upward.

Similarly, OPPR will shift upward when a rise in the marginal cost of quality improvement forces price to rise to re-equate price and marginal cost. In figure 13.1, OPPR shifts upward to OPPR', and a new equilibrium $[p',x']$ emerges with a lower quality but with a price that may rise, fall, or remain the same.

In short, a rise in the marginal cost of quality improvement will, in all but the most extreme cases of convexity of the demand function in price, force the firm to move price upward to re-equate marginal revenue and marginal cost. When the demand function is strictly concave ($D_{pp} < 0$) this will be partially countered by the need to re-equate marginal benefit–cost ratios of the policies, which will reduce price. When $D_{pp} \geqslant 0$, MBCE will slope positively, will shift upward with a rise in C_x, and will reinforce the upward price force from OPPR's shift. When $D_{pp} = 0$, MBCE will be vertical, and its leftward shift with a rise in C_x will have no effect on the rise in price brought about by OPPR's upward shift.

4 The Firm in a Rivalrous Context

4.1 Rival Quality Improvement, Slopes of Demand Function Unaffected

Consider, now, the reaction of a firm to a rise in the quality level of one of its rivals' products when the firm completely neglects any reactions by rivals to its policy response. Suppose, first, that such a change impacts only the position of firm 1's demand curve, but that D_p and D_x are everywhere unaffected. MBCE will not be affected by dx^* (where starred variables denote a rival's policy choices) whereas OPPR will shift to the right when D is jointly concave in p and x. Policy will unambiguously consist of a reduction in p and an increase in x. When D is convex in p ($D_{pp} \geqslant 0$) but concave in x, MBCE will slope positively, but in nonpathological cases OPPR will slope upward. An outward shift of OPPR, therefore, will *raise* price as well as quality if the slope of MBCE is less than the slope of OPPR, and lower both if OPPR is less steeply sloped at the equilibrium than MBCE.

Assume that $D_{pp} < 0$. From (13.18) and (13.19), as D_{pp} becomes larger in absolute value, MBCE becomes flatter and OPPR becomes steeper. Because demand is less responsive to price changes as $|D_{pp}|$ grows, the firm adjusts to rivals' quality policies by emphasizing the quality of its product. If $D_{xx} < 0$, as it grows in absolute size MBCE grows more steeply negative. Lessened responsiveness of sales to quality changes leads the firm to adjust to rivals' quality changes by greater price adjustments. In the limit, as D_{pp} approaches 0, all adjustment is made via price, but as D_{xx} approaches 0 a mix of price and quality adjustments will be used. This latter result occurs because even if D_x does not change with changes in x, C_x does change (in general) and hence a quality adjustment will occur.

When $D_{pp} \geqslant 0$, sales responses to price reductions rise more than linearly and MBCE will be positively sloped. As x rises and D_x/C_x in (13.16-1) falls, $-D_p$ must fall. To effect this, p must rise. Hence, when demand functions are convex in price, equation of marginal policy benefit–cost ratios requires that x and p rise and fall together. So, of course, does the requirement that the marginal profit from price policy be zero. Hence, both MBCE and OPPR will slope positively.

From (13.18), the *degree* of positive slope of MBCE when $D_{pp} \geqslant 0$ will be greater, (1) the larger the absolute value of D_p, (2) the smaller D_{pp}, (3) the larger the fall in D_x (i.e. $|D_{xx}|$), (4) the larger the rate of rise in the marginal cost of quality as x rises, and (5) the smaller that marginal cost of quality. These are motivated by (13.16-1). A rise in x leads to a fall in D_x/C_x the greater the rise in C_x and the fall in D_x, and the smaller the initial value of C_x. To match the fall in D_x/C_x, $-D_p$ must fall an equivalent amount, forcing p to rise. The smaller D_{pp}, the greater the price rise required to effect the change in $-D_p$. And, of course, the larger the initial $-D_p$, the higher is initial price, and the greater the required price rise.

The net effect upon the firm's policy responses depends upon the relative sizes of the positive slopes of MBCE and OPPR. On figure 13.2a, the case is illustrated where MBCE intersects OPPR from above because its slope is less steep. In this case the firm increases the quality standard of its product and increases price as well. The rise in a rival's quality shifts D leftward and, if price is maintained, leads to a rise in x to re-equate marginal profit from price policy to zero. The rise in x, however, raises C_x and lowers D_x, calling for a rise in p to re-equate marginal policy benefit–cost ratios.

When MBCE is below OPPR, that rise in p is less than what is required to equate the marginal profit of price policy at the higher x to zero, so quality is enhanced once more to bring that equality about at the higher p.

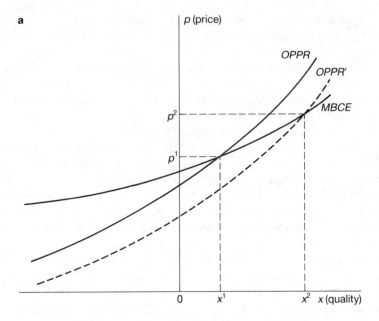

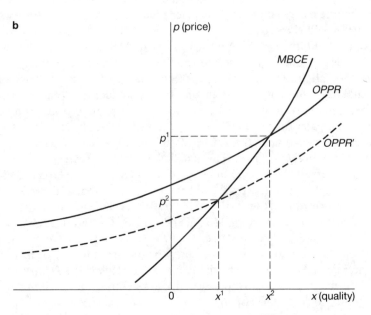

Figure 13.2 The firm's policy reaction to a rival's quality enhancement, $D_{pp} \geqslant 0$, when D_p and D_x are unaffected.
a, Slope of MBCE less than slope of OPPR; **b**, slope of MBCE greater than slope of OPPR.

A succession of such adjustments converges to the $[p^2, x^2]$ equilibrium of figure 13.2a. For any suboptimal x, the p dictated by the need to equate the marginal profit of price policy to zero is "pulled up" by the need to equate marginal policy benefit–cost ratios.

On the other hand, figure 13.2b illustrates the adjustment process when *MBCE* intersects *OPPR* from below. The shift downward of *OPPR* resulting from the initial shift in D requires that p fall at x'. The fall in p requires a rise in D_x / C_x obtained by lowering x. But the marginal profit of the price policy condition continuously pulls price downward as x falls.

Hence, the final result in the two cases that can occur when $D_{pp} \geqslant 0$ is somewhat paradoxical. In the case where a rise in x requires a weaker rise in p to re-equate marginal policy benefit–cost ratios price rises along with quality (figure 13.2a). When price must move upward by large amounts to balance marginal policy benefit–cost ratios when x rises, the final response is a fall in both prices and quality (figure 13.2b).

The paradox is readily understood. In the first case price response is weak relative to quality response, so the greater burden of adjustment must fall upon the latter. As it rises by large amounts, the demand curve shifts rightward, requiring p to rise to re-equate marginal profit of price policy to zero. In the second case, price changes must bear the brunt of the adjustment. As p falls by large amounts, D shifts rightward, requiring that quality be lowered to meet the marginal profit condition.

Let us summarize our results for the case of a rival's quality improvement when it does not affect D_p and D_x for firm 1.

1 In the "normal" case, when D_{pp} and $D_{xx} < 0$, the intuitive responses will occur. Firm 1 responds by raising the quality of its product and reducing its price, the exact mix of which policies will depend upon the degree of negative slope of *MBCE*. Price policy will play the larger role when demand is price elastic, closer to linearity in the price dimension, the marginal cost of quality change is small but responds in strong positive fashion to such changes, and D is strongly concave in x, indicating rapidly diminishing sales returns to increases in quality improvement. Oligopolistic quality competition under these conditions should lead to quality improvement and price reductions.

2 In the "abnormal" case, when $D_{pp} \geqslant 0$ (but $D_{xx} < 0$) increasing sales returns to price reductions characterize firm 1's demand. Under these conditions two outcomes are possible in both of which price and quality move in the same directions. When the tradeoff between price and quality dictated by the need to equate marginal policy benefit–cost ratios is less than that enforced by the need to equate the marginal profit of price policy to zero, quality adjustment plays the greater role. Quality will be improved but price will also be raised somewhat. In the opposite circumstance both price and quality will fall, with the former playing the dominant role.

If we accept diminishing sales returns to quality improvement, *the crucial element in determining which of these results emerges is the linearity, concavity, or convexity with respect to price of the firm's demand function.* This is conditional on the hypothesis that demand slopes are not affected by rival's decisions on quality changes.

4.2 Rival Quality Improvement, Slopes of Demand Functions Affected

Suppose, now, that a change in x^*, or a rival's quality position, does affect the slopes of firm 1's demand function in addition to its position. We assume D_{x^*} (i.e. $\delta D/\delta x^*$) is negative, and that D_{xx^*} can be positive or negative depending upon whether dx^* moves the rival brand in such direction as to become less or more substitutable for brand 1. And a similar statement holds for D_{px^*} which, under the same conditions, may be positive or negative.

When $D_{pp} < 0$, $D_{xx} < 0$, and $C_{xx} \geqslant 0$, for the most part the impact of a rival's quality change on p and x is ambiguous. When D_{px^*} and D_{xx^*} are positive, making demand more price elastic and quality inelastic, both p and x will rise if

$$\frac{D_{px^*}/D_p}{D_{x^*}/D} < 1 - C_D D_p, \qquad (13.20)$$

or if the ratio of the percentage change in D_p divided by the percentage fall in sales because of dx^* is less than unity minus the marginal cost of D_p. Broadly, then, if dx^* impacts demand more percentagewise than it moves the price slope of demand, firm 1 will increase both price and quality. Condition (13.20) is necessary and sufficient to shift *OPPR* upward, and *MBCE* will always move upward with an increase in dx^*.

When D_{px^*} and D_{xx^*} are both negative, *MBCE* and *OPPR* shift down, so that p falls but x moves ambiguously depending upon the degree of shift in both functions. With $D_{px^*} \geqslant 0$ and $D_{xx^*} < 0$, the shifts in *MBCE* and *OPPR* are ambiguous, and thus the movement of p and x not predictable. And when $D_{px^*} < 0$ and $D_{xx^*} \geqslant 0$, *MBCE* will shift down, but *OPPR*'s direction of movement is not determinable.

4.3 The Importance of Second-order Derivatives

Perhaps the most important general result of this analysis of oligopolistic price–quality policy which does not feature rivalrous consonance (to be defined in the next section) is the dominant role played by the second-order partial derivatives D_{pp}, D_{xx}, D_{px^*}, and D_{xx^*}. Their signs and magnitudes determine dp/dx slopes of *MBCE* and *OPPR* and the direction and amounts of shifts in these functions. Because most firms cannot be expected to know the signs and magnitudes of these derivatives or to feel their effects even in the intermediate term, we are entitled to some skepticism that firms' price and quality responses will follow the general patterns outlined above. Rather more rough-hewn patterns of response may be expected to hold in practice, more attuned to first-order effects. And, equally importantly, it is to be expected that many of these first-order swamping effects will be the result of firms' taking into account the impacts of their actions upon rivals' welfares, as well as other goals of their own not exclusively defined by profit maximization.

5 The Firm in Rivalrous Consonance

It follows that to come to grips with the true complexities of interdependence that characterize oligopolistic market structure, we must extend the firm's decision processes in dimensions that permit the inclusion of the sociological matrix of the industry or product group. Given the nonanonymity that small numbers impose upon rivals, and the expectations of each that others will react to his initiatives, the price–quality choice must be modelled to conform to the compulsions that push the firm simultaneously towards competition and cooperation. The mature oligopoly, at least, must be expected to experience drives in both directions, and the challenge to the theorist is to discover techniques to blend the policy motivations that result from such associations.

Elsewhere, and at some length, I have argued that a framework for experimentation for analysis of such socially conditioned egoism is "rivalrous consonance" employing crippled optimization techniques.[9] In the modelling, each firm is assumed to maximize the sum of its own and its rivals' profits (or other objectives) when the latter have been discounted by a "consonance factor," θ_{ij}. In rival i's maximization of such an "extended profit function," \$1 of rival j's profit (or loss) is treated as the equivalent of θ dollars of rival i's profit (or loss).

In a duopoly, suppose firms 1 and 2 have primary objectives of maximizing own-profits, but subject to the desire of taking into account the impact of their policies upon the rival's profit. We ignore other goals – expressible as constraints – for simplicity. Continue to suppose only one quality exists for firms to adjust, and let us continue to use unstarred variables and functions for firm 1 and starred for firm 2. Then, for example, firm 1's objective function may be written from (13.10), after suppressing Y as constant:

$$\text{Max} Z = D(p,x,p^*,x^*)(p - C(x,D)) + \theta_{12}[D^*(p^*,x^*,p,x)$$
$$(p^* - C^*(x^*,D^*)),\tag{13.21}$$

where Z is firm 1's *extended profit function*, which includes own-profit and consonance-factor discounted rival-profit. Define the average profit margins, $m = p - C(x,D)$ and $m^* = p^* - C^*(x^*,D^*)$. Then, first-order necessary conditions for an extended profit maximum are:

1. $D_p(m - C_D D) + \theta_{12} D_p^* (m^* - C_{D^*}^* D^*) + D = 0$ (13.22)

2. $D_x(m - C_D D) + \theta_{12} D_2^* (m^* - C_{D^*}^* D^*) - C_x D = 0.$

The expressions in parentheses are the marginal profits on brands 1 and 2, and we shall symbolize them M and M^* hereafter. Then (13.22–1) simply requires the marginal extended profit attendant to a slight fall in p to just offset the fall in revenue from previous sales caused by the price drop. And (13.22–2) requires the marginal extended profit from a slight enhancement of brand 1's quality to be equal to the increase in cost on previous sales caused by the quality change. As in section 4, this translates into the requirement that per dollar of direct policy cost, each policy must return the same marginal extended profit. Indeed, section 4's analysis is a special case of (13.22) for $\theta_{12} = 0$.

For firm 1, the analog of (13.16–1) – marginal policy benefit–cost equality as captured in *MBCE* of figure 13.1 – in rivalrous consonance is

1. $-\dfrac{D_p C_x + D_x}{D_p^* C_x + D_x^*} = \dfrac{\theta_{12} M^*}{M}.$ (13.23)

When $\theta_{12} = 0$, (13.23–1) becomes (13.16–1). Also, the analog of (13.16–2), or *OPPR* in figure 13.1, is

2. $D_p M + \theta_{12} D_p^* M^* + D = 0,$ (13.23)

which simply states the necessity of marginal extended profit on price policy to be zero. And, of course, for firm 2, the first-order necessary conditions may be written explicitly:

1. $-\dfrac{D_{p^*}^* C_{x^*}^* + D_{x^*}^*}{D_{p^*} C_{x^*}^* + D_{x^*}} = \dfrac{\theta_{21} M}{M^*}$ (13.24)

2. $D_{p^*}^* M^* + \theta_{21} D_{p^*} M + D^* = 0.$

For given values of p^* and x^* (p and x) the analysis of section 4 holds in its entirety for firm 1's (firm 2's) optimal policy-making. The novel elements are the complications introduced in the p/x (p^*/x^*) slopes of the *MBCE* and *OPPR* functions by p^* and x^* (p and x), and the shift effects on those functions of the rival prices and quality values.

For example, for firm 1, the slope of *MBCE* as defined in (13.23–1) is

$$\left(\frac{dp}{dx}\right)_{MBCE} =$$

$$-\frac{[D_{xx} + D_p C_{xx}]M + [D_x + D_p C_x]M_x}{[D_{pp}C_x]M + [D_x + D_p C_x]M_p}$$

(13.25)

$$+\frac{\theta_{12}([D_{xx}^* + D_p^* C_{xx}]M^* + [D_x^* + D_p^* C_x]M_x^*)}{+\theta_{12}([D_{pp}^* C_x]M^* + [D_x^* + D_p^* C_x])M_p^*}$$

where we continue to ignore second-order cross-derivatives, and where

$$M_p = 1 - 2C_D D_p > 0 \qquad M_{p^*}^* = 1 - 2C_{D^*}^* D_{p^*}^* > 0$$

$$M_x = -C_x - 2C_D D_x < 0 \qquad M_{x^*}^* = -C_{x^*}^* - 2C_{D^*}^* D_{x^*}^* < 0$$

$$M_{p^*} = -2C_D D_{p^*} < 0 \qquad M_p^* = -2C_{D^*}^* D_p^* < 0$$

$$M_{x^*} = -2C_D D_{x^*} > 0 \qquad M_x^* = -2C_{D^*}^* D_x^* > 0.$$

From (13.25) it can be seen that two complicating factors intrude when it is compared with the determination in (13.17) for the nonconsonance analysis. First, because M cannot be factored out, in both numerator and denominator bracketed terms modify M_x and M_p, whose signs are determined by the marginal impacts on amount demanded of price and quality changes as well as the marginal cost of quality change. Second, in numerator and denominator the existence of the second firm's profits in firm 1's extended profit calculations results in bracketed terms multiplied by θ_{12} which are indeterminate as to sign. On the assumption that $D_{pp} < 0$, it is no longer possible to assert unequivocally that $MBCE$ slopes negatively in the p–x plane as in figure 13.1.

However, in the numerator and denominators the first bracketed terms should dominate the second, so that the net sums are negative. This is because (1) M is expected to be greater than M_x, and (2) the second bracketed terms are opposite in sign and therefore offsetting. In the numerator, within the parentheses, both bracketed terms have offsetting elements signwise; they involve impacts of firm 1's variables upon firm 2's demand, which should be weaker than own-demand impacts; and the sum of the terms is multiplied by θ_{12}, which, given realistic values, should reduce the impact of D^* and M^* responses greatly. Hence, it is to be expected that the numerator will be negative.

In the denominator's parenthesized terms, the first bracket should be negative and the second, containing offsetting terms signwise and being multiplied by M_p^*, which may be relatively small, has a high probability of being negative. In any event, after multiplication by θ_{12}, it should pose no threat to the negativity of the denominator.

Therefore, we expect that *MBCE* will retain the negative slope it had in figure 13.1 (when $(D_{pp} < 0, \; D_{xx} < 0, \; D^*_{pp} < 0, \; D^*_{xx} < 0)$. However, we should also expect that rivalrous consonance will reduce the absolute size of the numerator somewhat and increase the absolute size of the domoninator, so that the absolute slope value will be smaller. A rise in quality will lead firm 1 to reduce price less under rivalrous consonance to re-equate the relevant benefit–cost ratios of price and quality policies.

On the other hand, *OPPR*'s slope is unambiguously positive:

$$\left(\frac{dp}{dx}\right)_{OPPR} = -\frac{D_p M_x + \theta_{12} D^*_p M^*_x + D_x}{D_{pp}M + D_p M_p + \theta_{12}D^*_p M^*_p + D_p}. \tag{13.26}$$

The denominator is unambiguously negative and the numerator positive. That is, when x rises, the need to re-equate the marginal extended profit to zero will require price to rise, as in the case of marginal own profit (i.e. $\theta_{12} = 0$). However, under rivalrous consonance, the denominator of (13.26) is expected to rise more in absolute value than the numerator, so the slope of *OPPR* should also be less steep than in the Cournot environment of section 4.

To make notation a bit more compact, let us define

1. $f_1(D_p, D_x, C_x, D^*_p, M^*, M, \theta_{12}) = M(D_p C_x + D_x) + \theta_{12} M^*(D^*_p C_x + D^*_x)$

2. $f_2(D_p, D^*_p, M^*, M, D, \theta_{12}) = D_p M + \theta_{12}D^*_p M^* + D. \tag{13.27}$

Then, defining $\delta f_1/\delta x = f_{1x}$, etc., we may rewrite (13.25) and (13.26) more compactly as:

$$1. \quad (dp/dx)_{MBCE} = -(f_{1x}/f_{1p}) \tag{13.28}$$

$$2. \quad (dp/dx)_{OPPR} = -(f_{2x}/f_{2p}).$$

Consider, now, the impact of a change in p^* upon *MBCE* for constant x when we continue to assume that other-variable second derivatives $(D^*_{pp}$, etc.) approximate zero:

$$\left(\frac{dp}{dp^*}\right)_{MBCE} = -\frac{AM_{p^*} + \theta_{12}M^*_{p^*}}{AM_p + \theta_{12}M^*_p + (D_{pp}C_x M/(D^*_p C_x + D^*_x))} = -(f_{1p^*}/f_{1p}), \tag{13.29}$$

where $A = (D_p C_x + D_x)/(D^*_p C_x + D^*_x)$. From (13.23-1), $A < 0$. Therefore, when $D^*_p C_x + D^*_x \geqslant 0$, $dp/dp^* \geqslant 0$, and *MBCE* shifts upward when p^* rises. Only when $D^*_p C_x + D^*_x < 0$ and is small enough to make the bracketed term in the denominator positive and larger than the absolute value of the first two terms will *MBCE* shift down. We treat the first case as more likely, and assume $dp/dp^* \geqslant 0$ for *MBCE*.

For *OPPR*:

$$\left(\frac{dp}{dp^*}\right)_{OPPR} = -\frac{D_p M_{p^*} + \theta_{12} D_p^* M_{p^*}^* + D_{p^*}}{D_{pp} M + (1 + M_p) D_p + \theta_{12} (D_p^* M_p^*)} = -(f_{2p^*}/f_{2p}),$$

(13.30)

which is unambiguously positive.

Hence, a rise in firm 2's price will raise firm 1's price in rivalrous consonance. But firm 1's quality will rise if *MBCE* rises more than *OPPR* and fall if the opposite is true, when p^* rises.

As for shifts in *MBCE* and *OPPR* when x^* changes, we obtain:

1. $$\left(\frac{dp}{dx^*}\right)_{MBCE} = -\frac{AM_{x^*} + \theta_{12} M_{x^*}^*}{AM_p + \theta_{12} M_p^* + (D_{pp} C_x M / D_p^* C_x + D_x^*)} = -(f_{1x^*}/f_{1p})$$

(13.31)

2. $$\left(\frac{dp}{dx^*}\right)_{OPPR} = -\frac{(D_p + \theta_{12} D_p^*) M_{x^*}^* + D_{x^*}}{D_{pp} M + (1 + M_{pp}) D_p + \theta_{12} (D_p^* M_p^*)} = -(f_{2x^*}/f_{2p}).$$

Since $f_{1x^*} < 0$ and we hypothesize $f_{1p} < 0$, *MBCE* should shift down when rival quality is improved. That is, if firm 1 were constrained to hold its quality constant, the need to re-equate marginal benefit per unit of marginal cost for its policies would lead it to lower price. We expect $f_{2x^*} \geqslant 0$ and $f_{2p} < 0$, so *OPPR* should shift up when a rival raises quality of product. If firm 1 could not change policy, the need to equate the marginal profit from price policy to zero should lead the firm to raise price. Hence x must fall, but p can rise or fall depending upon whether *OPPR* moves up by more or less than *MBCE*, respectively. Since the downward shift is tempered by the consonance term and D_{x^*} in f_{2x^*}, we expect the second alternative to occur.

This result is most dependent upon the sign of f_{2x^*}, and, specifically, assumes that firm 1's demand is more sensitive to own-price than other-quality. If the reverse is true, and firm 1's product demand is highly affected by firm 2's quality, then *OPPR* will shift down when x^* changes, and the shift will be enhanced by consonance. Quality then rises if the absolute size of *OPPR*'s shift is greater than that of *MBCE*, or falls with the reverse, whereas price falls unambiguously.

In section 4, when rivalrous consonance did not affect firm 1's responses and other-variable second derivatives were ignored, $dp/dp^* \geqslant 0$, $dx/dp^* < 0$, $dp/dx^* < 0$, and $dx/dx^* \geqslant 0$. Changes in rivals' parameters shift *MBCE* and, in both rival parameter changes shifted *OPPR* downward. When rivals' profit consequences are taken into account *à la* rivalrous consonance, this determinateness disappears. The problem arises because rivalrous consonance removes the immunity of *MBCE* from feeling the impacts of rival parameter changes. Under the same assumptions in both cases, the signs of $f_{2p}, f_{2x}, f_{1p^*}, f_{2p^*}, f_{1x^*}$, and f_{2x^*} are unambiguous, but where $f_{1p} = f_{1x} = 0$ in the nonconsonance case, these terms are ambiguously signed in rivalrous consonance.

Thus, rivalrous consonance affects the price–quality policy reaction of a firm by requiring it to re-equate the marginal benefit/marginal cost ratios in response to policy changes by rivals. The movement direction of price and quality to reachieve this equality depends upon the relative strength of the slopes of demand with respect to price and quality and the marginal cost of quality improvements for *both* firms to firm 1's p and x. If both firms show price-insensitivity in demands, a rise in $p*$ will require most of the adjustment to be made with a rise in x; quality-insensitivity leads to the opposite result.

6 Conclusion

Heuristic methods of measuring quality differentials should be tested empirically as a first step in the analysis of policy-making in differentiated oligopoly. This chapter offers some suggested procedures that may have merit. The availability of more than one policy dimension to the oligopolist raises the question of tradeoffs between them, and complicates the task of the economist who seeks to interpret realistic oligopolistic behavior. This is especially true when rivalrous consonance frameworks are used to incorporate rivals' concerns for the impacts of their policies upon other industry members.

The crucial relation in the interdependence analysis is the need to trade off price and quality changes to re-equate marginal profit per unit of marginal cost for both policy variables. Explicit results depend upon the first- and second-order partial derivatives of all firms' demand functions in the price–quality complex of the firm under analysis. Industry equilibrium occurs when these marginal benefit/marginal cost ratios are equal and the marginal extended policy profit for either the price or quality is zero for all firms.

The interdependence among firms' sales functions is so entangling that comparative statics analyses of parameter changes in unspecified systems is very difficult even when restrictive assumptions are made concerning relevant partial derivatives. In the general case it will be necessary at this point to examine specific industry relationships and resort to simulative theorizing in order to gain insights.

Notes

[1] "Mr Sraffa's article must be regarded as the fount from which my work flows, for the chief aim of this book is to attempt to carry out his pregnant suggestion that the

whole theory of value should be treated in terms of monopoly analysis" [12], p. v.

[2] Robinson points out the same asymmetry as Chamberlin between the polar analogs of pure competition and pure monopoly, with the latter requiring control over the supply of *all* commodities [12], p.x4.

[3] I have discussed this distinction between Chamberlin's product differentiation and its implied interproduct competition versus Robinson's interfirm competition in [10], pp. 299–30. See [12], pp. 50–1, 86, 89, 90n., 93, and 170. She does refer on p. 50 to "closely similar commodities," and several times she speaks of buyers' preferences for seller "for whatever reasons," which would seem to embrace product differentiation. Nonetheless, the reader is struck with her refusal to explicitly relate these preferences to qualities of the product. For example, on pp. 89–90 in her most extensive discussion of the issue, she lists as reasons for these preferences transport costs; guarantees of quality through a known seller's name, differences in facilities for service, credit, or customer complaints; and advertising. All of these are associated with the firm. And, in a curious footnote on p. 93, she compares the producer of a branded product with a pub owner given a limited monopoly by a license whose upper bound on profit is unlimited. This case is obviously not the typical one she has in mind in her analysis of imperfect markets. And, I believe, this emphasis upon the seller and purposeful ignoring of product differentiation is one of the reasons Chamberlin felt (unfairly) that she never truly blended monopoly and competition at the level of the firm.

[4] Robinson evinces no interest in the firm's choice of a quality complex for its product and dismisses advertising as equivalent to a reduction in price (p. 21). The comparison above does not imply that Chamberlin made great progress in the analysis of product quality choice of selling costs. But he did introduce them as dimensions of equivalent importance to price in the firm's decision-making.

[5] Cf. [4], pp. 204–11; [6], pp. vii, 26–30, 66–9, 74, 95, 141–2, 221–2, 274, 311–12. Indeed, in chapter 3, where he rewrites monopolistic competition theory as he would if he were to present it in 1951, his presentation in terms of spatially differentiated firms selling a homogeneous product is the Robinson paradigm.

[6] Cf. [6], pp. 33, 61–2, 195–6.

[7] [10], pp. 228–32. To my arguments could be added the lack of clarity about which cross-elasticity measures are appropriate for the task. See [1–3, 5, 7–9, 14].

[8] That is, unique up to a linear or a positive multiplicative factor transformation.

[9] See, for example, [11] for an extensive discussion of the framework and a motivation for its usage.

References

[1] Bishop, R. L., "Elasticities, Cross-elasticities, and Market Relationships", *American Economic Review*, 42 (1952), 781–803.

[2] ——, "Reply", *American Economic Review*, 43 (1953), 916–24.

[3] ——, "Reply", *American Economic Review*, 45 (1955), 382–6.

[4] Chamberlin, E. H., *The Theory of Monopolistic Competition*, 6th edn, Harvard University Press, Cambridge, MA, 1948.

[5] ——, "Elasticities, Cross-elasticities, and Market Relationships: Comment", *American Economic Review*, 43 (1953), 910–16.

[6] ——, *Towards a More General Theory of Value*, Oxford University Press, New York, 1957.

[7] Fellner, W., "Elasticities, Cross-elasticities, and Market Relationships: Comment", *American Economic Review*, 43 (1953), 898–910.

[8] ——, "The Adaptability and Lasting Significance of the Chamberlin Contribution", in R. E. Kuenne (ed.), *Monopolistic Competition Theory: Studies in Impact*, John Wiley & Sons, New York, 1967.

[9] Heiser, R., "Elasticities, Cross-elasticities, and Market Relationships: Comment", *American Economic Review*, 45 (1955), 373–82.

[10] Kuenne, Robert E., "Quality Space, Interproduct Competition, and General Equilibrium Theory", in Robert E. Kuenne (ed.), *Monopolistic Competition Theory: Studies in Impact*, John Wiley & Sons, New York, 1968, chapter 10. [Reprinted as chapter 11 in this volume.]

[11] ——, *Rivalrous Consonance: a Theory of General Oligopolistic Equilibrium*, Contributions to Economic Analysis No. 157, North-Holland, Amsterdam, 1986.

[12] Robinson, J., *The Economics of Imperfect Competition*, Macmillan, London, 1933.

[13] Sraffa, P., "The Laws of Returns under Competitive Conditions", *Economic Journal*, 26 (1926), 535–50.

[14] Triffin, R., *Monopolistic Competition and General Equilibrium Theory*, Harvard University Press, Cambridge, MA, 1949.

14

Price–marketing Competition and Information Flows in Spatial Oligopoly

1 The Emerging Industrial Structure

Within the past decade or two, developments within advanced economies' industrial structures and practices, spurred largely by technological innovation, led to an expectation that different approaches to the theory of location and spatial competition may be required to analyze economic activity in the future. The dominance of service industries argues for a lessening of the importance of transportation costs and an increasing decentralizing orientation to markets, in many instances to highly specialized markets.

Computer integrated manufacturing technology and enhanced use of robotics imply that the factory of the future will be smaller, more specialized in its outputs, and capable of retooling rapidly to produce smaller lot-sizes of goods closely tailored to customer needs. The rigid mass production of the assembly line will be doomed to a much smaller role, its huge concentrations of productive capacity dispersed in smaller, more flexible complexes in close contact with the special needs of their markets with emphasis upon rapid delivery and servicing of their product. Managerial concerns with labor cost will lessen as attention is paid to throughput time for product, new product development, and access to rapidly changing technological information.

Interaction of firms with customers on a continuous basis will become more important. Joint design of customers' products and a concern to keep them informed of new technological advances and products relevant to their needs will heighten the importance of close personal contacts. Information flows between firms and customers, firms and centers of research and innovation, and among firms to assess increasingly important qualitative

Originally published as chapter 3 in M. Chatterji and R. Kuenne (eds), *New Frontiers in Regional Science: Essays in Honour of Walter Isard*, and reproduced with permission of The Macmillan Press Ltd.

advantages of rivals will be more strategic than in the age of mass production of standardized outputs.

Of greatest importance in setting new structural forces in train has been the telecommunications revolution. Information technology makes feasible the decentralization of a firm's planning, management, production, marketing, and finance functions, and permits their dispersion to separate centers of attraction. The assurance of cheap, rapid, certain, extensive flows of information among such centers will increasingly permit the necessary interactions among internal firm resources to occur to the same time that it increases the opportunity for and quality of relevant external interactions, be they with customers, financial consultants, strategic planners, or others.

Emerging industrial structure will then be typified by small groups of highly specialized firms competing intensely in terms of product quality, customer desires, and information control. Personal and impersonal interactions will integrate a network of decentralized decision-making centers, with information flows moving along well-defined nodes on intensively used communications arcs. The intensification of interactions among firms and their suppliers, customers, advisers, and rivals, made possible by greater spatial proximity and the quantum leap in the ability to transmit and process information, should be confronted by regional scientists and spatial economists in order to understand its implications for spatial structure.[1]

This paper is a small first step in integrating product market activities and price competition into the newer spatial tableau by viewing marketing expenditures as fostering information flows with varying intensities and effectiveness. Marketing is used to embrace a variety of interactions between firm and consumer with a frequency that may be taken to vary with intensity and distance from source and an effectiveness that varies with quality. We will use the term as a surrogate for a wide variety of firm–customer interactions, therefore, that may be encompassed in "marketing activities." These may include consultations with the customer on design, on delivery schedules, on newly available products or technologies, servicing or maintenance of the customer's prior purchases, and so forth. Equally important are expenditures on all forms of advertising and sales promotions designed to enhance the firm's impersonal interactions with potential customers. All of these activities may be included in what Johannson and Karlsson [1] term the firm's "contact network" and we will use "marketing" as a convenient term to encompass these increasingly important activities.

Space affords a friction to information flow and to meaningful personal and impersonal interactions, but the lesser resistance offered to advertising permits it to substitute to some degree for the frequency of personal interactions. Of course, space fulfills its traditional role of resisting goods flows, and transport costs will continue to play their role in limiting commodity flows and restricting market areas for services. But they can no longer be given an exclusive function in determining spatial structure or functioning.

Some of the important issues that will challenge the regional scientist in the future are the integration of these spatial impedances; their dictates for the future location of firms and the decentralization of firms' divisions; the implications of the ability to substitute information flows for physical interactions over space; and the increase or decrease in the importance of networks to channel movement.

This paper will treat the price and marketing decisions of spatial duopolists who are fixed in their locations at opposite ends of a linear market of variable length. At the point of origin – taken to be the firms' locations – marketing expenditure is assumed to have a given effectiveness in (1) generating sales for the firm and (2) reducing the sales of its rival. That effectiveness decays with distance, on the assumption that the frequency of interaction of consumer with the message or messenger lessens over space. In addition forces generated by spatial proximity foster loyalty to brands that diminishes as distance increases, quite independent of the rise in delivered price.

It will be assumed that the duopolists offer a differentiated product at an f.o.b. price over the length of the linear market when movement of the product requires an expenditure of $\$T$ per unit distance for both brands. We are interested in the behavior of prices, sales, profits, and marketing expenditures as the length of the market, the transport rate, marketing effectiveness, and the spatial decay factors for marketing effectiveness are varied. Theoretical and simulation analyses will be employed to obtain insights into firm behavior in these areas.

2 A Simple Model of Price–marketing Competition

Assume that a rival's sales at a point s of the market line are a function of (1) the delivered price of its product, (2) its duopolist competitor's delivered price, (3) its marketing expenditure, and (4) its rival's marketing expenditure. Rival 1 is located at $s = 0$ and rival 2 at $s = L$ of the linear market, where L is the length of that market. Demand for firm i's product is at a maximum at its location but falls with distance because of (1) rising delivered price and (2) diminishing marketing payoff. Marketing costs of firm i are variable and are assumed to be a fraction, M_i, of the firm's revenue – an assumption that seems in conformance with actual practice.

For firm 1, demand in the neighborhood of point s is defined as:

$$X_1(s)\mathrm{d}s = a_1\,\mathrm{d}s - b_{11}(p_1 + sT)\mathrm{d}s + b_{12}(p_2 + (L-s)T\mathrm{d}s)$$
$$+ K_{11}(R_1M_1)^{\beta_{11}}e^{-\alpha_{11}s}\mathrm{d}s - K_{12}(R_2M_2)^{\beta_{12}}e^{-\alpha_{12}(L-s)}\mathrm{d}s,$$
$$(14.1)$$

where:

b_{11} = the response factor to firm 1's f.o.b. price, p_1, plus transportation costs;

b_{12} = the response factor to firm 2's f.o.b. price, p_2, plus transportation cost;

$K_{11}(R_1 M_1)^{\beta_{11}}$ = the net sales generated by firm 1's marketing expenditure $R_1 M_1$, at $s = 0$, when R_1 is firm 1's revenue and M_1 the fraction of it used for marketing, and where β_{11} is the elasticity of sales with respect to marketing costs;

$e^{-\alpha_{11}s}$ = the spatial decay factor for net sales due to marketing programmes at s;

$K_{12}(R_2 M_2)^{\beta_{12}}$ = the net sales lost due to firm 2's marketing efforts at $s = L$, or "attritional" effects of firm 2's marketing effort on firm 1's sales;

$e^{-\alpha_{12}(L-s)}$ = the decay factor for firm 1's net sales lost to firm 2's marketing expenditure;

c_1 = constant marginal and average cost of production for firm 1's product;

T = the transport cost per unit of firm 1 (and firm 2) product for $L = 1$, with such cost proportional to L.

If we integrate (14.1) over the line interval we obtain firm 1's sales curve:

$$X_1 = A_1 - B_{11}(p_1 + 0.5TL) + B_{12}(p_2 + 0.5TL) + K_{11}R_1^{\beta_{11}}\alpha_{11}^{-1}$$
$$(1 - e^{-\alpha_{11}L})M_1^{\beta_{11}} - K_{12}R_2^{\beta_{12}}\alpha_{12}^{-1}(1 - e^{-\alpha_{12}L})M_2^{\beta_{12}} \qquad (14.2)$$

where:

$$A_1 = a_1 L$$
$$B_{11} = b_{11} L$$
$$B_{12} = b_{12} L$$

Profits are then

$$\pi_1 = X_1(p_1 - c_1) - M_1 R_1 \qquad (14.3)$$

and first-order necessary conditions for a profit maximum are:

1. $\dfrac{\partial \pi_1}{\partial p_1} = X_1 + (p_1 - c_1)(-B_{11}) = 0$

2. $\dfrac{\partial \pi_1}{\partial M_1} = (p_1 - c_1)(\beta_{11}K_{11}R_1^{\beta_{11}}\alpha_{11}^{-1}(1 - e^{-\alpha_{11}L})M_1^{\beta_{11}-1} - R_1 = 0 \qquad (14.4)$

To simplify notation, define

$$D_{11} = K_{11} R_1^{\beta_{11}} \alpha_{11}^{-1} (1 - e^{-\alpha_{11} L}) M_1^{\beta_{11}}$$

so (14.4–2) can be written

$$\frac{(p_1 - c_1) \beta_{11} D_{11}}{M_1} - R_1 = 0 \qquad (14.5)$$

The second-order sufficient condition for a profit maximum, given R_1, R_2, p_2, and M_2 are that the following Hessian be negative definite:

$$[H] = \begin{bmatrix} -2B_{11} & \dfrac{\beta_{11} D_{11}}{M_1} \\ \dfrac{\beta_{11} D_{11}}{M_1} & \dfrac{(\beta_{11}^{-1}) R_1}{M_1} \end{bmatrix} \qquad (14.6)$$

The first-order nested principal minor is negative. Through use of the first-order conditions (14.4) the determinant of $[H]$ can be shown to be positive if

$$\beta_{11} < 1 - \frac{0.5 M_1 R_1}{\pi_1 + M_1 R_1} \qquad (14.7)$$

Thus, the elasticity of marketing-generated sales resulting from own-marketing must be less than the complement of one half the ratio of marketing expenditure to the sum of such expenditure and profits. For example, when profits are zero, β_{11} must be less than 0.5. Realistically, if marketing expenditures are about 3 percent of sales revenue and profits are about 3 percent of sales, β_{11} must be less then 0.88. We expect β_{11} to be in the neighborhood of 0.40, so that with nonnegative profits the second-order sufficient conditions for a profit maximum should be achieved.

Given symmetrical functions to (14.4) derivable for firm 2, the duopoly solution and the reaction functions can be sought. From (14.4):

1. $\quad p_1 = \dfrac{Q_{11} + B_{11} c_1}{2 B_{11}}$

2. $\quad M_1 = \left[\dfrac{R_1}{Q_{12} \beta_{11} (p_1 - c_1)} \right]^{(\beta_{11} - 1)^{-1}} \qquad (14.8)$

where

$$Q_{11} = A_1 - 0.5 B_{11} TL + B_{12} (p_2 + 0.5 TL) + K_{11} R_1^{\beta_{11}} \alpha_{11}^{-1} (1 - e^{-\alpha_{11} L}) M_1^{\beta_{11}} -$$

$$K_{12} (R_2 M_2)^{\beta_{12}} \alpha_{12}^{-1} (1 - e^{-\alpha_{12} L})$$

$$Q_{12} = K_{11} R_1^{\beta_{11}} \alpha_{11}^{-1} (1 - e^{-\alpha_{11} L}) = \frac{D_{11}}{M_1^{\beta_{11}}}$$

Analogous equation hold for the optimal price/marketing solution for firm 2. Then substituting (14.8.–2) into (14.8–1), and substituting like expressions for firm 2 into firm 1's price equation, and repeating the process for firm 2, we obtain the reaction functions:

1. $2B_{11}p_1 - V_{12}[\beta_{11}V_{12}(p_1 - c_1)]^{\beta_{11}/(1-\beta_{11})}$

$$= B_{12}p_2 - V_{13}(\beta_{22}V_{22}(p_2 - c_2))^{\beta_{12}/(1-\beta_{11})} + W_{11} \quad (14.9)$$

2. $2B_{22}p_2 - V_{22}[\beta_{22}V_{22}(p_2 - c_2)]^{\beta_{22}/(1-\beta_{22})}$

$$= B_{21}p_1 - V_{23}(\beta_{11}V_{12}(p_1 - c_1))^{\beta_{21}/(1-\beta_{11})} + W_{21}$$

where

$$V_{11} = A_1 - 0.5TL(B_{11} - B_{12}) \qquad V_{12} = K_{11}\alpha_{11}^{-1}(1 - e^{-\alpha_{11}L})$$

$$V_{21} = A_2 - 0.5TL(B_{22} - B_{21}) \qquad V_{22} = K_{22}\alpha_{22}^{-1}(1 - e^{-\alpha_{22}L})$$

$$W_{11} = V_{11} + B_{11}c_1 \qquad V_{13} = K_{12}\alpha_{12}^{-1}(1 - e^{-\alpha_{12}L})$$

$$W_{21} = V_{21} + B_{22}c_2 \qquad V_{23} = K_{21}\alpha_{21}^{-1}(1 - e^{-\alpha_{21}L})$$

The clumsiness of solving the reaction functions in (14.9) by closed methods makes their analysis difficult, but differentiation reveals that they are positively sloped and rise by increasing amounts, although they tend to be near-linear in relevant domains. I have resorted to simulation teachniques to obtain insights into the price–quantity–marketing–profit impacts of parametric changes, using a simple diagonalisation algorithm to solve equations (14.4) and a modified Taylor-series based algorithm to derive the reactions functions in (14.9). The results of those simulations are discussed in the following sections.

3 Case 1: Transportation Costs Dominant

As a baseline, I have chosen a parameter set which conforms to traditional spatial oligopoly competition models in the sense that price rivalry and transprtation costs are the dominant factors in economic space. The parameters are reproduced in table 14.1.

Firm 1 is at a disadvantage in terms of its price-relevant demand curve factors in that its sales are more sensitive to own-price and other-price than firm 2's. Moreover, its function intercept is about one-third lower than its rival's. In marketing position, however, it has some clear advantages in that although the initial effectiveness of the marketing dollar at its site – K_{11} – is less than its rival's, the decay rate of that effectiveness – α_{11} – is lower and the elasticity of sales with respect to marketing budget is higher. The sales

Table 14.1 Case 1 parameters

Firm 1	Firm 2	Both firms
$a_1 = 1{,}500$	$a_2 = 2{,}000$	$T = 5$
$b_{11} = 24$	$b_{12} = 20$	
$b_{12} = 10$	$b_{21} = 6$	
$\alpha_{11} = 0.10$	$\alpha_{22} = 0.15$	
$\alpha_{12} = 0.20$	$\alpha_{21} = 0.20$	
$\beta_{11} = 0.40$	$\beta_{22} = 0.38$	
$\beta_{12} = 0.20$	$\beta_{21} = 0.25$	
$K_{11} = 4$	$K_{22} = 5$	
$K_{12} = 10$	$K_{21} = 4$	
$c_1 = 25$	$c_2 = 30$	

of firms' rivals do not enter into their objective functions and so are irrelevant to their marketing decisions, but firm 1 is much more effective at its site in reducing firm 2's sales, although decay rates of that effectiveness are equal. Finally, the transport cost per unit of distance L is quite high relative to production costs in which latter firm 1 has an advantage.

Hence, the ability of firm 1 to raise price is somewhat less than firm 2's, but it has a distance-sensitive marketing advantage which should grow as L rises. Overall, given the importance of the price sensitivities and the transport rate in the parameters of case 1, its solutions should reveal the price impacts dominant with marketing subordinate, with firm 2 therefore somewhat favored.

In interpreting the solutions, consider the interactions of prices and marketing expenditures in the firms' demand functions. The own-price elasticity of firm 1's sales curve (14.2) is (in absolute terms)

$$-\epsilon_{p_1} = \frac{B_{11}p_1}{X_1} \tag{14.10}$$

and

$$\frac{\partial\left(-\epsilon_{p_1}\right)}{\partial L} = -\frac{\epsilon_{p_1}}{L}\left(1 - \epsilon_L\right) \tag{14.11}$$

where ϵ_L is the elasticity of sales with respect to L, or $(\partial X_1/\partial L)(L/X_1)$.

Hence, when $\epsilon_L < 1$, the sales curve for given p_1, p_2, $R_1 M_1$, and $R_2 M_2$ becomes more elastic and for $\epsilon_L > 1$ more inelastic. But

$$\epsilon_L = 1 - \left\{ \frac{0.5TL\left(B_{11} - B_{12}\right) + K_{11}\left(M_1 R_1\right)^{\beta_{11}}\left[\alpha_{11}^{-1}\left(1 - e^{-\alpha_{11}L}\right) - Le^{-\alpha_{11}L}\right]}{X_1} \right.$$
$$\left. - \frac{K_{12}\left(M_2 R_2\right)^{\beta_{12}}\left[\alpha_{12}^{-1}\left(1 - e^{-\alpha_{12}L}\right) - Le^{-\alpha_{12}L}\right]}{X_1} \right\} \tag{14.12}$$

For the terms in square brackets to be positive, $e^{\alpha L} > 1 + \alpha L$, which is true for all real $\alpha L \neq 0$. Hence, when own-price and own-marketing effects outweigh their other-price and other-marketing effects, the numerator of the expression in curly brackets will be positive and clearly less than X_1, so $0 < \epsilon_L < 1$. From (14.11), at all p_1, the *ceteris paribus* sales curve will become more elastic as L rises.

Therefore, were marketing expenditures to remain constant as L rose, the firms should be led to reduce prices. But $M_1 R_1$ and $M_2 R_2$ will tend to rise as L rises, and

$$\frac{\partial^2 (-\epsilon_{p_1})}{\partial L \partial (M_1 R_1)} = \frac{\epsilon_{p_1}}{X_1} \left[\left(1 - \epsilon_L - \frac{\epsilon_L}{L} \right) \frac{\partial X_1}{\partial (M_1 R_1)} + \beta_{11} K_{11} (M_1 R_1)^{\beta_{11}-1} e^{-\alpha_{11} L} \right]$$

(14.13)

This expression is negative for $0 < \epsilon_L < 1$, except possibly for small values of L coupled with large ϵ_L and small own-advertising effects. In general, however, it will be negative. Thus the rise in own-price elasticity as L increases is decreased with increases in $M_1 R_1$. With a large increase in $M_1 R_1$ as L increases this renders the *mutatis mutandis* sales function less elastic at the price ruling before L increases and price should tend to rise.

The case 1 features emphasize relatively small marketing expenditures by both firms so that elasticities should increase as L rises. This does in fact happen in all four solutions for case 1 variants reproduced in table 14.2. We will consider each variant in turn.

3.1 Variant 1: Both Firms Have Marketing Programs

In this case with the solution displayed in part A of table 14.2 when both firms have modest marketing programs, prices decline by increasing amounts as L rises and transportation costs mount. Firm 1's relative pricing disadvantage keeps its price at 78 to 80 percent of firm 2's, its distance-dependent marketing advantage being unable to compensate over this domain of L. Nonetheless, modest as both marketing programs are, they account for a rising proportion of sales as transport costs limit the market, increasing on a net basis (own-marketing effects less other-marketing effects) from 25 to 55 percent of sales for firm 1 and firm 2. Marketing costs reflect current economic conditions in being 1.5 to 3 percent of sales revenue. They rise somewhat for firm 1 over the range of L but decline as L rises from 5 to 10 for firm 2 as its marketing effectiveness declines over space.

The net effect of firm 1's relative price-effect disadvantage and marketing-effect advantage is to yield much larger profits to firm 2 than to itself. Indeed, the disadvantage widens with L as the percentage that firm 1's profit bears to firm 2's falls from 70 to 66 percent. The relative competitive

Table 14.2 Case 1 solutions for selected L

L	X_1	X_2	P_1	P_2	M_1 / M_1R_1	M_2 / M_2R_2	π_1	π_2	Firm 1 Own	Firm 1 Other	Firm 2 Own	Firm 2 Other
											Marketing sales effects	
A. Both firms have marketing programs												
1	811	883	$58.80	$74.15	0.0140 / $669	0.0160 / $1,045	$26,745	$37,942	283	83	314	54
5	3,764	4,126	56.37	71.26	0.0276 / 5,865	0.0259 / 7,720	112,204	162,639	2,126	392	2,105	271
10	6,433	7,187	51.80	65.94	0.0293 / 9,750	0.0241 / 11,400	162,671	246,874	4,096	590	3,715	415
B. Firm 1 only has a marketing program												
1	822	850	59.24	72.54	0.0140 / 683	0 / 0	27,453	36,194	285	0	0	53
5	3,794	3,854	56.62	68.54	0.0277 / 5,945	0 / 0	114,033	148,526	2,137	0	0	272
10	6,460	6,718	51.92	63.59	0.0293 / 9,822	0 / 0	164,093	225,669	4,103	0	0	416
C. Firm 2 only has a marketing program												
1	786	889	57.76	74.47	0 / 0	0.0160 / 1,057	25,764	38,498	0	83	315	0
5	3,503	4,152	54.19	71.52	0 / 0	0.0259 / 7,699	102,284	164,683	0	393	2,112	0
10	5,910	7,212	49.62	66.06	0 / 0	0.0241 / 11,466	145,500	248,594	0	591	3,723	0
D. Neither firm has a marketing program												
1	797	857	58.20	72.85	0 / 0	0 / 0	26,452	36,731	0	0	0	0
5	3,532	3,879	54.44	68.79	0 / 0	0 / 0	103,974	150,469	0	0	0	0
10	5,935	6,742	49.73	63.71	0 / 0	0 / 0	146,792	227,269	0	0	0	0

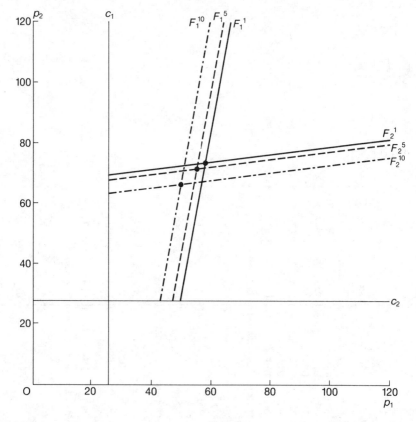

Figure 14.1   Reaction functions: case 1, variant 1, $L = 1$, 5, and 10.

disadvantage for firm 1 is depicted in figure 14.1, where reactions functions for the L values are drawn. The function for firm 1, F_1, shifts downward more rapidly, as L rises, than F_2, the function for firm 2.

The competitive interaction of the firms captured in the simulation brings about a stronger relative performance for firm 2 than could be surmised from the parameters. Marketing-effect sales are stronger than expected for $L = 5$ and 10 and the attritional effects upon firm 1's sales are also greater than anticipated. Firm 2's market share remains rather steady at about 52 percent as L rises, but its profits rise from 142 percent of firm 1's to 152 percent. Its stronger price advantages (including the intercept parameter a_2L) give firm 2 a decided total advantage over firm 1 with its slight marketing advantages over this domain of L.

3.2 Variant 2: Firm 1 Only Has a Marketing Program

When firm 1 only engages in marketing activity, it performs somewhat better at the expense of firm 2, as shown in part B of table 14.2. Sales of firm 1 do not improve dramatically and its prices are raised only slightly above those of variant 1. Its freedom from firm 2's attritional marketing results in higher sales potential, part of which is exploited in higher price instead of increased sales. However, firm 2 lowers prices substantially below those of variant 1 where both engage in marketing, limiting firm 1's ability to raise prices and expand sales. Overall, firm 1 does not benefit dramatically from firm 2's failure to market.

On the other hand, firm 2 suffers profit-wise from its cessation of marketing, and increasingly so as L increases. Prices drop substantially but sales decline nonetheless, even though firm 1's attritional damage is not materially changed. Failure to market is far more disadvantageous to firm 2 than being sole marketer is advantageous to firm 1. Nonetheless, firm 2 still does very well without such activity, compensating in large part for its loss in induced sales by increasing them via price reductions and benefiting from firm 1's price increases.

3.3 Variant 3: Firm 2 Only Has a Marketing Program

The conclusions concerning this variant are mirror images of those in the case where firm 1 only had a marketing program and need not be repeated. What is interesting for the three variants displayed in parts A, B, and C of table 14.2 is that M_1 and M_2 – the marketing expenditure fractions of sales revenues – remain constant. Optimal expenditures on those accounts are a constant proportion of changing gross receipts. It will be interesting to see that this continues in all other cases and variants to follow. Is this stability a mere happenstance in this set of cases, or is it a peculiarity of the model, or does it reflect a deeper tendency in marketing costs?

3.4 Variant 4: Neither Firm Has a Marketing Program

Finally, part D of table 14.2 presents the variant of case 1 where neither firm engages in marketing activity. When compared with the outcomes of variant 1, both firms survive well without the activity but do suffer significantly in terms of profits. Both firms reduce prices to maintain sales lost from marketing, and prices fall as L rises as they do in the three previous variants. Both firms do better than they do when their rival has a marketing program and they do not, but not by great amounts in terms of profits.

To summarize, these four variants of case 1 reflect conditions where marketing efforts have important impacts on sales but where price reductions are highly substitutable for such efforts without great profit sacrifices. Marketing expenditures when made are modest compared with revenue and profit and, interestingly, are in constant proportion to sales revenue. Firm 2 is slightly more disadvantaged as market grows but benefits from a bit more pricing power than firm 1. Overall, however, market share is remarkably stable in all four cases, with firm 1 controlling about 48 percent of the sales and firm 2 about 52 percent.

4 Case 2: Marketing Dominant

In order to model the newly emerging spatial economy described in section 1, I have altered case 1 parameters to (1) reduce the price sensitivities of sales, (2) reduce the transportation cost, and (3) increase the effectiveness of marketing programmes. Specifically, T is reduced from 5 to 1, the B coefficients are halved, and the K coefficients are doubled. The solutions for the four variants are reproduced in table 14.3.

4.1 Variant 1: Both Firms Have Marketing Programs

Net sales due to marketing now comprise a larger and increasing proportion of sales, and marketing expenditures have risen to between 7 and 13 percent of revenue from case 1 levels of 1 to 3 percent. Sales and profits have risen by large multiples of those in the case 1 counterpart in table 14.2, part A. Prices of firm 1 rise by decreasing amounts as L rises instead of falling, although p_2 declines when $L = 10$ after rising from $L = 1$ to $L = 5$ as marketing effectiveness falls off. In summary, prices, sales, marketing expenditures, and profits behave in expected manners. The reaction functions for this variant are graphed in figure 14.2 for $L = 1$, 5, and 10.

4.2 Variant 2: Firm 1 Only Has a Marketing Program

When firm 1 only actively engages in marketing, some interesting developments occur. Firm 2 is now greatly reduced in profitability and acts to counteract firm 1 by greatly reducing prices for all three L values. This restricts firm 1's ability to raise prices and indeed forces it for $L = 5$ to reduce price below the corresponding value for variant 1. Its sales actually decline from variant 1 values for $L = 5$ and 10, so that its profits are *reduced* below

Table 14.3 Case 2 solutions for selected L

					M_1 / M_1R_1	M_2 / M_2R_2			Firm 1		Firm 2	
L	X_1	X_2	P_1	P_2			π_1	π_2	Own	Other	Own	Other
					A. Both firms have marketing programs							
1	1,060	1,167	$113.37	$146.69	0.0718 $8,633	0.0730 $12,504	85,077	$123,666	819	202	905	135
5	6,608	6,695	135.14	163,91	0.1213 108,303	0.1059 116,229	619,525	780,371	7,557	1,021	6,944	777
10	13,755	13,188	139.63	161.88	0.1286 247,089	0.1013 246,157	1,329,712	1,523,015	16,492	1,595	13,165	1,288
					B. Firm 1 only has a marketing program							
1	1,080	983	114.97	128.31	0.0718 8,907	0	88,220	96,650	830	0	0	136
5	6,506	4,951	133.43	129.02	0.1213 105,319	0	600,144	490,257	7,472	0	0	772
10	13,418	9,945	136.82	129.45	0.1287 236,289	0	1,264,096	989,070	16,197	0	0	1,273
					C. Firm 2 only has a marketing program							
1	906	1,187	100.54	148.69	0	0.0729 12,872	68,468	128,007	0	203	915	0
5	4,655	6,711	102.58	164.23	0	0.1059 116,713	361,119	784,167	0	1,022	6,955	0
10	9,292	13,045	102.43	160.45	0	0.1013 212,104	719,543	1,489,638	0	1,589	13,066	0
					D. Neither firm has a marketing program							
1	924	1,001	101.96	130.12	0	0	71,108	100,239	0	0	0	0
5	4,573	4,965	101.21	129.31	0	0	348,475	493,085	0	0	0	0
10	9,032	9,829	100.27	128.29	0	0	679,847	966,099	0	0	0	0

Marketing sales effects

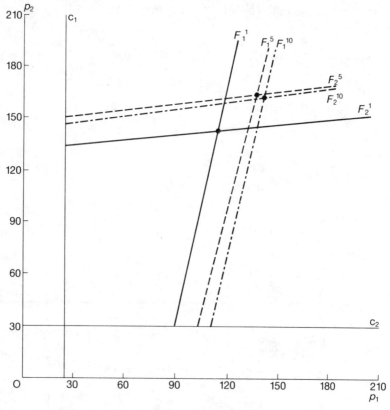

Figure 14.2   Reaction functions: case 2, variant 1, $L = 1$, 5, and 10.

that variant's values. This occurs despite the elimination of substantial firm 2 attritional effects. Finally, the marketing monopoly leads firm 1 to reduce its marketing expenditures for $L = 5$ and 10.

The new economy has created a synergism between the firms in which generally both are more profitable, especially in larger market areas when both engage in active marketing. This is because a rival's efforts increase its demand and permit it to raise its prices, which in turn allow others to raise prices. Marketing and price competition are inseparably linked, even when the latter's role is restricted.

4.3 Variant 3: Firm 2 Only Has a Marketing Program

When the firms exchange marketing monopoly roles, the same patterns emerge as in variant 2 with firms interchanged. Firm 1 reduces prices below variant 1 levels by even greater amounts than firm 2 did in variant 2. Nonetheless it suffers large reductions in sales and profits. Firm 2 does raise price slightly above variant 1 levels for $L = 1$ and 5 but reduces it slightly for $L = 10$. Firm 2's profits rise above those in the joint marketing case for $L = 1$ and 5 but fall in the case where market size grows to 10. Similarly, marketing budget for firm 2 rises slightly for $L = 1$ and 5 but falls for $L = 10$, but slightly.

In both variants 2 and 3, therefore, the tradeoff between price and marketing is that firm 1's price falls such that the marketing rival changes marketing budget only slightly, and then, especially for larger market sizes, downward. Synergism is revealed in the mutually beneficial effects of both firms' marketing efforts for larger L because of the tempering of price competition that it effects.

Finally, it is interesting once more in the new environment to observe the stability of M_1 and M_2 in variants 1, 2, and 3. Where nonzero, they are essentially identical, as they were in table 14.2, even in the face of rather different market shares in table 14.3. It is an intriguing recurrence of an unexplained regularity.

4.4 Variant 4: Neither Firm Has a Marketing Program

Profit-wise, both firms do worse when neither has a program than when both do, and much worse, of course, than in case 1. For lower values of L, each prefers that neither have a program than that only its rival does, but for higher values of L this is reversed. As marketing's incremental contributions to the sales of a firm decline with market size and the sales function becomes less elastic, that firm's price tends to rise or to fall less rapidly. Attrition losses to the rival taper off as well, and the rival finds that part B's higher price and sales yields higher profits than part D's lower price and sales.

For these four variants of case 2, marketing efforts play a dominant role in dictating prices, sales, and profits. Firm 2's advantages in pricing power are diminished rather rapidly as L rises and the marketing advantage of firm 1 asserts itself. Marketing costs rise from the 1 to 3 percent of case 1 revenues to 7 to 13 percent – an indication of the shift in costs away from labor and transportation that will characterize the new economy.

5 Case 3: Marketing Dominant with Assimilated Attrition

In cases 1 and 2, the firms' losses to a rival's marketing program were assumed to be lost to the duopolistic industry, either as aborted sales or as purchases of substitute products or services. In case 3, I assume that those "attrition" quantities are added to the causing firm's sales, so that a firm's marketing effort results in attracting sales that would not eventuate in the absence of the effort as well as diverting sales that would have benefited the rival seller. In this manner each firm is given a beneficial interest in its attritional effects which it does not have in the earlier cases. The solutions of the variants of the model's competitive environment are presented in table 14.4. They may be summarized briefly.

5.1 Variant 1: Both Firms Have Marketing Programs

The enhanced incentives to spend on marketing are revealed in both firms' increasing their marketing budgets by about 50 percent above case 2 levels and lifting M_1 and M_2 for all L values by a percentage point or more. Interestingly, the profits of both firms rise above case 2 counterparts and sales increase for both in the face of substantially higher prices. The diminishing returns to marketing expenditures result in only small gains in marketing-induced sales over case 2 levels, but their impact on prices is profit-effective.

5.2 Variant 2: Firm 1 Only Has a Marketing Program

Both firms' profits are higher in all L cases than they were in variant 2 of case 2, but for firm 1 all the L values yield smaller profits than when both firms have marketing programs. Its marketing budgets are reduced below corresponding variant 1 levels. The cause, of course, is that firm 2 reduces prices to close to their case 2 values, and firm 1 must respond by reducing p_1 to levels below variant 1 values. Marketing synergism is extremely strong for firm 1 in this "closed" sales model in that it prefers to have firm 2 compete in marketing than not to compete.

5.3 Variant 3: Firm 2 Only Has a Marketing Program

The results are broadly the same as those for the case where firm 1 had the sole marketing program. Firm 2 improves its position over variant 1 for $L = 1$, but then falls below the profitability levels of that variant for higher L values. The same forces are operating as were discussed in the summary of variant 2.

Table 14.4   Case 3 solutions for selected L

| | | | | | | | | | | Marketing sales effects | | | |
| | | | | | | | | | | Firm 1 | | Firm 2 | |
L	X_1	X_2	P_1	P_2	M_1 / M_1R_1	M_2 / M_2R_2	π_1	π_2		Own	Other	Own	Other
A. Both firms have marketing programs													
1	1,146	1,272	$120.49	$157.21	0.0872 / $12,038	0.0908 / $18,155	$97,392	$143,660		866	208	906	140
5	7,261	7,349	146.01	176.97	0.1347 / 147,751	0.1204 / 156,633	735,871	923,408		8,094	1,056	7,406	811
10	14,858	14,196	148.82	171.96	0.1392 / 307,836	0.1130 / 275,940	1,531,891	1,739,252		17,448	1,638	13,853	1,334
B. Firm 1 only has a marketing program													
1	1,143	988	120.24	128.80	0.0872 / 11.983	0 / 0	96,858	97,606		865	0	0	140
5	6,991	4,995	141.52	129.91	0.1350 / 133,510	0 / 0	681,021	499,065		7,873	0	0·	797
10	14,251	10,027	143.76	130.27	0.1395 / 285,824	0 / 0	1,406,699	1,005,502		16,923	0	0	1,309
C. Firm 2 only has a marketing program													
1	926	1,287	102.20	158.71	0 / 0	0.0906 / 18,510	71,528	147,143		0	209	968	0
5	4,783	7,308	104.71	176.17	0 / 0	0.1205 / 155,172	381,217	913,069		0	1,054	7,378	0
10	9,441	13,946	104.09	169.46	0 / 0	0.1130 / 750,598	750,598	1,677,242		0	1,628	13,684	0
D. Neither firm has a marketing program													
1	924	1,001	101.96	130.12	0 / 0	0 / 0	71,078	100,239		0	0	0	0
5	4,573	4,965	101.21	129.31	0 / 0	0 / 0	348,475	439,089		0	0	0	0
10	9,032	9,829	100.27	128.29	0 / 0	0 / 0	679,847	966,099		0	0	0	0

5.4 Variant 4: Neither Firm Has a Marketing Program

Both firms are heavily penalized at all L levels when marketing programs are denied them. Indeed, except for $L = 1$, both prefer their rival to engage in marketing if they do not – a change from case 2. Variant 4 solutions reveal very sharp reductions of prices and sales, as well as profits, below variant 1 levels: deprivation of marketing activities is especially punishing in this "new economic environment."

Finally, we note once more the meager variability of M_1 and M_2 in variants 1, 2, and 3. It would be most interesting to probe into the causes of this regularity which has emerged in the three cases treated.

6 Conclusions and Future Research Directions

Using some simple models of integrated price/marketing competition in space by oligopolists, this chapter has made a start in analyzing the characteristics of emerging economic structure in developed nations. The term "marketing" is used as an umbrella term for increasing personal and impersonal interactions between firms and customers. That characteristic, with its implications for competition within a differentiated oligopoly, will be crucial in analyzing the economy, including its spatial characteristics.

Extensions of the models presented and parametric displacements of the present models will be examined in the future. Models which include rivals' sales or market shares as a negative factor in the firms' objective functions should be constructed. The implications of improving the effectiveness of marketing (the β factors) and reducing the spatial impedance to interactions (the α factors) will be studied. Also, the strengths of the motive to decentralize locations to effectively reduce these α factors will be especially interesting.

At this point, some interesting results can be listed. Marketing costs should rise to become a significant portion of firms' costs in the new economy as marketing effects on sales rise to new levels of importance or even dominate prices and transport costs. The degree of tradeoff between price and marketing competition will be an important determinant of prices, profits, and market share. Firms' marketing expenditures may well be synergistically related, especially in large market areas, in so far as they increase demand functions and result in mutually supportive price rises. Price changes as a function of market size should tend to decrease as the market grows spatially, since marketing effectiveness in decreasing the elasticity of the demand functions declines and their "inelasticizing" effects diminish. Finally, the models' solutions in three quite different cases yield, within each case's variants, a surprising constancy of marketing costs as a proportion of revenue, and that tempts toward investigation of causes.

Note

[1] The work of Börje Johansson and his collaborators [1, 2, 3] is a notable pioneering effort to analyze these newer bases for spatial organization, and explicitly challenges the theory community to develop a framework for their analysis. Much of the work is devoted to the dynamics of information flow concerning process and product innovation in a network, and their impact upon spatial structure, but its basic conceptual framework is similar to the one developed in static mode in this chapter.

References

[1] Johansson, B. and C. Karlsson, *Industrial Applications of Information Technology*, CERUM Working Paper 1985, 4, University of Umeå, 1985.
[2] Johansson, B. and J. Larsson, "Characteristics of the Firm and the Spread of Technology Adoption", *Ricerche Economiche*, 60 (1986), 675-95.
[3] Johansson, B. and L. Westin, "Technical Change, Location, and Trade", *Papers of the Regional Science Association*, 62 (1987), 13-25.

15

Spatial Oligopoly: Price–location Interdependence and Social Cost in a Discrete Market Space

1 Introduction

The literature of spatial oligopoly is small in volume and constricted in scope – but, analytically, it is an elegant and imaginative one. Its substantive complexity is witnessed by its content of pioneer usages in economics of the calculus of variations, the theory of functional equations, and simulation. Yet, its results are largely confined to duopoly, and the applicability of theorems is severely limited by the simplifications made in their hypotheses.

In these respects the literature mirrors the general failure of synthetic economic theory to cope with interdependent variation. *A priori* reasoning is incapable of placing sufficiently restrictive limits upon function characteristics to permit derivation of interesting generalizable theorems. The modern theorist must no longer ignore the record: a century of advanced economic theory, adapting some initially most promising mathematical techniques to interdependence models, has taken us little distance in deriving insights into realistic economic variation. It is time to reorient both the aims and methodology of theoretical endeavor, away from the search after unattainable universals and toward a quest for useful insights of more limited applicability.

The theorist must reduce his ambitions to designing relevant analytical frameworks for solving specified relations for numerical answers and to deriving from these solutions the greatest amount of useful information they are capable of yielding. These results must be the product of a far more rigorous body of selection techniques than we now have. We need more systematic procedures to determine which parameters are critical in a model specification; for placing upper and lower bounds upon such parameters for

Originally published in *Regional Science and Urban Economics*, 7 (1977), 339–58, and reproduced with permission.

sensitivity analyses; and, given the outputs of such "efficient" parametric ranging, we require an "econometrics of simulation" to permit us to derive maximally the insights into economic reality they contain.

In this chapter I have sought to apply the rudiments of this methodology of "simulative theorizing" [8–11] to the oligopolistic industry in its inter-related price–location decision-making. Section 2 contains a brief review of the relevant literature. Section 3 indicates in detail the extension of the spatial oligopoly problem discussed in the present paper and the methods and models employed. Instrumentally, section 4 seeks to generalize a linear measure of the absolute size of a market to a similar measure for the plane. In section 5 we derive measures of the social costs of oligopoly and isolate the parameters on which it depends. Section 6 illustrates all the techniques with a simple case. Finally, we conclude with a brief summary in section 7.

2 A Brief Survey of the Literature

The environment within which the existing body of spatial oligopoly theory has been developed – with some exceptions to be noted – is that which frames Hotelling's seminal analysis [7] and Smithies's [14] extensions and modifications of it. Following Gannon [4, 5] we define that context as "simple spatial duopoly," with the following characteristics:

1 Two profit-maximizing firms exist which:
    (a) produce at identical constant costs, frequently taken to be zero for convenience;
    (b) price f.o.b. their locations at potentially different values, with neither rival's delivered price lower everywhere;
    (c) charge a uniform transport rate t per unit of product-distance, so that transport costs are proportional to distance moved;
    (d) sell at a positive unit profit;
    (e) have zero relocation costs;
    (f) adopt varying but simple assumptions of rival response to their price–location initiatives.
2 Consumers exist who:
    (a) are distributed continuously and uniformly along a bounded line segment of length L;
    (b) have identical demand functions in terms of delivered price;
    (c) treat both products as qualitatively homogeneous;
    (d) buy that product (if any) whose delivered price is smaller.

The open ends of the market's linear configuration imply that each rival's market area can be divided into two parts. The first is an exclusive, protected *hinterland* that lies between his location and that end with no intervening rival. The second is the area he shares with his rival – *the rivalrous region* – between his and his rival's location with a boundary marked by equal delivered prices. Hence, his optimal location is the resultant of two sets of forces: (1) centripetal, which draw him toward the center of the line to exploit the hinterland, and (2) centrifugal, which induce him to move toward the pole. The literature is almost wholly concerned with the isolation of the factors that generate these force sets, as well as rigorous or informal judgements of their relative strengths in order to gauge the resultant.

In Hotelling's paper [7] the critical special assumptions were (1a) zero marginal costs, (1b) identical f.o.b. prices, (1f) Cournot-like conjectures of rivals' nonreactions to price or locational initiatives, and (2b) infinitely inelastic demand functions. The first assumption merely simplifies the mathematics without sacrifice of generality; the second is a necessary condition for central concentration of the firms, for otherwise one firm must undersell the other at all points; the third creates the simplest of oligopolistic interdependence environments; and the fourth permits both firms to move toward the center without penalty of sales losses in the hinterlands. Centrifugal forces are nonexistent, and centripetal forces lead to Hotelling's famous concentration of rivals at the midpoint of the line.

Criticism of the results on the basis of these special postulates was fast to appear. Chamberlin [1] eliminated the hinterland by bending the linear market into a circle, showing that under Hotelling's conditions rivals' locations would be indeterminate but 180° apart. [He also believed that within Hotelling's environment that the introduction of a third firm gives rise to centrifugal forces and leads to a socially optimal location pattern with one rival at the center and the others at distances $1/6L$ from the end points of the line. He was incorrect in this, however, as no solution exists for this number. See chapter 16 of this volume.]

Hotelling appreciated the possibility of aggressive price cutting by one rival to force the other out of business in his "equilibrium" and that tacit collusion between the firms might lift prices without limit to the rivals' joint and individual benefits. Lerner and Singer [13] assumed infinite elasticity of the demand function to the finite price limit and finite elasticity above, but for the most part remained with his Cournot myopia assumption (although they did expand upon the war-of-survival case).

It was Smithies [14] who broadened and deepened spatial duopoly analysis by introducing (2b) linear demand functions with finite elasticities everywhere (which we write $X = a - bP^*$, where P^* is delivered price), and (1f) three alternative nonmarginal conjectural variation assumptions:

Case 1. Price-locational symmetry. Rivals expect their competitors to match exactly their f.o.b. price initiatives and to move symmetrically about the origin in response to locational moves.

Case 2. Price symmetry, fixed locations. Rivals expect price changes to be matched but the other firm's location to be unchanged.

Case 3. Fixed prices, fixed locations. The Hotelling and Lerner–Singer assumptions of Cournot myopia.

Finally, he retains the assumption of zero marginal costs (1a).

Assume the rivals are located where hinterlands and a rivalrous region exist, and that a rival contemplates a marginal movement toward the center, initially without an f.o.b. price change. His net increase or decrease in profit (proportionate to sales and equal to revenue) is the resultant of what he expects to gain in the amount of rivalrous region he controls offset by his losses in sales in the original hinterland. The conjectural gross gain in sales in the rivalrous region will be larger (1) the smaller his rival's expected price–location responses; (2) the smaller the transport rate, t; and (3) the more inelastic the demand curve, for average transport costs in the old firm-controlled rivalrous region will not have changed, and sales increase will be greater the less responsive demand is to delivered price in the newly acquired territory. The loss in sales in the old hinterland will be less (1) the smaller the absolute size, which correlates with L; (2) the smaller the transportation rate, t; and (3) the more inelastic the demand.

For his assumed conditions of linear demand and zero marginal costs, in his s-measure Smithies has neatly isolated the relationship of t, L, and a surrogate for elasticity. Setting $X = 0$ in the demand function, we define the price-axis intercept of the demand as

$$P_{max} = a/b. \tag{15.1}$$

Note that P_{max} includes both aspects of demand elasticity – position and slope – although, of course, it is an imperfect surrogate.[1] Then, define

$$s = t \cdot L/P_{max}. \tag{15.2}$$

The larger is s, the more punishing upon hinterland sales is the marginal move into the rivalrous region, and, in general, the less rewarding is the impact upon revenue of the enhanced rivalrous region. Therefore, s serves as an index of the strength of the centrifugal forces in the environments of cases 1 through 3.

In case 1, centrifugal forces totally dominate Hotelling's centripetal forces, as, regardless of the value of s, firms locate at the points that minimize transport costs: i.e. at the quartiles. Neither firm can hope to obtain more than half the market, so that each settles for the half he cannot be denied and charges an f.o.b. monopoly price (taking into account t as it affects demand in the definition of that price).

For case 2, a movement toward the center is expected to gain some rivalrous region increment and the rise in average transport costs dictates as well a fall in price from case 1 levels (even though it is expected that the price cut will be met). Location will be symmetrical about the center between it and the quartiles. When $s = 8/3$, location is at the quartile with $P = P_{max}$; when $s > 8/3$, location is at the quartiles with $P > P_{max}$ toward the extremities, so that all of the market will not be served; and when $s \leqslant 4/7$, location is at the center. Between these critical values centripetal and centrifugal forces balance at intervening locations, with the strength of the latter varying directly with s.

Case 3 differs from Hotelling's case (where $P_{max} = \infty$ and $s = 0$) only in the presence of a finite elasticity of demand. It assures that a move toward the center "costs" sales in the hinterland and will, therefore, introduce centrifugal forces (except where $s \leqslant 8/11$, when central location rules). For $s > 8/11$, the firm expects to hold rivalrous region from marginal moves outward and to reduce average transport costs in the hinterland, and firms will locate as in case 2 but closer to the center and with lower prices because of rivals' price matching. When $s \geqslant 8/3$ location will be at the quartiles.

One of Smithies's notable contributions was to focus upon optimal pricing and its interdependence with location. The relation of prices to s is more complicated and could not be subjected to closed analysis by Smithies. In general, it will pay firms to absorb freight by charging f.o.b. prices that are below the profit-maximizing levels where $t = 0$, and this tendency to swallow freight cost will rise with the degree of expected competition.

Devletoglou [2] introduced some novel elements to challenge the Hotelling centrality theorem, but narrows the framework as well. In the latter respect he assumes prices are fixed at a common level (1b) and that all rival moves are symmetrical about the center of a line (2a). We ignore his generalization of the market from a line to a bounded area as unimportant for the purpose of this survey.

His fundamental departure is to assume that consumers' preferences are characterized by "thick" indifference curves as they relate to distance; i.e. that distances d and $d + \varepsilon$, $\varepsilon > 0$, are indifferent to the consumer for some ε sufficiently small. Since distance translates into transport cost (not merely "disutility," which Devletoglou uses to develop his analysis), this implies that he ignores differences in transport costs below some threshold level. Hence, the consumer is only a qualified minimizer of delivery costs (2d).

From this assumption he establishes a "doubtful" region in which consumers are indifferent between producers. Since this region increases as the rivals near each other, a desire to minimize its size dictates movement toward the poles. Devletoglou provides this desire by arguing that inventory costs rise with the size of the doubtful region, and that "swarm effects" among consumers in it may prevent an even distribution of sales between rivals. Although the doubtful region is minimized at the poles, he argues inconclusively that the firms will drift to points where average transport costs are minimized, somewhat inward of the poles.

More recently, Gannon [4, 5] has extended the Hotelling–Smithies analysis in some novel and imaginative ways. In his most general work Gannon weakens Smithies's assumption of linear demand functions to general, well-behaved functions (1b), and introduces explicit *marginal* expectations of rivals' price–locational responses (1f). One unsatisfactory assumption he makes is that rivals respond only in similar mode: a price change leads only to a price response and a location change only to a location response.[2]

The central theorem deriving from his work is that a necessary condition for central location when conjectural variation is present is that both rivals must expect that a locational move on their part will lead the rival to move in their direction by less than the initiating move. Such conjectural variation, explicitly present in the first-order conditions, eliminates the determinateness of the Hotelling–Smithies work. Location can be anywhere on the line [4], p. 100: "In short, we can conclude nothing at all a priori about the equilibrium arrangement of the firms; although this is somewhat disconcerting from a theoretical standpoint, it is really not that surprising."

In a further analysis, with the more limited aim of establishing conditions on the demand functions that will yield Hotelling's central location, Gannon [5] employed functional analysis with similarly inconclusive results. With prices neutralized by assuming them equal (since central location can occur only if neither rival undercuts the other), and with the same condition on conjectural variation noted above, Gannon finds that a subset of negative exponential demand functions will yield central concentration, where the degree of convexity is crucial. The complexity of the conditions for linear and constant-elasticity demand curves is such that the results go little beyond Smithies's isolation of t, L, elasticity of demand (or a surrogate in Smithies's case), and degree of conjectural variation as crucial elements.

Gannon [5], p. 374, concludes: "Unfortunately, it does not appear to be possible to establish richer properties of general individual consumer demand functions that relate to global location and price equilibria involving central concentration. Rather, such properties must be catalogued for specific price-setting postulates and families of demand functions, and, in this way, their generality tested."

This is an important conclusion, and, as I have argued elsewhere [9–11], must be extended to most large-scale and/or complex economic interdependence modelling. We must begin to develop a body of methods to permit us to model situations of general interest with specified structural relations in a manner that maximizes the generalizability of the results, as well as to solve families of specific problems. Closed analysis is of limited usefulness in gaining insight into events that reflect complicated patterns of causation among the variables, and its glossy but largely false promise of overarching universals must not blind us to more effective if humbler means of obtaining knowledge.

3 An Extension of the Spatial Oligopoly Framework

In this spirit we shall extend spatial oligopoly analysis in several directions. First, we generalize the number of rivals from 2 to m. Second, we recognize the existence of markets at discrete points in space, permitting the rivals to locate at any point on the plane to serve those markets. Third, we generalize the Euclidean distance metric to a "pseudo-Euclidean" metric in order to permit closer approximations to realistic transportation costs.

The approach employs nonlinear programming and combinatorial programming techniques to solve specified models, and displaces these models' solutions with strategic parameter changes in order to gain insights into their impacts. Our present knowledge of methods of isolating the important parameters, of setting bounds upon them for sensitivity analysis, and of deriving theorems of limited generalizability is primitive. Hence, we do not assert that we have designed or manipulated these models in any definably efficient manner; but we have derived hypotheses and conjectures that will be useful to practitioners in the analysis of specific realistic spatial oligopoly problems, not to mention designing a framework for the solution of such problems.

We assume, therefore, n markets ("sinks"), with coordinates $[u_j, v_j]$ in the plane, and m rivals, each of whom will locate at a "source" with unknown coordinates $[x_i, y_i]$, not necessarily distinct. Demand functions at the sinks are the linear equations

$$X_j = a_j - b_j P_j^* \,, \tag{15.3}$$

where P_j^* is the minimum delivered price from all sources,

$$P^* = \min_i (P_{ij}) \,, \tag{15.4}$$

and, with d_{ij} equal to the distance between source and sink,

$$P_{ij} = P_i + t \cdot d_{ij} \,, \tag{15.5}$$

with d_{ij} a pseudo-Euclidean metric,

$$d_{ij} = [(u_j - x_i)^2 + (v_j - y_i)^2]^\alpha, \qquad 0 < \alpha < 1. \tag{15.6}$$

Costs at each source are constant at the average and marginal value of C_j. Moreover, weights W_j are applied to the consumption at each source to reflect differential importance in some dimension. In the absence of any such differentiation all $W_i = 1$, an assumption we make in this paper.

In this study we begin by seeking a straightforward joint profit maximization for the rivals, wherein the firms agree tacitly to permit that locational equilibrium and price configuration that optimizes joint profits. Formally,

$$\text{Max } Z = \sum_i \sum_j \sigma_j W_j \left(X_{ij} \left(P_i - C_i \right) \right), \tag{15.7}$$

where

$$X_{ij} = a_j - b_j \left(P_i + t \cdot d_{ij} \right), \qquad \text{all } i,j; \tag{15.8}$$

$$\sigma_{ij} = 1, \text{ if } P_i = P_j^*,$$

$$= 0, \text{ otherwise}, \qquad \text{all } i,j;$$

$$\sum_i \sigma_{ij} = 1, \qquad \text{all } j;$$

$$P_i, X_{ij} \geqslant 0, \qquad \text{all } i,j.$$

The model, therefore, is a 0–1 programming problem, with an objective function which is not jointly concave in σ, P and d, and we are faced with a nonconvex nonlinear programming problem.

It should be pointed out that it is possible to include behavioral inequality or equality constraints, and/or to alter the first-order maximization conditions, to limit the rivals' willingness to undergo losses or profit opportunities for the sake of the joint industry welfare. I have developed at length elsewhere [9–11] the advantages of this framework for oligopoly modelling, including cases with conjectural variation, and in sections 5 and 6 we will consider such oligopolistic behavior explicitly. At present, however, we concentrate upon the joint-profit maximization case.

We compute solutions to (15.7) and (15.8) by iterative sequences of two algorithms, SPATOL and SUMTOL, using the first to obtain a first approximation to source locations, then using the second on the basis of these locations to obtain optimal prices. These prices are then used to re-enter SPATOL for new locations of the sources, and these new locations are fed back to SUMTOL for another price configuration. This iterative process continues until a convergence criterion is met for locations. We shall describe each algorithm in turn.

3.1 SPATOL

We assume that prices and (constant) costs are given for the production units that locate at the sources, where both variables may differ among the units.

Further, the linear demand functions at each sink are specified, and again may differ from one another. The problem is then to locate a given number m of sources among the n sinks in such a manner as to optimize (15.7) subject to (15.8). These nonconvex problems are forms of the generalized multi-source Weber problem, for whose solution when the objective function is transport costs Kuenne and Soland [12] have devised a branch-and-bound algorithm, MULTIWEB. SPATOL is an alteration of MULTIWEB to accommodate the new objective function, demand functions, and price-cost parameters. Some changes were made in the manner of branching and bounding, but these are unduly technical and will be provided to those interested.[3]

Finally, the pseudo-Euclidean metric $[(u_j - x_i)^2 + (v_j - y_i)^2]^\alpha$ has been included, where $0 < \alpha < 1$. Permitting α to depart from 0.5 allows us to approach closer to the nonlinear distances and non-proportional transport charges of the real world.

Given f.o.b prices at sources, SPATOL yields the global optimum for (15.7) in the manner of yielding source locations. It is important to empha-size that SPATOL is capable of solving realistic problems with econometric-ally fitted functions and realistic market locations, even though we limit our usage in this study to simple examples for our simulative theorizing experiments.

3.2 SUMTOL

Consider (15.7) in the case where σ_{ij}, W_j, and $t \cdot d_{ij}$ are given. In this case Z is the sum of a set of concave functions in P_i, where i is the relevant source. We have used Fiacco and McCormick's [3] Sequential Unconstrained Minimization Technique (SUMT) to solve for the optimal source prices given the specified variables as parameters. The only constraints on the maximization are nonnegativity limitations for the prices, and hence the problem is a convex nonlinear programming problem which yields a global maximum.

Note that in each solution by SPATOL and SUMTOL we are obtaining a global minimum or maximum for the partial problem at hand; however, there is no guarantee that the joint product of the algorithms working in tandem will be a global optimum for the original problem. However, we have found that for problems of realistic size – with n in the neighborhood of 8 or 10 and m equal to 4 to 6 – widely differing choices of initial starting points will lead quickly to the same solution, which gives strong confidence that the global optimum has been attained.

4 The Index of Circular Compactness

SPATOL and SUMTOL have an obvious capability of treating realistic problems in spatial oligopoly, and a great deal of potentiality for tailoring to the specifics of the particular situation being studied. In this paper, however, we neglect the latter aspect to study the applicability of the framework to extending the theoretical insights derived from closed analysis in section 2. We exploit Smithies's insights into the nature of spatial duopoly with linear demand functions and organize our parameterization about his measure $s = t \cdot L/P_{max}$, since we will find in section 5 that the social cost of oligopoly is linked to its value. We assume the n sinks have identical demand functions $X_j = 1000 - 5P_j^*$, which implies $P_{max} = 200$. Distance is measured by the pseudo-Euclidean metric d_{ij}.

The variable L in Smithies's definition of s must be generalized from the line to the polygon and from continuous to discrete markets. We have done so by defining two magnitudes: (1) an *index of circular compactness*, to capture the relative dispersion of the sinks in a given polygonal form, and (2) the *area* of the polygon as a measure of absolute distances. Neither is a perfect surrogate for its intended measure, and both together do not fulfill L's function in the definition of s, but we feel they have performed reasonably well in our limited experiments. Moreover, the measure derived here may have an independent interest for those interested in spatial analysis.

Consider the convex hull of an arbitrarily scattered set of markets. Define, first the radius of a circle whose area equals that of the hull, and symbolise this r_A. Next, define the radius of a circle, r_P, whose circumference equals the perimeter of the hull. The index of circular compactness, or a measure of the scatter of the points, is then defined as

$$I = r_A^2/r_P^2 = 4\pi A/P^2,$$

where A is the area and P the perimeter of the convex hull. In table 15.1 we

Table 15.1   Index of circular compactness for polygons

Regular polygon	Index value
Straight line	0.000
Equilateral triangle	0.609
Rectangle, sides a and b	$\pi(ab)/(a + b)^2$
Square	0.785
Pentagon	0.865
Hexagon	0.907
Octagon	0.948
Dodecagon	0.977
Circle	1.000

display the value of I for regular polygons varying along the unit interval from 0.00 for the straight line to 1.00 for the circle.

We shall assume $n = 8$, so that the convex hull of the markets will have no more than eight extreme points. We have chosen equally arbitrarily to analyze spatial oligopoly within the square, and to place the eight sinks at the corners and midpoints of the sides. For absolute dispersion we have chosen $A = 100$, which yields sides of 10. Finally, we permit m to take the values 1, 2, 3, and 4. Ideally, we should like to treat I as a parameter of the analysis of profit-maximization location, rivalrous competition, pricing, and social cost to follow. At the present time, however, we shall employ the square to simplify the presentation of the framework.

5 The Social Cost of Oligopoly

We use as the index of social cost of oligopolistic market structure the reduction in social surplus – consumers' surplus plus producers' surplus – imposed by that market structure. We treat three cases, the first of which is the purely competitive one (with implied free entry of firms) in which each sink is supplied from local firms at marginal cost C with zero transport costs. The social surplus at any sink, which we symbolize $\bar{S}_c$, is then

$$\bar{S}_C = 0.5\,\bar{X}_C\,(P_{\max} - C),\qquad(15.9)$$

where $\bar{X}_C$ is the sales at any sink under the purely competitive conditions.

In figure 15.1 for any sink, with demand function AA' and costs CC', the purely competitive price will be OC, output $O\bar{X}_C$, and social surplus the triangle ABC.

In case 2 we assume pure competition yields to joint profit-maximization among m optimally located sources with their subsets of sinks. By means of SPATOL and SUMTOL optimal locations, sink allocations, and prices are obtained, which inflict two burdens upon the typical sink: (1) transport costs exist which did not exist in pure competition, and (2) prices depart from marginal costs and force the consumer to take less than he did when price equalled marginal cost. Both characteristics reduce social surplus. Consider, first, source i with its subset n_i sinks. Because of the linearity and symmetry of the problem we may deal in terms of the average distance of the source from the sinks, $\bar{d}_J$, and the average quantity taken, $\bar{X}_J$.

On figure 15.1 if we treat the functions graphed as those of the *average* sink in subgroup i, the demand curve falls by the amount of average transport cost per unit of product, $t\bar{d}_j$, or DE. From the firm's viewpoint the new sales function is FF', showing virtual sales at f.o.b. prices. The profit-maximizing f.o.b. price is obtained by locating the intersection of marginal revenue and marginal cost, so that price is P_J, average delivered price is $P_J + t\bar{d}_J$, and average sales per sink are $\bar{X}_J$. Further, the average change in

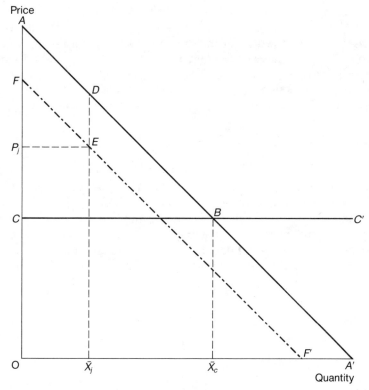

Figure 15.1 Purely competitive and joint-profit maximization solutions for a typical sink.

social welfare associated with oligopolistic joint profit maximization in group i is

$$\Delta \bar{S}_J = -[\bar{X}_J t \bar{d}_J + 0.5(P_J + t\bar{d}_J - C)(\bar{X}_C - \bar{X}_J)]$$

$$= -0.125b[(P_{max} - C)^2 + 6(P_{max} - C)t\bar{d}_J - 3t^2\bar{d}_J^2].$$

(15.10)

When $(P_{max} - C) > 0$ and equal to $t\bar{d}_J$, $\bar{X}_J = 0$ and $\Delta S_j = -\bar{S}_C < 0$. For $\Delta \bar{S}_J = 0$, $P_{max} = 0.464102t\bar{d}_J$ and $\bar{X}_J < 0$. Hence, $\Delta \bar{S}_J < 0$ for $(P_{max} - C) > 0$.

As a relative measure of the social burden of oligopolistic joint-profit maximization we employ

$$\phi = \Delta \bar{S}_J / \bar{S}_C = -0.25(1 + 6z - 3z^2),$$

(15.11)

where $z = t\bar{d}_J/(P_{max} - C)$ or transport cost per unit of maximum average profit. Hence, the relative burden depends upon: (1) transport costs per unit of output, (2) $P_{max} = a/b$, and (3) C. The measure z is similar to Smithies's s (where $C = 0$), although its function in our work is somewhat different; Smithies used it as a measure of the strength of centrifugal forces, whereas we employ it as a measure of the burdensomeness of oligopolistic location and pricing.

The measure ϕ ranges from -0.25 when $z = 0$ ($t\bar{d}_j = 0$ and P_j is the monopoly price) to -1.0 ($t\bar{d}_j = P_{max} - C$ and $\bar{X}_j = 0$). Moreover,

$$d\phi/dz = -1.5(1 - z) . \qquad (15.12)$$

Hence, a rise in z increases the social loss. Therefore, a rise in average distance from source to sinks in the group and/or a rise in the transport rate; a fall in a and/or a rise in b; or a rise in C will increase relative social loss. But the increase becomes smaller as the initial value of z rises. Note from (15.10) that the *absolute* social loss rises with a and falls with rises in b and C.

We may seek to gauge the relative importance of a, b, C, and $t\bar{d}_j$ in contributing to relative social burden in the only meaningful manner available to us – by going to the margin. We find

$$\partial\phi/\partial a = -(1.5)(1 - z)z/b(P_{max} - C) ,$$

$$\partial\phi/\partial b = -P_{max}(\partial\phi/\partial a) ,$$

$$\partial\phi/\partial C = -b(\partial\phi/\partial a) ,$$

$$\partial\phi/\partial t\bar{d}_j = -(b/z)(\partial\phi/\partial a) . \qquad (15.13)$$

Remembering that $0 \leqslant z \leqslant 1$, for small changes in these variables, $t\bar{d}_j$ has the largest impact, with b, C and a following in importance in that order. Note also that

$$\partial\phi/\partial t\bar{d}_j = (1/z)(\partial\phi/\partial C) . \qquad (15.14)$$

That is, an equal change in transport costs and marginal cost have distinctly different impacts; this occurs, of course, because a change in $t\bar{d}_j$ does not affect the base of the percentage, $\bar{S}_C$, whereas a rise in C reduces it as well as increases the incremental loss $\Delta\bar{S}_j$. The impact of a small change in $t\bar{d}_j$ is between 1 and 4 times as large as the impact of the same small change in C.

As a final step in the case 2 analysis we shall derive average relationships over all source groups. We define

$$P^* = \sum_i P_i/m, \qquad X^* = \sum_i X_i/m, \qquad d^* = \sum_i \bar{d}_j/m;$$

that is, we define the mean prices, outputs, and distances for the source groups. Then the optimal prices and outputs for the average sink in the analysis are defined in the same ways when related to d^* as to $\bar{d}_j$ in the analysis above, and all of the relationships above remain unaltered when that simple substitution is made in the relations. Hence we have an effective analysis of the social burden of oligopolistic joint-profit maximization upon the average sink of the n in the problem, and total output, profits, and transportation costs can be derived by multiplying X^*, average profit, and td^* by n. Therefore,

$$P^* = (0.5/b)\,(a - btd^* + bC)\,, \qquad X^* = 0.5\,(a - btd^* - bC)\,. \quad (15.15)$$

Now the introduction of an $(m + 1)$th source into the joint-profit maximization problem is wholly characterized in our model by a fall in d^* by an amount, unfortunately, that our combinatorial techniques can determine but not generalize. And, from (15.12), we know that the reduction of td^* in $(P_{\max} - C)$ units will decrease the social costs by increasing amounts as it approaches the limit of -0.25. We have graphed this relationship in figure 15.2, converting social loss to a positive value for ease of graphical presentation.

In case 3 we permit joint-profit maximization to be compromised by the aggressive interplay of m firms in seeking to better their individual profits. We assume that firms will move in a search for higher individual profits until

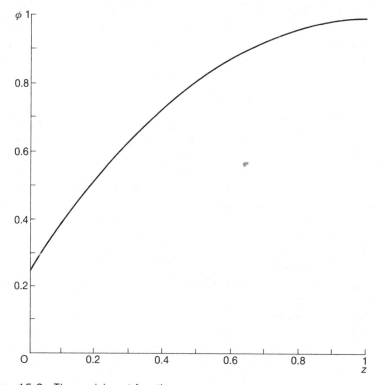

Figure 15.2   The social cost function.

a stable equilibrium is achieved in which no rival can relocate – given the others' locations – without hurting his position. The "wholly rivalrous" oligopolistic solutions are also completely characterized, in terms of their social costs, by the impact on d^* and ϕ of the departure from the joint-profit equilibrium with m firms. Hence, in spatial oligopoly theory such rivalrous competition is the exact equivalent, in social cost terms, of a reduced number of sources in a joint-profit equilibrium, as described by the degree of departure from the purely competitive equilibrium.

The missing link in the creation of a generalizable theory from this framework is the determination of d^* for a given number m of sources and firms, under joint-profit maximization or wholly rivalrous assumptions. For this we must employ the techniques of simulative theorizing via SPATOL and SUMTOL, within the contexts of convex hulls with differing indices of circular compactness, varying t values, changed P_{max} values and differing costs C. To illustrate, we present a simulation for the square in section 6.

6 An Experiment in Simulative Theorizing

We assume the spatial configuration is a square with length of side 10 miles and that eight sinks exist spaced about the perimeter at the four corners and the midpoints of the sides. At each sink j, the demand function is $X_j = 1000 - 5P_j^*$. Marginal and average costs at all sources are set at \$84, and $P_{max} = \$200$.

We parameterize the model by permitting the number of sources m to vary from 1 to 4, by setting the metric parameter α at 0.5 or 0.75, and by setting the transport rate, t, to 1 or 2. The optimal locations of sources and sink allocations were independent of t in our limited experiments, and are graphed in figure 15.3. In table 15.2 we list the 16 cases and relevant solution variable values. For all cases, $\bar{S}_C$, the consumer surplus at each sink under pure competition, is 33,640 and hence for all sinks is 269,120. For absolute losses, ϕ_i should be compared to the former figure and ϕ to the latter, where we continue to treat these variables as positive for ease of presentation.

Were m to be set equal to 8, monopoly would rule at each sink and $\phi_i = \phi = 0.25$: as noted in section 5, therefore, ϕ_i and ϕ have lower bounds of 0.25. In our example, where distances range from 0 to 6 miles, or 4 to 15 "extended miles" under the pseudo-Euclidean metric, losses ascribable to joint-profit maximization oligopoly are quite modest. With four rivals, for example, they are 0.281 for $\alpha = 0.5$, $t = 1$; 0.310 for $\alpha = 0.5$, $t = 2$; 0.300 for $\alpha = 0.75$, $t = 1$; and 0.349 for $\alpha = 0.75$, $t = 2$. The duopoly case causes these to rise to only 0.304, 0.356, 0.369, and 0.480, respectively.

Because z rises proportionately with $t \cdot \bar{d}$, a doubling of transport costs will double z, but ϕ rises substantially less. For example, if $z = 0.5$, a doubling

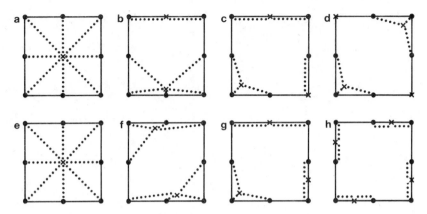

Figure 15.3 Optimal sink allocations and source locations.
a, $m = 1$, $\alpha = 0.5$, $t = 1$ or 2; **b**, $m = 2$, $\alpha = 0.5$,
$t = 1$ or 2; **c**, $m = 3$; $\alpha = 0.5$, $t = 1$ or 2; **d**, $m = 4$,
$\alpha = 0.5$, $t = 1$ or 2; **e**, $m = 1$, $\alpha = 0.75$, $t = 1$ or 2;
f, $m = 2$, $\alpha = 0.75$, $t = 1$ or 2; **g**, $m = 3$, $\alpha = 0.75$,
$t = 1$ or 2; **h**, $m = 4$, $\alpha = 0.75$, $t = 1$ or 2.

of transport costs will make $z = 1$, but ϕ rises by only 23 percent; if $z = 0.25$, the same operations increase ϕ by only 40 percent. Hence, even though we have seen that ϕ is more sensitive to changes in $t \cdot \bar{d}$ than in other variables, practically speaking it is quite robust with respect to such transport costs.

Suppose, now, that we permit the rivals to move from their joint-profit maximum locations whenever they felt, on a Cournot or non-Cournot expectational basis, that they can improve their profits, and that we permit prices to adjust to the optimal profit level for the new locations. What additional costs does this rivalrous action impose upon society?

Consider the cases of duopoly for $\alpha = 0.5$ (figure 15.3b). The rival controlling only three sinks can capture two now allocated to his competitor by moving along the line connecting their present locations sufficiently to just reduce the present distance (6.45) of the sinks from their source. But this will induce like movement from the original source until both sources are located at the center (or very close to one another at [5, 5]) and each has four sinks. At this stable rivalrous solution, when $t = 1$, each will price at \$138.98 and sell 1,099.65 units. Total sales, therefore, fall from 2,235.01 to 2,199.29, and total profits from \$124,889 to \$120,922. Also, $\bar{d}_1 = \bar{d}_2 = 6.04$, $z_1 = z_2 = 0.052$, $\phi_1 = \phi_2 = \phi = 0.326$. The latter measure compares with $\phi = 0.0304$ for joint-profit maximization. When $t = 2$, each rival sells 1,039.28 units at an f.o.b. price of \$135.96; total profits are \$108,001.97, compared with \$115,590.00 initially. Finally, $z_1 = z_2 = 0.194$ and $\phi_1 =$

Table 15.2 The solutions

m	Exponent	t	Source	Location	No. of sinks	$\bar{d}_J$	z_i	P_J	$\bar{X}_J$	ϕ_J	$\bar{P}$	$\bar{X}$	ϕ
1	0.5	1	1	[5.0,5.0]	8	6.04	0.052	138.98	274.91	0.326	138.98	274.91	0.326
2	0.5	1	1	[5.0,10.0]	3	3.33	0.029	140.33	281.67	0.293	139.97	279.84	0.304
			2	[5.0,0.75]	5	4.80	0.041	139.60	278.00	0.310			
3	0.5	1	1	[10.0,0.00]	2	2.50	0.022	140.33	283.75	0.283	140.49	282.46	0.290
			2	[1.60,1.06]	3	3.22	0.028	140.39	281.95	0.291			
			3	[5.00,10.00]	3	3.33	0.029	140.75	281.67	0.293			
4	0.5	1	1	[1.06,1.06]	3	3.22	0.028	140.39	281.95	0.291	141.20	267.93	0.281
			2	[8.94,8.94]	3	3.22	0.028	140.39	281.95	0.291			
			3	[0.00,10.00]	1	0.00	0.000	142.00	290.00	0.250			
			4	[10.00,0.00]	1	0.00	0.000	142.00	290.00	0.250			
1	0.75	1	1	[5.0,5.0]	8	14.99	0.129	134.50	253.40	0.431	134.50	253.40	0.431
2	0.75	1	1	[6.05,0.59]	4	9.68	0.083	137.16	265.82	0.369	137.16	265.82	0.369
			2	[3.95,9.41]	4	9.68	0.083	137.16	265.82	0.369			
3	0.75	1	1	[1.25,1.25]	3	6.01	0.052	138.99	274.94	0.326	139.09	275.49	0.326
			2	[10.0,2.50]	2	3.95	0.034	140.02	280.14	0.300			
			3	[5.0,10.0]	3	7.45	0.064	138.27	271.38	0.343			
4	0.75	1	1	[2.50,0.00]	2	3.95	0.034	140.02	280.12	0.300			
			2	[7.50,10.00]	2	3.95	0.034	140.02	280.12	0.300			

		2	[10.00,2.50]	3	2	3.95	0.034	140.02	280.12	0.300	140.02	280.12	0.300
		2	[0.00,7.50]	4	2	3.95	0.034	140.02	280.12	0.300			
1	0.5	2	[5.0,5.0]	1	8	6.04	0.104	135.96	259.82	0.398	135.96	259.82	0.398
2	0.5	2	[5.0,10.0]	1	3	3.33	0.058	138.67	273.33	0.334	138.19	269.67	0.356
			[5.0,0.75]	2	5	4.80	0.082	137.20	266.01	0.368			
3	0.5	2	[10.0,0.00]	1	2	2.50	0.044	139.50	277.50	0.315	138.98	274.91	0.328
			[1.06,1.06]	2	3	3.22	0.056	138.78	273.90	0.332			
			[5.0,10.00]	3	3	3.33	0.058	138.67	273.33	0.334			
4	0.5	2	[1.06,1.06]	1	3	6.44	0.056	138.78	273.90	0.332	140.39	281.95	0.310
			[8.94,8.94]	2	3	6.44	0.056	138.78	273.90	0.332			
			[0.00,10.00]	3	1	0.00	0.000	142.00	290.00	0.250			
			[10.00,0.00]	4	1	0.00	0.000	142.00	290.00	0.250			
1	0.75	2	[5.0,5.0]	1	8	29.98	0.258	130.74	233.70	0.587	130.74	233.70	0.587
2	0.75	2	[6.05,0.59]	1	4	9.68	0.167	132.33	241.63	0.480	132.33	241.63	0.480
			[3.95,9.41]	2	4	9.68	0.167	132.33	241.63	0.480			
3	0.75	2	[1.25,1.25]	1	3	6.01	0.104	135.98	259.89	0.398	136.19	260.92	0.398
			[10.0,2.50]	2	2	3.95	0.068	138.05	270.14	0.349			
			[5.00,10.0]	3	3	7.45	0.128	134.55	252.73	0.430			
4	0.75	2	[2.50,0.00]	1	2	3.95	0.068	138.05	270.24	0.349	138.05	270.24	0.349
			[7.50,10.0]	2	2	3.95	0.068	138.05	270.24	0.349			
			[10.0,2.50]	3	2	3.95	0.068	138.05	270.24	0.349			
			[0.00,7.50]	4	2	3.95	0.068	138.05	270.24	0.349			

$\phi_2 = \phi = 0.398$, with $\phi = 0.356$ in joint-profit maximization. Hence, when $m = 2$, social burden rises by 7 percent when $t = 1$ and 12 percent when $t = 2$.

When $m = 2$ and the metric exponent is 0.75, $\bar{d}_1 = \bar{d}_2 = 14.99$. For $t = 1$, $z_1 = z_2 = 0.129$ and $\phi_1 = \phi_2 = \phi = 0.431$, compared with 0.369 for joint-profit maximization. Prices fall from an average of \$137.16 to \$134.50 on an f.o.b. basis, sales fall from 2,126.56 to 2,027.2, and profits fall from \$112,115.81 to \$102,373.60. Social burden, therefore, as measured by ϕ, rises by 17 percent. For $t = 2$, $z_1 = z_2 = 0.258$ and $\phi_1 = \phi_2 = \phi = 0.587$, the latter contrasting with a joint-profit maximization level of 0.480. Prices f.o.b. fall from \$132.33 to \$130.74, sales from 1,933.04 to 1,869.60, and profits from \$93,421.79 to \$87,385.12. Social burden, measured by ϕ, therefore, rises by 22 percent.

Next, consider the cases where $m = 3$ (figure 15.3c, g). These locational configurations are unstable under the new assumptions, and locational moves will continue until sources are located at [5.0, 0.0], [5.0, 5.0], and [5.0, 10.0], or like positions which can be obtained by rotation of the square. When $\alpha = 0.5$, $t = 1$, these new locations yield $\phi = 0.290$, or a 2.4 percent increase in social burden. Also $\bar{d}_1 = \bar{d}_3 = 3.33$, $\bar{d}_2 = 0.5$; $\bar{X}_1 = \bar{X}_3 = 271.38$, $\bar{X}_2 = 270.25$; $z_1 = z_3 = 0.064$, $z_2 = 0.068$; and $\phi_1 = \phi_3 = 0.343$, $\phi_2 = 0.349$, so $\phi = 0.344$. In joint-profit maximization, $\phi = 0.326$, so the social burden of rivalry is a rise of about 6 percent. Finally, when $t = 2$, $\bar{X}_1 = \bar{X}_3 = 252.73$, $\bar{X}_2 = 250.50$; $z_1 = z_3 = 0.128$, $z_2 = 0.136$; and $\phi_1 = \phi_3 = 0.430$, $\phi = 0.440$. This yields a $\phi = 0.432$, compared with a joint-profit value of 0.398, for a degradation of about 8.5 percent.

As a final case, consider that of $m = 4$ for $\alpha = 0.5$. In the conditions of rivalry, the only stable configuration is that in which each source serves two sinks from a position where distance to both sinks sums to 5. For example, the pattern of figure 15.3h will satisfy the condition. When $t = 1$, $\bar{d}_1 = \bar{d}_2 = \bar{d}_3 = \bar{d}_4 = 2.5$; $\bar{X}_1 = \bar{X}_2 = \bar{X}_3 = \bar{X}_4 = 283.75$; $z_1 = z_2 = z_3 = z_4 = 0.022$; and $\phi_1 = \phi_2 = \phi_3 = \phi_4 = \phi = 0.283$. Under joint-profit maximization, $\phi = 0.281$ so the rivalrous competition inflicts costs of only 0.7 percent. When $t = 2$, $\bar{X}_1 = \bar{X}_2 = \bar{X}_3 = \bar{X}_4 = 273.90$; $z_1 = z_2 = z_3 = z_4 = 0.022$; and $\phi_1 = \phi_2 = \phi_3 = \phi_4 = \phi = 0.332$. The last figure implies an increased social burden of about 7 percent. For $\alpha = 0.75$, the joint-profit maximization attains the stable configuration, the nature of the metric penalizing longer distances and forcing a decentralization.

The social waste of rivalrous competition among oligopolistic competitors, therefore, is quite sensitive to transport costs, including in the latter transport rate, pseudo-Euclidean metric miles, and "roundaboutness" of realistic transport systems. However, it would appear from our analysis that it declines rapidly with the number of rivals.

7 Conclusion

In this paper we have extended the classic analyses of Hotelling and Smithies to the location of oligopolistic rivals in a discrete, nonlinear space. Our model features joint price–locational decisions in both a joint-profit maximization and a wholly rivalrous context. Our models are capable of altering or eliminating the tacit collusion implied by joint-profit maximization, although in this paper we have stepped outside the model to do so. In all of this analysis we have employed nonlinear and combinatorial programming approaches whose results are nongeneralizable in other than simulative terms. We have argued for a sustained effort in the research of the present and similar interdependence problems in economics to determine the promise of such methods as sources of insight into reality. Finally, we have developed a measure of compactness for convex hulls and a measure of social cost of spatial oligopoly, and have devoted some effort to analyzing the implications of the latter.

Notes

[1] The relation of a to elasticity in Smithies's measure s was pointed out by Gannon [4].
[2] Hartwick [6] has also criticized this aspect of Gannon's analysis.
[3] SPATOL is available in two versions, one of which maximizes joint profits with the possibility of eliminating sources that have low profit margins, and the other of which forces all sources into the problem. SUMTOL is available in both a joint profit and consumer welfare-maximizing form. All are in FORTRAN IV and are available at the cost of mailing.

References

[1] Chamberlin, E. H., *The Theory of Monopolistic Competition*, 6th edn, Harvard University Press, Cambridge, MA, 1948, appendix C.
[2] Devletoglou, N. E., "A Dissenting View of Duopoly and Spatial Competition", *Economica*, 32 (1965), 140–60.
[3] Fiacco, A. V. and G. P. McCormick, *Nonlinear Programming: Sequential Unconstrained Minimization Technique*, John Wiley & Sons, New York, 1968.
[4] Gannon, Colin A., "Consumer Demand, Conjectural Interdependence, and Location Equilibria in Simple Spatial Duopoly", *Regional Science Association Papers*, 28 (1972), 83–107.
[5] ——, "Central Concentration in Simple Spatial Duopoly: Some Behavioral and Functional Conditions", *Journal of Regional Science*, 13 (1973), 357–75.

[6] Hartwick, John M., "Comments on Colin A. Gannon's Paper", *Regional Science Association Papers*, 28 (1972), 109-10.

[7] Hotelling, Harold, "Stability in Competition", *Economic Journal*, 39 (1929), 41-57.

[8] Kuenne, Robert E., "Interproduct Distances in a Quality-space: Inexact Measurement in Differentiated Oligopoly Analysis", *Applied Economics*, 6 (1974), 255-73. [Reprinted as chapter 12 in this volume.]

[9] ——, "Toward a Usable General Theory of Oligopoly", *De Economist*, 122 (1974), 471-502. [Reprinted as chapter 1 in this volume.]

[10] ——, "Towards an Operational General Equilibrium Theory with Oligopoly: Some Experimental Results and Conjectures", *Kyklos*, 27 (1974), 792-820. [Reprinted as chapter 2 in this volume.]

[11] ——, "General Oligopolistic Equilibrium: a Crippled-optimization Approach", in *Pioneering Economics: Essays in Honor of Giovanni Demaria*, Cedam, Padua, 1978, 537-77. [Reprinted as chapter 3 in this volume].

[12] —— and Richard M. Soland, "Exact and Approximate Solutions to the Multisource Weber Problem", *Mathematical Programming*, 3 (1972), 193-209.

[13] Lerner, A. P. and H. W. Singer, "Some Notes on Duopoly and Spatial Competition", *Journal of Political Economy*, 45 (1937), 145-60.

[14] Smithies, Arthur, "Optimal Location in Spatial Competition", *Journal of Political Economy*, 49 (1941), 423-39.

16

The Dynamics of Oligopolistic Location: Present Status and Future Research Directions

1 Introduction

The purpose of this paper is a modest one. It is to review the rather small body of literature on spatial oligopoly, judge the degree of progress it has made in yielding insights into spatially conditioned decision-making in relevant economic contexts, and suggest some lines of departure for research in the light of its present revealed deficiencies.

By "dynamic" I simply mean strategic reaction through time on the part of knowledgeable rivals that may or may not converge to a steady solution. Spatially conditioned decisions are locations and prices. Relevant contributing characteristics of the environment are number of firms, configurations of the space involved, demand function characteristics and the spatial density of demand, and firms' conjectures about their rivals' reactions.

After an extremely rich research history, which has seen pioneering applications of the calculus of variations, simulation, and catastrophe theory, among other innovations in economics, where does the theory of spatial oligopoly stand today? Why has so little been done in the past ten years? Have the various strands of investigation converged to common conclusions about the desirable path of future research? What are the paths indicated? It is these questions I should like to address in this paper, with an emphasis upon the bearing of past research upon the future.

Originally published as chapter 2 in Å. E. Andersson, D. F. Batten, B. Johansson and P. Nijkamp (eds), *Advances in Spatial Theory and Dynamics*, North-Holland, Amsterdam, 1989, and reproduced with permission. The paper was given at a conference on dynamic models in spatial economics sponsored by the International Institute for Applied Systems Analysis, Laxenburg, Austria, in September 1984.

2 The Present Status of Spatial Oligopoly Analysis

In existing spatial oligopoly analysis interest focuses upon two questions: (1) the locational structure of the steady state equilibria, if they exist, and (2) the convergence or nonconvergence of the reactive process to such steady state. Most of the early work centers upon the first question, but as the inherent complexity of the real oligopoly market structure intruded into later analysis, simulation techniques had to be used. In such modelling the two problems merge. If, in a reaction sequence, when each firm is given the opportunity to adjust while its rivals remain quiescent, the solution cycles without converging, doubt is cast on the existence of a steady state that closed analysis cannot isolate. If it does converge consistently to one or a few configurations from widely different starting points, some support is given to the hypothesis that they are equilibria.

Following the lead of Gannon [3, 4], although generalizing his concept, I may define one body of research that originated in Hotelling's classic article [5] as "simple spatial oligopoly." Its notable features are simplicity of demand structure and of conjectures of rival responses to initiating moves. This set of models was treated definitively in Eaton and Lipsey [2] for the following assumptions:

1 The spatial configuration is linear, circular, or a disc, with consumers distributed uniformly or as a density function that is integrable.
2 Each consumer purchases one unit of good from the firm with lowest delivered price, so that sales are proportionate to consumers in the firms' market areas.
3 All firms charge the same f.o.b. prices, with transport costs that increase with distance, and with identical, fixed marginal profit.
4 No more than one firm can occupy a location and relocation costs are zero.
5 Firms locate to maximize profits subject to two alternative conjectures:
   (i) Cournot, or that rivals will not respond to initiating actions;
   (ii) game theoretic, or that rivals will respond in manners that maximize the loss of the initiating firm's market.
6 Firms relocate in a dynamic quiescent sequence with the steady state identified with a Nash equilibrium.

The results of the Eaton–Lipsey analysis are too complex to be related in complete detail in this short paper, but the broad outlines are relevant for my later conclusions. For linear or circular market spaces, under Cournot expectations, the necessary and sufficient conditions for a steady state solution may be stated quite simply. Each firm will have a long side and a short side to its market segment. Then the conditions are as follows:

Condition 1: No firm's total sales are less than some firm's longside sales.

Condition 2: Peripheral firms are always paired when they occur, so their short sides are (nearly) zero in size.

Condition 3: For every unpaired firm the number of customers at its left- and right-hand boundaries are equal.

Condition 4: For every paired firm the number of customers at the short-side boundary is no less than the number at the long-side boundary.

Hotelling left the impression that spatial oligopoly competition had a tendency to cluster firms in space, or, more generally, to minimum differentiation in any dimension with spatial analog (political programs, product brands, etc.), a hypothesis that Chamberlin [1] sensed would not be general. Eaton and Lipsey reveal that Hotelling's pairing of firms at the center of the linear market does occur for $n = 2$ under Cournot expectations. But for $n = 3$ no equilibrium exists: Chamberlin, in asserting a contrary position, failed to grasp the significance of condition 2. For $n = 4$ pairing occurs at the first and third quartiles, and for $n = 5$ a steady state exists with pairs at locations $1/6$ and $5/6$ and an unpaired firm at the center. But, for $n > 5$ an infinite number of steady state exists under simple oligopoly. If, following the suggestion of Chamberlin, we bend the line into a circle, for $n = 2$ all configurations are equilibria and for $n > 2$ an infinite number of solutions exists. By no means, therefore, is there a general tendency toward the pairing of rivals or of minimum differentiation.

As the models are increased in complexity, the indeterminacy becomes more general. In 2-space, when the market area is confined to a disc with uniform population distribution and Cournot conjectures, the solutions, if they exist, could not be obtained for $n \geqslant 3$, and simulation was necessary. Löschian hexagons, squares, and rectangles were not sustainable as steady state market area patterns. For $3 \leqslant n \leqslant 17$ the dynamic adjustment process failed to converge, and Eaton and Lipsey conjecture that no Nash equilibrium exists for $n > 2$ in simple spatial oligopoly. Shaked [11] has provided a nonexistence proof for $n = 3$.

The first step to what I shall call "complex spatial oligopoly" models was taken by Lerner and Singer [10] and, more importantly, by Smithies [12], with the introduction of more complicated demand assumptions and the consequent introduction of price as an endogenous variable simultaneously determined with location.

Smithies's research broadened and deepened the Hotelling analysis by introducing linear demand functions, joint determination of prices and locations, and more complicated patterns of price and location conjectures, although these latter remained symmetrical for both rivals. He derives a measure of the strength of the forces pulling duopolists toward the poles of a linear market by combining the transport rate, the size of market, and a surrogate for demand elasticity into a single parameter s. He related location to values of this measure under three different conjecture assumptions. The relation of price to s was too complex to be subject to closed analysis, although he found a general tendency for firms to absorb freight costs as they anticipated greater competitive reactions from rivals.

Gannon [3, 4] extended Smithies's work by introducing nonlinear demand functions and explicit marginal expectations of rivals' responses. In general, like Smithies, the burden of Gannon's work is that Hotelling's determinateness disappears with the introduction of these complications and general propositions in the absence of specified functions and parameters are not possible. Once more, in a framework of essential simplicity, the resources provided by general deductive frameworks are insufficient to yield insights.

Another predictable line of attack for spatial oligopolistic analysis in both one-space and two-space has been more extensive applications of game theory than the minimax conjectural variation assumption of Eaton and Lipsey permits. Stevens [13] modified the Hotelling problem by assuming a finite number of points on the line at which location could occur, and, to make the game zero-sum, assumed that the payoff function to firms was the difference in their sales at alternative locations. Straightforward two-person, zero-sum attack upon the spatial duopoly problem concludes that a minimax solution with pairing at the center is consistent with Hotelling's results. The work was an interesting introduction of game-theoretic conjectures into an essentially Hotelling framework.

More extensive applications of game theory were made by Isard and Smith [6, 7]. In a Hotelling economy with linear demand curves, they use standard isoprofit contour analysis to derive a Cournot solution to the duopoly problem with each firm located one-third of the distance from the end-points of the linear market. Of course, both firms can benefit from a collusive agreement, and the authors consider various plausible dynamic procedures to attain such agreement. They also analyze the possibility of side payments, beginning at the joint-profit maximization solution (at one of the quartiles) and negotiating over the division of the spoils. The Weber agglomeration economies problem is melded with the Hotelling case by introducing the former into the analysis. Most interestingly, the Weber agglomeration case is analyzed on its own, with various cooperative dynamic movement schemes discussed that iteratively reduce the space within which agglomeration can occur. The later article introduces the possibility of coalition formation into this agglomeration analysis.

As in all realistic oligopoly analysis, the strength of game theory ironically inheres in its disappointing results, for it succeeds in highlighting the richness of realistic processes through the methodology's general indeterminateness. It serves to reinforce the conclusions of our earlier discussions: spatial oligopoly presents dynamic adjustment potentialities that in the general case are essentially indeterminate in outcome. Hence, such problems must be accepted as *sui generis*, work is most profitably confined to specific cases via simulation, and the theoretical ambitions of the analyst should be constrained to the limited applicability of the theorems and conjectures that emerge from such analysis.

Such conclusions are not happy ones for the economic theorist. We are too much fascinated by the universal theorems of the physical scientist. The role of pure theory in illuminating applied research is a different one in the simpler universe of the physicist. When, in our own field, it points in the direction of simulation by indicating the essentially noncorrectible oversimplicity of our methods, we simply walk away. When, so to speak, we find our theory of hydrodynamics cannot explain the flow of air around an aircraft, we do not stoop to build wind tunnels. We simply do without aircraft as not worth the condescension from respectable abstraction necessary to achieve them.

3 Suggested Research Directions

A rather compelling theme emerges from this record of research progress, in my opinion. It is that pure theory has reached the limits of its ability to illuminate spatial oligopoly using the traditional frameworks available to the oligopoly analyst. Newer methodologies must build upon the foundation of the old, but wisely. These methods must include specific assumptions about demand functions and costs, sacrificing generality of results for evaluable solutions. They must be operational, with parameters capable of estimation. And they should be flexible – more so than the rigid models of traditional oligopoly theory – with the capability of treating a broad spectrum of industry mixtures of competition and cooperation and of tailoring to comply with specific industry structures and folkways. And, lastly, perhaps more susceptible of indictment as pure personal preference, I should like to see the insights obtained when spatial oligopoly is placed within the matrix of stochastic processes, or at least when random behavior is incorporated into spatial demand.

I have some ideas about each of the three directions – simulative theorizing, cooperative rivalry, and stochastic process – but they are only investigatory beginnings or contemplations. I discuss each briefly below.

3.1 Simulative Theorizing

In a published article [8] I experimented with a simulation using n firms serving m discrete market points in space, where the firms can locate anywhere within the convex hull of the market points. Various metrics were also used to permit economic distances to approach more closely those resulting from concave transport cost functions over distance. Costs are constant for each firm but may differ among firms, linear demand functions are assumed at sinks in terms of delivered prices, which in turn are f.o.b. prices at sources plus transport costs proportionate to distance.

The resulting model is a very complicated nonlinear programming model with no constraints other than definitional identities and nonnegativity constraints. The objective function – arbitrarily chosen as the maximization of joint profit – is not jointly convex in the endogenous variables and hence yields only local optima. Moreover, it is very difficult to solve, owing entirely to the presence of the spatial dimension. It was solved by iterative use of two algorithms. The first assumes prices fixed and employs a multisource Weber point branch-and-bound algorithm to derive tentative source locations. The second assumes those locations to be fixed and determines optimal prices in a straightforward nonlinear programming application. Each of the two algorithms will converge to optimal solutions given the fixity of price or source location, since branch-and-bound is an exhaustive search technique and the programming problem is convex in prices. The iterative processes are stopped when convergence criteria are met.

At least, the branch-and-bound algorithm converges for small to medium-size numbers of sources and sinks, and obtains very good answers for larger numbers. The price model was solved by the Sequential Unconstrained Minimization Technique (SUMT), a penalty function algorithm which is readily adapted to sequential quiescent sequences. Our solutions converged well for 4 to 6 firms and 8 to 10 sinks, approaching the same solutions for widely varying initial assumptions.

The model was used to exploit Smithies's insight into the importance of transport rate, size of market, and demand elasticity in spatial oligopoly, or the s measure discussed in section 2. Also the model was used to measure changes in locational patterns and prices when joint-profit maximization is compared with purely competitive pricing and Cournot-myopic expectations of rivals' responses.

One difficult problem occurs in extending this framework to permit multi-objective decision-making in a spatial context by including constraints *in the spatial dimension*. Those objectives that impact only prices directly are easily handled, but combinatorial programming algorithms like branch-and-bound find it difficult to deal with constraints. Hence, constraints on location, which exist in the realistic location decisions of firms, are difficult to include. Research into means of incorporating them into branch-and-bound algorithms, or into developing alternative heuristic algorithms as substitutes, would be extremely valuable.

In a deeper sense, we also need a better framework for efficient parameter manipulation of such simulations to derive insights of maximum generalizability. Are there general methods for quickly discerning the sensitive parameters in such models? Can the notion of Smithies's artificial s parameter that economically combines the influences of several parameters be generalized? Are there general methods for placing upper and lower bounds on parameters? Must each sensitivity analysis be an *ad hoc* procedure without general principles of structure, formulation, or interpretation, or can general frameworks be found to generalize such analysis?

We truly require an "econometrics of simulation" that specifies general guidelines for structuring and codifying models and post-optimality analysis, if simulative theorizing is to become a tool of theoretical research.

3.2 Rivalrous Consonance

In recognition of the varying mixtures of rivalry and cooperation that characterize market structures, ranging from joint-profit maximization through Cournot disregard of rivals' profits into active warfare, the simulative joint-profit maximization objective can be decentralized to permit each firm to maximize its own profit plus the weighted sum of rivals' profits. The weights reflect the firm's conception of the industry power structure in the broadest sense from its own viewpoint. Other goals can be incorporated as constraints if the algorithmic difficulties discussed above were solved.

I have advocated this framework in nonspatial oligopolistic studies for a variety of reasons, ranging from its ability to model mature oligopolistic industry behavior more realistically to the possibility of developing a theory of general oligopolistic equilibrium [see chapter 5 in this volume]. It would be most interesting to see what its application in the spatial dimension would imply. How is tacit cooperation or bounded competition reflected in location patterns? In what manners do they change as rivalry increases? What is the locational equivalent of active price war, set off when firms value rivals profits at negative values? At the present time I am most interested in making this extension of the rivalrous consonance framework, with and without the multi-objective complication. For example, as a start, it would be interesting to model the Eaton–Lipsey cases on the disc for n between 3 and 17. One could approximate the assumption of a uniform continuous distribution of demand by increasingly dense evenly distributed discrete demand points, and use the multisource Weber point and optimal pricing algorithms in tandem for solutions. This might confirm or refute the conjecture of nonequilibrium.

3.3 Stochastic Process Theory

Stochastic process theory has been extensively used in spatial economics only in the adoption of diffusion theory to explain the spread and patterning of innovations and similar phenomena over space. My surmise is that it could be usefully employed in explaining the nature of certain types of contingency demand over space, the evolution of market areas, the sequence of rival entries, and the resulting spatial patterning of locations and prices. No doubt, as is true of stochastic processes with any degree of complexity, simulation would have to be resorted to once more. However, the discernment of steady state patterns and their changes under different parametric regimes could be quite rewarding.

My only excursion into such areas has been an investigation of an elementary Poisson demand process in space and its implications for the market area of a single firm [9]. If the ocurrence of demands in a time period over space were Poisson (which I assumed) and the amount of demand with such an occurrence followed a geometric distribution (which I did not assume), then demand over space is a "stuttering Poisson" process with a negative binomial probability function. It is well known that for a sufficiently large number of occurrences the normal distribution approximates this function, and it would be relatively simple to study the nature of oligopolistic decision-making under such regimes, when joint-profit maximization, Cournot conjectures, or, more broadly, rivalrous consonance is assumed.

4 Conclusion

Spatial oligopoly theory developed along several paths from Hotelling's original formulation of a linear economy with perfectly inelastic demand. These included differently shaped spaces, with and without interiors, elastic demand functions, game theoretical rivalry, the endogenization of prices, and non-Cournot conjectural variation. Some of the efforts were definitive, notably that of Eaton and Lipsey's extension and generalization of the Hotelling problem. All have explicitly or implicitly reached the conclusion that general deductive analysis with nonspecified models could go no further profitably.

The field of spatial oligopoly analysis, as a consequence, has been dormant for the past decade or so. There is a clear need to stimulate analysis in this most relevant market structure as it relates to space. The need to investigate simulative alternatives with specified parameters and functions seems clear. Among other advantages it will permit the investigation of differentiated oligopoly, blends of rivalry and cooperation, multi-objective decision making and larger numbers of rivals. Most importantly, it offers the only presently perceived route out of the impasse that current methods have engendered.

References

[1] Chamberlin, E. H., *The Theory of Monopolistic Competition*, 6th edn, Harvard University Press, Cambridge, MA, 1948, appendix C.

[2] Eaton, B. C. and R. G. Lipsey, "The Principle of Minimum Differentiation Reconsidered: Some New Developments in the Theory of Spatial Competition", *Review of Economic Studies*, 45 (1975), 27–49.

[3] Gannon, C. A., "Consumer Demand, Conjectural Interdependence, and Location Equilibria in Simple Spatial Duopoly", *Regional Science Association Papers*, 28 (1972), 83–107.

[4] ——, "Central Concentration in Simple Spatial Duopoly: Some Behavioral and Functional Conditions", *Journal of Regional Science*, 13 (1973), 357–75.

[5] Hotelling, H., "Stability in Competition", *Economic Journal*, 39 (1929), 41–57.

[6] Isard, W. and T. E. Smith, "Location Games: with Applications to Classic Location Problems", *Papers of the Regional Science Association*, 19 (1968), 45–80.

[7] ——, "Coalition Location Games: Paper 3", *Papers of the Regional Science Association*, 20 (1969), 95–107.

[8] Kuenne, R. E., "Spatial Oligopoly: Price–Location Interdependence and Social Cost in a Discrete Market Space", *Regional Science and Urban Economics*, 7 (1977), 339–58. [Reprinted as chapter 15 in this volume.]

[9] ——, "Economic Decision Making in a Poisson Demand Space", in Å. E. Andersson, W. Isard, and T. Puu (eds), *Regional and Industrial Development Theories, Models and Empirical Evidence*, North-Holland, Amsterdam, 1984, 331–46.

[10] Lerner, A. P. and H. W. Singer, "Some Notes on Duopoly and Spatial Competition", *Journal of Political Economy*, 45 (1937), 145–60.

[11] Shaked, A., "Non-existence of Equilibria for the Two-dimensional Three-firm Location Problem", *Review of Economic Studies*, 45 (1975), 51–5.

[12] Smithies, A., "Optimal Location in Spatial Competition", *Journal of Political Economy*, 49 (1941), 423–39.

[13] Stevens, B. H., "An Application of Game Theory to a Problem in Location Strategy", *Papers of the Regional Science Association*, 7 (1961), 143–57.

17

Modelling Price and Nonprice Competition in Spatial Oligopoly

1 Introduction

Important movements in the reshaping of firm and industry structure and function are afoot in developed economies. These changes seem clearly destined to have important implications for the microeconomist in at least three dimensions:

1 They will increase the frequency and intensity of oligopolistic competition within such economic systems.
2 The notion of "marketing" will come to embrace a much wider spectrum of firm–customer intercommunications and relationships than are currently connoted by that term, with greater stress upon continuing personal communication than presently prevailing.
3 The role of space as a factor in impeding economic interaction among agents and thereby shaping regional and national spatial structure will evolve from one whose primary influence is felt in restricting goods flow to one of imposition of limitations on information transmission and on other forms of personal and impersonal interaction.

Each of these implications has a bearing upon the motivation and aims of this chapter. The expectation that oligopolistic market structure will become even more prevalent and give rise to more intense rivalry arises from the relocation of lower technology, metal-bashing, production line industries to less developed nations. The small or medium-sized firm is emerging as the archetype of the developed economy's producer. Instead of requiring large agglomerations of highly specialized capital equipment dedicated to long runs of standardized products, the newer firm is oriented to smaller niche markets with specialized and technologically challenging needs.

An unpublished paper delivered at the International Symposium on Economic Modelling, University of Urbino, Urbino, Italy, July 23–25, 1990.

The production needs of such firms put a premium on facilities and skills that are capable of producing small lots of goods that are tailored to customers' individualized needs. Such products will have to be produced quickly and with minimum retooling times and costs, frequently with the help of equally specialized suppliers of components. In both services and industrial production the typifying industry should consist of rather small numbers of small to medium-sized firms in active competition for limited numbers of customers with high technological standards of quality. Competition for their trade will be based upon price, quality, delivery schedule and dependability, servicing, and continuing provision of information and recommendations for product or process design.

The nature of that competition will alter somewhat, therefore, to place more emphasis upon nonprice competition as a supplement to and, to some extent, a substitute for price rivalry. The marketing function, defined broadly as the provision of information to potential customers in a wide variety of personal and impersonal intercommunications, will be a centerpiece of nonprice competition. Although advertising in the usual meaning of the term will play an important role, other forms of marketing stressing the maintenance of close relations with customers and potential customers through personal consultations and joint design efforts, as well as continuous flows of tailored information, become more significant in the new economy. I shall use the term "advertising" in this chapter to mean marketing effort in this more inclusive meaning of the term.

The altered structure of production will place a great premium upon the closeness of contacts with both customers and suppliers and the need for cheap and dependable flows of information. The telecommunications advances of the past 20 or 30 years permit the various functions of the firm to be split apart, with production, marketing, finance, research and development, and so forth, to be performed at locations that are optimal for the performance of their functions. "Nearness" to customers, defined more broadly than mere spatial proximity but including it, will become more important in the competitive process. Transport costs on components and final product will decline somewhat in importance in the face of the rising costs of maintaining this communications or information proximity.

One of the most challenging features of researching the implications of such movements as outlined above is that they involve three of the most difficult areas of microeconomic theory: oligopoly theory, the theory of nonprice competition, and spatial theory. The presence of all three problems in the task we set ourselves is rather daunting, and any attempt to scale the glass mountain must be expected to result in slow progress and a good deal of slippage.

Nonetheless, this chapter takes a first step in seeking insights into the nature of this highly rivalrous form of competition in which price and nonprice components are employed both to enhance one's own sales and to reduce those of one's competitors. Space is assumed to impede sales in two ways: by inflicting transportation costs in an f.o.b pricing regime and by reducing the effectiveness of marketing effort. The first is effected through the transportation rate r and the second through parameters α_{ij} to inflict exponential decay. As distance increases the frequency and intensity of personal contacts between producer and consumer must be expected to decline, the number of impersonal contacts between customers and advertising messages to lessen, and the indirect effects of marketing endeavor that spread by word-of-mouth in a diffusion process to weaken.

2 Model 1: Aggregated Demand Effects of Marketing

Model 1 is a variant of a model which I have published and used in an earlier analysis [3]. In section 2 of this chapter I would like to undertake some of the tasks that were suggested for future work at the end of that earlier article.

Suppose firms 1 and 2 compete duopolistically without collusion for sales along a linear market of length L. Firm 1 is located at point $s = 0$ and firm 2 at $s = L$, and both firms have no option to move from these end-point sites. They sell a differentiated product to consumers with uniform density along the line, and compete through price and marketing ("advertising") expenditures to maximise their own individual profits without taking their rival's welfare into account.[1] As noted in section 1, demand for its product is greatest at a firm's site and diminishes with distance because of (1) a rise in the f.o.b. price of the product due to transport costs, which are proportionate to the transport rate, r, and distance, and (2) a decay factor, α_{ij}, which reduces the effects on demand of its marketing effort in an exponential fashion.

Specifically, then, each firm in each iteration assumes the mill price of its rival, P_j, and its marketing expenditure, A_j, constant and maximizes its profit, π_i. For example, for firm 1:

$$\underset{P_1, A_1}{\text{Max}} \; \pi_1 = X_1 (P_1 - C_1) - A_1 \qquad (17.1)$$

subject to the definition of its demand, X_1. To obtain that, we define the demand function at any point $s \in L$ as follows:

$$X_1(s)\mathrm{d}s = a_1 \mathrm{d}s - b_{11}(P_1 + rs)\mathrm{d}s + b_{12}(P_2 + r(L-s))\mathrm{d}s$$
$$+ K_{11} A_1^{\beta_{11}} e^{-\alpha_{11} s} \mathrm{d}s - K_{12} A_2^{\beta_{12}} e^{-\alpha_{12}(L-s)} \mathrm{d}s \qquad (17.2)$$

where:

b_{11} = the own-price response factor to delivered price

b_{12} = the other-price response factor to rival 2's f.o.b. price

$K_{11}A_1^{\beta_{11}}$ = the sales generated by marketing expenditure A_1 at firm 1's site, s, with β_{11} the elasticity of sales with respect to marketing costs

$e^{-\alpha_{11}s}$ = the spatial decay factor for net sales to firm 1's marketing programs at s

$K_{12}A_2^{\beta_{12}}$ = sales lost at s to firm 2's advertising efforts, or the "attritional effect" suffered by firm 1

$e^{-\alpha_{12}(L - s)}$ = the decay factor for the attritional effect of firm 2's marketing program

c_1 = the constant marginal and average cost of firm 1's product.

Firm 1's demand function is obtained by integrating over the line of length L:

$$X_1 = \int_0^L X_1 ds = a_1 - b_{11}(P_1 L + 0.5rL^2) + b_{12}(P_2 + 0.5rL^2)$$

$$+ K_{11}A_1^{\beta_{11}}\alpha_{11}^{-1}(1 - e^{-\alpha_{11}L}) - K_{12}A_2^{\beta_{12}}\alpha_{12}^{-1}(1 - e^{-\alpha_{21}L}). \quad (17.3)$$

First-order necessary conditions for a constrained maximum are then:

1. $\dfrac{\delta \pi_1}{\delta P_1} = X_1 + (P_1 - C_1)(-b_{11}L) = 0$

2. $\dfrac{\delta \pi_1}{\delta A_1} = (P_1 - C_1)\beta_{11}K_{11}A_1^{\beta_{11}-1}\alpha_{11}^{-1}(1 - e^{-\delta_{11}L}) - 1 = 0.$

$$(17.4)$$

In [3] I have performed a detailed analysis of the conditions under which the Hessian matrix of the problem will be negative definite, and hence when a global maximum is guaranteed.[2]

When the model is solved iteratively for firms 1 and 2, convergence to the optimal strategies $[P_i^0, A_i^0]$ occurs rapidly and from the solutions it is possible to derive the firms' reaction functions:

1. $2b_{11}P_1 L - V_{12}(\beta_{22}V_{12}(P_1 - c_1))^{\beta_{11}/(1 - \beta_{11})}$

$= b_{12}P_2 L - V_{13}(\beta_{22}V_{22}(P_2 - c_2))^{\beta_{12}/(1 - \beta_{22})} + W_{11}$

2. $2b_{22}P_2 L - V_{22}(\beta_{22}V_{22}(P_2 - c_2))^{\beta_{22}/(1 - \beta_{22})}$

$= b_{21}P_1 L - V_{23}(\beta_{11}V_{12}(P_1 - c_1))^{\beta_{21}/(1 - \beta_{11})} + W_{21}. \quad (17.5)$

where

$V_{11} = a_1 L - 0.5rL(b_{11} - b_{12})L$ $\qquad V_{12} = K_{11}\alpha_{11}^{-1}(1 - e^{-\alpha_{11}L})$

$V_{21} = a_2 L - 0.5rL(b_{22} - b_{21})L$ $\qquad V_{22} = K_{22}\alpha_{22}^{-1}(1 - e^{-\alpha_{22}L})$

$$W_{11} = V_{11} + b_{11}c_1 L \qquad\qquad V_{13} = K_{12}\alpha_{12}^{-1}\left(1 - e^{-\alpha_{12}L}\right)$$

$$W_{21} = V_{21} + b_{22}c_2 L \qquad\qquad V_{23} = K_{21}\alpha_{21}^{-1}\left(1 - e^{-\alpha_{21}L}\right).$$

Simulation is necessary to derive insights into the interdependent variation inherent in the model. A simple diagonalization algorithm was used to solve for the optimal strategies and a modified Taylor-series based algorithm to obtain the reaction functions.

2.1 Case 1: The Symmetric Case

In my previous employment of the model I analyzed three cases: a classic case where transportation costs dominated marketing effectiveness in restricting sales; a case where marketing effectiveness was not much impeded by transportation costs; and a case where each firm captured in its own sales a fraction of the attrition effect it wrought on its rival. Within each case four variants were analyzed: both firms had marketing programs; one firm had a marketing program and the other did not; and neither firm had a marketing program. In all cases and variants, the parameters were chosen so that firm 1 was disadvantaged with respect to its demand conditions but had a slight advantage in marketing effectiveness and a smaller spatial decay function.

One of the most interesting results of the simulations was that for a given case firms tended to have a constant ratio of advertising budgets to revenues over all variants. The source of this constancy still eludes detection.[3]

More fundamentally, the results suggested that marketing budgets should rise to become a significant portion of firms' costs in the new economy – to the extent the model captures that regime. Optimization required a great deal of tradeoff between prices and advertising, with firms lowering price to counter rivals' higher advertising budgets and raising price to take advantage of rivals' less effective marketing. These implications clash with the relative stability of prices in present-day oligopoly, and may augur more flexibility in the future. And price tended to decrease or at least rise more slowly as the size of market L grew, since market effectiveness decayed and its "inelasticizing" effect weakened.

In case 1 an attempt is made, via simulation, to study the interactive effects of duopolistic competition between two rivals with exactly the same parameters. Hence, I am dealing with competitors of equal strength whose advertising to a large extent tends to cancel out and be wasteful from the viewpoint of their joint welfare. I am interested in the behavior of prices and profits under such conditions as well as isolation of the primary driving parameters.

To supplement the previous analysis, therefore, I have solved the symmetrical case for a large number of different parameter sets, varying one parameter at a time, in a sensitivity analysis. A continuing interest of mine is in encouraging the development of an "econometrics of simulation," or a body of techniques that are designed to derive insights from a set of simulation results in an efficient manner using statistical techniques. In furtherance of this aim as well as to isolate those insights from the present model, I have applied regression analysis to the simulation "observations" in an attempt to extract generalizations from the data.

Below I list the parameter set which constituted the base case for the symmetrical problem:

$$
\begin{aligned}
L &= 10 & r &= 2 \\
a_1 &= a_2 = 2{,}000 \\
b_{11} &= b_{22} = 10 & b_{12} &= b_{21} = 6 \\
\alpha_{11} &= \alpha_{22} = 0.1 & \alpha_{12} &= \alpha_{21} = 0.2 \\
\beta_{11} &= \beta_{22} = 0.4 & \beta_{12} &= \beta_{21} = 0.2 \\
K_{11} &= K_{22} = 4 & K_{12} &= K_{21} = 10 \\
c_1 &= c_2 = 25
\end{aligned}
$$

Two solutions are of interest as providing important baselines for the analysis: they are the base case solution and the solution when marketing programs are not possible:

Solution	$P_1 = P_2$	$A_1 = A_2$	$X_1 = X_2$	$\pi_1 = \pi_2$
Base case	$73.01	$29,994	9,601	$430,929
Zero marketing	69.43	0	8,887	390,882

If both firms refrained from advertising their individual profits would decrease when compared with the base case solution. Price would be lower to the consumer although sales of each firm would decline. As we shall see, however, were one firm to refrain from advertising and the other employ a marketing campaign the advertiser would enjoy higher profits and the non-advertiser lower when compared with the base case solution. Hence, in the symmetrical case it is in the individual interests of both rivals to advertise. Note that in the base case the marketing budget is about 4.3 percent of firms' revenues, which is a realistic value for many firms which base their marketing budget on a fixed percentage of receipts.

To obtain insights into firms' behavior in the symmetrical case I generated 56 different "observations" by varying each of the parameters singly and identically for both firms to maintain symmetry. I then regressed price, advertising outlay, quantity, and profits against all of the parameters to isolate the fundamental relationships of each of the parameters. Although the regression model is linear and many of the relationships are nonlinear, the parameter values employed were kept within limits where the linear approximation was not overly distorting. Therefore, the quantitative values of the regression coefficients are in most instances representative of the impacts registered in the solutions.

2.1.1 The Marketing Budgets

The regression equation derived for advertising budgets is the following:

$$A_i = -28{,}872 + 153L - 2{,}300T + 35a_i - 9{,}975b_{ii} + 3{,}662b_{ij}$$
$$-94{,}716\alpha_{ii} - 38{,}083\alpha_{ij} - 1{,}281\beta_{ii} - 39{,}588\beta_{ij} + 48{,}182K_{ii}$$
$$- 133K_{ij} - 397c_i \quad (\text{adjusted } R^2 = 0.824)$$

A visual impression of the fit may be found in figure 17.1, which contains the absolute values with base case at observation 1, and in figure 17.2, which has the values normalized as percentages of the base case value. In the latter figure, observation 15 on figure 17.1 was eliminated because it resulted from a b_{ii} value judged to be unrealistically low.

All of the signs of the regression coefficients are in the proper direction. The numerical value of the regression coefficient for L is much too small, however, with a value of about 3,000 closer to the observation values. The magnitudes of the other coefficients are reasonable.

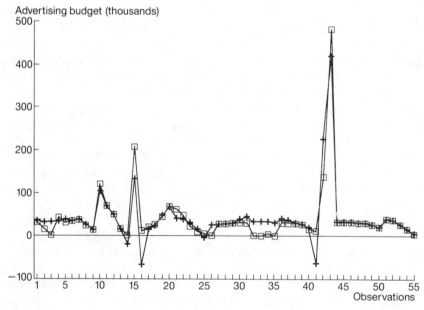

Figure 17.1   Advertising regression, symmetrical case.
□, actual advertising; +, fitted advertising.

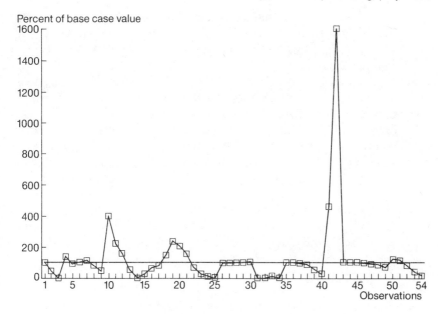

Figure 17.2   Normalized advertising values.
□, actual advertising; ————, base case norm.

Taking into account the size of the units in which the parameters are calibrated, the strength of other-price coefficient influence on own-firm advertising was unexpected. Each unit rise in the other-price sensitivity coefficient (b_{ij}) induces about \$3,662 in additional advertising by the benefiting firm, which, in a sample of observations in which the mean of the marketing budgets was \$40,155, is a substantial amount. The motivation is clear from the Dorfman–Steiner theorem:[4] a rise in b_{ij} shifts firm i's demand curve to the right, reducing its elasticity. Firm i then raises price but the own-price elasticity of demand at the new price is less than at the old. The marginal revenue of own advertising must therefore fall to the lower value of the elasticity, which requires increased advertising. In the given sample, own-price elasticity (= marginal revenue of advertising) fell by about 0.025 points for each unit rise in b_{ij}. Hence, the advertising budget rose about \$1,472 for each fall of 0.01 in own-price elasticity. Of course, I have neglected the chain of interaction that begins with firm j's reaction to firm i's initiating moves, the results of which are included in the regression coefficients.

The other-advertising effectiveness coefficient (β_{ij}) also demonstrates surprising strength: each 0.1 rise in its value induces the suffering firm to reduce its own advertising budget by about \$3,959. A rise in β_{ij} shifts firm i's demand function leftwards, increasing its elasticity, leading firm i to reduce price and raise the optimal elasticity. This leads the firm to reduce its marketing budget to raise its marginal revenue productivity, which sets off a complicated sequence of reactions between the firms before the new equilibrium is achieved.

Figure 17.1 and 17.2 reveal the goodness of fit of the regression equation and show the displacements that resulted in large impacts on the advertising budget. Observations 10–13 incorporate successive reductions in a_1 from 4,000 to 500, and demonstrate an expected sensitivity to the intercept of the demand function. The next departure from the typical displacement level for advertising occurs with observation 15, which depicts the result of a fall in b_{ii} from 20 to 10. As noted above, this observation was eliminated from figure 17.2. Observations 17–20 depict the results of the rise in b_{ij} from 1 to 15, and 21 the rise in α_{ii} from 0.02 to 0.5. Finally, the huge impacts of observations 42 and 43 (41 and 42 on figure 17.2) are the results of jumps in K_{ii} from 2 to 8 and 12 respectively.

2.1.2 Prices

The regression equation for prices is reproduced below and in figure 17.3:

$$P_i = 126.79 - 0.50L - 2.41T + 0.03a_1 - 6.54b_1 + 3.08b_2 -$$
$$16.61\alpha_{ii} + 7.55\alpha_{ij} + 0.18\beta_{ii} - 41.18\beta_{ij} + 3.9K_{ii} - 0.13K_{ij} +$$
$$0.53c_i \ (\text{adjusted } R^2 = 0.796)$$

The solution values are depicted graphically in figures 17.3 and 17.4 is absolute and normalized forms. Observation 15 in figure 17.3 is eliminated in figure 17.4. All of the coefficients are correctly signed.

As a_i decreases from 4,000 to 500 in observations 10–14 the demand function becomes more elastic, leading the firm to initiate price reductions. Indeed, it is one of the more important price movers, as the figures show, and the regression coefficient captures the departures quite well. Observations 15–17 (16–17) reveal the own-price sensitivity (b_{ij}) of the equation, 19–20 (18–19) that of b_{ij}, 42–43 (41–42) that of K_{ii}, and, at the end of the chart, the sensitivity of price to c_i.

The strategic parameters for A_i and P_i in the symmetrical case, therefore, are the same for the most part: a_i, b_{ii}, b_{ij}, and K_{ii}. To a somewhat lesser degree they share c_i as an important mover, although it is stronger for P_i than A_i. For both variables β_{ij} is a surprisingly important factor in the variation and reveals that influence in observations 36–40 (35–39). One interesting result from a study of figures 17.2 and 17.4 is the greater relative movement of prices when compared with marketing budgets when solutions vary in response to parameter changes.

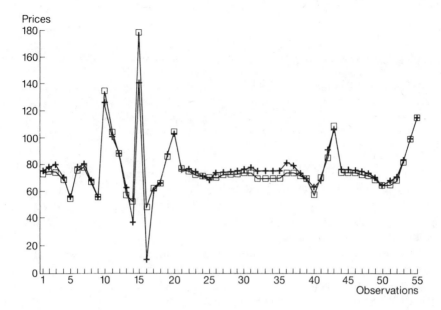

Figure 17.3 Price regression, symmetrical case.
□, actual prices; +, fitted prices.

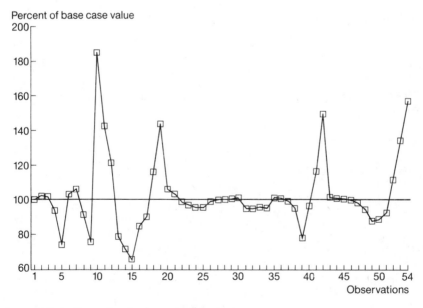

Figure 17.4 Normalized prices, symmetrical case.
□, actual prices; ———, base case norm.

2.1.3 Sales

The sales regression is the following and is drawn on figure 17.5:

$$X_i = -2325 + 533L - 429T + 6a_i - 426b_{ii} + 636b_{ij} - 2{,}179\alpha_{ii}$$
$$+ 1{,}214\alpha_{ij} + 35\beta_{ii} - 7{,}356\beta_{ij} + 833K_{ii} - 19K_{ij} - 87c_i$$

$$(\text{Adjusted } R^2 = 0.951)$$

The absolute and normalized patterns of sales response are graphed in figures 17.5 and 17.6. The revealed sensitivity to parameter changes repeats that discussed for advertising and prices. The extreme sensitivity to changes in transportation cost, T, and the intercept a_i is noteworthy. Also, sales and advertising reveal parallel directional moves in every case, while for prices and sales contrary directional moves are recorded for changes in L, T, K_{ij}, and c_i. A rise in L tends to shift demand functions rightward, which can be expected to reduce price elasticity and therefore increase price. But such a change also increases the slopes of the function, increasing own-price elasticity, and this effect outweighs the shift effect to lead to price reductions, especially as the latter are increasingly diminished by the rising decay level for the new and more distant markets.

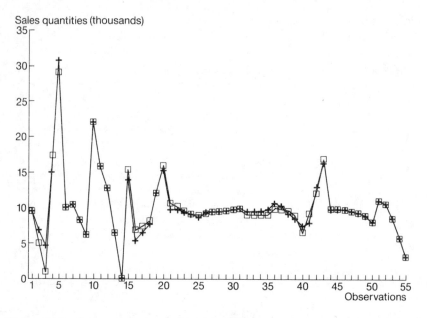

Figure 17.5 Sales regression, symmetrical case.
□, actual sales; +, fitted prices.

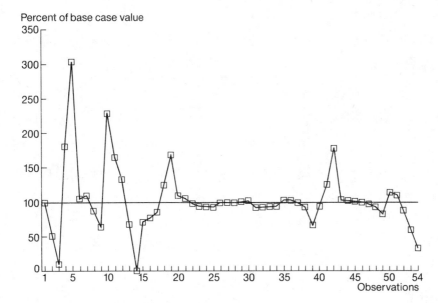

Percent of base case value

Figure 17.6   Normalized sales, symmetrical case.
□, actual sales; ———, base case norm.

2.1.4 Profits

Finally, the regression equation, depicted in figure 17.7, for profits in the symmetrical case is

$$\pi_i = 771{,}589 + 11{,}564L - 38{,}902T + 688a_i - 100{,}067b_{ii}$$
$$+ 68{,}830b_{ij} - 267{,}114\alpha_{ii} + 112{,}191\alpha_{ij} + 4{,}424\beta_{ii}$$
$$- 670{,}839\beta_{ij} + 51{,}609K_{ii} - 2{,}367K_{ij} - 6{,}370c_i$$
$$(\text{adjusted } R^2 = 0.807)$$

Figures 17.7 and 17.8 reproduce the absolute and relative profits values.

Profits, of course, are a derivative variable from sales and prices, and so reflect their movements. When a parameter change causes opposite movements in X_i and P_i one cannot project the general movement in profits, and this happens in the case of L, K_{ij}, and c_i. However, the relative sizes of the movements in the two variables in these cases, as shown in figures 17.4 and 17.6, lead to the expectation of the signs in the regression equation. No new insights into the relative strength of parameter-induced changes in the solutions are revealed in the figures.

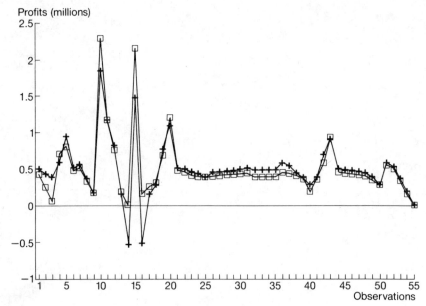

Figure 17.7 Profits regression, symmetrical case.
□, actual profits; + fitted profits.

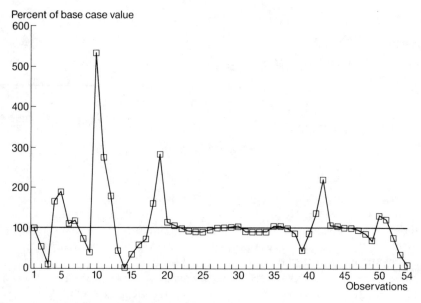

Figure 17.8 Normalized profits, symmetrical case.
□, actual profits; ———, base case norm.

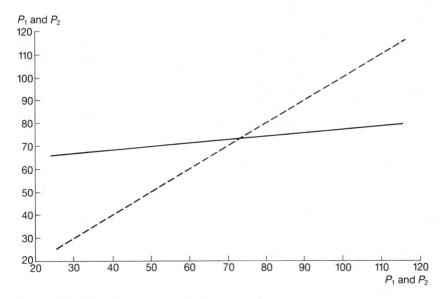

Figure 17.9 Reaction curves and solution.
——————, reaction curves; — — — —, 45 degree line.

Finally, in figure 17.9 I reproduce the reaction functions of the two firms in the base case, depicting firm i's price reaction to firm j's price (and, in the symmetrical case, firm j's reaction to firm i's price). Their intersection with the 45° line yields the price solution. These price reaction functions are drawn with advertising changing optimally for the firms.

2.2 Case 2: The Dominant Firm Case

The symmetrical case is interesting as a point of departure in the study of oligopolistic equilibrium because it reveals patterns of adjustment among firms when they all have equal constraints upon and freedoms in their strategy spaces. Parallel movements in all variables shed light upon the kinds of changes that would occur in a world where numbers of firms alone determine the degree of competition.

In the real world, however, to this component of the competitive process must be added the relative strengths and weaknesses of rivals and the movements in the variables that are ascribable to the need to react with compensations for these differences. The next case, therefore, introduces an environment in which one firm is dominant, and the weaker firm must react to competitive initiatives with nonparallel strategies that minimize its weak position.

The observations for this case were obtained by beginning with the symmetrical base case and changing each parameter for firm 1 by 10, 20, 30, 40, and 50 percent from its base case value in the direction of profit advantage, while firm 2's parameter set remains unchanged at base case values. On figure 17.10 to 17.21 the horizontal axis lists the relevant parameter being changed at the left-most observation representing its displacement. Movements to the right are always in the direction of improvement of firm 1's competitive position. The base case observation is labelled B on the graphs. Finally, two observations have been omitted from the graphic displays because they result in large deviations which require the scales to be so enlarged that the movements of other solution values are reduced in amplitude and difficult to discern. Those observations are for $b_{11} = 10$ and $\beta_{11} = 0.48$. The normalized variable values for those omitted parameters will be given in the discussion below.

2.2.1 The Marketing Budgets

The regression equations for the firms' marketing budgets are the following:

$$A_1 = -2{,}307{,}404 + 49a_1 - 10{,}903b_{11} + 5{,}928b_{21} - 638{,}814\alpha_{11}$$
$$- 166{,}322\alpha_{21} + 5{,}956{,}205\beta_{11} + 164{,}588\beta_{21} + 26{,}427K_{11}$$
$$+ 3{,}325K_{21} - 1{,}892c_1 \quad (\text{adjusted } R^2 = 0.849)$$
$$A_2 = 4{,}789 + 5a_1 - 1{,}146b_{11} + 2{,}595b_{21} - 13{,}013\alpha_{11}$$
$$- 157\alpha_{21} + 57{,}801\beta_{11} - 11{,}128\beta_{21} + 476K_{11} - 9K_{21}$$
$$+ 48c_1 \quad (\text{adjusted } R^2 = 0.963)$$

Figures 17.10 and 17.11 respectively depict the fit of these regression equations to the solution values. Figure 17.12 presents the solution values for the firms' advertising budgets normalized by division by the base case values. The omitted normalized solution values for $b_{11} = 10$ were 484.7 for firm 1 and 143.7 for firm 2; for $\beta_{11} = 0.48$ they were 1,922.8 and 116.5 respectively.

The most striking feature of the solutions and the regression equations describing them is that the almost universal response of firm 2 to parameter changes that favor firm 1 is to follow firm 1 in increasing its advertising budget, albeit by smaller amounts. As firm 1's advantage increases and its marketing expenditures rise, firm 2 in general follows suit. Similarly, when α_{21} falls to make firm 1's impact on firm 2's sales stronger, if firm 1 reduces its advertising budget so also does firm 2. The only exception to the rule is when c_1 declines.

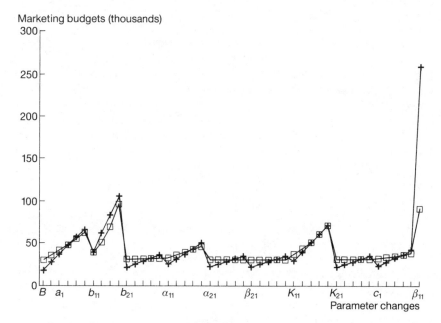

Figure 17.10 Dominant firm regression, firm 1, marketing.
□, actual marketing; +, fitted marketing.

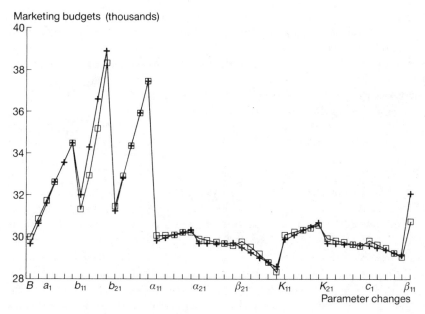

Figure 17.11 Dominant firm regression, firm 2, marketing.
□, actual marketing, +, fitted marketing.

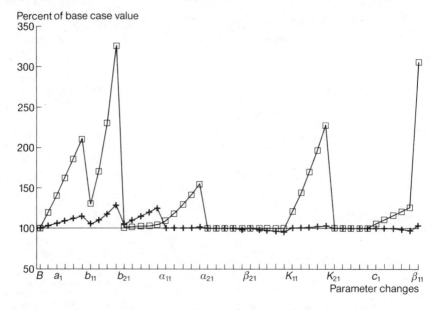

Figure 17.12   Dominant firm model, marketing values.
□, firm 1 marketing; +, firm 2 marketing.

The general motivation of this competitive result is in itself interesting. When firm 1's parameters change in its favor, it leads in general to a decline in the price elasticity of its demand, and to a new optimum in which that elasticity has declined. By the Dorfman–Steiner theorem, firm 1's advertising increases to lower the marginal revenue of marketing to the lower price elasticity. The conflicting forces of a rise in firm 1's price and an increase in its advertising lead to a smaller decline in the price elasticity of demand for firm 2's product, and therefore to some rise in price and some responsive rise in advertising budget.

There develops, therefore, in oligopolistic competition that involves price and marketing strategies, a synergism – even in the case of zero cooperation – that results in some advantage accruing initially to one competitor advancing the profit interest of the other. Absent advances in one competitor's ability to enhance the negative impacts on his rival's sales – α_{21}, β_{21}, and K_{21} in our model – or relative increases in production technology that lower production costs – c_1 – the indirect effects upon rivals of parameter changes that enhance own-profits directly generally increase the welfare of rivals and decrease public welfare. I shall note these points more explicitly in the discussion of profit solutions, but their foreshadowing can be denoted in the behavior of induced advertising expenditures by firm 2 noted above.

In these respects, from the regression equations note that a rise in b_{11}, increasing the price sensitivity of firm 1's demand function, decreases its advertising by about \$11,000 per unit, but it also decreases firm 2's by about \$1,146. An increase in b_{21} benefits firm 2 by enhancing its sales at any level of P_1, and leads to an *increase* in firm 1's advertising, dutifully followed by firm 2. For both firms β_{21} has a surprisingly large impact upon the advertising budget, as does α_{21} upon firm 1's marketing. These are results that were unexpected, given the indirect nature of the benefits a firm derives from affecting its rival's sales negatively.

2.2.2 Prices

As would be expected these patterns are repeated in the regression equations describing the price solutions:

$$P_1 = -33.02 + 0.03a_1 - 6.74b_{11} + 1.17b_{21} - 85.75\alpha_{11}$$
$$- 24.15\alpha_{21} + 392.05\beta_{11} + 22.47\beta_{21} + 3.31K_{11}$$
$$+ 0.48K_{21} + 0.29c_1 \quad (\text{adjusted } R^2 = 0.968)$$
$$P_2 = 49.39 + 0a_1 - 1.03b_{11} + 2.38b_{21} - 11.12\alpha_{11} + 0.53\alpha_{21}$$
$$+ 53.23\beta_{11} - 11.51\beta_{21} + 0.42K_{11} - 0.02K_{21} + 0.05c_1$$
$$(\text{adjusted } R^2 = 0.968)$$

Figures 17.13 and 17.14 depict the very close fits of the regressions to the solution values and figure 17.15 displays those solution values as percentages of base case values. For the omitted observations, the normalized value for P_1 was 203.1 and 146.0 for b_{11} and β_{11} respectively, and P_2 was 115.9 and 106.3.

These three charts make clear the nature of the response of a weaker rival to a stronger rival's enhanced competitiveness. In every case firm 2 follows firm 1's price lead, sheltering under the latter's elevation of prices to enhance its own, always staying beneath those prices, or reducing price below its stronger rival when that rival lowers price. Only when α_{21} falls (firm 1's advertising decays more slowly over space as a factor in reducing firm 2's sales), b_{21} rises (firm 2's sensitivity to firm 1's price rises), K_{21} rises (firm 1's advertising effectiveness in reducing firm 2's sales is raised), or c_1 falls does firm 1 lower price in its profit-maximizing strategy. In the first three cases, firm 1 follows firm 2's lead, since the latter is forced, by virtue of shifts in its demand curve and consequent rises in its elasticity, to lower price. In the case of lower firm 1 costs, that firm finds it to its

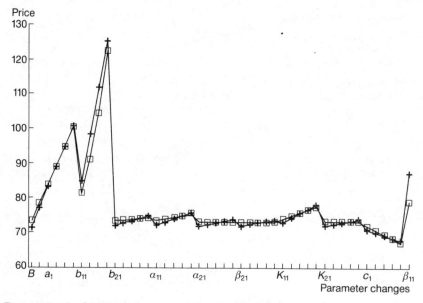

Figure 17.13 Dominant firm regression, firm 1, price.
□, actual firm 1 price; +, fitted firm 1 price.

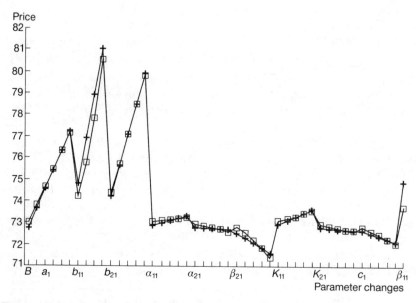

Figure 17.14 Dominant firm regression, firm 2, price.
□, actual firm 2 price; +, fitted firm 2 price.

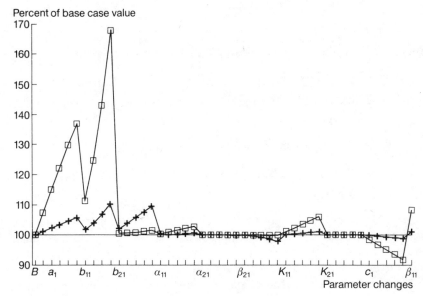

Figure 17.15   Dominant firm model, actual prices.
□, actual firm 1 price; +, actual firm 2 price.

advantage to lower price, and firm 2 must follow.

A rather surprising characteristic of advertising expenditures and prices in these solutions is that, except for cost changes, the two variables move in parallel fashion: each firm either raises marketing budgets and prices together, or reduces both. They are not used as substitutes. If the model is a good depiction of reality, this would go far to explain why prominent brands in oligopolistic industries fail to compete on price to gain market share, but rather tend to meet rivals' advertising campaigns with similar expenditures.

Those parameters which are most forceful in bringing about price changes are those which are most effective in reducing price elasticity of demand: obviously, a_1 and b_{11}, and, among those directly involved in advertising, K_{11} and β_{11}. Interestingly, these reductions in the optimal price elasticities for firm 1 persist even after firm 2's reactions. Indeed, one of the persistent patterns in the data is the small movement of the elasticity of the optimal solution point on firm 2's demand curve. Throughout all 48 solutions its price elasticity varies only between 1.42 and 1.53, whereas firm 1's ranges between 1.20 and 1.52.

2.2.3 Sales

The sales regressions of solutions on firm 1 parameters are the following:

$$X_1 = -24,921 + 6a_1 - 280b_{11} + 120b_{21} - 9,367\alpha_{11} - 1,392\alpha_{21}$$
$$+ 74,633\beta_{11} - 1,057\beta_{21} + 491K_{11} + 27K_{21} - 115c_1 \quad \text{(adjusted}$$
$$R^2 = 0.951)$$

$$X_2 = 4,870 + 1a_1 - 207b_{11} + 477b_{21} - 2,230\alpha_{11} + 108\alpha_{21}$$
$$+ 10,668\beta_{11} - 2,294\beta_{21} + 85K_{11} - 4K_{21} + 10c_1 \quad \text{(adjusted}$$
$$R^2 = 0.969)$$

Figures 17.16 and 17.17 record the excellent fit of both regressions to solution values and figure 17.18 maps solution sales in normative fashion. Omitted normalized observations for firm 1 are 128.9 and 170.0 for b_{11} and β_{11} respectively and 124.3 and 109.6 for firm 2.

The normalized values for X_1 and X_2 move in close synchronization with their firms' prices, both in direction and in percentage magnitude, with the exception of those resulting from changes in a_1 which affect sales proportionately more than price, and the inverse movement of firm 1's price and

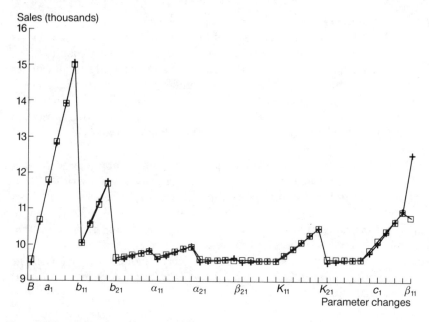

Figure 17.16 Dominant firm regression, firm 1, sales.
□, actual firm 1 sales; +, fitted firm 1 sales.

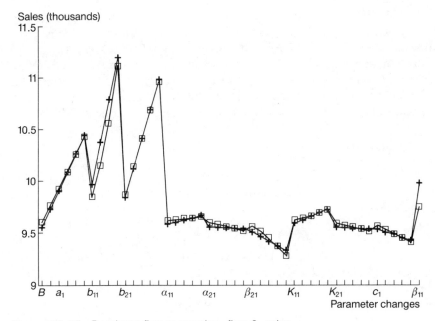

Figure 17.17 Dominant firm regression, firm 2, sales.
□, actual firm 2 sales; +, fitted firm 2 sales.

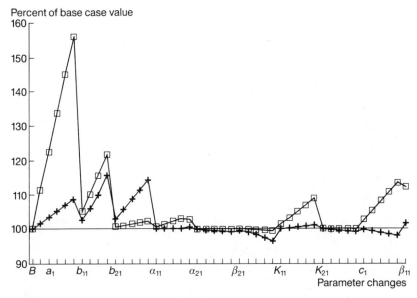

Figure 17.18 Dominant firm model, actual sales.
□, actual firm 1 sales; +, actual firm 2 sales.

sales with cost reductions. Since it was seen in the analysis of price movements that both firms' prices moved in parallel directions for the most part, this tandem movement of prices and quantities implies that *both* firms raise prices and increase sales as a result of the competititve process when either firm obtains an advantage which directly affects its own demand function. The result of the competition may in fact be to limit price increases accruing to both, but it is not strong enough to result in price reductions.

2.2.4 Profits

Finally, the results discussed above for the other three variables prepare us for the path of profits in the parametric displacements. The regressions are given below:

$$\pi_1 = -668{,}326 + 641a_1 - 84{,}357b_{11} + 18{,}337b_{21}$$
$$- 1{,}121{,}537\alpha_{11} - 348{,}843\alpha_{21} + 3{,}917{,}259\beta_{11} + 318{,}614\beta_{21}$$
$$+ 41{,}176K_{11} + 6{,}945K_{21} - 12{,}558c_1 \quad (\text{adjusted } R^2 = 0.964)$$

$$\pi_2 = -14{,}027 + 86a_1 - 20{,}688b_{11} + 46{,}354b_{21} - 240{,}690\alpha_{11}$$
$$- 9{,}647\alpha_{21} + 1{,}030{,}157\beta_{11} - 185{,}873\beta_{21} + 8{,}649K_{11}$$
$$- 14K_{21} + 779c_1 \quad (\text{adjusted } R^2 = 0.960)$$

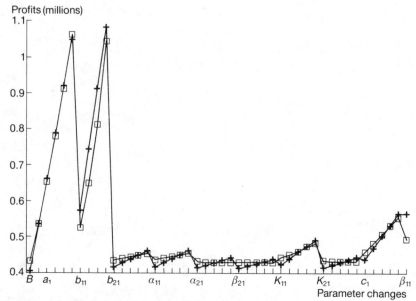

Figure 17.19 Dominant firm regression, firm 1, profits.
□, actual firm 1 profits; +, actual firm 2 sales.

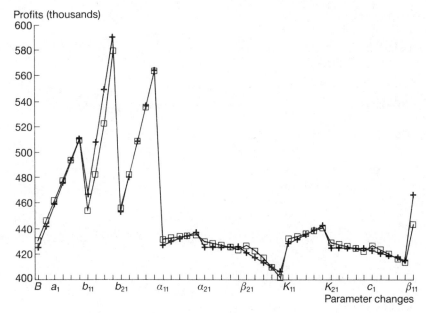

Figure 17.20 Dominant firm regression, firm 2, profits.
□, actual firm 2 profits; +, fitted firm 2 profits.

Figures 17.19 and 17.20 depict the regressions and the solution values and figure 17.21 displays the normalized values of the solution values. For the excluded observations, firm 1's normalized values were 321.7 and 175.1 for b_{11} and β_{11}, while firm 2's values for these observations were 155.2 and 120.3 respectively.

The most interesting feature of the solutions, as shown most clearly on figure 17.21, is that firm 2's profits, with few exceptions, rise above the base case level. Only for those changes that directly impact its demand function – α_{21}, β_{21} and K_{21} – and for falls in c_1 do firm 2's profits fall below base case values and in these cases *only by quite small amounts*. Duopolistic competition employing price and advertising strategies permits both firms to benefit from the gains in advantage of either as long as such gains do not directly impact the rival's demand function or the initiating firm's costs.

2.2.5 Conclusion

Of course, these conclusions come as no surprise after our noting the parallel movements of advertising, prices, and sales in the previous analysis, but they are nonetheless rather startling results. Such firms, even when they compete fully, are led to solutions that possess the surface characteristics of

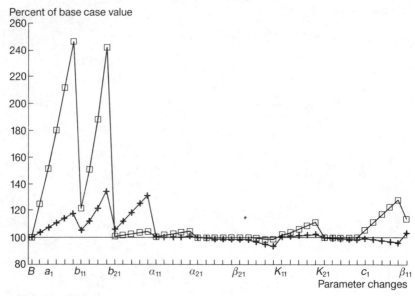

Figure 17.21   Dominant firm model, actual profits.
□, actual firm 1 profits; +, actual firm 2 profits.

cooperative or collusive strategies. Each shelters under the price increases of the other and lessens the need for the initiating firm to temper the price advantages gained. And the nature of the solutions is such that a great temptation toward overt collusion and cooperation or tacit coordination of strategies exists. Indeed, it would require a good deal of nonrationality for firms in such industries not to develop cooperative relationships that temper the rather limited role of competition and permit even greater joint benefits from coexistence.

Nor does the introduction of advertising as a second strategy to complete price policy lead to more intensive competition. From the symmetric case, when both firms are denied the advertising tool prices tend toward a value of 69.41 and sales to 8,882 per firm. Profits approach $394,481. If we use the base case values with advertising, these are normalized at 0.95, 0.93, and 0.92 respectively. Advertising does permit a rise in sales to the public of about 7 percent, but only at the cost of a 5 percent rise in price and substantial devotion of resources to advertising.

I have analyzed a variety of other parameter sets with model 1 type systems for the derivation of other insights which I will not take space to repeat here [3]. Despite the simplicity of its structure the model seems rich in the potential to yield hypotheses concerning the extremely complex decision-making of spatial oligopoly with nonprice competition. I shall close the chapter with a discussion of some ongoing and future research topics that have been suggested by the work to date.

3 Research in Progress and Prospect

3.1 Model 2: Disaggregated Demand Effects of Marketing

One of the less satisfying features of model 1 is that it does not distinguish the different paths of impact "advertising" may take in the search for profit and their connections with price as a competitive instrument. it aggregates all of the effects upon rivals' demands of their own and their competitors' marketing expenditures in the two relevant terms of the demand function in (17.2). However, it is possible to specify seven separate demand effects that a firm's marketing efforts can exert in an oligopolistic industry. In an effort to extend the analysis by identifying each of these impacts with a separate term in the demand equations, therefore, I constructed model 2, with the basic environmental features of model 1, but with demand functions (specified arbitrarily for firm 1) possessing the following form:

$$
\begin{aligned}
X_1(s)ds = \{ &A_1 + (U_{111}A_1 - U_{112}A_1^2)e^{-\delta_1 s} - (U_{121}A_2 - U_{122}A_2^2) \\
&e^{-\delta_2(L-s)} - (b_{11}(P_1 + rs) - (V_{111}A_1 - V_{112}A_1^2)e^{-\delta_1 s} \\
&+ (V_{121}A_2 - V_{122}A_2^2)e^{-\delta_2(L-s)}) + (b_{12}(P_2 + r(L-s))) \\
&+ (W_{111}A_1 - W_{112}A_1^2)e^{-\delta_1 s} - (W_{121}A_2 - W_{122}A_2^2)e^{-\delta_2(L-s)}) \\
&+ b_{13}(U_{211}A_1 - U_{212}A_1^2)e^{-\delta_1 s} \\
&+ b_{13}(V_{211}A_1 - V_{212}A_1^2)(P_2 + r(L-s))e^{-\delta_1 s} \\
&+ b_{13}(W_{211}A_1 - W_{212}A_1^2)(P_1 + rs)e^{-\delta_1 s}\}ds
\end{aligned}
\tag{17.6}
$$

The novel terms in this formulation define the separate demand effects of marketing:

1 The *own-demand, price-neutral market share effect*, which is effected by U_{111} and U_{112} (U_{221} and U_{222}). It impacts the intercept of the demand function without affecting the slopes, and it increases the market share of the firm regardless of prices ruling for both products.
2 The *own-demand, own-price market share effect*, which acts to reduce the price-sensitivity of the firm's demand. It is exercised by V_{111} and V_{112} (V_{221} and V_{222}). This is the classic goal of advertising to make the demand function more own-price inelastic to increase the firm's pricing power and profits.
3 The *own-demand, other-price market share effect*, enhancing the sales

accruing to the advertiser when the rival firm raises its price. It is quite conceivable that negative advertising may have an indirect effect on one's sales by leading a rival's customers to desert the rival when he raises prices without affecting the own-price sensitivity of the benefiting firm. The parameter involved is W_{111} and W_{112} (W_{221} and W_{222}).

4 The *other-demand, price-neutral attritional effect*, which acts, through U_{212} and U_{222} (U_{121} and U_{122}), to reduce a rival's market share by shifting the intercept of its demand function downwards. This attrition may result in a loss of demand by the industry through a reduction in consumption of both firms' products or may be partially or wholly captured by the advertising firm (see effect 7 below).

5 The *other-demand, other-price attritional effect*, which impacts the rival's demand by increasing the sensitivity of its demand to its own price. The rival's own-price coefficient (b_{11} or b_{21}) is incremented positively, resulting in lost sales with price increases. These lost sales may be lost to both firms or may be partially or wholly captured by the advertising firm. The effect is activated by parameters V_{121} and V_{122} (V_{211} and V_{212}).

6. The *other-demand, own-price attritional effect*, which, via W_{121} and W_{122} (W_{211} and W_{212}), reduces the sales of a rival that accrue when the advertising firm raises its price. By treating this effect independently of the own-demand, own-price effect I assume that when firm 1 raises its price firm 2 may gain fewer sales than it would if firm 1's advertising level fell but that firm 1 need not experience increased sales as a result. If it does it will do so through the next and last effect.

7 The *recapture-of-rival-attrition effect*, which is contained in the last term of the demand function and whose magnitude is specified by b_{13} (b_{23}). This parameter determines how much of the attrition wrought by firm 1's (2's) marketing effort through the effects in 4, 5, and 6 is captured as increased sales of its own product.

To obtain firm 1's demand function we integrate (17.6) by parts over the linear market of length L. Define $U_{11}^* = U_{111}/\delta_1$, etc., and $U_{21}^* = U_{121}/\delta_2$, etc. Then:

$$\int_0^L X_1 ds = a_1 L + (U_{111}^{2*}A_1 - U_{112}^{2*}A_1^2)(1 - e^{-\delta_1 L}) - (U_{121}^*A_2 - U_{122}^*A_2^2)$$
$$(1 - e^{-\delta_2 L}) - b_{11}(P_1 L + 0.5rL^2) + (V_{111}^*A_1 - V_{112}^*A_1^2)$$
$$\{P_1(1 - e^{-\delta_1 L} + (r/\delta_1)(1 - e^{-\delta_1 L}(1 + \delta_1 L)))\} - (V_{121}^*A_1$$
$$- V_{122}^*A_2^2)\{P_1(1 - e^{-\delta_2 L} + (r/\delta_2)(1 - e^{-\delta_2 L}(1 + \delta_2 L)))\}$$
$$+ b_{12}(P_2 + 0.5rL^2) + (W_{111}^*A_1 - W_{122}^*A_2^2)\{P_2(1 - e^{-\delta_1 L}$$
$$+ (r/\delta_1)(1 - e^{-\delta_1 L}(1 + \delta_1 L)))\} - (W_{121}^*A_2 - W_{122}^*A_2^2)$$
$$\{P_2(1 - e^{-\delta_2 L} + (r/\delta_2)(1 - e^{-\delta_2 L}(1 + \delta_2 L)))\} + b_{13}(U_{211}^*A_1$$

$$- U_{212}^* A_1^2)(1 - e^{-\delta_1 L}) + b_{13}(V_{211}^* A_1 - V_{212}^* A_1^2)\{P_2(1 - e^{-\delta_1 L}$$

$$+ (r/\delta_1) \ (1 - e^{-\delta_1 L}(1 + \delta_1 L)))\} + b_{13}(W_{211}^* A_1 - W_{212}^* A_1^2)$$

$$\{P_1(1 - e^{-\delta_1 L} + (r/\delta_1) \ (1 - e^{-\delta_1 L}(1 + \delta_1 L)))\}. \tag{17.7}$$

The model consists, then, of maximizing (17.1) subject to (17.7) and given P_2 and A_2, and to do so iteratively with a symmetrical maximization for firm 2. First partial derivatives of the profit functions with respect to P_1 (P_2) and A_1 (A_2) were set equal to zero, and the algorithm used to solve the model successively set one pair of the variables constant at the values of the prior iteration, solved for P_1 (or P_2) analytically and employed a Newton–Raphson technique to solve for A_1 (or A_2) holding A_2 (or A_1) constant.

Unfortunately to this point I have not been able to get consistent convergence to a solution. Whether this is a calibration problem or structural is now being studied. But I am convinced that some such decomposition of advertising's impacts upon the demand curves of the rivals is desirable.

3.2 Introduction of Three or More Firms

One desirable innovation which is feasible because of the simplicity of the model's structure is to introduce a third firm at the mid-point of the linear market and study the impact it would have upon the competitive process. It would then be desirable to move the locations of firms 1 and 2 from the endpoints to $0.166L$ and $0.833L$ positions where their locational advantages are equalized. This research is also in progress.

3.3 Cooperative Tempering of the Competition

As indicated in the analysis of section 2, important rewards to both rivals would attend a tacit agreement to cooperate in rational recognition of a consonance of self-interest. This feature can be readily built into the model through the use of *rivalrous consonance* analysis, which intrudes this cooperation by having each rival maximize the sum of own-profits and other-profits, when the latter is discounted by a *consonance factor*, $\theta_i \in [0, 1]$. Model 1 is a limiting case where $\theta_i = \theta_j = 0$, whereas joint-profit maximization occurs when both factors are unity. By choosing values of the θ factors that lie in the interior of the interval we can study the impacts of varying degrees of tacit cooperation.

Notes

[1] Within the context of rivalrous consonance this implies that each firm maximizes own-profits plus rival profits multiplied by a consonance factor, θ_i, equal to zero. By allowing this consonance factor to vary between 0 and 1 it is possible to intrude into the model any degree of reasonable collusion between the two up to and including joint profit maximization when both θ_i are equal to 1. See [2]. See section 3.3 for its application to models of the type presented in this chapter.

[2] See [3], pp. 42–5. Briefly, the diagonal elements are both negative and the determinant of the Hessian will be positive when

$$\beta_{11} < 1 - \left(\left(0.5A_1/\pi_1 \right) + A_1 \right).$$

That is, the elasticity of sales with respect to own-marketing budgets must be less than the complement of the ratio of one-half the advertising budget to the sum of profits plus that budget. When profits are zero, then, β_{11} must be less than 0.5, and when profits are positive the upper bound rises substantially. When advertising budgets are equal to profits, that bound becomes 0.75, and when it is one quarter of profits it becomes 0.9. Since it is difficult to imagine a productivity factor much above 0.5, the sufficient condition for a global profit maximum for each firm, given the other's strategy, is achieved except for special pathological parameter sets introduced for particular reasons.

[3] By manipulating the Dorfman–Steiner theorem (see note 4) the proportion of revenue spent on advertising is the ratio of the revenue elasticity of advertising to the negative of the price elasticity of demand. For firm 1, for example, this may be reduced to the expression.

$$M_1 = \frac{K_{11}\beta_{11}A^{\beta_{11}}\left(1 - e^{-\alpha_{11}L}\right)}{-\varepsilon_1\alpha_{11}X_1},$$

where M_1 is the advertising ratio and ε_1 the price elasticity of demand. It is not clear why in the instances referenced this expression remained nearly constant.

[4] See [1]. Briefly, Dorfman and Steiner showed that at a joint-profit optimum for price and advertising the absolute value of the price elasticity of demand must equal the marginal revenue of advertising. This can be motivated by observing that the price elasticity of demand is the increase in revenue from the increased sales obtained by a price decrease (PdX) divided by the cost of that price decrease as measured by loss on intramarginal sales (XdP). Hence, it is the marginal revenue obtained by a dollar of price reduction cost. This must be equated to the marginal revenue obtainable by spending the $1 on advertising as an alternative strategy.

References

[1] Dorfman, Robert and Peter O. Steiner, "Optimal Advertising and Optimal Quality", *American Economic Review*, 44 (1954), 826–36.

[2] Kuenne, Robert E., *Rivalrous Consonance: a Theory of General Oligopolistic Equilibrium*, North-Holland, Amsterdam, 1986.

[3] ——, "Price-Marketing Competition and Information Flows in Spatial Oligopoly", in Manas Chatterji and Robert E. Kuenne (eds), *New Frontiers in Regional Science: Essays in Honour of Walter Isard*, Macmillan, London, 1990, 38–56. [Reprinted as chapter 14 in this volume.]

Part IV

Oligopolistic Decision-making under Uncertainty

Introduction to Part IV

The three selections in this part reflect the most recent theoretical interest of mine in the introduction of uncertainty and imperfect information into the analysis of oligopoly, and the extension of the logic of decision-making in oligopoly to noneconomic bargaining situations. Game theoretic approaches are quite generally employed in these areas: can the rivalrous consonance theory of mature oligopoly make contributions?

The theory of decision-making under uncertainty and imperfect or asymmetric information are currently receiving much attention from economists, following pioneering work by Kenneth Arrow in the 1950s. His concept of *contingency states* is fundamental to the field. In the specific application to the decision involved in auction bidding other pioneers must be noted, including a group of operations research specialists (cited in chapter 18) and economists like William Vickrey and John Harsanyi.

Chapter 18 was originally published in a *Festschrift* honoring Kenneth Arrow and builds upon his use of subjective probability in decision-making to analyze optimal bidding procedures by oligopolistic suppliers in government procurement. My interest in the subject was a result of my consulting in defense management and the difficulties the US Department of Defense had in getting oil companies to bid on contracts for the provision of jet fuel during the petroleum shortage of 1979. However, as made clear in the paper, I believe the analysis has much broader application in bidding situations than this one.

One of the difficulties in applying to oligopoly analysis the game-theoretic bidding theory that most analysts use in one form or another is that it assumes that rivals' knowledge of their competitors' costs or reservation prices is essentially nil. Also, each bidder is assumed to use the same bidding function, with bids determined from it by competitors' opportunity costs of submitting bids. This is not an adequate description of the knowledge and imperfect information base for rivals in industries in which small numbers of participants engage, such as is characteristic in bidding

425

auctions for specialized government needs. The paper seeks to model such bidding in manners that approximate more closely the oligopoly environment using subjective probabilistic tools. Rivals' bidding functions become derivatives of such probabilistic expectations of competitors's behavior, given those rivals' costs of bidding. In a sense, this is an extension into an uncertain environment of my insistence upon a specified power structure in oligopoly theory without explicit uncertainty.

The analysis – using Weibull probability density functions – is quite intricate and results are not easily summarized. But I feel the framework offers an operational alternative to oligopolistic bidding models whose assumptions concerning rivals' information ignore the subjective notions founded upon experience with their competitors.

Chapter 19 turns to another issue involving uncertainty in oligopoly: the role of information flows over space and the implications they have for pricing. This issue arises in a nonstochastic environment in chapters 14 and 17, where I analyzed space as an impediment to marketing information effectiveness. As I noted in those papers, I believe information flow and its implications for oligopolistic decision-making will come increasingly under scrutiny by theorists.

This paper is concerned with its impact upon pricing, the notion being that contrary to the belief that a reduction in the space separating rivals should increase price competition and reduce prices, proximity may in fact enhance information flow and encourage rivalrous consonance. Tacit cooperation may occur to raise prices instead of lower them.

Such pricing information is largely conjectural and probabilistic, and its perception by a rival is best treated as a subjective probability density function over a competitor's price changes. The firm also has a similar probability function over its rival's (I analyze duopoly in this paper for ease of presentation) reactions to its own pricing initiatives. *Reactive uncertainty*, or conjectural variation, therefore, is also probabilistic. Once more, for reasons of mathematical tractability and flexibility in approximating familiar distributions, I use Weibull distributions in the analyses.

In a mature oligopoly, the expected range in which rivals' prices can fluctuate is narrow if exogenous shocks are absent. As distance from rivals decreases, information flows are faster and reactions more certain, so proximity also limits the range of expected price change initiations. I have defined ranges I believe to be realistic and derived expected values for the Weibull distributions. A major assumption is that in mature rivalry, characterized by rivalrous consonance, the expected value for a rival's price today is higher than or equal to its price yesterday: the belief is that a rival is more likely to lift price than lower it. This expected value should rise as distance between rivals decreases because of information flow considerations mentioned above.

Hence, in mature oligopoly there is endemic an expectation that rivals will raise prices slightly over time, and that belief intensifies as firms cluster in information nodes. Thus the *initiating* uncertainty on rivals' parts is conducive to a cooperative pricing policy. Reactive expectations by competitors to a rival's initiating price changes are treated in the paper by obtaining that rival's expectations of changes in the parameters of his own probability function and hence induced changes in this expected value of the competitor's price. Thus, if firm 1 raises price, firm 1 expects firm 2 to follow suit, which raises the expected value of p_2 in firm 1's planning. Thus, *reactive* uncertainty enhances the buoyant price expectations endemic to rivalrous consonance, and that buoyancy increases as proximity of location increases.

I conjecture that part of the motivation for rivals to locate in agglomerations may be to enhance pricing information flow and with it higher expected prices and profits. A deficiency of the model is that it fails to take into explicit account the narrowing of the dispersion of the subjective probability density functions as experience accumulates supporting the mature rivalry hypothesis.

Chapter 20 is a frontal assault on the role of uncertainty in oligopoly analysis. It lists a set of conditions requisite for mature rivalry and rivalrous consonance to exist and then, through an application of techniques similar to those of chapter 19, moves to analyze the implications of uncertainty in such an environment. Autonomous and reactive pricing decisions are included in the analysis and in the same subjective probabilistic framework as that in the previous selection. Under conditions of such rivalry, uncertainty is seen to impart an upward bias in prices over time. Autonomous price change expectations are linked to the characteristic of mature oligopoly. Reactive price change expectations are assumed once more to affect the parameters of the firm's subjective probability density function, and enhance the expectation of favourable rival price changes. Hence, perhaps paradoxically, uncertainty in the mature rivalrous environment enhances cooperative motivation.

The suggestion is made that this framework could be applied with useful results to the analysis of relations between the Soviet Union and NATO members. The recent thawing of the Cold War and the capacity for open negotiations (unavailable in oligopoly) makes the possibility of cooperative rivalry promising. And, finally, rivalrous consonance is introduced into the model to add enhanced strength to the implicit drive in the uncertainty model toward cooperation.

The three selections in this part of the volume are experimental sallies into the highly important fields of uncertainty and information flows. Both phenomena are obviously extremely important in oligopolistic decision-making. The most important result, I believe, is the counterintuitive notion that uncertainty may enable a greater amount of tacit cooperation to exist in interdependent pricing than would exist in its absence. In the years to come, I am sure, these fields will receive a great deal of attention from microtheorists and permit more extensive insights to be obtained.

18

Oligopolistic Uncertainty and Optimal Bidding in Government Procurement: A Subjective Probability Approach

Kenneth Arrow's early and continuing interest in the economics of risk and uncertainty and his contributions to the literature it inspired were pivotal in the developments that have characterized the field in the past 20 years. A re-reading of the *Essays in the Theory of Risk Bearing* – some of which date back a quarter century or more – confirms in detail the impressions they created at first reading. In them Arrow moves effortlessly between the rigor of mathematical analysis and the brilliantly intuitive and conjectural.

At the core of his interest is the desire to integrate risk and uncertainty into the theory of general equilibrium, with the implied need to create universal futures markets or other institutions for risk-shifting. The seminal question emerges from his analysis: why has the market economy failed to provide these opportunities for the risk-averse? The search for answers leads Arrow into imaginative and insightful discussion of moral hazard, the economics of health care, the role of and demand for information, the conceptual foundations of insurance, and the nature of research and development activities. The contributions in these fields are characterized by an ease of brilliance: effortless movement from insight to insight at a pace that exhausts the reader. As a concrete example, essay 5 – *"Insurance, Risk and Resource Allocation"* – must surely rank among the most insightful ten pages in economic literature.

One of Arrow's pioneering contributions to the field was the acceptance of subjective probability as a valid and primitive conceptual basis for the analysis of choice under uncertainty. The notion that agents' attitudes toward uncertain events are shaped by intuitive and experiential feelings of obscure origin and with little prospect of successful explanation is still a

Originally published as chapter 21 in George Feiwel (ed.), *Arrow and the Ascent of Modern Economic Theory*, Macmillan, London, 1987, and reproduced by permission.

difficult one to accept for some economists. The attitude that unless one can derive the probability density function ruling over an outcome space from the objective evidence of the phenomena one does not have the basis for a fruitful analysis is still apparent in such fields as the theory of bidding.

Despite the fact that the early interest of Arrow in the economics of uncertainty arose from a concern with government procurement contracting (notably cost-plus contracts as a means of shifting risk to the government at some cost in moral hazard), the theory of bidding was one of the few topics in the theory of decision-making under uncertainty that escaped his scrutiny. The present paper does not arrogate itself to an assertion of lineal descent from Arrow's seminal work, but it does attempt to work within frameworks that are clearly indicated by that work to analyze oligopolistic bidding strategies using subjective probability as the core concept. It acknowledges, therefore, its debt to Arrow in pointing to untravelled routes into difficult territory for exploratory excursions.

1 Bidding in a Competitive Market Structure

Modern optimal bidding theory reveals two distinct sources. The earlier strand of research interest originated in operations research, and was given initial form in the seminal work of Friedman [6]. Indeed, that term is peculiarly appropriate because the article was abstracted from Friedman's dissertation, which earned him the first PhD degree awarded in the field of operations research. That work, and subsequent work by operations research specialists, quite naturally focused upon the strategic decision-making of the firm, largely abstracting from the interdependence of rival bidders' expectations (see, for example, [2, 3, 10]). It did, however, incorporate the economic theoretic work of Arrow [1] and Pratt [14] in preferences under risk – notably risk aversion.

The second stream of contributions was originated by economists, with pioneering work by Vickrey [15] and the development of games with incomplete information by Harsanyi [8]. It shifts the emphasis to the game-theoretic interdependence of bidders, employing the notion of a Nash non-cooperative equilibrium among their expectations of rivals' behavior. Impressive work in the development of these competitive auction behavior theories has been contributed by Wilson [16–19], Engelbrecht-Wiggins [5], Harris and Ravio [7], Holt [9], Baron [4], Milgrom [12], Milgrom and Weber [13], and Kuhlman and Johnson [11].

Paradoxically, the adoption of a game-theoretic orientation leads to an impersonality and state of ignorance about rivals' costs and opportunities that are inappropriate in many oligopolistic bidding contexts. Although they may vary somewhat among authors, the following assumptions about competitive bidding environments in a procurement contract auction[1] are characteristic of the literature:

1 Each bidder knows the value of the contract to himself (equal to his opportunity cost or reservation price) but he is ignorant about his rivals' valuations and reservation prices in the small – that is, rival by rival.[2]
2 The reservation prices for all firms are independently drawn realizations from a sample space under the regime of the same probability density function.
3 All bidders have symmetric preferences and information concerning rival bidders, and hence it is assumed (in order to obtain a Nash equilibrium) that all bidders will determine a bid from a common bidding function with opportunity cost the argument.
4 The bidder's specific bid will be affected by his expectation of the lowest bid of his rivals as a body, derivable by order statistics from 2 and 3.

In major government procurement contracts, as well as in many other auction contexts, these assumptions do not permit an adequate analytical description of the rivalry among bidders. Rivals may be few in the oligopolistic sense, with rather accurate knowledge of their competitors' opportunity costs, attitudes toward risk, management styles, desires to establish a continuing relation with the contractor, normal profit margins, and so forth. In no sense can the reservation prices – which may depart from strict opportunity costs in these circumstances – be treated as independent drawings from a common probability density function. Moreover, the relevance of a Nash equilibrium for expected bids is questionable, given the limited scope for conjectural variation reasoning, the once-for-all and secret nature of the bidding, and the rival-specific bidding functions forthcoming in oligopolistic bidding structures.

This chapter seeks to model oligopolistic bidding in sealed tenders for government contracts in manners that approach more closely the practices, states of knowledge and strategic thinking of oligopolists. That implies a return to the interests of earlier researchers when oligopoly was featured rather than anonymous competition. It incorporates knowledge and belief held by the bidder as subjective probabilistic "hunches" about rivals' bids that can be approximated by families of familiar probability functions. And, lastly, it attempts to derive some policy implications for government in designing its contracting requirements and conventions.

2 The Firm's Bidding Decision

We assume that a government purchasing agent requests bids from producers for delivery of q units of product over a specified time period. It is further assumed that the firm has alternative private sector markets for the product and that its industry is oligopolistic. For the time period in question the firm's capacity to produce the good sets an upper bound of k units, all of which could be sold in the private sector market at positive profit levels. How would the profit-maximizing firm decide whether to bid on the contract, and if it does decide to bid, how does it determine the size of that bid in its state of imperfect but existent knowledge of its rivals' cost, profit, market share, and management profiles?

Rival 1 – whose bidding decisions we analyze – has expectations about its private sector sales potential in the form of a family of conditional probability density functions

$$h(p|w), \qquad 0 < w \leqslant k, \qquad (18.1)$$

which state, for each hypothetical sales level w, the subjective expectations about prices p at which it could be sold. We will not be more specific about these functions except to say that they are expected to be unimodal, strongly peaked, and with small variances, given rival 1's extensive experience in its primary market.

More important for our immediate interests is the stochastic structure of rival 1's decision-making in the bidding procedure. Central to our modelling of that process are four assumptions:

1 Given its acquaintance with the demand and cost structure of the industry, and perhaps formal or informal maximum bid signals from the government, firm 1 formulates a lower bound L and upper bound U, within which it is certain the successful bid will lie.
2 For each of its perceived rival bidders, firm 1's expectations of the bidder's circumstances can be expressed as probabilities the bid will be a given price or less. Rival 1 can formulate several such defining probabilities for given bid levels for each of its perceived rivals.
3 For each of rival 1's competitors, the defining probabilities can be used by firm 1 to approximate its subjective expectations with a cumulative density function of simple form over the domain $b_j \in [L, \infty]$, where b_j, $j \neq 1$, are the bids of rivals j. For convenience, we may normalize the bids with the transformation,

$$x = \frac{b_j - L}{U - L}, \qquad (18.2)$$

and define the cumulative functions over $x \in [0, \infty]$.
4 A preference function for choices under risk can be calculated for rival 1, and its bid will be determined by its desire to maximize the expected utility of profits. For purposes of simplicity, these preferences will be

taken to be approximately risk-neutral, given the "normal" income levels anticipated under the contract, so that they are linear in profits.

Because we are interested in modelling oligopolistic decision-making in an operational manner that approximates the capabilities and habits of the actual decision-makers, attention is called to an important feature of (18.2). It is not supposed that rival 1 constructs or is in command of a probability distribution over rival j's bids, specifying the "probability" of any particular bid. Rather, the much more realistic assertion is that rival 1 can specify hunches about several critical values: the most likely (modal) bid, the value below which rival 1 is 95 percent certain that rival j will bid, the likelihood of rival j bidding rival 1's estimate of his opportunity cost or less, and so forth. After fitting a cumulative density function to this subjective information, the underlying rival's probability density function can be *derived* from the operational information, but it is not presumed to have a meaningful pre-existence in the active decision process of the decision-maker.[3]

Consider, now, rival 1's appraisal of rival j's decision process. In the framework assumed in (18.2) a cumulative probability density function, $G_j(x)$, is determinable, where $x = (b - L)/(U - L), x \in [0, \infty]$. Although x is unbounded, firm 1 expects that $G_j(x)$ can be approximated by a Weibull cumulative density function,

$$G_j(x) = 1 - e^{-(x/a_j)^{c_j}}, \qquad 0 \leqslant x \leqslant \infty, \qquad (18.3)$$

where a_j is a scale parameter and c_j a shape parameter.

The Weibull is adopted because it is a flexible two-parameter distribution with convenient mathematical properties. With (say) $G_j(0.995) = 0.995$, one degree of freedom in fitting $G_j(x)$ is used. If firm 1 can specify its guess as to firm j's most likely bid, it may be used as the mode,

$$\text{Mode} = \begin{cases} a_j \left(1 - \dfrac{1}{c_j}\right)^{1/c_j}, & c_j > 1 \\ 0, & c_j \leqslant 1, \end{cases} \qquad (18.4)$$

in firm j's underlying estimated *bidding density function*,

$$g_j(x) \equiv G_j'(x) = \frac{c_j}{a_j^{c_j}} x^{c_j - 1} e^{-(x/a_j)^{c_j}}. \qquad (18.5)$$

This function is a Weibull distribution yielding the *implied* probabilities of firm j bidding in the small interval about x.

When $c_j = 1$, the Weibull is the negative exponential function, and when $c_j = 2$ it is the Rayleigh distribution. Note that the mode is nonzero for $c_j > 1$. Given the inverse of the cumulative function,

$$G_j(x)^{-1} = a_j \left(In \frac{1}{1-\alpha} \right)^{1/c_j}, \tag{18.6}$$

where α is a specified probability, and either a second point that can be put in (18.6), or the mode in (18.4), the values for a_j and c_j can be solved for. The flexibility of the Weibull is illustrated in table 18.1, where the values of $G_j(x)$ are recorded for a wide range of c_j, a_j, and implied modes. This flexibility, its two-parameter nature, and its ease of mathematical manipulation make the Weibull an ideal distribution for the approximation of firm 1's subjective notions of its rivals' behavior.

Table 18.1   Values of the cumulative Weibull distribution for a variety of parameter and modal values

x	[2,0.43]	[3,0.57]	[4,0.66]	$[c_j, a_j]$ [5,0.71]	[10,0.84]	[15,0.89]	[20,0.92]
0.10	0.05	0.01	–	–	–	–	–
0.25	0.29	0.08	0.02	0.01	–	–	–
0.50	0.74	0.49	0.28	0.16	0.01	–	–
0.75	0.95	0.90	0.81	0.73	0.28	0.07	0.02
0.85	0.98	0.96	0.94	0.91	0.68	0.39	0.19
0.95	0.99	0.99	0.99	0.99	0.97	0.93	0.85
Mode	0.30	0.50	0.61	0.68	0.83	0.89	0.92

The probability firm 1's normalized bid x will win over rival j's bid is

$$f_j(x) = 1 - G_j(x) = e^{-(x/a_j)^{c_j}}, \tag{18.7}$$

and the probability x will win the contract, when firm 1 considers each rival in similar fashion, is

$$f(x) = \prod_j f_j(x) = \prod_j (1 - G_j(x)) = e^{-\Sigma_j (x/a_j)^{c_j}}. \tag{18.8}$$

It is noted that for all $c_j > 0$, and realistic $0 < a_j \leqslant 1$, $f(x)$ is continuous, negatively sloped, with second-order derivatives.

For simplicity we will assume that variable costs, v, per unit of firm 1's product are constant. Further, we assume that the increasingly burdensome costs of doing business with the federal government are capable of being monetized by the firm, and may be approximated by m dollars per unit of q. Among such costs are the legal costs of coping with voluminous contracts and of submitting to potential litigation for violations of Equal Opportunity Employment, Affirmative Action, Minority Business, Small Business, and so on, statutes; the costs of submitting to specified cost escalation indices that do not accurately track market costs; the costs of being unable to allocate to the government on a fractional basis in periods of shortage; the costs of being unable to invoke *force majeure* in times of raw material unavailability; the burdens of testing and retesting the product to assure its conformance to government specifications; and so forth.[4]

The expected profit of the firm in its total operations may be written as a function of its actual bid, b_1, on the contract, and its normalized value x_1 :

$$E(\pi_1) = f(x_1)\left\{q(b_1 - v - m) + (k - q)\left(\int_0^\infty p \cdot h(p|k - q)\,dp - v\right)\right\}$$
$$+ (1 - f(x_1))\{k(E(p|k) - v)\}, \tag{18.9}$$

where $E(p|k - q)$ and $E(p|k)$ are the expected prices obtained from sales of $k - q$ and k units respectively on the private market. Expected total profits are the sum of (1), the probability of winning the contract times the contract's net revenue and net revenue from the sale of remaining output in the private market and (2), the probability of losing the contract times the expected net revenue from sale of capacity output in the private market. More compactly,

$$E(\pi) = f(x)[q(x \cdot (U - L) + L - v - m)] + f(x)[E(\bar{\pi}_{k-q}) -$$
$$E(\bar{\pi}_k)] + E(\bar{\pi}_k), \tag{18.10}$$

where $E(\bar{\pi}_{k-q})$ and $E(\bar{\pi}_k)$ are expected profits in the private market from the sale of $k - q$ and k units respectively.

Then, first order conditions for a maximum are

$$\frac{dE(\pi)}{dx} = f(x) \cdot q \cdot (U - L) + f'(x)[q \cdot (x \cdot (U - L) + L - v - m)] +$$
$$f'(x)[\Delta E(\bar{\pi})] = 0 \tag{18.11}$$

From (18.11),

$$x^0 = r^0 - \left(\frac{L - v - m}{U - L}\right) - \frac{\Delta E(\bar{\pi})}{q \cdot (U - L)}, \tag{18.12}$$

where $r^0 = f(x^0)/ - f'(x^0)$. A necessary and sufficient condition that $E(\pi)$ be strictly concave is that $f'(x) < -0.5f''(x)r$. Since $f'(x) < 0$, a sufficient condition for strict concavity is $f''(x) \leq 0$, but it cannot be expected to be met in some relevant domains of $f(x)$. Hence, the quantitative relationships for specific forms of $f(x)$ must be evaluated. For the Weibull formulation, $f'' > 0$ in its upper domain, but strict concavity will hold for all $x > 0$.

Note that (18.12) is on a normalized per unit of q basis, and that multiplication of both sides by the normalizing factor $(U - L)$ converts to dollars per unit of q. Indeed, condition (18.12) is more readily interpretable after conversion to

$$b^0 = v + m - \frac{\Delta E(\bar{\pi})}{q} + r^0(U - L) \qquad (18.13)$$

$$= v + m - \frac{\Delta E(\bar{\pi})}{q} + s^0 \qquad (18.14)$$

$$= o + s^0.$$

The optimal bid price per unit of q by firm 1 will be (1), unit variable and contracting cost (2), less the net gain or plus the net loss in private market profit per unit of contract quantity because $k - q$ units instead of k are sold, plus (3), s^0, or an *oligopoly bidding surplus* per unit of q. We will term (1) + (2) the opportunity cost of a unit of q, or o.

In an oligopolistic bidding context there may exist in the typical bidder's tender a positive rent over and above any oligopoly surpluses that are present in $\Delta E(\bar{\pi})$ *(and therefore o).* Its source lies wholly in the uncertainty that inheres in a bidding rivalry in which the market structure does not lead bidders to expect rivals to bid opportunity cost. Consider (18.13):

$$b^0 - o = s^0 = r^0(U - L) \qquad (18.15)$$

$$= \frac{f(x^0)}{-f'(x^0)} (U - L) = \frac{f(x^0)dx}{-f'(x^0)dx} (U - L).$$

The first order condition may be written

$$q(b^0 - o)(-f'(x^0)dx = q \cdot f(x^0)dx(U - L). \qquad (18.16)$$

At the maximum, a slight rise in b, $db = (U - L)dx$, the probability of losing the contract rises by $(-f'(x)db)/(U - L)$, the marginal risk of loss. The left-hand side of (18.16), therefore, is the marginal expected loss with a rise in b. The right-hand side is the marginal expected gain from the rise. Hence, (18.16) states the requirement that b be set at the level that equates marginal expected loss to marginal expected gain from small changes in b. Thus, s *is the marginal expected benefit per unit of contract sales per unit of marginal risk.*

For convenience, henceforth we will use normalized bids x and r, which is s per unit of normalized bid. It is a summary index of firm 1's perceived information about its opportunity cost advantages or disadvantages relative to rivals, the aggressiveness of rival managements, and these managements' capabilities of perceiving similar situations and attitudes of their rivals.[5]

The existence of r (and s) is not recognized in competitive bidding theory as summarized in section 1. Consider, for example, the competitive bid derivation of firm 1's tender as depicted in figure 18.1. We graph $r(x)$ on

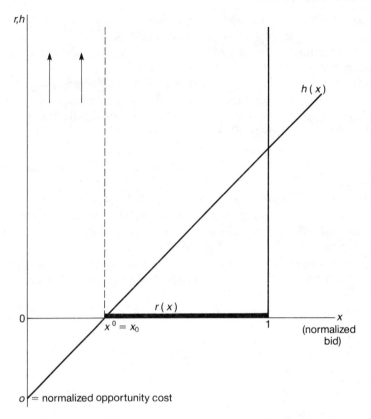

Figure 18.1 The firm's optimal bid in an identical cost industry.

the vertical axis as a function of x on the horizontal axis. The function $r(x) = f(x)/-f'(x)$ is drawn as quite large in the early phases since for very low bids firm 1 views $f(x)$ as close to 1 and $-f'(x)$ as close to zero. If all firms were viewed as having the same opportunity costs, then $r(x)$ would be near-infinite over the domain $x \in [0, x_0]$, with x_0 the normalized bid transformation of the common opportunity cost. At x_0 in this identical cost case $r(x)$ would fall discontinuously to the horizontal axis and then coincide with it in the interval $x \in [x_0, 1]$, on which domain $f(x) = 0$.

The normalized unit surplus function, $h(x) = x - [(v + m - L - \Delta E(\bar{\pi})/q)/(U - L)$, depicting the excess above costs any bid is in normalized units, is positively sloped at a unitary value and intersects the horizontal axis at normalized opportunity cost. In the identical cost case this would be at x_0, and firm 1 (and all firms) would find the intersection of $r(x)$ and $h(x)$ at x_0, with $r = 0$.

Figure 18.1 may also be used to depict the monopoly bid. In the interval $x \in [0, 1]$, r is "infinitely" large, then drops discontinuously to 0 at $x = 1$. The $h(x)$ function "intersects" $r(x)$ in this discontinuity and determines the optimal bid at $x^0 = 1$.

Figure 18.2, by contrast, depicts the more realistic oligopolistic decision process. The bid x_c is now firm 1's (normalized) opportunity cost, and $r(x)$ is depicted as negatively sloped. The optimal (normalized) bid, x^0, occurs where $h(x^0) = r(x^0)$, with $r^0 > 0$. From the definition of $r(x)$,

$$\frac{dr(x)}{dx} = \frac{f(x) \cdot f''(x)}{(f'(x))^2} - 1 = r\frac{f''(x)}{-f'(x)} - 1. \qquad (18.17)$$

In interpreting this expression it is useful to recall that $f''(x)$ is the (negative of the) slope of $-f'(x)$. The function $f(x)$ will typically be concave in its lower domain and convex in its upper domain, so that $-f'(x)$ will rise to a modal value (where $f''(x) = 0$) and fall from that value.

From (18.17), in the concave portion of $f(x)$, where $-f'(x)$ is rising, $dr/dx < 0$. Where $f(x)$ is convex, it is possible for $dr/dx \geqslant 0$. From (18.17),

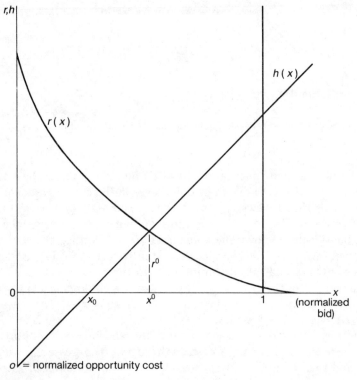

Figure 18.2   The oligopolistic firm's optimal bid.

$$\frac{dr(x)}{dx} \geqslant 0 \rightarrow \frac{f''(x)}{-f'(x)} \geqslant \frac{-f'(x)}{f(x)}. \tag{18.18}$$

That is, when the percentage fall in $-f'(x)$ is greater than or equal to the percentage fall in $f(x)$ as x rises, (18.18) will hold.

Consider, now, the Weibull approximations to the firms' perceived $f_j(x)$ functions. From (18.8), for firm 1,

$$r(x) = \left[\sum_j \frac{c_j}{a_j^{c_j}} x^{c_j - 1} \right]^{-1}, \tag{18.19}$$

and, suppressing identifying firm subscripts to reduce clutter,

$$\frac{dr(x)}{dx} = -r^2 \left[\sum_j \frac{c(c-1)}{a^c} x^{c-2} \right], \tag{18.20}$$

A sufficient condition for $dr(x)/dx = 0$ is that all $c_j = 1$, in which case all $G_j(x)$ (see 18.3) are the cumulative negative exponential function. From (18.8) then, $-f'(x)$ will be a negative exponential density function. The characteristic of such functions is that the equality of (18.18) holds, and $r(x)$ is a horizontal linear function. Of course, in this case, $f(x)$ is strictly convex on $x \in [0, \infty]$.

However, from (18.20) where all $c_j > 1$, $dr(x)/dx < 0$ as drawn in figure 18.2. Also,

$$\frac{d^2r(x)}{dx^2} = \frac{2(r'(x))^2}{r} - r^2 \left\{ \sum_j \frac{c(c-1)(c-2)}{a^c} x^{c-3} \right\}, \tag{18.21}$$

where r is the initial value of $r(x)$ and j-subscripts have been suppressed. When $1 < c_j \leqslant 2$, all j, $r(x)$ will be convex as drawn. When all $c_j > 2$, $r(x)$ can be shown to be convex as well.

As a last example, suppose $-f'(x)$ is a normal density function, and $\bar{x}$ is in terms of standard deviation units. Then

$$\frac{dr(\bar{x})}{d\bar{x}} = \bar{x}r - 1, \tag{18.22}$$

and $\bar{x}r$ reaches a maximum of 0.978 for $\bar{x} = +3.27$, well beyond the value where $f(\bar{x})$ attains 0.99. The function $r(x)$, therefore, is everywhere negatively sloped.

3 Parametric Displacement Analyses

To understand better the nature of the firm's decision-making, and as a prelude to the analysis of appropriate policy actions by government procurement officials to reduce r in bidders' tenders, it will be useful to analyse the impact of changes in a_j and c_j upon $r(x)$. Recall that these are the *perceptions* by firm 1 of the parameters of the probability density functions of firms j underlying firm 1's confidence-of-winning function $f(x)$.

3.1 Displacement of a Scale Parameter, a_k

Consider rival k's probability density function over x as given in (18.5) and as derived from firm 1's perceptions, with mode defined in (18.4) and

$$\text{Mean} = a_k \Gamma\left(\frac{c_k + 1}{c_k}\right) \qquad (18.23)$$

$$\text{Variance} = a_k^2 \left\{ \Gamma\left(\frac{c_k + 2}{c_k}\right) - \left[\Gamma\left(\frac{c_k + 1}{c_k}\right) \right]^2 \right\}.$$

The role of a_k is clear: when it is increased the mode and mean rise proportionately and the variance as the square of the factor of change. A rise in a_k "shifts" the distribution to the right, increasing the variance as a consequence of the enlarged scaling unit.

If firm 1 believes that firm k's level of confidence has risen generally or that its management has become somewhat less concerned to win the contract, perhaps because of increased demand in the private market, this may be depicted as a rise in a_k. If for every normalized bid x the probability that firm k will bid no more than x falls, the change may be interpreted as a rise in a_k, at least in relevant domains of x.

From (18.8),

$$\dot{f'}\big|_{a_k} = \frac{df(x)/da_k}{f(x)} = \frac{c_k}{a_k}\left(\frac{x}{a_k}\right)^{c_k} > 0. \qquad (18.24)$$

The perceived rise in a_k (and firm k's confidence) increases firm 1's expectations of winning with a bid x. Also,

$$-\dot{f'}\big|_{a_k} = \frac{d(-f'(x)/da_k)}{-f'(x)} = \frac{c_k x^{c_k-1} r}{a_k^{c_k+1}}(x - c_k r) \qquad (18.25)$$

$$= \dot{f'}\big|_{a_k} - \frac{c_k^2 x^{c_k-1} r}{a_k^{c_k+1}}$$

which is ambiguous as to sign. But

$$\dot{r}\big|_{a_k} = \frac{dr(x)/da_k}{r(x)} = \frac{c_k^2 x^{c_k-1}}{a_k^{c_k+1}} r = \dot{f}\big|_{a_k} - (-\dot{f}\big|_{a_k}) > 0. \qquad (18.26)$$

Hence, if $(-\dot{f}'|_{a_k})$ is positive it will be smaller in absolute size than $\dot{f}|_{a_k}$. A rise in a_k may increase the probability that dx will lose a bid for firm 1, but it will be swamped by the rise in firm 1's probability of winning with bid x. A rise in any or all a_j's in firm 1's field of perception will shift its $r(x)$ function upward in figure 18.2 and lead to a rise in its bid and its bidding surplus.

This proposition underscores an interesting aspect of the oligopolistic bidding context. Every oligopolistic bidder determines its own probability of winning the contract *indirectly* by formulating expectations of its rivals' attitudes and opportunities. Subject to the constraint of its opportunity cost and judgement of L and U, each rival formulates a bid as a composite reflection of others' perceived potential actions. Government contracting policies will impact a rival, therefore, not directly, but via their imagined impacts upon competitors. It is the anomaly of oligopolistic bidding in this probabilistic context that such *direct* reactions cannot occur, for there are no functions defining each firm's probability density functions over bids. Such functions have only a shadow existence in the expectations of rivals, since even that existence derives from the cumulative density functions subjectively perceived by those rivals.

3.2 Displacement of the Shape Parameter, c_k

The shape parameter, c_k, in a Weibull distribution permits the study of the impact of perceived changes in the variance of a rival's density function by firm 1 rather well, isolated from changes in the expected value of the function. Table 18.2 reveals the behavior of the expected value, the mode, and the variance of the $g_j(x)$ Weibull functions as c_j varies within relevant ranges with a_j constant.

Note from table 18.1 that the domain of c_j that seems most relevant for realistic choices of U and L is between 10 and 20. Over this domain the expected values and modes of the $g_j(x)$ maintain a rather constant absolute relationship and rise moderately in value as c_j rises with a_j constant. Most

Table 18.2 Values of expected value, mode, and variance of Weibull probability density functions for relevant c_j values

	c_j				
	2	4	10	15	20
Expected value	$0.8862a_j$	$0.9064a_j$	$0.9514a_j$	$0.9687a_j$	$0.9735a_j$
Mode	$0.71a_j$	$0.93a_j$	$0.99a_j$	$0.99a_j$	$0.99a_j$
Variance	$0.2146a_j^2$	$0.0647a_j^2$	$0.0131a_j^2$	$0.0103a_j^2$	$0.0036a_j^2$

notable, however, is the fall in variance that occurs over the interval. It is not possible to dissociate changes in c_j from changes in central tendency; however, the largest impact of changes in c_j with a_j constant is upon the variance of the distribution.

What does a rise in rival 1's perception of a single competitor's c_k do to its bid, when expected value does not change much but the variance contracts greatly about a somewhat larger mode? From (18.19)

$$\dot{r}\big|_{c_k} = \frac{dr(x)/dc_k}{r(x)} = \frac{-rx^{c_k-1}}{a_k^{c_k}}\left(1 + c_k[\ln x - \ln a_{kk}]\right). \qquad (18.27)$$

The $r(x)$ function of figure 18.2 "pivots" at $x_p = a_k e^{-c_k-1}$ with *ceteris paribus* changes in c_k.[6] To the left of this value $(x < x_p)$, the new $r(x)$ function lies above the old, so that if $h(x)$ intersects $r(x)$ in this region the bid and oligopoly surplus will rise. But for $x > x_p$ the new function will lie below the old, and x^0 and $r(x^0)$ will fall. From table 18.1, for $c_k \in [10, 20]$, a_k will range between 0.84 and 0.92, yielding values for x_p between 0.76 and 0.88. In most instances bids must be expected to occur above such levels, and, therefore, bids and surpluses to fall with a rise in any c_k.

Hence, even though a rise in c_k raises firm 1's expectation of the modal bid of firm k, and would be expected to raise firm 1's bid, the decrease in the variance of firm k's bidding density function overcomes this tendency for realistic bid values. The fall in the risk of losing with the bid enhancement is not large enough to outweigh the expected fall in $f(x)$:

$$\dot{f}\big|_{c_k} = \frac{df(x)/dc_k}{f(x)} = -\left(\frac{x}{c_k}\right)^{c_k}[\ln x - \ln a_k], \qquad (18.28)$$

so that for $x > a_k$, $f(x)$ falls.

It follows that decreases in the variance of firms' expectations of rivals' bidding density functions should reduce bids and the associated surplus if such firms receive accurate information about the maximum bid the government is willing to consider. Formally or informally this should be communicated to all potential bidders. Also, the publication of past winning and losing bids by the bidders may have this effect, for example, of reducing variance. In mature oligopolies, where rivals have had the opportunity to experience each others' bids and pricing policies over long periods, the variances of expected bidder density functions should be smaller than in newer industries, and hence should yield bids closer to opportunity costs with smaller oligopoly surpluses.

3.3 The Expected Value of Information

Suppose firm 1 were able to purchase information on rival k's bidding intentions. How would it value the information?

If the nature of the intelligence were simply whether or not firm k would bid, the answer is straightforward. If firm 1 has no additional information, its subjective view of firm k's intentions are included in $f(x)$ and optimal bid x^0 and unit surplus r^0 are as determined in (18.12) and on figure 18.2. If firm 1 knew that firm k would bid, then its own bid is unaltered at x^0 and *ex post facto* the information is of no value. If firm 1 learns that firm k will not bid, then the $r(x)$ function of figure 18.2 shifts upward, and the optimal bid rises to x^* with $r(x^*) = r^*$. *Ex post facto* the value of the information is $r^* - r^0$ (per unit of contract sales).

Firm 1's willingness to pay – given the risk neutrality we have assumed throughout – is the convex combination of the payoff in firm k bids times the probability of its bidding and the payoff of knowing firm k will not bid times the probability of that, or

$$\text{EVI (expected value of information)} = p \cdot 0 + (1 - p)(r^* - r^0),$$
(18.29)

where p is the perceived probability of firm k's bidding. If, *ex ante facto*, the best guess must be based on $g_k(x)$, then

$$\text{EVI} = \int_0^1 g(x) \cdot 0 \, dx + \int_1^\infty g(x)(r^* - r^0) \, dx.$$
(18.30)

For the Weibull formulation

$$\text{EVI} = e^{-a_k^{-c_k}}(r^* - r^{*0}).$$
(18.31)

This value may be termed the *exclusionary component* of the value of information, determined by the reduction in uncertainty the elimination of a bidder causes, as registered in other bidder's oligopoly surpluses and the perceived probability the rival will exclude himself.

Suppose, now, the information offered is x_k, rival k's bid. Let us assume that the cost of bidding for rival 1 is zero. The potential elimination of uncertainty by the exclusion of $g_k(x)$ from $f(x)$ will shift $r(x)$ upward to $r^*(x)$ as in the exclusionary component. However, this potential knowledge also will truncate $f(x)$ at x_k, rival k's potentially knowable bid, and $f(x) = 0$ for $x > x_k$.

Let x^* and $r^* = r^*(x^*)$ be the bid and expected oligopoly rent that would occur in the exclusionary component. The truncation effect must now be included as a *participating component* of the value of information. If $x_k < o$, firm 1's opportunity cost, firm 1 will leave the bidding and the value of the information will be zero. If $o \leqslant x_k < x^*$, then firm 1 must alter its bid to (slightly under) x_k, and the expected value of the information to firm 1 is $r(x_k)$. If $x_k > x^*$, firm 1's bid will be x^*, and the value of the information will be $r^* - r$.

In deciding whether to purchase the information, firm 1 must apply some probabilities that x_k lies within each of these regions, and, for the region $o \leqslant x_k < x^*$, probabilities for each potential bid. If its best available information is that encapsulated in $g_k(x)$, then EVI (the expected value of information) is

$$\text{EVI} = \int_0^o g_k(x) \cdot 0 \, dx + \int_o^{x^*} g_k(x) r^*(x_k) \, dx + \int_{x^*}^{\infty} g_k(x) (r^* - r^0) \, dx$$

$$= \int_o^{x^*} g_k(x) r^*(x_k) \, dx + \int_{x^*}^{\infty} g_k(x) (r^* - r^0) \, dx. \tag{18.32}$$

In the Weibull formulation,

$$\text{EVI} = \int_0^{x^*} \left[\frac{\dfrac{k_k}{a^{ck}} \left(\dfrac{x}{a_k}\right)^{c_k - 1} e^{-(x/a_k)^{c_k}}}{\Omega_{j \neq k} \dfrac{c_j}{a^{cj}} \left(\dfrac{x}{a_j}\right)^{c_j - 1}} \right] dx + e^{-(x^*/a_k)^{c_k}(r^* - r^0)} \tag{18.33}$$

which yields meagre results in this general form. If firm 1 has n rivals with $a_j = a, c_j = c$, for all j, and $c = 2$, then (18.33) simplifies to

$$\text{EVI} = \frac{a}{2(n-1)} \left(e^{-(o/a)^2} - e^{-(x^*/a)^2} + e^{-(x^*/a)^2} (r^* - r^0) \right). \tag{18.34}$$

4 Conclusion

More than two decades ago, Arrow wrote:

> With some inaccuracy, descriptions of uncertain consequences can be classified into two major categories, those which use exclusively the language of probability distributions and those which call for some other principle, either to replace or to supplement. The difference in viewpoints is related, though not perfectly, to the dispute between those who interpret probability as a measure of degree of belief (e.g., I. Fisher or Lord Keynes . . .) and those who regard probability as a measure (objective) of relative frequency . . . The latter concept clearly cannot encompass certain types of ignorance. [1], pp. 8–9.

He goes on to point out that if an event is to happen only once, the degree of belief interpretation is the only one acceptable.

I have argued in this paper that to move bidding theory into an oligopolistic context requires the acceptance of cumulative subjective probability functions as primitive constructs, much as consumer preferences are accepted as data in conventional theory. Bidding theory at the hands of economists suffers the same fate as general equilibrium analysis: a flight to the comforting confines of competitive analysis and its deceptive, faceless universals.

But buried deep within the Arrovian canon, suitably parenthesized (after all, this is Arrow, the future co-author with Hahn of *General Competitive Analysis*) and decades before the first light awakened some of us, is another significant insight of relevance to this last criticism:

> In my judgment, this will be an increasingly common situation in economic theory; broad general theorems of the kind we admire can usually only be found under undesirably restrictive conditions. What theory can imply in a broad range of cases is a computing algorithm. To test theory, then, we need econometric evidence or at least well-informed quantitative judgments as inputs into the computing process. [1]

This observation is peculiarly relevant to oligopoly analysis, whose distinctive feature is its *sui generis* essence. In this paper I have urged a step in the direction of moving the analysis of oligopolistic bidding toward operational frameworks by experimenting with flexible and manipulable probability functions that require a few obtainable observations. For some time I have believed that the measurement of power structures in oligopolistic industries is essential to the analysis of their pricing decisions. Indirectly, in oligopolistic bidding theory, that is also central to the determination of bids and their component rents, via subjective probability.

Notes

[1] We deal with a sealed bid procurement contract tender which awards the contract to the lowest bidder at its price, provided it is at or below the reservation price of the buyer. This is a *first-price* or *discriminatory* auction with a buyer reservation price.

[2] Alternatively, the value of the contract to all bidders is assumed to be identical and known to all as such.

[3] Compare Arrow's consumer: "the consumer cannot seriously be expected to write down in any explicit way his maximand. Rather the process of optimization consists of a series of comparisons among alternative ways of spending marginal dollars; the utility function is revealed to the consumer in the process" [1], p. 229. Insufficient attention has been devoted to deriving underlying objective functions that are being optimized unconsciously by an economic agent following intuitive rules of conduct.

[4] These costs and their inspired reluctance on the part of firms to bid on government contracts in periods of strong private economy demand or material shortages are well known to government contracting personnel. A recent experience was in the

petroleum shortage of 1979, when government purchasers of jet fuel confronted reluctant bidders with patriotic appeals and threats of invoking the Defense Production Act.

[5] Kortanek et al. [10] term a similar term a "competitive advantage fee." As indicated in the discussion, this does not adequately convey its origin in oligopoly structure, its perceptual basis, nor its functioning as an economic rent. Another interpretation of r is that it is the "force of survival," akin to the "forces of mortality" in reliability theory, in that in the neighborhood of a bid it measures the "cover" firm 1 has in raising its bid slightly.

[6] To a good approximation for values of c_k between 10 and 20, the mode of $g_k(x)$ approximates $a_k e^{-c_k \tau - 2}$. Hence,

$$x_p \approx \text{Mode}\left(\exp\left[-c_k^{-1}\left(1 - c_k^{-1}\right)\right]\right)$$

and, in the domain of c_k cited x_p will lie below the mode of the underlying density function for rival k.

References

[1] Arrow, K. J. *Essays in the Theory of Risk-Bearing*, Markham, Chicago, 1971.

[2] Attanasi, E. D. and S. R. Johnson, "Expectations, Market Structure, and Sequential Bid Pricing", *Southern Economic Journal*, 42 (1975), 18-32.

[3] —— "Sequential Bidding Models: a Decision Theoretic Approach", *Industrial Organization Review*, 14 (1977), 234-45.

[4] Baron, D. P., "Incentive Contracts and Competitive Bidding", *American Economic Review*, 62 (1972), 384-94.

[5] Engelbrecht-Wiggins, R., "Auctions and Bidding Models: a Survey", *Management Science*, 25 (1980), 1272-7.

[6] Friedman, L., "A Comparative Bidding Strategy", *Operations Research*, 4 (1956), 104-12.

[7] Harris, M. and A. Ravio, "Allocation Mechanisms and the Design of Auctions", *Econometrica*, 49 (1981), 1477-99.

[8] Harsanyi, J. C., "Games With Incomplete Information Played by 'Bayesian' Players", *Management Science*, 14 (1967), 159-82; 15 (1968) 320-34, 486-502.

[9] Holt, C. A. Jr, "Competitive Bidding for Contracts Under Alternative Auction Procedures", *Journal of Political Economy*, 88 (1980), 433-45.

[10] Kortanek, K. O., J. V. Soden and D. Sodaro, "Profit Analysis and Sequential Bid Price Models", *Management Science*, 20 (1973), 396-417.

[11] Kuhlman, J. M. and S. R. Johnson, "The Number of Competitors and Bid Prices", *Southern Economic Journal*, 50 (1983), 213-20.

[12] Milgrom, P. R., "Rational Expectations, Information Acquisition, and Competitive Bidding", *Econometrica* 49 (1981), 921-44.

[13] —— and R. J. Weber, "A Theory of Auctions and Competitive Bidding", *Econometrica*, 50 (1982), 1089-122.

[14] Pratt, J. W., "Risk Aversion in the Small and in the Large", *Econometrica*, 32 (1964), 122-36.

[15] Vickrey, W., "Counterspeculation, Auctions, and Competitive Sealed Tenders", *Journal of Finance*, 16 (1961), 8-37.

[16] Wilson, R., "Competitive Bidding With Asymmetrical Information", *Management Science*, 13 (1967), A816-20.

[17] ——, "Competitive Bidding With Disparate Information", *Management Science*, 15 (1969), 446-8.

[18] ——, "A Bidding Model of Perfect Competition", *Review of Economic Studies*, (1977), 511-18.

[19] ——, "Auctions of Shares", *Quarterly Journal of Economics*, 93 (1979), 675-98.

19

Uncertainty, Spatial Proximity, and the Stability of Oligopoly Pricing

1 Introduction

One of the commonplaces of spatial economic theory is that proximity heightens the interaction of economic agents and the interdependence among their decisions. Distance impedes the flow of goods and information, on the one hand, insulating economic actors against the undesirable consequences of competition and close monitoring of their decision environment, but on the other, interfering with their access to markets and information about rivals. Gravity and entropy models are macroincorporations of the intensifying interactions born of proximity. Diffusion models treat the interactions in microsystems as random processes, and spatial pricing models feature their enhanced competitive effects.

Oligopolistic price analysis is distinctive in that it features interdependence among the decisions of firms as well as interactions between firms and customers. A general theory of the net resultant of these interactions upon pricing strategies in oligopoly is an unwritten treatise in microeconomic theory. Spatial oligopoly behavior is an even more difficult subject for analysis – a missing chapter in the handbook.

One of the contributions to analytical complexity that springs from the intrusion of rivalrous interdependence is the important role played by information about the actions and intentions of rivals in oligopolistic pricing decisions. And because that information is in the largest part speculative and expectational, its introduction brings in its train the necessity to deal with uncertainty.

In this paper I attempt to apply uncertainty analysis to spatial oligopolistic pricing decisions in order to gain insight into a seeming departure from the general implication discussed above. If spatial proximity is expected to

Originally published in *Environment and Planning A*, 21 (1989), 1001–3, and reproduced with permission of Pion Limited.

increase price competition among firms, why in so many cases of oligopoly does it seem to leseen it? In the pricing behavior of local oligopolies providing goods and services, for example, with which we are all familiar, why is active competition so rare or confined to announced occasions of short duration ("sales")?

One thinks of price behavior among service stations; medical, legal, and real estate practices; department and other retail stores; supermarkets; banks; and so forth. Why are prices so similar and price movements so uniform in timing and extent? Can they be driven in such remarkably conformist fashion by marginal cost? Or can some partial explanations be found in the effects which spatial proximity exercise on the extent and nature of uncertainty as it affects information flows? In more general terms, does proximity tend to enhance the "rivalrous consonance of interests"[1] that dampens price competition in mature oligopolies?

My approach is limited in its ambition, as, I believe, any fruitful attempt to gain insights into oligopoly must be. In particular, it does not seek to endogenize two aspects of the firm's reasoning under uncertainty that other analysts believe should be endogenized. First, a primitive concept in the theory is a notional subjective probability function that characterizes a firm's probabilistic expectations of the pricing initiatives of a rival. That is, I hypothesize that firm 1 has subjective hunches about the propensity of firm 2 to initiate autonomous price changes. Those guesses spring from firm 1's knowledge of firm 2's management, firm 1's strength relative to other firms in the industry, its experience with the pricing history of firm 2, its familiarity with the cost structure of the industry, and so forth. I do not assert, of course, that firm 1 has an explicit well-defined probability density function which it consults in its pricing strategy. Rather, the assertion is that the fuzzy perceptions that firm 1 has about the likelihood of firm 2 initiating price changes can be approximated by such a function. The analogy with the consumer's utility function is an exact one. It too is the concoction of the economist in order to represent, for analytical convenience, a set of attitudes held by an individual toward consumer goods.

The analogy with the utility function holds in one other respect; the probability function represents attitudes which are taken as exogenous, and which are not to be explained by the model. My feeling is that any attempt to derive that probability function from assumptions about firm 1's attitude formation would be fruitless within the *sui generis* environment of oligopoly. Those who argue that such functions should be derived endogenously lament the loss of power which the theory suffers as a consequence. To be consistent, it seems to me that they should criticize the theory of consumption for failing to explain the formation of consumer attitudes to goods. Derivation of the latter should be considerably simpler than mapping the formative forces behind the subjective probability views of rivalrous firms.

Similarly, I accept the firm's probabilistic judgements of the induced price reactions of its rivals to its own autonomous price initiatives – that is, its probabilistic conjectural variation – as being exogenous for the same reasons. I do hypothesize about the relation of spatial proximity to the nature of such expectations, but these are only partial explanations of the state of the firm's views about the reactive potential of its rivals.

2 The Firm's Autonomous Expectations

For simplicity, but without sacrificing generality, I restrict the analysis to the case of duopoly. Firm 1 has at the start of the period an expected sales function, $E(X_1)$, which is assumed to be linear:

$$E(X_1) = a_1 - g_{11}p_1 + g_{12}E(p_2), \qquad a_1, g_{11}, g_{12} > 0, \qquad (19.1)$$

where $g_{12} = g_{12}(s_{12})$, with s_{12} being the distance between the firms, measured in some appropriate metric, and p_1 is firm 1's price. It is assumed, in accordance with conventional theory, that $dg_{12}/ds_{12} < 0$. E is the expectations operator. We assume that firm 1 has a constant unit cost, k_1, so that its expected profit function is,

$$E(\pi_1) = E(X_1)(p_1 - k_1),$$

which is to be maximized with respect to p_1. Differentiated products are implicit in the statement of equation (19.1), and these and selling costs are assumed to be constant during the analysis.

Two types of uncertainty confront firm 1 in planning its pricing decisions. The first concerns firm 2's autonomous price changes in the current period from its price set last period, p_2^*. The second concerns changes in its current price that would be made in response to firm 1's own autonomous price changes, or $E(dp_2/dp_1)$. This *reactive uncertainty* is frequently termed "conjectural variation."

$E(p_2)$ (hereafter $\bar{p}_2$) is taken to be the expected value of a subjective probability density function which exists implicitly in the consciousness of firm 1's decision-makers. This view has been discussed in section 1 with the goal of clarifying the content of the assumption. On the basis of its knowledge of the industry and of firm 2's relevant characteristics, firm 1's management formulates subjective expectations that can be translated into certain critical fractile values of the probability density function. In reality, the exact form of this density function, were it capable of being extracted from the attitudes of decision-makers, would be empirical, following no known form, and would be limited to a rather narrow relevant price domain.

I have assumed that it can be rather closely approximated in that relevant domain by the Weibull density function.

The Weibull distribution has certain features which recommend its use in the formal analysis of the decision process of firm 1. It is a two-parameter distribution of transcendental form:

$$f(p_2) = \frac{c_1 p_2^{c_1-1}}{b_1^{c_1}} \exp\left[-\left(\frac{p_2}{b_1}\right)^{c_1}\right], \qquad p_2 \in [0, \infty],$$

where b_1 is a *scale* parameter establishing the scale of measurement of the price fractiles, and c_1 is a *shape* parameter, determining most importantly the "peakedness" of the density function. In order to reduce notational clutter, I will suppress the subscripts 1 on b and c parameters where their reference to firm 1 is implicitly clear.

Through appropriate choice of c, a wide variety of configurations can be obtained from the Weibull function. When $c = 1$, it becomes the exponential probability density function, falling monotonically from a maximum value where the fractile equals zero. When $c = 2$, the Weibull function is the Rayleigh distribution. When $c \approx 3.34$, it approaches a bell-shaped curve.[2] One advantage of the Weibull function in its use in oligopoly analysis is that when $c > 3.34$, the mean of the distribution is less than the mode, and the Pearsonian coefficient of skewness (S) is negative,

$$S = \frac{\text{mean} - \text{mode}}{\sigma} = \frac{\bar{p}_2 - \hat{p}_2}{\sigma},$$

so the distribution is skewed moderately to the left. This is viewed as an advantage because I assume that, in situations of active oligopolistic rivalry, firm 1 will believe it more likely that firm 2 will reduce its price autonomously by a given amount than that it will increase it by that amount. Typically, I believe, there is a downward bias in firm 1's expectations of firm 2's autonomous price moves in active rivalry.

An instrumental advantage of the Weibull function is its ability to be manipulated mathematically, largely because of its simple structure. For example, its distribution function (or cumulative density function) has the form

$$F(p_2) = 1 - \exp\left[-\left(\frac{p_2}{b}\right)^c\right],$$

the inverse of which can be written as

$$\tilde{p}_\alpha = F^{-1}(\alpha) = b\left(\ln\frac{1}{1-\alpha}\right)^{1/c},$$

where α is a specified probability.

Consider now the subjective expectations of firm 1. It knows the price, p_2^*, set by its rival in the previous period. It is important to assume that the nature of firm 1's speculation about firm 2's autonomous price changes takes the form of estimating brackets within which firm 1 believes firm 2's price will fall with a certain level of confidence in the absence of any change in its own price. That is, firm 1 estimates a lower bound, $\tilde{p}_2^-$, and an upper bound, $\tilde{p}_2^+$, within which it is $100(2\alpha - 1)$ percent confident that firm 2's price will fall if p_1^* is unchanged. For the purpose of this analysis, I have set α equal to 0.95, and the lower and upper bounds on the interval may be written as ratios to p_2^*:

$$\tilde{p}_2^- = (1 - r_1^-)p_2^*, \qquad \tilde{p}_2^+ = (1 + r_1^+)p_2^*. \qquad (19.2)$$

If the implied notional subjective probability density function over this interval can be approximated by a Weibull distribution, then the b and c parameters of that function are defined from the inverse distribution function:

$$\left.\begin{array}{l} \tilde{p}_2^- = b\left[\ln\dfrac{1}{1 - 0.05}\right]^{1/c} = b(0.05129)^{1/c}, \\[3mm] \tilde{p}_2^+ = b\left[\ln\dfrac{1}{1 - 0.95}\right]^{1/c} = b(2.99573)^{1/c}. \end{array}\right\} \qquad (19.3)$$

With $\tilde{p}_2^-$ and $\tilde{p}_2^+$ known from equation (19.2), it follows from equation (19.3) that

$$c = 4.06745\left[\ln\frac{\tilde{p}_2^+}{\tilde{p}_2^-}\right]^{-1},$$

$$b = \tilde{p}_2^-/0.05129^{1/c} = \tilde{p}_2^+/2.99573^{1/c}.$$

I have termed $[\tilde{p}_2^-, \tilde{p}_2^+]$ the *range bracket* of firm 1's autonomous price expectations, and $\tilde{p}_2^+/\tilde{p}_2^-$ the *range ratio*. Note that the shape parameter, c, of the distribution is determined by the range ratio alone, given the probability level defining the range bracket. The scale parameter, b, is dependent on c and the limits of the range bracket.

If we assume that firm 1's expectation of firm 2's price if $p_1 = p_1^*$ (and if all other rivals do not change their prices) may be at least approximated by the expected value of the distribution[3], then firm 1's expectation is given by

$$\bar{p}_2 = b\Gamma\left(\frac{c + 1}{c}\right), \qquad (19.4)$$

where Γ is the gamma function. A good polynomial approximation to this gamma function [1] is the following:

$$\Gamma\left(\frac{c+1}{c}\right) \approx 1 - 0.5748646c^{-1} + 0.9512363c^{-2} - 0.6998588c^{-3}$$

$$+ 0.4245549c^{-4} - 0.1919678c^{-5} + \epsilon(c^{-1}), \quad (19.5)$$

where $|\epsilon(c^{-1})| \leqslant 5 \times 10^{-0.5}$. Therefore, in the analysis to follow

$$\bar{p}_2 \approx b(1 - 0.5748646c^{-1} + 0.9512363c^{-2} - 0.6998588c^{-3}$$

$$+ 0.4245549c^{-4} - 0.1010678c^{-5}) .$$

I define a mature oligopoly as one in which constituent firms form narrow range brackets on the autonomous price movements of their rivals, given the absence of exogenous impacts such as changes in cost conditions. I associate this gestalt with "maturity" because it tends to emerge when rivals have been conditioned by extensive experience with each other, perhaps after suffering painful learning episodes with price instability. Within spatial oligopolies whose rivals are in close proximity, such as those in the examples of local service industries cited, impacts of autonomous changes are quickly transmitted, information about rivals' attitudes and circumstances is readily available, and punishment for excessive autonomy is rather swift and personal.

Let us be more precise about realistic range brackets that might apply in mature oligopoly. I would suggest that changes of ±10 percent would set outer limits on autonomous change. In table 19.1 I have assumed that $p_2^* = 1$ and have listed eight range brackets within these limits in order to obtain values for b and c that are applicable to mature oligopoly, and in order to observe the $\bar{p}_2$ that results from the Weibull distributions defined by them.

Within this set of realistic range brackets, the c parameter varies between

Table 19.1   Representative range brackets for mature oligopoly autonomous price changes, with implied Weibull function parameters

Bracket	b	c	$\bar{p}_2(p_2^* = 1)$	σ	$V (=\sigma/p_2)$	A [a]	$\hat{p}_2$ [b]	S [c]
[0.97, 1.03]	1.01346	67.77049	1.00491	0.01920	0.01910	98.97	1.01324	−0.434
[0.95, 1.03]	1.00821	50.30729	0.99646	0.02520	0.02530	98.93	1.00781	−0.431
[0.95, 1.05]	1.02203	40.64058	1.00790	0.03181	0.03156	99.01	1.02140	−0.425
[0.97, 1.10]	1.06331	32.34054	1.04527	0.04085	0.03908	98.99	1.06228	−0.416
[0.90, 1.03]	0.99319	30.14728	0.97531	0.04030	0.04132	98.94	0.99208	−0.416
[0.95, 1.10]	1.05735	27.74457	1.03669	0.04671	0.04506	98.98	1.05595	−0.412
[0.90, 1.05]	1.00723	26.38620	0.98654	0.05130	0.05204	99.34	1.00576	−0.375
[0.90, 1.10]	1.04204	20.26928	1.01494	0.05805	0.05718	98.72	1.03944	−0.419

[a] Percent of area captured by $\bar{p} \pm 3\sigma$.
[b] Mode $= b(1 - 1/c)^{1/c}$.
[c] Pearson coefficient of skewness $\in [-1, +1]$.

20 and 70, with values between 40 and 50 for brackets of [0.95, 1.03] and [0.95, 1.05] which we would accept as typical of mature oligopolistic autonomous price change potentials in steady state conditions. When range brackets have greater downside than upside discrepancies from previous prices, then $\bar{p}_2 < p_2^*$, whereas when brackets are symmetrical about p_2^* or have greater upside unbalance, then $\bar{p}_2 > p_2^*$. In mature oligopoly, where we expect rivals to discount downside movements by their rivals, we assume bracket imbalance on the upside, and hence that firm 1 would adopt an expected value of p_2 that was greater than p_2^*. Rivals in mature oligopolies will therefore have expectations that normally rivals will be more likely to lift prices above present levels than to reduce them. Autonomous uncertainty therefore plays a type of phantom collusive role in this sense.

Within this realistic range of autonomous uncertainty, the coefficient of variation is between 2 and 6 percent so that standard deviation is a small proportion of expected value. The Weibull distribution in these precincts has a scatter close to that of the normal distribution, with the mean $\pm 3\sigma$ including about 99 percent of the area. In addition, in every case the mode exceeds the mean so that the distribution is skewed negatively to a moderate degree of -0.38 to -0.43.

My thesis is that the range ratio is positively correlated with distance, where

$$z_1 = z_1(s_{12}), \quad z_1' \frac{dz_1}{ds_{12}} > 0, \quad \frac{d^2 z_1}{ds_{12}^2} < 0,$$

$$z_1 = \frac{\bar{p}_2^+}{\bar{p}_2^-} = \frac{1 + r_1^+}{1 - r_1^-}.$$

Information flow and reluctance to act autonomously increase as distance decreases, and the expectations of rivals react accordingly. The impact of a reduction in distance is an increase in c:

$$\frac{dc}{dz_1} = - \left[\frac{(4.06745) z_1'}{z_1 (\ln z_1)^2} \right] < 0.$$

The rise in c increases the peakedness of the distribution and reduces the scatter of the distribution relative to the mean.

Further, I hypothesize that z_1 is narrowed primarily by upward movement of its lower bound. That is,

$$\left| \frac{d\bar{p}_2^l}{ds_{12}} \right| > \left| \frac{d\bar{p}_2^+}{ds_{12}} \right|. \tag{19.6}$$

Because $d\bar{p}_2^-/ds_{12}$ is negative, as distance falls $\bar{p}_2^-$ rises, and $d\bar{p}_2^+/ds_{12}$ may be positive or negative but is less in absolute value than $d\bar{p}_2/ds_{12}$. From equation (19.4)

$$1. \quad \frac{d\bar{p}_2}{d\tilde{p}_2^-} = b\frac{d\Gamma_1}{dc}\frac{dc}{d\tilde{p}_2^-} + \Gamma_1\frac{db}{d\tilde{p}_2^-},$$

$$2. \quad \frac{d\bar{p}_2}{d\tilde{p}_2^+} = b\frac{d\Gamma_1}{dc}\frac{dc}{d\tilde{p}_2^+} + \Gamma_1\frac{db}{d\tilde{p}_2^+},$$

(19.7)

where $\Gamma_1 = \Gamma[(c+1)/c]$.

Differentiation of equations (19.3) yields:

$$\frac{db}{d\tilde{p}_2^-} = 0.26975\,(0.05129)^{-1/c},$$

$$\frac{dc}{d\tilde{p}_2^-} = 0.24585b^{-1}c^2(0.05129)^{-1/c},$$

$$\frac{db}{d\tilde{p}_2^+} = 0.73025\,(2.99573)^{-1/c},$$

$$\frac{dc}{d\tilde{p}_2^+} = -0.24585b^{-1}c^2(2.99573)^{-1/c}.$$

From the approximation in equation (19.5),

$$\frac{d\Gamma_1}{dc} \approx 0.5748646c^{-2} - 1.9024726c^{-3} + 2.0995764c^{-4} - 1.6982196c^{-5}$$
$$+ 0.505339c^{-6}$$

(19.8)

Consider now equation (19.7-2):

$$\left.\begin{array}{l}
\dfrac{d\bar{p}_2}{d\tilde{p}_2^+} > 0, \quad \text{iff} \quad b\dfrac{d\Gamma_1}{dc}\dfrac{dc}{d\tilde{p}_2^+} + \Gamma_1\dfrac{db}{d\tilde{p}_2^+} > 0, \\[2ex]
\text{or} \quad \dfrac{1}{b}\dfrac{db}{d\tilde{p}_2^+} \Big/ \dfrac{dc}{d\tilde{p}_2^+} < -\dfrac{1}{\Gamma_1}\dfrac{d\Gamma_1}{dc}, \\[2ex]
\text{or} \quad -\dfrac{1}{b}\dfrac{2.97026}{0.05129^{1/c}}\dfrac{\tilde{p}_2^-}{c^2} < \dfrac{1}{\Gamma_1}\dfrac{d\Gamma_1}{dc}, \\[2ex]
\text{or} \quad 2.97026 > c^2\dfrac{1}{\Gamma_1}\dfrac{d\Gamma_1}{dc}.
\end{array}\right\}$$

(19.9)

But, from equations (19.5) and (19.8)

$$\frac{1}{\Gamma_1}\frac{d\Gamma_1}{dc} \approx 0.5748646c^{-2} - 1.5720033c^{-3} + 0.649055c^{-4}.$$

Substituting in the last inequality in relation (19.9) yields

$$\frac{d\bar{p}_2}{d\tilde{p}_2^+} > 0, \quad \text{iff} \quad 2.3953954c^2 + 1.5720033c - 0.6490553 > 0. \quad (19.10)$$

This inequality will be true for $c > 0.240$, so that for realistic values in mature oligopoly $d\bar{p}_2/d\tilde{p}_2^+ > 0$.

Also, evaluation of equation (19.7–2) reveals that

$$\frac{1}{\Gamma_1} \frac{d\Gamma_1}{dc} > 0,$$

where $c \notin [0.507, 2.228]$, so that $d\bar{p}_2/d\tilde{p}_2^- > 0$ in relevant domains of c. From these evaluations of equations (19.7) and (19.8) it follows that

$$\frac{d\bar{p}_2}{d\tilde{p}_2^-} - \frac{d\bar{p}_2}{d\tilde{p}_2^+} \approx (0.6490553 - 1.572003c - 0.52235c^2)(0.05129)^{1/c}$$
$$+ (0.6490553 - 1.572033c + 3.5451746c^2)(2.99573)^{1/c}, \quad (19.11)$$

which will be positive for the relevant interval $c \in [20, 70]$. Hence

$$\left(\frac{d\bar{p}_2}{dp_2^-} \frac{d\tilde{p}_2^-}{ds_{12}}\right) - \left(\frac{d\bar{p}_2}{d\tilde{p}_2^+} \frac{d\tilde{p}_2^+}{ds_{12}}\right) < 0,$$

when $dp_2^+/ds_{12} < 0$ and when $dp_2^+/ds_{12} > 0$ and inequality (19.6) holds.

The net impact of proximity upon autonomous uncertainty under such expectations is, therefore, to increase the expected value of the rival's price in current decision-making. In terms of the density function, c increases to make it more peaked, and b rises to shift it to the right. Moreover, the relative dispersion of the function, as measured by the coefficient of variation, V, falls, for

$$V = \frac{\sigma}{\bar{p}_2} = \left(\frac{\Gamma_2}{\Gamma_1^2} - 1\right)^{1/2},$$

where $\Gamma_2 = \Gamma[(c+2)/c]$.

Since

$$\left(\frac{c+2}{c}\right) \approx 1 - 1.1497292c^{-1} + 3.8049452c^{-2} - 5.5988704c^{-3}$$
$$+ 6.7928784c^{-4} - 3.2341696c^{-5}, \quad (19.12)$$

and

$$\frac{dV}{dc} = 0.5\left(\frac{\Gamma_2}{\Gamma_1^2} - 1\right)^{1/2}\left(\frac{1}{\Gamma_1^2}\frac{d\Gamma_2}{dc} - \frac{2\Gamma_2}{\Gamma_1^3}\frac{d\Gamma_1}{dc}\right),$$

it follows that

$$\frac{\mathrm{d}V}{\mathrm{d}c} < 0, \qquad \text{iff} \quad \frac{\Gamma_2}{\Gamma_1}\frac{\mathrm{d}\Gamma_1}{\mathrm{d}c}\bigg/\frac{\mathrm{d}\Gamma_2}{\mathrm{d}c} > 0.5, \qquad (19.13)$$

or, from approximations in expressions (19.5) and (19.12)

$$\frac{\mathrm{d}V}{\mathrm{d}c} < 0, \qquad \text{iff} \quad (1 - 0.5748646c^{-1} + 2.52324c^{-2})$$
$$\times\ (0.5 + 1.65471c^{-1} + 5.47386c^{-2}) > 0.5.$$

But the left-hand side of the inequality approaches 0.5 from above as $c \to \infty$, so that V falls as the range ratio falls in the indicated manner because of increased proximity.

It is interesting in this scheme of translating the implications of uncertainty that the expected values of rivals' prices will typically depart from their going values. Expectations of autonomous price increases are endemic to formation of price strategy by virtue of uncertainty. A continuous force is acting to upset the status quo. In mature oligopoly we expect that these departures will be proportionately small but biased upward, so that rivals are expected to lift prices slightly, unless the lower limit of the range bracket is quite low relative to the upper.

Proximity, primarily via enhanced information flow, tends to reduce the range ratio by raising the lower bound. This reinforces the tendency of expected rival prices to rise above going price, reduces the relative scatter of the density function over rival prices, and makes it more peaked.

3 The Firm's Reaction Expectations

The second component of firm 1's uncertainty is that induced by its own autonomous price actions. This is encompassed in the well-known *conjectural variations* of oligopoly theory that are the focus of the uncertainty analysis in standard approaches. The manner in which I shall incorporate these expectations is to assume that firm 1 has determinate expectations of the way in which its price actions impact the bounds on the range bracket, and that those expectations are functions of proximity:

$$\frac{\mathrm{d}\tilde{p}_2^-}{\mathrm{d}p_1} = m_1^-\,(s_{12}), \quad \frac{\mathrm{d}\tilde{p}_2^+}{\mathrm{d}p_1} = m_1^+\,(s_{12}).$$

These expectations are then used to determine changes in b and c in its density function, which in turn alter $\bar{p}_2$.

In mature oligopolistic industries, where autonomous uncertainty is contained within narrow bounds, reactive uncertainty can be expected to dominate autonomous uncertainty. For given promixity values, firm 1 treats firm

2's induced reaction as (locally) a constant proportion of its price-change initiatives.

By differentiating equation (19.3), we obtain

$$
\begin{bmatrix} 0.05129^{1/c} & 2.97026(0.05129)^{1/c}\,bc^{-2} \\ 2.99573^{1/c} & -1.09719(2.99573)^{1/c}\,bc^{-2} \end{bmatrix} \begin{bmatrix} db \\ dc \end{bmatrix} = \begin{bmatrix} d\tilde{p}_2^- \\ d\tilde{p}_2^+ \end{bmatrix},
$$

the solution of which yields

$$
\begin{bmatrix} db \\ dc \end{bmatrix} = \begin{bmatrix} 0.26975 & 0.73025 \\ 0.24585b^{-1}c^2 & -0.24585b^{-1}c^2 \end{bmatrix} \begin{bmatrix} (0.05129)^{-1/c}d\tilde{p}_2^- \\ (2.99573)^{-1/c}d\tilde{p}_2^+ \end{bmatrix}
$$

Therefore

$$
\left.
\begin{aligned}
\frac{db}{dp_1} &= \left(\frac{0.26975 m_1^-}{0.05129^{1/c}} + \frac{0.73025 m_1^+}{2.99573^{1/c}} \right), \\
\frac{dc}{dp_1} &= 0.24585 b^{-1} c^2 \left(\frac{m_1^-}{0.05129^{1/c}} - \frac{m_1^+}{2.99573^{1/c}} \right),
\end{aligned}
\right\}
\tag{19.14}
$$

which identify the impacts of reactive uncertainty upon firm 1's subjective probability density function over p_2.

My hypothesis is that in a mature oligopoly m_1^- and m_1^+ will be positive, with $m_1^- > m_1^+$. Firm 1 will feel some assurance that if it raises p_1, firm 2 will not reduce price and will tend to take large proportionate advantage of the opportunity to follow suit. The lower bound of the bracket would tend to rise more than the upper, in that firm 1 will be less confident in believing that firm 2 will surpass its price rise.

I further hypothesize that spatial proximity, fostering the flow of information, will narrow $m_1^+ - m_1^-$, primarily by raising m_1^-. Hence

$$
\frac{d(m_1^+ - m_1^-)}{ds_{12}} > 0,
$$

$$
\frac{dm_1^-}{ds_{12}} < 0, \qquad \frac{dm_1^+}{ds_{12}} \geqslant 0;
$$

$$
\left| \frac{dm_1^-}{ds_{12}} \right| > \frac{dm_1^+}{ds_{12}}.
$$

With s_{12} fixed, it follows from equation (19.14) that $db/dp_1 > 0$, and $dc/dp_1 > 0$, since $m_1^-/m_1^+ > 1$. Also, from relation (19.13) $dV/dp_1 < 0$, so that relative dispersion will fall. From relation (19.11)

$$\frac{d\tilde{p}_2}{dp_1} = \frac{d\bar{p}_2}{d\bar{p}_2^-} m_1^- - \frac{d\bar{p}_2}{d\tilde{p}_2^+} m_1^+ > 0, \qquad c \in [20, 70].$$

Therefore, reactive uncertainty under conditions of close spatial proximity acts to increase $E(p_2)$ above the value determined by autonomous uncertainty. It enhances firm 1's willingness to increase prices above the level that autonomous expectations would. The general bias toward price rise in the industry is given a substantial boost by this second form of uncertainty.

4 The Firm's Maximum Expected Profits and Reaction Function

Consider the firm's expected profit function defined in equation (19.1) and the first-order conditions necessary for its maximization:

$$\frac{dE(\pi_1)}{dp_1} = E(X_1) + (p_1 - k_1) \left[-g_{11} + g_{12} \left(\Gamma_1 \frac{db}{dp_1} + b \frac{d\Gamma_1}{dc} \frac{dc}{dp_1} \right) \right]$$

$$= E(X_1) + (p_1 - k_1) \left\{ -g_{11} + g_{12} \left[\Gamma_1 \left(\frac{0.26975m_1^-}{0.05129^{1/c}} + \frac{0.73025m_1^+}{2.99573^{1/c}} \right) \right. \right.$$

$$\left. \left. + 0.24585c^2 \left(\frac{m_1^-}{0.05129^{1/c}} - \frac{m_1^+}{2.99573^{1/c}} \right) \frac{d\Gamma_1}{dc} \right] \right\}$$

$$= 0.$$

This can be rewritten as

$$\frac{E(X_1) - (p_1 - k_1)g_{11}}{- (p_1 - k_1)g_{12}} = \frac{d\bar{p}_2}{dp_1}$$

$$= \frac{m_1^-}{0.05129^{1/c}} \left(0.26975\Gamma_1 + 0.24585c^2 \frac{d\Gamma_1}{dc} \right)$$

$$+ \frac{m_1^+}{2.99573^{1/c}} \left(0.73025\Gamma_1 - 0.24585c^2 \frac{d\Gamma_1}{dc} \right).$$

$$(19.15)$$

Let $R_1^- = m_1^-/\tilde{p}_2^-$, and $R_1^+ = m_1^+/\tilde{p}_2^+$, or the proportionate changes in the range-bracket bounds. As a result of the approximations in relations (19.5) and (19.8), it follows that

$$\frac{d\bar{p}_2}{dp_1} \approx [R_1^-(0.41108 - 0.62779c^{-1} + 0.25660c^{-2})$$

$$+ R_1^+ (0.58892 + 0.04793c^{-1} + 0.69464c^{-2})]$$

$$\times \left(\frac{\bar{p}_2}{1 - 0.57486c^{-1} + 0.95124c^{-2}} \right). \tag{19.16}$$

For our limiting cases,

$$\left. \begin{array}{ll} c = 20: & \dfrac{d\bar{p}_2}{dp_1} \approx (0.39089R_1^- + 0.60911R_1^+)\bar{p}_2, \\[3mm] c = 70: & \dfrac{d\bar{p}_2}{d\bar{p}_1} \approx (0.40549R_1^- + 0.59451R_1^+)\bar{p}_2, \end{array} \right\} \tag{19.17}$$

Thus the proportionate change in $\bar{p}_2$ caused by induced uncertainty approx-imates a convex combination of proportionate changes in the range-bracket bounds, in which such changes are weighted by about 0.4 with respect to lower and 0.6 with respect to upper bounds.

To interpret expressions (19.15) to (19.17) let us rewrite equation (19.5) as

$$[E(X_1) - (p_1 - k_1)g_{11}] + \left[(p_1 - k_1)g_{12}\frac{d\bar{p}_2}{dp_1} \right] = 0. \tag{19.18}$$

The expression in the first set of brackets is marginal profit when firm 1 takes only autonomous uncertainty into account. The term in the second set of brackets is the marginal profit as a result of firm 1 taking reactive uncertainty into account.

Expanding by means of equation (19.1), we obtain

$$p_1^0 = \left[a_1 + g_{11}k_1 + \bar{p}_2 - g_{12}k_1\frac{d\bar{p}_2}{dp_1} \right] / \left(2g_{11} - g_{12}\frac{d\bar{p}_2}{dp_1} \right). \tag{19.19}$$

The impact of proximity on p_1^0, the optimal p_1, is

$$\frac{dp_1^0}{ds_{12}} = \left(2g_{11} - g_{12}\frac{d\bar{p}_2}{dp_1} \right)^{-1}$$

$$\times \left[\bar{p}_2\frac{dg_{12}}{ds_{12}} + (p_1^0 - k_1)\frac{dg_{12}}{ds_{12}}\frac{d\bar{p}_2}{dp_1} + (p_1^0 - k_1)g_{12}\frac{d^2\bar{p}_2}{dp_1\,ds_{12}} + g_{12}\frac{d\bar{p}_2}{ds_{12}} \right]. \tag{19.20}$$

From equation (19.18) it is easily seen that the multiplicative factor in equation (19.20) is positive and that by assumption, all of the terms in brackets are negative. Hence, $dp_1^0/ds_{12} < 0$, so a fall in the distance sepa-rating two rivals raises the equilibrium prices set by rivals in duopoly under uncertainty.

This price enhancement is the result of three independent effects of spatial proximity:

1 The closer rival 2 is to rival 1, the greater the response of demands to changes in other prices. This reflects the classic competitive effect of proximity and acts to reduce expected price.
2 The closer rival 2 is to rival 1, the less uncertain will be autonomous price movements of rivals, and the higher expected prices will be on this account.
3 The closer rival 2 is to rival 1, the smaller will reactive uncertainty be (especially with respect to potential price reductions), and the higher expected prices will be.

Equation (19.19) is the firm's reaction function, R_{1u}, when both autonomous and reactive uncertainty are incorporated into firm 1's strategies. Although it is nonlinear in structure, it may be depicted as approximately linear for the purposes of our presentation. It may be contrasted with the reaction function derived from the expected profit function under conditions of certainty, when firm 1 assumes p_2 will be set at p_2^*:

$$p_1^c = \frac{a_1 + g_{11}k_1}{2g_{11}} + 0.5\frac{g_{12}}{g_{11}}p_2^*,$$

which we will term R_1^c, or the firm's reaction function under certainty.

By setting $d\bar{p}_2/dp_1 = 0$ in equation (19.15), we may eliminate reactive uncertainty but keep autonomous uncertainty in the first-order condition, to obtain R_{1a}, the reaction function of firm 1 under autonomous uncertainty only:

$$p_1^a = \frac{a_1 + g_{11}k_1}{2g_{11}} + 0.5\frac{g_{12}\bar{p}_2}{g_{11}}$$

$$= \frac{a_1 + g_{11}k_1}{2g_{11}} + 0.5\frac{g_{12}(1 - r_1^-)}{0.05129^{1/c}}\frac{c + 1}{c}.$$

The impact of the two types of uncertainty upon reaction functions is shown in figure 19.1. Corresponding reaction functions for the three cases are assumed for firm 2. R_{1c} and R_{2c} depict the responses of $p_{i,t}^*$ to $p_{j,t-1}^*$ when both firms assume that their rivals will hold price constant. The certainty equilibrium is at point C on the figure. For a given spatial proximity, s_{12}, R_{1a}, and R_{2a} represent the functions when both firms take into account autonomous uncertainty only. The rotations from R_{1c} and R_{2c} are drawn as relatively small for reasons developed in section 2, but because such uncertainty raises the expected value of rivals' prices, at any $p_{j,t-1}^*$ value firm 1 will react with a larger $p_{i,t}^*$ than it would under certainty. Prices will

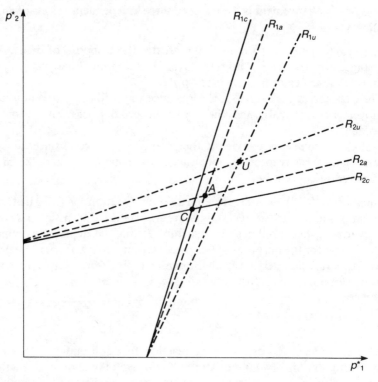

Figure 19.1 Reaction functions under conditions of autonomous and reactive uncertainty.

therefore tend to A, at which point both firms' prices are higher than at C. Last, functions R_{1u} and R_{2u} incorporate reactive uncertainty in close spatial proximity. The equilibrium price pair at U is the full uncertainty equilibrium with prices substantially above C and A price pairs.

As shown in equation (19.20), as s_{12} falls and proximity increases, R_{1a} and R_{1u} pivot in the direction of higher prices, if my analysis is correct. This raises the question of whether some of the motivating factors for the normal agglomeration of local retail outlets in shopping malls, or of service stations at traffic intersections, or of professional practitioners in professional buildings, may be the enhancement of information flow among rivals, the reduction which this brings about both in autonomous and in reactive price uncertainty, and the favorable price effects consequently enjoyed by all as a result.

5   Some Necessary Refinements

In this paper I have attempted to introduce the impact of uncertainty on oligopolistic pricing strategies in a simple but realistic way, using the notion of subjective probability and α probability intervals as encapsulating the strategy modes of rivals. The impact of such intervals upon the expected values of rivals' prices is the medium for transmission of uncertainty of price strategies.

One limitation of the paper is that the application of proportionality factors to going prices in order to derive such intervals exogenizes a process that should be responsive to historical experience. The factors r_i^-, r_i^+, m_i^-, and m_i^+ should vary with historical experience with rivals, these intervals tending to narrow if the spatially induced expected price stability does materialize. The intervals can never be expected to close completely, but should narrow, with the result that autonomous uncertainty should be lessened (R_{ia} should approach R_{ic} more closely in figure 19.1) although the impact of reactive uncertainty may be enhanced as both m_i^- and m_i^+ rise.

This need points up, perhaps, the ultimately dynamic nature of the adjustment process and the potential need to construct explicit dynamic models to depict the operation of the factors at work. I must confess to a basic skepticism about the usefulness of dynamic models in oligopoly analysis, despite the debate that rages about the usefulness of static model depictions of adjustment. Generally, it is the nature of the equilibrium that is of primary interest in the oligopoly problem, the process of its attainment being of secondary interest unless it affects the nature of that equilibrium. It seems to me that most dynamic models, when compared with their static counterparts, do not really demonstrate fundamental differences in the nature of the equilibria toward which they converge. The interest of the models in inherent in the trajectory of prices through time, and the nature of the trajectory is dependent upon the rigid specifics of the dynamic model adopted. In my opinion, one crosses into territory with more rigid demands in order to analyze phenomena of lesser concern which do not alter in essential respects the phenomena of primary concern.

I, and many others, have reservations about using expected values as unidimensional summaries of the effect of the uncertainty scatter of prices about the going price. The question is an empirical one: does the firm tend to design its stretegies *as if* it treated the expected value as a certainty equivalent? Or does it come closer to using the median or mode? Or does risk aversion bias it toward some value in the lower portion of the range interval? Surely the standard deviation of the subjective probability density function enters into the determination of a planning price in more subtle ways than merely affecting expected value. We continue to search for more satisfying measures and interpretations.

In conclusion, I suspect that oligopolistic tacit cooperation operates even more effectively than I have suggested in this paper which has concentrated on the roles of space and uncertainty. I have presented at some length elsewhere [2] the concept of "rivalrous consonance," or the theory that oligopolistic competition is in general a mixture of competition and cooperation which can be described by models in which each rival takes the profits of other firms into account in his or her profit-maximization strategies. That theory could be extended to the present case, but would prolong the paper unduly and obscure its central theses.

Notes

[1] The term denotes a pervasive consciousness among rivals that they form a community within which their interests at once converge and diverge. Relations among them are, therefore, mixtures of rivalry and cooperation, as determined by the number of firms, the nature of the products, personalities within the industry, and the flow of information. From the complex of such factors emerges a "power structure" which must be incorporated in models of price determination for the industry.

[2] It is well known that the Weibull distribution is a close approximation to the normal distribution of $c \approx 3.34$, although if interest focuses upon the tails of the normal distribution, slightly different c values are appropriate. It will be shown that the standard deviation of the Weibull distribution is close to that of the normal distribution for a wide domain of c values.

[3] Like many economists, I am suspicious about the reality of expected value reasoning, an argument I develop further in section 4. I follow the conventional procedure in the absence of a more convincing alternative.

References

[1] Hastings, J.R.C., *Polynomial Approximations for Digital Computers*, Princeton University Press, Princeton, NJ, 1955.
[2] Kuenne, R.E. *Rivalrous Consonance: a Theory of General Oligopolistic Equilibrium*, North-Holland, Amsterdam, 1986.

20

Conflict Management and the Theory of Mature Oligopoly

1 Introduction

In a decision process based wholly upon self-interest, community maturity is the product of a variety of factors, among which the following seem important:

1 The attainment of assured positions within the community of similarly situated rivals.
2 Rapid and extensive flows of information among rivals concerning their autonomous actions.
3 An assurance of rapid responses by rivals to one's autonomous actions with the potential to neutralize anticipated gains or render them negative in prospect.
4 Risk-averse attitudes by rivals to autonomous actions that may directly or indirectly threaten seriously their assured positions within the community.
5 A sufficient time span of coexistence to assure rivals of the indefinite maintainability of these community characteristics.

Within such communities egoistic rivalry tends to be tempered by attempts to establish mechanisms of tacit or overt cooperation. The mechanisms create an environment of restrained competition which, to use John Rawls's felicitous phrase, is motivated not by altruism but by prudence. When we relax the assumption that actors are driven solely by self-interest, and permit communitarian attitudes of pride and collective concern to intrude, these drives to cooperate may also incorporate a component that transcends narrow egoism.

This paper discusses two mechanisms which I believe operate in mature oligopolistic market structures to institute mixtures of rivalry and tacit

Originally published in *Conflict Management and Peace Science*, 10 (1988), 37–57, and reproduced with permission.

cooperation with respect to pricing policies. Within the oligopolistic market structure such mutually interdependent but independent strategy choices must be exercised in conflict management, and they are fruitfully approached as such. Unfortunately, the economist's occupational bias toward competitive processes and neglect of the communitarian matrices within which such processes occur have led to a neglect of the implicit cooperative impulses that move beneath the surface of such processes.

The first of such mechanisms is the response of mature oligopoly incumbents to uncertainty. Employing a subjective probability approach, I analyze the impacts of uncertainty about rivals' *autonomous* and *reactive* pricing decisions upon a firm's own decisions. It will be shown that under specific assumptions about the nature of a firm's probabilistic reasoning such uncertainty serves as a facilitator of tacit collusion, thereby aiding the conflict management function. This presentation is made in section 3.

My belief that tacit pricing cooperation in mature oligopoly is more deeply rooted that this probabilistic reasoning leads to the analysis of the second mechanism. The recognition of a "rivalrous consonance of interests" comes to pervade the mature oligopoly, and rivals shape their pricing strategies to take the welfare of their fellow incumbents as well as their own into account. The industry's interdependence of pricing decisions reflects a mixture of the competitive and the tacitly cooperative, providing a rich mine of experience in conflict management. Section 4 presents a flexible framework with which to analyze the interplay of pricing strategies within such a context.

Section 2 provides a brief introduction to the economist's methodology for dealing with conflict management and the peculiar problems in this regard presented by the oligopolistic market structure. Finally, section 5 contains a summary of the analyses and conclusions drawn from them.

2 The Economist's Models of Conflict Management

Economists who specialize in the pricing mechanisms of capitalism are, and are of right to be, students of conflict. The conflict of wills among economic agents occurs within markets and is of two forms: *competition*, when the actors on either side of the market vie with one another, and *bargaining*, when they clash across sides. The self-interest of every buyer clashes at once with that of every other buyer and of every seller, and the egoistic drives of such seller force similar orientations upon him or her. The context is the Hobbesian war of all against all.

The mechanisms of the market may be depicted as resolvers of conflict in this disintegrated battlefield in two sets of circumstances, and economists, in their quest for generalizable, determinate resolutions have been fond of both. The first occurs in conditions where the economic power over price is atomized, so that no agent on either side can take actions that have percep- tible impacts on the outcome of the conflict. Anonymous, faceless, unconcerted competiton and bargaining bring about a stalemate which no actor has the motive or power to disrupt. Diplomacy, strategy, alliance, compromise, imposition of will – terms that are familiar in arenas of human conflict – are irrelevant here. The equilibrium is a balance of powerlessness, the implications of which are acquiesced in by impotent actors.

The second set of circumstances occurs when one side of the market retains the atomistic structure just discussed, but a single agent on the other side attains unilateral power over price. The monopolist (or monopsonist) imposes a resolution by dictating a price of his choosing and offering to sell (buy) all of the good demanded at that price. Bargaining is eliminated and competition ineffective in the face of rigid prices.

Conflict resolution models of these types, fitting the purely competitive, monopolistically competitive, monopolistic, and monopsonistic market structures, are of dominant interest to economic theorists because their extreme assumptions concerning the distribution of power among agents permit them to be treated as anonymous automata motivated by a single simplistic goal within a socio-historical matrix of no consequence.

Such abstractions have relevance to a few realistic markets, it is true, and their dominance in economic theory has contributed to economists' sense of their distinctive professionalism. But the cost has been an isola- tion from other social sciences which must cope with the multi-objective strivings of goal-driven human agents in realistic contexts where power structures are endogenously determined. The economist's disinterest in such arenas of conflict has led him to a single-minded concern with the *efficiency* of conflict resolutions, which can be treated in a depersonalized fashion, and to a disdain for the *equity* of such resolutions, which cannot be so treated.

But there is one market structure which the economist realizes cannot be analyzed in such antiseptic manners – that of oligopoly. Unfortunately, much as he tries to hide the fact from his professional self it is the structure of dominant realistic relevance. Conflict occurs among rivals with signifi- cant but unequal power over price, these power structures change with per- sonality changes, a set of folkways and mores emerges in the industry, and subtle mixtures of conflict and cooperation develop over time. Multiple objectives, varying among the rivals, must be accommodated by the analysis, and such dimensions as potential entry, product and selling cost competi- tion, and the appeal to political power for industry support complicate the struggle on the market's playing field.

Fortunately, economists are devoting more effort to the analysis of con- flict in oligopoly. Game-theoretic approaches dominate the field, but one can quarrel with their bias toward searching for generalizable solutions using techniques that perpetuate the economist's abstraction from the socio-psychological dimensions. That bias leads to an overemphasis upon the competitive mechanisms active in conflict resolution at the expense of the subtler forces that temper rivalry with tacit cooperation and compromise. But for those who welcome the economist's interest in conflict resolution in contexts where realistic power structures, diplomacy, predation, tacit collusion, alliance, strategy, cultural folkways, conjectural uncertainty, and the force of personality are active factors, some rejoicing for his or her coming of age is in order.

This paper is a modest attempt to study some of the forces that restrain rivalrous competition in conditions of mature oligopoly. By that term – which I have attempted to define in section 1 – I mean to identify an industry whose major rivals have coexisted for long periods, so that each firm has had extensive experience with every other, and the information flows among them are rapid and unimpeded. In the absence of exogenous shocks, such industries can be expected to develop means of *conflict management* that permit a basic stability in prices and smoothness in price adjustment that escape less settled oligopolies.

My interest in such industries is in the study of (1) the nature of the balance between competition and cooperation that characterizes its price equilibrium, (2) the forces that inhere in such structures that facilitate the emergence of these resolutions, and (3) the development of techniques that capture the reaction patterns occurring in the structure and yield insights into the nature of the equilibria.

In section 3, I investigate the role that uncertainty may play in a mature oligopoly to stabilize the price structure, or, more accurately, give it a gentle upward momentum. To do so I employ the notion of a subjective probability density function over rivals' prices to analyze both autonomous and induced uncertainty.

3 The Role of Uncertainty

In its pricing decision the oligopolistic firm is susceptible to two types of uncertainty. The first is *autonomous* uncertainty, or the variance about rivals' going prices from which the current period realization of price will emerge. Rivals may act independently to alter their prior period's prices and so upset the industrial price structure. The second is *induced* uncertainty: i.e. rival i's expectations of rival j's reaction to rival i's autonomous price changes, or probabilistic conjectural variation.

I assume that firms begin the current period knowing rivals' last-period prices as parameters, and, in the face of both types of uncertainty, fix their prices for the current period. Firms' adjustments to rivals' actual prices during the current period will be made in the next period. This period's prices are determined by maximizing expected profits with autonomous and induced uncertainty components. The techniques I employ in this paper seek to unify the treatment of both types of uncertainty through the use of a subjective probability function over a rival's autonomous price changes. The parameters of that function are modified by that rival's anticipated induced reactions to the firm's own autonomous price initiatives.

3.1 The Subjective Probability Density Function

I hypothesize that firm 1's management has subjective hunches about its rivals' autonomous price changes in the current period, based upon its knowledge of industry costs; its familiarity with rivals' managements and their revealed objectives; its perception of the industry's power structure in the sense of precedence and deference in pricing decisions; and its experience with rivals' actions in previous periods. I further assume that these visceral expectations could be concretized as a subjective probability function with primary relevance over some relatively narrow domain of prices in a neighbourhood of going price.

The function is notional, in that it is not asserted that the firm actually consults such a density function in its decision-making, but rather that its expectations could be so formalized with appropriate interrrogation. In this sense the analogy with standard consumer utility functions is exact. In reality such formalizations, were they performed, would be likely to yield empirical density functions which are not exactly describable by standard functional forms. However, in the analysis to follow, I will assume that a sufficiently close approximation to the empirical function depicting firm i's expectations of firm j's price intentions in relevant domains will be given by the Weibull density function:

$$f_i(p_j) = (c_i p_j^{c_i-1}/b_i^{c_i})e^{-(p_j/b_i)^{c_i}}, \quad p_j \in [0, \infty]. \tag{20.1}$$

Henceforth, to simplify the analysis but without loss of generality, I will treat only the case of duopoly with firms 1 and 2, and will depict firm 1's decision process unless otherwise noted. Firm 2's reasoning will be symmetrical. Further, to reduce notational clutter, I will suppress the subscript 1 when reference to firm 1 is clear from the context.

The Weibull distribution is chosen for several reasons. First, it is a two parameter distribution with a *scale* parameter (b) and a *shape* parameter (c), which can be easily fitted to information concerning firm 1's expectations. A location parameter may also be specified, but we will assume the origin of the fractile axis is zero. Second, by proper choice of c, a rather large variety of function shapes is obtainable. When $c = 1$, the Weibull becomes the negative exponential function, declining monotonically with mode at fractile 0. When $c = 2$, the Weibull is the Rayleigh distribution. If $c \approx 3.34$, the Weibull is an excellent approximation of the normal curve [3].

More relevant for the analysis of oligopolistic expectations is the fact that for $c > 3.34$ the mean of the Weibull is less than the mode, so that the Pearsonian coefficient of skewness is negative, and the distribution is skewed to the left. The Weibull distribution is used primarily in reliability theory to depict the times to failure for components whose failure rate increases $(c > 1)$ with time of usage. Hence, the probabilities of times to failure above the mode fall off rather abruptly. In the general case of oligopolistic rivalry the subjective expectations of firms must include a larger domain of price reductions by a rival than price increases, since the temptations are to lower prices to achieve advantages at rivals' expense.

Finally, the distribution is relatively easy to manipulate mathematically because of the simplicity of its derivative functions. For example, the distribution or cumulative density function is

$$F(p_2) = 1 - e^{-(p_2/b)^c}, \tag{20.2}$$

with inverse

$$F^{-1}(\alpha) = \tilde{p}_\alpha = b \left(\ln \left[\frac{1}{1-\alpha} \right] \right)^{c^{-1}}, \tag{20.3}$$

where α is a specified probability value.

My hypothesis is that firm 1's subjective hunches about firm 2's price initiatives can be approximately represented as the definition of a price bracket within which firm 1 is effectively certain that p_2 will be placed by firm 2's strategy. For the present analysis I will assume that "certainty" is a 95 percent confidence that firm 2's price this period will fall within the bracket $[\tilde{p}_2^-, \tilde{p}_2^+] = [(1 - r^-)p_2^*, (1 + r^+)p_2^*]$, where p_2^* is last period's price, and r^- and r^+ are proportion parameters.

From (20.3)

$$1. \quad \tilde{p}_2^- = b \left(\ln \left[\frac{1}{0.95} \right] \right)^{c^{-1}} = b(0.05129)^{c^{-1}}$$

$$\tag{20.4}$$

$$2. \quad \tilde{p}_2^+ = b \left(\ln \left[\frac{1}{0.05} \right] \right)^{c^{-1}} = b(2.99573)^{c^{-1}},$$

where $[\tilde{p}_2^-, \tilde{p}_2^+]$, which I will term the *range bracket*, are the limits of the 0.95 price bracket existing in firm 1's subjective expectations. Its views of firm 2's autonomous price changes are encompassed with 0.95 probability within this bracket. Hence, from (20.4), the parameters of the underlying density function (20.1) are

1. $c = \dfrac{4.06745}{\ln(\tilde{p}_2^+/\tilde{p}_2^-)}$ (20.5)

2. $b = \dfrac{\tilde{p}_2^-}{(0.05129)^{c^{-1}}} = \dfrac{\tilde{p}_2^+}{(2.99573)^{c^{-1}}}.$

I will call the ratio of prices in the denominator of c the *range ratio*.

Note that in the Weibull distribution the shape parameter c is determined (given the probability level of the range bracket) by the range ratio, or, effectively, $(1 + r^+)/(1 - r^-)$, rising as the ratio approaches 1. Given c, b is dependent upon the absolute values of the range bracket bounds.

If we assume that firm 1's expected value of p_2 is the expected value of the Weibull function, then

$$E\{p_2\} \equiv p_2 = b\Gamma\left(\frac{c+1}{c}\right) = b\Gamma(z),$$ (20.6)

where $\Gamma(z)$ is the gamma function. A good polynomial approximation of the gamma function is the following [1]:

$$\Gamma(z) = 1 - 0.5748646c^{-1} + 0.9512363c^{-2} - 0.6998588c^{-3} + 0.4245549c^{-4}$$
$$- 0.1919678c^{-5} + \varepsilon(c^{-1}),$$ (20.7)

where $|\varepsilon(c^{-1})| \leqslant 5 \times 10^{-0.5}$. Therefore, for the analysis to follow, from (20.6) and (20.7),

$$\tilde{p}_2 \approx b(1 - 0.5748646c^{-1} + 0.9512363c^{-2} - 0.6998588c^{-3} + 0.4245549c^{-4}$$
$$- 0.1919678c^{-5}).$$ (20.8)

3.2 Autonomous Price Expectations

My definition of a mature oligopoly is centered upon the range ratio and its bounds and the anticipated reactions of those bounds to firm 1's autonomous price moves. Thus, it embraces the firms' subjective notions of their rivals' autonomous price moves and their reactive price changes. In this section, which deals with autonomous uncertainty, we define two characteristics of a mature oligopoly that concern anticipated autonomous price change:

Characteristic 1. In mature oligopoly the range brackets that encompass rivals' price movements around p^* tend to be narrow. Rivals expect their fellows to move prices by relatively small proportions.

Characteristic 2. In mature oligopoly the range brackets about going prices are unbalanced to the right. That is, the upper bound is farther above p^* than the lower bound is below it. Rivals believe that within the narrow limits of the range bracket an upward bias in their fellows' price intentions exists.

In terms of the framework within which I am casting oligopolistic pricing uncertainty these are significant manifestations of maturity. Rivals who have coexisted for long periods, whose information about each others' decision environment is extensive, and who may have experienced the ravages of price instability in the industry, should exhibit notional density functions over each other's prices with these characteristics.

To fix ideas, I suggest that in mature oligopoly the range brackets will be no more than ± 10 percent of p^*, and more typically will be within ± 5 percent of going prices. In table 20.1, I have chosen eight range brackets that fall within the outer limits for brackets, three of which lie within the narrower limits. For $p_2^* = 1$, b and c parameters are calculated, along with the mean, mode, standard deviation, coefficient of variation, and skewness coefficient for the relevant density functions.

Note that when the range brackets have bounds that are equidistant from p^* (i.e. $r^- = r^+$) the expected value of the distribution is greater than unity, so $\bar{p}_2 > p_2^*$. When they conform to characteristic 2 and are unbalanced to the right, they yield a $\bar{p}_2$ that is larger than p_2^* by even larger amounts. Only when they are unbalanced to the left is $\bar{p}_2 < p_2^*$. In mature oligopoly the expectation is that rivals' attitudes toward potential autonomous price changes will be biased upward slightly.

It is interesting to note the rather close correspondence of the percentages of the density function areas captured within the $\bar{p}_2 \pm 1\sigma$, $\pm 2\sigma$, and $\pm 3\sigma$ fractile brackets to those of the normal distribution. The Weibull is a bit more highly concentrated in the first of these brackets than the normal except for the limiting range bracket [0.90, 1.10] for which it is rather close. In all cases, however, the second and third fractile brackets correspond closely to their normal curve complements in area contained.

The values of the mode are quite close to $\bar{p}_2$ in all instances. For the three range brackets within the narrow limits of $p_2^* \pm 5$ percent the mean percentage increment of mode above mean is 1.1 percent, and for all eight brackets it averages 1.61 percent. For the limiting bracket of [0.90, 1.10] it rises to a maximum of 2.41 percent. Interestingly, if firm 1 were to employ the modes of its notional density function as the expectation of p_2, it would always expect firm 2 to raise its price in its autonomous price decision phase. The skewness coefficients are moderate in the range of -0.375 to -0.434, falling as c approaches 3.34.

In terms of conflict management in mature oligopoly these deductions suggest that uncertainty makes an independent contribution to a stable strategic environment by lessening price rivalry. Firm 1 will price its product in the expectation that firm 2 may raise its price slightly, and firm 2 will share the same expectation of firm 1's pricing. Both firms, therefore, will be

Table 20.1 Representative range brackets for mature oligopoly autonomous price changes, with implied Weibull function parameters

Bracket	b	c	$\bar{p}_2(\bar{p}_2^* = 1)$	σ	$V(\sigma/\bar{p}_2)$[a]	$\bar{p}_2 \pm 3\sigma$	$\hat{p}_2$[b]	S[c]	$\bar{p}_2 \pm 1\sigma$	$\bar{p}_2 \pm 2\sigma$	$[(\hat{p}_2/\bar{p}_2) - 1] \times 100$
[0.97, 1.03]	1.01346	67.77049	1.00491	0.01920	0.01910	98.97%	1.01324	−0.43	72.88%	95.98%	0.82%
[0.95, 1.03]	1.00821	50.30729	0.99646	0.02520	0.02530	98.93	1.00781	−0.43	71.57	95.88	1.14
[0.95, 1.05]	1.02203	40.64058	1.00790	0.03181	0.03156	99.01	1.02140	−0.43	72.28	95.96	1.34
[0.97, 1.10]	1.06331	32.34054	1.04527	0.04085	0.03908	98.99	1.06228	−0.42	71.64	95.81	1.63
[0.90, 1.03]	0.99319	30.14728	0.97531	0.04030	0.04132	98.94	0.99208	−0.42	70.95	95.62	1.72
[0.95, 1.10]	1.05735	27.74457	1.03669	0.04671	0.04506	98.98	1.05595	−0.41	71.11	95.70	1.86
[0.90, 1.05]	1.00723	26.38620	0.98654	0.05130	0.05204	99.34	1.00576	−0.38	75.78	96.86	1.95
[0.90, 1.10]	1.04204	20.26928	1.01443	0.06294	0.05718	98.72	1.03944	−0.42	67.36	94.61	2.41

[a] Coefficient of variation.
[b] Mode $= b(1 - c^{-1})c^{-1}$.
[c] Pearson coefficient of skewness $\in [-1, +1]$.

led to set higher current prices for any given going price, p^*, of their rival than they would if $\bar{p} = p^*$, and their mutual action should reinforce the individual drives to raise prices. Gently rising prices over time in mature oligopoly should result from this noncollusive cooperative environment created by the existence of restrained uncertainty concerning autonomous price changes.

Moreover, as maturity grows over time, the range bracket is expected to react in one of two ways. It may narrow, with the lower bound rising and the upper bound falling by a smaller absolute amount or remaining fixed, or else it may rise with a rise in the lower bound and a larger rise in the upper bound. Consider the Weibull function for both cases. From (20.6)

$$1. \quad \frac{d\bar{p}_2}{d\tilde{p}_2^-} = b\frac{d\Gamma(z)}{dc}\frac{dc}{d\tilde{p}_2^-} + \Gamma(z)\frac{db}{d\tilde{p}_2^-}$$

$$2. \quad \frac{d\bar{p}_2}{d\tilde{p}_2^+} = b\frac{d\Gamma(z)}{dc}\frac{dc}{d\tilde{p}_2^+} + \Gamma(z)\frac{db}{d\tilde{p}_2^+}.$$

(20.9)

Differentiation of (20.4) yields

$$1. \quad \frac{db}{d\tilde{p}_2^-} = 0.26975\,(0.05129)^{-c-1}$$

$$2. \quad \frac{dc}{d\tilde{p}_2^-} = 0.24585b^{-1}c^2(0.05129)^{-c-1}$$

(20.10)

$$3. \quad \frac{db}{d\tilde{p}_2^+} = 0.73025\,(2.99573)^{-c-1}$$

$$4. \quad \frac{dc}{d\tilde{p}_2^+} = -0.24585b^{-1}c^2(2.99573)^{-c-1}.$$

From the approximation of (20.7)

$$\frac{d\Gamma(z)}{dc} \approx 0.574864c^{-2} - 1.9024726c^{-3} + 2.0995764c^{-4} - 1.6982196c^{-5}$$

$$+ 0.505339c^{-6}.$$

(20.11)

Consider now equation (20.9-2):

$$\frac{d\bar{p}_2}{d\tilde{p}_2^+} > 0 \quad \text{iff} \quad \frac{bd\Gamma(z)}{dc}\frac{dc}{d\tilde{p}_2^+} + \Gamma(z)\frac{db}{d\tilde{p}_2^+} > 0$$

(20.12)

$$\text{or} \quad \frac{1}{b}\frac{db/d\tilde{p}_2^+}{dc/d\tilde{p}_2^+} < \frac{d\Gamma(z)/dc}{\Gamma(z)}$$

$$\text{or} \quad -\frac{1}{b}\frac{(2.97026)}{(0.05129)^{c-1}}\frac{\tilde{p}_2^-}{c^2} < \frac{d\Gamma(z)/dc}{\Gamma(z)}$$

$$\text{or} \quad 2.97026 > c^2\frac{d\Gamma(z)/dc}{\Gamma(z)}.$$

From (20.7)

$$\frac{d\Gamma(z)/dc}{\Gamma(z)} \approx 0.574864c^{-2} - 1.5720033c^{-3} + 0.649055c^{-4}, \quad (20.13)$$

which substituted into the last inequality in (20.11) yields

$$\frac{d\bar{p}_2}{d\tilde{p}_2^+} > 0 \text{ iff } 2.3953954c^2 + 1.5720033c - 0.6490553 > 0. \quad (20.14)$$

This inequality will hold for $c > 0.24$, so for the realistic values of $c \in [20, 70]$ it follows that $d\bar{p}_2/d\tilde{p}_2^+ > 0$.

Also, evaluation of (20.12) reveals that

$$\frac{d\Gamma(z)/dc}{\Gamma(z)} > 0 \text{ for } c \notin [0.507, 2.23].$$

hence, from (20.9-1) given $db/d\tilde{p}_2^- > 0$, and $dc/d\tilde{p}_2^- > 0$, $d\bar{p}_2/d\tilde{p}_2^- > 0$ in the relevant domain of c for mature oligopoly.

The net result of changes in $\tilde{p}_2^-$ and $\tilde{p}_2^+$ is then:

$$d\bar{p}_2 = \left[\left(\frac{dc}{d\tilde{p}_2^-} + \frac{dc}{d\tilde{p}_2^+}\right)\frac{bd\Gamma(z)/dc}{\Gamma(z)} + \left(\frac{db}{d\tilde{p}_2^-} + \frac{db}{d\tilde{p}_2^+}\right)\right](d\tilde{p}_2^- + d\tilde{p}_2^+)\Gamma(z).$$

$$(20.15)$$

From (20.10-2) and (20.10-4) the first parenthesized term within the brackets will be positive for all $c > 0$, and from (20.13), the first term will be positive for all positive $c \notin [0.507, 2.228]$. From (20.10-1) and (20.10-3) the second term in brackets will be positive for all $c > 0$. Therefore, within the relevant domain of c the bracketed term will be positive. Since $\Gamma(z) > 0$, the sign of (15) depends on the sum of the differentials. Only when $d\tilde{p}_2^+$ is negative and larger in absolute value than $d\tilde{p}_2^-$ will $d\bar{p}_2$ be negative. Because this latter case is not expected in mature oligopoly, changes in the range bracket over time should favor a rising price vector for rivals.

Autonomous price uncertainty exerts two forces, therefore, which act continuously to support a suppression of conflict by giving a gentle upward impetus to prices. Even if rivals retain fixed range brackets over time, expected prices should rise above going prices period after period. If those brackets change in the indicated manners, the rise in expected prices should be enhanced. Whether or not these upward impulses will be manifested in actual price rises depends, of course, on other factors, such as demand and cost functions and firms' objectives other than profit maximization. But the decision making environment is made somewhat more conducive to peaceful coexistence by the forces of uncertainty.

3.3 Reaction Expectations

The second type of uncertainty that enshrouds the firm's decisions in oligopoly is that concerning rivals' reactions induced by a firm's autonomous actions. These expectations are the *conjectural variations* of standard oligopoly theory. I assume that firm 1 incorporates this uncertainty in its strategies by altering the parameters of its density function via its anticipations of rivals' range brackets. Specifically, I assume that the firm has notions about the responses of the bracket bounds of firm 2 to firm 1's autonomous price changes:

$$\frac{d\tilde{p}_2^-}{dp_1} = m^-, \qquad \frac{d\tilde{p}_2^+}{dp_1} = m^+,$$

where m^- and m^+ are constants. These expectations are in turn used to determine changes in parameters b and c, which alter the subjective probability density function held in firm 1 over firm 2's prices. This treatment unifies the treatment of autonomous and reactive uncertainty using the subjective probability density function as a vehicle. Such changes are expected to alter the forces affecting $\bar{p}_2$ thereby.

Because autonomous change in a mature oligopoly is expected to be tightly bounded, reactive changes are taken to dominate the firm's uncertainty. I specify two characteristics of m^- and m^+ in a mature oligopoly.

Characteristic 3. In a mature oligopoly m^- and m^+ will be nonnegative, with rivals expected to follow the directional leads of autonomous changes rather than running counter to them. Opposition will be registered in the degree to which the initiatives are followed to avoid confrontation in contrarian strategies.

Characteristic 4. Oligopolies in general are more concerned about incumbents' price reductions than increases. This will be reflected in firm 1's expectations of firm 2's responses by $m^- > m^+$.

If firm 1 reduces price, risking the destabilization of the industry's price structure, the probability that firm 2 will lower its price must rise, and the probability that it will raise its price must fall. With the skewed nature of the density function, $\tilde{p}_2^-$ must fall by more than $\tilde{p}_2^+$.

These induced movements in $\tilde{p}_2^-$ and $\tilde{p}_2^+$ will in turn effectively change b and c firm 1's notional subjective probability density function. Differentiation of (20.4) yields

$$\begin{bmatrix} (0.05129)^{c-1} & (2.97026)(0.05129)^{c-1bc-2} \\ (2,99573)^{c-1} & -(1.09719)(2.99573)^{c-1bc-2} \end{bmatrix} \begin{bmatrix} db \\ dc \end{bmatrix} = \begin{bmatrix} d\tilde{p}_2^- \\ d\tilde{p}_2^+ \end{bmatrix}$$

(20.16)

whose solution is

1. $\dfrac{db}{dp_1} = \dfrac{0.26975m^-}{(0.05129)^{c-1}} + \dfrac{0.73025m^+}{(2.99573)^{c-1}}$

(20.17)

2. $\dfrac{dc}{dp_1} = 0.24585b^{-1}c^2 \left(\dfrac{m^-}{(0.05129)^{c-1}} - \dfrac{m^+}{(2.99573)^{c-1}} \right).$

It follows from characteristics 3 and 4 that db/dp_1 and dc/dp_1 are positive. From (20.15), therefore, and the analysis accompanying it, $dp_2/dp_1 > 0$ within the relevant domain of c values for mature oligopoly.

Reactive uncertainty, therefore, acts to reinforce the impulses originating in autonomous uncertainty to raise $\bar{p}_2$ above p_2^*, enhancing firm 1's motivation to increase p_1 – a motivation that has already been strengthened by $\Delta p_2 = \bar{p}_2 - p_2^* > 0$. These observations can now be formalized.

3.4 The Firm's Maximum Expected Profits and Reaction Functions

Assume that firm 1's expected sales function is

$$E\{X_1\} = a_1 - g_{11}p_1 + g_{12}E\{p_2\}, \qquad a_1, g_{11}, g_{12} > 0 \qquad (20.18)$$
$$= a_1 - g_{11}p_1 + g_{12}(p_2^* + \Delta p_2),$$

and that, with constant average cost, k_1, its expected profits are

$$E\{\pi_1\} = E\{X_1\}(p_1 - k_1). \qquad (20.19)$$

The first-order necessary condition for an expected profit maximum is

$$\frac{dE\{\pi_1\}}{dp_1} = [g_{11}(p_1 - k_1) - E\{X_1\}] - \left[(p_1 - k_1)g_{12}\frac{d\bar{p}_2}{dp_1} \right] = 0.$$

(20.20)

The terms in the first set of brackets constitute marginal expected profit, taking into account only autonomous uncertainty. If reactive uncertainty were zero, this marginal expected profit would be equated to zero. The optimal p_1 in this case will be higher than it would be in the absence of autonomous uncertainty by $0.5(g_{12}/g_{11})\Delta p_2$. But if reactive uncertainty is incorporated in the firm's decision-making, the term in the second bracket must be positive. Hence, the first bracket must be positive, or marginal expected revenue must exceed marginal cost. Thus, p_1 must be above the level dictated by autonomous uncertainty alone. In summary,

$$p_1^c = \frac{(a_1 + g_{11}k_1)}{2g_{11}} + 0.5\frac{g_{12}}{g_{11}}p_2^*, \qquad (20.21)$$

where p_1^c is the optimal price under certainty. Hence the reaction function under certainty is linear in p_2^*.

Under autonomous uncertainty, the reaction function is

$$p_1^a = \frac{(a_1 - g_{11}k_1)}{2g_{11}} + 0.5\frac{g_{12}}{g_{11}}\bar{p}_2$$

$$= \frac{(a_1 + g_{11}k_1)}{2g_{11}} + 0.5\frac{g_{12}}{g_{11}}b\Gamma(z) \qquad (20.22)$$

$$= \frac{(a_1 + g_{11}k_1)}{2g_{11}} + 0.5\frac{(g_{12}(1 - r^-)\Gamma(z))}{(0.05129)^{c-1}}p_2^*.$$

Define

$$A = a_1 + g_{11}k_1 + g_{12}\bar{p}_2$$

$$A' = \frac{dA}{dp_2^*} = \frac{g_{12}(1 - r^-)\Gamma(z)}{(0.05129)^{c-1}}.$$

Then

$$p_1^a = \frac{a_1 + g_{11}k_1}{2g_{11}} + \frac{0.5A'}{g_{11}}p_2^*. \qquad (20.23)$$

Further,

$$\frac{dp_1^a}{dp_2^*} = \frac{0.5A'}{g_{11}}, \qquad \frac{d^2p_1^a}{dp_2^{*2}} = 0. \qquad (20.24)$$

When reactive uncertainty is added to autonomous uncertainty the reaction function may be written

$$p_1^u = \frac{Ap_2^* - k_1B}{2g_{11}p_2^* - B}, \qquad (20.25)$$

which derives from (20.20), where

$$B = g_{12}M\bar{p}_2.$$

The derivation of M follows from $d\bar{p}_2/dp_1$ in (20.20). That is,

$$\frac{d\bar{p}_2}{dp_1} = \Gamma(z)\frac{db}{dp_1} + b\frac{d\Gamma(z)}{dc}\frac{dc}{dp_1}, \qquad (20.26)$$

which may be approximated from (20.7) and (20.13) by

$$\frac{d\bar{p}_2}{dp_1} \approx \frac{\bar{p}_2}{p_2^*}\left\{ [0.41108 - 0.38648c^{-1} + 0.15957c^{-2}]\frac{m^-}{(1-r^-)} \right.$$
$$\left. - 0.15957c^{-2}\frac{m^+}{(1+r^+)}\right\} \qquad (20.27)$$
$$\approx \frac{\bar{p}_2}{p_2^*}\{M\} .$$

Note that M is a convex combination of $(m^-/(1-r^-))$ and $(m^+/(1+r^+))$.

The three reaction functions (20.21), (20.22), and (20.25) are linear in structure, in general, for relevant range brackets, $p_1^u > p_1^a > p_1^c$ for given p_2^* values. For example, given the following data for firms 1 and 2,

$$E\{X_1\} = 200 - 5p_1 + 1.6\bar{p}_2, \quad k_1 = 7, \quad r^- = 0.65, \quad r^+ = 0.35$$
$$E\{X_2\} = 350 - 7p_2 + 3.5\bar{p}_1, \quad k_2 = 0.5, \quad r^- = 0.65, \quad r^+ = 0.35,$$
$$(20.28)$$

and for the range bracket [0.97, 1.03] for both firms, the reaction functions are

$$p_1^c = 23.5 + 0.16p_2^* \qquad P^c = [28.69, 32.42]$$
$$p_2^c = 25.25 + 0.25p_1^*$$
$$p_1^a = 23.5 + 0.1608p_2^* \qquad P^a = [28.72, 32.46] \qquad (20.29)$$
$$p_2^c = 25.25 + 0.2512p_1^*$$
$$p_1^u = 24.86 + 0.1741p_2^* \qquad P^u = [31.40, 37.57]$$
$$p_2^u = 28.61 + 0.2853p_1^* .$$

The relations are graphed in figure 20.1. The price vector under certainty, $P^c = [p_1^c, p_2^c]$ is smaller than P^a, which in turn is dominated by P^u. In mature oligopoly reactive uncertainty is expected to have a larger impact upon the equilibrium prices than autonomous uncertainty, and this is illustrated in the reaction functions, R_1^c, R_1^a and R_1^u of figure 20.1.

In summary, in a mature oligopolistic industry, the contribution of autonomous and reactive uncertainty, when firms' incorporation of such concerns can be approximated by our price bracket construction, is to facilitate conflict management. Uncertainty in such circumstances conduces to mutually beneficial but tacit cooperation because of the manner in which it structures the expectations of rivals. Paradoxically, perhaps, uncertainty conditions the environment in a positive or conflict-lessening manner.

This suggests the extension of the analysis to such mature rivalrous

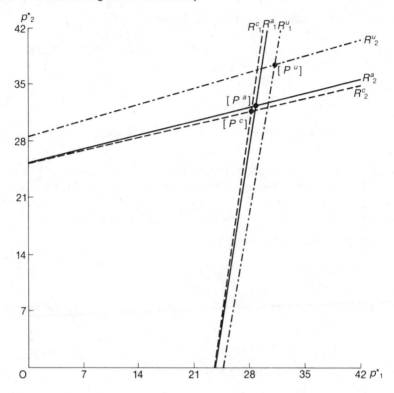

Figure 20.1   The reaction functions under certainty, autonomous uncertainty, and full uncertainty.

relationships as the current military postures of Warsaw Pact and NATO coalitions. As coexistence extends into its fifth decade, the range brackets on both antagonists' autonomous expectations can be expected to have narrowed and to possess some bias in the direction of mutual benefit. Rival reactions will be expected to be within relatively tight intervals, with relatively greater responses in the noncooperative direction but nonetheless significant reinforcing moves in the cooperative direction.

The distinctive difference between diplomatic moves and pricing decisions is the opportunity to negotiate openly in the former and the necessity for tacit collusion in the latter. Because uncertainty is so sensitive to information flow in its impacts on decisions and because such flow is facilitated in general by face-to-face bargaining, one would expect that range brackets would tend to be narrowed in such negotiations compared with those ruling in mature oligopoly. However, in both autonomous and reaction uncertainty, the same biases in range brackets and range bound reactions should rule. Therefore, rivals should be led to arrive at solutions which are of benefit over the status quo to both parties.

4 Rivalrous Consonance

In mature oligopoly uncertainty is expected to play the role of a passive cooperation facilitator, and thereby to enhance the cooperative characteristics of the industry's price solutions. However, over time, mature oligopolies must be expected to initiate more active cooperative procedures designed to manage conflict. This section presents a framework for studying the motivation and impacts of such noncollusive strategies to enhance cooperative outcomes.

I start from the simple notion that mature oligopolies are established communities of decision-making units whose selfish interests imply both competition and cooperation. In their pricing decisions, industry members view their relations as a "rivalrous consonance of interests," or a mixture of the competitive and the cooperative. They see rivals as occupying a hierarchical relationship in terms of the degree of rivalry they present and, therefore, the extent of deference that self-interest dictates they be accorded. In short, there exists a *power structure* in the industry which defines, for each firm, the mix of competition and cooperation that should shape its strategic attitudes to each of its rivals. The ensemble of these binary relations defines the effective power structure within which the industry's pricing decisions are made.

Hence, within mature oligopolies as in other social communities, informed self-interest leads to conflicts in goal-seeking as well as to cooperation in their attainment. Conflict is managed by institutions that seek to instill a balance between both motivations. Where overt cooperative agreements are forbidden, as in oligopoly, these institutions will emerge informally through signalling via behavior patterns. Analyses of their implications requires the simulation by formal models of the outcomes of informal procedures. That is what the techniques of this section seek to do. (See Kuenne [2] for a detailed presentation of this concept.)

Let us remain with duopoly for purposes of simplifying the model. I assume that a notional encapsulation of the power structure can be depicted in the vector $\theta = [\theta_1, \theta_2]$. The parameter θ_1 is the *consonance coefficient* which defines the deference firm 1 pays to firm 2 in its decision making. More specifically, θ_1 is the valuation firm 1 places upon firm 2's profits, calibrated in units of its own (firm 1's) profits, in making its pricing decisions.

By virtue of such factors as the degree of substitutability of firm 2's product for firm 1's, the aggressiveness of firm 2's management, the ability to respond reactively to firm 1's autonomous price changes springing from firm 2's financial position, and so forth, firm 1 forms a judgement of the degree of cooperative deference it should pay to firm 2's welfare in setting its price. It does this by adding to its expected profit function of (20.19) the expected profit function of firm 2 discounted by θ_1. The *extended profit function* is

$$E\{Z_1\} = E\{X_1\}(p_1 - k_1) + \theta_1[E\{X_2\}(E\{p_2\} - k_2)], \quad (20.30)$$

and from the first-order necessary condition the reaction function, R_1^r, may be written

$$p_1^r = \frac{Ap_2^* - (k_1 B - \theta_1(\bar{p}_2 - k_2)g_{21})p_2^* + \theta_1 C}{2g_{11}p_2^{*2} - Bp_2^* - \theta_1 g_{12}\bar{p}_2 M}, \quad (20.31)$$

where

$$C = (a_2 - 2g_{22}\bar{p}_2 + k_2 g_{22})M\bar{p}_2.$$

Note that when $\bar{p}_2$ is near k_2, so firm 2's profits are near zero, the positive consonance terms in the numerator of (20.31) become small, while the negative consonance term in the denominator remains relatively large. Therefore, in the lower price domains of p_2^*, R_1^r may be backward bending. This occurs because firm 1 is led to give little cooperative deference to firm 2 when its profits are low, so that its own profit enhancement of a drop in p_1 may outweigh the discounted other-profit impact of that action.

For the case where the data are those of (20.28) and where $\theta_1 = \theta_2 = 0.35$, the reaction functions are drawn in figure 20.2. Their specifications are given in (20.32):

$$1. \quad p_1^r = \frac{1.608p_2^{*2} + 228.525p_2^* + 50.556}{9.235p_2^* - 0.268}$$

$$\quad (20.32)$$

$$2. \quad p_2^r = \frac{3.517p_1^{*2} + 351.545p_1^* + 39.589}{12.327p_1^* - 0.585}$$

The tacit cooperation exercised in mature oligopoly via rivalrous consonance results in higher prices enjoyed by both firms than those forthcoming under certainty or uncertainty. The solution vector for the reaction functions of (20.32) is $P^r = [31.81, 37.75]$, which may be compared with the solutions of (20.29). Such price solutions rise with θ-values. Practical values of θ_1 and θ_2 will vary between 0 and 1, where 0 denotes a complete absence of cooperation (the "Cournot" solution) and yields P^u, and 1 is complete cooperation and results in joint-profit maximization (the "Chamberlin" solution).

Clearly, varying θ-mixes index different mixtures of rivalry and cooperation in the industry's pricing decisions, and mature oligopolies may be

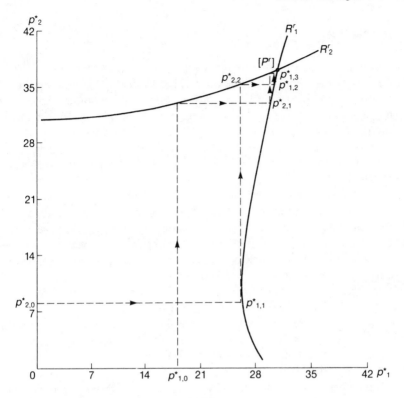

Figure 20.2   The reaction functions under rivalrous consonance.

expected to exhibit substantial amounts of such deference. My view is that it is a potent means of conflict management that arises spontaneously from extensive periods of coexistence of rivals who must respect one another's survivability and must deplore short-sighted price actions that threaten profit stability.

The extension to broader areas of human conflict is rather straight-forward. In such arenas rivals frequently have the advantage of face-to-face negotiations, so that subtle signalling does not play an exclusive role. Anticipation of other participants' reactions to one's own actions in terms of some welfare measure, and judgements of the importance of such impacts to one's own welfare are central to conflict management. Perhaps the greatest generalizable lesson from the economic application is the demonstration of its potential when no formal negotiations are permissible.

5 Conclusion

Economists must confront the thorny problems of conflict management within the body of their discipline only in the context of bargaining theory. Frequently, such theory confronts rather short-run situations that require rapid conflict *resolution* (e.g. labor–management bargaining, contract negotiations). In such confrontations, short-run self-interest can be assumed to dominate, and the economist's bent to interpret human behavior as exclusively competitive can be applied properly through game-theoretic frameworks.

In oligopolistic decision-making, however, where short-run interests are tempered by long-term concerns, and especially in conditions I have termed "mature oligopoly," conflict resolution yields to conflict management, a nonorganic association of individual decision-makers becomes a community, and competition must be melded with prudent cooperation. Game-theoretic frameworks serve us poorly as vehicles of entry into the analysis of such contexts, even though they may serve as convenient scaffolding on which to present the results of more useful theories.

The search for insights into communitarian management of conflict within the special confines of tacit cooperation is vital, in my judgement. Mechanisms of two types are of interest: (1) those that arise from unavoidable characteristics of the environment, fostering cooperative solutions in the normal process of decision-making, and (2) those which emerge from the conscious signalling of the actors.

This chapter has dealt with conflict management mechanisms of both types. It has been demonstrated that certain features of oligopolistic uncertainty in an environment with "mature" patterns of behavior enhance cooperative solutions and mitigate conflict. Foremost among such characteristics are the common expectation that the probabilities of autonomous price actions are biased in the upward direction, and the expectation that rivals will both follow such upward price movements with reactive changes in the same direction and respond with even greater alacrity to price cuts by similar moves.

The second type of mechanism is exemplified by a type of tacit collusion among firms in mature oligopoly which is notionalized as a discounted inclusion of rivals' profit functions in the decision-making of each firm. The matrix of such discount factors defines an industry power structure, or pattern of deference, which operates through motives of prudence to induce a form of cooperative pricing.

Each such mechanism serves to restrain the conflict inherent in oligopolistic relations – conflict which must always outweigh the cooperative by the nature of the community's purpose. But it is most interesting that there exist such mechanisms to temper or stablize such conflict even in the absence of the ability to establish such institutions formally.

References

[1] Hastings, C., Jr, *Polynomial Approximations for Digital Computers*, Princeton University Press, Princeton, NJ, 1955.

[2] Kuenne, Robert E., *Rivalrous Consonance: a Theory of General Oligopolistic Equilibrium*, Contributions to Economic Analysis 157, North-Holland, Amsterdam, 1986.

[3] Makino, Toji, "Mean Hazard Rate and Its Application to the Normal Approximation of the Weibull Distribution", *Naval Research Logistics Quarterly*, 31, no. 3 (1984), 1–8.

Index